# Mauritius, Réunion & Seychelles

Jean-Bernard Carillet

Brandon Presser

# MAURITIUS

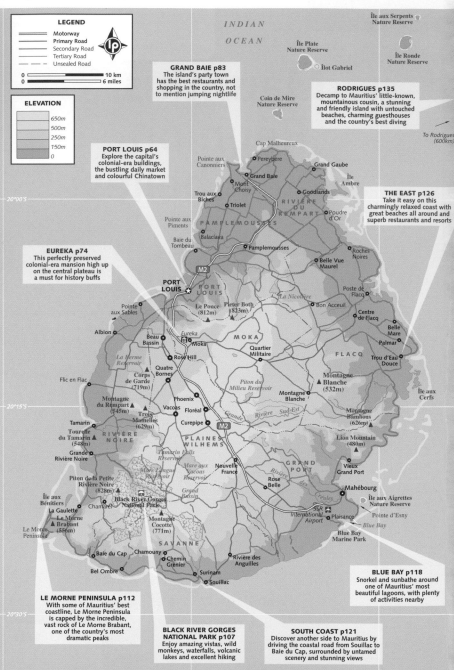

**LEGEND**

Motorway
Primary Road
Secondary Road
Tertiary Road
Unsealed Road

0 ———— 10 km
0 ———— 6 miles

**ELEVATION**

650m
500m
250m
150m
0

**GRAND BAIE p83**
The island's party town has the best restaurants and shopping in the country, not to mention jumping nightlife

**RODRIGUES p135**
Decamp to Mauritius' little-known, mountainous cousin, a stunning and friendly island with untouched beaches, charming guesthouses and the country's best diving

**PORT LOUIS p64**
Explore the capital's colonial-era buildings, the bustling daily market and colourful Chinatown

**THE EAST p126**
Take it easy on this charmingly relaxed coast with great beaches all around and superb restaurants and resorts

**EUREKA p74**
This perfectly preserved colonial-era mansion high up on the central plateau is a must for history buffs

**BLUE BAY p118**
Snorkel and sunbathe around one of Mauritius' most beautiful lagoons, with plenty of activities nearby

**LE MORNE PENINSULA p112**
With some of Mauritius' best coastline, Le Morne Peninsula is capped by the incredible, vast rock of Le Morne Brabant, one of the country's most dramatic peaks

**BLACK RIVER GORGES NATIONAL PARK p107**
Enjoy amazing vistas, wild monkeys, waterfalls, volcanic lakes and excellent hiking

**SOUTH COAST p121**
Discover another side to Mauritius by driving the coastal road from Souillac to Baie du Cap, surrounded by untamed scenery and stunning views

INDIAN OCEAN

INDIAN OCEAN

To Rodrigues (600km)

# RÉUNION

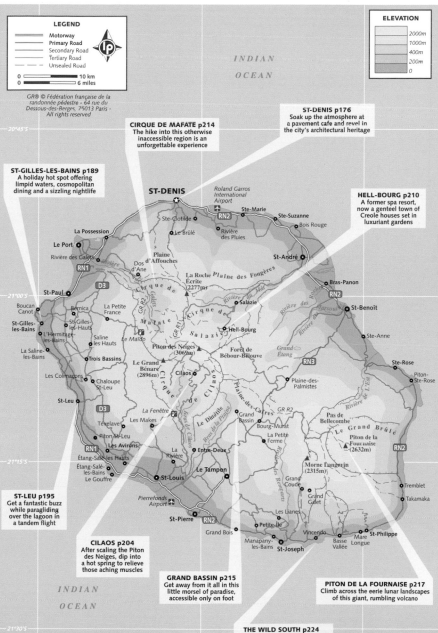

**ST-DENIS p176**
Soak up the atmosphere at a pavement cafe and revel in the city's architectural heritage

**CIRQUE DE MAFATE p214**
The hike into this otherwise inaccessible region is an unforgettable experience

**ST-GILLES-LES-BAINS p189**
A holiday hot spot offering limpid waters, cosmopolitan dining and a sizzling nightlife

**HELL-BOURG p210**
A former spa resort, now a genteel town of Creole houses set in luxuriant gardens

**ST-LEU p195**
Get a fantastic buzz while paragliding over the lagoon in a tandem flight

**CILAOS p204**
After scaling the Piton des Neiges, dip into a hot spring to relieve those aching muscles

**GRAND BASSIN p215**
Get away from it all in this little morsel of paradise, accessible only on foot

**PITON DE LA FOURNAISE p217**
Climb across the eerie lunar landscapes of this giant, rumbling volcano

**THE WILD SOUTH p224**
Secluded hamlets where time has stood still, secret coves and wave-whipped headlands typify the Wild South

LEGEND
Motorway
Primary Road
Secondary Road
Tertiary Road
Unsealed Road

0 — 10 km
0 — 6 miles

ELEVATION
2000m
1000m
400m
200m
0

INDIAN OCEAN

INDIAN OCEAN

ST-DENIS
Roland Garros International Airport
Ste-Marie
Ste-Clotilde
Le Brûlé
Ste-Suzanne
Bois Rouge
Rivière des Pluies
La Possession
Le Port
Rivière des Galets
Plaine d'Affouches
Dos d'Ane
La Roche Écrite (2277m)
Plaine des Fougères
St-André
Bras-Panon
St-Paul
Boucan Canot
Bernica
La Petite France
Salazie
St-Benoît
St-Gilles-les-Bains
St-Gilles-les-Hauts
Hell-Bourg
Ste-Anne
L'Hermitage-les-Bains
Saline les Hauts
Le Maïdo
Piton des Neiges (3069m)
Forêt de Bébour-Bélouve
Grand Étang
La Saline-les-Bains
Trois Bassins
Le Grand Bénare (2896m)
Cilaos
Ste-Rose
Les Colimaçons
Chaloupe St-Leu
Plaine-des-Palmistes
Piton-Ste-Rose
St-Leu
La Fenêtre
Les Makes
Le Dimitile
Grand Bassin
Bourg-Murat
Pas de Bellecombe
Le Grand Brûlé
Tévelave
Piton St-Leu
La Petite Ferme
Piton de la Fournaise (2632m)
Les Avirons
Étang-Salé-les-Hauts
La Rivière
Entre-Deux
Morne Langevin (2315m)
Étang-Salé-les-Bains
Le Gouffre
Le Tampon
St-Louis
Grand Coude
Tremblet
Pierrefonds Airport
Grand Galet
Takamaka
St-Pierre
Grand Bois
Les Lianes
Petite-Île
Vincendo
Manapany-les-Bains
St-Joseph
Basse Vallée
Mare Longue
St-Philippe

20°45'S
21°00'S
21°15'S
21°30'S
55°15'E
55°30'E
55°45'E

# SEYCHELLES

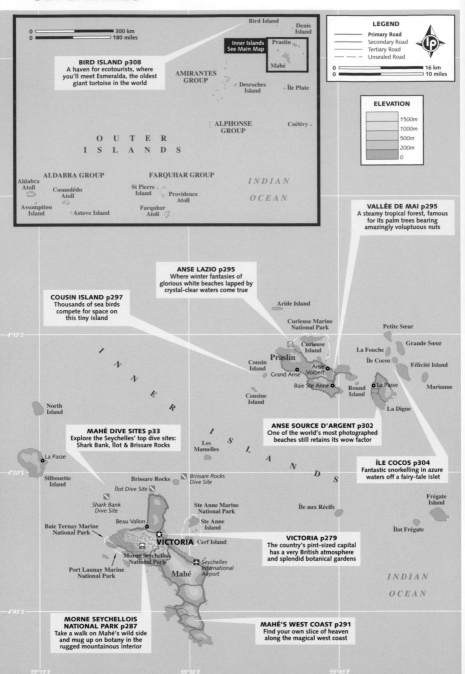

**LEGEND**

— Primary Road
— Secondary Road
— Tertiary Road
- - - Unsealed Road

0 ⸻ 16 km
0 ⸻ 10 miles

**ELEVATION**

1500m
1000m
500m
200m
0

0 ⸻ 300 km
0 ⸻ 180 miles

**BIRD ISLAND p308**
A haven for ecotourists, where you'll meet Esmeralda, the oldest giant tortoise in the world

Bird Island
Denis Island

Inner Islands
See Main Map

Praslin
Mahé

AMIRANTES GROUP

Desroches Island

Île Plate

ALPHONSE GROUP

Coétivy

O U T E R
I S L A N D S

INDIAN OCEAN

ALDABRA GROUP

Aldabra Atoll

Cosmolédo Atoll

Assomption Island

Astove Island

FARQUHAR GROUP

St Pierre Island

Providence Atoll

Farquhar Atoll

**VALLÉE DE MAI p295**
A steamy tropical forest, famous for its palm trees bearing amazingly voluptuous nuts

**ANSE LAZIO p295**
Where winter fantasies of glorious white beaches lapped by crystal-clear waters come true

**COUSIN ISLAND p297**
Thousands of sea birds compete for space on this tiny island

Aride Island

Curieuse Marine National Park

Petite Sœur

Grande Sœur

Curieuse Island

La Fouche

Île Cocos

Félicité Island

Cousin Island

Praslin

Anse Volbert

Grand Anse

Baie Ste Anne

Round Island

La Passe

Marianne

La Digue

Cousine Island

I N N E R

North Island

I
S
L
A
N
D
S

**MAHÉ DIVE SITES p33**
Explore the Seychelles' top dive sites: Shark Bank, Îlot & Brissare Rocks

**ANSE SOURCE D'ARGENT p302**
One of the world's most photographed beaches still retains its wow factor

**ÎLE COCOS p304**
Fantastic snorkelling in azure waters off a fairy-tale islet

La Passe

Silhouette Island

Les Mamelles

Frégate Island

Brissare Rocks
Îlot Dive Site

Brissare Rocks Dive Site

Shark Bank Dive Site

Île aux Récifs

Îlot Frégate

Baie Ternay Marine National Park

Ste Anne Marine National Park

Ste Anne Island

Beau Vallon

VICTORIA

Cerf Island

**VICTORIA p279**
The country's pint-sized capital has a very British atmosphere and splendid botanical gardens

INDIAN OCEAN

Morne Seychellois National Park

Seychelles International Airport

Port Launay Marine National Park

Mahé

**MORNE SEYCHELLOIS NATIONAL PARK p287**
Take a walk on Mahé's wild side and mug up on botany in the rugged mountainous interior

**MAHÉ'S WEST COAST p291**
Find your own slice of heaven along the magical west coast

4°15'S

4°30'S

4°45'S

55°15'E

55°30'E

55°45'E

# On the Road

## JEAN-BERNARD CARILLET Coordinating Author

Hawaii? No, Réunion. Here I'm standing at the Pas de Bellecombe viewpoint. The big volcano you see in the background is the Piton de la Fournaise (p217), Réunion's iconic attraction. That day I got up at the crack of dawn to climb up to the rim of the caldera and gaze into the jaws of the giant, but I was not lucky – it started raining soon after I set off. I completed the hike, though, and by the time I came back to the car park, conditions got brighter, just in time for that picture!

---

**BRANDON PRESSER** It's a guide to Mauritius, of course it's a beach photo! Except this isn't Mauritius, it's Rodrigues (p135). My trip to this sleepy sister island was the perfect antidote to the aggravating traffic jams on the mainland. On Rodrigues I could zip around on a scooter, and when the roads faded away I'd continue my mission on foot. The island's wild eastern shores were particularly rugged, but the technicolour lagoon called out to me with its inspiring tapestry of sapphire, emerald and topaz. I couldn't help but take a little break in the powder-soft sand to jot down a few notes and reflections. Welcome to my office.

*For full author biographies see p338.*

# Mauritius, Réunion & Seychelles Highlights

Beaches that defy all superlatives, wild landscapes that will forever be etched into your memory, loads of adventure options, excellent opportunities for wildlife watching and a glimpse of history – there are countless attractions in Mauritius, Réunion and Seychelles. Paradise found? You be the judge.

We asked our authors and travellers what they love most about the region. Share your highlights at www.lonelyplanet.com/mauritius.

JEAN-BERNARD CARILLET

## 1 PARAGLIDING IN ST-LEU

The first time I tried paragliding was in St-Leu (Réunion; p196). I arranged a tandem flight with a reputable outfit. I felt utterly confident; the instructors were highly professional and they gave me a proper briefing before we drove to the platform at an altitude of 800m. The take-off site was very reassuring as there were no obstacles and the slope was very gentle. After the take-off, I was overwhelmed by a sensation of silence and freedom. We glided for about 20 minutes – I can't really judge it, as I had lost all notion of time. I was totally gobsmacked by the views of the lagoon below. We landed softly on a small beach. Unforgettable.

**Jean-Bernard Carillet, Lonely Planet Author**

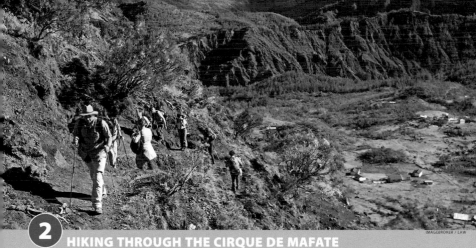

## 2 HIKING THROUGH THE CIRQUE DE MAFATE

Mafate (Réunion; p214) is an absolute gem. It feels like the world's end. There's no road, just walking paths. I spent almost a week exploring the Cirque, staying at the *gîtes* (self-catering accommodations). My favourite places are Aurère and Îlet à Bourse; these hamlets are frozen in time. I always found the welcome warm and genuine. And the scenery blew my mind, with waterfalls, soaring peaks and lush vegetation. Three days is a minimum to soak up the atmosphere.

**Marie Mosnier, Traveller, France**

## 3 THE MIGHTY VOLCANO

I didn't climb up the Piton de la Fournaise (Réunion; p217), but just seeing it from Pas de Bellecombe is memorable. It's otherworldly because there's not an ounce of vegetation, only huge expanses of solidified lava; it looks like a set from a sci-fi movie. Next time I'll definitely climb up to the viewpoint in order to see the inside of the caldera.

**Jean-Paul Diana, Teacher, Réunion**

IMAGEBROKER / GER

## **4** ARCHITECTURAL GEMS IN ST-DENIS

St-Denis (Réunion; p177) has a wide array of architectural wonders (including the town hall). I was amazed by the Creole mansions that flank Rue de Paris and Ave de la Victoire; most have been taste-fully restored and now shelter administrative offices. They lend an air of elegance to St-Denis.

**Anne-Lise Semaesse, Traveller, France**

IMAGEBROKER / LAW

## **5** MORNE SEYCHELLOIS NATIONAL PARK

In their quest for the perfect beach, many travellers are oblivious to the fact that there's a splendid national park on Mahé (Seychelles; p287). It's a sad mistake, because they miss out on fantastic experi-ences in this lush park. Take a guided tour and I guarantee you'll feel like you're on the set of *Lost*. You'll come across rare species of birds, reptiles and plants. Not to mention breathtaking viewpoints.

**Jean-Bernard Carillet, Lonely Planet Author**

## DENIS

We stayed a week on Denis (Seychelles; p308). This was the most romantic trip in my life. This private island resort had all the ingredients to get away from it all. No TV. No phones. Just nature. We felt like Robinson Crusoe. The hotel was elegant yet simple and defined 'barefoot luxury'. We enjoyed the nature walks with the conservationist, who showed us numerous species of birds as well as giant tortoises.

**Dorothée Pasqualin, Traveller, France**

6

JEAN-BERNARD-CARILLET

## ANSE LAZIO

It was like an apparition: the water was so scintillating and the sand so dazzling white that I rubbed my eyes. It was picture-postcard perfect wherever I looked. Backed by big granite boulders and lush vegetation, Anse Lazio (p295) feels raw and untamed, despite the fact that it's the most renowned beach in the Seychelles. I did some snorkelling in gin-clear, bath-warm waters.

**Céline Bellini, Traveller, France**

7

HOLGER LEUE

JEAN-BERNARD-CARILLET

## 8 LA DIGUE & ÎLE COCOS

Peace. Serenity. All in the Seychelles. La Digue (p302) is special. It's wild, quiet and ecofriendly. I hired a bike and explored the island at leisure. I also walked to Anse Marron (p304), a secluded beach at the southern tip of La Digue. The next day, I took a boat excursion to Île Cocos (p304) and snorkelled in a subaquatic paradise with lots of colourful critters in crystal-clear waters.

**Fabien Forget, Traveller, Mauritius**

IMAGEBROKER / RDB

## 9 DIVING NEAR FLIC EN FLAC

The architecture of the underwater rock formations and the substantial schools of fish make Mauritius a haven for scuba buffs. The best sites are the walls and drop-offs on the edge of the turquoise lagoon. La Cathédrale (p29), near Flic en Flac is a personal favourite.

**Gérald Rambert, Scuba Pro, Mauritius**

## CHAMBRES & TABLES D'HÔTES

Whether it's along the west coast of Mauritius or in the quiet highlands of Rodrigues, the *chambres d'hôtes* (family-run B&Bs; p147) experience is the best way to learn about local life. The highlight, of course, is the nightly *tables d'hôtes* (meal served at a *chambre d'hôte*; p153) where the guests and hosts gather together for a traditional meal. Authenticity is the new luxury in Mauritius!

**Josette Marchal-Vexlard, Guesthouse Owner, Mauritius**

JOHN HAY

## BEACHSIDE BLISS

Choosing your favourite beach on Mauritius is like trying to pick a flavour of ice cream – they're all so good! Although I have a particular affinity for the rugged eastern and southeastern shores – particularly the beaches at Pointe d'Esny (p118) and Belle Mare (p131) – any quiet slice of paradise will do the trick. Nothing beats toeing the sand from your private seaside villa.

**Brandon Presser, Lonely Planet Author**

JEAN ROBERT

OLIVER STREW

## 12 SIGHTS, SOUNDS & SMELLS OF PORT LOUIS

Your first few moments on the streets of Port Louis (Mauritius; p64) are a feeling you'll never forget. The cacophony of honking horns and cajoling vendors feels wildly overwhelming at first, then suddenly you find your rhythm among the chaos and start wandering through labyrinthine alleyways in search of the legendary *dhal puris* (Indian snacks).

**Brandon Presser, Lonely Planet Author**

# Contents

# Regional Map Contents

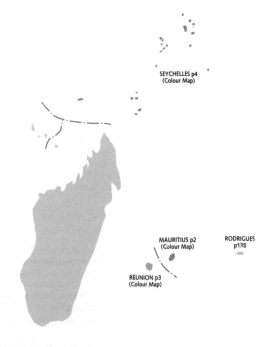

SEYCHELLES p4
(Colour Map)

MAURITIUS p2
(Colour Map)

RODRIGUES
p13S

RÉUNION p3
(Colour Map)

# Destination Mauritius, Réunion & Seychelles

Raise your hand: who wants to go to Mauritius, Réunion or the Seychelles? We thought so. Three unique destinations cast in the warm azure waters of the Indian Ocean, Mauritius, Réunion and Seychelles can all stake a convincing claim to being a piece of paradise. Indeed, there are worse things in life than splashing about in glinting turquoise seas, sampling gourmet fare in a fancy restaurant and sipping a cocktail on your private terrace. While you'll probably see some of the best beaches you've ever come across, there's so much more to each destination that any trip will be an exciting experience, whether it be trekking in the lush volcanic landscape or Réunion's steamy interior, exploring Mauritius' fascinating colonial past or just island hopping between deserted islands in the Seychelles.

On top of offering sexy attractions, what this trio of islands also has in common is French influence. Despite the British being the last colonial power to dominate the region, it's actually the French influence that permeates and informs the experience of Mauritius, Réunion and Seychelles today. While Réunion remains a part of France, independent Mauritius and Seychelles retain so much of their French past (mixed in with their equally beguiling Afro-Asian cultural influences) that even the most cosmopolitan traveller will be impressed.

The comparison ends there. Each country is confronted with specific issues. In Réunion, the major concerns are related to raising the capacity of the transport system. The island is congested, and the local political leaders plan to build new expressways. But these projects, given the tortuous terrain of the island, involve massive investments; small wonder that the métropole (mainland France) is somehow dragging its feet when it comes to subsidising such herculean civil engineering in a context of global recession and public debt. At the same time, such projects would be beneficial to the local workforce and sustain growth. A dilemma.

The Seychelles, which has long billed itself as a paradise, is now experiencing the reality principle. Gone are the good old times of the welfare state. As of November 2008, the country was forced to enter global competition under the tight control of the IMF and accept the fact that it can't live beyond its means and finance its lifestyle by continuously borrowing internationally. It was decided to float the rupee, and prices rose by 30%. The population was hard hit but suffered in silence. Paradisiacal Seychelles has also recently realised that hell is on its doorstep. Since 2008 the area has been increasingly unsafe due to regular attacks led by Somali pirates on vessels cruising in the Seychellois territorial waters. To alleviate the fears of the population (and the foreign tour operators), the government has established defence agreements with the USA and other Western fleets to improve the safety of the Seychellois waters. Don't fret, though; at the time of writing, only the Outer Islands, including Aldabra, were off-limits to travellers.

And now, Mauritius. Paradise on the wane? Maybe. Government corruption and an increase in crime are the order of the day in Mauritius. The tourist industry remains afloat but the destination has partially lost its image of exclusivity. Why? Cheaper package deals are increasingly available, and now that China is crushing the textile industry and tourism isn't booming like a few years ago, Mauritius has no other choice than to hard sell its assets.

# Getting Started

Travel to Mauritius, Réunion and Seychelles is exceptionally safe and easy. There are superb tourism infrastructures in each country, excellent planning resources online, a good level of English is spoken everywhere (bar, maybe, in Réunion) and the choice of activities, hotels and eating is hard to rival anywhere. Of course islands this beautiful are rarely free of crowds and development, so it's important to read up on specific destinations to see if they'll provide the kind of holiday you're looking for – divers looking for social life and entertainment should avoid honeymooner magnets (and vice versa), while those looking to get away from crowds should steer clear of big resorts and head off the beaten path.

Outside the busiest periods of the high season, it's not necessary to book everything, especially if you're a bit flexible.

## WHEN TO GO

Nestled between the Tropic of Capricorn and the equator, all three countries offer year-round heat and there's almost no time in any country when travel isn't advised. However, there are of course nuances, and depending on what you're interested in doing there are considerations to take into account. For example, if you're planning a hiking trip to Réunion, the best time is during the dry season, which runs from late April until October. Likewise, diving in Mauritius is best from October to December and March to April.

The time of year perhaps best avoided is January to February when it's the peak of the cyclone season. Although direct hits are rare, cyclones way offshore can still bring grey days and strong winds, even to the Seychelles, which technically lies outside the cyclone belt.

The climate in all three destinations is broadly similar: a hot, rainy summer from December to April (October to April in the Seychelles) is followed by a cooler, drier winter from May to November (May to September in the Seychelles). Rainfall levels are much higher in the mountains, particularly in Réunion, which boasts a number of world records. Cilaos holds the world record for most rain in a single day – a total of 1870mm fell on 16 March 1952.

Coastal temperatures rarely drop below 20°C in Mauritius and Réunion, or below 24°C in the Seychelles, making these islands a truly year-round destination.

For all three destinations you are advised to plan your travel well in advance, especially during the French holidays when hotels can be booked up months before. Ask your travel agent for advice on the dates of school holidays in France, which vary slightly from year to year. The Christmas to New Year period is also particularly busy. Airline reservations may be difficult to get at this time, so book well ahead to avoid disappointment. Keep in mind that many hotels hike up their room rates during the peak seasons.

For more information on the best times to travel, see p64 for Mauritius, p176 for Réunion and p279 for the Seychelles.

## COSTS & MONEY

For climate charts for Mauritius see p150, Réunion p260 Seychelles p313.

None of these destinations are ever going to be bargains, the main expense being the flights needed to cover the huge distances most visitors have to travel to get here. However, despite enjoying a reputation for opulence and exclusivity, it's perfectly possible to visit all three countries on a limited budget.

Seychelles has traditionally been the most expensive of the lot, and while it remains the most exclusive today, its tourist board is now keen on promoting cheaper accommodation options such as guesthouses; as a result the country has become a far better destination for independent travellers. Réunion is the next most expensive, while Mauritius is a budget-friendly option for those who want to backpack, although five-star hotels also proliferate, making the huge choice of accommodation options part of the island's attraction.

You can keep accommodation costs down by staying in self-catering apartments or small guesthouses and by basing yourself in one place; the longer you stay (and the more of you there are), the cheaper it becomes. It helps to travel off-season as well: prices are generally discounted and there's more chance of being able to bargain.

On the positive side, it's possible to eat reasonably cheaply, even in the Seychelles, by patronising snack stands and getting takeaway meals – or, of course, by self-catering. Restaurants cover a huge scope of price ranges, from barely more expensive than takeaways to almost as expensive as those in London or Paris. In four- and five-star resorts and hotels, restaurants tend to be very pricey, although most guests are on half-or full-board packages, the costs are reduced. Buses in all three destinations provide a cheap method of getting around, although car hire is reasonably priced everywhere too.

It's also worth investigating package holidays, including flights and accommodation, since these can often work out cheaper than travelling independently.

## Mauritius

Due to the unstable fluctuations in the global economy, many tourist-focused establishments – namely accommodation – have priced their rooms in euros. Restaurants tend to charge Mauritian rupees (with the exception of several ultra-upmarket options found at high-end resorts). As far as a daily budget is concerned, backpackers staying in the barebones guesthouses and eating meals at street stands can expect to spend in the region of €25 to €35 per person. Opting for a midrange hotel and smart restaurants will push it up

---

### DON'T LEAVE HOME WITHOUT...

- Getting any necessary vaccinations and visas.

- Nonbeach clothing: some of the best restaurants in all three countries are smart affairs and shorts or bikini tops simply won't do – think lightweight but smart clothing, decent shoes and nondenim trousers for men. Also if you plan to go into the mountains, bring a long-sleeved top for the cool night air.

- Plenty of sun cream, after-sun lotion and bug repellent. Since the Chikungunya epidemic (see p325) most hotels will provide free electronic mosquito repellents to put on at night, but an extra layer of protection is always good, especially for evening dining outside or for long walks.

- Walkers should bring binoculars, walking boots, a lightweight waterproof jacket, a compass and a basic medical kit.

- Divers should bring their certification and log, as well as any equipment they want to use for diving.

- Even nondivers will save money and time bringing their own mask, snorkel and flippers so they can dive right in and start exploring.

- Everyone should bring flip flops, a sun hat and good sunglasses with UV protection.

- Bring a driving licence if you want to hire a car and travel insurance details to know what activities are and aren't included in your policy.

to at least €60. These costs are calculated on the basis of two people sharing a room; single travellers will need to budget extra. Travellers interested in three-, four- and five-star hotels should consider booking at discounted rates through a travel agent or online. Most resorts now include half-board meal plans. Figure anything between €90 and €650 per person.

## Réunion

Prices in Réunion are roughly similar to those found in mainland France. The absolute minimum daily budget, possible if you're staying in the cheapest guesthouses and eating takeaway meals or self-catering, will be €40 per person on the basis of two people sharing a room. For a reasonably comfortable midrange hotel, with a light lunch and dinner in a decent restaurant, you're looking at around €70 to €100 per person.

## Seychelles

Visitors to the Seychelles on a tight budget will struggle to get by on less than €80 per person per day (on the basis of two people sharing a room in a guesthouse or self-contained bungalow), without excursions and activities. A more realistic budget, allowing you to stay at a moderately priced hotel and treat yourself to a few good restaurants, will come in at around €100 to €150 per person per day. Living it up in a top-end resort will usually cost at least €250 per person per day, but will shoot up very quickly with meals and activities. Island hopping and indulging in excursions and other activities also jacks up costs considerably.

## TRAVELLING RESPONSIBLY

As well as creating much of the region's wealth, tourism has cost local people and, most particularly, the local environment dearly. Worst affected are the coasts and particularly the fringing lagoon, where areas of the coral reef and the fragile marine environment are seriously degraded. The sheer number of tourists also makes extra demands on water supplies, electricity and other resources; creates problems of waste management; and puts more vehicles on the roads.

The good news is that all three countries are now taking these problems seriously and generally as a result development has been curtailed to a more considered pace. Ecotourism has been expanded enormously too, although in many places it is more of a buzzword than anything particularly beneficial to the environment.

Not that tourism can be blamed for all of the region's environmental woes of course, but there are positive steps that we as individual travellers can take to lessen our impact on the environment (see the boxed text, p21).

For further guidelines regarding the underwater world see the boxed text, p35; for tips on low-impact hiking, see the boxed text, p248.

## TRAVEL LITERATURE

There's a surprisingly small amount of literature about each island, although there are definitely some interesting writings available if you persevere. Bernardin de St-Pierre's 1773 *Journey to Mauritius* describes Mauritius in its early colonial period, complete with a horrendous account of the treatment of slaves, the experience of which would inform Bernardin de St-Pierre's later works, including his classic *Paul and Virginie* (1787), the now deeply unfashionable love story of two young French émigrés brought up in Mauritius (see the boxed text, p131).

A more recent addition to the writing about the island is Patrick O'Brian's enjoyable historical novel *The Mauritius Command* (1977), a swashbuckling

---

**HOW MAURI**

Scuba dive Rs

Meal in an upma restaurant Rs 1000

Car hire per day Rs 95

One night in a *chambre d'hôte* on Rodrigues Rs 1500

A six-pack of Phoenix beer Rs 320

---

**HOW MUCH IN SEYCHELLES?**

One night in a swish resort -- the sky's the limit

Local bus ride €0.50

Boat excursion €110

One dive €50

Bottle of Seybrew beer €1.50

---

**HOW MUCH IN RÉUNION?**

Tandem flight paragliding in St-Leu €75

Car hire per week €220

Stodgy *carri* (curry) €10

One night in a *chambre d'hôte* (double) €45

Glass of local rum €3

adventure in the Aubrey-Maturin series, which sees Captain Jack Aubrey sent on a mission to rid Mauritius and Réunion of the French during the Napoleonic Wars. It's considered by some to be the best of the entire Aubrey-Maturin series.

In his funny and informative book *Golden Bats & Pink Pigeons*, naturalist Gerald Durrell tells of his time spent rescuing a number of Mauritian species from the brink of extinction. Durrell was too late for the dodo, but Errol Fuller does the bird proud with his comprehensive and quirky *Dodo: From Extinction to Icon*, which covers the history and the myths surrounding this endearing creature.

# TOP 10                                    MAURITIUS

## BEACHES IN THE REGION

Competition is stiff in this department. Here's a list of our favourites.

1 Anse Source d'Argent, La Digue, Seychelles (p302)

2 Anse Lazio, Praslin, Seychelles (p295)

3 Anse Intendance, Mahé, Seychelles (p291)

4 Baie Laraie, Curieuse, Seychelles (p297)

5 Étang-Salé-les-Bains, Réunion (p199)

6 L'Hermitage-les-Bains, Réunion (p189)

7 Eastern Beaches, Rodrigues (p135)

8 Île aux Cerfs, Mauritius (p130)

9 Pointe d'Esny, Mauritius (p118)

10 Île Plate, Mauritius (p86)

## FESTIVALS & EVENTS

Festivals in the Indian Ocean are always spectacular and often unusual. For other events, see Festivals & Events in the individual country directories.

1 Teemeedee – December and January, Mauritius (p152) and Réunion (p236)

2 Maha Shivaratri – February or March, Grand Bassin (p109)

3 National Day – 12 March, Mauritius (p153)

4 FetAfrik – May, Mahé, Seychelles (p314)

5 Independence Day – 29 June, Seychelles (p314)

6 Sakifo – August, St-Pierre (p261)

7 Festival Kreol – last week in October, Seychelles (p314)

8 Divali (Dipavali) – late October or early November, Réunion (p236) and Mauritius (p152)

9 Grand Raid – October or November, Réunion (p262)

10 Abolition of Slavery Day – 20 December; Réunion (p262)

## GREEN FORAYS

Go slow, go green and buzz sustainable in these havens off the tourist track.

1 Îlet des Salazes, Réunion (p205)

2 Cirque de Mafate, Réunion (p212)

3 Grand Bassin, Réunion (p213)

4 Rivière des Remparts, Réunion (p228)

5 Morne Seychellois National Park, Seychelles (p287)

6 Cousin Island, Seychelles (p297)

7 Bird Island, Seychelles (p308)

8 South Coast, Mauritius (p121)

9 Black River Gorges National Park, Mauritius (p107)

10 François Leguat, Rodrigues (p137)

**TIPS FOR RESPONSIBLE TRAVEL**

■ Be careful not to damage coral reefs when diving or snorkelling.

■ Never buy souvenirs made from materials such as turtleshell, seashells or coral.

■ Never drop litter anywhere and bring a bag to pick up any litter left by less considerate people.

■ Buy locally made produce, souvenirs and other day-to-day objects whenever possible.

■ Don't light fires and be very careful when disposing of cigarette butts, particularly during droughts or the dry season.

An unusual book about Réunion's social history is Françoise Verges' *Monsters and Revolutionaries*, which looks at the complex relationship between the colonisers and colonised on the island through a number of different prisms.

Seychelles travel lit is best represented by Athol Thomas' *Forgotten Eden*. Though written in the 1960s and now out of print (but available as an ebook), it still paints a vivid picture of the beauty and magic of these islands.

*Beyond the Reefs* by William Travis takes a look back at the Seychelles of the 1970s, before conservation issues came to the fore, when Travis saw plenty of action as a shark fisher and latter-day adventurer.

*Empires of the Monsoon* by Richard Hall is the most informative and entertaining history of the Indian Ocean. It only touches briefly on Mauritius, Réunion and the Seychelles, but it does place them in a broader context.

## INTERNET RESOURCES

**Lonely Planet** (www.lonelyplanet.com) Summaries on travel to Mauritius, Réunion and the Seychelles; the Thorn Tree forum; travel news and links to useful travel resources.

**Mauritius Government Portal** (www.gov.mu) This huge and multifaceted site contains all the information you could ever need about Mauritius including a huge selection of links.

**Mauritius Tourism Promotion Authority** (www.tourism-mauritius.mu) Has a great selection of hotels, activities and other useful information including plenty of ecotourism suggestions.

**Réunion Tourisme** (www.reunion.fr) Réunion's official tourist website is an encyclopedia of things to see and do.

**Seychelles.com** (www.seychelles.com) Official home of the Seychelles Tourism Board, this website overflows with great tips and ideas.

**Nature Seychelles** (www.natureseychelles.org) An excellent resource for anyone interested in environment-related matters and conservation issues in the Seychelles.

# Itineraries

## CLASSIC ROUTES

### JAUNT AROUND MAURITIUS                                            Two Weeks

Start near the airport along the stunning sands of **Pointe d'Esny** (p118). Snorkel through the sparkling azure lagoon at **Blue Bay** (p118), eco-explore **Île aux Aigrettes** (p118), then slip up to sleepy **Mahébourg** (p113) for the Monday market.

Drive north along the coast. Embrace the fisherman lifestyle in **Trou d'Eau Douce** (p128) then glide through the crystal lagoon to **Île aux Cerfs** (p130).

Pass through the endless acreage of sky-reaching sugarcane before emerging on the north coast to take in the views at **Cap Malheureux** (p94). Hop on a catamaran bound for the scenic **northern islands** (p86) then treat yourself to a round of repasts in lively **Grand Baie** (p88).

The wonderfully chaotic streets of **Port Louis** (p64) are next on the itinerary. Then head south through urban sprawl that stretches along the **Central Plateau** (p73).

Emerge on the west coast for a spot of diving in **Flic en Flac** (p119) then base yourself around **Black River** (p103). From here, there are plenty of exhilarating options to get the blood flowing: canyoning through the **Black River Gorges** (p107), biking in **Chamarel** (p108) or climbing the iconic **Morne Brabant** (p112). Don't miss a morning of dolphin-watching just off the coast of **Tamarin** (p104).

**The two-week circuit of Mauritius will take you to sun-drenched beaches, botanical gardens, idyllic islands and lively market towns, all packed into just 300km.**

## TOUR OF RÉUNION                                          Two Weeks

In two weeks, you can loop around the island, take a couple of jaunts into the interior and even visit a volcano.

Spend the first day sampling the infamous nightlife of **St-Gilles-les-Bains** (p189) before heading to the beach to recover at **L'Hermitage-les-Bains** (p189). Allow three days to make the most of the area's botanical gardens, museums and water sports.

Head next to the **Cirque de Cilaos** (p202), where you should allow at least two days to soak up the rugged mountain scenery and the laid-back atmosphere.

The volcano awaits at **Piton de la Fournaise** (p217). Base yourself at the Gîte du Volcan, ready to make a dawn ascent for stunning views.

Next make for the bright lights of **St-Pierre** (p220) – if possible, get here for the huge Saturday market and stay the night near **St-Joseph** (p227). Don't miss **Ste-Rose** (p239), where lava laps at the door of a church and narrowly misses the Virgin Mary.

As you head back to the north of the island, go inland and stay at least two nights in **Hell-Bourg** (p210), exploring the **Cirque de Salazie** (p209). Finally, set off towards the capital via the Indian-influenced **St-André** (p235) and end your trip sampling cafe-culture and Creole architecture in the capital, **St-Denis** (p176).

From sophisticated beach resorts to mountain villages, art galleries to volcanoes, two weeks is perfect to sample the variety Réunion has to offer. Get hooked on the hiking, and you could easily fill a month. This tour covers around 400km.

## ESSENTIAL SEYCHELLES                                    Two Weeks

Two weeks is fine for a taster of the Seychelles' islands – allowing plenty of time for enjoying the very best of the country's superb beaches.

On the first day, tune into island life in the capital, **Victoria** (p279), checking out the market and strolling among the palm trees in the botanical gardens. Move on to **Beau Vallon** (p283), where three days can easily be spent messing around in and on the water – schedule in a day's diving or a boat trip to **Ste Anne Marine National Park** (p288). Devote the next two days to the beaches and byways of **Mahé** (p279), and walking in the **Morne Seychellois National Park** (p287).

Next, cruise over to **Praslin** (p294). Ogle curvaceous coco-de-mer nuts in the **Vallée de Mai** (p295), before flaking out on the perfect, sugar-white sands at **Anse Lazio** (p295). Fill the next four days with snorkelling, diving and swimming off **Anse Volbert** (p295), getting up close and personal with giant tortoises on **Curieuse Island** (p297) and walking among cacophonous clouds of sea birds on **Cousin Island** (p297).

From Praslin, make sail for **La Digue** (p302). Three days is the perfect amount of time to lapse into La Digue's slow vibe. Visit **Anse Source d'Argent** (p302) – the archetypal paradise beach. Get there late afternoon for the best atmosphere. Take a snorkelling trip around nearby islands, then find solitude on the beaches of **Grand Anse** (p302) and **Petite Anse** (p303). All too soon, it will be time to tear yourself away for the trip back to Victoria.

**In just 200km and two weeks, this tour will cover the three main islands and a smattering of satellite islands, plus a sampler of marine parks, bird reserves and native forests. There's even time for boat trips and water sports.**

# ROADS LESS TRAVELLED

## RODRIGUES – THE OTHER MAURITIUS          One Week

Some call Rodrigues a mini-Mauritius, even though it's different in almost every way. What they really mean is that this is the closest you can get to what Mauritius was like before tourism took off, with an almost total lack of development compared to the mainland, and few tourists make it out this far on the 1½-hour flight into the Indian Ocean. A week is ample time to discover the delights of this small, mountainous island. Depending on the weather you can divide the days between walking, diving and taking boat trips to nearby islands.

First, though, spend half a day strolling the streets of **Port Mathurin** (p137). The island's endearingly sleepy 'capital' springs into life on Saturday morning when it seems the entire population descends for the weekly market.

The classic coastal hike starts at **St François** (p139), then heads south via a gem of a beach at **Trou d'Argent** (p139) to **Graviers** (p139), from where there are buses back to Port Mathurin.

You're spoilt for choice when it comes to diving. Top spots include the channel off St François, **La Passe St François** (p30), on the edge of the lagoon, with more options beyond the reefs. As for boat trips, first choice should be **Île aux Cocos** (p137) for its wealth of birdlife. There's good snorkelling around the little-visited **Île aux Chats** and **Île Hermitage** (p137) off the south coast.

On your last day, treat yourself to a seafood feast at one of the great family-run restaurants scattered around the island.

Leave behind the commercialism of Mauritius' main island for a week to discover a more traditional way of life among the fishing and agricultural communities of Rodrigues. Divers are in for a treat, too, exploring the underwater world of the massive, encircling lagoon.

## RÉUNION'S SUD SAUVAGE        One Week

Réunion's 'Wild South' offers volcanic landscapes, massive ravines, wave-lashed cliffs and sensational hiking trails. You can discover the best of the region in a reasonably leisurely week.

Start at **Ste-Rose** (p239) and head south to find the first tongues of lava tumbling down to the sea. Pay a quick visit to the **Vierge au Parasol** (p240) before crossing the threatening lava fields of **Le Grand Brûlé** (p232), to spend a night or two near **St-Philippe** (p231) or **St-Joseph** (p227); stay up in the hills for a real taste of rural life. From here you can visit a spice garden, learn about vanilla and local crafts or hike the spectacular **Rivière des Remparts** (p228).

Pass quickly through **St-Pierre** (p220) en route to the high plateau of **Plaine-des-Cafres** (p214) to visit the **Maison du Volcan** (p215). Take the magnificent forest road up to **Piton de la Fournaise** (p217), Réunion's restless volcano. Climb to the top at the crack of dawn to leave the crowds behind.

Now drop back down to Plaine-des-Cafres, where you could spend a couple of days hiking to **Grand Bassin** (p215), a village at the end of the world. Finally, head for **Plaine-des-Palmistes** (p218), where the hikes through the **Forêt de Bébour-Bélouve** (p219) and to **Trou de Fer** (p220) provide unforgettable experiences.

**This one-week tour of southern Réunion takes you across lava fields, past breathtaking coastal scenery and up a volcano to gaze into the jaws of the giant. It ends 200km later among the quiet rural villages of the high plains.**

# TAILORED TRIPS

## THE ADRENALIN RUSH

Réunion rightly markets itself as the 'intense isle'; almost every conceivable stomach-churning, heart-pumping activity is on offer. With a bit of planning – and a fair amount of cash – adventure sports enthusiasts can test their stamina in an action-packed week. Check your insurance policy, take a deep breath and go for it!

Kick off day one in **St-Gilles-les-Bains** (p202) with an ear-popping helicopter ride, ducking and weaving around the three Cirques. On landing, hotfoot it up to **Le Maïdo** (p187), grab a mountain bike and hurtle down to the coast again along vertiginous biking trails.

Later that day push on to **Cilaos** (p204). Make a crack-of-dawn start to scale the almost vertical **Piton des Neiges** (p206); to really enjoy the experience, spread the climb over two days. On day four, there's a choice between slithering down canyons, bouncing down rivers on a raft or galloping amid forests and pastures in the Hautes Plaines in Réunion's heartland.

At the end of day four, head for **St-Leu** (p195). Spend days five and six swooping high above the lagoon by paraglider, plunging off the reef to scuba dive with sharks, or surfing the world-famous left-hander – La Gauche de St-Leu – at the mouth of the **Ravine des Colimaçons** (p196); less-experienced surfers will find thrills and spills aplenty riding the area's quieter waves.

Day seven? Definitely the day of rest!

## DIVER'S & SNORKELLER'S DELIGHT

You could spend a lifetime diving the reefs and granite outcrops of the Seychelles, but a week is enough time to sample a range of sites, including some of the very best in the Indian Ocean.

Jump in at the deep end at **Shark Bank** (p33) off the northwest coast of **Mahé** (p33). No prizes for guessing what's in store here: sharks aplenty with their stingray sidekicks, barracuda and other bruisers. Off Mahé's north tip, **Îlot** (p33) offers an unbelievable variety of smaller fish in shimmering shoals. Nearby, **Brissare Rocks** (p33) is ablaze with fire coral.

On day four, head over to **Praslin** (p33) for a change of scene. The waters around **Curieuse Island** (p297) are teeming with fish life in dazzling, dizzying displays.

Spend your last day exploring the islands northwest of **La Digue** (p33). The rock formations around **Île Cocos** (p304), **Marianne** (p34) and the sisters, **Petite** and **Grande Sœur** (p304), are out of this world. Marine turtles are common, while stingrays, eagle rays and reef sharks add a touch of spice. Even the odd manta and whale shark cruise through from time to time.

# Diving in Mauritius, Réunion & Seychelles

A growing number of travellers come to the Indian Ocean for the mother lode of dive sites, and justifiably so. Though largely overshadowed by the iconic Maldives, scuba diving in Mauritius, Réunion and Seychelles is increasingly popular. Beneath the clear turquoise waters is a trove of unbelievable riches: rainbow-coloured fish and large pelagic species (and yes, sharks are part of the package!), a dramatic seascape, a few wrecks and a host of drop-offs and reefs. It's not the cheapest place on earth to dive (Thailand or the Red Sea it ain't) but it's a great place to learn, and in turn love, scuba diving. Good news: bar a few areas, the dive sites are never crowded.

The dive sites presented here (see the relevant regional maps for their location) are only a sampling of hundreds of sites available.

**HOW MUCH?**

Introductory dive: €40-65

Single dive: €40-65 (including equipment rental)

Open Water certification course: €300-450

## MAURITIUS

So, you want variety? Abundant marine life, dramatic seascapes, atmospheric wrecks – Mauritius has it all, not to mention well-established, high-quality dive operators. Mauritius is almost entirely surrounded by a barrier reef, within which turquoise lagoons provide great possibilities for snorkellers, swimmers and novice divers. And there is the pièce de résistance: Rodrigues, which has virgin sites and outstanding fish life.

### Dive Sites

#### THE NORTH

The north coast is a magnet for divers of all levels, and it's no wonder – there's a good balance of thrilling dives, wrecks, drop-offs and easy dives.

The islands off the coast (Île Plate, Coin de Mire) are the main highlights, with splendid sites and diverse fish life – not to mention a sense of wilderness. **La Fosse aux Requins** will make your spine tingle. On the northwestern side of Île Plate, a bowl-shaped basin carved into the cliff is home to an eerie concentration of blacktip sharks (numbering from five to about 30 on certain days) that keep swirling around. Why? Possibly because the waters here are rich in oxygen thanks to the swell. Good news for novice divers in search of excitement: this shallow dive (12m) is accessible with an Open Water certificate, though the current can be a bit tricky. One proviso: the encounter with the sharks is probable but cannot be guaranteed!

Coin de Mire is another diver's treat, with a few stunning drop-offs – we recommend **Carpenters** and the aptly named **The Wall**. Both have fairly good coral formations and tons of fish life. Near the Wall, the shipwreck **Djabeda** is a former Japanese freighter that was scuttled in 1998 in 30m. It's more atmospheric than fishy.

To the northwest, Trou aux Biches is the main jumping-off point to a variety of superb dives. Be sure to fill your logbook with **Holt's Rock** (also known as Stenopus), which features two rocky domes and big boulders; **Lobster Rock**, in about 20m, geared to novice divers; and **Tombant de la Pointe aux Canonniers**, between Holt's Rock and Lobster Rock, suitable for experienced divers, with an exhilarating drop-off that tumbles from 32m to about 60m. Other reputable walls in the area: **Caravelle**, **Corsaire Wall** and **Kingfish**, all embellished with black coral and seafans. In the mood for wrecks? Make a beeline for **Waterlily** and **Emily**, as well as the photogenic, 45m-long **Stella Maru**, all of which are accessible to novice divers.

See under the various Activities headings in the North Mauritius section (p78) for local dive centres.

## THE WEST

The Flic en Flac area ranks among the best in Mauritius when it comes to diving. Conditions are optimal year-round – it's protected from the prevailing winds – and visibility is usually excellent. We can't gush enough about **Rempart Serpent** (Snake Rampart), possibly the quirkiest dive in Mauritius. Located a 15-minute boat trip from Flic en Flac, it takes its name from the sinuous rock lying about 25m below the surface, which attracts perhaps the greatest concentration in the world of weird and wonderful scorpion fish, stonefish, moray eels and lionfish. Another fave is **La Cathédrale**, with a memorable seascape – think a warren of cavelets, stipples, passages and ledges. It's full of reef species, including fusiliers, surgeonfish, groupers, snappers, angelfish and lobsters. One downside: it's so popular that it's fairly congested. **Couline Bambou** and **Manioc** are less crowded but no less attractive.

Wreck fans will be spoiled here too, with a handful of atmospheric wrecks, including the **Kei Sei 113**, scuttled in the 1980s. Resting at about 35m, it's accessible to seasoned divers only. Beginners might try the **Tug II**, a 20m-long tugboat scuttled in 1981 that sits on the sand in about 20m. It's now home to thousands of colourful fish. Hint: lie without moving on the sandy bottom and you'll see swaying conger eels slip down into their burrows.

And the southwest coast? The area between Le Morne Peninsula and Rivière Noire (Black River) has a few diving hot spots, including the fishy **Passe St Jacques** and **Casiers**. The weak points are the average visibility and the fairly dull topography.

See p99 for local dive centres.

## THE SOUTHEAST

Off the southeast coast it's the dramatic underwater terrain that impresses more than anything, making for unique profiles. You'll be rewarded with a profusion of caves, tunnels and giant arches – it's very scenic – as well as large numbers of pelagics thrown in for good measure. The hitch? From June to August most sites are exposed to the prevailing winds – expect choppy seas in rough weather.

**Colorado** is the magic mantra. As befits its name, this site looks like an underwater version of the famous American valley. This 400m-long canyon is peppered with chasms, tunnels, crevices and boulders where masses of lobsters, jacks, groupers and barracuda seek shelter. Another must-dive is **Roches Zozo**, close to Colorado. It features a huge rock that rises from the sea-

Don't worry too muc... about the effects of th... 2004 tsunami – most sites in Mauritius, Réunion and the Seychelles are not coral dives.

---

### THE FIRST TIME

You've always fancied venturing underwater on scuba? Now's your chance. Mauiltius, Réunion and the Seychelles are perfect starting points for new divers, as the warm waters and shallow reefs are a forgiving training environment. Most dive centres offer courses for beginners and employ experienced instructors.

Just about anyone in reasonably good health can sign up for an introductory dive (from €40), including children aged eight and over. It typically takes place in shallow (3m to 5m) water and lasts about 30 minutes. It's escorted by a divemaster.

If you choose to enrol in an Open Water course, count on it taking about four days, including a few classroom lectures and open-water training. Once you're certified, your C-card is valid permanently and recognised all over the world.

bed to about 12m, pocked with crevices where lobsters hide. To the south, **Grotte Langouste** is a cave brimming with lobsters.

Wreck buffs will explore the **Sirius**, a 19th-century vessel that rests in the 20m range off Mahébourg, but it's not in good shape.

For beginners, **Blue Bay** is a safe, lovely spot to learn to dive, with a parade of reef fish to be observed on the sprawling reef. Blue Bay is the only place in Mauritius where you'll find patches of thriving coral.

See p119 for local dive centres.

### THE EAST

There is a fantastic parade of pelagic and reef fish to be observed in the **Belmar Pass**. Strong tidal currents push the deep water back and forth through the passage, providing nutrients for a staggering array of species. The seascape is another draw; the passage is peppered with numerous chasms, gullies, coral canyons and sandy valleys. Sharks, especially bull sharks and grey sharks, regularly patrol the area. There are at least five different sites in the Passe.

Towards the south, off Trou d'Eau Douce, the **Passe de Trou d'Eau Douce** is another worthwhile site, though it's less spectacular than Passe de Belle Mare. It's usually done as a drift dive.

See p131 for local dive centres.

Before embarking on a scuba-diving trip, be sure to obtain reliable information about the physical and environmental conditions of the dive site and dive only at sites within your realm of experience.

### RODRIGUES

This is the Indian Ocean at its best. A true gem, Rodrigues boasts numerous untouched sites for those willing to experience something different. There's a profusion of coral that you won't see anywhere else in Mauritius, and the density of fish life is astounding. The underwater scenery is another pull, with a smorgasbord of canyons, arches and caves.

Rodrigues' signature dives include **La Passe St François** and **Le Canyon**, off the east coast. La Passe St François is a kilometre-long channel teeming with tuna, unicorn fish, groupers, turtles, rays and jacks (of the *Caranx ignobilis* variety) the size of a small car. Le Canyon is a truly atmospheric dive site – you'll dive in a canyon that runs under the reef, with openings that allow beams of sunlight to pass through. If you're after Tolkienesque scenery, ask for **La Basilique**, which is like an underwater medieval castle carved into the reef, full of galleries, faults and archways (but no coral). **Karlanne** is another hot favourite, offering dense marine life and healthy coral formations, especially those of the *Acropora* and *Porites* genuses.

The south coast has its fair share of thrilling dives, too. Most sites are in the area of **La Grande Passe**. To say it's fishy is an understatement, and you don't need to go below 20m to admire the full gamut of reef species.

See p140 for local dive centres.

## Practicalities

In Mauritius, look out for the *Field Guide to Corals of Mauritius* by Ruby Moothien Pillay, Hiroaki Terashima, Atmanun Venkatasami and Hiro'omi Uchida. In Réunion, look out for *Fonds Sous-Marins de l'Île de la Réunion* by Eric Dutrieux (in French).

### DIVING CONDITIONS

Although Mauritius is diveable year-round, the most favourable periods are October to December, March and April (January and February are peak months for cyclone activity). During July and August, when the southeast trade winds are at their strongest, the seas are too rough and murky for diving all along the east coast and around Rodrigues. Visibility is heavily weather dependent and thus varies a lot – from a low of 10m at certain sites at certain periods of the year to 40m at others.

Current conditions vary a lot, from imperceptible to powerful. Water temperatures range from a low of 22°C in August to a high of 28°C between December and February.

## DIVE OPERATORS

There are at least 40 professional dive centres in Mauritius. Most belong to the **Mauritius Scuba Diving Association** (MSDA; ☎ 454 0011; www.msda.mu), which is affiliated with CMAS and makes regular and rigorous checks. Most dive centres are also affiliated with one or more of the internationally recognised certifying agencies, usually PADI or CMAS. Many dive centres in Mauritius are hotel-based, but they all welcome walk-in clients. In general, you can expect well-maintained equipment, good facilities and professional staff, but standards may vary from one centre to another, so it pays to shop around.

## RÉUNION

Who said that diving in Réunion wasn't interesting? OK, the island is mostly famous for its trekking options, but it shouldn't be sneezed at. You'll be positively surprised: there's a wide choice of shallow dives inside the lagoon for novices and deeper dives (mostly 25m to 40m) just outside for more experienced divers, as well as a few purpose-sunk wrecks thrown in for good measure.

### Dive Sites

Most dive sites are located off the west coast between Boucan Canot and Grand Bois.

#### ST-GILLES-LES-BAINS

If you want relaxed diving, St-Gilles will appeal to you. Diving here is focused on the reefs, which slope gently away in a series of valleys to a sandy bottom in about 25m – very reassuring. Pelagics are rare, but small reef species are prolific.

Colourful sites such as **Tour de Boucan** and **Le Pain de Sucre**, none of which are deeper than 20m, offer great opportunities off Boucan Canot. The setting is the strong point, with a contoured terrain and lots of small critters in the recesses (damselfish, parrotfish, triggerfish, lobsters), as well as a few seafans. On **Petites Gorgones** (also known as Saliba), keep an eye out for leaf scorpion fishes and turtles. Straight off L'Hermitage-les-Bains, **La Passe de L'Hermitage** is an exciting dive. The terrain is nicely sculpted, with little canyons and large boulders that act as magnets for a wealth of species. Sadly, visibility is often reduced.

If you have a hankering for wrecks, the **Haï Siang** (maximum depth 55m) and the **Navarra** (maximum depth 55m) will keep you entertained, though at such depths they are accessible to very experienced divers only. Novice divers will head to **La Barge**, off St-Paul, a relaxing wreck dive in less than 22m. See p189 for local dive centres.

#### ST-LEU

St-Leu features splendid wall diving and good coral fields. Here walls tumble steeply to several dozen metres. Be sure to bookmark **Tombant de la Pointe au Sel**, south of St-Leu, which is widely regarded as Réunion's best all-round dive site. In addition to great scenery, this stunning drop-off offers a fabulous array of fish life and seldom fails to produce good sightings of pelagics, especially tuna, barracuda and jacks, as well as hammerhead sharks between October and November.

**Les Pyramides** is another stunner, with two seamounts rising from 70m to 38m. For novices, nothing can beat the very secure yet atmospheric **Le Jardin des Kiosques**, with a depth ranging from 3m to 18m. It's all about little canyons and grooves. Another relaxing site, **La Maison Verte** is blessed with good coral formations.

For identification of tropical fish and corals, refer to *Reef Fishes & Corals* and *More Reef Fishes & Nudibranchs* by Dennis King, or the *Indian Ocean Reef Guide* by Helmut Debelius.

Wreck enthusiasts will enjoy the **Antonio Lorenzo**, a well-preserved vessel that rests in about 35m on a sandy bottom off Pointe des Chateaux. Fish life is not dynamic – it's the ambience that's the pull.

Whales can be seen cruising past the area from October to November. See p195 for local dive centres.

### ST-PIERRE

Savvy divers, this area is for you. It's unhyped and that's why we enjoy it so much. There are a host of untouched sites between St-Pierre and Grand Bois. The main drawcard here is the topography, with numerous ridges, canyons and drop-offs. Sites well worth bookmarking include **Petit Tombant Très Poissonneux, Japonicus, Demotel** and **Cap Thérèse**, to name a few.

See p222 for the local dive centre.

## Practicalities

### DIVING CONDITIONS

While it is possible to dive all year, the best time is October to April, when the water is at its warmest (about 28°C). However, you might want to avoid February through March, which is the cyclone season. Water temperatures can drop to about 21°C in August.

### DIVE OPERATORS

The dive centres are concentrated around St-Gilles-les-Bains, St-Leu and St-Pierre. The standard of diving facilities is high. You'll find professional dive centres staffed with qualified instructors catering to divers of all levels. Staff members usually speak English. Most dive centres are affiliated with PADI, SSI or CMAS – all internationally recognised dive organisations.

Take note that a simple medical certificate stating you are fit enough to dive is compulsory for diving in France. You can get one from your doctor in your home country or have it faxed or emailed to the dive centre. Otherwise, you can get one from any doctor in Réunion (€23).

## SEYCHELLES

The Seychelles is sure to elicit strong emotions. Billed as one of the Indian Ocean's great diving destinations, it almost rivals the Maldives, though it's

---

### SNORKELLING

If the idea of total immersion doesn't appeal to you, snorkelling is possible in the three countries. It's a great way to explore the underwater world with minimal equipment and without the costs associated with diving. Even the shallowest reefs are home to many colourful critters. In all three destinations, rental gear is widely available from dive centres.

In Mauritius, top spots include the marine park at Blue Bay and along the west coast off Flic en Flac and Trou aux Biches, not forgetting the lagoon around Rodrigues. Companies running trips on glass-bottomed boats will often include snorkelling in the deal.

In Réunion, the lagoon along the west coast between St-Gilles-les-Bains and La Saline-les-Bains offers great snorkelling, with particularly good marine life off L'Hermitage-les-Bains. Take advice before leaping in as the currents can be dangerous.

In the Seychelles, the sheltered lagoons provide safe havens for swimming and snorkelling. The Ste Anne and Port Launay Marine National Parks are firm favourites in the waters around Mahé. In September and October, divers have a chance to snorkel alongside whale sharks. Around Praslin, try off Anse Lazio and Anse Volbert beaches, or take a boat trip from Anse Volbert to St Pierre islet. Close to La Digue, the submerged granite boulders around Coco, Grande Sœur and Marianne islands are teeming with fish life.

much less hyped – all the better for you. Good news: you don't need to be a strong diver – there are sites for all levels.

There's excellent diving off Mahé, Praslin and La Digue, the three main islands, as well as off the other inner islands. The strong point is the underwater scenery, complete with big granite boulders and seamounts – it's as atmospheric as on land. If you have the chance to embark on a live-aboard, you'll dive the outer island.

## Dive Sites

### MAHÉ

If you are based in the north, whet your appetite with **Shark Bank**, Mahé's signature dive, for experienced divers only. As the name suggests, sharks are a fairly common sight around this 30m-tall granite plateau 9km off Beau Vallon (Mahé) – they're generally reef sharks, but you may also see whale sharks between February and November. Expect to encounter brissant rays the size of Mini Mokes, eagle rays, barracuda, batfish and teeming yellow snapper and big-eyes. The plateau is covered with bright orange sponges and white gorgonians. There is nearly always a strong current at this site. **Îlot** is a granite outcrop just off north Mahé which consists of several large boulders topped by a tuft of palm trees. The current in the channel can be quite strong, but the cluster of boulders yields one of the highest densities of fish life in the Seychelles. Golden cup coral festoons the canyons and gullies, and gorgonians and other soft corals abound. You're sure to see yellow-spotted burr fish, turtles, anemones and clownfish, peppered moray eels, Spanish dancer nudibranchs and thousands of hingeback shrimps. Îlot is about a 15-minute boat ride from Beau Vallon. It's suitable for all levels of divers. About 5km north of Mahé, and accessed from Beau Vallon, **Brissare Rocks** is another granite pinnacle. The site features abundant fire coral and great concentrations of yellow snapper, wrasse, parrotfish and fusiliers, as well as groupers and eagle rays. Reef sharks and whale sharks are also known to visit the area. The Baie Ternay Marine National Park and the Ste Anne Marine National Park also offer great opportunities for experienced divers and novices alike.

If you need a break from offshore dives, a few shipwrecks will keep you happy, including the **Twin Barges**, which sit upright on the seabed in about 20m in Beau Vallon bay. A hot favourite used to be the **Ennerdale**, a massive 216m-long vessel sunk in 1970 on a sandbank, to the northeast, but local dive centres now seem to prefer the **Aldebaran**, which was recently scuttled and is much more easily accessible.

If you're based in the southwest, you'll probably have the following sites on your menu:

**Alice in Wonderland** Famous for its healthy coral formations.

**Intendance Rock** Same features as Jailhouse Rock.

**Jailhouse Rock** A high-voltage drift dive for experienced divers. Prolific fish life.

**Shark Point** Whitetips and grey reef sharks are commonly sighted here.

See p284 and p292 for local dive centres.

### PRASLIN & LA DIGUE

There are superb dive sites off Aride Island, including **Aride Bank**, which can be accessed from Praslin if you don't mind the tedious 30-minute boat trip to get to the sites. Closer to Praslin, approximately halfway between Aride and Praslin, **Booby Islet** is an exposed seamount that consistently sizzles with fish action.

Local divemasters also recommend the following sites:

**Anse Sévère** An easy site, close to the shore of La Digue.

**Ave Maria Rocks** A seamount northwest of La Digue. Noted for its shark sightings.

If you're a certified diver, don't forget to bring your C-card from a recognised scuba-diving instructional agency and your logbook with you.

**Cousin** An easy site.
**Marianne Island** An islet east of La Digue, famous for its dense fish life (including grey sharks) and contoured seascape.
**South Cousine Island** A dive site similar to Cousin.
**White Bank** About 200m west of Ave Maria Rocks. Stunning seascape (tunnels, arches) and prolific fish life, including shoals of jacks.

See p298 for local dive centres.

### OTHER INNER ISLANDS & OUTER ISLANDS

For wealthy divers, the private islands of Desroches, Frégate, North, Silhouette and Denis offer fantastic diving options, with absolutely pristine sites, and only one dive boat: yours. One step beyond, you'll find Aldabra, Cosmoledo and Astove, which are the stuff of legend. They feature the best sites in the eastern Indian Ocean, with electric fish action in a totally virgin territory and high-voltage drift dives. The catch? They were not accessible at the time of writing due to the presence of Somali pirates in the area. When the situation normalises, they will be served by one live-aboard, the **Indian Ocean Explorer** (www.ioexpl.com). Stay tuned.

> Make sure you allow 24 hours between diving and taking a flight, to minimise the risk of residual nitrogen in the blood that can cause decompression injury.

## Practicalities

### DIVING CONDITIONS

Diving in the Seychelles heavily hinges on the weather conditions, currents and direction of the wind, but it can be sampled over all of the seasons as there are always sheltered conditions. Dive sites are chosen according to the prevailing winds. The calmest seas are from April to May and October to November. Due to currents and wind, visibility is temperamental and can drop to 5m. But in normal conditions you can expect 25m.

### DIVE OPERATORS

The Seychelles' 15-odd diving centres have first-rate personnel and facilities. You'll find dive centres in Mahé, Praslin, La Digue, Ste Anne, Silhouette, Frégate, Denis, North and Desroches. Most centres are affiliated with PADI.

## MARINE LIFE

Let's be honest: the western Indian Ocean is not the richest marine realm in the world – some parts of the Caribbean, the South Pacific and the Red Sea boast more prolific fish life. But it's far from being poor – in fact, it has everything from tiny nudibranchs (sea slugs) to huge whale sharks. It's just a matter of quantities, not diversity.

Like technicolour critters? You'll encounter a dizzying array of reef species darting around the reef, including clownfish, parrotfish, angelfish, emperor-fish, butterfly-fish and various types of grouper. Moray eels are also frequently encountered.

Pelagic fish – larger beasts that live in the open sea, such as tuna and barracuda – sometimes cruise quite close to the reef in search of prey. Of the shark species inhabiting these waters, the most common are the whitetip reef shark, the hammerhead shark and the reasonably docile nurse shark.

The most common species of ray found around the Seychelles and Mauritius is the manta ray. One of the larger stingray species, often encountered at Shark Bank off Mahé, is the brissant (or round ribbon-tailed) ray. It can grow up to 2m across. The blue-spotted stingray is quite common in the sandy areas between the granite boulders of the Seychelles.

The best place to see turtles in the wild is the Seychelles, where there are a number of important breeding grounds for hawksbill and green turtles.

And coral? It's not the strongest point. The Indian Ocean's shallow-water reefs were badly hit by 'coral bleaching' in 1997 and 1998. In parts of the Seychelles, up to 90% of hard corals (the reef-building corals) were wiped out. They are still struggling, but there are encouraging signs of new growth. Fortunately, the fish and other reef creatures don't appear to have been affected.

## MARINE CONSERVATION

The main pressures on the marine environment are pollution, over-exploitation and inappropriate activities such as the use of drag anchors and explosives for fishing. In recent years Mauritius, Réunion and the Seychelles have introduced laws banning destructive practices, such as shell and coral collection, shark finning and spear-fishing. Each has also established marine reserves to protect at least some of their coral reefs. If you're willing to help, there are good volunteering opportunities, especially in Mauritius and the Seychelles.

> Coral bleaching is triggered by unnaturally high temperatures that cause the polyps to expel the symbiotic algae that give them their colour. If the temperature does not drop quickly enough, the coral eventually dies from the loss of the protective algae.

### Mauritius

The most active groups are the **Mauritius Marine Conservation Society** (MMCS; ☎ 696 5368; www.mmcs-ngo.org) and the **Mauritius Underwater Group** (MUG; ☎ 696 5368; www.mug.mu), both of which were founded by concerned local divers. They run education, research and monitoring programs, campaign for the control of water pollution and reef destruction and the installation of pavement mooring buoys, and have created artificial reefs (the wrecks along the west coast) to enhance the marine environment. Both groups are also pushing for more marine parks.

In Rodrigues, **Shoals** ( ☎ 831 1225; www.shoalsrodrigues.net) is campaigning for the installation of 'environmentally friendly' mooring buoys and working with local authorities to establish marine reserves as part of a sustainable fisheries project. It also runs volunteering programs.

Supported by the **Mauritius Scuba Diving Association** (MSDA; ☎ 454 0011; www.msda.mu), an increasing number of dive operators now regularly clean 'their' stretch of lagoon. If you find an operator polluting or destroying the reef, report it to the MSDA.

### Réunion

The **Association Parc Marin de la Réunion** ( ☎ 0262 34 64 44; http://parcmarin.chez.com, in French) is charged with managing and protecting the lagoon. After many years

---

### DIVING WITH A CONSCIENCE

Please consider the following tips when diving, to help preserve the ecology and beauty of reefs:

- Encourage dive operators to establish permanent moorings at appropriate dive sites.
- Practise and maintain proper buoyancy control.
- Avoid touching living marine organisms with your body and equipment.
- Take great care in underwater caves, as your air bubbles can damage fragile organisms.
- Minimise your disturbance of marine animals.
- Take home all your trash, and any litter you may find as well.
- Never stand on corals, even if they look solid and robust.
- Do not buy or collect seashells, or buy any seashell or turtleshell products.
- Dive with a local dive operator that follows high safety, ethical and professional standards.

According to the Convention on International Trade in Endangered Species (CITES), marine turtles are among the world's most endangered species, threatened by pollution and human exploitation. Their downfall has been their edible flesh and eggs, as well as their shell, which is used for jewellery and ornaments.

campaigning for the park to be upgraded to a nature reserve, it succeeded in early 2007 – the park's now a fully fledged nature reserve.

## Seychelles

The **Marine Conservation Society Seychelles** (MCSS; ☎ 713500; www.mcss.sc) monitors and promotes marine habitats and biodiversity. Current projects include whale-shark, turtle and coral-reef monitoring. Visitors are welcome to participate in the monitoring programs (see the website). To add to the fun, you can also adopt a whale shark or a turtle through MCSS.

**Nature Seychelles** ( ☎ 601100; www.natureseychelles.org) also works to improve biodiversity. Its conservation projects include the restoration of island ecosystems and a recent wide-reaching project to study the effects of coral bleaching on fish life.

**Seychelles Island Foundation** ( ☎ 321735; www.sif.sc) concentrates its efforts on studying and protecting Aldabra, a marine biodiversity hot spot.

TIM ROCK

# ACTIVITIES & ECOTOURISM

Sure, these divine islands strewn across the peacock-blue Indian Ocean were designed for lounging on a beach or luxuriating in sensuous nature. But we feel certain you didn't come all this way merely to rest on your elbows. When you've finished sipping your cocktail, you may want to get the blood flowing a little more. Hiking, diving, snorkelling and other adventure options are all readily available, with the added appeal of fantastic settings. Wildlife lovers will get a buzz too. A variety of charismatic species can easily be approached, especially in the Seychelles.

# Aquatic Delights

Consider diving and snorkelling anywhere in the Seychelles, Mauritius or Réunion to be nothing less than a privilege. Healthy reefs, canyonlike terrain, shallow shelves, exciting shipwrecks, seamounts and quick shoreline drop-offs give snorkellers and divers almost instant access to a variety of environments. The water is warm and clear, and teeming with life from the tiniest juvenile tropical to the largest pelagic creature.

REINHARD DIRSCHERL/PHOTOLIBRARY

Southeast of Mauritius, Blue Bay Marine Park (p118) offers fantastic snorkelling conditions. Imagine a huge swimming pool with pristine turquoise water dotted with a multitude of coral heads and a profusion of small reef fish.

### ❷ Shark Bank

Mahé's iconic dive is Shark Bank (p33), where (harmless!) reef sharks are a fairly common sight around a vast granite plateau in the Seychelles. Between February and November you may also spot a whale shark cruising by.

### ❸ Praslin & La Digue

There's a host of splendid dive sites between Praslin and La Digue in the Seychelles, but if it's fish action you're after, White Bank (p34) will top your wish list.

### ❹ St-Leu

Réunion is more famous for its hiking trails than its diving opportunities, but St-Leu, on the west coast, has some cracking sites. Tombant de la Pointe au Sel (p31) is especially good, with stunning underwater scenery and frequent sightings of pelagic fish.

### ❺ Rodrigues

Ah, Rodrigues (p135). So many good surprises below the surface. Dense fish life. Giant-sized jacks. Atmospheric sites. A dramatic seascape. Healthy coral formations. And no crowds. Top spots include La Basilique and Le Canyon.

### ❻ Flic en Flac

Diving at La Cathédrale (p29) off Flic en Flac, Mauritius, is an unforgettable experience. With its signature stone arches and cavern, this site has a highly aesthetic appeal.

### ❼ Île Cocos & St Pierre Islet

It's the dream Indian Ocean snapshot: two confetti islands marooned in azure waters. Easily accessed from Praslin in the Seychelles, St Pierre Islet (p298) offers tip-top conditions – it's gin-clear, bath-warm and packed with technicolour fish. North of La Digue, Île Cocos (p304) is equally impressive.

# Hiking

Crisscrossed with a fabulous network of paths ranging from simple nature trails to more challenging itineraries, Réunion has all the flavours of superlative hiking. Mauritius and Rodrigues also boast excellent walking options. The biggest surprise? The Seychelles. On top of world-renowned beaches, this archipelago offers divine coastal ambles and lovely jungle walks.

JEAN-BERNARD CARILLET     JEAN-BERNARD CARILLET

### ❶ Coastal Walks

On La Digue in the Seychelles you can walk to Anse Marron (p304), a beach few people know exist. If there's more than a handful of people here, register a complaint. On Rodrigues, you can follow the coast to the beach at Trou d'Argent (p139)

### ❷ Nature Walks in the Morne Seychellois National Park

The best way to experience the most secretive parts of the Seychelles' Mahé is on foot. Take a guided walk in the jungly Morne Seychellois National Park (p289) and say hello to the cute *Sooglossus sardineri*, the smallest frog on earth.

### ❸ Conquer a Volcano

Inevitably, it is Réunion's iconic attraction, Piton de la Fournaise (p219), which receives the most attention. Few experiences can compare with walking across fields of solidified lava and up to a viewpoint on the rim of the main crater.

### ❹ Cirque de Mafate

To really escape it all, head to the magical Cirque de Mafate (p214), which is only accessible on foot and feels like the world's end. Spending a few days hiking through the Cirque will also give you a taste of authentic rural Réunionnais life.

### ❺ The Roof of Réunion

For a real challenge launch an assault on Piton des Neiges (p254), Réunion's highest summit (3070m). It's an arduous one- or two-day hike, but the sensational 360-degree view is more than worth the blisters. Giddy up and get goin'!

### ❻ Le Morne

Wow, the views! Lording over the turquoise sea, the 500m-high Le Morne (p112) is a sensational vantage point. The (guided) ascent to get there is worth every bead of sweat. Keep an eye out for the *boucle d'oreille* (earring), Mauritius' national flower.

# Adrenaline Fix

With its extraordinarily varied terrain, Réunion is an incredible stage for the action seeker in search of anything from canyoning and paragliding to white-water rafting and horse riding. Mauritius, Rodrigues and the Seychelles aren't just about quiet walks and gentle snorkelling; when it comes to recharging adrenaline levels, they have a few good surprises up their sleeves.

JEAN-BERNARD CARILLET

### 1 Canyoning

Immerse yourself in grandiose scenery and explore the canyons in the Cirque de Cilaos (p206) or Cirque de Salazie (p211) in Réunion; expect various jumps, leaps in crystal-clear natural pools and rappelling. In Mauritius, adventurers abseil down the seven chutes at Tamarin (p108).

### 2 Horseback Riding

Saddle up! It's a fun and ecofriendly way to enjoy the long sandy beaches and glorious hinterlands, far from the crowds. In Réunion, take a ride to Grand Étang (p238). In the Seychelles, what about cantering along Grand Anse beach (p292)?

### 3 Paragliding

Picture yourself, comfortably seated, gracefully drifting over the azure waters of the lagoon, feeling the caress of the breeze on your face… Paragliding from the slopes above St-Leu (p196) on Réunion is a memorable experience. For beginners, local operators offer tandem flights.

### 4 Kitesurfing

Did you know? Mauritius and Rodrigues offer world-class kitesurfing and windsurfing. At Le Morne (p112) beginners can take classes while experts can take off to perform spectacular aerials at One Eye, one of the meanest, moodiest spots on the planet. On Rodrigues, the place to go is Mourouk (p140).

### 5 White-Water Rafting

The raging torrent of the Rivière des Marsouins (p238) on Réunion was designed to be plunged down, screaming, in a rubber raft. Perfect for when playing sardines on the beach ceases to do it.

### 6 Surfing

The wicked Gauche de St-Leu (p196) is Réunion's signature wave. For beginners, St-Gilles-les-Bains (p189) and Étang-Salé-les-Bains (p199) offer some much easier breaks. Mauritius has a modest surfing scene around Tamarin (p103).

SIME/RIPANI MASSIMO/4CORNERS IMAGES

HOLGER LEUE

# Ecotourism & Wildlife Spotting

Charge up your camera batteries, people – the Seychelles, which some have dubbed 'The Galápagos of the Indian Ocean', has got some truly shutter-blowing wildlife-spotting opportunities just begging for pixelation. Scratch the neck of a giant tortoise, swim alongside a photogenic whale shark or observe thousands of nesting sooty terns. The best part is you don't even need a tele-photo lens to capture such scenes.

### ❶ Turtles & Giant Tortoises

Watching sea turtles nesting on Bird Island's sandy beaches (p308) or giant Aldabra tortoises roaming freely on Curieuse (p297) in the Seychelles is one of those once-in-a-lifetime, tell-the-grandkids-about-it experiences.

### ❷ Whale-Shark Spotting

No doubt you'll impress your friends when you get home with stories of close encounters with whale sharks. In September and October you can swim alongside these harmless, blue-grey giants off Mahé's coast (p285) in the Seychelles – a truly exhilarating experience.

### ❸ Feathered Paradise

The bird sanctuaries of Cousin (p297), Aride (p298) and Bird Islands (p308) in the Seychelles should figure heavily in your planning if you're hoping to spot sooty terns, tropicbirds, warblers and magpie robins. For some bird-watchers, the dream of a lifetime is to witness a pair of flycatchers on La Digue (p304).

### ❹ Vallée de Mai

Praslin's World Heritage–listed Vallée de Mai (p295) is a slice of Eden where you can see the very rare coco de mer palms in their natural state. If you're lucky, you might also glimpse the elusive black parrot of the Seychelles.

### ❺ Black River Gorges National Park

Growing weary of roasting on the beach? Head to Black River Gorges National Park (p107), Mauritius' sole (and largely underrated) national park. The best way to appreciate the area is a guided walk.

# Mauritius

JEAN-BERNARD CARILLET

# Mauritius Snapshots

Mauritius is squaring up to be one of the Indian Ocean's most progressive and dynamic nations, with an increasingly impressive and malleable economic model, and a liberal democratic political culture that has become the envy of many African neighbours.

With its traditional industries of sugar, tea, tobacco and textiles bottoming out after a long decline, Mauritius is in the process of reorienting itself towards the private sector with advancements in IT and banking to ensure its long-term economic viability. Mauritius also has close relationships with the two economic and political powerhouses of the region, South Africa and India, and its unique position both culturally and geographically between Africa and Asia has allowed Mauritius to punch well above its weight internationally. Although tourism numbers have dipped due to the shifting economic climate, locals are optimistic that rampant consumerism will resume once the financial dark cloud lifts.

Despite this positive outlook, Mauritius is not a place without problems. Racial conflict simmers in some urban areas, particularly between Hindu and Muslim populations, creating an atmosphere of tension in and around Port Louis which, while unnoticeable to most visitors, rather goes against the culture of tolerance and mutual respect that underpins Mauritian society – officially at least.

Internationally, tensions continue between Mauritius and its former colonial master, Britain, over the shabby British treatment of both Mauritius and the Chagos Islanders in the dispute about ownership of the Chagos Archipelago. The British-owned islands are leased until 2016 to the US, which uses the main island, Diego Garcia, as one of its major air bases (see p52). Mauritius claims the archipelago as its own territory, and the British, who have removed some 2000 Chagossians to Mauritius and the Seychelles (despite several international legal cases that have deemed this illegal), are refusing to budge an inch. Legal battles continue to wage regarding whether or not to allow the Chagossians to lawfully return to their homeland.

Domestically, corruption remains a big issue in all walks of life – it brought down the first government of current prime minister, Navin Ramgoolam, in 2000 when two of his senior ministers were accused of taking huge backhanders. Ramgoolam is back in power now after a brief hiatus when Paul Bérenger, the first non-Hindu prime minister of Mauritius, led the country. The same names conspicuously crop up again and again in Mauritian politics – Navin Ramgoolam is, after all, the son of Sir Seewoosagur Ramgoolam, Mauritius' independence leader and the island's first prime minister. Politics is definitely a family affair, as exhibited once more on 5 May 2010 when Ramgoolan once again defeated Bérenger.

In 2005 an epidemic of Chikungunya (a viral disease spread by mosquitoes) swept across Mauritius and the neighbouring nations in the Indian Ocean. This resulted in a sharp drop in hotel reservations, but the numbers bounced back by the end of 2006. The Ministry of Health promptly eradicated the problem and an emergency action plan was put in place should a similar situation happen in the future. Tourist numbers fell once again in 2009 – this time because of the global economic recession. Nonetheless, the luxury travel market seems to be slowly turning back in the right direction and construction and refurbishment have forged forward with full force to accommodate the projected numbers once the world's markets realign.

Despite Mauritius making economic progress in recent years, this isn't felt at all levels of society. Patches of extreme poverty still exist throughout

## FAST FACTS

Population: 1,277,300

Area: 2040 sq km

Total coastline: 177km

Highest point: Mt Piton (828m)

Literacy rate: male 88.4%, female 80.6%

Unemployment rate: 7.8%

Life expectancy: 72.6 years

Annual GDP: US$16.1 billion

Population living below the poverty line: 10%

Languages: English, Creole, Bhojpuri & French

After a mostly steady increase in tourism over the last 20 years, Mauritius' tourist numbers dropped by a noticeable 5.7% from 2008 to 2009 due to the global economic recession.

the island (particularly in Port Louis, some shanty towns around the country and – most pronounced – in Rodrigues), although most visitors are unlikely to witness this firsthand.

All in all, things are looking up today for this buoyant and ambitious island nation, aware of its problems but fiercely proud of its multiculturalism, tolerance and stability, just off the coast of a continent where these traits are in all too short a supply.

# HISTORY

Mauritius had no native population predating the European colonisers (unless you count the ill-fated dodo), and so unlike many other small islands for which colonisation resulted in the savage destruction of the native inhabitants a short period later, Mauritius' initial history is pleasantly guilt-free (again, unless you count the dodo). This historical point is vastly important to understanding the country's inclusive culture of tolerance and easy acceptance of all people: there's nobody in the ethnic melting pot able to claim precedence over the others. Broadly speaking, Mauritius experienced four distinct historical periods in its colonisation leading up to full independence from the UK in 1968.

## THE FIRST COLONISERS

Although Arab traders knew of Mauritius – which they rather unfairly called Dina Arobi (Isle of Desolation) – perhaps as early as the 10th century, the first Europeans to discover these uninhabited islands were the Portuguese, around 1507. They, too, were more interested in trade and never attempted to settle.

In 1598, a group of Dutch sailors landed on the southeast coast of the island and claimed it for the Netherlands. For the next 40 years the Dutch used Mauritius as a supply base for Batavia (Java), before deciding to settle near their original landing spot. Settlement ruins can still be seen at Vieux Grand Port, near Mahébourg.

The colony never really flourished, however, and the Dutch abandoned it in 1710. Nevertheless, they left their mark: the Dutch were responsible for the extinction of the dodo and for introducing slaves from Africa, deer from Java, wild boar, tobacco and, above all, sugar cane.

*Mauritius was originally named in honour of the Dutch prince Maurits van Nassau by the Dutch explorers who first settled the island in the 17th century.*

## ÎLE DE FRANCE

Five years later it was the turn of the French, when Captain Guillaume Dufresne d'Arsel sailed across from what is now Réunion and claimed Mauritius for France. The island was rechristened Île de France, but nothing much happened until the arrival in 1735 of the dynamic governor Bertrand François Mahé de Labourdonnais, Mauritius' first hero. He not only transformed Port Louis into a thriving seaport, but also built the first sugar mill and established a road network.

It was around this time that Mauritius' best-known historic event occurred when the *St Géran* went down during a storm off the northeast coast in 1744. The shipwreck inspired Bernardin de St-Pierre's romantic novel *Paul et Virginie*, an early bestseller (see p131).

As the English gained the upper hand in the Indian Ocean in the late 18th century, Port Louis became a haven for pirates and slightly more respectable corsairs – mercenary marines paid by a country to prey on enemy ships. The most famous Franco-Mauritian corsair was Robert Surcouf, who wrought havoc on British shipping.

In 1789, French settlers in Mauritius recognised the revolution in France and got rid of their governor. But they refused to free their slaves when the abolition of slavery was decreed in Paris in 1794.

*During the early colonial periods before they were made extinct, the indigenous Mauritian giant tortoise was so large that two adult men could comfortably sit on its back and enjoy a (slow) ride.*

## BRITISH RULE

In 1810, during the Napoleonic Wars, the British moved in on Mauritius as part of their grand plan to control the Indian Ocean. Things started badly when they were defeated at the Battle of Vieux Grand Port, the only French naval victory inscribed on the Arc de Triomphe in Paris. Just a few months later, however, British forces landed at Cap Malheureux on the north coast and took over the island.

The new British rulers renamed the island Mauritius, but allowed the Franco-Mauritians to retain their language, religion and legal system, and the all-important sugar-cane plantations on which the economy depended. The slaves were finally freed in 1835, by which time there were over 70,000 on the island. They were replaced or supplemented by labour imported from India and China. As many as 500,000 Indians took up the promise of a better life in Mauritius, often to find themselves living and working in appalling conditions on minimum pay.

By sheer weight of numbers, the Indian workforce gradually achieved a greater say in the running of the country. Their struggle was given extra impetus when Indian political and spiritual leader Mahatma Gandhi visited Mauritius in 1901 to push for civil rights. However, the key event was the introduction of universal suffrage in 1959, and the key personality Dr (later Sir) Seewoosagur Ramgoolam. Founder of the Labour Party in 1936, Seewoosagur Ramgoolam led the fight for independence, which was finally granted in 1968.

## INDEPENDENCE

The prime minister of newly independent Mauritius was, not surprisingly, Sir Seewoosagur Ramgoolam. He remained in office for the next 13 years and continued to command great reverence until his death in 1986, since when a host of public buildings have been named in his honour.

The political landscape has largely been dominated by the trio of Anerood Jugnauth, the Indian leader of the Mouvement Socialiste Mauricien (MSM), the Franco-Mauritian Paul Bérenger, with his leftist Mouvement Militant Mauricien (MMM), and Navin Ramgoolam, son of Sir Seewoosagur and leader of the Mauritian Labour Party. The former two parties formed their first coalition government in 1982, with Jugnauth as prime minister and Bérenger as finance minister. In the years that followed, the two men were in and out of government, sometimes powersharing, at other times in opposition to each other, according to the complex and shifting web of allegiances which enlivens Mauritian politics. In 1995 and again in 2005, Navin Ramgoolam beat the MSM-MMM coalition with his Alliance Sociale coalition.

On the economic front meanwhile, Mauritius was undergoing a minor miracle. Up until the 1970s the Mauritian economy could be summed up in one word – sugar. Sugar represented more than 90% of the country's exports, covered most of its fertile land and was its largest employer by far. Every so often, a cyclone would devastate the cane crop, or a world drop in sugar prices would have bitter consequences.

From the 1970s the government went all out to promote textiles, tourism and financial services, much of it based on foreign investment. Soon Mauritius was one of the world's largest exporters of textiles, with Ralph Lauren, Pierre Cardin, Lacoste and other famous brands all manufactured on the island. Income from tourism also grew by leaps and bounds as the government targeted the luxury end of the market.

The strategy paid off. The 1980s and 1990s saw the Mauritian economy grow by a remarkable 5% a year. Unemployment fell from a whopping 42% in 1980 to less than 6% by 2000 and overall standards of living improved. Even

---

**KAYA**

It was a black day for Mauritius, and a blacker one still for the Creole community. On 21 February 1999, the singer Joseph Topize (aka Kaya) was found dead in his police cell, seemingly a victim of police brutality, after being arrested for smoking cannabis at a prolegalisation rally.

As the pioneer of *seggae*, a unique combination of reggae and traditional *séga* beats, Kaya provided a voice for disadvantaged Creoles across the country. His death in the custody of Indian police split Mauritian society along racial lines, triggering four days of violent riots that left several people dead and brought the country to a standstill.

An autopsy cleared the police of wrongdoing, but the events have forced the Indian-dominated government to acknowledge *le malaise Créole,* Creoles' anger at their impoverished status in a country that has been dominated by Indians since independence.

In contrast to these violent scenes, Kaya's music is full of positive energy. The classic album *Seggae Experience* is a tribute to the singer's unique vision.

---

so, rates of unemployment and poverty remained high among the Creole population (people of mixed Afro-European origin), many of whom also felt frustrated at their lack of political power in the face of the Indian majority. These tensions spilled out onto the streets of Port Louis in 1999, triggered by the death in police custody of the singer Kaya, an ardent campaigner for the rights of the disadvantaged Creole population. The riots brought the country to a standstill for four days and forced the government to make political concessions.

# THE CULTURE

Mauritius is often cited as an example of racial and religious harmony, and compared with most other countries it is. On the surface, there are few signs of conflict. However, racial divisions are still apparent, more so than in Réunion or the Seychelles. Tensions between the Hindu majority and Muslim and Creole minorities persist despite the general respect for constitutional prohibitions against discrimination, and constitute one of the country's few potential political flash points.

## THE NATIONAL IDENTITY

Despite being a relatively young country with a diverse population, there is a surprisingly strong sense of national identity in Mauritius that transcends racial and cultural ties. Of the various forces binding Mauritians together, the most important is language. Not the official language of English, but Creole, which is the first language of 70% to 80% of the population and understood by virtually all Mauritians. Another common bond is that everyone is an immigrant or descended from immigrants. Food and music are also unifiers, as is the importance placed on family life. Mauritius is a small, close-knit community. Living in such close proximity breaks down barriers and increases understanding between the different groups. Respect for others and tolerance are deeply ingrained in all sectors of society, despite the occasional flare up of racial tension.

Mauritians place great importance on education – not just to get a better job, but as a goal in its own right. Lawyers, doctors and teachers are regarded with tremendous respect. The pinnacle of success for many is to work in the civil service, though this is beginning to change as salaries rise among artisans and businesspeople.

As individuals, Mauritians live up to their reputation of being friendly, laid-back, hospitable and generous. Many go out of their way to help strangers, and there's nothing a Mauritian likes more than a good chat. They are gentle people, more likely to make a joke about something than get angry. Cultural differences do occur, however: the Chinese tend to be more reserved than the happy-go-lucky Creoles, who work hard but do love a good party.

## LIFESTYLE

In general, each ethnic group maintains a way of life similar to that found in their countries of origin, even if they are second- or third-generation Mauritian. Several generations typically live together under one roof and the main social unit is the extended family – as witnessed by the size of family parties on a Sunday picnic. Mauritians are usually married by the age of 25. The majority of wives stay home to raise the family, while the husband earns the daily bread. Arranged marriages are still the norm among Indian families, while the Hindu caste system has also been replicated to some degree. Among all groups, religion and religious institutions continue to play a central role in community life.

As with elsewhere, this very traditional pattern is starting to break down as the younger generation grows more individualistic and more Westernised. They are far more likely to socialise with people from other communities, and intermarriage is on the rise. Other forces for change are the rise in consumerism and the emergence of a largely Indian and Chinese middle class. Middle-class couples are more likely to set up their own home and to have fewer children, while the wife may even go out to work. Statistics also show a slight decline in the number of marriages, while the divorce rate has doubled over the last 20 years.

Women's equality still has a long way to go in Mauritius. Many women have to accept low-paid, unskilled jobs, typically in a textile factory or as a cleaner. Even highly qualified women can find it hard to get promotions in the private sector, though they do better in the public service. In 2003 the government passed a Sex Discrimination Act and set up an independent unit to investigate sex discrimination cases, including sexual harassment at work. The unit's also charged with raising awareness levels and educating employers about equal opportunities.

There is little evidence of premeditated discrimination against gays and lesbians in Mauritius. Nevertheless, it's a very macho society, and gays and especially lesbians tend to keep a low profile. In fact most Indo-Mauritian homosexuals often marry someone of the opposite sex and clandestinely engage in same-sex activity through internet meet-ups and arranged parties.

Despite the fact that all forms of discrimination are illegal under the Mauritian constitution, it is widely recognised that the Creole minority has been socially, economically and politically marginalised. It's a vicious circle. Creoles find it harder to get work, partly because of low levels of literacy, but few Creole children complete secondary school because they're needed to help support the family. Expectations are also lower – and so it goes on. Creole poverty is particularly noticeable in the almost exclusively Creole island of Rodrigues.

As a result of the economic boom, overall living standards have improved in recent years and the majority of houses now have piped water and electricity. However, the gap between rich and poor is widening. It is estimated that the top 20% of the population earns 44% of the total income and that 10% lives below the poverty mark. A labourer's wage is just Rs 6000 per month, while a teacher might earn Rs 12,000. There is minimal social-security provision in Mauritius; people rely on their family in times of need. You'll find a few beggars around the markets and mosques, but the visible presence of poverty on the streets is relatively discreet.

Acts of violent crime remain relatively low, though petty crime is sharply on the rise. Burglaries and break-ins are common, and tourists are a target for thieves. Although drug use isn't a serious problem, small amounts of heroin are smuggled in from South Africa en route to Réunion and elsewhere and some is consumed locally.

One thing that is rife is corruption, though the only form likely to affect tourists is the commission system prevalent among taxi drivers. Local drivers fume about police 'fines'; connections are used to the maximum; and newspapers are full of financial scandals in the cosy, closed world of the Hindu-dominated administration. In 2002 the government set up the Independent Commission Against Corruption, which has unearthed some pretty dirty dealings. Among a number of high-profile cases, two senior bank officials were arrested for embezzling Rs 866 million and a former cabinet minister for accepting Rs 4.5 million in bribes.

## ECONOMY

Former prime minister Paul Bérenger envisaged Mauritius enjoying a 'quantum leap' to a 'knowledge island' during his brief premiership, making Mauritius the Indian Ocean's internet hub, and while progress continues to be made along these lines, traditional agricultural activities, tourism and textiles continue to provide most of the jobs in the country.

But Mauritius has effectively run out of coastline to develop its tourism industry significantly further, with all the best beaches having been taken. Attention is now focused on developments like La Balise Marina (p104) in the west, which will open the nation to a new dimension of luxury sea travel.

Meanwhile, the sugar industry is being downsized; vast work forces have been laid off because of increased mechanisation or factory closures. In light of these developments it's clear that Mauritius needs a sound economic vision for the future to stave off continued unemployment during the global recession. You can expect to see lots more call centres here (with much of the population speaking fluent Hindu or Mandarin there's lots of scope for service industries for both China and India being based here) as well as IT free-trade zones.

The banking industry – Mauritius' secret world of international money transfers and tax loopholes – continues to see huge benefits for the economy despite the global downturn.

For the moment Mauritius still hums along nicely. Its people, many of them naturally mercantile traders by heritage, love to barter, haggle and hawk – and if a stroll through Port Louis or Curepipe can be seen as a microcosm of the country in general, then it's clear that Mauritians are eager workers who highly value material success.

Search YouTube for 'Navin Ramgoolam' and you'll find his speech (in French and Creole) for using government funds to purchase an Aston Martin – the footage of Ramgoolam crashing the vehicle during a drag race at the airport has been mysteriously removed from the internet…

## POPULATION

Mauritius is made up of five ethnic groups: Indo-Mauritian (68%), Creole (27%), Sino-Mauritian (3%), Franco-Mauritian (1%) and the new kids on the block – South African expats (1%). Another small group you might come across are the Chagos Islanders (see p52).

Although the population growth rate (currently 0.9%) is quite low, a quarter of Mauritians are under 15 years of age. The country also has one of the world's highest population densities, with an average of nearly 600 people per sq km, rising to a staggering 3000 per sq km in urban areas. Worst are Port Louis and the Central Plateau towns, which developed in the wake of the malaria epidemics that hit the coast in the 1860s. Even more people are drifting to urban areas in search of work as the sugar factories mechanise or close down altogether. The vast majority of Mauritians now work in construction, industry and the service sector – all very urban activities.

## DIEGO GARCIA & THE CHAGOSSIAN BETRAYAL

One of the most prolonged betrayals in British colonial history is that surrounding the secret exile of the Chagos Islanders from their homeland in the 1960s and 1970s, in order to lease the main island, Diego Garcia, to the USA for use as a military base.

The islanders were 'resettled' in Mauritius and the Seychelles between 1965 and 1973. Some 5000 now live in abject poverty in the slums of Port Louis, where they continue to fight for their right to return home. The islanders won derisory compensation of £4 million from the British in 1982, which was paid out to the poverty-stricken islanders in return for them signing away their rights – many of them not realising at the time what the legal documents they were signing meant.

In 2000 the High Court in London ruled that the Chagossians had been evicted illegally and upheld their right to be repatriated. Nothing happened, so the Chagossians went back to court. In October 2003 the judge rejected their claim for further compensation, though he acknowledged that the British government had treated the islanders 'shamefully' and that the compensation had been inadequate. In May 2007 the Chagossians won a further case at the Court of Appeal in London, in which the government's behaviour was condemned as unlawful and an abuse of power. The judges in the case also refused to place a stay on the ruling, meaning the Chagossians were free to return to all islands (with the exception of Diego Garcia itself) with immediate effect. In 2008 the case was overturned. The Chagos Archipelago has now been ceded to the US military until 2016.

John Pilger's superb 2004 documentary is essential viewing for anyone who wants to learn the truth behind the British government's claims to respect human rights. You can watch it online here: www.jonhs.net/freemovies/stealing_a_nation.htm. Further information and ways to help the Chagossians can be found here: www.chagossupport.org.uk. For additional information on the Chagos Islanders, check out David Vine's new book *Island of Shame*.

The Indian population (the majority of which is Hindu) is descended from the labourers who were brought to the island to work the cane fields. Nowadays, Indians form the backbone of the labouring and agricultural community and own many of the island's small- and medium-sized businesses, typically in manufacturing and the retail trade. Central Plateau towns such as Rose Hill have a strong Indian flavour.

Indians also tend to be prominent in civic life. Local elections are always racially aligned, and since the Indians are in the majority, Hindus always win at the polls. The prime minister between 2003 and 2005, Franco-Mauritian Paul Bérenger, was the first non-Indian at the helm in the country's history, and he only managed that through a deal struck with his predecessor, Indian Anerood Jugnauth (see p48).

After the Indo-Mauritians, the next largest group is the Creoles, descendants of African slaves, with varying amounts of European ancestry. Creoles as a whole form the most disadvantaged sector of society. The majority work in low-paid jobs or eke out a living from fishing or subsistence farming, most notably on Rodrigues, where Creoles make up 98% of the population.

Mauritius' 30,000 Sino-Mauritians are involved mostly in commerce. Despite their small numbers, the Chinese community plays a disproportionate role in the country's economy, though they tend to avoid politics. Most came to the country as self-employed entrepreneurs and settled in the towns (particularly Port Louis), though most villages have at least one Chinese store.

Franco-Mauritians, the descendants of the *grands blancs* (rich whites), have their hands on Mauritius' purse strings. Most of the sugar mills, banks and other big businesses are still owned by Franco-Mauritians, who tend to screen themselves off from their former labourers in palatial private residences in the hills around Curepipe, and own almost all the luxurious holiday homes along the coast. Many others have decamped completely to

Mauritius is the most densely populated country in Africa.

live in South Africa and France. In fact, there are now more South African expats living on the island (congregated on the west coast) than there are Franco-Mauritians.

## RELIGION

There is a close link between religion and race in Mauritius and a remarkable degree of religious tolerance. Mosques, churches and Hindu temples can be found within a stone's throw of each other in many parts of the country.

Over half the population is Hindu, all of whom are of Indian origin. Festivals play a central role in the Hindu faith and the calendar's packed with colourful celebrations. See p152 for a rundown of the most important ones.

There's a certain amount of resentment against the Hindus in Mauritius, not for religious reasons but because the Hindu majority dominates the country's political life and its administration. Up until now, with the economy in full swing, this has merely resulted in grumbling about discrimination and 'jobs for the boys', but there's a fear this might change if the economy really begins to falter.

Nearly one-third of the population is Roman Catholic. Catholicism is practised by most Creoles, and it has picked up a few voodoo overtones over the years. Most Franco-Mauritians are also Catholic and a few Chinese and Indians have converted, largely through intermarriage.

Muslims make up roughly one-fifth of the population. Like the Hindus, Mauritian Muslims originally came from India. In Mauritius, where Islam co-exists in close proximity to other religions, it tends to be fairly liberal, though attendance at mosque is high and many Muslim women wear the hijab.

Sino-Mauritians are the least conspicuous in their worship. The one big exception is Chinese New Year, which is celebrated in Port Louis with great gusto. There are a few Chinese temples in Port Louis.

> Grand Bassin in southern Mauritius is the largest Hindu pilgrimage outside India. Believed to have been created when Shiva spilled some water from the Ganges that he was carrying on his head, the lake is visited by half a million pilgrims each year.

## ARTS

Mauritian architecture, literature and fine arts are all firmly based in the French tradition. The country's music, however, is African in origin and is very much alive and kicking.

### Literature

Mauritius' most famous contribution to world literature – one that has become entangled in the island's history – is the romantic novel *Paul et Virginie* by Bernardin de St-Pierre, which was first published in 1788 (see p131). An English translation of the novel is widely available in Mauritius.

---

**RESPONSIBLE TRAVEL**

The people of Mauritius have a well-deserved reputation for being exceptionally tolerant. That said, there are a few 'rules' of behaviour to abide by.

Although beachwear is fine for the beaches, you will cause offence and may invite pestering if you dress skimpily elsewhere. Nude bathing is forbidden, while women going topless is tolerated around some hotel pools, but not on the beaches.

Mauritius has many temples and mosques. You are welcome to visit, but should dress and behave with respect: miniskirts and singlet tops are a no-no, and it is normal to remove your shoes – there's usually a sign indicating where to leave them. Many temples and mosques also ask you not to take photos, while some Hindu temples request that you remove all leather items, such as belts. At mosques, you may be required to cover your head in certain areas, so remember to take along a scarf. Never touch a carving or statue of a deity. If at any time you're unsure about protocol, the best thing to do is ask.

The author captures the landscapes beautifully, though his ultramoralistic tearjerker is less likely to appeal to modern tastes.

Joseph Conrad's oblique love story *A Smile of Fortune*, collected in '*Twixt Land and Sea* (1912), is set in Mauritius, although it's hardly very flattering about the place. Set in the late 19th century it does, however, give a taste of the mercantile activity of the time and the curious mix of 'negroes', Creoles, 'coolies' and marooned Frenchmen who populated the island then. Visitors to the island will certainly identify with Conrad's description of Mauritius as the '"Pearl of the Ocean"… a pearl distilling sweetness on the world', but will undoubtedly find the current inhabitants far more pleasant to deal with than the characters described in the story.

Those who want to read a 20th-century Mauritian novel should try something by Malcolm de Chazal, whose most famous works are *Sens Plastique*, available in translation, and *Petrusmok*. Chazal was an eccentric recluse, but he inspired a whole generation of local writers. His works are a highly original blend of poetry and philosophy, and are peppered with pithy statements, such as 'Avoid clean people who have a dirty stare'.

Of living writers, perhaps the best-known internationally is Carl de Souza. In his novel *Le Sang de l'Anglais* he looks at the often ambivalent relationship between Mauritians and their countries of origin, while *La Maison qui Marchait Vers le Large*, set in Port Louis, takes intercommunity conflict as its theme. *Les Jours Kaya* is a coming-of-age book set against the violence following Kaya's death (see p49).

Other contemporary novelists to look out for include Ananda Devi, Shenaz Patel and Natacha Appanah-Mouriquand. Unfortunately, their works as yet are only available in French, regarded as the language of culture.

In more recent times, the French author JMG Clézio, whose father was Mauritian, has also set a number of novels in Mauritius, of which *Le Chercheur d'Or* (The Prospector) has been translated into English.

## Music & Dance

You'll hear *séga* everywhere nowadays, but in the early 20th century it fell seriously out of fashion. Its revival in the early 1950s is credited to the Creole singer Ti-Frère, whose song 'Anita' has become a classic. Though he died in 1992, Ti-Frère is still the country's most popular *séga* star. More recent

---

Unlikely to be at your local multiplex any time soon is Mauritius' first ever film, *Benares*, made on the island in 2005. It's a touching portrait of two friends from the country travelling to Port Louis to find wives.

---

### SÉGA!

*Séga* is the powerful combination of music and dance originally conceived by African slaves as a diversion from the injustice of their daily existence. At the end of a hard day in the cane fields, couples danced the *séga* around campfires on the beach to the accompaniment of drums.

Because of the sand (some say because of the shackles), there could be no fancy footwork. So today, when dancing the *séga*, the feet never leave the ground. The rest of the body makes up for it and the result, when the fire is hot, can be extremely erotic. In the rhythm and beat of *séga*, you can see or hear connections with the Latin American salsa, the Caribbean calypso and the African origins of the people. It's a personal, visceral dance where the dancers let the music take over and abandon themselves to the beat.

The dance is traditionally accompanied by the beat of the *ravanne*, a primitive goatskin drum. The beat starts slowly and builds into a pulsating rhythm, which normally carries away performers and onlookers alike. You may be lucky enough to see the dance being performed spontaneously at beach parties or family barbecues. Otherwise, you'll have to make do with the less authentic *séga* soirees offered by some bars and restaurants and most of the big hotels, often in combination with a Mauritian buffet. Nonresidents are usually welcome, though may have to pay (generally around Rs 200/100 per adult/child, which is then deducted from the food or drink bill).

Creole groups and singers with a wide following include Cassiya, Fanfan and the prolific Jean-Claude Gaspard.

Séga evolved slightly differently in Rodrigues. Here the drum plays a more prominent role in what's known as séga tambour. The island's accordion bands are also famous for their surprising repertoire, which includes waltzes, polkas, quadrilles and Scottish reels. Over the years these were learned from passing European sailors and gradually absorbed into the local folk music. They're now an essential part of any Rodriguan knees-up.

A newer Mauritian musical form was invented by Creole musician Kaya in seggae, which blends elements of séga and reggae. With his band Racine Tatane, Kaya gave a voice to dissatisfied Creoles around the island. Tragically, the singer died in police custody in February 1999 (see p49). Following in Kaya's footsteps, Ras Natty Baby and his Natty Rebels are one of most popular seggae groups; sales gained an extra boost when Ras Natty Baby was imprisoned for heroin trafficking in 2003.

Recently, ragga, a blend of house music, traditional Indian music and reggae, has been gaining a following. Mauritian ragga groups include Black Ayou and the Authentic Steel Brothers.

## Architecture

Caught up in the need to develop its economy, Mauritius paid little attention to its architectural heritage until recently. As a result many splendid colonial mansions and more humble dwellings have been lost under the sea of concrete. Those still standing may be luckier. In 2003 the government set up a National Heritage Fund charged with preserving the country's historic buildings.

Those which have fared best are the plantation houses dating from the 18th and 19th centuries, which you'll still see standing in glorious isolation amid the cane fields. Many are privately owned and closed to the public, such as Le Réduit, near Moka, which is now the president's official residence. Others have been converted into museums and restaurants, including Eureka (p74), a beautifully restored mansion also near Moka. But rescuing these houses is expensive and time-consuming. Many of the raw materials, such as tamarind wood, are in short supply. It's easier and cheaper to rip down the old timber frames, and throw up brand-new concrete blocks on the sturdy foundations beneath.

The majority of Mauritians now live in nondescript concrete apartment blocks in the towns and cities. Middle-class families might possibly afford a seaside apartment or villa. The coast around Trou aux Biches and Flic en Flac is lined with these uninspiring boxes, all cheek by jowl. A few more enlightened developers are beginning to add traditional flourishes, such as lambrequins (decorative wooden borders) and bright paintwork. Hotels and restaurants are also getting better at incorporating a bit of local colour.

As for major civic projects, the most prestigious in recent times has been Port Louis' Caudan Waterfront development. Given its location at the very heart of the capital, the architects decided to incorporate elements of the traditional architecture found around nearby Place d'Armes. Further inspiration came from the nearby stone-and-steel dockyard buildings to provide another link with the past. Plans are now underway to build a Caudan-like complex in sleepy Mahébourg, and the country's first luxury yacht port, La Balise Marina (p104), has broken ground in Black River.

## Visual Arts

Historically, Mauritian artists took their lead from what was happening in Europe and, in particular, France. Some of the 18th- and 19th-century

The website www.sega.mu is devoted entirely to Mauritius' much loved national music, which developed from the songs and dances of slaves. You can listen to séga here as well as read a very detailed history.

Another great music website is www.radio-moris.com, where you can listen to the radio station live and hear lots of great séga, seggae and ragga.

---

**THE ARCHITECTURAL HERITAGE**

The first French settlers naturally brought with them building styles from home. Over the years the architecture gradually evolved until it became supremely well suited to the hot, humid tropics. It's for this reason that so many of the grand plantation houses have survived the ravages of time.

Flourishes that appear to be ornamental – vaulted roofs and decorative pierced screens, for example – all serve to keep the occupants cool and dry. The most distinctive feature is the shingled roof with ornamental turrets and rows of attic windows. These wedding-cake touches conceal a vaulted roof, which allows the air to circulate. Another characteristic element is the wide, airy *varangue* (verandah), where raffia blinds, fans and pot plants create a cooling humidity.

The roofs, windows and overhangs are usually lined with delicate, lace-like *lambrequins* (decorative wooden borders), which are purely ornamental. They vary from simple, repetitive floral patterns to elaborate pierced friezes; in all cases a botanical theme predominates.

*Lambrequins,* shingle roofs and verandahs or wrought-iron balconies are also found in colonial-era town houses. The more prestigious buildings were constructed of brick, or even stone, and so are better able to withstand cyclones and termites. In Port Louis, Government House and other buildings lining Place d'Armes are all fine examples.

At the other end of the scale, traditional labourers' houses typically consist of two rooms (one for sleeping, one for eating) and a verandah; because of the fire risk the kitchen is usually separate. Nowadays they are built of corrugated iron rather than termite-resistant hardwood, but are still painted in eye-catching colours that offset the white *lambrequins*. The garden overflowing with edible and ornamental plants is almost as important as the house itself.

---

engravings and oils of Mauritian landscapes you see could almost be mistaken for Europe. The classical statue of Paul and Virginie in Port Louis' Blue Penny Museum and the one of King Edward VII at the city's Champ de Mars Racecourse were both created by Mauritius' best-known sculptor, Prosper d'Épinay.

In the 20th century, the surrealist writer and painter Malcolm de Chazal injected a bit of local colour into the scene. Inspired by the island's prolific nature, his paintings are full of light and energy. You'll see numerous copies of the *Blue Dodo* and other Chazal works around, but originals are extremely rare. A gallery in Pereybère features some of his work (p91).

Contemporary Mauritian art tends to be driven by the tourist market. One artist you'll find reproduced everywhere is Vaco Baissac, instantly recognisable from the blocks of colour outlined in black, like a stained-glass window. His gallery is in Grand Baie (p91).

Other commercially successful artists include Danielle Hitié, who produces minutely detailed renderings of markets as well as rural scenes, and Françoise Vrot, known for her very expressive portraits of women fieldworkers. Both artists are exhibited in galleries in Grand Baie, where Vrot also has her studio (p91).

Keep an eye out for exhibitions by more innovative contemporary artists, such as Hervé Masson, Serge Constantin, Henri Koombes and Khalid Nazroo. All have had some success on the international scene, though are less visible locally.

# FOOD & DRINK

The rich and diverse heritage of Mauritius makes for some good reading on restaurant menus, with Indian, Chinese, French and African cuisine all having a 'greatest hits'–like showing in most places you'll visit. Mauritian, or Creole, cuisine takes various elements from each when preparing the fish and seafood dishes that are the national staple. For food-related vocabulary and expressions, see p331.

## STAPLES & SPECIALITIES

Mauritian cuisine is very similar across the island – a rich and delicious mix of Indian spices and fresh local seafood and fish prepared with strong influences from Chinese, French and African cuisine. The cuisine of Rodrigues is quite different – less spicy but with more fresh fruit and beans used as ingredients.

In Mauritius, rice, noodles, fish and seafood are the staples of everyday life, although to a great extent what people eat depends on their ethnic background. A Sino-Mauritian may well start the day with tea and noodles, a Franco-Mauritian with a *café au lait* and croissant, and an Indo-Mauritian with a chapatti. However, come lunchtime nearly everyone enjoys a hot meal – whether it be a spicy seafood *carri* (curry) or *mines* (noodles) and a cooling beer. Dinner is the main meal of the day and is usually eaten *en famille* (with family). The Mauritians love their cocktail hour, and so you'll nearly always have an *apéro* (aperitif) or a *ti punch* (small punch) – usually a rum-based fruit cocktail. While meat is widely eaten (especially in Chinese and French cuisine), the most common mainstays are fish and seafood. Marlin is a big favourite, as are mussels, octopus and calamari.

## DRINKS

Unsurprisingly the national drink is rum, and although most agree that Mauritian rum isn't up to the standard of the Caribbean equivalent, there are still some excellent brands produced, particularly Green Island – the dark variety of which is superb. Despite a long history of rum production in Mauritius, the socially preferred spirit tends to be whisky – a hangover from the 150-year British rule.

The national beer is Phoenix, an excellent pilsner produced at the Phoenix Brewery since the 1960s and a regular prizewinner at festivals around the world. The other premium brand of the brewery, Blue Marlin, is also very good.

The Mauritians are also great tea drinkers and you shouldn't miss trying the range of Bois Chéri teas on sale throughout the country. The vanilla tea is the most famous and is quite delicious and refreshing even in the heat of the day. You'll have a chance to see it being made and can taste it at the Bois Chéri tea plantation in southern Mauritius (p122).

During Hindu and Muslim festivals, deliciously flavoured drinks such as *lassi* (Indian yoghurt drink) and almond milk (almond- and cardamom-flavoured milk) are prepared.

## WHERE TO EAT & DRINK

There tends to be quite a bit of segregation between 'tourist' restaurants and 'local' ones, particularly around bigger resort areas. In places such as Port Louis and the central highlands this is a lot less pronounced, and most places have a mixed clientele.

Throughout the Mauritius chapter we've tried to avoid including solely tourist eateries unless they are very special or the only things on offer. Nearly all restaurants have menus in English, or at least staff who speak English, so communication difficulties are kept to a minimum.

Most restaurants have several cuisines served up cheek by jowl, although they're nearly always separated from each other on the menu. While in better restaurants this will mean each cuisine is prepared by a different expert chef, on the whole most chefs are decent at cooking one cuisine and prepare the remaining dishes with something approaching indifference. The rule is a fairly obvious one – don't go to a Chinese restaurant for a good curry.

Bat curry is a speciality in some restaurants in Mauritius, although you won't see it on the menu; it tends to be a speciality the islanders keep to themselves.

Look out for the delicious, thirst-quenching almond-based drink *alouda* while visiting Mauritius. Topped with ice cream, it's the perfect antidote to the midday heat or after enjoying a particularly hot curry...

The best places to eat throughout the country tend to be *tables d'hôtes*, privately hosted meals often given by people who run guesthouses as well, but just as often offered alone. These give you a unique insight into local life, as you'll usually dine with the host couple and often their children, plus any other travellers who've arranged to come by (or people staying in the guesthouse). It's nearly always necessary to book a *table d'hôte*, preferably a day in advance, although it's always worth asking – bigger operations will sometimes be able to accommodate last-minute additions.

Opening hours tend to be quite flexible (and unpredictable in smaller places!), although as a rule it's good not to leave eating too late – even though many places are officially open until 11pm, if they're empty by 10pm there's a chance they'll shut early. Port Louis is a ghost town for everything, including eating, in the evening as the middle classes tend to live out of town, so it's usually the Caudan Waterfront or nothing after dark.

## Quick Eats

Places to enjoy eats on the run are in plentiful supply in Mauritius. Street vendors are at every bus station and town square, and takeaway shops can be found in numerous shopping centres and markets; both offer inexpensive local treats, including Indian, French and Chinese delicacies. Almost all restaurants, except the most upmarket, will do takeaway. In Mauritius, roadside food stalls serving dinner dishes such as *biryani* (curried rice), Indian rotis and *farattas* (unleavened flaky flour pancakes) are popular.

The atmospheric markets are worth visiting for the popular *gâteaux piments* (deep-fried balls of lentils and chilli), which are cooked on the spot. You should also try the delicious *dhal puris* (Indian snacks), rotis, samosas and *bhajas* (fried balls of besan dough with herbs or onion).

Indian and Chinese restaurants offer quick and inexpensive meals and snacks. Remember to buy some Indian savouries such as *caca pigeon* (an Indian nibble) or the famous Chinese *char siu* (barbecue pork).

## VEGETARIANS & VEGANS

Vegetarians will fare well in Mauritius, although they may be disappointed by the lack of variety. Indian restaurants tend to offer the best choice, but often this is limited to a variation on the theme of *carri de légumes* (vegetable curry). Chinese restaurants are also good for vegetarians, while Creole and French places are much more limiting, although almost everywhere has a vegetable curry on the menu. Pescatarians will be spoiled for choice as almost every eatery in the country offers fresh seafood and freshly caught fish cooked to perfection.

Vegans will find things harder, but not unassailably so – most resorts will be able to offer vegan options with advance warning, and again Indian restaurants will offer the most choice.

## HABITS & CUSTOMS

Eating habits vary across ethnic groups. Some groups eat with their fingers, others don't eat meat on Fridays and some abstain from eating pork – it's hard to generalise across the community.

Breakfasts are normally very quick and informal. Lunch is also a fairly casual affair, although at the weekend it tends to be more formal, when family and friends gather to share the pleasures of the table. In restaurants, special menus are offered for weekend lunches. Before dinner, which is a very formal occasion, *gajacks* (predinner snacks) and *un apéro* or *un ti punch* (predinner drinks) are commonly served; during the meal, wine or beer is usually served.

As eating and drinking are important social activities, behaviour at the table should be respectful. Locals can be strict about table manners, and it's

*Les Délices de Rodrigues* (in French), by Françoise Baptiste, presents recipes from Rodrigues. Madame Baptiste also arranges bespoke Rodrigues cookery courses at her guesthouses in Grande Montagne, Rodrigues. Contact her for details (see p141).

To make a 'millionaire's' salad' you must cut down a whole palm tree, just to use the edible heart of palm. Once the heart of palm is removed, the plant dies.

considered rude to pick at your food or mix it together. You are also expected to be reasonably well dressed. Unless you are in a beach environment, wearing beachwear or other skimpy clothing won't be well received – casual but neat clothing is the norm. When invited to dine with locals, bring a small gift (perhaps some flowers or a bottle of wine).

If you are attending a traditional Indian or Chinese meal or a dinner associated with a religious celebration, follow what the locals do. Generally, your hosts will make you feel comfortable, but if you are unsure, ask about the serving customs and the order of dishes. Definitely attend an Indian or a Chinese wedding if you get the opportunity – these celebrations are true culinary feasts.

# ENVIRONMENT

## THE LAND

Mauritius is the peak of an enormous volcanic chain that also includes Réunion, though it is much older and therefore less rugged than its neighbour.

The island's highest mountains are found in the southwest, from where the land drops slightly to a central plateau before climbing again to the chain of oddly shaped mountains behind Port Louis and the Montagne Bambous to the east. Beyond these mountains a plain slopes gently down to the north coast.

Unlike Réunion, Mauritius has no active volcanoes, although remnants of volcanic activity abound. Extinct craters and volcanic lakes, such as the Trou aux Cerfs crater in Curepipe and the Grand Bassin holy lake, are good examples. Over the aeons, the volcanoes generated millions of lava boulders, much to the chagrin of the indentured farm labourers who had to clear the land for sugar cane. Heaps of boulders dot the landscape. Some that have been piled into tidy pyramids are listed monuments!

Mauritius also includes a number of widely scattered inhabited islands, of which the most important is Rodrigues, 600km to the northeast. Rodrigues is another ancient volcanic peak and is surrounded by a lagoon twice the size of the island itself. Mauritius also owns the sparsely inhabited islands of Cargados Carajos, northeast of the mainland, and the Agalega Islands, two islands adjacent to the Seychelles.

Mauritius also stakes territorial claim to the Chagos Archipelago, officially part of the British Indian Ocean Territory and controversially ceded to the US military until 2016 (see p52).

> You must be a holder of a Mauritian passport to visit the wildly remote island of St Brandon.

## WILDLIFE

Mauritius is a haven for botanists, zoologists, ornithologists and all sorts of other 'ologists'. To experience some of what's on offer in the way of flora and fauna, visitors should visit the botanical gardens at Pamplemousses and Curepipe; Casela Nature & Leisure Park and the Black River Gorges National Park in the west; and Île aux Aigrettes, La Vanille and the various *domaines* in the south and southeast.

The best source of information is the **Mauritian Wildlife Foundation** (MWF; ☎ 631 2396; www.ile-aux-aigrettes.com/pages/mwf.htm), which was founded in 1984 to protect and manage the country's many rare species. The MWF vigorously supports the creation of national parks and reserves, and the monitoring of whales, dolphins and turtles. It has had significant success in restoring the populations of several endangered bird species and in conserving endemic vegetation. Nevertheless, there is still a long way to go.

For information on marine life, see p34.

## Animals

Mauritius has only one native mammal, the wonderful fruit bat – a common sight at twilight each evening as they come to life and begin their night's foraging. All other mammals present on the island were introduced with varying degrees of success by colonists. Mongooses are typical of the slapdash ecological management of the past – they were introduced from India in the late 19th century to control plague-carrying rats. The intention was to import only males, but some females slipped through and soon there were mongooses everywhere. They remain fairly common, as are the bands of macaque monkeys that hang out around Grand Bassin and the Black River Gorges. Java deer, imported by the Dutch for fresh meat, and wild pigs also roam the more remote forests.

Native reptiles include the beautiful turquoise-and-red Ornate Day gecko and Telfair's skink, a clawed lizard, both of which can be seen on Île aux Aigrettes. You can rest easy if you see a slithering critter – there are no dangerous reptiles in Mauritius.

As for bird life, the best-known representative was the dodo, the super-sized pigeon that found its docility rewarded with extinction (see p69). The dodo was only the first of the many now extinct victims of Mauritius' colonisation. Several other local bird species looked doomed until a few years back, although thanks to phenomenal conservation efforts, some now have a chance of survival.

The Mauritius kestrel was the victim of pesticide poisoning, habitat destruction and hunting. By 1974 just six birds remained: four in the wild and two in captivity. A captive-breeding program established in 1973 has led to an amazing recovery, with numbers now just under 1000. With luck, you might see kestrels in the Black River Gorges and at the many *domaines* north of Mahébourg.

The lovely pink pigeon has also been pulled back from the brink thanks to captive breeding. From a mere 10 or so individuals in 1990 there are now over 400. A colony has been established on Île aux Aigrettes, off Mahébourg, safe from egg-stealing rats and monkeys and human poachers.

Similar captive-breeding programs are helping to preserve the echo parakeet, found mainly in the Black River Gorges, and the Rodrigues fruit bat, among other endangered species.

The birds you're most likely to see, however, are the introduced songbirds, such as the little red Madagascar fody, the Indian mynah (its yellow beak and feet giving it a cartoon-character appearance) and the most common bird of all on Mauritius – the red-whiskered bulbul. Between October and May the Terre Rouge estuary north of Port Louis provides an important wintering ground for migratory water birds such as the whimbrel, the grey plover, and the common and curlew sandpipers.

## Plants

Almost one-third of the 900 plant species found in Mauritius are unique to these islands. Many of these endemic plants have fared poorly in competition with introduced plants such as guava and privet, and have been depleted by introduced deer, pigs and monkeys. General forest clearance and the establishment of crop monocultures have exacerbated the problem, so that less than 1% of Mauritius' original forest is intact.

Mauritius' forests originally included the *tambalacoque* tree, which is also known as the dodo tree and is not far from extinction itself. It's a tall tree with a silver trunk and a large, tough seed that supposedly only germinates after being eaten by, and passing through the stomach of, a dodo. Scientists are sceptical about this rumour, but there's no denying the tree is extremely

Errol Fuller's *Dodo: From Extinction to Icon* is a fascinating history of how the demise of this one species due to human behaviour has become such a powerful worldwide metaphor for the dangers humans pose to their environment.

Gerald Durrell's highly readable account of his adventures in Mauritius, *Golden Bats and Pink Pigeons*, remains a great companion to any trip, especially given that many of the species Durrell describes are extremely rare and even extinct today.

difficult to propagate. The easiest place to find this and other rare plant species is in the botanical gardens at Pamplemousses.

For a tropical island, Mauritius is not big on coconut palms. Instead, casuarinas (also known as *filaos*) fringe most of the beaches. These tall, wispy trees act as useful windbreaks and grow well in sandy soil. The government planted them along the shores to help stop erosion; eucalyptus trees have been widely planted for the same reason.

Other impressive and highly visible trees are the giant Indian banyan and the brilliant red flowering flamboyant (royal poinciana).

Staying with shades of red, one flower you will see in abundance is anthurium, with its single, glossy petal and protruding yellow spadix. The plant originated in South America and was introduced to Mauritius in the late 19th century. The flower, which at first sight you'd swear was plastic, can last up to three weeks after being cut and is therefore a popular display plant. Now grown in commercial quantities for export, it is used to spruce up hotels and public meeting places.

Mangroves are enjoying a renaissance in Mauritius today. Originally cut down to reduce swamp areas where malarial mosquitos could breed, they've been discovered to be an important part of the food chain for tropical fish, and thus large projects to develop mangrove areas have been undertaken, particularly on the east coast.

All the indigenous giant tortoises of Mauritius and similar Aldabra giant tortoises from Madagascar have been reintroduced in captivity to the islands in recent decades.

## NATIONAL PARKS

Since 1988, several international organisations have been working with the government to set up conservation areas in Mauritius. About 3.5% of the land area is now protected either as national parks, managed mainly for ecosystem preservation and for recreation, or as nature reserves.

The largest park is the Black River Gorges National Park, established in 1994 in the southwest of the island. It covers some 68 sq km and preserves a wide variety of forest environments, from pine forest to tropical scrub, and includes the country's largest area of native forest. Two of the most important nature reserves are Île aux Aigrettes and Île Ronde, both of which are being restored to their natural state by replacing introduced plants and animals with native species.

In 1997 marine parks were proclaimed at Blue Bay (near Mahébourg on the southeast coast) and Balaclava (on the west coast), but the number of visitors to the area makes it difficult to establish rigorous controls and there is a need to encourage local fishermen to use less destructive techniques.

## ENVIRONMENTAL ISSUES

The environment of Mauritius has paid a heavy price for the country's rapid economic development. And despite the recent economic setbacks, the government seems more keen than ever to encourage more tourists – at least, the rich ones – to continue plugging the gap left by a declining sugar industry and waning textile industry. However, the expansion of tourist facilities is straining the island's infrastructure and causing problems such as environmental degradation and excessive demand on services such as electricity, water and transport.

For many species it is already too late, but there is a growing awareness of the need for conservation among decision makers and the general public. The difficulty is to achieve a balance between protecting the immensely fragile island ecosystems and easing the ever-increasing pressure on land and other natural resources.

One area of particular concern is the amount of construction along the coast – almost every beach has been developed, most of it tourist related.

## IMPORTANT NATIONAL PARKS & RESERVES

| Park | Features | Activities | Best time to visit |
| --- | --- | --- | --- |
| Balaclava Marine Park (p80) | lagoon, coral reef, turtle breeding grounds | snorkelling, diving, glass-bottomed boat tours | all year |
| Black River Gorges National Park (p107) | forested mountains, Mauritius kestrel, black ebony trees, macaque monkeys | hiking, bird-watching | Sep–Jan for flowers |
| Blue Bay Marine Park (p118) | lagoon, corals, fish life | snorkelling, diving, glass-bottomed boat tours | all year |
| Île aux Aigrettes Nature Reserve (p118) | coral island, coastal forests, pink pigeons, Aldabra giant tortoises | ecotours | all year |

Luckily, Mauritians are very keen to put environmental concerns first: a proposal for a hotel on Île des Deux Cocos in Blue Bay, for example, met with such fierce resistance that it has been abandoned. Tree huggers also fervently combated plans to construct a highway through the old forests in the southeast.

The government now requires an environmental impact assessment for all new building projects, including coastal hotels, marinas and golf courses, and even for activities such as undersea walks. Planning regulations for hotel developments on Rodrigues are particularly strict: they must be small, single storey, built in traditional style and stand at least 30m back from the high-tide mark. Since water shortages are a problem on Rodrigues, new hotels must also recycle their water.

To combat littering and other forms of environmental degradation, the government has established a special environmental police force charged with enforcing the legislation and educating the local population. To report wrongdoers, there is even a **hotline** ( ☎ 210 5151).

If anything, the marine environment is suffering even more from over-exploitation. The coast off Grand Baie is particularly affected by too many divers and boats concentrated in a few specific locations. In addition, silting and chemical pollution are resulting in extensive coral damage and falling fish populations. In the west, dolphin-watching is an extremely popular activity for tourists; however, the sudden increase in operators has called the sustainability of it into question. Choose your tour boat carefully – companies who do not have the dolphins' wellbeing at heart should be avoided. For more information on marine conservation in Mauritius, see p35.

The Mauritian Wildlife Foundation (MWF) is heavily involved in raising awareness of conservation issues among the local population and tourists. A visit to see MWF's work on Île aux Aigrettes (p118) is highly recommended.

# Mauritius

Famed for its sapphire waters, powder-white beaches and large swaths of tropical forest, Mauritius is a slice of paradise that has long been synonymous with immeasurable luxury. But step away from your package holiday and you'll quickly find a whole other world. The *real* Mauritius is almost the exact opposite of the tranquil oceanic Eden depicted in postcards. Horns honk, tractors belch smoke, and pedestrians scramble through the streets in traffic-choked Port Louis, the nation's chaotic capital. Beyond the urban buzz, clusters of fishing villages and shanty towns dot the seaside in the nooks between the pearly gates of the island's heavenly hotels.

Travellers who explore will discover that Mauritius is much more complex and intriguing than a simple dichotomy between the tourist and nontourist bubbles. The Island is a crucible of wildly dynamic and diverse peoples. Sometimes these cultural differences blend together in magical harmony. At other times, however, ethnic differences are caricatured, and allegiances are clearly drawn. The Hindu majority controls the government, the Chinese have a strong mercantile influence, the fraction of Franco-Mauritians maintain their vestigially aristocratic influence, and the Creoles infuse island life with an intoxicating live-and-let-live attitude.

Ultimately, Mauritius is the kind of place that rewards even the smallest attempts at exploration. So, if your biggest discovery is the beach butler service at your hotel, then you'll need to plan a second visit!

---

### HIGHLIGHTS

- Enjoying *chambre d'hôte* charm along the stunning beach in **Pointe d'Esny** (p118) then savouring street fare in **Mahébourg** (p113)

- Spotting breaching dolphins in **Tamarin** (p103) then diving in the sea to explore the cavernous drop-offs below the turquoise lagoon at **Flic en Flac** (p99)

- Fruit bats in **Black River Gorges National Park** (p107), or hoofing it over cracked rock and delicate flowers for spectacular views from the top of **Le Morne** (p112)

- Uncovering the island's plantation past with a visit to **Eureka** (p74) then sampling the Creole cuisine served along **La Route du Thé** (p122)

- Exploring the back streets of the charismatic and chaotic capital **Port Louis** (p64)

---

- Population: 1.28 million
- Telephone code: 230
- Area: 2040 sq km

## CLIMATE & WHEN TO GO

Mauritius enjoys a typically tropical climate with year-round heat. The summer months are from December to April, when it can be extremely humid, and the cooler winter, such as it is, runs from May to November.

Peak cyclone months are January and February, and although offshore storms rarely hit Mauritius (Rodrigues suffers far more regularly than the mainland), they can bring days of squally rain.

Coastal temperatures range between 25°C and 33°C in summer and between 18°C and 24°C in winter. On the plateau it will be some 5°C cooler. The highlands are also the wettest part of the island – it can rain here at any time of year, and even when it's not raining the area can be cloaked in low-lying cloud.

Apart from the Christmas–New Year peak, Mauritius doesn't really have high and low seasons. The situation is more dependent on outside factors (such as the French school holidays, which cause a big increase in demand and prices in August).

# PORT LOUIS

**pop 155,700**

Forget what you've heard about Port Louis (*por* loo-ee) – it's the kind of place that can only be understood when you experience it in person. Although regularly compared to other African cities (and lauded for its advancements in the economic sector), the island's capital often feels like a kaleidoscope of countries and cultures, with flashes of India, Africa, Europe, China and the Middle East.

Despite being the national capital, the main economic hub and the biggest city in the country, Port Louis occupies a rather strange place in the psyche of modern Mauritius. Its low-lying position has historically made it an undesirable locale – disease swept through in the 18th and 19th centuries, prompting the professional classes to live in the towns of the Central Plateau. The trend continues today as thousands of commuters descend upon the capital, then rumble out of town at sunset giving the city centre a depressingly impoverished feel after dark.

This impression is totally false, however. Port Louis has plenty going for it, but it's a city that profits from exploration – those who only visit the Disney-esque Caudan Waterfront will get a very bland impression of the national capital. The bustle and chaos of the streets, the labyrinthine ethnic quarters and some wonderfully preserved colonial buildings make Port Louis far more than a place to come for some pricey shopping away from the beach.

## HISTORY

Port Louis was first settled in the 17th century by the Dutch, who called it Noordt Wester Haven. It was the French governor Bertrand François Mahé de Labourdonnais, however, who took the initiative and developed it into a busy capital and port after 1736. Labourdonnais is commemorated with a much-photographed statue at the seaward end of Place d'Armes, the square that marks the city centre.

Few cities have bounced back from as many natural disasters as Port Louis, or Port Napoleon as it was known briefly in the early 19th century before the British took the island. Between 1773 and 1892 a series of fires, plagues and tropical storms all tried, and failed, to level the town. In 1819 cholera arrived from Manila on the frigate *Topaz*, killing an estimated 700 Port Louis residents. Things quietened down until 1866, when malaria suddenly appeared on the scene, causing a further 3700 fatalities. Around this time people started heading for the cooler (and healthier) Central Plateau, so the town's population was mercifully small when the 1892 cyclone whipped through and destroyed 3000 homes.

The 20th century saw Port Louis become one of Africa's most important financial centres and ports – to which the ever-growing number of high-rise glass-fronted banks in the city centre attest.

## ORIENTATION

Port Louis is divided by Mauritius' only motorway, which runs by the harbour and Caudan Waterfront. The Caudan side is a sanitised city with smart shops and bars, but little in the way of atmosphere, while the vast majority of the city is on the other side of the road – dirty, colourful, chaotic and much more fun.

The centre of the city is hard to pin down exactly – the natural centre is Place d'Armes, a picturesque palm-lined avenue that runs from the harbour to Government House. From here nearly all the sites of interest are within easy walking distance. The main banks have their offices around Place d'Armes or along Sir William Newton St nearby. Royal St runs northeast through Chinatown and is also of interest to travellers.

Port Louis' two main bus stations are located either side of the city centre, each a few minutes' walk from Place d'Armes. Arriving from the airport, you'll be dropped at the more southerly Victoria Square bus station.

# INFORMATION
## Bookshops
**Bookcourt** ( ☎ 211 9146; Caudan Waterfront; ☪ 10am-6pm Mon-Sat) The country's best bookshop sells a broad range of English, French and Creole books, including guidebooks.

## Emergency
**Ambulance** ( ☎ 114)
**Fire services** ( ☎ 995)
**Police** ( ☎ emergency 999, headquarters 203 1212; Line Barracks, Lord Kitchener St)

## Internet Access
**Internet Cafe** ( ☎ 213 2435; Port Louis Waterfront; per 15/40min Rs 35/70; ☪ 9am-10pm Mon-Sat, 10am-4pm Sun) Decorated like a primary school. Twelve computer terminals.

## Medical Services
**Dr Jeetoo Hospital** ( ☎ 212 3201; Volcy Pougnet St) Provides 24-hour medical and dental treatment and has a 24-hour pharmacy. Staff speak English and French.
**Medical Trading Pharmacy** ( ☎ 294 0440; Chaussée St) One of the best pharmacies in the city, just by Company Gardens.

## Money
You'll find ATMs throughout Port Louis, while all the main banks are concentrated around Sir William Newton St. Standard banking hours are 9am to 3.15pm Monday to Thursday and 9am to 3.30pm Friday. Some banks are open on Saturday mornings, while those at the airport are open whenever flights arrive.
**Barclays** ( ☎ 207 1800; Sir William Newton St)
**HSBC** ( ☎ 203 8333; Place d'Armes)
**Mauritius Commercial Bank** (MCB; ☎ 202 5000; 9-15 Sir William Newton St)
**State Bank of Mauritius** ( ☎ 202 1111; State Bank Tower, Place d'Armes)

## Post
**Central post office** ( ☎ 208 2851; Place du Quai; ☪ 8.15am-4pm Mon-Fri, 8.15-11.45am Sat) The last 45 minutes before closing are for stamp sales only.

## Tourist Information
**Mauritius Tourism Promotion Authority** (MTPA; ☎ 210 1545; www.tourism-mauritius.mu; 4-5th fl, Victoria House, St Louis St; ☪ 9am-4pm Mon-Fri, 9am-noon Sat) Distributes maps of Port Louis and Mauritius, and can advise on car hire, excursions and hotels throughout the country.

# DANGERS & ANNOYANCES
Port Louis is a city with a big underclass and as such is not safe at night. After dark all travellers should stick to well-lit main streets and avoid Company Gardens, favoured hang-out of pimps and drug dealers. If you don't know your exact route, take a taxi. During the daytime it's a very safe city but beware of pickpockets anywhere, particularly in the market and around the bus stations.

# SIGHTS & ACTIVITIES
Port Louis has a wide assortment of wonderfully interesting sights; however, the best way to get a feel for the city is to wander through the streets and get lost in the labyrinth of back alleys and winding lanes.

Most of the following sights can be reached on foot – consider a taxi or bus to reach the citadel and Père Laval's shrine.

## Central Market
Port Louis' rightly famous **Central Market** ( ☪ 5.30am-5.30pm Mon-Sat, 5.30am-11.30pm Sun), the centre of the local economy since Victorian times, was cleaned up considerably in a 2004 renovation. Many comment that it's lost much of its dirty charm and atmosphere (you're far less likely to see rats, although it's possible), but it's still a good place to get a feel for the everyday life of many locals, watch the hawkers at work and buy some souvenirs. Most authentic are the wonderful fruit and vegetable sections (including herbal medicines and aphrodisiacs).

If you're looking for souvenirs, a wide variety of Malagasy handicrafts are available, along with souvenir T-shirts of varying quality. The level of hustling here can be tiresome, however, and you'll have to bargain hard; start by slashing the price quoted by about 30%.

## Place d'Armes
The city's most imposing boulevard, Place d'Armes – the Champs-Élysées of Port Louis – is lined with royal palms and leads up to **Government House**, a beautiful French colonial

MAURITIUS

# PORT LOUIS

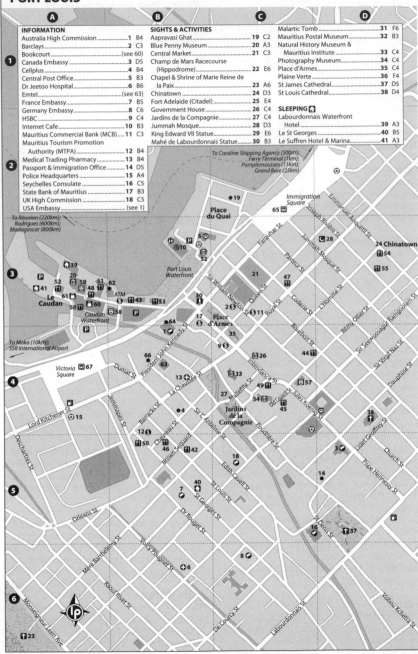

**INFORMATION**
| | |
|---|---|
| Australia High Commission | **1** B4 |
| Barclays | **2** C3 |
| Bookcourt | (see 60) |
| Canada Embassy | **3** D5 |
| Cellplus | **4** B4 |
| Central Post Office | **5** B3 |
| Dr Jeetoo Hospital | **6** B6 |
| Emtel | (see 63) |
| France Embassy | **7** B5 |
| Germany Embassy | **8** C6 |
| HSBC | **9** C4 |
| Internet Cafe | **10** B3 |
| Mauritius Commercial Bank (MCB) | **11** C3 |
| Mauritius Tourism Promotion Authority (MTPA) | **12** B4 |
| Medical Trading Pharmacy | **13** B4 |
| Passport & Immigration Office | **14** D5 |
| Police Headquarters | **15** A4 |
| Seychelles Consulate | **16** C5 |
| State Bank of Mauritius | **17** B3 |
| UK High Commission | **18** C5 |
| USA Embassy | (see 1) |

**SIGHTS & ACTIVITIES**
| | |
|---|---|
| Aapravasi Ghat | **19** C2 |
| Blue Penny Museum | **20** A3 |
| Central Market | **21** C3 |
| Champ de Mars Racecourse (Hippodrome) | **22** E6 |
| Chapel & Shrine of Marie Reine de la Paix | **23** A6 |
| Chinatown | **24** D3 |
| Fort Adelaide (Citadel) | **25** E4 |
| Government House | **26** C4 |
| Jardins de la Compagnie | **27** C4 |
| Jummah Mosque | **28** D3 |
| King Edward VII Statue | **29** E6 |
| Mahé de Labourdonnais Statue | **30** B3 |

| | |
|---|---|
| Malartic Tomb | **31** F6 |
| Mauritius Postal Museum | **32** B3 |
| Natural History Museum & Mauritius Institute | **33** C4 |
| Photography Museum | **34** C4 |
| Place d'Armes | **35** C4 |
| Plaine Verte | **36** F4 |
| St James Cathedral | **37** D5 |
| St Louis Cathedral | **38** D4 |

**SLEEPING**
| | |
|---|---|
| Labourdonnais Waterfront Hotel | **39** A3 |
| Le St Georges | **40** B5 |
| Le Suffren Hotel & Marina | **41** A3 |

To Coraline Shipping Agency (500m);
Ferry Terminal (1km);
Pamplemousses (11km);
Grand Baie (25km)

To Réunion (220km);
Rodrigues (600km);
Madagascar (800km)

Place du Quai

Immigration Square

Port Louis Waterfront

Le Caudan

Caudan Waterfront

ATM

To Moka (10km);
SSR International Airport

Place d'Armes

24 Chinatown

Victoria Square

Jardins de la Compagnie

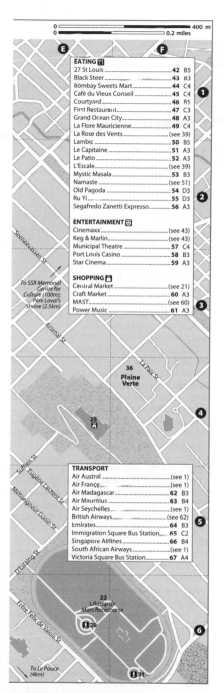

0 ——————— 400 m
0 ——————— 0.2 miles

**EATING** 🍴
27 St Louis ........................................ **42** B5
Black Steer ...................................... **43** B3
Bombay Sweets Mart ................... **44** C4
Café du Vieux Conseil ................. **45** C4
Courtyard ......................................... **46** B5
First Restaurant .............................. **47** C3
Grand Ocean City .......................... **48** A3
La Flore Mauricienne .................... **49** C4
La Rose des Vents ..................... (see 39)
Lambic ............................................... **50** B5
Le Capitaine .................................... **51** A3
Le Patio ............................................ **52** A3
L'Escale ........................................ (see 39)
Mystic Masala ................................ **53** B3
Namaste ...................................... (see 51)
Old Pagoda ...................................... **54** D3
Ru Yi ................................................... **55** D3
Segafredo Zanetti Expresso ....... **56** A3

**ENTERTAINMENT** 🎭
Cinemaxx ..................................... (see 43)
Keg & Marlin ................................ (see 43)
Municipal Theatre ......................... **57** C4
Port Louis Casino ........................... **58** B3
Star Cinema ..................................... **59** A3

**SHOPPING** 🛍
Central Market ............................ (see 21)
Craft Market .................................... **60** A3
MAST ............................................. (see 60)
Power Music ..................................... **61** A3

Seeneevassen St

To SSR Memorial
Centre for
Culture (100m);
Père Laval's
Shrine (2.5km)

Arsenal St

**36**
**Plaine**
**Verte**

La Paix St

**25**

Suffren St

Eugène Laurent St

Monseigneur Gonin St

**TRANSPORT**
Air Austral ................................... (see 1)
Air France ..................................... (see 1)
Air Madagascar ............................. **62** B3
Air Mauritius .................................. **63** B4
Air Seychelles .............................. (see 1)
British Airways ............................ (see 62)
Emirates ........................................... **64** B3
Immigration Square Bus Station .. **65** C2
Singapore Airlines ........................ **66** B4
South African Airways ................ (see 1)
Victoria Square Bus Station ........ **67** A4

D'Estaing St

**22**
Champ de
Mars Racecourse

**29**

Frère Felix de Valois St

To Le Pouce
(4km)

**31**

structure dating from 1738. Outside there's a typically solemn statue of Queen Victoria in full 'we are not amused' mode. The **statue of Mahé de Labourdonnais** at the quayside end of the avenue is the best-loved in the city and has become Port Louis' emblem throughout Mauritius.

One of the major intersections is named after Sookdeo Bissoondoyal, a senior Mauritian politician, independence leader and, eventually, opposition leader against Navin Ramgoolam, who died in 1977.

## Jardins de la Compagnie

It's a real pity that Jardins de la Compagnie (Company Gardens) has such a sleazy atmosphere as it's by far the most attractive park in the city, with its vast banyan trees, huge number of statues, quiet benches and fountains. During the day it's perfectly safe, but you should avoid it at night when it becomes the city's favoured hang-out for prostitutes and drug addicts. In early colonial times, the gardens were the vegetable patch of the French East India Company. Today, it's best known for its statues of local sculptor Prosper d'Épinay and the much-loved musician Ti-Frère (see p54).

## Chinatown

The Chinese have traditionally occupied a quietly industrious position in the life of Port Louis. The region between the two 'friendship gates' on Royal St forms the centre of Port Louis' Chinatown. Here you'll see the rich mercantile life of the hard-working Chinese community, the busy Chinese restaurants and grocery stores, and the streets echoing with the unmistakable clatter of mah-jong tiles.

## Fort Adelaide (Citadel)

Fort Adelaide, also known as the Citadel, resembles a Moorish fortress. Built by the British, the fort sits high on the crown of a hill, offering splendid views over the city and its harbour. The old barracks have been restored and transformed into a row of intriguing boutiques – good for a few minutes of window-shopping. The quickest route up is via Suffren St. Allow around 10 minutes for the climb.

## Blue Penny Museum

Whether or not you fully understand the philatelic obsession with the Mauritian one-penny and two-pence stamps of 1847, the **Blue Penny Museum** ( ☎ 210 8176; www.bluepennymuseum.com;

MAURITIUS

---

**A MILLION-DOLLAR STAMP?**

Philatelists (that's 'stamp collectors' to the rest of us) go weak at the knees at the mention of the Mauritian 'Post Office' one-penny and two-pence stamps. Issued in 1847, these stamps were incorrectly printed with the words 'Post Office' rather than 'Post Paid'. They were recalled upon discovery of the error, but not before the wife of the British governor had mailed out a few dozen on invitations to one of her famous balls.

These stamps now rank among the most valuable in the world. The 'Bordeaux cover', a letter bearing both stamps which was mailed to France, was last sold for a staggering US$3.8 million. In 1993 a consortium of Mauritian companies paid US$2.2 million for the pair of unused one-penny and two-pence stamps now on display in Port Louis' Blue Penny Museum. This is the only place in the world where the two can be seen together on public view.

---

Caudan Waterfront; adult/child Rs 225/100; 10am-5pm Mon-Sat) is far more wide ranging than its name suggests, taking in the history of the island's exploration, settlement and colonial period. It's Port Louis' best museum, with a fantastic selection of antique maps, photographs and engravings from different periods in history. There's a room dedicated to temporary exhibits and a small gift shop as well.

The pride of the museum's collection is two of the world's rarest stamps: the red one-penny and blue two-pence 'Post Office' stamps issued in 1847 (see the boxed text, p68). To preserve the colours, they are only lit up for 10 minutes at a time: every hour, on the half-hour. They were returned to the island after being purchased by a consortium of Mauritian companies (including Beachcomber and Air Mauritius). The stamps are considered a national treasure and are probably the most valuable objects on the entire island.

On the ground floor you'll see the country's most famous work of art: a superbly life-like statue by the Mauritian sculptor Prosper d'Épinay, carved in 1884. Based on Bernardin de St-Pierre's novel *Paul et Virginie* (see p131), the sculpture depicts the young hero carrying his sweetheart across a raging torrent.

### Natural History Museum & Mauritius Institute

There's only one real attraction at this small but proud **museum** ( 212 0639; La Chaussée St; admission free; 9am-4pm Mon, Tue, Thu & Fri, 9am-noon Sat): the famous (though somewhat grubby) reconstruction of a dodo. Scottish scientists assembled the curious-looking bird in the late 19th century, using the only complete dodo skeleton in existence (see p69). The rest of the museum's three halls get marks for trying, but

the majority of the other exhibits are a sad testimony to the fact that fish don't readily lend themselves to the process of taxidermy. Look out, however, for the stuffed birds, including the solitaire and red rail, both also now extinct.

### Mauritius Postal Museum

This interesting **museum** ( 213 4812; www.mauritiuspost.mu; Place du Quai; adult/child Rs 150/90; 9.30am-4.30pm Mon-Fri, 10am-4pm Sat) beside the central post office houses a mishmash of commemorative stamps and other postal paraphernalia from around the world. A new exhibit details the history of the Mauritius post using a rich assortment of photographs and artefacts. Of particular interest is the display about mail delivery to the remote dependencies of Agaléga and St Bandon. The museum shop sells replica first-day covers of the famous 'Post Office' stamps of 1847 (see the boxed text, p68), which make unusual souvenirs.

### Photography Museum

This small but engaging **museum** ( 211 1705; www.voyaz.com/musee-photo; Old Council St; admission Rs 150; 9am-3pm Mon-Fri), down a cobbled lane opposite the Municipal Theatre, is the labour of love of local photographer Tristan Bréville. He's amassed a treasure trove of old cameras and prints, including several daguerreotypes (the forerunner of photographs) produced in Mauritius in 1840, just a few months after the technique was discovered in France. The museum also contains a vast archive of historical photos of the island (however, only a fraction are on display).

### Père Laval's Shrine

The **shrine** (Map p75; 242 2129; 8.30am-noon & 1-4.45pm Mon-Sat, 10am-noon & 1-4pm Sun) of the French Catholic priest and missionary Père Jacques Désiré Laval is something of a Lourdes of the Indian Ocean, with many miracles attributed to visits to the priest's grave. The padre died in 1864 and was beatified in 1979 during a visit by Pope John Paul II. He is credited with converting 67,000 people to Christianity during his 23 years in Mauritius.

Today Père Laval is a popular figure for Mauritians of all religions. Pilgrims come here from as far afield as South Africa, Britain and France to commemorate the anniversary of his death on 9 September. Notice the coloured plaster effigy of the priest on top of the tomb – it's been rubbed smooth by miracle-wishing pilgrims.

At other times of year the shrine is fairly quiet, though the services held on Friday at 1pm and 5pm attract a reasonable crowd. In the same complex is a large modern church and a shop with a permanent exhibition of Père Laval's robe, mitre, letters and photographs. The shrine is slightly removed from the city centre. To get there, take a bus signed 'Cité La Cure' or 'Père Laval' from the Immigration Square bus station.

## Cathedrals & Churches

Notable places of worship include **St James Cathedral** (Poudrière St) and **St Louis Cathedral** (Sir William Newton St). Inaugurated in 1850, St James is the oldest Anglican church in Mauritius, and has a peaceful, wood-panelled interior with plaques commemorating local worthies. The more austere, but also busier, St Louis

Cathedral dates from 1932 and is popular with the Chinese community.

The modern **chapel and shrine of Marie Reine de la Paix** (Monseigneur Leen Ave) is a popular spot for prayers, and the ornamental gardens offer views over the city. During Pope John Paul II's visit to the island he officiated his first Mass here. The most important place of pilgrimage for Mauritian Christians is the shrine of Père Laval on the city's northern outskirts (p68).

## Aapravasi Ghat

If you've spent at least a day driving around the island then you've probably noticed the dozens of large brown signs cryptically mentioning this cultural site without providing any further information. Aapravasi Ghat is a small complex of buildings located on the seafront – it served as the island's main immigration depot for indentured labourers from India. Britain pioneered their indentured servant scheme in Mauritius and from 1849 to 1923 over half a million immigrants were processed here before being shipped to various plantations or other colonial islands. Today, almost 70% of Mauritius' citizens can trace their roots back to Aapravasi Ghat. The Aapravasi Ghat Trust Fund manages the property, and although there isn't heaps to see besides having a wander around and taking in the surroundings, there are plans underway to fully restore all of the structure. The ghat was listed a World Heritage Site by Unesco in 2006 for its important role in the island's social history.

---

**DEAD AS A DODO**

Illustrations from the logbooks of the first ships to reach Mauritius show hundreds of plump flightless birds running down to the beach to investigate the newcomers. Lacking natural predators, these giant relatives of the pigeon were easy prey for hungry sailors, who named the bird *dodo*, meaning 'stupid'. It took just 30 years for passing sailors and their pets and pests (dogs, monkeys, pigs and rats) to drive the dodo to extinction; the last confirmed sighting was in the 1660s.

Just as surprising as the speed of the dodo's demise is how little evidence remains that the bird ever existed. A few relics made it back to Europe during the 18th century – a dried beak ended up at the University of Copenhagen in Denmark, while the University of Oxford in England managed to get hold of a whole head and a foot – but until recently our knowledge of the dodo was mainly based on sketches by 17th-century seamen.

However, in 1865 local schoolteacher George Clark discovered a dodo skeleton in a marshy area on the site of what is now the international airport. The skeleton was reassembled by scientists in Edinburgh, and has formed the basis of all subsequent dodo reconstructions, one of which is on display in the Natural History Museum in Port Louis.

For the full story of the dodo's demise, read Errol Fuller's fascinating book *Dodo: From Extinction to Icon*.

MAURITIUS

## Jummah Mosque

The **Jummah Mosque** (Royal St; ◷ 8am-noon & 2-4pm Mon-Thu, Sat & Sun), the most important mosque in Mauritius, was built in the 1850s, and is a delightful blend of Indian, Creole and Islamic architecture – it would look equally at home in Istanbul, Delhi or New Orleans! Visitors are welcome in the peaceful inner courtyard except on Fridays and during the month of Ramadan.

## Champ de Mars Racecourse (Hippodrome)

This racecourse, also known as the Hippodrome, was a military training ground until the **Mauritius Turf Club** ( ☎ 211 2147; www.mau ritiusturfclub.com) was founded in 1812, making it the second-oldest racecourse in the world. Mauritian independence was proclaimed here in 1968. Within the racecourse stands a statue of **King Edward VII** by the sculptor Prosper d'Épinay, and the **Malartic Tomb**, an obelisk to a French governor.

The racing season lasts from around April to late November, with meetings usually held on a Saturday or Sunday. The biggest race of all is the Maiden Cup in September. If you're here on a race day, it's well worth joining the throng of betting-crazy locals. Tickets for the stands and loges range from Rs 50 to 100, but admission to the rest of the ground is usually free. For race dates, contact the Mauritius Turf Club or check the local media.

## SSR Memorial Centre for Culture

This simple **house museum** ( ☎ 242 0053; Sir Seewoosagur Ramgoolam St; admission free; ◷ 9am-4pm Mon-Fri, 9am-noon Sat) near the Jardin Plaine Verte was home to Mauritius' father of independence, Sir Seewoosagur Ramgoolam, from 1935 until 1968. It's an interesting exhibit on his life, with some fascinating photographs, a collection of his personal belongings and even films about the great man, beloved by all Mauritians.

## Plaine Verte

Located on the far side of the citadel, Plaine Verte is the Muslim quarter of the city and strongly contrasts the glass towers in central Port Louis. Very little care is given to the area's facades – construction materials (usually concrete) are always left exposed – which gives the neighbourhood a certain dilapidated feel despite the lively bustle. After snooping around some of the alleyways for tucked-away

bakeries, make your way to the vibrant fabric shops lining **Papillon St**.

## SLEEPING

We do not particularly recommend staying in Port Louis – the selection of quality sleeps is minimal and the city is practically a ghost town after sunset. The following choices (the only places that don't feel like dosshouses) are all upmarket.

**Le St Georges** ( ☎ 211 2581; 19 St Georges St; r incl breakfast from Rs 2000; ⊠ ◻ ⍮ ) Towering above the surrounding residential neighbourhood, Le St Georges is excellent value for money. The rooms are fairly unexciting but they are clean and equipped with all the necessary comforts. There's a decent breakfast and a pool for relaxing by, as well as a pleasant bar and restaurant. The location is also good, just a five-minute walk from the centre of town.

**Le Suffren Hotel & Marina** ( ☎ 202 4000; www. lesuffrenhotel.com; Caudan Waterfront; d Rs 6000-9000; ⊠ ◻ ⏃ ⍮ ) Le Suffren is the trendier sister hotel to the Labourdonnais, just a short complimentary boat ride away. For better or for worse you feel like you're almost out of the city despite being just a couple of minutes from the waterfront. The rooms are smaller than at the Labourdonnais but the place has a very pleasant, convivial feel, with an excellent bar and restaurant.

**Labourdonnais Waterfront Hotel** ( ☎ 202 4000; www.labourdonnais.com; Caudan Waterfront; d incl breakfast Rs 8000-12,000; ⊠ ◻ ⏃ ⍮ ) Definitely the best option in town, the Labourdonnais is an ultrasmart business hotel on the Caudan Waterfront. The rooms are excellent – even the standards are huge. All are bathed in light, with cavernous bathrooms, and most have excellent views of the city and harbour, particularly the so-called 'turret rooms' at each top corner. Facilities include a gym, pool and business centre, and there are a number of eateries.

## EATING

Port Louis has a great eating scene where the ethnic diversity of the city again comes up trumps. As the middle classes tend to reside outside the city many places are only open for lunch – head to the Caudan Waterfront in the evenings and on weekends.

## City Centre

Central Port Louis features an endless assortment of eating establishments at both ends of the dining spectrum – from frenetic roadside vendors to atmospheric restaurants set within the city's last remaining colonial homes.

The Central Market, Chinatown and the bus stations provide happy hunting grounds for street-side nibbles, but you'll find stalls all over town peddling *samousas, gâteaux piments* and *dhal puri*. The general rule of thumb is to queue behind the longest line – gossip travels fast and everyone seems to simultaneously know who's serving up the best stall grub. **Bombay Sweets Mart** (7 Rémy Ollier St) is famous for the Indian nibbles colourfully known as *caca pigeon* (literally, 'pigeon droppings'). In Chinatown, locals line up for honey-glazed pork at the **old pagoda** (Emmanuel Anquetil St; 100g pork Rs 30; ✆ 9am-1pm).

**Ru Yi** (32 Joseph Rivière St; mains Rs 90-290; ✆ 11am-2pm & 6-10pm) You can't go wrong with any of the restaurants in Chinatown, but this one is a favourite for its commitment to high-quality dishes. The atmosphere is a bit lacking, but then again when has an inner-city Chinese restaurant ever been featured in a design magazine?

**First Restaurant** ( ☎ 212 0685; cnr Royal & Coderie Sts; mains from Rs 120; ✆ lunch & dinner Tue-Sun) If the age-old rule that a good Chinese restaurant is full of Chinese diners applies, then First is a winner. Packed with large family groups enjoying vast feasts of delicious Cantonese cooking, this is one of Chinatown's finest and prices are surprisingly reasonable for the quality of the fare.

**La Flore Mauricienne** ( ☎ 212 2200; 10 Intendance St; mains Rs 250; ✆ 7.30am-5pm Mon-Fri, 8.30am-1pm Sat) There's something rather Parisian about the bustle and brusque service here, but then this is a long-standing favourite lunchtime haunt of the local business and political elite as well as tourists. The daily specials are always good value, and there's a big selection of dishes including a good vegetarian choice. Inside it's a more formal setting, whereas the terrace is a great place to people-watch.

**27 St Louis** ( ☎ 212 5823; 27B St Louis St; mains Rs 250-800; ✆ noon-3pm daily, dinner Fri) Recognised as one of the top addresses in Port Louis (if not all of Mauritius) for a high-end spin on local cuisine, 27 St Louis promises delicious homages to Creole fusion fare served up in a charmingly restored plantation-era manse. Bistro eats – think scrumptious croissant sandwiches – are available for tighter budgets.

**our pick** **Lambic** ( ☎ 212 6011; 4 St Georges St; mains Rs 500; ✆ 8am-10.45pm Mon-Sat) Set in a refurbished colonial home in the heart of the capital's chaos, Lambic is a beer buff's paradise. If the dark-wood bar, antique timber beams and fanned napkins don't win you over, then you'll surely be impressed by the glass-faced pantries covering all the interior walls – they reveal hundreds upon hundreds of alcoholic imports. Waiters are well versed in the high art of matching platters to pints (yes, that's right – you match your meal *to* your beer here). If you're thinking about sticking around for a while, why not join the beer club – it meets regularly to wax philosophic about brewing styles.

**Courtyard** ( ☎ 210 0810; cnr St Louis & Chevreau Sts; mains Rs 600-1300; ✆ 9am-5pm) Set around an eponymous courtyard, this European-style restaurant also features a stylish indoor dining space built in a restored stone structure. The impressive menu focuses on a memorable assortment of fusion tastes and fresh cuisine, such as steaming seafood and finely sliced carpaccios.

**Café du Vieux Conseil** ( ☎ 211 0393; Old Council St; mains Rs 1200; ✆ 8am-4pm Mon-Sat) Down a charming side street, this lunchtime institution must have the most delightful location of any restaurant in Port Louis. The food is nothing spectacular, and somewhat pricey, but there's a good choice from crêpes and salads to octopus curry and smoked marlin.

## Caudan Waterfront

There's a wide variety of restaurants and cafes in the Caudan complex, from bustling food courts to upscale seaside dining. Lunching locals gravitate towards takeaway eats or Pizza Hut; you'll find the cruise crowd enjoying overpriced fare at the hotels.

**Mystic Masala** (snacks & mains Rs 60-210; ✆ lunch & dinner) Tasty Indian snacks and light meals are the order of the day at this harbourfront kiosk with its handful of trestle tables.

**Le Patio** ( ☎ 213 5353; mains from Rs 120; ✆ lunch) A favourite for those seeking salads and sandwiches instead of street stalls.

**Segafredo Zanetti Expresso** ( ☎ 211 7346; snacks & mains from Rs 120; ✆ 9.30am-5.30pm) Finally a decent cup of joe! Salads and pastries also refresh the curry-jaded palate.

**Grand Ocean City** ( ☎ 211 8357; mains Rs 180-380; ✆ noon-2pm) Excellent Shanghainese treats. Hands down the best place in Port Louis for dim sum (on Thursday and Sunday).

**Namaste** ( ☎ 211 6710; mains from Rs 200; ✆ lunch & dinner, closed lunch Sun) Namaste manages to be atmospheric despite its location in the sanitised Caudan complex. The specialities here are North Indian.

**MAURITIUS**

**Black Steer** ( ☎ 211 9147; mains Rs 250; ✓ lunch & dinner) This link in the popular steakhouse chain overlooks the harbour and offers great steaks, mixed grills, combos and the like.

**Le Capitaine** ( ☎ 213 0038; mains Rs 280-500; ✓ 11.30am-4pm & 6-10pm) Small, stylish and reasonably priced. Seafood and Mauritian classics are on offer. A terrace full of tables offers great views back to the city centre.

**L'Escale** ( ☎ 202 4017; mains from Rs 300; ✓ 6.30am-11pm) The main restaurant of the Labourdonnais Waterfront Hotel. A refined and elegant option serving superb local creations like prawn stew.

**La Rose des Vents** ( ☎ 202 4017; mains Rs 400-800; ✓ lunch & dinner, closed Sat lunch & Sun) The Labourdonnais Waterfront Hotel boasts this upmarket seafood restaurant, famed for its lobster dishes.

## DRINKING & ENTERTAINMENT

Port Louis is not exactly a happening place at night and come sunset the city is virtually silent as commuters retire to the Central Plateau towns. What evening life there is tends to be concentrated on the Caudan Waterfront. A movie, a cocktail or a gamble are about all that's available; for nightlife you'll be better off in Grand Baie or Flic en Flac.

### Casino

**Port Louis Casino** ( ☎ 210 4203; Caudan Waterfront; ✓ 10am-4am, gaming tables 8pm-4am; 🕱 ) The mighty popular city casino is about the liveliest place in town after midnight – its salient feature externally is its ship-shaped design, crowned at its prow by the campest lion imaginable. Miaow. There are slot machines downstairs and blackjack and American roulette on the 1st floor. Smart-casual dress is required.

### Cinemas

**Star Cinema** ( ☎ 211 5361; Caudan Waterfront; tickets Rs 150; 🕱 ) This is Port Louis' biggest and best cinema, with three screens offering mainstream international releases. Films are generally dubbed in French and there are usually four or five screenings a day.

**Cinemaxx** ( ☎ 210 7416; Caudan Waterfront; tickets Rs 100; 🕱 ) The two-screen Cinemaxx usually shows one Hindi or Tamil film and one international release daily. Again, most films are dubbed in French, though occasionally you'll find one with English subtitles.

### Live Music

**Keg & Marlin** ( ☎ 211 6821; Caudan Waterfront; ✓ noon-midnight Mon-Thu, to 3am Fri, to 1am Sat & Sun; 🕱 ) At the weekends the Keg & Marlin transforms into Port Louis' only live-music venue. Standards vary enormously from rock outfits to *séga* (Mauritian folk dance).

### Theatre

The appealing **Municipal Theatre** (Jules Koenig St) has changed little since it was built in 1822, making it the oldest theatre in the Indian Ocean region. Decorated in the style of the classic London theatres, it seats about 600 over three levels, and has an exquisitely painted dome ceiling with cherubs and chandeliers. Performances are in the evenings – usually at 8pm, and cost upwards of Rs 100. Look for announcements in the local press or call the tourist office to find out what's on. Theatre tickets can be purchased at the box office in the theatre itself.

## SHOPPING

Most of the city centre's main streets have clusters of merchants selling similar items. Bourbon St has swarms of flower sellers, Coderie St (also spelt Corderie St) has silk and fabric vendors, and La Chaussée St is where locals go to buy electronics.

Port Louis' **Central Market** ( ✓ 5.30am-5.30pm Mon-Sat, 5.30am-11.30pm Sun) has a wide selection of T-shirts, basketry, spices and souvenirs; bargain to get a decent price.

Based in the Caudan Waterfront, **Craft Market** ( ☎ 210 0139; ✓ 9.30am-3.30pm) is less fun but also less hassle than Central Market. You'll find more-upmarket souvenirs, such as Mauritius glass and essential oils, from the Domaine de l'Ylang Ylang. The model ship manufacturer **MAST** ( ☎ 211 7170; ✓ 9.30am-3.30pm) also has an outlet here.

The Caudan Waterfront is also the place to go for trendy knick-knacks and designer boutiques, including Floreal, Maille St, Shibani, IV Pl@y and Habit. **Power Music** ( ☎ 211 9143; ✓ 9.30am-3.30pm) stocks a good selection of CDs by local artists.

## GETTING THERE & AWAY

All of the main airlines serving Mauritius have offices near the waterfront.

**Air Austral** ( ☎ 202 6677; Rogers House, 5 President John Kennedy St)

**Air France** ( ☎ 202 6747; Rogers House, 5 President John Kennedy St)

**Air Madagascar** ( ☎ 203 2150; IBL House, Caudan Waterfront)

**Air Mauritius** ( ☎ 207 7212; Air Mauritius Centre, President John Kennedy St)

**Air Seychelles** ( ☎ 202 6655; Rogers House, 5 President John Kennedy St)

**British Airways** ( ☎ 202 8000; IBL House, Caudan Waterfront)

**Emirates** ( ☎ 213 9100; Harbour Front Bldg, Place d'Armes)

**Singapore Airlines** ( ☎ 208 7695; 3 President John Kennedy St)

**South African Airways** ( ☎ 202 6737; Rogers House, 5 President John Kennedy St)

### Bus

Port Louis' two bus stations are both located in the city centre. Buses for northern and eastern destinations, such as Trou aux Biches, Grand Baie and Pamplemousses, leave from Immigration Square, northeast of the Central Market. Buses for southern and western destinations, such as Mahébourg, Curepipe and Quatre Bornes, use the Victoria Square terminus just southwest of the city centre.

The first departure on most routes is at about 6am; the last leaves at around 6pm.

### Ferry

Ferries to Rodrigues and Réunion dock beside the passenger terminal on Quai D of Port Louis harbour, 1km northwest of town. For more information about boats to and from Rodrigues, see p144; for Réunion, see p322.

### Taxi

Taxis from Port Louis to Grand Baie cost Rs 800. To Flic en Flac it's Rs 950, to Mahébourg it's Rs 1200 and to Belle Mare it's Rs 1500. If you'd prefer a private vehicle, contact any of the island's rental agencies (p159) – they'll deliver the car to your hotel.

### GETTING AROUND
#### To/From the Airport

There are no special airport buses, but regular services between Port Louis and Mahébourg call at the airport; the stop is roughly 300m from the terminal buildings, near the large roundabout. Heading to the airport from Port Louis, allow two hours to be on the safe side and make sure the conductor knows where you're going, as drivers occasionally skip the detour down to the airport.

Expect to pay Rs 1000 for a taxi from Port Louis to the airport – the ride takes one hour

if you're taking one of the morning flights back to Europe.

### Car

Given the number of traffic snarls, it's not worth trying to drive around Port Louis. Daytrippers are advised to leave their car in one of the car parks at the Caudan Waterfront. These are open from 7am to 11pm and cost Rs 30 for the first four hours plus Rs 30 for each additional hour. The turn-off to the Caudan is located at a marked roundabout south of the city centre. Thus, if you are coming from the north part of the island, you must drive all the way through the city, pass the waterfront complex, then make a U shape back towards the city on a signposted side road.

Cars can be parked on the street for a maximum of two hours at a time; a marked parking coupon, available at any filling station, must be displayed on the dashboard. See p159 for more about street parking.

### Taxi

As a general rule, do not take a taxi around the city centre during daylight hours. The traffic jams are perpetual and you'll quickly notice that the pedestrians are moving faster than the cars. If for some reason you find yourself needing to get around Port Louis after dark, expect to pay Rs 100 for a short taxi ride across town. And, as usual, always agree to a price beforehand.

# CENTRAL PLATEAU

Home to a large majority of Mauritians, the cool and rainy centre of the island feels like a continuation of the urban chaos in Port Louis. There's very little to see in the corridor of towns that runs almost unbroken from the capital to Curepipe; in fact, it's pretty much the opposite of that postcard your friends sent you from their trip here last year.

For tourists interested in learning about life on the island beyond the sand and sun, there are a few worthwhile attractions hidden among the gridiron – the best is Eureka, a charming plantation home and museum. Visitors looking for retail therapy will also enjoy an afternoon of snooping around the local markets and factory outlets for discounted apparel, diamonds and model ships.

The urban sprawl quickly dissipates after Curepipe, leaving way for a variety of natural wonders – such as Black River Gorges National Park and Grand Bassin, a sacred pilgrimage sight for Hindus – that should definitely feature on your to-do list. These hot spots can be found in our coverage of the west part of the island (p96).

## Getting There & Around

The Central Plateau towns are serviced by frequent bus connections with Port Louis. Other useful routes include the direct services between Quatre Bornes and Flic en Flac, on the west coast, and between Curepipe and Mahébourg, to the southeast; the latter service passes the airport.

As usual, the best way to get around the island is by private vehicle. Cars can be arranged through your accommodation. If you take a taxi, you're looking at Rs 1200 from Quatre Bornes to Grand Baie, Rs 700 to Flic en Flac and Rs 1000 to the airport.

## PAILLES
pop 10,100

Just a few miles outside of the capital, the strange sugar-estate-turned-theme-park **Domaine Les Pailles** (Map p75; ☎ 286 4225; www.do mainelespailles.net; ☸ 10am-4.30pm) has been transformed into a cultural and heritage centre that makes for an enjoyable half-day excursion. The facilities include rides in horse-drawn carriages, a miniature railway, a working replica of a traditional ox-driven sugar mill, a rum distillery producing the estate's own brew, a spice garden, a quad-biking circuit and a children's playground. On weekdays it's also possible to horseback ride around the estate. Call the riding centre, **Les Écuries du Domaine** ( ☎ 286 4240; ☸ 8am-5.30pm Mon-Fri, 8am-noon Sat), to make a reservation.

The Domaine also has a great selection of upmarket restaurants – expect to pay upwards

of Rs 500 for your meal. Best of the bunch is the **Clos St Louis** ( ☸ lunch Mon-Sat, dinner Fri & Sat), which serves French and Mauritian cuisine in a charming plantation home. At the pillow-strewn **Indra** ( ☸ lunch & dinner Mon-Sat), diners will savour a Mauritian twist on traditional Indian cuisine amid ambient thumps of a tabla and languid strums of a sitar. Try **Fu Xiao** ( ☸ lunch Sun-Fri, dinner daily) for Chinese cuisine, and **La Dolce Vita** ( ☸ lunch daily, dinner Wed, Fri & Sat) for pool-side Italian dining with a spot of minigolf.

To get to the Domaine, take any bus running between Port Louis and Curepipe and ask to be let off at the turn-off for Domaine Les Pailles (it's clearly signposted). From the main road it takes less than half an hour on foot to the reception. Alternatively, it's a 10-minute taxi ride from Port Louis or Moka.

## MOKA & AROUND
pop 8800

The most charming of the Central Plateau towns, the country's academic centre and official home to the president of Mauritius, picturesque Moka is a great place to visit for a taste of Mauritian history. The scenery is dramatic here, too, with waterfalls, valleys and the towering Le Pouce (812m; p74) in the background. Moka's main attraction, though, is the captivating colonial mansion of Eureka. Almost perfectly preserved from the mid-19th century, it provides an interesting window to the island's plantation past.

### Eureka

If you're only going to visit one attraction related to Mauritius' rich colonial history, choose **Eureka** (Map p75; ☎ 433 8477; www.maisoneu reka.com; admission house Rs 175, house & waterfall Rs 300; ☸ 9am-5pm Mon-Sat, 9am-3pm Sun). This perfectly preserved Creole mansion was built in the 1830s and today it's a museum and veritable

---

**HIKING THE CENTRAL PLATEAU**

The mountain ranges fringing the Central Plateau offer a variety of memorable rambles and hikes. Two of the best introductions to hiking in Mauritius are **Le Pouce** (812m), a thumb-shaped peak on the plateau's northern edge, and **Corps de Garde** (719m), a wedge-like ridge to the southwest that makes for a slightly more challenging endeavour.

Both hikes offer resplendent views down to the coastal plains, but are best appreciated when tackled with a local guide who can annotate the hike with detailed information about the local flora and history. See p149 for suggested operators. If you decide to go at it alone, check out www.fitsy.com, a brilliant website that has mapped out the walks with extensive GPS and satellite detail. For planning purposes, allow about two hours for each hike if you're starting at the trailhead.

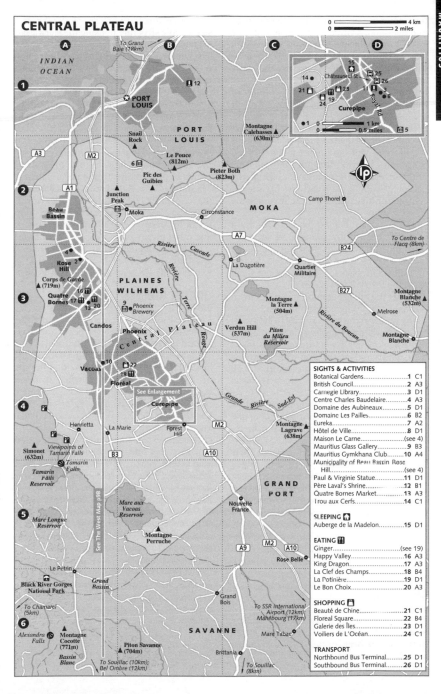

# CENTRAL PLATEAU

**SIGHTS & ACTIVITIES**
Botanical Gardens......................1 C1
British Council...........................2 A3
Carnegie Library........................3 D1
Centre Charles Baudelaire..........4 A3
Domaine des Aubineaux.............5 D1
Domaine Les Pailles..................6 B2
Eureka.....................................7 A2
Hôtel de Ville............................8 D1
Maison Le Carne....................(see 4)
Mauritius Glass Gallery..............9 B3
Mauritius Gymkhana Club........10 A4
Municipality of Beau Bassin Rose
 Hill......................................(see 4)
Paul & Virginie Statue..............11 D1
Père Laval's Shrine...................12 B1
Quatre Bornes Market..............13 A3
Trou aux Cerfs.........................14 C1

**SLEEPING**
Auberge de la Madelon............15 D1

**EATING**
Ginger.................................(see 19)
Happy Valley..........................16 A3
King Dragon...........................17 A3
La Clef des Champs.................18 B4
La Potinière............................19 D1
Le Bon Choix..........................20 A3

**SHOPPING**
Beauté de Chine.....................21 C1
Floreal Square........................22 B4
Galerie des Îles.......................23 D1
Voiliers de L'Océan.................24 C1

**TRANSPORT**
Northbound Bus Terminal........25 D1
Southbound Bus Terminal.........26 D1

time machine providing incredible insight into the island's vibrant plantation past. The estate's unusual name is believed to have been the reaction of Eugène Le Clézio when he successfully won a bid to purchase the house at auction in 1856.

The main manor house is a masterpiece of tropical construction, which apparently kept the interior deliciously cool during the unbearably hot summers, and boasts 109 doors and more rooms than a Cluedo board. Rooms are adorned with an impeccably preserved collection of period furniture imported by the French East India Company – take special note of the antique maps and a strange shower contraption that was quite the luxury some 150 years ago.

The courtyard behind the main mansion contains beautifully manicured grounds surrounded by a set of stone cottages – the former servants quarters and kitchen. Follow the trail out the back for 15 minutes and you'll reach the lovely Ravin waterfall.

To get the full experience, we recommend planning your visit around noon to enjoy a relaxing repast at the in-house **table d'hôte** (menu Rs 600; ☺ noon-3pm). Sample an assortment of Mauritian classics like *marlin fumée* (smoked fish), lentils and curried fish while enjoying the delightful throwback atmosphere. Call ahead as sometimes the restaurant is closed for tour groups.

If you wish to spend the night on the plantation, there are two authentic cottages on the property that have been converted into lovely bedrooms with en suite facilities and kitchenettes. Both rooms at this so-called **maison d'hôte** (r incl breakfast Rs 3450) have period furnishings from the French East India Company. The St George cabin, the smaller of the two units, was once the cell for the estate's priest. At the time of research plans were underway to convert a third cottage into accommodation.

To get to Eureka, take a bus from Curepipe or Victoria Square in Port Louis and get off at Moka. Eureka is signed about 1km north of the bus stop.

## ROSE HILL
pop 106,000

Rose Hill (pronounced row-zeel by locals), wedged between Beau Bassin and Quatre Bornes in the heart of the Central Plateau's conurbation, is virtually a suburb of Port Louis and a major cultural centre for Mauritius.

Architecture buffs will appreciate the unusual Creole structure housing the **Municipality of Beau Bassin-Rose Hill** (Map p75) on St Jean Rd. The building was constructed in 1933 as a municipal theatre. The attractive Creole manse next door – **Maison Le Carne** (Map p75) – houses the Mauritius Research Council.

Two of Mauritius' most important cultural centres are also located in Rose Hill. The **British Council** (Map p75; ☎ 403 0200; general.enquiries@mu.britishcouncil.org; St Jean Rd; ☺ 11am-5pm Tue-Fri, 9am-2.30pm Sat) is across the main road from the bus station. It has a regular program of events in English and a good library. Behind Maison Le Carne is the **Centre Charles Baudelaire** (Map p75; ☎ 454 7929; ccb@intnet.mu; 15/17 Gordon St; ☺ 10am-5.30pm Tue-Fri, 9am-3pm Sat), which puts on an impressive schedule of plays, concerts and other events promoting French culture.

There are regular buses from Port Louis and Curepipe to Rose Hill, and from Rose Hill to Centre de Flacq on the east coast.

## QUATRE BORNES
pop 81,000

For most tourists, Quatre Bornes is nothing more than a continuation of Port Louis' haphazard urban sprawl – its main street, St Jean Rd, is always choked with traffic. Despite the vehicular setback, it's worth visiting the city on Thursdays and Sundays when scores of locals flock to the city to rummage through stall upon stall at the bustling produce and textile **market** (Map p75); there's also a popular vegie market on Saturdays.

After an exhausting jaunt through the market, check out one of following restaurants: **King Dragon** (Map p75; ☎ 426 0223; St Jean Rd; mains Rs 160-1000; ☺ noon-2pm & 6.30-10pm) If you liked Domaine Anna in Flic en Flac, then you'll love this local favourite owned by the same family. Expertly prepared Chinese fare is served up to contented locals. **Happy Valley** (Map p75; ☎ 454 9208; 79 St Jean Rd; mains from Rs 250; ☺ noon-2pm & 7-10.30pm) Another big-hitter serving Chinese mains. Hugely popular with the local Asian population. **Le Bon Choix** (Map p75; ☎ 465 3856; 76 St Jean Rd; mains from Rs 250; ☺ 11am-midnight) The self-aggrandising name ('the right choice', in French) attracts a steady stream of locals and tourists. Seafood is the house speciality.

Frequent bus services operate between Rose Hill, Port Louis and the bus station in Quatre Bornes beside the town hall. Buses for Curepipe, Floréal and Flic en Flac stop at regular intervals along St Jean Rd. See p74 for taxi details.

## VACOAS & PHOENIX
**pop 110,000**
The industrial centre of Phoenix is home to the Phoenix Brewery, located beside the M2 motorway. While Phoenix doesn't hold much interest for visitors (sadly the brewery is not open to the public), the **Mauritius Glass Gallery** (Map p75; ☎ 696 3360; Pont Fer, Phoenix; admission Rs 50; ☒ 8am-5pm Mon-Sat) produces unusual souvenirs made from recycled glass. You can see them being made using traditional methods in the workshop, which also doubles as a small museum.

Golf enthusiasts will be interested to learn that the oldest golf course in the Indian Ocean, **Mauritius Gymkhana Club** (Map p75; ☎ 696 1404; www.mgc.intnet.mu; Suffolk Close, Vacoas), is found in Vacoas. It's the fourth-oldest fairway in the world (the three older courses are in Britain and India).

## FLORÉAL
The 'Beverly Hills' of Mauritius is a rather posh suburb northwest of Curepipe. The area has become synonymous with the high-quality knitwear produced by the Floreal Knitwear Company. Fill your suitcase with clothes at **Floreal Square** (Map p75; ☎ 698 8011; Swami Sivananda Ave; ☒ 9.30am-5.30pm Mon-Sat) on the main road from Curepipe.

If you're in the neighbourhood, we highly recommend seeking out **La Clef des Champs** (Map p75; ☎ 686 3458; Queen Mary Ave; menu per person Rs 1000; ☒ noon-2pm & 7-11pm Mon-Fri), the *table d'hôte* – and pet project – of Jacqueline Dalais, chef to the stars. Known for her impressive library of self-created recipes, Jacqueline has earned quite the reputation on the island for her unparalleled cuisine – she is regularly called upon to cater government functions, especially when foreign dignitaries are in town. Dishes served in her quaint dining room lean towards Provençal flavours; the presentation is exquisite.

## CUREPIPE
**pop 84,200**
Effectively Mauritius' second city, Curepipe is a bustling highland commercial centre famous for its rainy weather, volcanic crater and retail shopping. Its strange name reputedly stems from the malaria epidemic of 1867 when people fleeing from lowland Port Louis would 'cure' their pipes of malarial bacteria by smoking them here (although it's more likely that the area was named after a fondly remembered town in France).

Curepipe is the highest of the plateau towns. At 550m above sea level, temperatures are refreshingly cool in summer, but the town is often swathed in cloud. The damp climate gives the buildings an ageing, mildewed quality. Bring an umbrella, as it can rain without warning at any time of year. According to lowlanders, Curepipe has two seasons: the little season of big rains and the big season of little rains.

### Orientation & Information
Curepipe is bisected by Royal Rd, which runs approximately north–south. Most of the city's banks, shops and restaurants gather around the junction of Royal Rd and Châteauneuf St. Head east along Châteauneuf St for the bus station. Most of the sights, such as the Trou aux Cerfs crater and the botanical gardens, are within walking distance of the town centre.

### Sights
#### TOWN CENTRE
Overlooking a small park in the centre of Curepipe, the **Hôtel de Ville** (Map p75; town hall) is one of Mauritius' best surviving structures from its colonial era. Notice the gable windows, verandah and decorative wooden friezes known as *dentelles* – all are signature traits of the island's early plantation architecture. The building was moved here from Moka in 1903.

Nearby, you'll find a bronze copy of Prosper d'Épinay's famous **statue of Paul and Virginie** (see p131). The original is on display in Port Louis' Blue Penny Museum.

Next to the town hall, the stone building with the distinctive neoclassical porch houses the municipal **Carnegie Library** (Map p75; ☎ 674 2278; ☒ 9.30am-6pm Mon-Fri, 9.30am-3pm Sat). Its collection includes rare books on Mauritius dating back to the 18th century.

#### DOMAINE DES AUBINEAUX
The manor house of the **Domaine des Aubineaux** (Map p75; ☎ 676 3089; Royal Rd; adult/child Rs 300/150; ☒ 8am-4pm Mon-Fri, 8am-1pm Sat) was built in 1872 in a classic colonial style, and in 1889 it was the first residence on the island to be outfitted

with electricity. The plantation was transformed into a museum in 2000, and today it marks the first stop on the historical La Route du Thé (p122). Keep an eye out for old photographs preserving the memory of the local colonial manses that have fallen victim to harsh weather and the relentless passage of time. Exotic plants fill the garden under the shade of camphor trees, and when you're ready for a break you can sip savoury teas in the converted billiard parlour.

### TROU AUX CERFS

About 1km west of central Curepipe, the **Trou aux Cerfs** (Map p75) is an extinct volcanic crater some 100m deep and 1km in circumference. The bowl is heavily wooded, but from the road around the rim – a favourite spot for joggers and walkers – you get lovely views of the plateau. There are benches for rest and reflection, and a radar station for keeping an electronic eye on cyclone activity.

### BOTANICAL GARDENS

The well-kept **gardens** (Map p75; admission free; 8am-6pm May-Sep, 7am-7pm Oct-Apr) of Curepipe were created in 1870 to foster foliage that thrived in cooler weather – the grounds in Pamplemousses (p95) proved far too sweltering for certain species.

## Sleeping & Eating

Unless you're on business or visiting family, it's hard to imagine why you'd want to stay in Curepipe. There are, however, a couple of good-quality restaurants (including a famous *table d'hôte* in nearby Floréal) should you be passing through the centre of the island around lunchtime. Believe it or not, the cafeteria at the local hospital (Clinique de Lorette) serves a mean quiche at lunchtime – it's a local secret.

**Auberge de la Madelon** (Map p75; 670 1885; www.aubergemadelon.com; 10 Sir John Pope Hennessy St; d Rs 1200; ) Excellent value and centrally located, this well-run place is simple, small and surpringly stylish, boasting comfy en suite rooms and a very helpful management.

**La Potinière** (Map p75; 670 2648; Sir Winston Churchill St; crêpes Rs 150-400, mains from Rs 200; 10am-3pm & 6.30-10pm Tue-Sat) Curepipe's most obviously upmarket restaurant hides in an unassuming concrete block, but inside all is starched linen and gleaming tableware. The menu features a selection of quintessential Mauritian eats – hearts of palm, wild boar and seafood.

**Ginger** (Map p75; 676 0250; Garden Village, 21 Sir Winston Churchill; mains Rs 300-400; 9am-10pm Mon-Sat) Undeniably trendy, Ginger mixes East and West in a more playful and forward-thinking way than traditional Mauritian recipes. Try tender steaks and mouth-watering crab salads served at lacquered teak tables.

## Shopping

Curepipe is where the locals go to shop; you can find an incredible assortment of discounted items just by walking from the Royal College to the Galerie Currimjee. Try **Galerie des Îles** (Map p75; 670 7516; Arcade Currimjee; 9.30am-5.30pm Mon-Sat) for a generous selection of local designs and artisans. **Beauté de Chine** (Map p75; Les Arcades, Rue du Jardin; 9.30-5.30 Mon-Fri, to 1pm Sat), one of the longest-running stores on the island, sells an assortment of old-world relics like copper, jade, silk and antique porcelain.

Travellers looking for model-ship showrooms and workshops should join the circuit and stop by **Voiliers de L'Océan** (Map p75; 676 6986, 674 6764; www.voiliersocean.intnet.mu; Sir Winston Churchill St; 9am-6pm). Roughly 200 models are produced per month and visitors can watch the artisans at work. Forest Hill, just beyond central Curepipe, has a small collection of notable craft houses – worth a look if you're interested in model ships.

## Getting There & Away

Curepipe is an important transport hub, with frequent bus services to Port Louis (Victoria Square), Mahébourg, Centre de Flacq, Moka and surrounding towns such as Floréal, Phoenix, Quatre Bornes and Rose Hill. There are two terminals – the northbound and the southbound. Most services go from the northbound (Port Louis, Rose Hill, Quatre Bornes); Mahébourg is served from the southbound. The terminals lie on either side of Châteauneuf St, at the junction with Victoria Ave.

From Curepipe, expect to pay Rs 800 for a taxi ride to the airport, Rs 1500 to Grand Baie, Rs 1400 to Belle Mare, Rs 1000 to Port Louis, Rs 950 to Flic en Flac and Rs 500 to Black River.

# THE NORTH

Mauritius' tourism panache started in the north, and today there's plenty on offer for visitors. Although most of the area's spectacular beaches have been claimed by hotel construction, it's never hard to get away from it all and discover the little nooks that remain largely untouched by development.

Grand Baie is the eye of the tourist storm, boasting Mauritius' best nightlife and some of the island's most excellent restaurants. The small beachside villages around Grand Baie – Trou aux Biches, Mont Choisy and Pereybère – are quickly developing in a similar fashion.

The inland plain of sugar-cane fields – pocked with piles of volcanic boulders stacked by indentured servants – is known as Pamplemousses and gently slopes towards the sea. Here you'll find the wonderful Sir Seewoosagur Ramgoolam Botanical Gardens and the rightly popular L'Aventure du Sucre –

a museum dedicated to Mauritius' traditional colonial export.

## Getting There & Around

The most useful bus routes in and around this area are those running from Port Louis' Immigration Square bus station up the coast to Trou aux Biches, Grand Baie, Pereybère and Cap Malheureux. There are also express services direct from Port Louis to Grand Baie. Port Louis is the starting point for buses via Pamplemousses to Grand Gaube.

To reach this area from the airport, change buses in Port Louis. Alternatively, a taxi costs Rs 700 from Port Louis to Balaclava, Rs 800 to Grand Baie and Rs 900 to Grand Gaube. Add an additional Rs 1000 to reach the airport.

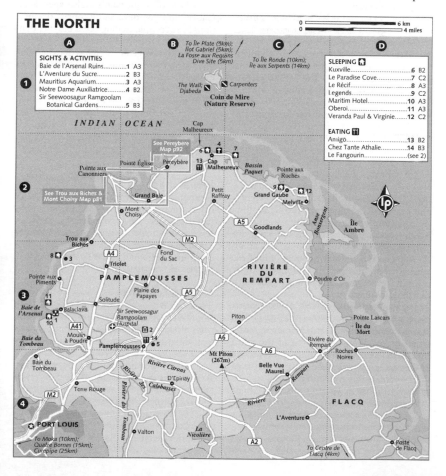

**THE NORTH**

SIGHTS & ACTIVITIES
Baie de l'Arsenal Ruins..............1 A3
L'Aventure du Sucre..................2 B3
Mauritius Aquarium....................3 A3
Notre Dame Auxiliatrice.............4 B2
Sir Seewoosagur Ramgoolam
  Botanical Gardens....................5 B3

SLEEPING
Kuxville....................................6 B2
Le Paradise Cove.......................7 C2
Le Récif....................................8 A3
Legends....................................9 C2
Maritim Hotel...........................10 A3
Oberoi.....................................11 A3
Veranda Paul & Virginie........12 C2

EATING
Amigo......................................13 B2
Chez Tante Athalie.................14 B3
Le Fangourin...................(see 2)

Most hotels and guesthouses have bikes for hire and can help organise car hire. Otherwise, you can approach the rental agencies directly. The largest concentration is in Grand Baie, and there is a smattering of outlets in and around Trou aux Biches and Pereybère.

## BALACLAVA TO POINTE AUX PIMENTS

Balaclava is named after the region's black-lava rocks, not the Crimean battlefield, in case you were wondering. You can still see the **ruins** of the French arsenal – along with a flour mill and a lime kiln – within the grounds of the Maritim Hotel at Baie de l'Arsenal. Nonguests can obtain permission to visit the ruins from the security guard at the hotel entrance; the track begins about 30m inside the gate to the right.

Also of interest is the **Mauritius Aquarium** (Map p79; ☎ 261 4561; www.mauritiusaquarium.com; Coastal Rd, Pointe aux Piments; adult/child/family Rs 250/125/650; ☽ 9.30am-5pm Mon-Sat, 10am-4pm Sun), which offers nondivers and children the chance to see the incredible marine life of the Indian Ocean up close. There's daily fish feeding at 11am.

This long stretch of sand features a wide range of three-, four- and five-star retreats. The following resorts are our favourites.

**our pick** **Le Récif** (Map p79; ☎ 261 0444; www.lere cif.com; Coastal Rd, Pointe aux Piments; s/d incl half board €120/180; ☒ ☐ ☎ ☒) is a wickedly stylish resort that proves the jetsetter lifestyle doesn't always have to come with an exorbitant price tag. Vibrant greens – like radioactive celery – and smooth ocean blues liven the plantation-style slatting on the crisp white walls. The public areas leading down to the sand are riddled with pillow-strewn nooks. And, along the sea, guests lie in various states of undress while soaking in the stylish plunge pool or reclining under one of the island's trademark thatch umbrellas.

The **Maritim Hotel** (Map p79; ☎ 204 1000; www.mar itim.de; Balaclava; r incl breakfast €170-745; ☒ ☐ ☎ ☒) is a well-established German-owned hotel with an enviable position out of the wind on Turtle Bay. Its main plus points are a 25-hectare park, complete with a nine-hole golf course, tennis courts and riding stables. It has a great beach where guests can indulge in everything from snorkelling to waterski-ing, and there's a choice of three restaurants, including a fantastic venue in a refurbished colonial manse. Don't miss the old arsenal that used to be a powder magazine.

Set in copious gardens, the **Oberoi** (Map p79; ☎ 204 3600; www.oberoihotels.com; Pointe aux Piments; r incl breakfast €950-1280, with private pool €1760-3050; ☒ ☐ ☎ ☒) boasts a gorgeous beach and stunning grounds including a high-flowing waterfall that dominates the ensemble. The best villas here have their own pools and gardens, enjoying total privacy and making them perfect for honeymooners. Inside it's all understated luxury, an inventive mix of African and Asian design.

There are no bus services to Balaclava or Baie de l'Arsenal. A taxi from Port Louis will cost Rs 400 to 500.

## TROU AUX BICHES & MONT CHOISY

Relaxed Trou aux Biches and the neighbour-ing village of Mont Choisy (also spelt Mon Choisy) are fast-developing tourist destina-tions full of people seeking better beaches than Grand Baie. Trou aux Biches (Does' Watering Hole) enjoys gorgeous stretches of casuarina-lined sand that continue almost unbroken all the way to sleepy Mont Choisy.

There's no doubt that the ongoing develop-ment has rather robbed the area of its quiet, unspoilt feel, but it's still cheaper and far less hectic than Grand Baie. Even the beaches are pleasantly uncrowded during the week, al-though there's fierce competition for picnic spots on weekends.

### Information

Neither Trou aux Biches nor Mont Choisy offer much in the way of shops and other facilities. There are a few grocery stores scat-tered around and a branch of the **Mauritius Commercial Bank** (MCB; Royal Rd, Mont Choisy), with a 24-hour ATM and a **bureau de change** (☽ 9am-5pm Mon-Fri, 9am-noon Sat).

### Sights & Activities

Trou aux Biches and Mont Choisy are both important watersports centres. Activities on offer range from touring the lagoon in a glass-bottomed boat to parasailing, waterskiing, deep-sea fishing and diving.

Snorkelling equipment (Rs 150 per day) can be rented at the **boat house** (☎ 728 4335; ☽ 9am-5pm) on Trou aux Biches' public beach. It also rents out pedalos and kayaks (Rs 400 per hour), and offers a variety of other activities, including glass-bottomed boat tours (Rs 500 per hour per person), waterskiing (Rs 550 per 12 minutes) and parasailing (Rs 1000 per 10 minutes).

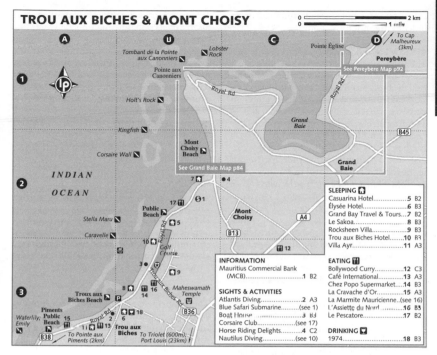

## DIVING

Dive centres that are consistently recommended for their professional and friendly service include **Nautilus Diving** ( ☎ 265 5495; www.nautilusdivers.com; 🕑 10am-4pm Mon-Sat), at the Trou aux Biches Hotel, and **Atlantis Diving** ( ☎ 265 7172; www.atlantis.freewebspace.com; 🕑 8am-5pm), located further south along the main road. Nautilus Diving is the oldest operator on the island – the owner, Richard Lai Cheong, and his staff run a great school for beginners. For more information on diving in Mauritius, see p28.

## HORSEBACK RIDING

There's an excellent riding school, **Horse Riding Delights** ( ☎ 265 6159; guylaine.sophie@montchoisy.com; Mont Choisy Sugar Estate; 🕑 daily by reservation) on the edge of Mont Choisy, just after the junction by the Tarisa Resort. Here you can ride in over 200 hectares of land, populated with deer and giant tortoises. There is also horseback riding at the Maritim Hotel (p80) in Balaclava.

## DEEP-SEA FISHING

Deep-sea anglers should head for the **Corsaire Club** ( ☎ 265 5209; fax 265 6267; 🕑 9am-5pm) beside Le Pescatore restaurant in Mont Choisy. A half-day's boat charter costs around Rs 15,000. For more information on deep-sea fishing, see p148.

## SUBMARINE RIDES

If you fancy diving but don't want to get wet, **Blue Safari Submarine** ( ☎ 263 3333; www.blue-safari.com; Royal Rd, Mont Choisy, adult/child Rs 3900/2300; 🕑 9am-4pm) takes you down among the coral and fishes to a depth of 35m. The ride lasts roughly two hours, of which 40 minutes are spent underwater, with departures every hour according to demand. Reservations are recommended at least a day in advance.

## Sleeping

It seems almost every building along this stretch of coast is available for rent in some shape or form. Much of the accommodation is in the midrange bracket and consists of self-catering apartments, villas and bungalows, often with terraces or balconies for viewing the sunset. We strongly advise sticking to the main road that carves a path near the coast – we ventured inland hoping to find tucked-away treasures but instead stumbled upon filthy by-the-hour bedrooms.

## APARTMENTS & VILLAS

The usual suspects of the villa-renting business manage a slew of properties in apartment-ridden Trou aux Biches and Mont Choisy. **EasyRent** ( ☎ 452 1010; www.easyrent.mu) offers an excellent selection of fully serviced villas in Trou aux Biches, including the charming Case Creole (from €150), a traditional house with bamboo ceilings and a charming beachside garden. It also manages four seaside apartments in the lovely Cerisier complex. Further north in Mont Choisy, **Grand Bay Travel & Tours** ( ☎ 265 5261; www.gbtt.com; Royal Rd) manages a cluster of poolside studios and apartments at very reasonable prices . The accommodation is comfy, if a bit sterile. A block of slightly threadbare apartments can also be found at **Élysée Hotel** ( ☎ 265 6946; www.elyseehotelgroup.com; cnr Royal Rd & Pére Laval St, Trou aux Biches; studio/6-person apt €49/62; 🅿 🕹 ).

**Villa Ayr** ( ☎ 709 3453, 265 5555; www.apartment strouauxbiches.com; 1 Carangue Ave, Trou aux Biches; studio/6-person apt €75/114; 🅿 💻 � ), a stack of modern apartments, is managed by doting Brigitte and her husband (both avid scuba divers originally from the UK), with big smiles and a genuine flair for making guests feel welcome – in fact, it's almost as though you were staying at a *chambre d'hôte* (family-run B&B).

## GUESTHOUSES & CHAMBRES D'HÔTES

**Rocksheen Villa** ( ☎ 265 5043; www.rocksheenvilla.com; 161 Morcellement Jhuboo, Trou aux Biches; studios €26-30; 🅿 ) Down a quiet side street about 300m back from the beach is this homey guesthouse run by a charming Scottish-Mauritian couple. It has proven so popular that they've built an extension. Well run and spotlessly clean, the place receives consistently good reports from travellers.

## HOTELS & RESORTS

**Casuarina Hotel** ( ☎ 204 5000; www.hotel-casuarina.com; Royal Rd, Trou aux Biches; d incl breakfast from €115; 🅿 🕹 � ) Definitely one of the more interesting midrange places, Casuarina's Moorish style is matched by equally inventive apartment layouts. It's also pleasantly small and feels very relaxed. The only minus is having to cross the road to the beach, but otherwise this place is great.

**Le Sakoa** ( ☎ 265 5244; www.lesakoa.com; Royal Rd, Trou aux Biches; d incl breakfast/half board from €168/218; 🅿 💻 � 🕹 ) Easily the most stylish option in

Trou aux Biches, Le Sakoa is instantly recognisable by its signature high-pitched roofs that match the neighbouring palms both in height and grandeur. Spacious accommodation is in wonderful two-storey thatched blocks radiating out from the fantastic beach. A charming dark-marble infinity pool anchors the hotel's centre, providing a luxurious setting for couples and families.

**Trou aux Biches Hotel** ( ☎ 204 6565; www.trouaux biches-hotel.com; Royal Rd, Trou aux Biches; s/d incl half board from €336/448; 🅿 💻 � 🕹 ) After an exhaustive renovation, the newly completed Trou aux Biches Hotel has reset the standards for five-star luxury in Mauritius with its clutch of traditionally inspired beachside suites and villas. The resort's design scheme incorporates rustic elements – like thatch, wicker, and hand-cut boulders – into the unquestionably modern surrounds. Spas, pools and two kilometres of sand make this the most desirable address in Trou aux Biches.

## Eating

The competitive nature of Grand Baie's dining scene has begun to trickle down the coast – the increasingly broad selection of outlets caters for most tastes.

### RESTAURANTS

**Bollywood Curry** ( ☎ 261 7028; Royal Rd; mains Rs 90-200; 🕒 lunch & dinner) Bollywood Curry serves out-of-this-world curries in uberbasic surrounds (think buzzing neon bulbs and cracked tiles) – it doesn't get more authentic than this! To find the restaurant from the Grand Baie area, follow signs to the M2 Hwy and veer around the first roundabout towards Triolet. After passing the turn-off to Mont Choisy go 500m – it's on the left side in the first plaza after the rows of cane.

**La Marmite Mauricienne** ( ☎ 265 7604; Trou aux Biches Rd; mains Rs 150-400; 🕒 lunch & dinner) This basic but sweet place down the road beyond L'Assiette du Nord has a pleasant outdoor feel, with lots of tables on the terrace (although sadly it's on a rather busy road). The menu is Mauritian, featuring mostly seafood, noodles and curries.

**Café International** ( ☎ 723 9214; Royal Rd; mains Rs 190-400; 🕒 5.30-11.30pm Mon, 9.30am-3pm & 5.30-11pm Tue-Fri, 9.30am-6pm Sat) As the name suggests, this popular South African–run spot serves up an excellent assortment of dishes from around the world – burgers, curries and sandwiches are the stars of the menu.

**L'Assiette du Nord** ( ☎ 265 7040; Trou aux Biches; mains Rs 200-340; ☺ lunch & dinner) A popular option where you can opt for the terrace or a slightly smarter dining area behind the fish-tank partition. Seafood features strongly, served in Chinese, Indian and Creole style. Try fish cooked in banana leaf with madras sauce or perhaps prawns in garlic butter.

**La Cravache d'Or** ( ☎ 265 7021; Trou aux Biches; mains Rs 500; ☺ lunch & dinner Mon-Sat) La Cravache d'Or enjoys an absolutely gorgeous setting right on the beach, making it perfect for a romantic meal. The small daily changing menu features meat and fish dishes, although vegetarians can be catered for. Reserve in advance on weekends, and at any time you'd like to be sure of sitting at one of the sea-view tables.

**Le Pescatore** ( ☎ 265 6337; Mont Choisy; mains Rs 700; ☺ lunch & dinner) Wonderfully chic, light decor and a great terrace overlooking the fishing boats in the sea below set the scene for a truly superior eating experience. Dishes such as lobster in ginger and sake sauce, and St Brandon Berry fish with carrot juice and cardamom give you an idea of what to expect.

### SELF-CATERING
Self-caterers should head for the well-stocked **Chez Popo Supermarket** (Royal Rd) in Trou aux Biches. If you spend more than Rs 2000 the owner will deliver your purchases to your accommodation upon request. Around Mont Choisy, **Persand Royal Supermarket** (Royal Rd) is your best bet.

## Drinking
Although the area's dining scene is steadily growing, nightlife options are thin. You'll have to head to Pointe Aux Canonniers nearby, or Grand Baie just beyond. The only notable option is **1974** ( ☎ 265 7400; Royal Rd, Ex-Aquarium Bldg; ☺ 11am-midnight), a popular local haunt in Trou aux Biches serving pub grub and Italian ice cream. There's live music on Friday and Saturday, and great sunset cocktails any day of the week.

## Getting There & Around
Trou aux Biches and Mont Choisy are served by nonexpress buses running between Port Louis' Immigration Square bus station and Cap Malheureux via Grand Baie. There are bus stops about every 500m along the coastal highway.

Figure on Rs 200 for a taxi ride in the Trou aux Biches/Mont Choisy area. A taxi to Grand Baie costs between Rs 400 and Rs 500 depending on the destination. It's Rs 600 to Pereybère.

## GRAND BAIE
**pop 2800**
In the 17th century the Dutch used to call Grand Baie 'De Bogt Zonder Eynt', which meant the 'Bay Without End'. Today it appears as though it's the development – not the bay – that is without end. Although the term 'tourist hub' may frighten many away, Grand Baie actually has a lot of virtues. There are several quiet nooks in the area (like charming Pointe aux Canonnier) to escape the noise and hustle, accommodation options are wide ranging, there are convenient transport connections and you'll never tire of the myriad dining options. It's no St-Tropez, but it still has its charms.

## Orientation
Orientation in Grand Baie is easy, as almost everything is strung out along the coastal highway. The centre point of the town is the Sunset Blvd shopping complex (including the jetty) at the junction of the coastal highway (known here as Royal Rd) and La Salette Rd – the road inland to Goodlands and the M2 motorway via the Super U Hypermarket.

## Information
### BOOKSHOPS
The best selection of books (specifically Mauritius-related titles) can be found in the Super U Hypermarket.

**Papyrus** ( ☎ 263 0012; Richmond Hill Bldg, La Salette Rd; ☺ 9am-7pm Mon-Sat, 9.30am-noon Sun) A small bookshop with a range of mainly French-language books and magazines.

### INTERNET ACCESS
**Cyber Pirate** (Galeries Espace Ocean Bldg; per 30mins Rs 30; ☺ 9.30am-8pm Mon-Sat)

**Grand Baie Cyber Café** (Royal Rd; per hr Rs 180; ☺ 9am-11pm) Below Ti Fleur Soleil.

**Internet Cafe** ( ☎ 263 2478; Super U Hypermarket, La Salette Rd; per hr Rs 180; ☺ 9am-8.30pm Mon-Fri, 9am-9.30pm Sat, 9am-1.30pm Sun) Next to the checkouts.

### MONEY
**Mauritius Commercial Bank** (MCB; Royal Rd; ☺ bureau de change 8am-6pm Mon-Sat, 9am-noon Sun)

**State Bank** (Royal Rd; ☺ bureau de change 8am-6pm Mon-Sat, 9am-noon Sun)

**Thomas Cook Exchange Bureau** (Royal Rd; ☺ 8am-8pm)

MAURITIUS

# GRAND BAIE

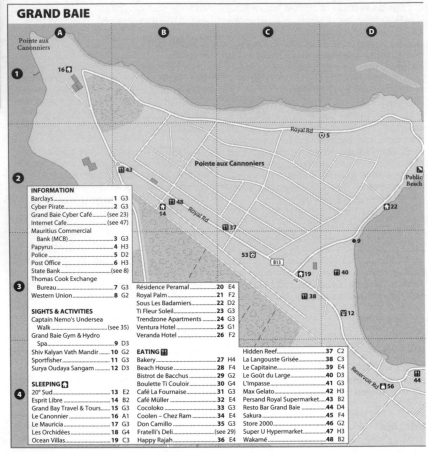

**INFORMATION**

| | |
|---|---|
| Barclays | **1** G3 |
| Cyber Pirate | **2** G3 |
| Grand Baie Cyber Café | (see 23) |
| Internet Cafe | (see 47) |
| Mauritius Commercial Bank (MCB) | **3** G3 |
| Papyrus | **4** H3 |
| Police | **5** D2 |
| Post Office | **6** H3 |
| State Bank | (see 8) |
| Thomas Cook Exchange Bureau | **7** G3 |
| Western Union | **8** G2 |

**SIGHTS & ACTIVITIES**

| | |
|---|---|
| Captain Nemo's Undersea Walk | (see 35) |
| Grand Baie Gym & Hydro Spa | **9** D3 |
| Shiv Kalyan Vath Mandir | **10** G2 |
| Sportfisher | **11** G3 |
| Surya Oudaya Sangam | **12** D3 |

**SLEEPING**

| | |
|---|---|
| 20° Sud | **13** E2 |
| Esprit Libre | **14** B2 |
| Grand Bay Travel & Tours | **15** G3 |
| Le Canonnier | **16** A1 |
| Le Mauricia | **17** G3 |
| Les Orchidées | **18** G4 |
| Ocean Villas | **19** C3 |
| Résidence Peramal | **20** E4 |
| Royal Palm | **21** F2 |
| Sous Les Badamiers | **22** D2 |
| Ti Fleur Soleil | **23** G3 |
| Trendzone Apartments | **24** G3 |
| Ventura Hotel | **25** G1 |
| Veranda Hotel | **26** F2 |

**EATING**

| | |
|---|---|
| Bakery | **27** H4 |
| Beach House | **28** F4 |
| Bistrot de Bacchus | **29** G2 |
| Boulette Ti Couloir | **30** G4 |
| Café La Fournaise | **31** G3 |
| Café Müller | **32** E4 |
| Cocoloko | **33** G3 |
| Coolen – Chez Ram | **34** E4 |
| Don Camillo | **35** G3 |
| Fratelli's Deli | (see 29) |
| Happy Rajah | **36** E4 |
| Hidden Reef | **37** C2 |
| La Langouste Grisée | **38** C3 |
| Le Capitaine | **39** E4 |
| Le Goût du Large | **40** D3 |
| L'Impasse | **41** G3 |
| Max Gelato | **42** H3 |
| Persand Royal Supermarket | **43** B2 |
| Resto Bar Grand Baie | **44** D4 |
| Sakura | **45** F4 |
| Store 2000 | **46** G2 |
| Super U Hypermarket | **47** H3 |
| Wakamé | **48** B2 |

## POST

**Post office** (Richmond Hill Bldg, La Salette Rd; 8.15am-4pm Mon-Fri, 8.15am-11.45am Sat) Out near the Super U Hypermarket; the last 45 minutes before closing are for stamp sales only.

## Sights & Activities

Grand Baie's prime attraction is the range of water-based activities on offer. Otherwise, the only specific sights are a couple of vividly colourful Tamil temples.

### TEMPLES

**Surya Oudaya Sangam** ( 8am-5pm Mon-Sat), located at the west end of town, and the older **Shiv Kalyan Vath Mandir**, towards Pereybère, are both are dedicated to Shiva. Visitors are

welcome but shoes should be removed before entering.

### CATAMARANS & CRUISES

Catamaran day trips are the most popular activity in the north – most cruises depart from Grand Baie. Perhaps the most interesting of the options on offer is the trip offered by **Yacht Charters** ( 263 8395; www.isla-mauritia. com). Its magnificent sailing ship, the *Isla Mauritia*, was built in 1852 and is claimed to be the world's oldest active schooner. **Magic Sails** ( 262 7188; www.magicsails.mu) offers a unique product as well – a two-day liveaboard boat trip that takes in the island's mountain-backed western coast. Also worth checking out are the day trips with **Maeva**

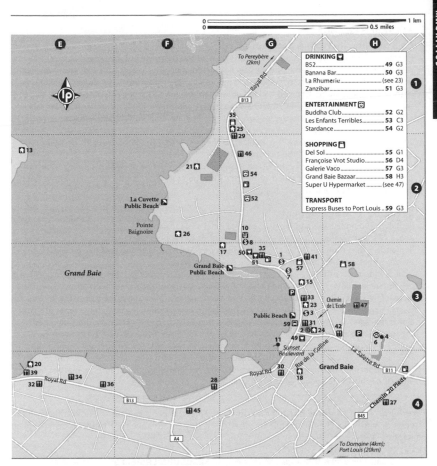

DRINKING
B52 .......................................... 49 G3
Banana Bar ............................. 50 G3
La Rhumerie ...................... (see 23)
Zanzibar .................................. 51 G3

ENTERTAINMENT
Buddha Club ........................... 52 G2
Les Enfants Terribles .............. 53 C3
Stardance ............................... 54 G2

SHOPPING
Del Sol ..................................... 55 G1
Françoise Vrot Studio ........... 56 D4
Galerie Vaco ........................... 57 G3
Grand Baie Bazaar .................. 58 H3
Super U Hypermarket .......... (see 47)

TRANSPORT
Express Buses to Port Louis .. 59 G3

(www.maeva.mu), **Croisières Australes** ( ☎ 670 4301; www.mttb-mautourco.com) and **20° Sud** (p87).

In general, we advise booking with a company that is licensed to set foot on one of the northern islands. You shouldn't pay more than Rs 1500 for one of the party-prone cats, and your day trip should include a full lunch, drinks and snorkelling apparel. Check out www.mauritiuscatamaran.com for a list of operators.

### SKYDIVING

'Wanna get high?' asks **Skydive Austral** ( ☎ 499 5551; www.skydiveaustral.com; sky dive €250) with a winked eye. This new adventure outfit offers travellers a whole new way to check out the island – from 3000m in the air as you zoom towards the earth after jumping from a plane. It's based at a clearing towards Roches Noires in the east, but touts and transfers make Grand Baie a good departure point.

### DEEP-SEA FISHING

Based beside the Sunset Blvd jetty, **Sportfisher** ( ☎ 263 8358; www.sportfisher.com; Royal Rd; half-/full day from Rs 13,000/15,000 per boat; 🕑 7am-6pm) has four boats, each taking up to six people (three anglers and three companions). For more information on deep-sea fishing, see p148.

### SWIMMING & SPAS

The beach at Grand Baie is nothing special and the bay here is congested with boats. Instead, you're better off heading for **La Cuvette public beach** beside the Verandah Hotel towards

## NORTHERN ISLANDS

### Coin de Mire, Île Plate & Îlot Gabriel

The distinctive Coin de Mire (Gunner's Quoin), 4km off the coast, was so named because it resembles the quoin (wedge) used to steady the aim of a cannon. The island is now a nature reserve and home to a number of rare species, such as the red-tailed tropicbird and Bojer's skink. None of the major catamarans stop here as landing is often difficult. Despite the island's striking shape there's not much to see here anyway – it's the kind of place that looks far better from far away.

Most operators take you to the lagoon between Île Plate and Îlot Gabriel, 7km further north, which offers good snorkelling. Barbecue lunches are served on a sandy patch of Îlot Gabriel, while 20° Sud's luxury cruiser (see p87) currently has the sole right to land on Île Plate – day-trippers eat in the charming ruins of the Governor's House.

Boats to the islands depart from Grand Baie. You can book online at www.mauritiuscatamaran. com, through any local tour agent or directly with the cruise companies (p84). Prices are from Rs 1200 to 1500 per person, including lunch.

### Île Ronde & Île aux Serpents

Île Ronde (Round Island) and Île aux Serpents (Snake Island) are two significant nature reserves about 20km and 24km respectively from Mauritius. It is not possible to land on them. Ironically, Île Ronde is not round and has snakes, while Île aux Serpents is round and has no snakes; the theory is that an early cartographer simply made a mistake.

Île Ronde covers roughly 170 hectares and scientists believe it has more endangered species per square kilometre than anywhere else in the world. Many of the plants, such as the hurricane palm (of which one lonely tree remains) and the bottle palm, are unique to the island. The endemic fauna includes the keel-scaled boa and the burrowing boa (possibly extinct), three types of skink and three types of gecko. Among the sea birds that breed on the island are the wedge-tailed shearwater, the red-tailed tropicbird and the gadfly (or Round Island) petrel. Naturalist Gerald Durrell gives a very graphic description of the island in his book *Golden Bats and Pink Pigeons*.

The smaller Île aux Serpents (42 hectares) is a renowned bird sanctuary. The birds residing on the island include the sooty tern, the lesser noddy, the common noddy and the masked (blue-footed) booby. Nactus geckos and Bojer's skinks are also found here.

Pereybère. If you continue north, you'll find a series of sandy beaches accessible by small passages between the seemingly continuous string of private villas.

The **Grand Baie Gym & Hydro Spa** ( ☎ 263 4891; www.grandbaiegym.com; 3 X Club Rd; day membership Rs 690) has a fabulous pool and gym, and you can indulge in a huge range of spa treatments, steam yourself in the *hammam* (Turkish bath) or enjoy low-fat dishes at the cafe across the street.

### UNDERSEA WALKS

For nondivers, **Captain Nemo's Undersea Walk** ( ☎ 263 7819; Royal Rd; per person Rs 1200; ☼ 8.30am-5pm) provides the unique experience of walking underwater wearing a diver's helmet and weight belt. Solar-powered pumps on the boat above feed oxygen to you during the 25-minute 'walk on the wet side'. Walks are available to everyone over the age of seven. There are trips every few hours from 9am to 3pm. In peak season it's advisable to book a day in advance. For more information on undersea walks, see p150.

### SEMISUBMERSIBLES

A number of semisubmersible vessels offer coral-viewing tours. *Le Nessee* (adult/child €24/14) is a distinctive yellow semisubmarine run by Croisières Australes. It departs from Grand Baie's Sunset Blvd jetty several times daily and the trip lasts just under two hours, with 30 minutes of snorkelling for those who wish. Tickets are available from hotels and tour agents.

## Sleeping

Much of the budget and midrange accommodation in Grand Baie takes the form of self-catering studios and apartments. There are some excellent deals around, especially if you arrive with friends in tow at a quiet time of the year. A clutch of smart hotels occupies the east side of the bay, but Grand Baie is not necessarily a centre for luxury.

## APARTMENTS & VILLAS

You can't go wrong with any of the following. Don't forget to check out additional choices in Pereybère nearby (p92).

**CG Villas** ( ☎ 262 5777; www.villas-maurice.com) Offers access to a collection of villas and apartments directly on the bay.

**EasyRent** ( ☎ 452 1010; www.easyrent.mu) High-quality villas are on offer.

**Grand Bay Travel & Tours** ( ☎ 263 8771; www.gbtt. com; Royal Rd) Runs several multi-apartment properties from basic digs to luxury sleeps.

**Idyllic Villas** (www.idyllic-mauritius.com) Manages a gaggle of private seaside villas – good deals can be scouted in the charming Pointe aux Canonniers neighbourhood.

**Résidence Peramal** ( ☎ 263 8109; www.residence peramal.com; Royal Rd; studios €25, apt €30-40; ☒ ) Excellent-value self-catering accommodation on a little promontory plum in the centre of Grand Baie.

**Trendzone Apartments** ( ☎ 263 8277; trendzoneapart ments@gmail.com; La Salette Rd; apt €40-50; ☒ 🛜 ) Modern apartment units above the Trendzone boutique in the heart of town between Super U and the sea.

## GUESTHOUSES & CHAMBRES D'HÔTES

**our pick Sous Le Badamiers** ( ☎ 263 4391; www.sou-slebadamiers.com; Royal Rd, Pointe aux Canonniers; s/d from €34/46; ☒ 🖳 ) Once known as Chez Vaco for the artist's enchanting paintings that adorn almost every wall, this wonderful li'l guesthouse now takes its name from the looming *badamier* trees that shade the charming cloister at the entrance. The delightful rooms are sponge painted in soothing neutral tones and furnishings are accented with patterns of woven rattan – there's a certain warm minimalism here that feels stylish yet homey. This place is a real find.

**Esprit Libre** ( ☎ 269 1159; www.espritlibremaurice.com; rue Bourdet, Pointe aux Canonniers; r incl breakfast €60-110; ☒ 🛜 ) Easily one of the best values for money on the island, this charming guesthouse is run by two friendly Québécois, Stéphane and André, who run their enclave of 'free spirits' with one mantra in mind: customer service. Rooms are simple and tastefully decorated and the on-site restaurant offers up an inventive menu that has lured in a faithful crowd of locals. To reach the guesthouse, turn left at the large elephant statue (you can't miss it) when coming from Grand Baie.

**Ocean Villas** ( ☎ 263 6788; www.ocean-villas.mu; Royal Rd, Pointe aux Canonniers; r incl breakfast from Rs 2200, apt from Rs 3700; ☒ 🖳 🛜 🛋 ) Ocean Villas is recommended for its broad range of accommodation, from straightforward hotel rooms to self-catering units for up to eight people and sleek honeymoon suites with sunken baths. Facilities include an excellent pool plus a small strip of beach (with limited watersports on offer), a restaurant and the love nest – a private house on the beach.

**Les Orchidées** ( ☎ 263 8780; www.mauritius-island. com/orchidees; Route de la Colline; s/d incl half board from €52/82; ☒ 🛋 ) Highly recommended and extremely popular (book ahead), this small hotel is set back from the coast in a quiet location just a short walk from the centre of town. Sweet, simple, brightly coloured rooms and a charming pool area make this a great option.

## HOTELS & RESORTS

Grand Baie has two distinct classes of hotels: the grandiose resorts and the street-side inns belonging to a somewhat bygone era of affordable sleeps. Despite Grand Baie's reputation as 'tourist central' there are less luxury resorts in the area than one might think.

**Ventura Hotel** ( ☎ 263 6030; www.hotelventura.com; Royal Rd; s/d incl breakfast €39/60; ☒ 🛋 🛜 ) It may look virtually deserted but this is a decent central option with a surprisingly pleasant pool and public area once you get through the indifferent exterior. You have a choice of double rooms and family rooms, which sleep four. All have TV, air-con, phone and a view onto the pool.

**Ti Fleur Soleil** ( ☎ 269 3380; www.tifleursoleil.com; Royal Rd; d incl breakfast €68; ☒ 🛜 ) The 'little sunflower' is a sweet, friendly hotel that can't be beat for its location right in the heart of Grand Baie. You'll find chocolates on your pillow at bedtime, chilled handtowels when you check in and discounted massages (Rs 1200 for 90 minutes) at the in-house spa. It's these little touches that make the extra difference with travellers.

**our pick 20° Sud** ( ☎ 263 5000; www.20degressud. com; Royal Rd, Pointe aux Canonniers; d incl half board from Rs 220; ☒ 🖳 🛜 🛋 ) The boutiquiest boutique resort on the island, 20° Sud has a cache of chic, plantation-inspired rooms. Walls are lavished with generous coats of prim white paint; draped linen and elegant dark-wood mouldings perfectly accent the surrounds. Palatial oak doors initiate guests into the

MAURITIUS

vine-draped public area, a lush palm grove with an inviting swimming pool and a cosy lodge-style library. 20° Sud also operates a popular catamaran day trip to Île Plate (p86) for snorkelling, sunbathing and an elegant barbecue feast in the stylishly half-renovated ruins of the old Governor's House (nonguests can join in as well, although you must book several days in advance as the trip is exceedingly popular).

**Verandah Hotel** ( ☎ 209 8000; www.verandah group.com; Royal Rd; s/d incl half board from €139/198; ❌ ▣ ⛶ ☑ ) The rather elegant public areas here give the Verandah a sense of exclusivity unusual for the price. The two pools, good facilities and a recent refit of the rooms also help. The beach is fine, but no great shakes, although the location is handy for town and there's a full-service Seven Colours spa here to help with relaxation.

Grand Baie also has three wildly popular Beachcomber resorts representing the opposite ends of the resort spectrum:

**Le Canonnier** ( ☎ 263 7000; www.lecanonnier-hotel. com; Pointe aux Canonniers; d incl half board from €360; ❌ ▣ ⛶ ☑ ) The location here is one of the best in the country: a headland with attractive beaches on all sides – there's even a ruined lighthouse (now rather sacrilegiously housing a kids club) on the grounds. It's a pity then that the accommodation is in rather uninspiring beige blocks. Inside the rooms are small (and equally beige) but the guests seem delighted with the experience.

**Le Mauricia** ( ☎ 209 1100; www.lemauricia-hotel.com; d incl half board from Rs €360; ❌ ▣ ⛶ ☑ ) With *Titanic* proportions (the hotel's design was inspired by the shape of an oceanliner), this option boasts an endless array of activities from watersports to the on-site nightclub.

**Royal Palm** ( ☎ 209 8300; www.royalpalm-hotel.com; d incl half board from Rs €1100; ❌ ▣ ⛶ ☑ ) The world-famous flagship of the Beachcomber group is the pinnacle of luxury and a veritable playground for the rich and famous. Staff don safari-butler uniforms (stylish pith helmets!) and meticulously arranged flower bouquets are the centrepiece of every room.

## Eating

For a lazy beach town lost in the Indian Ocean, Grand Baie has an incredible assortment of restaurants. While the centre of town is packed with eateries, the very best tend to be slightly outside the heart of Grand Baie, particularly towards Pointe aux Canonnier and Pereybère. You'll have no end of choice, though; the following are just the best of a good bunch.

### BUDGET

**Boulette Ti Couloir** ( ☎ 263 5645; Royal Rd; boulettes Rs 6; ❇ lunch & dinner Mon-Sat, lunch Sun) Follow the low-slung billboard for Paparazzi down a back alley to reach this tucked-away snack shop. As the name suggest, this microscopic joint really is just a *ti couloir* (li'l hallway) where a couple of women cook up savoury *boulettes* (steamed balls) to unending lines of locals.

**Café La Fournaise** ( ☎ 263 4589; Grand Bay Plaza, Royal Rd; coffee Rs 80; ❇ 7.30am-midnight) Right at the junction of La Salette and Royal Rds, this popular coffee and snack shop has attempted a Starbucks-esque design scheme with trendy-yet-comfy catalogue furniture. The coffee earns top marks and it's a great place to escape the heat with cool blasts of air-con.

**Max Gelato** ( ☎ 732 0304; www.maxgelato.com; La Salette Rd; small cone Rs 90; ❇ noon-7pm Mon-Sat, 10am-7pm Sun) Widely considered the best *gelataria* on the island, Max whips up a scrumptious assortment of flavours to cool you down after a day in the sun. We especially liked the vanilla cream and nutella. A half-kilo case of takeaway treats costs Rs 250.

**Café Müller** ( ☎ 263 5230; Royal Rd; salads & sandwiches from Rs 120; ❇ 9.30am-5pm Mon-Sat) This charming option is a great place to fill the belly for breakfast or lunch. As the name suggests, it's a German-run cafe and bakery that rustles up great sandwiches in a lovely grassy garden.

**Domaine** ( ☎ 263 5286; Narainen St, Upper Vale, The Vale; mains Rs 100-340; ❇ 11am-1pm) 'Domaine' is the answer every local offers when travellers ask where to go to savour some Mauritian home cookin' while escaping the throngs of vacationers. So, naturally this inland haunt is starting to fill up with tourists. Go quick before someone else lets the cat out of the bag or tells the owner that his prices are remarkably low!

**Coolen – Chez Ram** ( ☎ 263 8569; Royal Rd; mains Rs 150-200; ❇ lunch & dinner Thu-Tue) The clear local favourite among Royal Rd's endless parade of restaurants, Coolen is situated smack in the centre of tourist town but is usually filled to the brim with Mauritians. Customers are welcomed with fish cakes and a splash of rum while they thumb through the menu of Creole and seafood staples. Go for the fish in banana leaves (Rs 175) and make sure to save room for the banana flambé.

**L'Impasse** ( ☎ 263 3137; Dodo Sq, Royal Rd; lunch/dinner menu Rs 185/235; ❇ 9am-11pm Mon-Sat) Homemade teas, fresh French and Thai-inspired salads, and fish from the Seychelles makes this little eatery well worth finding. Follow the signs down a back alley – it's next door to the Vaco gallery in 'Dodo Square'.

### MIDRANGE

**Don Camillo** ( ☎ 263 8540; Royal Rd; pizzas Rs 250-390; ⏰ dinner daily, lunch Mon-Sat) Despite its unpromising location beside the Caltex petrol station, Don Camillo is a great place to taste real pizza. In the evening it's positively buzzing – either get there early or reserve.

**Happy Rajah** ( ☎ 263 2241; Royal Rd; mains Rs 160-600; ⏰ lunch & dinner) Near one of the Tamil temples in a large wooden structure, Happy Rajah satisfies costumers with a large selection of surprisingly filling curries and stews. Lunches are served in the vestibule – if you come in the evening you'll eat in the more atmospheric dining room draped in oriental tapestries.

**Hidden Reef** ( ☎ 263 0567; Royal Rd, Pointe aux Canonniers; mains Rs 180-450; ⏰ 10am-3pm & 6pm-midnight Mon-Sat) Pronounced 'Eden Reef' by most locals, this popular spot features a dozen tables spread around a garden of lazy palms sprouting up from the crushed coral underfoot. The ambience is dimly lit and romantic – you'll need a torch to thumb through your menu (provided, of course), and when you can't decide what to order the waiter will let you try half-and-half appetiser samplers to go with your seafood main. The complimentary shot of homemade coffee rum is the perfect way to end the meal.

**Sakura** ( ☎ 263 8092; Royal Rd; mains from Rs 270; ⏰ 11.30am-2.30pm & 6.30-10.30pm Mon-Sat, 5.30-10.30pm Sun) Despite Grand Baie's wishy-washy dining scene, Sakura has managed to hold its own for 22 years – the faded decor is living proof. The friendly owners are present every evening waving to repeat customers and watching their skilled chefs fling ingredients in the air during the exhilarating teppanyaki shows. Reservations are essential if you want your meal cooked at your table.

**Cocoloko** ( ☎ 263 1241; Royal Rd; coffee Rs 70, mains Rs 270-550; ⏰ 11am-11pm; 🛜 ) Arranged around an inviting pebble-strewn courtyard across the street from the beach, Cocoloko has firmly established itself as one of Grand Baie's premiere *it* spots for lounging jetsetters. Familiar international fare – salads, steaks and pizza (or 'Pizzaloko' as it's known) – won't inspire devotion, but the atmosphere is very conducive to coffee sipping and cocktail clinking. There's free wi-fi for customers.

**Beach House** ( ☎ 263 2599; Royal Rd; mains Rs 275-475; ⏰ lunch & dinner) Owned by a famous South African rugby player, this lively joint bustles with about as much energy as a sports match in overtime. The owner is often seen roaming around shirtless signing autographs, and the expat staff is usually just as surly. There is, however, a major draw: an unbeatable location smack dab along the lapping waves of Grand Baie's emerald lagoon. Skip the uninspired pub grub and come early for sunset cocktails – you'll have front-row seats and get to carouse with the other patrons before everyone's soused. There's live music on Sunday afternoons.

**Resto Bar Grand Baie** ( ☎ 292 0797; Royal Rd; steak Rs 300; ⏰ lunch & dinner) 'The dilemma of having a successful restaurant is that it's always swamped with customers' said the cantankerous owner – a veritable Dr House of restaurateurs. 'So I closed my place in the centre of Grand Baie and moved here where it's nice and quiet.' We're not surprised that the diner-phobic chef once ran a popular joint – you won't find a better steak for the price. Order your beef bloody or rare – a well-done piece of meat is a 'crime against humanity'.

**Le Goût du Large** ( ☎ 263 3116, 752 1866; Royal Rd; mains Rs 320-480; ⏰ 7.30am-late) Let your nose guide you past the nightmarishly cramped parking lot – once you round the corner you'll find a scrumptious steaks and seafood served in a seaside pavilion. The Astroturf and tiki umbrellas feel a bit out of place, but you hardly notice them when the mood lighting kicks on after sunset.

**Wakamé** ( ☎ 263 9888; Royal Rd, Pointe aux Canonniers; mains Rs 330; ⏰ noon-2.30pm & 7-11pm Wed-Mon) Decorated with the usual Japanese austerity, this popular joint specialises in (yup, you guessed it) sushi and teppanyaki. A word to the wise: on Friday's all-you-can-eat-sushi night it's best to arrive late in the evening so all of the sushi saved from the night before has been eaten by earlier diners. To reach Wakamé follow the main road out to Pointe aux Canonnier beyond Hidden Reef – if you hit the giant plaster elephant you've gone too far.

### TOP END

**Le Capitaine** ( ☎ 263 6867; Royal Rd; mains Rs 420-710; ⏰ 11.30am-3pm & 6.30-10.30pm) This is a popular place serving good standard seafood and fish dishes in a pleasant convivial space that combines style with informality and great bay views. Fresh lobster is the pick of the menu, while other delicious mains include whole crab cooked in white wine, and lobster ravioli with fresh mushroom and cucumber quenelles. Reservations are essential in the evening.

**Bistrot de Bacchus** ( ☎ 263 3203; Ventura Plaza, Royal Rd; mains Rs 470-740; ☺ noon-3pm & 7-10.30pm Mon-Sat) Styled like an old cellar with rounded brick arches and alcoves, this wine bar and restaurant features a small menu of brasserie-inspired dishes. But here's the real beauty: all by-the-glass wine is served at retail rather than restaurant prices.

**La Langouste Grisée** ( ☎ 263 1035; Royal Rd; mains Rs 1000; ☺ lunch & dinner) This is a restaurant frequented by the great and the good of Grand Baie, offering very stylish dining overlooking an attractive garden and a swimming pool–like pond. As a winner of the Fourchette d'Or in 2005, 'the Tipsy Lobster' is generally recognised as one of the best restaurants on the island. Dishes from its imaginative Franco-Mauritian menu include Dorado fillet with peanut sauce and banana slices. Lobster is obviously the speciality and vegetarians really shouldn't bother coming.

### SELF-CATERING

Located 200m inland from Grand Baie's main drag, the vast **Super U Hypermarket** (La Salette Rd; ☺ 9am-8.30pm Mon-Fri, 9am-9.30pm Sat, 9am-1.30pm Sun) is, by far, the best supermarket on the island and sells almost everything self-caterers could want. You can also buy groceries and other essentials at **Store 2000** (Royal Rd; ☺ 7.30am-7.30pm Mon-Sat, to noon Sun). **Fratelli's Deli** ( ☎ 263 2793; Ventura Plaza, Royal Rd; ☺ 9am-6.30pm Mon-Thu, 9am-10pm Fri & Sat) has an excellent assortment of freshly prepared Italian faves (and its cappuccinos are divine). There's also an excellent 24-hour **bakery** ( ☎ 263 7000) on Rte B45 near the turn-off to La Salette Rd.

Street vendors and vegetable stands can be found all along Royal Rd. They tend to congregate near the public beaches. There are several fast-food vendors near the entrance to Super U – the best stall food, however, is a roti stand located directly across La Salette Rd from the megamart.

## Drinking & Entertainment

If you're looking for a party in Mauritius, you'll find it in Grand Baie. Many of the area's restaurants – like Beach House and Cocoloko – have buzzing nightlife as well. There's also a discotheque at Le Mauricia hotel where smoking laws apparently don't apply.

**our pick** **Les Enfants Terribles** ( ☎ 263 8117; Royal Rd, Pointe aux Canonniers; ☺ 7pm-3am Tue, Fri & Sat) The top pick for a night out on the town, the 'little terrors' has a roaring dance floor, a chilled-out lounge and a special VIP section that overflows with champagne. Walls bedecked with hundreds of crinkled photos of partiers confirm the sociable local vibe.

**Banana Bar** ( ☎ 263 0326; Royal Rd; admission Rs 150; ☺ 10am-3am Mon-Sat, 6am-3am Sun) In the Caltex parking lot near Don Camillo, this is one of the best spots to grab a drink and catch up with friends.

**Buddha Club** ( ☎ 263 7664; Royal Rd; admission Wed & Thu free, Fri & Sat Rs 250; ☺ 11.30pm-5am Wed-Sat; ☒ ) Grand Baie's top nightspot positively sizzles on a Friday and Saturday night when all three dance floors are packed. Smart-casual dress is required.

**Stardance** ( ☎ 263 6388; Royal Rd; admission Tue-Thu & Sun free, Fri free for women, Fri & Sat Rs 250; ☺ 11pm-5am Tue-Sun; ☒ ) Near the Buddha Bar, its rival also has three dance floors with a choice of techno, tropical and '60s to '80s music. It's slightly more relaxed and less selective as well.

**Zanzibar** ( ☎ 263 3265; Royal Rd; admission Rs 100; ☺ 11.30pm-5am Mon, Wed, Fri & Sat) There's a nicely intimate, clubby atmosphere to this small bar-disco decked out with sofas and African artefacts. The most relaxed place in town.

**B52** ( ☎ 263 0214; La Salette Rd; ☺ 10am-midnight Mon-Sat) This large, popular spot serves up great cocktails all day long in its al fresco setting back from the main coastal road.

**La Rhumerie** ( ☎ 263 7664; Royal Rd; ☺ 7am-midnight) Friendly bar and restaurant with a lethal selection of *rhum arrangés* (flavoured rums).

## Shopping

**Sunset Boulevard** (Royal Rd) is home to chic boutiques, including knitwear specialists Floreal, Maille St and Shibani; Harris Wilson for menswear; and Hémisphère Sud for fabulous leather goods. Cheaper clothing stores, such as Red Snapper and IV Pl@y, are concentrated in and around the **Super U Hypermarket** (La Salette Rd). Intriguing light-sensitive **Del Sol** (www.delsol. com) products are sold at a friendly boutique in Ventura Plaza.

**Grand Baie Bazaar** ( ☺ 9.30am-4.30pm Mon-Sat, 9am-noon Sun) A craft market hidden down an inland street away from Royal Rd. There's a broad range of touristy Mauritian and Malagasy crafts. Prices aren't fixed, but it's not expensive and there's minimal hassling from vendors.

To purchase some original art, visit the studio of **Françoise Vrot** ( ☎ 263 5118; Reservoir Rd; ⏰ 10am-1pm & 3-6.30pm) to see her expressive portraits of women fieldworkers, or head to **Galerie Vaco** ( ☎ 263 6862; Dodo Sq, Royal Rd; ⏰ 10am-5pm Mon & Wed-Sat, to 1pm Tue) to buy one of Vaco Baissac's instantly recognisable works.

## Getting There & Away

There are no direct buses to Grand Baie from the airport, so it's necessary to change in Port Louis and transfer between two bus stations to do so. Almost all people will have a transfer provided by their hotel and for others arriving after a 12-hour flight, we definitely suggest taking a taxi – or better still, ordering one in advance via the hotel.

Express buses run directly between Immigration Square in Port Louis and Grand Baie every half-hour, terminating near the junction of Royal and La Salette Rds. Nonexpress buses en route to Cap Malheureux will also drop you in Grand Baie. Buses between Pamplemousses and Grand Baie leave roughly every hour. The terminus for express buses to and from Port Louis is on Royal Rd about 100m north of the intersection of Royal and La Salette Rds. Nonexpress services via Trou aux Biches stop every few hundred metres along the coast road.

For taxi rides from Grand Baie, expect to pay between Rs 400 and Rs 500 to Trou aux Biches, Rs 800 to Port Louis and Rs 1800 to the airport. A return trip to Pamplemousses, including waiting time, should set you back Rs 500 or so.

## Getting Around
### BICYCLE

Many hotels and guesthouses can arrange bicycle hire. Rates vary, but expect to pay between Rs 150 and 250 per day, less if you hire for several days. Most of the local tour operators have bikes for rent; just walk down Royal Rd and see what's on offer.

### CAR

There are numerous car-hire companies in Grand Baie, so you should be able to bargain, especially if you're renting for several days.

Prices generally start at around Rs 1200 per day for a small hatchback. Find out whether the management of your hotel or guesthouse has a special discount agreement with a local company. Motorbikes of 50cc and 100cc are widely available in Grand Baie; rental charges hover at around Rs 500 per day, less if you rent for several days.

## PEREYBÈRE

As development continues to boom along the north coast, it's becoming rather difficult to tell where Grand Baie ends and Pereybère (peu-ray-bear) begins. This area is very much the second development on the north coast after Grand Baie and has found the sweet spot between being a bustling tourist hub and a quiet holiday hideaway.

## Information

Pereybère boasts an efficient internet cafe, the **Hard Drive Café** ( ☎ 263 1076; Royal Rd; per min Rs 2; ⏰ 8am-9.30pm). The **Mauritius Commercial Bank** (MCB; Royal Rd) has an **bureau de change** ( ⏰ 8am-6pm Mon-Sat, 9am-noon Sun) open outside regular banking hours.

## Sights & Activities
### GALERIE DU MOULIN CASSÉ

Housed in a charmingly restored sugar mill, the **Galerie du Moulin Cassé** ( ☎ 727 0672; Old Mill Rd; ⏰ 10am-6pm Fri) features the vibrant floral scenes of painter Malcolm de Chazal (1902–82) and a collection of photographs by Diane Henry. The most impressive display, however, is the collection of over 20,000 terracotta pots lining the vaulted arcs of the ceiling.

### DIVING

Divers can organise expeditions either through **Ocean Spirit Diving** ( ☎ 263 4428; Royal Rd; www.osdiving.com; ⏰ 8am-8pm Mon-Sat, 8am-noon Sun) or with Wolfgang Clausen at **Orca Dive Club** (www.orca-diveclub-mauritius.com) on the grounds of the Hibiscus Hotel. For more information on diving in Mauritius, see p28.

### SPAS

For some indulgent relaxation, head to the very smart **Surya Ayurvedic Spa** ( ☎ 263 1637; www.spasurya.com; Royal Rd; ⏰ 9am-8pm) and treat yourself to an Indian massage or a steam in the *hammam*. Your other option is **Chi** (The Spa; ☎ 263 9621; Old Mill Rd; ⏰ 9am-7pm), located near the Baptist church. The 90-minute 'Chi

MAURITIUS

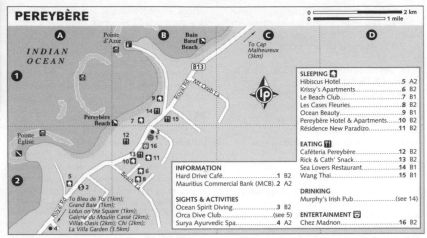

**PEREYBÈRE**

Balance' (a footbath with five essential elements oils) costs Rs 1325 – quite reasonable when compared to the in-house spas at the surrounding hotels.

## Sleeping

While there are a few larger hotels on the beach side of the main road, the majority of accommodation here is made up of charming guesthouses and little hotels in the back streets, a short walk from the town centre and public beach.

### APARTMENTS & VILLAS

Several rental companies in Grand Baie (p87) also manage a slew of lodging in Pereybère.

**Krissy's Apartments** ( ☎ 263 8859; limfat@bow.intnet.mu; Beach Lane; studios/apt €15/35; ☒ ) This complex of self-catering units is dirt cheap without too much dirt. The sterile neon lighting doesn't make for a sexy beach holiday, but who can complain with the bargain-basement prices.

**Les Cases Fleuries** ( ☎ 263 8868; casefle@intnet.mu; Beach Lane; studios/apt €30/40; ☒ ) There's something surprisingly rarefied in the air here considering the perfectly reasonable prices. A variety of studios and apartments for up to six people are set in a flower-filled garden, and the crowd is a wealthy French one for the most part. Go for one of the prim white studios – the apartments are dour.

**Villas Oasis** ( ☎ 422 8435; www.evaco.mu; villas from €175; ☒ ☒ ☒ ) These villas – the most luxurious on the north coast – are a steal if you're travelling with family or friends. Trendy Asian-inspired decor permeates the lavish open-air floorplans. Security is tight, privacy is held sacred and there's a real sense of being a VIP. The only downside is that you'll need a private vehicle to get to the beach. Evaco, the development company responsible for these beautiful residences, is currently constructing yet another property, Domaine Des Alizées – visit the website for details.

Also worth a look:

**Résidence New Paradizo** ( ☎ 263 7413; www.newparadizo.com; Royal Rd; studios €35-60, apt €90-125; ☒ ☒ ) Set slightly back from the main road. A complex of spick-and-span apartments.

### GUESTHOUSES & CHAMBRES D'HÔTES

**Bleu de Toi** ( ☎ 269 1761; www.hotelbleudetoi.com; Royal Rd; r €90; ☒ ☒ ☒ ☒ ) Owned by friendly Belgians, this lovely B&B is the area's only worthy contender in the guesthouse category. Rooms are done up with simple yet tasteful furnishings and adorable arched doorways abound. Don't miss the charming *table d'hôte* (€12 to €18) in the evenings. Blue de Toi is quite pricey compared to the *chambres d'hôtes* in Pointe d'Esny, but it's highly recommended if you want to stay in the north.

### HOTELS & RESORTS

**Pereybère Hotel & Apartments** ( ☎ 263 8320; www.pereyberehotel.com; Royal Rd; r/ste €49/69; ☒ ☒ ☒ ) Right in the thick of things, this old-timer may look rather dated from the front but the rooms are surprisingly prim. The hotel is, however, guilty of false advertisement – signs

RITIUS

boast sea views (possible if there wasn't a forest of giant *filao* trees in the way) and Jacuzzis (which are actually just showers with fancy nozzles and buttons).

**Ocean Beauty** ( ☎ 263 6039; www.ocean-beauty.com; Pointe d'Azur; r incl breakfast €55-220; ❄ ⬜ � 🖥 ) Ocean Beauty is a boutique hotel aimed squarely at honeymooners. This is boutique basic though, which means the rooms are stylish and atmospheric, but there's very little else to the hotel. Despite this, it's a great spot for romance; breakfast is served on your balcony and there's direct access to the lovely town beach. Beware of the pool that plays Enya at you while you swim.

**Le Beach Club** ( ☎ 263 5104; www.le-beachclub.com; Royal Rd; studios €76-87, apt €107-122; ❄ ) This complex of studios and two-bedroom apartments is one of the few places on the seafront and has a great little beach, perfect for swimming. Rooms have festive tropical colours, but the common areas are so tiny they feel like storage spaces for stacked furniture. Plan your check-in time before arriving – the reception has limited hours.

**Hibiscus Hotel** ( ☎ 263 8554; www.hibiscushotel.com; Royal Rd; s/d incl half board €145/220; ❄ 🖥 🛜 ) Hibiscus boasts a stone path that wends past thick jungle-like gardens, a super pool and a private beach of sorts (although there's quite a bit of rock to negotiate). Accommodation is in clean, comfortable rooms in three-storey blocks.

## Eating & Drinking

Like in Grand Baie, most of Pereybère's restaurants also double as good places for a drink, though the neighbourhood is generally much quieter. The following options are some of the top spots amid the frenzy of ever-growing eating options.

**Lotus on the Square** ( ☎ 263 3251; Royal Rd; snacks & mains from Rs 90; 🕑 9.30am-5pm Mon-Sat) The garden of this small, arty cafe on the road to Pereybère makes a nice place to linger over a latte or cappuccino. It also does refreshing fruit juices and homemade sorbets in unusual flavours such as tamarind, basil and cinnamon.

**Caféteria Pereybère** ( ☎ 263 8539; Royal Rd; mains Rs 110-225; 🕑 10.30am-10pm) This friendly all-day cafe-restaurant behind the public beach offers grilled fish, octopus curry, and steak and chips from an extensive menu. Portions are on the small side.

**Rick & Cath' Snack** ( ☎ 741 4374; Royal Rd; mains Rs 150-190; 🕑 7am-9pm Mon-Fri, to 2pm Sat) A cluster

of plastic chairs painted in primary colours welcomes customers when they swing by for a tasty breakfast or a cone of locally made ice cream.

**Wang Thai** ( ☎ 263 4050; Royal Rd; mains Rs 250; 🕑 lunch Tue-Sun, dinner daily) Long the best restaurant in town and a pioneer of authentic Thai food in Mauritius, Wang Thai is a sophisticated, airy place with Buddha statues and raw silks setting the scene for surprisingly affordable cuisine. Treat your taste buds to such classics as *tom yum thalay* (lemongrass-laced seafood soup), green curry and *phad thai* (mixed fried noodles).

**Murphy's Irish Pub** ( ☎ 263 6299; Royal Rd; mains Rs 350-500; 🕑 11am-midnight) What were the odds that Mauritius' first Irish pub would land in tiny Pereybère? Perhaps more suited to Grand Baie, Murphy's makes an unusual bedfellow for the swanky Sea Lovers Restaurant, run by the same team. In true Irish-pubs-abroad style, it looks nothing like an Irish pub, but has cold beer and big-screen sports.

**Sea Lovers Restaurant** ( ☎ 263 6299; Royal Rd; mains Rs 350-700; 🕑 lunch & dinner) This is, without a doubt, the smartest spot in the area. There's a gorgeous terrace built right into the sand and the furniture is unquestionably stylish. The food, however, is nothing to write home about and the service can be a bit lacking as well. It's worth stopping by to take in the atmosphere – just stick to the drinks list.

**La Villa Garden** ( ☎ 262 7552; 1331 20 Pieds Rd; menu Rs 1500; 🕑 dinner Tue-Sat, lunch Sun) A stylishly austere gate suddenly cuts across a patch of sugar cane revealing this lauded addition to the north's dining scene. This bastion of *haute cuisine* proudly peddles gastronomic tributes to a variety of faraway lands that have inspired the acclaimed chef; the French countryside, Morocco and Vietnam.

## Entertainment

You'll find *séga* shows at the restaurant **Chez Madnon** ( ☎ 269 1457; Royal Rd; drinks Rs 80-350) every night from 7.30pm and 11.30pm – if you're looking for something rowdier you'll have to hit up the clubs in Grand Baie.

## Getting There & Around

Buses between Port Louis and Cap Malheureux stop in Pereybère as well as Grand Baie. Services run roughly every 30 minutes.

You can rent cars, motorbikes and bicycles through the local tour agents. Cars start at Rs

900 per day and motorbikes at Rs 500 for a 50cc or 100cc bike. Pedal bikes cost upwards of Rs 150 per day. Most of Grand Baie's car-hire companies will also drop off and pick up cars in Pereybère.

## CAP MALHEUREUX

The northern edge of Mauritius has stunning views out to the islands off the coast beyond, most obviously of the dramatic slopes of Coin de Mire. Although it feels like rather a back-water today, 'Cape Misfortune' (thus named for the number of ships that foundered on the rocks here) is a place of great historical importance for Mauritius: it was here that the British invasion force finally defeated the French in 1810 and took over the island.

A little further on lies the minuscule fishing village also known as Cap Malheureux, with its much-photographed church, the red-roofed **Notre Dame Auxiliatrice**. It's worth a quick peek inside for its intricate woodwork and a holy-water basin fashioned out of a giant clamshell. A sign strictly prohibits newlyweds 'faking' a church wedding for the photographers here – really, some people, eh? You can attend Mass here at 6pm on Saturday and 9am on Sunday.

Heading around the coast the landscape becomes wilder and more rugged. A clutch of hotels occupies the few decent beaches in be-tween the rocky coves and muddy tidal creeks. They offer a perfect hideaway for those who want to get away from it all.

### Sleeping

**Kuxville** (Map p79; ☎ 262 8836; www.kuxville.com; studios from €33, apt from €54; ☒ ☜ ) There's a huge choice of accommodation on offer at this perennially popular apartment complex about 1.5km west of Cap Malheureux village. Accommodation is in impeccably clean studios or apartments sleeping up to four people; 'gardenside' units are in a newer compound across the road. There's a fine little beach and a small kite-boarding school headed up by the affable owner Nico Kux.

**Le Paradise Cove** (Map p79; ☎ 204 4000; www.para disecovehotel.com; Anse la Raie; s/d/ste incl half board from €462/616/952; ☒ ☐ ☜ ☒ ) Paradise Cove is a five-star boutique resort aimed at honeymooners. Terribly understated but as utterly luxurious as its name suggests, it's built on an attractive small cove – the beach is at the end of an inlet from the sea, which gives it remarkable privacy. Other great touches include a golf course, tennis

courts, free watersports, a dive centre, brightly painted and delightful rooms and 'love nests' on the promontory overlooking the northern islands. With three restaurants, a Cinq Mondes spa and award-winning gardens, this stylish place is a great destination for couples.

### Eating

Outside the hotel restaurants there are just a few eating options in the area, the best being Amigo.

**our pick** **Amigo** ( ☎ 262 8418; Royal Rd; mains Rs 230-800; ☜ 11.30am-3.30pm & 6.30-11.30pm Mon-Sat) Everyone adores this friendly joint tucked behind the township near the cane farms. The writing's on the wall (literally) – contented customers have left myriad messages of love and affection on every flat surface in the restaurant. The tables, however, are graffiti free – they're reserved for the excellent seafood specialities. Side note: the letters in the restaurant's name are the first ini-tials of the owner (sadly now deceased) and his four sons. Ironically, the owner didn't speak a lick of Spanish. Delivery available.

### Getting There & Away

Buses run roughly every half-hour between Port Louis' Immigration Square bus station and Cap Malheureux, via Grand Baie. A taxi to Port Louis will cost Rs 800, to Grand Baie Rs 400 and to the airport Rs 2000.

## GRAND GAUBE

Grand Gaube is where the development of northern Mauritius currently ends, although it has itself become a flash point for hotel building in recent years. Despite this, it re-mains a tiny fishing village with a good beach about 6km east of Cap Malheureux. Beyond the small rocky bays of Grande Gaube there are almost no beaches until a long way down the east coast, making any trip beyond here an illuminating glimpse into traditional Mauritian life without the tourists. In 1744 the *St Géran* foundered off Grand Gaube in a storm, inspiring the famous love story *Paul et Virginie* by Bernardin de St-Pierre (see the boxed text, p131).

It's possible to explore **Île Ambre** offshore on a sea kayaking trip with **Yemaya** ( ☎ 752 0046, 283 8187; www.yemayaadventures.com).

### Sleeping & Eating

**Verandah Paul & Virginie** (Map p79; ☎ 266 9700; www. paul-et-virginie-hotel.com; s/d incl half board from Rs 139/198;

 ⊠ ▢ ⊚ ⊠ ) The longest-established hotel in Grande Gaube is a pleasant surprise. It's small enough not to be overwhelming yet offers all the services and comforts required for luxury: two pools, a couple of restaurants, a Seven Colour's 'wellness' spa, plenty of entertainment and activities, and a kids club. The style is colonial, although the atmosphere is very relaxed. The rooms are stylishly fitted out and spacious, all with sea views, and there's a small but attractive beach.

**Legends** (Map p79; ☎ 698 9800; www.naiade.com; s/d incl half board from €330/488; ⊠ ▢ ⊚ ⊠ ) This very large, stylish establishment enjoys an idyllic location miles from the mass tourism found further down the coast. Guests here are welcomed with a drum-banging ceremony, and have the run of the pretty bay and the hotel's well-appointed surroundings. The hotel is Feng Shui themed (God help us) but don't be distracted by the waffle about metal elements, Chi flow or the mirror being a 'reflection of serenity' – at the end of the day Legends is a smart beach hotel whose marketing people have just got a little bit over-excited.

### Getting There & Away

Buses run roughly every 15 minutes between Port Louis' Immigration Square bus station and Grand Gaube. A taxi to Port Louis will cost Rs 900, to Grand Baie Rs 500 and to the airport Rs 2100.

## PAMPLEMOUSSES

Most visitors to northern Mauritius take the time to visit Pamplemousses for its fa-mous botanical gardens, which are worth a diversion if you fancy an afternoon away from the beach. Officially known as the Sir Seewoosagur Ramgoolam Botanical Gardens (and occasionally referred to as the Royal Botanical Gardens), they feature a stunning variety of endemic and foreign plant species. Also of interest is the decommissioned Beau Plan sugar factory nearby, which has been converted into a fascinating museum.

Pamplemousses itself was named for the grapefruit-like citrus trees that the Dutch introduced to Mauritius from Java. The town is typically Mauritian and feels a million miles away from Grand Baie or Trou aux Biches.

### Sir Seewoosagur Ramgoolam Botanical Gardens

Don't be put off if you've never been particularly interested in botany – after London's Kew Gardens the **SSR Botanical Gardens** (Jardins de Pamplemousses; Map p79; admission Rs100; ☺ 8.30am-5.30pm) is one of the best places in the world to learn about plants, trees and flowers. It's also one of the most popular tourist attractions in Mauritius and is easily reached from almost anywhere on the island.

Named after Sir Seewoosagur Ramgoolam, the first prime minister of independent Mauritius, the gardens also house the funerary platform where he was cremated. His ashes were scattered on the Ganges in India.

The plants are gradually being labelled and map boards installed, but this is still very patchy and thus the gardens are best seen with a guide (guided golf-buggy tours cost Rs

---

**PAUL & VIRGINIE**

Mauritius' most popular folk tale tells the story of two lovers, Paul and Virginie, who encounter tragedy when the ship that is carrying Virginie founders on the reef. Although Paul swims out to the wreck to save her, Virginie modestly refuses to remove her clothes to swim ashore, and drowns; Paul dies of a broken heart shortly after.

The story was written by Bernardin de St-Pierre in the 18th century, but was inspired by a real-life tragedy that took place some years earlier. In 1744, the ship *St Géran* was wrecked during a storm off Île Ambre, to the southeast of Grand Gaube, with almost 200 lives lost. Among them were two female passengers who refused to undress to swim ashore and were dragged down by the weight of their clothes. The true story is more a tragedy of social mores than one of romance!

The *St Géran* was carrying a hoard of Spanish money and machinery from France for the island's first sugar refinery. A French dive expedition explored the wreck in 1966 and many of their finds are on display in Mahébourg's National History Museum and the Blue Penny Museum in Port Louis.

You'll run into Paul and Virginie everywhere in Mauritius. The statue by Prosper d'Épinay is perhaps the most famous memorial. The original is in the Blue Penny Museum and there's a copy near the town hall in Curepipe.

250/100 per adult/child), as you'll miss many of the most interesting species if you go alone.

The gardens were started by Mahé de Labourdonnais in 1735 as a vegetable plot for his **Mon Plaisir Château** (which now contains a small exhibition of photographs). The landscape came into its own in 1768 under the auspices of the French horticulturalist Pierre Poivre. Like Kew Gardens, the gardens played a significant role in the horticultural espionage of the day. Poivre imported seeds from around the world in a bid to end France's dependence on Asian spices. The gardens were neglected between 1810 and 1849 until British horticulturalist James Duncan transformed them into an arboretum for palms and other tropical trees.

Palms still constitute the most important part of the horticultural display, and they come in an astonishing variety of shapes and forms. Some of the more prominent are the stubby bottle palms, the tall royal palms and the talipot palms, which flower once after about 40 years and then die. Other varieties include the raffia, sugar, toddy, fever, fan and even sealing-wax palms. There are many other curious tree species on display, including the marmalade box tree, the fish poison tree and the sausage tree.

The centrepiece of the gardens is a pond filled with giant Victoria amazonica water lilies, native to South America. Young leaves emerge as wrinkled balls and unfold into the classic tea-tray shape up to 2m across in a matter of hours. The flowers in the centre of the huge leaves open white one day and close red the next. The lilies are at their biggest and best in the warm summer months, notably January.

Various international dignitaries have planted trees in the gardens, including Nelson Mandela, Indira Gandhi and a host of British royals.

While you're in the neighbourhood it's worth grabbing a delicious Creole lunch at **Chez Tante Athalie** ( ☎ 243 9266; Centre de Flacq Rd, Mont Gout; menu Rs 450; ☼ lunch Mon-Sat) – the best-known *table d'hôte* in the area.

## L'Aventure du Sucre

On the other side of the motorway's roundabout from the botanical gardens, the former Beau Plan sugar factory now houses a fascinating **museum** (Map p79; ☎ 243 0660; www.aventuredusucre.com; adult/child Rs 350/175; ☼ 9am-5pm). It not only tells the story of sugar in great detail, but also covers the history of Mauritius, slavery, the rum trade and much, much more. Allow at least a couple of hours to do it justice.

The original factory was founded in 1797 and only ceased working in 1999. Most of the machinery is still in place and former workers are on hand to answer questions about the factory and the complicated process of turning sugar cane into crystals. There are also videos and interactive displays as well as quizzes for children. At the end of the visit you can taste four of the 15 different varieties of unrefined sugar, two of which were invented in Mauritius.

If all that's set your taste buds working, you could sup a glass of sugar cane juice at **Le Fangourin** ( ☎ 243 0660; mains Rs 245-945; ☼ 11.30am-4pm), a stylish cafe-restaurant in the grounds of the museum. It specialises in sophisticated Creole cuisine and all sorts of sugary delights.

## GETTING THERE & AWAY

Pamplemousses can be reached by bus from Grand Baie, Trou aux Biches, Grand Gaube and Port Louis. Services from Grand Baie and Trou aux Biches run approximately every hour and stop near the sugar museum on the way to the botanical gardens.

Buses from Port Louis' Immigration Square bus station and Grand Gaube operate every 10 to 15 minutes. These buses only stop at the botanical gardens, from where it takes about 15 minutes to walk to the museum.

# THE WEST

A world away from the shores of the north, Mauritius' western wonderland is the nation's most diverse coast. The bustling tourist hub of Flic en Flac may be an inauspicious welcome mat, but the treasures that lie just beyond will satisfy even the pickiest holidaymaker. A veritable swatch book of lush greens and light browns, the area of Black River has scalloping sandy bays that dimple the arable farmland. Development is rampant here as expats arrive in droves to build their dream villa amid sleepy fishing villages. Then, further on, the tic-tac-toes of Tamarin's shimmering salt flats perfectly reflect the beaming sun and soaring hills of fauna-filled Black River Gorges National Park. Next is bucolic Chamarel nestled in the highlands, followed by the last iteration of sky-reaching stone, Le Morne

Brabant; an awesomely photogenic crag that caps the coastline's southern tip.

## Getting Around

The main bus routes in west Mauritius are those from Port Louis down to the southern end of Rivière Noire, and from Quatre Bornes to Baie du Cap. There is also a regular service between Quatre Bornes and Chamarel.

Your hotel or guesthouse should be able to arrange bike and car hire. Otherwise, one of the outlets in Flic en Flac or La Gaulette should be able to help.

Note that there are only two petrol stations in the west – one at Flic en Flac, and one in Black River near La Preneuse.

## ALBION

pop 3300

A small dent of coral-strewn tranquillity between Port Louis and Flic en Flac, the quiet waters of Albion are home to a lovely house reef offshore and the surprisingly charming **Club Med La Plantation d'Albion** ( ☎ 206 0700; www.clubmed.com; d per week incl full board €3000; 🅿 🖳 🛜 🏊 ). Forget what you know about the Club Med chain, this is one of the finest resorts on the island, with acres of groomed gardens and a savvy design scheme that fuses African and Zen motifs. The beach isn't tops here, but the luxurious swimming pools more than make up for it. Quirky side note: during particularly tumultuous rainstorms guests often find fragments of Ming dynasty china from a merchant vessel that ran aground in the reef many moons ago.

After a few too many days of beachside lethargy, get the blood rushing again with an invigorating half-day rock-climbing session on the Belle Vue cliffs, about a 10-minute walk from the lighthouse. Contact **Vertical World** ( ☎ 697 5430; www.verticalworldltd.com) for details.

## FLIC EN FLAC

pop 2000

As wonderful and whimsical as the name sounds, Flic en Flac isn't quite the picture of paradise you saw on your travel agent's website. The area's moniker is thought to be a corruption of the old Dutch name Fried Landt Flaak (meaning 'Free and Flat Land'); the endless acreage of sandy shoreline was undoubtedly striking when explorers first arrived in the 18th century. Today, the public beach is peppered with weeping *filao* trees (a bit of rubbish, too, unfortunately), and the area is exploding with apartment complexes, souvenir shops, moneychangers and pinch-a-penny holiday rentals. Although development in Flic en Flac has gone the way of Grand Baie, it's still about a dozen clubs and restaurants short of attracting a party crowd in earnest.

All is not lost, however; if you stay at any of the high-end resorts in the Wolmar area outside the town, you'll uncover some stellar stretches of sand, glorious diving and a handful of palate-pleasing restaurants.

## Orientation

The centre of Flic en Flac is dominated by Pasadena Village, a large shopping complex with a couple of restaurants, shops, a supermarket and a hotel on top. North of Pasadena the main road weaves through an inland cluster of guesthouses and souvenir shops; south of the shopping complex the road hugs the coastline with a vast public beach on one side and rows upon rows of holiday housing on the other. As the road continues south, the endless blocks of concrete apartments and ever-changing restaurants fades into far-more-refined Wolmar, a suburb of Flic en Flac, where all the luxury hotels congregate.

## Information

### EMERGENCY

The police station is well positioned in the centre of Flic en Flac beside the post office and across the street from the Pasadena Village complex.

### INTERNET ACCESS

**Internet Cafe** (Royal Rd; per 15min Rs 25; 🕑 8am-8pm Mon-Sat, 8am-5pm Sun) Inside the Spar supermarket at Pasadena Village.

**Zub Express** ( ☎ 434 8868; Royal Rd; per 5min Rs 10; 🕑 11am-3pm & 6-10pm Sat-Thu) Update your blog at this restaurant-cum-grocery-store in the Wolmar area of Flic en Flac.

### MONEY

Due to the pedestrian and resort-less atmosphere in central Flic en Flac, you'll find ATMs and moneychangers every 70m along the main drag. There's a Western Union on Royal Rd just north of Pasadena Village.

### POST

**Post office** ( 🕑 8.15am-11.15am & noon-4pm Mon-Fri, 8.15-11.45am Sat) In a light-blue *case*-style house across the street from the Pasadena Village complex.

MAURITIUS

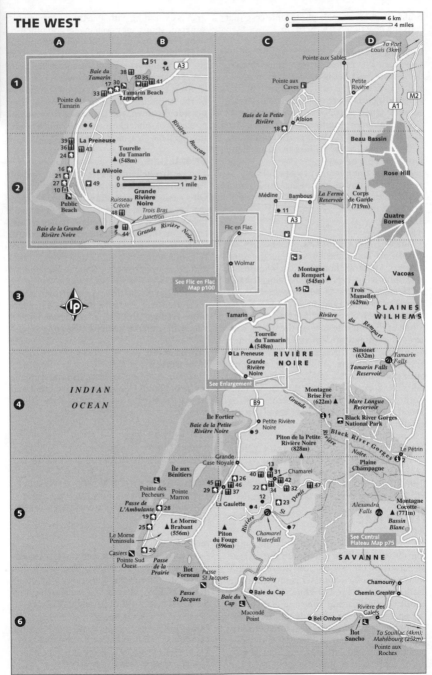

THE WEST

MAURITIUS

## TOURIST INFORMATION

**Mauritius Tourism Promotion Authority** (MTPA;
☎ 453 8860; www.tourism-mauritius.mu; ☽ 9am-5pm
Mon-Sat) There's a small MTPA office inside Pasadena
Village where you can get general information about Mauritius or organise car hire, although every time we stopped
by the kiosk was empty save for a couple of ornery hornets.

## TRAVEL AGENCIES

Local travel agencies are more than abundant
in the area, especially along the main road
between the entrance to town and Pasadena
Village. Most offer the exact same products
and swipe identical commission.

**Flic en Flac Tourist Agency** ( ☎ 453 9389; www.
fftourist.com; Royal Rd; ☽ 8.30am-5pm Mon-Sat,
8.30am-1pm Sun) Has been around for many years and
offers well-priced sightseeing packages and vehicle hire.

**Mr Concierge** ( ☎ 498 2233; www.mrconcierge.mu)
Pickier travellers should try contacting Mr Concierge.

## Sights

### CASELA NATURE & LEISURE PARK

This 14-hectare **nature park** (Map p98; ☎ 452 0693,
727 6076; www.caselayemen.mu; adult/child Rs 270/170;
☽ 9am-5pm May-Sep, 9am-6pm Oct-Apr) is on the main
road 1km south of the turn to Flic en Flac. The
beautifully landscaped reserve is a haven for
animals and offers a variety of heart-pumping
'rando fun' like zip-lines, suspension bridges,
hiking, swimming spots hidden in canyons
and quad-bike 'safaris' around the neighbouring 45-sq-km **Yemen Reserve** (Map p98; ☎ 452 0693;

2hr quad-bike trips Rs 2775), where deer, wild pigs,
fruit bats and monkeys can be seen in their
natural habitat. Children are well catered for
with a petting zoo, a playground, giant tortoises, fishing and minigolf.

The park's most popular attraction is **walking
with lions and cheetahs** ( ☎ 452 5546; www.safari-adventures-mauritius.com; 1hr walk Rs 2000). You'll be amazed
at how large and powerful these felines really
are – this is not an activity for the little ones
(you must be at least 150cm tall). The park also
has a popular restaurant, Mirador (p102), with
sweeping views of the coastal plain.

### MÉDINE SUGAR FACTORY

Rather unattractively spewing out smoke into
the countryside around Flic en Flac is the **Médine
Sugar Factory** (Map p98; ☎ 452 0400, 401 6000), one of
the country's biggest. During the cutting season
(July to early November) it's possible to take a
guided one-hour tour of the factory. You can
also visit the distillery, where the 'waste' molasses is turned into rum. The visit ends with a tasting session. Call ahead for details. The factory is
6km northeast of Flic en Flac. If you get stuck
behind a sugar-cane trucks overburdened by
harvested crops, you can bet it's heading here.

## Activities

In addition to the activities at Casela Nature &
Leisure Park and golfing at Tamarina further
south (p105), the main activities in Flic en Flac
are watersports.

MAURITIUS

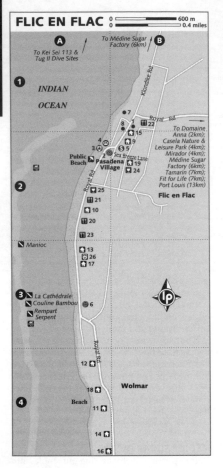

Some of Mauritius' best dive sites can be found just beyond the emerald lagoon near Flic en Flac where the shallow waters suddenly give way to the deep. The most popular site in the area is La Cathédrale, with its signature stone arches and tucked-away cavern. For more information on diving in Mauritius, see p28.

The top dive operator in the area is **Sun Divers** ( ☎ 453 8441; www.sundiversmauritius.com; ☺ 8am-4pm Mon-Sat, 8pm-noon Sun), based at La Pirogue hotel. It is one of the oldest outfits on the island and Gerald, one of the instructors, is an internationally recognised underwater photographer who has published a thoroughly researched book about Mauritian sea life. Three daily dives are scheduled at 9am, noon and 2.30pm with a minimum of three participants. One dive costs Rs 1675 with discounts for those who have their own equipment.

Like La Pirogue, most of the other upmarket hotels in Wolmar have their own diving operators (all are open to participants from outside the hotel). There are also several operators with storefronts in central Flic en Flac, including **Exploration Sous-Marine** ( ☎ 453 8450; www.pierre-szalay.com; ☺ 8.30am-4pm Mon-Fri, 8.30am-2pm Sat), based just beyond the entrance to Club Eden, an Italian-run private vacation property. **Sea Urchin Diving Centre** ( ☎ 751 2235; www.sea-urchin-diving.com; ☺ 9am-1pm Mon-Fri, 10am-2pm Sat) is on the main road. Figure around Rs1200/3500 for a one-/three-dive package. Check out www.msda.mu for a list of licensed and insured dive operators.

## Sleeping

Central Flic en Flac is decidedly *not* upmarket, with condos and apartment complexes flanking every street. South of Flic en Flac, in the Wolmar area, you'll find several charming luxury options directly on the sand.

## APARTMENTS & VILLAS

Flic en Flac trumps all of the island's other beach towns when it comes to cheap holiday rentals. None of the options are located directly on the beach as the coastal road cuts a line between development and the sandy shore, but there are still plenty of beach views to be had.

**EasyRent** ( ☎ 452 1010; www.easyrent.mul; apt per night €250) Leases a small variety of rental options including the only single-family villa in the area.

**Escale Vacances** ( ☎ 453 9389, 453 5002; www.fftourist.com; Royal Rd; apt per night €60-150) A justifiably popular apartment complex across the coastal road from the public beach. The fully equipped, one-bedroom duplexes represent excellent value for money; those in the front get sea views, though cop some road noise.

**Jet-7** ( ☎ 453 9600, 467 7735; www.jet-7.com; apt per night €50-150) The most popular rental operator in the area manages a handful of expansive multi-unit properties, including the Datier, Tamarinier, Latanier and Grenadier complexes.

## GUESTHOUSES & CHAMBRES D'HÔTES

**Résidence Art** (Little Acorn; ☎ 453 5277; fax 453 5278; Royal Rd; s/d/apt Rs 650/850/1000; 🍴 ) Peeping out from behind a rusty wrought-iron gate and overgrown foliage, this ramshackle guesthouse is the first place you should look if you're serious about pinching pennies. The rooms are basic – we'd say bare if it weren't for the one coy mosaic on the wall – but everything's clean and most of the bathroom fixtures are sparkling new. If you can, go for a room with a terrace on the 2nd floor. Laundry costs Rs 200, and, if you ask with a smile, the owner will let you borrow her bicycle.

**Villa Paul & Virginie** ( ☎ 453 5537; www.villa-paul-et-virginie.com; Sea Breeze Lane; d incl breakfast €50; 🍴 🛜 🐾 ) This eccentric hotel (which feels more like a guesthouse) was under renovation when we stopped by. Things look promising – it's definitely worth keeping an eye on this place.

If everything else is full:

**Easy World Hotel** ( ☎ 453 8557; easyworld@intnet.mu; Royal Rd; r/studios Rs 800/1000; 🍴 ) Basic, cheap, though rather threadbare. Set slightly back from the main drag, but impossible to miss.

## HOTELS & RESORTS

The hotels in the Flic en Flac area can be sharply divided into two categories – small midrange sleeps and grandiose top-end resorts stretched across the flaxen sand. If you're considering one of the pricier options, it is best to book through a travel agent who can marry your accommodation to a discounted airline ticket. Rack rates are represented here, but large discounts can be scouted, especially at Sugar Beach and La Pirogue.

**Aanari** ( ☎ 453 9000; www.aanari.com; Royal Rd; d incl half board from €72; 🍴 🖥 🛜 🐾 ) Perched atop the Pasadena Village, Aanari is attempting boutique sophistication with a clutch of oriental statues and special 'VIP perks' for guests. Rooms feel distinctly Asian in theme with lacquered furnishings, errant flower petals and silk bed runners. The hotel's biggest drawcard is the window-filled spa and fitness centre on the roof.

**Seavilla Resort & Spa** ( ☎ 453 8880; seavillahotel@yahoo.com; Royal Rd; s/d incl breakfast €95/136; 🍴 🖥 🐾 ) A local management group has taken over this defunct apartment complex and turned it into a comfortable hotel. The spacious rooms, many with sweeping sea views, have plasma TVs, modern kitchenettes, tropically inspired bedding and loads of wicker furniture. A great option for families.

**Manisa Hotel** ( ☎ 453 8550; www.manisahotel.com; Royal Rd; d incl half board €120; 🍴 🐾 🛜 ) Like a relic from a bygone era, this stalwart midranger is in desperate need of an overhaul. The dour faux-marble entrance and faded facade leave little to write home about, but if you temper your expectations (and focus your attention on the tended garden and pool) Manisa represents fairly good value for money.

**Sands Resort** ( ☎ 403 1200; www.thesandsresort.mu; Royal Rd, Wolmar; s/d incl half board €220/320; 🍴 🖥 🛜 🐾 ) With gorgeous views from the beachside pool out onto Tamarin Bay and towards Le Morne, this sophisticated yet unpretentious option enjoys an airy, tropical elegance which permeates the open, timber-frame lobby. The bedrooms sport subtle earthy tones, generous bathrooms and sea-view balconies. There are two restaurants, a spa and plenty of sports activities, including a dive centre.

**our pick** **La Pirogue** ( ☎ 403 3900; www.lapirogue.com; Royal Rd, Wolmar; r incl half board €340; 🍴 🖥 🛜 🐾 ) Mauritius' oldest resort shares the same management as Sugar Beach next door, but there's a completely different feel here. Rather than a colonial manse theme, La Pirogue opts for a charming fishing village vibe with semicircle clusters of adorable hut-villas arranged along the 500m of spectacular sandy beach. The resort was built around the same time as the Sydney Opera House and if you look carefully you'll notice that the thatch roofing is arranged in a similar fashion to the trademark cavalier helmet-like roofing on the iconic opera house. To some, it may feel like the resort is starting to show its age, but to most visitors, La Pirogue represents a classic paradigm of Mauritius' beachside hospitality.

**Sugar Beach Resort** ( ☎ 453 9090; www.sugar beachresort.mu; Royal Rd, Wolmar; d incl half board €710; ✖ 🖳 🛜 🏊 ) With its mock-plantation mansion look and wonderfully colonial lawns, Sugar Bay is a well-run resort catering to a huge number of people coming to enjoy the smart settings and great beach. It's a very family-friendly resort (think lots of kids in the pool and live entertainment at dinner) and shares facilities with La Pirogue next door.

Other favourites:

**Hilton** ( ☎ 403 1000; www.mauritius.hilton.com; Royal Rd, Wolmar; d incl half board from €368; ✖ 🖳 🛜 🏊 ) Exotic tropical charm is manifested through sublime gardens and rambling waterways. The rooms themselves subscribe to a more standard international design scheme.

**Maradiva** ( ☎ 403 1500; www.maradiva.com; Royal Rd, Wolmar; villas incl breakfast €1000-5000; ✖ 🖳 🛜 🏊 ) Perfectly manicured grounds sprinkled with luxurious villas. Oozes jet-set charm from the entry gate to the sleek seaside resto-lounge. Half-board rates are available for an additional €60 per person.

## Eating

Flic en Flac has quite a paradoxical dining scene. Wealthier vacationers tend to stay on the grounds of their upmarket hotels to take advantage of their 'half-board' holiday packages, while budgetarians usually opt to self-cater or nibble on street fare. This leaves a strange void in the middle of the dining spectrum, and as a result there's a noticeable lack of out-of-this-world establishments in central Flic en Flac.

Foodies should consider booking a reservation at an in-house restaurant on the grounds of one of the top-end hotels, or drive down to Black River for a more memorable and eclectic assortment of eats.

### RESTAURANTS

**Ah-Youn** ( ☎ 453 9099; Royal Rd; mains from Rs 100; ✇ 11am-10pm) We're not sure how much of a compliment it is to say that Ah-Youn's best features are its swift service and generous portions, but alas it's true. Don't worry though, the food is perfectly palatable and, frankly, a much better choice than many of the other restaurants in town (not listed here). The kitchen's focus is mainly Chinese fare, but Mauritian flavours have crept onto the menu as well.

**Le Papayou** ( ☎ 453 9826; Royal Rd; mains Rs 130-280; ✇ 9.30am-3pm & 6-10pm Mon-Sat) Service can come with a smile or a scowl at this tiny local joint, but that's all just part of the charm. You'll find scores of local vendors flocking here on their lunch break for the cheap eclectic menu (paella, pizza etc) at pinch-a-penny prices. Try the signature 'papayou' (cooked payapa sweetened with sugar and ice cream) with a cup of fresh coffee – Flic en Flac's finest.

**Restaurant de L'Ouest** ( ☎ 453 8726; Royal Rd; mains from Rs 160; ✇ lunch & dinner) Right in the thick of things, this is a fine place for a meal. While the crowd is almost exclusively foreign and the nightly entertainment (including *séga* on Sundays) is sometimes unwelcome, the Mauritian food is imaginatively prepared and beautifully presented.

**Mirador** ( ☎ 452 0845; Casela Nature & Leisure Park; mains Rs 200; ✇ 10.30am-4pm) It's well worth planning your visit to Casela around lunchtime to grab a bite at the on-site restaurant. This charming open-air cafe has photogenic views of the sea and western plains, and serves a variety of international and local dishes (including a scrumptious heart of palm salad sourced from within the reserve).

**our pick Domaine Anna** ( ☎ 453 9650; Médine; mains from Rs 200; ✇ 11.30am-2.30pm & 6.30-10.30pm Thu-Sun) You'll need a taxi or rental car to get here, but you'll be really glad you made the trip. Flic en Flac's most refined dining experience sits in colonial-style pavilions with gauzy netting, wooden banisters and sky-scraping cane in the distance. The predominantly Chinese menu may seem surprising considering the surrounds, but the food is excellent – locals come from all over the island to get their frequent fix of crab, calamari and succulent lobster.

**Chez Pepe** ( ☎ 453 9383; Royal Rd; mains Rs 205-375; ✇ 11.30am-late) Undoubtedly the most popular option around, Chez Pepe is a lively spot serving up Italian faves like pizza, pasta and rustic Tuscan meats. It won't be a particularly memorable meal, but it's the best place for a bite along Flic en Flac's beachside road. Locals dig it for the reasonable prices and somewhat efficient service.

**Ginger Thai** ( ☎ 403 1000; Hilton, Royal Rd, Wolmar; meals €44, 🕑 7.30-10.30pm Tue-Sun) Transport your taste buds to the 'land of smiles' at this elegant option on the grounds of the lovely Hilton resort in Wolmar. The streamers woven through the slatted ceiling are undeniably Asian in theme, and the signature dishes (prawns in a rich green curry, roasted duck, spiced vegies etc) are refined and authentic.

### SELF-CATERING

Tucked in the basement of Pasadena Village, **Spar** (Royal Rd; 🕑 8am-8pm Mon-Sat, 8am-5pm Sun) is a large supermarket that will satisfy any self-caterer's needs.

If you're not in the mood to pack a picnic, you'll find a few fast-food trucks parked under the weeping *filao* trees along the sand at the northern part of the public beach. They serve fruit, chips, drinks and kebabs (chicken bits, lettuce, mayonnaise, hot sauce and ketchup unceremoniously mixed together and spread across a baguette) all for under Rs 60. You can't see Le Morne from this part of the beach, but it's a scenic spot to enjoy a bite nonetheless.

## Drinking & Entertainment

Although Flic en Flac is undoubtedly booming with development, it hasn't quite reached the grandeur of Grand Baie in the north. There are a handful of nondescript bars in addition to our list of faves following. Travellers are also welcome at most of the top-end hotels for sundowners and dancing (call ahead).

**KenziBar** ( ☎ 453 5259; 🕑 6.30pm-midnight Tue-Sat) On an inland road beside Villa Paul & Virginie, KenziBar is your best bet for nightlife in Flic en Flac. There's tongue-tingling *rhum arrangés,* fire-spurting torches, live music (on Fridays and Saturdays) and a mangy, pat-hungry dog that calls the bar home – welcome to Mauritius!

**Shotz** ( ☎ 453 8644; Royal Rd; 🕑 10.30am-11.30pm) At the Americanised Shooters Sports Pub & Grill, Shotz is about as jet-set as things get beyond the high walls of the upmarket resorts.

**Casino** ( ☎ 453 8022; Royal Rd; 🕑 10am-3am) Spend the evening amid slot machines and roulette tables at the local casino situated in the basement of Pasadena Village.

**90° Bar** ( ☎ 453 9080; Royal Rd; 🕑 11am-midnight) The unapologetic decor (think smoke and mirrors, literally) could not be mistaken for anything but a nightclub. It's popular with the same crowd that hangs out at Shotz.

## Getting There & Around

There is a bus from Port Louis to Flic en Flac and Wolmar every 15 to 20 minutes. Public buses constantly ply the coastal route in Flic en Flac and many tourists use it as a cheap and quick hop-on-hop-off service. A taxi from Port Louis to Flic en Flac will cost you Rs 900. Figure on Rs 2000 for a taxi to the airport, Rs 1400 to Le Morne and Rs 1700 to Belle Mare. A ride to Black River costs Rs 500.

All accommodation and travel agencies in the area can help arrange bicycle and car hire. Count on Rs 250 for a bike. Cars start at Rs 900 for a manual; Rs1200 for an automatic. Local car-hire outfits include the following:

**Easy Drive Rent a Car** ( ☎ 453 8557; easyworld@ intent.mu; Royal Rd) At the Easy World Hotel.

**Fit for Life** ( ☎ 452 2005; www.fflmauritius.com) Reputable bike hire. Located in the township of Bambous, nearby.

**Flic en Flac Tourist Agency** ( ☎ 453 9389; www. fftourist.com; Royal Rd; 🕑 8.30am-5pm Mon-Sat, 8.30am-1pm Sun) Cars and bikes.

## TAMARIN & RIVIÈRE NOIRE (BLACK RIVER)
pop 60,000

The large swath of beach-fringed land between Flic En Flac and Le Morne is known to most Mauritians as Rivière Noire (Black River). One of the island's last coastal areas to witness development, this constellation of townships has grown by leaps and bounds over the last few years as unsightly salt flats morph into stylish housing projects for South African expats, and traditional hunting grounds get reimagined as scenic zoos and cycling paths. Despite the sudden appearance of modern structures, Black River is a great place to base yourself for a more active and authentic experience. Sensational hiking, scenic shorelines, top-notch fishing and interesting historical relics are all within arm's reach.

## Sights
### TAMARIN BEACH

Locals like to wax nostalgic about Tamarin Beach, and in many ways this sandy cove still feels like a throwback to earlier times – especially since the centrally located Tamarin Hotel looks like it hasn't been renovated since *Jaws* was in cinemas.

MAURITIUS

Once upon a time the area was known as Santosha Bay (you'll still find the word 'Santosha' scribbled on a few buildings in faded paint) and offered wave hunters some of the best surfing on the planet. In fact, before the bay earned the name Santosha, locals refused to give the beach a moniker because they didn't want outsiders to discover their cache of surfable seas!

Today the waves and currents have changed and surfing at Le Morne (p112) has really taken off, but Tamarin – unmarred by high-walled resort compounds – remains a popular place for locals to hang out on weekends. On Saturdays there are always informal volleyball and football games in the sand (feel free to join in) and during the evening live jazz tunes waft through the air.

The best time to take advantage of the sea is between 8am and 9am when weather is clear and the kiosks have yet to open their shutters. The walk between Tamarin Beach and southern Wolmar is very scenic and not accessible by car (women are advised not to do it alone).

### MARTELLO TOWER
In the 1830s the British built five 'Martello' towers – copies of the tower at Mortella Point in Corsica (vowel order was apparently not a priority for the British) – to protect their young colony from predators (namely the French who were suspected of supporting a slave rebellion). Although the other towers have fallen into ruin, the one at La Preneuse has been converted into a small **museum** (Map p98; ☎ 583 0178; foemau@intnet. com; admission free; ⊙ 9.30am-5pm Tue-Sat, 9.30am-1.30pm Sun). Captions explain the tower's ingenious design – walls measure 3m in thickness and are crowned by a copper cannon that could apparently destroy a target 2km away.

### LA ROUTE DU SEL
Not quite a *route* like the Route du Thé, the salt flats along the main road in Tamarin are a popular stopping point for camera-happy travellers. The coterie of Creole women manually shifting buckets of salt makes for an excellent photo opp. At the time of research, plans were well underway for a small museum dedicated to the fading industry.

### LA BALISE MARINA
The billboards are everywhere – **La Balise Marina** ( ☎ 483 7272; www.labalisemarina.com) prom-ises to revolutionise the tourism industry in Mauritius by creating the island's first port welcoming luxury yachts. Construction of the marina and its adjoining complex of shops and apartments is barely underway, but once complete, Black River is expected to overflow with some serious tourist traffic.

## Activities
In addition to the following activities, there are ample hiking opportunities at Black River Gorges National Park (p108) further inland and Le Morne Peninsula (p112) to the south.

### DOLPHIN-WATCHING
Tamarin Beach's heyday as a surf hub may have subsided, but now tourists are flocking to the area to check out the friendly pods of bottlenose and spinner dolphins that swim by each morning. Speedboats departing from all over the island circle the western waters offering tourists a chance to jump in and swim with the gentle creatures.

The sudden increase in operators has called the sustainability of local dolphin-watching into question. Choose your tour boat carefully – companies who do not have the dolphins' well-being at heart should be avoided. Trips usually depart at 7am. Figure on around €40 for a two-hour excursion. **JP Henry Charters Ltd** ( ☎ 729 0901; www.blackriver-mauritius.com) offers highly recommended dolphin trips on either a catamaran or speedboat. Check out www. mauritiuscatamarans.com for a short list of tour operators, or visit www.mrconcierge. mu to arrange a private boat that will take you out before the crowds. Note that some dolphin-watching trips include a visit to Île aux Bénitiers – see p111 for details.

### DEEP-SEA FISHING
The estuary at Black River suddenly plunges 700m down to the ocean floor making it one of the island's deep-sea fishing hubs. The peak fishing season is between November and March when you can catch just about anything from blue marlin to hammerheads. Black marlin and barracuda can be caught throughout the year, while the yellowfin season is from March to May and the wahoo season is around September to December.

There are a number of fishermen in the area that offer outings on fully equipped boats. Many of them congregate at **Le Morne Anglers' Club** (Map p98; ☎ 483 5801; www.morneanglers.

com; ⊗ 6.30am-8.30pm), signposted beside the crumbling police station. In addition to fishing outings, it also offers boat charters and catamaran cruises along the coast for a spot of dolphin-watching, snorkelling and barbecue picnics. Outings can also be arranged with **La Pirogue Big Game Fishing** (Map p100; ☎ 483 8054; www.lapiroguebiggame.com) based at La Pirogue hotel in Flic en Flac. **Zazou Fishing** (Map p98; ☎ 729 9222, 788 3804; www.zazoufishing.com; Ave des Rougets, Tamarin) is a reputable operator offering an excellent deal: Rs 13,000 for a half-day at sea (from 7am to 1pm) that can be extended to 4pm for an additional Rs 2000. There's a six-person maximum.

For more information on deep-sea fishing, see p148.

### GOLF

The magnificent **Tamarina Golf, Spa & Beach Club** (Map p98; ☎ 401 3000; www.tamarina.mu; Tamarin Bay) is an 18-hole course designed by Rodney Wright. It sprawls across 206 hectares along an old hunting estate situated between the coastal townships and the looming spine of the inland hills. The property also features two inviting restaurants – La Madrague (p106) and Le Dix-Neuf (p107) – and over a hundred rentable villas.

### HORSEBACK RIDING

Located along the main road at the southern end of Black River towards Le Morne, **Le Ranch** (Map p98; ☎ 483 5478; www.mauritius-island.com/leranch; Ramdanee Lane, La Mivoie; ⊗ 7am-noon & 2-7.30pm Mon-Sat) offers competent riders the chance to do one- to three-hour trots along the sea or in the hills nearby. Beginner rides around the farm are available as well.

## Sleeping

Noticeably devoid of monstrous upmarket resorts, Black River prefers old-school inns, quiet villas and welcoming *chambres d'hôtes* tucked down narrow, tree-lined lanes.

### APARTMENTS & VILLAS

The residential vibe in Black River means that there's a wide selection of private apartments and villas for rent. Visitors who want to gain insight into the life of a Mauritian patrician should consider renting a home in the gated estate of Plantation Marguery up the hill from the stylish Ruisseau Créole shopping complex in Grande Rivière Noire.

**EasyRent** ( ☎ 452 1010; www.easyrent.mu) The managers live in the area and have their finger on the pulse when

it comes to local bargains. La Falaise (near the salt pans in Tamarin; apt €70), a gorgeous two-floor apartment, is one of the best deals on the island.

**Marlin Creek Residence** (Map p98; ☎ 483 7720; www.ilemauricelocation.com; 10 Colonel Dean Ave; d/bungalow incl breakfast €91/155; ⊠ ⦿ 🖘 ) This new addition to Black River's sleeping scene sits along the cerulean bay just a stone's throw from the local jetty. The buzzing fisherfolk next door give the property a wonderfully local feel.

**Royal Mauritius** ( ☎ 940 2169; www.royalmauritius.com; villa €450-600) Manages four luxurious properties in Black River (and two at Grand Gaube in the north). Each private villa comes with a mini army of butlers, a chef, a chauffeured vehicle and a speedboat (yes, a speedboat).

**Tamarina Golf, Spa & Beach Club** (Map p98; ☎ 401 3000; www.tamarina.mu; Tamarin; villa €400-700) Golf enthusiasts should consider leasing a luxurious villa here – rental packages include golfing privileges.

### GUESTHOUSES & CHAMBRES D'HÔTES

**Chez Jacques** (Lagane's Place; Map p98; ☎ 483 6445, 741 3017; www.chezjacques.mu; Tamarin Beach; r €31) Squeeze down a side road on the way to Tamarin Beach and you'll uncover the famous Chez Jacques. Forty years ago Jacques' parents opened their home to visiting surfers and although the number of wave hunters has dwindled, there's still a laid-back vibe here – this is as close as you'll get to a backpacker's hostel on the island. Jacques can help watersports enthusiasts get kitted up; he also hosts regular guitar jam sessions.

**our pick Les Lataniers Bleus** (Map p98; ☎ 483 6541; www.leslataniersbleus.com; La Preneuse; d incl breakfast €115-150; ⊠ ⦿ 🖘 ⓢ ) If you're hoping to partake in the Mauritian *chambre d'hôte* experience, look no further – Les Lataniers Bleus offers local hospitality at its finest. The formidable Josette Marchal-Vexlard is the head of the household, and she dotes upon her guests with effortless charm and an infectious smile. The darling rooms are spread across three houses situated on an ample, beachside orchard. Every comfort has been considered – there's even a powerpoint hidden in a tree trunk so you can update your blog while sitting in the sand! The evening *table d'hôte* on the verandah is a great way to meet other guests and learn about life on the island from the affable hostess.

### HOTELS & RESORTS

**Bay Hotel** (Map p98; ☎ 483 6525; www.the-bay-hotel-mauritius.com; Ave des Cocotiers, La Preneuse; s/d incl breakfast €61/132; ⊠ ⦿ 🖘 ⓢ ) What a find! The Bay comes pretty darn close to boutique chic while still keeping prices relatively low. The thoughtfully decorated rooms (think bright pillows and artsy wall hangings) are arranged on two floors around a white-walled courtyard. Don't miss the seaside restaurant and pool out the back. Half-board rates are available for an additional €20 per person.

**La Mariposa** (Map p98; ☎ 483 5048; www.lamariposa.mu; Allée des Pêcheurs, La Preneuse; apt incl breakfast €90-125; 🄽 🄰 🛜) Set directly along the sea and surrounded by a wild tropical garden, this quiet option features an L-shaped row of double-decker apartments. Rooms are breezy and simple, with cream-coloured walls, scarlet drapes and rounded balconies promising memorable sunset views.

**Tamarin Hotel** (Map p98; ☎ 483 6927; www.blue-season-hotels.com; Tamarin Beach; s/d/tr incl breakfast from €90/126/170; 🄽 🄻 🄰) This welcoming address should be an entry in all film location scouts' Rolodexes, 'cause no one does '70s retro quite like the Tamarin Hotel. Believe it or not the throwback colour scheme was a conscious choice during the renovation in 2002 – you'll either adore it or abhor it so it's best to click through a few pictures on the website before committing. Even if you don't decide to stay here it's well worth swinging by to take in the chilled-out atmosphere. There's a great pool, a sociable stretch of sand out front and a welcoming restaurant that usually hums with live beats. Watersports enthusiasts should ask at the front desk about surfing lessons (Rs 600).

## Eating

The townships of the Black River area have a respectable selection of dining choices. In general, prices are quite high relative to the rest of the island as the target customers are usually expat South Africans and wealthy Franco-Mauritians.

### RESTAURANTS

**Pavillon de Jade** (Map p98; ☎ 483 6151; Royal Rd at Trois Bras Junction, Grande Rivière Noire; dishes Rs 80-300; 🄽 lunch & dinner) You hardly ever see any diners at this no-frills Chinese joint above a faded supermarket, but the proud owner refuses to sell his land to the hungry developers of the Balise Marina project (smart guy!). If the owner caves, chances are high that you'll find this local haunt across the street from its original location.

**Le Cabanon Créole** (Map p98; ☎ 483 5783; Royal Rd, La Preneuse; mains Rs 180; 🄽 11am-9.30pm) Friendly service and spicy spins on Creole home cooking make this family-run place a perennial favourite. There's a limited range of daily dishes, such as *rougaille saucisses* (spicy sausages) and chicken curry; specials, like lobster or whole fresh fish, can be ordered in advance. It's best to reserve in the evenings as there are only a handful of tables. Delivery available.

**La Bonne Chute** (Map p98; ☎ 483 6552; Royal Rd, La Preneuse; mains Rs 250; 🄽 lunch & dinner Mon-Sat) Don't be dissuaded by the petrol-station-adjacent location, La Bonne Chute has built its reputation around its flavourful dishes and attractive garden setting. From venison and beef to steamed fish and crab, the kitchen always seems to get it right. And don't forget to save room for one of the homemade desserts.

**Cosa Nostra** (Map p98; ☎ 483 6169; cnr Anthurium Lane & Royal Rd, Tamarin; pizzas Rs 250-300; 🄽 lunch & dinner Tue-Sun) Two things make this popular pizza joint famous: the whisper-thin crust (you'll swear that you're just eating toppings) and the turtle-speed service (you'll think the servers went back to Italy to fetch your slice).

**Les Sirandanes** (Map p98; ☎ 483 6525; Bay Hotel, Ave des Cocotiers, La Preneuse; mains Rs 250-500; 🄽 lunch & dinner) Slide between the crisp white walls of the Bay Hotel to uncover Les Sirandanes perched directly along the sea under generous thatch awnings. Stare out to the bobbing fishing boats in the lagoon while savouring a delectable assortment of gourmet spins on Mauritian cuisine.

**OUR PICK La Madrague** (The Beach Club; Map p98; ☎ 483 0260; Tamarina Golf, Spa & Beach Club, Tamarin Bay; mains Rs 350-550, Sunday brunch Rs 700-1200; 🄽 noon-10pm) Adorned with loads of stylish wicker and sleek wooden slatting, this feels like a poolside restaurant at a posh resort, yet there's no hotel in sight. Only the locals know about La Madrague – it's hidden at the end of the dirt track that splinters off from the entrance gate to the Tamarina golf grounds. The menu features an assortment of standard international dishes (think club sandwiches and lamb chops), but the real draw is the inviting infinity-edge swimming pool bedecked with shimmering dark marble. While away a sunny day under the shade of a coconut palm and when you're ready for some sand, simply scamper down the stairs to the semiprivate beach below.

The following dining venues are located in the stylish Ruisseau Créole shopping complex in Grande Rivière Noire:

**Pizza De'lic** (Map p98; ☎ 483 7003; pizzas from Rs 210; ☺ 10.30am-2.30pm & 5.30-9.30pm) A scatter of outdoor tables orbits the brightly lit kitchen. Delicious pizzas are constructed atop thin crunchy crust.

**Zucca** (Map p98; ☎ 483 7005; mains Rs 300-500; ☺ 11.30am-2.30pm & 8-10pm) Owned by an Italian mama who saunters around her restaurant with a certain forceful alacrity. High-quality dishes like beef carpaccio, homemade pasta and osso bucco will have you wagging your hands like they do back in the Bootland.

**Niu** (Map p98; ☎ 483 7118; mains Rs 300-500; ☺ noon-11pm) Niu employs a minimalist design scheme befitting the hippest address in London or New York. Fresh sushi and sashimi is the name of the game, though continental treats, like spring rolls and fried rice, further spice up the menu.

### SELF-CATERING

There are two large supermarkets in the area. **London Way** (Map p98; ☎ 696 0088; Royal Rd, Grande Rivière Noire; ☺ 8.30am 7pm Mon-Tue & Thu, to 8pm Fri & Sat, to 12.30pm Sun) and **Kaddy Plus** (Map p98; Tamarin; ☺ 8.30am-7.30pm Mon-Thu, to 8pm Fri & Sat, to 1pm Sun). London Way looks a bit worn out, though locals prefer it to Kaddy Plus as it has a wider selection of items. It is, however, worth swinging by Kaddy Plus for the surplus of goods sold from a small *boulangerie* (bakery) kiosk just before the main entrance (to the left, under the Lavazza sign).

Those in search of street eats will usually find *boulette* (meatball) vendors at Tamarin Beach (across from the eponymous hotel) on Saturday and Sunday between 3pm and 7.30pm. Locals say that these are the best on the island. Quick street-side bites (fried rice and the like) are also available at the back of London Way.

At the other end of the spectrum, self-servers will find a delightful assortment of gourmet imports at **L'Epicerie Gourmande** (Map p98; ☎ 483 8735; Barachois St, Tamarin; ☺ 9.30am-6pm).

## Drinking & Entertainment

Noticeably quieter than the scene in Grand Baie or even Flic en Flac, the communities of Black River prefer house parties to loud nights out at the club. Still, there are a couple places to go out for the evening, and many of the area's restaurants have a great after-hours vibe. Do keep in mind, though, that Flic en Flac is only a 15- to 25-minute drive up the coast (depending on where you're coming from).

If you're looking for a bit of live music, try the Tamarin Hotel (p106). The owner is a jazz fanatic and plays the saxophone with his local band. It's best to call ahead – they only place twice a week and not always on weekends.

**Big Willy's** (Map p98; ☎ 483 7400; Tamarin; ☺ 3pm-2am Tue-Fri, 9am-2am Sat, 11am-2am Sun) Owned by a South African and perennially popular with the expat crowd, Big Willy's is the *it* spot for DJ-ed dance beats and rugby on the tube.

**Bali Copy** (Map p98; ☎ 483 8252; Tutti Frutti, La Preneuse; ☺ 9am-midnight) Set within what looks like an office building, this lively joint is precisely what its name suggests: a Bali copy. There's a chilled-out tropical vibe matched by thematic decor, and the ambient beats rev up on weekends to attract the local surfing crowd.

**Le Dix-Neuf** (Map p98; ☎ 483 0300; Tamarina Golf, Spa & Beach Club, Tamarin Bay; ☺ 7am-7.30pm) Hidden behind the walls of Tamarina's exclusive golfing grounds, this classy lodge-like venue, situated at the clubhouse, is a great place for a sundown snifter. Notice how the pentagonal window behind the dark-wood bar perfectly frames the sharp, rooflike ridges of the nearby hills. Golfers should swing by before tee-off – the breakfasts (Rs 350) are killer.

## Getting There & Around

Buses headed for Tamarin leave Port Louis roughly every hour and Quatre Bornes every 20 minutes. These buses also stop in La Preneuse. A taxi from Port Louis costs Rs 800. Expect to pay Rs 1500 for the airport, Rs 500 for Flic en Flac, Rs 600 for Le Morne and Rs 1500 to reach Belle Mare.

Although Black River is home to a large percentage of Mauritius' wealthiest citizens, the roads in the region are surprisingly ragged and ridden with potholes. This is not the place to test out any unfamiliar vehicles.

## BLACK RIVER GORGES NATIONAL PARK

Mauritius' sole national park is a wild expanse of rolling hills and thick forest covering roughly 2% of the island's surface. Once the island's prime hunting grounds, the area became a protected preserve in 1994 after scientists identified over 300 species of flowering plants, nine endemic species of bird and a population of giant fruit bats that numbered more than 4000. Wild boar, macaque monkeys and curious deer also wander through the vast swaths of old-growth ebony, and sightings are not uncommon.

Hiking and mountain biking are the two best ways to explore the national park and a tourism infrastructure has gradually developed over the years. The main **Black River Gorges Visitors Centre** (Map p98; ☎ 258 0057; ☽ 7am-5pm Mon-Fri, 9am-5pm Sat & Sun) is at the park's western entrance, about 7.5km southeast of Black River's Trois Bras Junction. The alternative is the **Pétrin Information Centre** (Map p98; ☎ 507 0128; ☽ 7am-3.15pm Mon-Sat) at the eastern entrance to the park. Staff at both can offer advice on the different trails, brief you about the area's wildlife through captioned displays, and hand out fairly sketchy maps.

## Hiking the Black River Gorges

There are numerous trails that crisscross Black River Gorges National Park like unravelling shoestrings. While all of the trailheads are clearly marked along one of the two roads running through the park, many of the paths can quickly get obscured in the brush, leaving hikers confused. It's well worth stopping at one of the visitors centres to grab a crude map and check in about the current state of the trails. We recommend hiring a guide if you're serious about exploring the park and uncovering the majestic viewpoints. See p149 for guide suggestions. You can also contact the visitors centres ahead of time to enquire about hiring a ranger.

If you decide to attempt a trip under your own steam, you'll need a private vehicle as getting to the trailheads can be near impossible with public transport. The best option is to get a taxi to drop you off at a trailhead and then pick up a bus at the lower end of the park; the coast road is well covered by buses travelling between the main towns.

We suggest checking www.fitsy.com before you head out into the wild. This handy website features detailed trail information using GPS and satellite coordinates.

Note that there is nowhere to buy food or drinks in the park. Make sure you bring plenty of water and energy-boosting snacks. You'll also need insect repellent, wet-weather gear and shoes with good grip – no matter how hot and sunny the coast may be it is usually wet and humid within the park. Consider binoculars for wildlife-watching.

The best time to visit the park is during the flowering season between September and January. Look for the rare *tambalacoque* (dodo tree), the black ebony trees and the wild guavas. Bird-watchers should keep an eye out for the Mauritius kestrel, pink pigeon, echo parakeet and Mauritius cuckoo-shrike.

## Tamarin Falls

Positioned on the outskirts of the Black River Gorges roughly 8km southwest of Curepipe in central Mauritius, this set of seven scenic cascades (some say 11) is a wonderful reward for those willing to take on a challenging hike.

Attempts to access the falls should not be done without a guide. Local guides (charging Rs 500 to 1000) usually wait around the bus station at Henrietta, a township near Curepipe, although we prefer linking up with Yanature (see p112).

For a truly unique and unforgettable experience, adventurers can abseil from chute to chute on a half- or full-day canyoning excursion with **Vertical World** ( ☎ 697 5430; www.verticalworldltd.com) or **Otélair** ( ☎ 696 6750; www.otelair.com). Both operators start their trips from Henrietta as well.

## CHAMAREL

**pop 700**

Known throughout the island for its hushed bucolic vibe and cool breezes, Chamarel is a hidden hamlet tucked into the western hills. But if you're expecting the heaven-reaching grandeur of the mountains on Réunion, then you'll be sorely disappointed. Chamarel's attractions are much more humble – most tourists come through to visit the famous coloured earths, others pass by during lunchtime to sample the gamut of *tables d'hôtes* repasts.

## Sights & Activities

### COLOURED EARTHS & CHAMAREL WATERFALL

The **Chamarel Coloured Earths** (Map p98; ☎ 483 8298; adult/child Rs 100/50; ☽ 7am-5.30pm), 4km southwest of Chamarel, has, for some unknown reason, become one of the sights on the island's usual tourist circuit, although most travellers find it quite underwhelming after a long journey. If you temper your expectations and approach an excursion here as a quirky side trip, then there's a greater chance of enjoying the variations of colourful sand – a result of the uneven cooling of molten rock. Tortoises roam the preserve providing a wonderful distraction if you have the tykes in tow.

About halfway (1.5km) between the entrance gate and the colourful sands is a scenic viewpoint over the **Chamarel waterfall**, which plunges more than 95m in a single drop. You can abseil with **Vertical World** ( ☎ 697 5430; www.verticalworldltd.com) from the top of the falls all the way into the pool at its base.

The entire property was once the private estate of Charles de Chazal de Chamarel, who entertained Matthew Flinders during Flinders' captivity in Mauritius during the Napoleonic Wars (p125).

### RHUMERIE DE CHAMAREL

Set among the vast hillside plantations of Chamarel, the **Rhumerie de Chamarel** (Map p98; ☎ 483 7980; www.rhumeriedechamarel.com; Royal Rd; adult/child incl tasting Rs 350/175; ⏰ 9.30am-5.30pm Mon-Sat) is a working distillery that doubles as a museum showcasing the rum-making process. The pet project of the Beachcomber hotel tycoon, the factory opened in 2008 and uses a special 'ecofriendly' production method ensuring that all materials are recycled. The rum is quite tasty and makes for a pleasant coda to a guided tour of the plant. It's best to time your visit with a lunchtime break at the on-site gourmet restaurant, L'Alchimiste (p110).

### MOUNTAIN BIKING

Chamarel and the Black River Gorges are the island's best spots to test your wits (and leg muscles) during a day of mountain biking. Full- and half-day adventures can be arranged with professional 'cycle-path' Patrick Haberland at his outfit, **Yemaya** ( ☎ 752 0046, 283

8187; www.yemayaadventures.com). Trips depart from La Vieille Cheminée.

### HORSEBACK RIDING

**La Vieille Cheminée** (Map p98; ☎ 483 5249; www.la vieillecheminee.com), a farm and rustic lodge, offers guided trots on horseback through the hilly countryside and along its shady ravines. Tumble down the far side of Chamarel, toward Souillac, and you'll find a second riding school at the Union Ducray Sugar Estate (see p122 for details), which cares for ageing equines rescued from the rigours of the island's rampant horseracing industry.

### PARC AVENTURE CHAMAREL

Tucked away in the forest, this **adventure park** (Map p98; ☎ 234 5385; adult/child Rs 500/200; ⏰ session 9.15am, 11.15am, 1.15pm) offers tourists a few fun thrills like zip-lines, mini suspension bridges and a ropes course. Reservations are required.

## Sleeping

The following options offer welcome respite from the gaggle of beachside accommodation options that fill the rest of this chapter.

**Le Coteau Fleurie** (Map p98; ☎ 733 3963; Royal Rd, Chamarel; d incl breakfast €80; 🅿 ) Plucked from the sky-scraping ridges of Réunion, this lovely *chambre d'hôte* feels miles away from anything else in Mauritius. A quaint Creole-style option, it embraces its traditional roots and offers travellers a welcome retreat among fruit trees and thick jungle trunks.

---

### GRAND BASSIN

According to legend, Shiva and his wife Parvati were circling the earth on a contraption made from flowers when they were dazzled by an island set in an emerald sea. Shiva, who was carrying the Ganges River on his head to protect the world from floods, decided to land. As he did so a few drops of water dripped from his head and landed in a crater to form a lake. The Ganges expressed unhappiness about its water being left on an uninhabited island, but Shiva replied that dwellers from the banks of the Ganges would one day settle there and perform an annual pilgrimage, during which water from the lake would be presented as an offering.

The dazzling island is, of course, Mauritius; the legendary craterlake is known as Grand Bassin (Ganga Talao). It is a renowned pilgrimage site, to which up to 500,000 of the island's Hindu community come each year to pay homage to Shiva during the Maha Shivaratri celebrations. This vast festival takes place over three days in February or March (depending on the lunar cycle) and is the largest Hindu celebration outside India.

The most devoted pilgrims walk from their village to the sacred lake carrying a *kanvar*, a light wooden frame or arch decorated with paper flowers. This is no easy feat – February is Mauritius' hottest month and it almost always rains during the festivities. Once the pilgrims arrive they perform a puja, burning incense and camphor at the lake shore and offering food and flowers.

**MAURITIUS**

**Chalets en Champagne** (Map p98; ☎ 483 6610; www.acoeurbois.com; 110 Route Champagne, Chamarel; d incl half board €115-190; ❀) These beautiful log cabins are tucked into the mountainside amid gnarled tropical trees. The decor stays true to the wooded theme (think thatch roofs and stone-lined bath tubs) while gently incorporating modern touches (air-con, DVD players etc). Hikers will appreciate the surrounding network of marked trails that weave across the tree-lined terrain like tangled shoestrings.

**Lakaz Chamarel** (Map p98; ☎ 483 5240; www.lakaz chamarel.com; Piton Canot; s/d incl half board from €132/215; ❀ ❀) This 'exclusive lodge' in the countryside around Chamarel is a wonderfully conceived collection of rustic (yet oh-so elegant) cabins offering a blissful getaway amid gorgeous forests, gardens and streams. Rooms are tastefully decorated with chic safari-style trimmings. Not to be missed is the serene spa and the charming swimming pool adorned with stone goddess statues.

## Eating

Over the last few years, Chamarel has gained an island-wide reputation for its clutch of charming *tables d'hôtes* sprinkled around the hilltops. Lately, unscrupulous taxi drivers are capitalising on the area's newfound notoriety among foodies by overcharging tourists and demanding hefty commissions from the local restaurants. We recommend navigating the area with a private vehicle and choosing a dining option at your leisure.

**Barbizon** (Map p98; ☎ 483 5078; Ste-Anne Rd; mains Rs 200-600; ❀ lunch) It may not look like much from the outside but Barbizon has made quite the name for itself in the area, namely due to the lively and smiley owners. Marie-Ange helms the pots and pans whipping up traditional Mauritian flavours from her family's cookbook while Rico L'Intelligent (what a name!) entertains at the tables. Delivery available.

**Le Chamarel Restaurant** (Map p98; ☎ 483 6421; La Crête; mains Rs 350-600; ❀ lunch) Perched on the hillside 1km west of Chamarel along the descending road to Black River, this local mainstay is best known for its cantilevered verandah delivering a postcard-perfect panorama of the west coast. The food is also worth a mention – the finely tuned menu features an assortment of surf and turf mains. Penny-pinchers should not be dissuaded by the high prices – visitors are still welcome to take in the views over beverages (Rs 80 to 120).

**Domaine du Cachet** (Map p98; ☎ 483 5259; www. visitdomaineducachet.com; La Montagne; mains Rs 450; ❀ 11am-4.30pm) Owned by the same people who run the ultrapopular Sirokan (p111) in La Gaulette, this newer contribution to Chamarel's intriguing dining scene oozes *table d'hôte* charm from behind the honey-tinged facade. The restaurant is situated along the Baie du Cap–Chamarel Rd beyond the post office but before the Coloured Earth.

**Varangue sur Morne** (Map p98; ☎ 483 6610; Plaine Champagne Rd; mains from Rs 700; ❀ 11am-4.30pm) This former hunting lodge is an institution, and it's not too hard to see why. Its stunning location offers great views over the national park towards the ocean, and the superb menu reads like a veritable ode to your taste buds: tender braised wild boar, prawns flambéed in Île de France Rum and a laundry list of clever cocktails. Reservations are advised.

**L'Alchimiste** (Map p98; ☎ 483 7980; Rhumerie de Chamarel, Royal Rd; menu €35; ❀ noon-3pm Mon-Sat) The Rhumerie de Chamarel's chic in-house restaurant boasts an impressive prix-fixe menu that promises to satisfy. The chef's philosophy is definitely gourmet; flavourful Mauritian favourites are whipped into eye-pleasing concoctions.

Locals joke that everyone and their sister has a *table d'hôte* in the area, so you'll really be spoilt for choice. The following options are also worth a look-see, but feel free to branch out and uncover your own hidden table. Figure on Rs 400 to 600 for a sizeable meal.

**Chez Pierre Paul** ( ☎ 483 5079; Royal Rd; ❀ lunch) No delusions of grandeur here, just simple Creole cuisine.

**Le Domaine de Saint-Denis** ( ☎ 728 5562; Chamarel; ❀ lunch) Features recipes from the kitchen of Jacqueline Dalais, the unofficial First Lady of Mauritian cuisine.

**Les Palmiers** ( ☎ 483 8364; Royal Rd; ❀ lunch) A step up from the kitchen table serving traditional eats like curries and *faratas* (pan-fried flat breads).

## Getting There & Around

Although there's bus service from Quatre Bornes to Chamarel, we highly recommend using private transport. Do not visit Chamarel by taxi – drivers are given exorbitant commissions for bringing tourists to the various attractions and *tables d'hôtes*. You can rent cars and bicycles from Ropsen (p111) in La Gaulette.

## LA GAULETTE

**pop 2000**

South of Black River, the mountains draw ever closer to the coast. You'll find pinewoods and mangroves mingling with the lapping waves, but little in the way of habitation besides the pockets of impoverished shanty towns along the road. Then, a small township emerges under the shade of the nearby hills – it's a quiet place where the lazy fisherfolk lifestyle effortlessly mixes with the carefree surfer vibe. Welcome to La Gaulette.

## Sights & Activities

The area's most notable attraction is the lovely **Île aux Bénitiers**, which floats just above sea level in the technicolour reef offshore. The islet is considerably larger than many of the other outcrops in the lagoon (keep an eye out for the interesting rocky projection that looks like the top half of an hourglass) and sports a beautiful picnic-worthy beach, a small coconut farm and a colony of migratory birds. The island's keeper is quite the local character – he travels around with an ever-growing pack of chipper dogs. Most of the fishermen docked at La Gaulette offer small excursions to the island – try **Kissen** ( ☎ 758 9849, 451 5156). The village's top tour operator, **Ropsen** ( ☎ 451 5763, 255 5546; www.ropsen. net), also organises catamaran excursions, as well as dolphin-watching tours, island tours, car rentals and accommodation. The number of boat operators that visit the island continues to grow each year and most of the products are identical: crowded catamarans and a picnic lunch on the sand. Check out www.mauritiusattractions.com to make heads or tails of the boat choices – try the Harris Wilson catamaran for a more luxurious (and less crowded) island experience. Note that many cruise operators combine a trip to Île aux Bénitiers with dolphin-watching (see p104).

## Sleeping

Gaining popularity among the kitesurfing crowd, La Gaulette represents an excellent price-value ratio. There are currently two notable options in the village and we suspect that this number will quickly grow over the next couple of years.

**ourpick** **Ropsen** (Map p98; ☎ 451 5763; www.ropsen. net; Royal Rd; apt from €30; ✸ ▢ ☞ ) From modern studios to large multibedroom apartments, friendly Ropsen proffers such a vast array of high-quality options that you'll start to think every building in La Gaulette is a rentable villa! Insist on a sea view and you'll be treated to some of the most spectacular vistas on the island. Almost all of Ropsen's properties have wi-fi, and guests without a laptop can check their email at the computer terminal in Ropsen's office.

**ourpick** **Maison Papaye** (Map p98; ☎ 752 0918; www.maisonpapaye.com; r €30-60; ✸ ▢ ☞ ▥ ) Set among imposing homes on a residential street away from the sea, this stately *chambre d'hôte* is a real find. Although the whitewashed facade, gabled roofs and periwinkle shutters may hint at a colonial past, the building is only a few years old. The owners designed their retirement getaway to invoke the island's plantation past and they keep tradition alive every evening with their Creole-inspired *table d'hôte* dinners (€12) served on the shaded verandah.

## Eating

The small superettes (a small self-service grocery store) that line the main street through town cater for the legions of self-caterers; there are only a few restaurants in the area. For more options consider driving up to Chamarel or Black River.

**La Kaz Do** (Map p98; ☎ 451 6128; Royal Rd; mains Rs 110-990; ⏲ lunch & dinner) Buzzing under a sun-soaked tin roof, little La Kaz Do welcomes diners on the *case*-like verandah. Well-priced platters include Chinese staples like steamy *mine frites* (fried noodles) or scrumptious curries (the eggplant is the owner's favourite). Ask about the 'magic bowl' if you're feeling a bit adventurous.

**Pointe Pecheur** (Map p98; ☎ 451 5910; Coastal Rd, La Gaulette; mains from Rs 200; ⏲ lunch & dinner) There's not much to distinguish this place from the scatter of superettes besides its well-deserved reputation. This busy little haunt churns out a wide variety of cuisine from Chinese to Mauritian, but most people come for the delicious pizza.

**Sirokan** (Map p98; ☎ 451 5115; Royal Rd; mains Rs 250-400; ⏲ lunch & dinner) Bedecked with a pastoral latticework of flowering twigs and bamboo branches, Sirokan (a bastardisation of '*sirop de cane*' or '*sugar cane*') is unquestionably La Gaulette's top dining spot despite its unassuming position along the main road at the far north end of town. You'll have your choice of perfectly prepared steak or seafood. Try either one, or both – you really can't go wrong. The owners of Sirokan also run Domaine du Cachet (p110) in Chamarel.

## Getting There & Around

Buses (every 20 minutes) between Quatre Bornes and Baie du Cap stop in La Gaulette. There are no direct buses from Port Louis. Instead you have to go via Quatre Bornes, or take the bus from Port Louis to Black River and change.

A taxi between Port Louis and La Gaulette will cost around Rs 1000; it's Rs 1600 to the airport. Do not take a taxi to Chamarel (see p110) – rent a vehicle instead.

## LE MORNE PENINSULA

Visible from much of southwestern Mauritius, the iconic Le Morne Brabant (556m) is a stunning rock crag from which this beautiful peninsula takes its name. Shaped like a hammerhead shark, the peninsula itself has some of the island's best beaches, now home to a number of upmarket hotels. Almost totally uninhabited by locals, the peninsula nevertheless has a particular resonance in Mauritian culture – according to legend, a group of escaped slaves fled to the peninsula in the early 19th century, hiding out on top of the mountain to remain free. The story goes that the slaves, ignorant of the fact that slavery had been abolished just before their escape, panicked when they saw a troop of soldiers making their way up the cliffs. Believing they were to be recaptured, the slaves flung themselves from the cliff tops to their deaths in huge numbers. And thus the crag earned its name – Le Morne means Mournful One. Although there are no historical records to substantiate the story, it's an important tale for Mauritians.

## Sights & Activities

Although the area's upmarket hotels have gobbled up most of peninsula's sand-front property, the beaches themselves are still open to the public. Travellers not staying in one of the local resorts can find several access points along the public roads.

### HIKING

Added to the Unesco World Heritage list in 2008, Le Morne is the star of many postcards as it slopes through the sky then plunges back down into the blue. Few tourists, however, realise that the view from the top is even more spectacular. As you ascend the crag you'll pass through an indigenous forest, which is the only place on the island where you'll find

Mauritius' national flower, the *boucle d'oreille* ('earring'). And when you reach 500m, you'll be treated to unobstructed vistas of the colourful reefs to the west and south. The trail increases in difficulty the higher up you go – those with limited mobility can still take in the views from a midway point (around 260m).

The best way to explore the heaping basalt mound is on a guided hike with **Yanature** ( ☎ 785 6177; www.yanature.com; half-/full day per person €40/50), a one-man operation headed up by friendly Yan. A nature enthusiast and eighth-generation Mauritian, Yan grew up at the base of Le Morne and wandered the snaking trails well into his teenage years; his father managed one of the five-star resorts nearby. Yan has exclusive permission from the Gambier family – the landowners of Le Morne – to bring tourists through. After Le Morne, consider tagging along on one of Yan's other hiking excursions through Black River Gorges National Park, or perhaps to Tamarin Falls and the Corps de Garde. Discounts are offered to those who participate in multiple outings.

### WINDSURFING & KITESURFING

The area is home to the ultimate surfing spot in all of Mauritius: **One Eye**, so named because surfers will see a small hole (or 'eye') appear in Le Morne's rockface when they are at the exact spot in the sea to catch the perfect wave. Beginners should start on the western side of the peninsula in the 'Kite Lagoon'; the southern winds are much more severe and unpredictable. Kiteboarders of every ilk (from newbies to pros) can sign up for a class with the recommended professionals at **Son of Kite** ( ☎ 972 9019; www.sonofkite.com). **Yoaneye Kite Centre** (Map p98; ☎ 737 8296; www.yoaneye.com; 114 Villa Mona, Le Petit Morne), an IKO-affiliated centre, offers courses as well. The worldwide surfing organisation **Club Mistral** (Map p98; ☎ 909 6010; www.club-mistral.com) operates intensive kitesurfing and windsurfing courses from their school at the Indian Resort. Figure on around €75 for a one-hour private course.

## Sleeping & Eating

Largely the domain of five-star properties (rumours are sprouting that a 'six-star' resort is in the works), the fan-shaped swath of sand below the looming Le Morne Brabant is a wonderful place to spend your days on Mauritius if you're looking for a lazy beach holiday. Despite the hefty price tags (from

€150 to €300) attached to most resorts, the area's **villa rentals** ( ☎ 499 2233; www.mrconcierge. mu) are surprisingly well priced due to their far-flung location. Renters will need to lease a private vehicle to get around.

You can't go wrong with any of Le Morne's resort options – they are all upmarket.

**Indian Resort** (Map p98; ☎ 261 8000; www.apavou -hotels.com; d incl half board €150; 🛠 🖳 🛜 🏋 ) Besides the remote stretch of gorgeous beach, Indian's strong suit is the wide range of activities, including kitesurfing.

**Paradis** (Map p98; ☎ 401 5050; www.paradis-hotel. com; d incl half board from €434-1050; 🛠 🖳 🛜 🏋 ) Stunning sea views, luxurious accommodation and endless activities. What more could you ask for? Not to be missed is the fresh seafood at Blue Marlin, one of the in-house restaurants. One of Beachcomber's best.

**Dinarobin** (Map p98; ☎ 401 4900; www.dinarobin -hotel.com; d incl half board from €534-1288; 🛠 🖳 🛜 🏋 ) Another ravishing Beachcomber beauty, with a sprawling campus of 172 suites. Named for the first moniker given to the island by Arab merchants in the 10th century. Rated 'five-star plus' – and it lives up to the expectations.

**Les Pavillons** (Map p98; ☎ 401 4000; www.naiade. com; d incl half board €750; 🛠 🖳 🛜 🏋 ) Much more intimate than many of the other luxury frontrunners on the island. Rooms are in attractive plantation-style pavilions. Managed by Naiade.

## Getting There & Away

Buses en route between Quatre Bornes and Baie du Cap stop on the main road by the junction for Le Morne. These buses run roughly every hour. A taxi from Port Louis to the Le Morne hotels costs Rs 1500; figure on Rs 1800 to the airport, Rs 1400 to Flic en Flac and Rs 2200 to Belle Mare.

# THE SOUTH & SOUTHEAST

With brilliant flashes of India, Ireland and the Caribbean, the wild unfolding south is an undeniable favourite for many. Long considered too harsh to develop due to its steep, wind-battered cliffs, the south coast has managed to stave off the encroaching hands of developers until quite recently. A few luxury resorts have popped up over the last few years, but the area remains mostly rugged, with a plantation estate or two hidden among the towering cane.

The jagged southern cliffs taper off at the shimmering reefs in Blue Bay, and just beyond you'll uncover the gorgeous beach of Pointe d'Esny with its cluster of homey *chambres d'hôtes*. The gritty gridiron of Mahébourg anchors the southeast, providing an interesting perspective on local life that starkly contrasts the unfurling streamers of sand stretching beyond the sleepy commercial centre. Then, the coastal road cuts north, passing endless forests of green – the stomping ground of the island's first settlers some 400 years ago.

## Getting There & Around

Mahébourg is the main transport hub in this region, with buses departing from here for destinations along both the east and south coasts. The Mahébourg–Blue Bay area is also the best place to arrange car and bike hire.

Useful bus services include a route from Souillac to Curepipe and Port Louis, and from Baie du Cap up the west coast to Quatre Bornes.

## MAHÉBOURG
**pop 17,000**

Founded in 1805, Mahébourg (my-boor) was named after the famous French governor Mahé de Labourdonnais. The town was once a busy port, but these days it's something of a backwater, with a small fleet of fishermen and a grid of dilapidated buildings.

There is, however, something relentlessly charming about this bite-size burg, and its Napoleonic bravado seems to have fooled most Mauritians into believing that it's the island's 'second city' (it's not). Big plans are in fact underway for a mammoth Caudan-like waterfront complex, but for now it's all about simple pleasures: an interesting naval museum, a buzzing market, spicy street food, pinch-a-penny lodging, and beautiful beaches to the north and south.

### Orientation

There's a decidedly colonial air to Mahébourg's grid of tree-lined streets, which spread north and east from the butter-coloured Catholic church. The main commercial area is found to the northeast, focused on the market and nearby bus station. Hotels and guesthouses are scattered among the quiet residential streets lying between Royal Rd and the seafront.

MAURITIUS

# THE SOUTH & SOUTHEAST

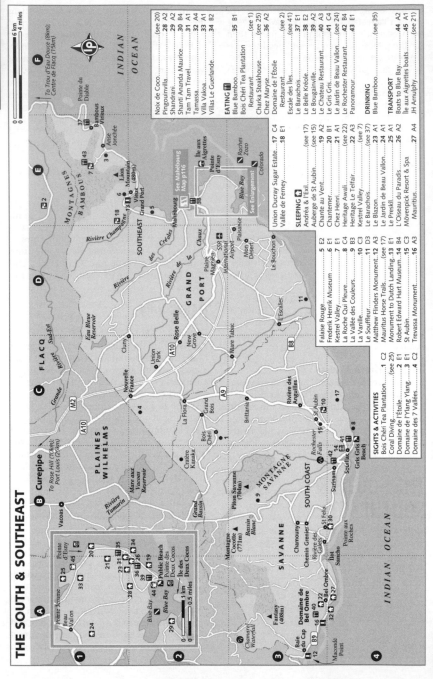

## Information

**Cybersurf** ( ☎ 631 4247; Rue de Labourdonnais; ⏰ 9am-8.30pm Mon-Sat, 9am-noon Sun; per 30 mins Rs 30)

**HSBC** ( ☎ 631 9633; Royal Rd)

**Mauritius Commercial Bank** (MCB; ☎ 631 2879; Rue des Délices)

**Post office** (Royal Rd; ⏰ 8.15am-4pm Mon-Fri, 8.15am-11.45pm Sat)

**Starnet Café** ( ☎ 631 3454; London Way Commercial Centre; ⏰ 10am-7pm Mon-Tue & Thu-Sat, 9.30am-1.30pm Wed & Sun; per 30 mins Rs 30)

## Sights

You can easily cover Mahébourg's smattering of sights in a day, leaving plenty of time to wander the back streets and take a stroll along the seafront. Everything can be tackled on foot, though you might want to hire a bike to get out to the biscuit factory.

### MONDAY MARKET

Don't miss the 'foire de Mahébourg' held every Monday in central Mahébourg near the waterfront. The initial focus was silks and other textiles, but these days you'll find a roaring produce section, rows of tacky bric-a-brac and steaming food stalls. It's the perfect place to try some of the local snacks – *gâteaux piments*, *dhal puris*, *samousa* and chilli bites – usually dispensed from boxes on the backs of motorcycles. It doesn't take long to navigate the snaking rows of vendors, but it's well worth visiting if you found the market in Port Louis far too touristy.

### NATIONAL HISTORY MUSEUM

The colonial mansion housing this **museum** ( ☎ 631 9329; Royal Rd; admission free; ⏰ 9am-4pm Wed-Mon), just beyond central Mahébourg, used to belong to the Robillard family and played an important part in the island's history. It was here in 1810 that the injured commanders of the French and English fleets were taken for treatment after the Battle of Vieux Grand Port (the only naval battle in which the French got the upper hand over their British foes). The story of the victory is retold in the museum, along with salvaged items – cannons, grapeshot and the all-important wine bottles – from the British frigate *Magicienne*, which sank in the battle.

The museum contains some fascinating artefacts, including early maps of the island and renderings of Mauritius' original fauna including, of course, the dodo. One real curio is a picture of Dutch gentlemen riding in pairs on the back of a giant tortoise, who also went the way of the dodo.

The bell and a cache of Spanish coins from the wreck of the *St Géran* are also on display. The ship's demise in 1744, off the northeast coast of Mauritius, inspired the famous love story *Paul et Virginie* by Bernardin de St-Pierre (p95).

New additions to the museum include a retrofitted train carriage out back and a replica of Napoleon's boat used in the infamous battle won against the English (a re-creation of the battle itself is in the works).

### NOTRE DAME DES ANGES

The butter-coloured tower of Notre Dame des Anges church provides a focal point in Mahébourg. The original church was built in 1849, but it has been restored several times over the years, most recently in 1938. Take a quick peek inside at the baronial roof timbers. Local people visit throughout the day to make offerings to Père Laval (p68), whose statue stands to your right immediately inside the door. It's worth a visit just for the priceless 'beware of children' sign outside.

### RAULT BISCUIT FACTORY

In 1870 the Rault family started producing manioc biscuits at their little **biscuit factory** ( ☎ 631 9559; admission Rs 150; ⏰ 9am-3pm Mon-Fri) on the northern outskirts of Mahébourg. It has changed hardly a jot since. The crispy, square cookies are made almost entirely by hand using a secret recipe passed down from generation to generation and baked on hotplates over stoves fuelled with dried sugarcane leaves. The short guided tour ends with a chance to sample the end result – with a nice cup of tea, of course. The factory is on the far side of the Cavendish Bridge; when you cross the bridge take a left and follow the signs.

## Activities

The most popular activity in the area is an excursion by boat to the offshore islands nearby (Île aux Aigrettes, Île de la Passe, Île aux Vacoas and Île au Phare), or the uber-popular Île aux Cerfs further on. Most of the trips involve snorkelling and include a lunch. Scores of boatswains park along the shores of Mahébourg and Blue Bay (p119) awaiting customers and offering relatively similar

MAURITIUS

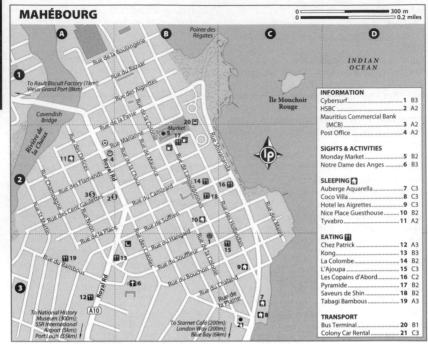

**MAHÉBOURG**

0 | 300 m
0 | 0.2 miles

experiences. Our operator of choice is **Jean-Claude Farla** ( ☎ 631 7090, 423 1322), a local fisherman and six-time national swimming champion who went on to compete in the Indian Ocean games. Not only is he somewhat of a local legend, he is the only person to offer sailing outings on a traditional 22ft pirogue (others have souped-up boats with motors). Figure on €20 for a half-day trip in the pirogue gliding through the blue and stopping periodically to snorkel and free dive. It's €50 for a full-day excursion to Île aux Cerfs with a stop at Île de Flamant and a BBQ lunch on Île aux Mangénie. It's best to call at least two days ahead to ensure that he's available (there's a six person minimum).

During the winter months when the winds are strong in the southeast, you can kitesurf in the bay with **Son of Kite** ( ☎ 972 9019; www.sonofkite.com). A one-hour private lesson costs €75.

## Sleeping

You won't come across any grand hotels in quaint Mahébourg, instead you'll find a reasonable proliferation of simple guesthouses. We recommend staying in Pointe d'Esny further down the coast.

**Hotel les Aigrettes** ( ☎ 631 9094; saidadhoomun@hotmail.com; cnr Rue du Chaland & Rue des Hollandais; s/d small Rs 800/1000, large incl breakfast Rs 1200/1600; ✗ 🖳 ) Seemingly always under construction, Hotel les Aigrettes feels a bit like a Jenga tower with its stack of bedrooms and protruding balconies winding several storeys high. The rooms are clean (some even have sea views), the owner has a big smile and plans are underway to create a restaurant on the lobby level.

**Tyvabro** ( ☎ 631 9674; www.tyvabro.com; Rue Marianne; d incl breakfast €25; ✗ 🛜 ) A newer addition to Mahébourg's sleeping scene, this family-run operation earns high marks for friendly and eager service. Little perks like DVD players, a dartboard and a welcoming roof deck more than make up for the past-their-prime furnishings in the rooms.

**Auberge Aquarella** ( ☎ 631 2767; www.aquarellamu.com; 6 Rue Shivananda; s/d incl breakfast from €50/75; ✗ 🖳 🖳 ) This small hotel is spread across three sparkling white buildings surrounding an inviting infinity pool that virtually spills into the sea. The owners, Gino and Véro, have a real knack for making travellers feel at home – we wouldn't stay anywhere else. The rooms are sparsely decorated so it's best to nab a spot with unobstructed sea views or go for the hobbit bungalow out the back (you'll see).

If everything else is full:

**Nice Place Guesthouse** ( ☎ 631 9419; Rue de Labourdonnais; s/d from Rs 800/1000; ❄ ) As the name suggests: nice rooms – if a bit faded – tended by a lovely Indian couple.

**Coco Villa** ( ☎ 631 2346; www.mahecocovilla.net; Rue Shivananda; s/d from Rs 1200/1500; ❄ ) Basic but clean rooms, some with sea views. Next door to Auberge Aquarella.

## Eating & Drinking

Like a microscopic Port Louis, Mahébourg has dozens of back alleys riddled with hidden eats known only to locals. If you're planning to swing by for a visit, make sure you come on a Monday when the local **market** (p115) is in full swing – you'll be treated to the colourful clanging of street stalls as vendors hawk savoury snacks to lines of lip-licking shoppers. We've included a few of our favourite street vendors below, but you can hunt down your own – Mahébourg's the perfect place to get lost and stumble upon your own tucked-away treasures.

The face of Mahébourg's dining and drinking scene is about to change drastically as developers have their eye on the town's port. Over the next few years a large waterfront complex will be developed to rival the Caudan in Port Louis.

An eclectic assortment of quality dining options also awaits the palate in Pointe d'Esny (p121), just south of Mahébourg.

**Tabagi Bambous** ( ☎ 796 0070; Rue du Bambous; rotis Rs 9; ❄ 7.30am-9.30pm) Dark, dimly lit and usually dingy, *tabagis* (convenience stores) line the streets of every town and township in Mauritius – they're an essential part of the local lifestyle. If you have yet to visit one, the unusually popular Bambous is the perfect place to lose your *tabagi* virginity. Customers come to visit Amrita, the proprietor, who is constantly dishing out her signature rotis while Bollywood heroines clink their bejewelled costumes on the TV screen. Amrita herself is quite the anomaly – it's very rare for a woman to run her own business in the less-developed parts of the country.

**Shyam** ( ☎ 764 2960; rotis & dhal puris Rs 9; ❄ lunch) For the best *dhal puri* in town, look no further than Shyam (you can call him 'Sam'). He scoots around town scooping out flavourful snacks from an empty aquarium tank on the back of his motorbike. On Monday you'll find him at the market, and he always makes an appearance at the public schools when the students are set free from class in the afternoon. If you're desperate for *dhal puri*, just give him a ring and he'll come find you.

**Pyramide** ( ☎ 631 9731; Rue de Labourdonnais; kebabs Rs 40; ❄ 10am-4.30pm Mon-Sat) This hero of the street-food scene is located beside the Caltex petrol station at the market grounds. Delicious *briani* (a rice dish cooked in a steel pot with various eastern spices and meat or fish) and 'kebabs' (salad, meat and sauce on a toasted baguette) seem to emerge from the kitchen in factory proportions as fishermen and hawkers queue for a midday nibble.

**L'Ajoupa** ( ☎ 290 1268; Rue du Souffleur; snacks & mains Rs 40-300; ❄ 10.30am-3.30pm & 6.30-9.30pm Thu-Tue) L'Ajoupa is worth an honourable mention for its homey tree-lined garden hidden behind a scratched picket fence – the perfect place to catch up with friends for a drink and some *poisson frit* (fried fish).

**Saveurs de Shin** ( ☎ 631 3668, 751 5932; Rue de Suffren; mains Rs 80-350; ❄ 10am-3pm & 6-10pm Wed-Mon) Locals are very excited about this recent addition to Mahébourg's dining line-up, namely due to the low prices and sizeable portions. Go for the chef's faves, like the *canard laqué* (duck), *ke fan* (roasted chicken with rice) or *lap mee fan* (smorgasbord of duck, chicken and prawns).

**La Colombe** ( ☎ 631 8594; Rue des Hollandais; mains Rs 200-390; ❄ lunch & dinner) Disco lights, kitsch decor and smiling staff await you at this lively venue located on a side street set back from the promenade. House specials include venison, wild boar and a smattering of seafood. Things liven up a bit on Saturday, which is occasionally *séga* night.

**Chez Patrick** ( ☎ 631 9298; Royal Rd; mains Rs 200-500; ❄ lunch & dinner) Patrick's is hugely popular with locals and tourists for its unpretentious atmosphere and authentic Creole cooking. The Phoenix beer banner out the front reads 'so delicious, so Mauritius' and we think the motto holds true for the restaurant, too.

**Les Copains d'Abord** ( ☎ 631 9728; Rue Shivananda; mains Rs 300-500; ❄ 9am-11pm) Hands down the most popular dining option in town (and the only one that has any real sense of nightlife), Les Copains d'Abord occupies an enviable position along the seafront promenade on the south side of town. Tasty Mauritian dishes

MAURITIUS

(think fresh seafood curry and flavourful *rougaille saucisses*), smart decor and frequent fits of live music will help you quickly forget that the menu is overpriced.

### SELF-CATERING
There are plenty of self-service options for villa renters and picnickers. Supermarkets and convenience stores are peppered throughout Mahébourg – try **Kong** ( ☎ 631 9252; 47 Royal Rd; 🕑 9am-7pm Mon-Sat, to noon Sun) in the city centre or the modern **London Way** ( ☎ 696 0088; 🕑 8.30am-7pm Mon-Tue & Thu, to 8pm Fri & Sat, to 12.30pm Sun) on the main road heading towards Pointe d'Esny.

### Getting There & Away
Mahébourg is an important transport hub. There are express buses every half-hour to and from Port Louis and at least every 15 minutes from Curepipe. Most but not all of these buses stop at the airport en route; check before boarding. A shuttle to Blue Bay runs roughly every 30 minutes.

Buses running north from Mahébourg go to Centre de Flacq via Vieux Grand Port every 20 minutes or so. Heading south, there are less frequent services to Souillac via Rivière des Anguilles.

A taxi for the 15-minute hop from SSR international airport to Mahébourg costs Rs 500. You'll pay Rs 1200 to reach Port Louis, Rs 1500 to reach Flic en Flac and Rs 1200 for Belle Mare.

### Getting Around
You'll find a variety of local car renters who also offer rides to the airport nearby. Your accommodation can hook you up with a vehicle or try **Colony Car Rental** ( ☎ 631 7062; Rue de la Colonie) for competitively priced leases and pick-ups. It's worth picking up a scooter or bicycle for a scenic ride up along the coast or down to Blue Bay.

## POINTE D'ESNY & BLUE BAY
Mahébourg may be short on sand but Pointe d'Esny and Blue Bay more than make up for it. With one of the most beautiful stretches of beach on the entire island, this area has become one of the favoured spots for private villas and charming *chambres d'hôtes*. Pointe d'Esny is also the jumping-off point for those interested in visiting the nature reserve on Île aux Aigrettes.

### Blue Bay Marine Park
In an effort to protect the area's rich underwater forest of rare corals from encroaching development, the government has given Blue Bay 'marine park' status. Besides a mandate barring high-speed watercrafts it seems that conservation plans are a bit laissez-faire, to put it gently. Local environmentalists fear that irreversible coral bleaching is inevitable, which is a shame as this is the best snorkelling spot on the island.

There are no 'official' tours of the marine park like on Île aux Aigrettes – the protected patches of coral can be easily explored on a snorkelling outing or on an excursion aboard a glass-bottom boat (figure on around Rs 200 per person for one hour). See p119 for more information.

### Île aux Aigrettes
This popular ecotourism destination is a nature reserve on an island roughly 800m off the coast. It preserves very rare remnants of the coastal forests of Mauritius and provides a sanctuary for animals and plants unique to the area, like Aldabra giant tortoises, ebony trees, wild orchids and the endangered pink pigeon.

Kudos should be given to the **Mauritian Wildlife Foundation** (MWF; ☎ 631 2396; www.ile-aux-aigrettes.com; admission incl transfer €20), which manages the reserve and conducts tours of the island (revenues are ploughed back into its conservation efforts). There are five daily departures during the week (between 9.30am and 2pm) and two or three morning departures on weekends. Tours start from Pointe Jérome, near Le Preskil hotel (Map p120). Bookings should be made a couple of days in advance by phoning MWF. The two-hour tour of the island involves a good deal of walking; wear comfortable shoes and bring a hat, sunscreen, water and insect repellent.

### Île des Deux Cocos
Île des Deux Cocos sits at the edge of the azure lagoon and was once used by Sir Hesketh Bell, the flamboyant British governor, to entertain guests. Today, the Naiade hotel group has maintained the tradition of entertaining visitors by offering tourists a relaxing day of swimming, beach lazing and snorkelling. Welcome drinks, an immense buffet lunch and rum tasting are also included. Travellers with serious cash to burn can rent out the

island's sole villa (constructed by Bell over a century ago) for an eye-popping €2100 per night. Transport to the island can be arranged by any of the Naiade hotels. An all-inclusive day on the island costs €60. Call ☎ 698 2222 for more information.

## Activities

### BOAT EXCURSION
Just like Mahébourg to the north, Blue Bay is home to a variety of boat operators that offer journeys on glass-bottom boats and excursions to the nearby islands. Travellers should be careful, however, when choosing a boatswain here – the area has seen an increased number of drug dealers and addicts in recent years, and several one-man operations are merely a front to support their narcotics habit. Also, the tides vary greatly in this part of the island; only a knowledgeable tour leader will know when the optimal times are for going to sea. Jean-Claude Farla in Mahébourg (see p116) is an excellent choice; in Blue Bay try **Totof** ( ☎ 790 3626, 754 8873; boatotof@yahoo.com), an exuberant character who promises a memorable day of snorkelling, island hopping and barbecues. He can also arrange evening cruises upon demand. **Arauld** ( ☎ 752 9722) is also a trustworthy pick. Alternatively you can ask at your accommodation for additional recommendations – Le Preskil, for example, runs outings on its private catamaran (available to nonguests as well). Note that all of these operators also run boat trips to Île aux Cerfs. For trips to Île aux Aigrettes, see p118.

### DIVING
There are several dive sites of note lurking off the southeastern coast of Mauritius. These scuba hot spots – mostly wall dives and dropoffs – have interesting rock formations that plunge to 40m and attract a good amount of colourful fish. The most noteworthy sites are **Colorado** and **Roches Zozo** ('zozo' is Creole for bird; the site was named for the swarms of avians that orbit the area while swooping down to snag shallow fish). For more information on diving in Mauritius, see p28.

Friendly Tony, one of the most knowledgeable divers in Mauritius, runs **Coral Diving** (Map p114; ☎ 604 1000, 604 1084; www.coraldiving.com; ☼ 9am-5pm Mon-Sat, 9am-1pm Sun), the southeast's main scuba operator. It is primarily located on the sandy grounds of Le Preskil hotel.

## Sleeping
The communities of Pointe d'Esny and Blue Bay are popular places to call home during a holiday. Blue Bay has a number of well-priced apartments, while Pointe d'Esny boasts a colourful array of excellent *chambres d'hôtes*. The area's one slight disadvantage is the rumble of departing planes from the nearby airport; there aren't many, but they can be awfully grumbly.

### APARTMENTS & VILLAS
The area in the south, slightly inland from the public beach at Blue Bay, is beginning to look like a mini Flic en Flac with its cluster of cheap holiday apartments often rented out by weekending locals.

Try any of the following:

**EasyRent** ( ☎ 452 1010; www.easyrent.mu) Manages a variety of high-quality properties in the area including the luxurious Azur Villas (€220 to €425).

**Pingouinvilla** ( ☎ 637 3051; www.pingouinvillas.com; Rue Daurades, Blue Bay; apt per week €225-400; ✹ ) Charming complex of fully equipped apartments. Maid service twice per week.

**Tam Tam Travel** ( ☎ 631 8642; tamtnt@intnet.mu; Coastal Rd) Friendly local travel agency that can set you up with a holiday pad in the neighbourhood.

**Villa Vakoa** ( ☎ 727 3216, 431 1099; villavakoa@ gmail.com; villa €150-300; ✹ ☒ ) Large two-storey property located 300m south of Le Preskil, with travertine floors, an American-style kitchen and spacious bedrooms. Sleeps six.

### GUESTHOUSES & CHAMBRES D'HÔTES
More so than anywhere else on the island, Pointe d'Esny has a smile-worthy assortment of memorable guesthouses and *chambres d'hôtes*. If you're planning on staying in different parts of the island during your holiday, then put this area at the top of your list.

**Le Blazon** (Map p114; ☎ 771 7917, 631 1699; www. residence-leblason.com; s/d incl half board €30/50; ✹ ☒ ) Set a block inland from the main coastal road, Le Blazon has a decidedly residential vibe since traffic rarely ever zooms by. There are four rooms spread across two floors, a guest kitchen and an inviting Japanese sauna.

**our pick** **Chez Henri** (Map p114; ☎ 631 9806; www. henri-vacances.com; Coastal Rd; s/d incl breakfast €35/40; ✹ ☒ ) Staying at Henri and Marie-Josée's welcoming *chambre d'hôte*, housed in a foliage-draped building befitting provincial France, feels like a trip to the countryside to visit your long-lost uncle and aunt. Rooms are lovingly filled with loads of wood and wicker, and each one sports a useful kitchenette. Don't miss the excellent three-course dinners (€15 to €20) served on the patio – it's a great opportunity to meet the other guests and listen to Henri recount his various adventures while rattling off an endless stream of double entendres (it helps if you speak French though).

**our pick** **L'Oiseau du Paradis** (Map p114; ☎ 631 5469, 729 3597; info@oiseauduparadis; Coastal Rd; s/d incl breakfast from €40/50, villa €180; ☒ ☒ ☜ ) The newest addition to Pointe d'Esny's coterie of guesthouses is undeniably stylish and remarkably homey. Rooms are coated in soothing tropical colours and feature an eclectic mix of rustic wooden touches (stylish lamps and nightstands) and thoroughly modern fixtures (bucket sinks and rain showers). Although it's located on the far side of the coastal road, guests have access to the stunning beach via the owner's private villa across the street (which you can also rent).

**Chante au Vent** (Map p114; ☎ 631 9614; www.chanteauvent.com; Coastal Rd; r from Rs 1800-3100, studios from Rs 2200-3000; ☒ ) Chante au Vent's only distinction is that it's the oldest B&B in Pointe d'Esny. Besides that superlative it's our least favourite spot among the options listed. The grounds themselves are quite charming but the main building feels weathered and worn. Rooms are sparsely decorated and feel like a monk's chamber. It's the sea views, however, that are the major perk – you can feel the ocean's spray from your balcony.

**Le Jardin de Beau Vallon** ( ☎ 631 2850; www.lejardindebeauvallon.com; Rue de Beau Vallon; s/d Rs 2500/3800, bungalows s/d 2300/3200; ☒ ☜ ) Beau Vallon is primarily known for its charming restaurant set on the ground floor of an 18th-century colonial manor house (see p121). There are, however, several rooms on the property that make for a memorable vacation experience. Perched above the restaurant are two welcoming suites that draw their decorative inspiration from Madagascar and East Asia – vibrant tapestries tumble down the walls and four-poster beds are ensconced in a tornado of silky streamers. Several newer bungalows are arranged in a row just beyond the main building and are adorned with plantation-style incarnations of wood and wicker.

**Villas Le Guerlande** (Map p114; ☎ 631 9882; www.leguerlande.com; Coastal Rd; s/d incl half board Rs 2640/4600; ☒ ☜ ) This German-run property features a campus of well-tended apartment-bungalows

sprawling across Pointe d'Esny's postcard-pretty coast. The theme is 'island life', with generous amounts of teak and wicker filling the sun-drenched rooms. Suites with high-pitched roofs and lofted beds are particularly charming.

These smaller spots, located next door to one another, are also worth a look:

**Noix de Coco** (Map p114; ☎ 631 9987; noixdecoco@intnet.mu; Coastal Rd; d incl breakfast €45-60; ☒ ) Dorette has opened her charming home to travellers. Several rooms have sea views, though you'll spend most of your time lounging on the sand-swept terrace.

**Chantemer** (Map p114; ☎ 631 3861; www.chantemer.mu; Coastal Rd; r incl breakfast €60-84) Attractive and well-run private guesthouse with a lovely garden leading down to the beach. All very tastefully decorated with family heirlooms and art.

### HOTELS & RESORTS

Amid the various accommodation types south of Mahébourg stand two excellent resorts.

**Le Preskîl** (Map p114; ☎ 604 1000; www.lepreskil.com; Pointe Jérome; d incl half board from €190; ☒ ☐ ☜ ☒ ) An unparalleled position on a secluded spit of sand? Check! A friendly staff that operates with Swiss efficiency? Check! Romantic views of the turquoise lagoon and rolling jungle mountains? Check! This four-star resort – with a subtle Creole design scheme – seems to have hit all the right notes, and, after an extensive renovation, we can't find a reason not to stay at this slice of paradise. In addition to the usual bevy of watersports and activities, Le Preskîl boasts a popular kids club, expert scuba diving, and a private catamaran shuttling vacationers to the nearby marine park and Île aux Cerfs.

**Shandrani** (Map p114; ☎ 603 4343; www.shandrani-hotel.com; d incl full board Rs €800; ☒ ☐ ☜ ☒ ) On the south side of Blue Bay, this relaxed and family-friendly resort rambles across a private peninsula garnished with luscious jungle foliage. It has no fewer than three beaches and boasts all the facilities you would expect from a heavy hitter in the top-end category: four restaurants, a golf course, tennis courts, a dive centre and more. It's the only five-star property on the island offering all-inclusive accommodation, which admittedly gives the hotel a slightly negative cruiseship-like stigma.

## Eating

Despite the palpable residential vibe, Pointe d'Esny and Blue Bay have a few noteworthy options spread along the coastal road.

**Blue Bamboo** (Map p114; ☎ 631 5801; Coastal Rd; mains Rs 180-430; ۞ 11.30am-3pm & 6-11pm) Blue Bamboo has many charms: a cosy plant-filled cloister, delicious pan pizza, friendly owners and an inviting lounge on the 2nd floor. The upstairs bar is open every day, except Monday, from 6pm to midnight. It's best to call ahead if you're eyeing a table in the bamboo-lined courtyard.

**Chez Maryse** (Map p114; ☎ 978 8211; Coastal Rd; mains from Rs 190; ۞ lunch & dinner) After winning a 'women's empowerment' grant from the Mauritian government, friendly Maryse and her two sisters opened a small restaurant in her backyard. Savoury Creole eats are stewed under her yellow tin roof and served to contented customers gathered around the haphazard collection of tables. Chez Maryse is across the street from L'Oiseau du Paradis.

**Le Jardin de Beau Vallon** (Map p114; ☎ 631 2850; Rue de Beau Vallon; mains Rs 190-560; ۞ noon-3pm & 7-10pm) Emerging from an inland thicket of trees and sky-scraping cane leaves, Beau Vallon is an enchanting colonial estate that has been carefully and lovingly refurbished over the last few decades. Romantic dark-wood panelling, flavourful island spices, and the lazy spin of frond-shaped ceiling fans elicit fantasies found on the pages of a Ripling passage. Now if only the staff could be as charming and demure as the surrounds – our welcome wasn't as pleasant as it could have been.

**Le Bougainville** (Map p114; ☎ 631 8299; Coastal Rd; mains Rs 200-300; ۞ 10am-10pm) Worth a mention for its breezy terrace, friendly atmosphere and convenient location across from Blue Bay beach, Le Bougainville is a popular hang-out for locals and tourists alike. The menu is vast – salads, pizza, fish, curries etc – but it's best to stick to the drink list when there's a crowd (a plethora of orders never fails to confuse the kitchen staff).

**La Belle Kréole** (Map p114; ☎ 631 5017; Cité la Chaux; mains Rs 250-1200; ۞ 10am-3pm & 6-10.30pm) Set on a mangrove and marked by a large pirogue, this popular option dishes out tasty Mauritian cuisine like venison curry and *rougaille saucisses*. The prices are very high, but the lagoon-side atmosphere is undeniably memorable.

**Charka Steakhouse** (Map p114; ☎ 604 1000; Le Preskîl, Pointe Jérome; mains Rs 600-1200; ۞ 7-10.30pm) Set deep within the grounds of Le Preskîl resort but billed as its own separate restaurant, Charka is a must for meat lovers. Fresh South African steaks of the highest quality are grilled

to perfection in modern surrounds sparsely accented by the odd African mask or hunting spear. Reservations are essential, especially if you aren't staying at the hotel.

## Getting There & Around

Buses to and from Mahébourg run every 30 minutes. A taxi there will cost Rs 300, and it's Rs 500 to the airport. See p118 for taxi fares to other parts of the island.

All of the area's guesthouses can arrange car hire or offer you a vehicle to lease from their private collection. Try Hernri at **JH Arnulphy** ( ☎ 631 9806; www.henri-vacances.com) who offers cars for €31 per day. Arnulphy can also help with bicycle hire; rates start at Rs 100 per day.

# SOUTH COAST

Mauritius' southern coast features some of the country's wildest and most attractive scenery. Here you'll find basalt cliffs, sheltered sandy coves, hidden falls and traditional fishing villages where fisherfolk sell their catch at roadside stalls. Beyond the shoreline lies endless sugar-cane fields and dense forests that clothe the hillsides in a patchwork of vibrant greens.

The region is known as Savanne and is noticeably devoid of any prominent towns save Rivière des Anguilles and Souillac. Both can be used as bases from which to explore the nearby parks and preserves, though we recommend staying elsewhere and visiting the far south during a day trip aboard a private vehicle.

## La Vanille

This exciting **zoo and reserve** (Map p114; ☎ 626 2503; www.lavanille-reserve.com; adult/child Rs 205/150; ۞ 9.30am-6pm) makes for a fantastic field trip with the kids. The park has the greatest number of giant tortoises in captivity (over 1000), a result of a wildly successful breeding program for the Aldabra and Radiata species. While the enormous farm of Nile crocodiles (population 2000) is undoubtedly impressive, nothing quite beats the unbelievably gigantic display of creepy-crawlies in the insectarium – it's worth coming to La Vanille just to check out this immense collection of mounted critters (over 23,000 species!). Allow at least 1½ hours for a complete visit.

Those with a taste for adventure (literally) should sample the croc croquette at the **Hungry Crocodile Restaurant** (mains Rs 165-425). It also does

MAURITIUS

more-conventional dishes like spaghetti bolognaise. Don't forget your mozzie repellent – you won't be the only one feasting at the lunch table...

La Vanille is clearly signposted 2km south of Rivière des Anguilles.

## Bois Chéri Tea Plantation

This 250-hectare **tea factory and museum** (Map p114; ☎ 507 0216; www.larouteduthe.mu; adult/child Rs 350/165; ☸ 8.30am-4.30pm Mon-Fri, 8.30am-2.30pm Sat) is located about 12km north of Rivière des Anguilles amid an endless acreage of cane. Visitors can take an hour-long tour of the tea-processing facility, which ends with a stop at a small exhibition space annotating the island's tea history through machines and photos. The best part of the visit is undoubtedly the sampling session at the end. It's advisable to plan your trip during the morning as most of the action takes place before noon. After your tour, stick around for lunch – the in-house **restaurant** (admission incl set menu Rs 600; ☸ 10.30am-3.30pm) takes a formidable stab at gourmet cuisine and uses locally sourced ingredients. The commanding views over the riverine plains are also quite captivating.

## St Aubin

If you're following La Route du Thé (p122), then the final stop after Bois Chéri is **St Aubin** (Map p114; ☎ 626 1513; www.larouteduthe.mu; admission incl set menu Rs 960.25; ☸ 8am-4pm Mon-Sat), an elegant plantation house that dates back to 1819. The estate no longer produces sugar, but in the gardens of the house there is a traditional rum distillery and a nursery growing anthurium flowers and vanilla – you'll learn all about the fascinating history of vanilla production on the guided tour.

The height of the St Aubin experience is a meal at the wonderfully charming **table d'hôte**

(☸ noon-3pm Mon-Sat) in the main manor house. The dining room is one of best throwbacks to colonial times – dainty chandeliers cast ambient light over the white tablecloths and antique wooden furniture. The set menu showcases the fruits of the plantation: hearts of palm, pineapple, mango and chilli, to name a few. Reservations are recommended.

If you wish to stay the night, the on-site **Auberge de St Aubin** (d incl half board Rs 3500; ⚡ ) has three rooms in the plantation manse across from the estate's main building. The bedroom at the front of the house perfectly captures the charming colonial ambience with creaky wooden floors and cotton gauzing over the four-poster bed – the two rooms in the back are noticeably more modern and have a bit less character.

## Union Ducray Sugar Estate

Though not necessarily a tourist attraction unto itself, the area around the Union Ducray Sugar Estate is a horseback-riding haven. **Mauritius Horse Trails** (Map p114; ☎ 725 7430; www.mauritiushorsetrails.com) is a friendly stable that takes in old horses that have been put out to pasture (so to speak) after years of rigorous racing at the hippodrome in Port Louis. Friendly Lindy, originally from South Africa, rehabilitates and retrains the horses into gentle trail equines. Scenic trots along the craggy shoreline are always on offer and half-day trips include a Creole-style lunch.

**Andréa & l'Exil** (Relais des Lodges; Map p114; ☎ 471 0555; www.relaisdeslodges.com; d incl half board Rs 3500; ⚡ ) The properties of Andréa and l'Exil each have a collection of 10 lovely cottages. The units at Andréa, along the sea, have gabled roofs and glass-panelled walls facing the rugged Ireland-esque coast. There's also an inviting swimming pool and reputable restaurant on-site. Perched high in the hills, l'Exil's

---

**LA ROUTE DU THÉ**

**La Route du Thé** (The Tea Route; www.larouteduthe.mu) offers tourists a window into the island's plantation past by linking together three of the island's remaining colonial estates. The first stop is the Creole manse-turned-museum at the Domaine des Aubineaux near Curepipe (p77). Then the route veers south to the vast Bois Chéri tea plantation (p122). The final stop is the stately St Aubin (p122), with its lush gardens and rum distillery. Despite the itinerary's name, the focus of the trip extends far beyond tea – each stop has a charming *table d'hôte*, a museum and the St Aubin even offers period-style accommodation.

True architecture buffs and historians should consider doing the route backwards and tacking on the resplendent Eureka estate (p74) at the end of the journey.

cache of serene bungalows has a distinctive adobe ranch-style architecture. Five rooms offer views of the distant sea while the other five face the rumbling waterfall nearby (a 20-minute walk) – all are surrounded by luscious fruit-bearing trees. Room rates include a guided hike through the interior forest beyond the sea of sugar cane. Guests can also arrange 4WD excursions, and tours of the neighbouring sugar estate can be organised between December and June. At the time of research only the lodges at Andréa were open for visitors, although l'Exil should be back up and running fairly soon – check the website for updates.

## Souillac
**pop 4400**
Continuing west along the seashore, the largest settlement along the south coast is Souillac, 7km from Rivière des Anguilles. The town itself is of little interest, but there's a clutch of (somewhat) interesting sights just beyond. Souillac is named after the Vicomte de Souillac, the island's French governor from 1779 to 1787.

### SIGHTS
**Rochester Falls** are by no means the country's most spectacular falls, but they are worth a detour if you're in the area. Follow the make-shift signs from Souillac – the route is rather circuitous but reliable nonetheless. Prepare yourself for hawkers who want a tip for telling you where to park your car. The gushing cascade will emerge from the cane fields after a five-minute walk from your vehicle.

Robert Edward Hart (1891–1954) was a renowned Mauritian poet, apparently appreciated by both the French and the English, although we've yet to meet anyone who's heard of him. His rather uninteresting house, La Nef, is an attractive coral-stone cottage which was opened to the public as the **Robert Edward Hart museum** (Map p114; ☎ 625 6101; admission free; ☒ 9am-4pm Mon & Wed-Fri, to noon Sat) in 1967. On display are some originals and copies of Hart's letters, plays, speeches and poetry, as well as his fiddle, spectacles and trusty Britannic toilet. His award from the National Institute of Sciences for services to 'telepathy, hypnotism and personal magnetism' could do with some explanation. Sadly the captions are only in French. This is definitely rainy-day tourism.

Continue east along the road past the museum and you come to a grassy cliff top, which affords a view of the black rocky coastline and broken reef. A path leads down to the wild and empty **Gris Gris beach**; a wooden sign warns of the dangers of swimming here. The term *gris gris* traditionally refers to 'black magic', and looking at the tortuous coastline, you can see how the area got its name.

Right at the end of the next headland, 600m further on, **La Roche Qui Pleure** (The Crying Rock; Map p114) resembles a crying man – you'll have to stand there puzzling it out for quite some time, and the waves really have to crash for the 'tears' to come out, but it's oddly satisfying when you finally get it.

**Le Souffleur**, a hidden attraction known only to locals, isn't exactly a stone's throw from Souillac like the other sights in this section. You'll need a bit of gumption (and a 4WD) to tackle this one, but if you ask anyone in the know, they'll all say that it's well worth the adventure.

Situated on the coast about halfway between Souillac and Blue Bay, this geological anomaly is a half-formed grotto on the side of a cliff that spouts a geyser-like fountain of water (up to 20m in the air!) when the seas are rough. As the waves crash against the cliff the seawater pushes through a crack in the bluffs like a blowhole on a whale. If the seas aren't particularly rough during your visit, there's a natural land bridge nearby that's worth a camera click or two. It was formed when the roof collapsed on another naturally formed grotto.

To reach the super-secret *souffleur*, head for the Savannah sugar estate near the village of L'Escalier, cross the estate, then follow the snaking track once you reach the sea. Even if you don't seek permission to cross the sugar estate, we highly recommend bringing a local with you otherwise you may never find the place.

### SLEEPING & EATING
The best sleeping option in the area is the Andréa lodges bordering the Union Ducray Sugar Estate (see p122). The other choices are rather lacklustre and attached to popular eating establishments. If you're eating by the sea in Gris Gris, opt for something with seafood – it was probably caught offshore about 12m away.

**Le Gris Gris** (Chez Rosy; Map p114; ☎ 625 4179; mains Rs 150-250; ☒ lunch) Rosy's place is a simple affair with a motley assortment of wicker and plastic furniture. The food, however, never misses the mark – locals and tourists rave about home-cooked Mauritian and Chinese dishes.

**Escale des Îles** (Map p114; ☎ 625 7014; mains Rs 200-450; ☺ lunch & dinner) Next door to Rosy's and slightly more serious (the staff wear uniforms), Escale des Îles is set within a brightly coloured building and has a popular sea-facing patio. There are a couple of rooms above the restaurant (doubles Rs 500), but we'd rather stay elsewhere.

**Le Rochester Restaurant** (Map p114; ☎ 625 4180; mains Rs 325; ☺ lunch & dinner, closed dinner Tue) The charming Madame Appadu, who once ran the Cabane en Paille restaurant at the Vallée des Couleurs, now has her own family restaurant in an old colonial building by the bridge to Surinam. A delightful mix of Creole, Indian and Chinese staples are served on a shady terrace situated atop a gushing ravine. Upstairs you'll find three small guest rooms (singles/doubles including breakfast Rs 900/1600), but they're nothing to write home about.

### GETTING THERE & AROUND

There are buses roughly every half-hour from Mahébourg to Souillac via the airport and Rivière des Anguilles. From Port Louis, buses run hourly, calling at Rivière des Anguilles en route. There are also frequent services to and from Souillac to Curepipe, with three buses a day taking the coast road via Pointe aux Roches. Buses heading along the coast to Baie du Cap depart hourly.

## La Vallée des Couleurs

Despite having 23 colours (as opposed to Chamarel's seven; p108), **La Vallée des Couleurs** (Map p114; ☎ 251 8666; Mare Anguilles; admission Rs 200; ☺ 9am-5pm) is the less impressive of the island's two 'coloured earths'. The reserve does, however, have a scenic nature trail that passes some trickling waterfalls, memorable vistas, crawling tortoises and blossoming tropical flowers. It takes about an hour to complete the reserve's circuit.

## Bel Ombre

Despite being miles from the bucket-and-spade atmosphere of Flic en Flac or Grand Baie, Bel Ombre has quickly developed into a cosy tourist bubble along the wild southern shores. The main attraction here is the **Domaine de Bel Ombre** (Map p114; ☎ 623 5615; www.

domainedebelombre.mu), an open nature reserve set on the old sugar plantation, which was developed by Charles Telfair between 1816 and 1833. Today it's a multifaceted venture with a brilliant golf course, Integrated Resort Scheme (IRS) properties, ruins from a colonial mill and the Valriche Nature Reserve – a haven for quad biking, hiking and touring on 4WDs.

The reserve has two lovely restaurants: an elegant dining venue at the golf club with views of the manicured greens, and the must-try **Le Château Restaurant** (Map p114; ☎ 623 5620; mains from Rs 1200; ☺ lunch Mon-Sat, dinner Fri & Sat). Dominique Blais, the head chef at Heritage Le Telfair, presides over this stunning conversion of the old Bel Ombre plantation house. This is *the* place for an exceptional meal of traditional Franco-Mauritian cuisine with contemporary flourish.

The sumptuous estate also features two five-star hotels, both run by Verandah Resorts. The **Heritage Le Telfair** (Map p114; ☎ 601 5500; www.heritageletelfair.com; s/d/tr incl half board €310/444/697; ✖ ▣ ⌨ ☂) has perfectly captured the luxury and grandeur of the island's colonial yesteryears, while the **Heritage Awali** (Map p114; ☎ 601 1500; www.heritageawali.com; s/d/tr incl half board €310/444/697; ✖ ▣ ⌨ ☂) prefers an African heritage, with abounding masks, drums and tribal art.

There are several other top-end resorts strung along the beach in the area:

**Shanti Ananda Maurice** (Map p114; ☎ 603 7200; www.shantiananda.com; St Felix; d incl breakfast €285; ✖ ▣ ⌨ ☂) The second development of the luxury masterminds behind the notoriously high-end Ananda in the Himalayas. A spa retreat theme has been recently abandoned for pure five-star comfort.

**Tamassa** (Map p114; ☎ 603 7300; www.naiade.com; s/d incl full board from €290/430; ✖ ▣ ⌨ ☂) The new kid on the block offering four-star luxury amid contemporary surrounds and bold colour schemes.

**Mövenpick Resort & Spa Mauritius** (Map p114; ☎ 623 5000; www.movenpick-hotels.com; d incl half board €554; ✖ ▣ ⌨ ☂) Wild *Temple of Doom*-like entry, stunning central avenue and charming accommodation in three-storey buildings facing the sea.

There is regular bus service from Curepipe to Bel Ombre via Nouvelle France and Chemin Grenier.

## Baie du Cap
pop 2300

The coastline between Baie du Cap and the stunning Le Morne Peninsula is some of the most beautiful in the country, and blissfully free of development. The only sights in the area besides the casuarina-lined beaches are a couple of low-key monuments. The first is the **Trevassa Monument** (Map p114), about 1km beyond Bel Ombre village, which commemorates the sinking of the British steamer *Trevassa* in 1923. She went down 2600km off Mauritius. Sixteen survivors were eventually washed ashore at Bel Ombre after surviving 25 days in an open lifeboat.

The second is the **Matthew Flinders Monument** (Map p114), which stands on the shore 500m west of Baie du Cap. It was erected in 2003 to honour the 200th anniversary of the arrival of Matthew Flinders, an English navigator and cartographer. He was less warmly received at the time; the poor bloke didn't know that England and France were at war and he was swiftly imprisoned for six years. For an interesting read on the subject, take a look at Huguette Ly-Tio-Fane Pineo's book *In the Grips of the Eagle: Matthew Flinders at the Île de France, 1803–1810.*

Bus services along here are limited. Baie du Cap is the terminus for buses from Souillac and Quatre Bornes (via Tamarin). Buses run approximately every 20 minutes.

## SOUTHEAST MAURITIUS

North of Mahébourg, the main road hugs the coast as it winds around the base of Lion Mountain (480m) and the Montagnes Bambous range. This area was the first settled by the Dutch early in the 17th century, and was one of the first parts of the country to lose its native ebony forest to the burgeoning sugar-cane industry. Nevertheless, dense forest still cloaks the mountains. In recent years, several wealthy locals have purchased large tracts of land and turned them into forest reserves, tourist attractions and designated hunting grounds. In addition to the following big-ticket preserves you'll also stumble across lesser-known parks like **Domaine des 7 Vallées** ( ☎ 631 3317; www.domaine7vallees.mu), **Falaise Rouge** ( ☎ 433 1010; www.cieletnature.com) and **Domaine de l'Ylang Ylang**, where essential oils are distilled using traditional methods.

The best way to explore the region is by private vehicle; most tour operators can hook you up with a half- or full-day visit to any of the region's *domaines*. Opting for public transport is also possible, though significantly less convenient. Buses between Mahébourg

and Centre de Flacq ply the coast road, passing through Vieux Grand Port, Anse Jonchée and Bambous Virieux. There are departures every 20 minutes or so.

## Vallée de Ferney

Run by the same folks as the Domaine de l'Étoile (p126), this **reserve** (Map p114; ☎ 433 1010/50, 729 1050; www.cieletnature.com) protects a 400-year-old forest. The Ferney Valley is perhaps best known as the site of a recent tree-hugging demonstration that ignited when a Chinese paving company sought to construct a highway directly through the protected hinterland. Attempts at development were unsuccessful and the reserve continues to offer guided 1½-hour tours departing from the well-curated visitors centre. Fill your belly at the on-site restaurant after working up an appetite on the trails.

The turn-off to the 200-hectare reserve is clearly marked along the coastal road, around 2km south of Vieux Grand Port.

## Vieux Grand Port
pop 2900

This is the 'cradle of Mauritian history', where the first human inhabitants of the island landed on 9 September 1598 under the command of Wybrandt Van Warwyck. The Dutch later built a fort 3km further north in what is now the town of Vieux Grand Port, although a monument marks the actual landing point as well (Map p114). It was the local headquarters of the Dutch East India Company until 1710, when the Dutch abandoned the island. The site was then taken over by the French.

The battered ruins of Fort Frederik Hendrik stand in a park near the church at the northern end of Vieux Grand Port and include the remains of an old Dutch church, a bakery, a prison, a forge, a powder magazine and a dispensary. A few clay pipes, wine bottles and other items left behind by both the Dutch and French occupants are now on display in the **Frederik Hendrik Museum** ( ☎ 634 4319; admission free; 🕑 9am–4pm Mon–Sat). The museum also outlines the history of the Dutch in Mauritius.

Vieux Grand Port is perhaps more famous as the site of the only French naval victory to be inscribed on the Arc de Triomphe in Paris. Relics of the 1810 battle with the English are on display at the National History Museum in Mahébourg.

## Lion Mountain

Overlooking Vieux Grand Port is Lion Mountain (480m), immediately recognisable from its sphinxlike profile. The mountain offers a splendid half-day hike with stunning views over the coast. It's a very challenging but rewarding walk that climbs up the lion's 'back' to finish at an impressive viewpoint on the 'head'. We recommend hiring a local guide (see p149 for details), though if you decide to go it alone you'll find the trailhead beside the police station at the north of Vieux Grand Port. Check out www.fitsy.com for detailed GPS information about the hike, though the main trail is fairly obvious and runs straight along the ridge and up over a rocky area to the peak. There are a few hairy scrambles over the rocks before you reach the flat area on the lion's head. From here you can see right across the interior of the island. Return the same way you came up. Allow three to four hours for the return trip.

## Kestrel Valley
## (Domaine d'Anse Jonchée)

The scenic **Kestrel Valley** (Map p114; ☎ 634 5011; www.kestrelvalley.com) is primarily a hunting reserve for Javanese deer. The 950 hectares of forested mountain terrain also act as a reserve for many endemic bird species, including the Mauritius kestrel – one of the world's rarest birds of prey. A portion of the reserve has been blocked off for hikers – there are four marked trails (from 2km to 6km long) that wind through the park.

The estate is equally famed for its restaurant, **Panoramour** (mains Rs 500; ⏲ 8.30am-4.30pm & 6-9pm), which looks like a thatch-covered treehouse perched atop a 500m hill. The helipad that adjoins the restaurant gives you an idea of the kind of people who drop by for lunch –the food is rightly delicious and extraordinary coastal views make the hefty bill worthwhile. All the meat is produced on the estate's farm or shot in the park – wild boar curry, venison steaks and honey pork ribs all feature on the menu.

Accommodation is provided near the restaurant in thatched **bungalows** (d incl half board Rs 4000). However, the feel is resolutely rustic and there are lots of bugs. If you like creature comforts, you'll be better off in a hotel on the coast.

Note that the reserve used to be known as the Domaine du Chasseur – the park now called Domaine du Chasseur is near the town of Nouvelle France.

## Bambous Virieux

This small settlement is the site of a pioneering project to restore the mangroves that were destroyed by the British following the malaria epidemic of 1866. There is little of interest tourist-wise, though there's a short nature trail through the mangroves at **Le Barachois** (Map p114; ☎ 634 5643; d incl breakfast €70), a hotel where you can stay in simple, rustic rooms with terraces overlooking the water. The in-house **restaurant** (menu from Rs 1000; ⏲ 9am-9pm) serves scrumptious seafood and local game (venison and boar) during hunting season.

## Domaine de l'Étoile

Teetering between the eastern and southeast realms of the island, this popular **forest reserve** (Map p114; ☎ 433 1010/50, 729 1050; www.cieletnature.com) is set on over 2000 hectares of unspoilt terrain – the perfect hinterland to explore by horse or rumbling quad bike. Mountain biking, guided hikes and archery are also on offer. Enjoy a bite at the on-site **restaurant** (meal per person Rs 720; ⏲ 11am-2pm), and if you're lucky, you'll spot several Javanese stags hiding in the forest – there are over 1000 living in the reserve.

# THE EAST

Lacking the touts, nightclubs and souvenir shacks of Flic en Flac in the west and Grand Baie in the north, the east face of Mauritius feels enviably untouched by mass tourism – a fantastic coincidence as the island's very best beaches line this quiet coast. This area is, however, the most exclusive side of the island, and the congregation of luxury hotels attracts the kind of crowd likely to take a helicopter transfer from the airport when they arrive. But fear not, budget-savvy traveller, the east still has several tricks up its sleeve. Start at Trou d'Eau Douce, which has retained the feel of a sleepy fishing village despite rubbing shoulders with the grand hotels next door. There are plenty of cheap digs around town and it's the jumping-off point for the wildly popular Île aux Cerfs. Vacationers looking for a private slice of paradise will be happy to know that there are dozens of reasonably priced beach houses dotting the shoreline.

## Getting There & Around

The main transport hub for east Mauritius is the inland town of Centre de Flacq. You'll

# THE EAST

0 —————— 5 km
0 —————— 3 miles

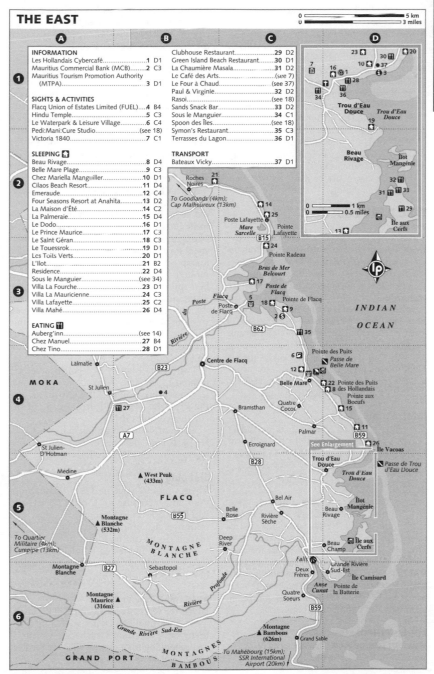

MAURITIUS

have to change here if you're arriving by bus from Port Louis, the Central Plateau towns or Mahébourg in the south. There are onward connections from Centre de Flacq to villages along the east coast, although some services are pretty infrequent. You can bank on bus transport from Centre de Flacq to Palmar and Poste Lafayette (with continuing service to Rivière du Rempart) but there are no buses to Belle Mare. Figure on around Rs 500 for a taxi between the coastal towns and Centre de Flacq.

Most hotels and guesthouses have bikes for rent. Otherwise, you can rent bikes from any of the travel agencies in Trou d'Eau Douce. Car rentals can easily be arranged through your accommodation.

## TROU D'EAU DOUCE
pop 5400

'Sweet water hole' sits at a set of major crossroads making it the unwitting tourism hub on this side of the island. It's a lovely little place, if a bit melancholic, where fishermen unravel their nets after a morning at sea and housewives walk around with baskets of vegies balanced on their heads. The sea is a stunning shade of blue here, but Trou d'Eau Douce's claim to fame is its easy access to the massively popular Île aux Cerfs, a favoured destination for day-tripping tourists. Despite the nagging heckles for an island-bound water taxi, this seaside township makes a great base for exploring the east coast – especially for those on a tighter budget.

### Information

The centre of Trou d'Eau Douce is marked by a large stone church, near which you'll find the post office, the police station and a small petrol station.

#### INTERNET ACCESS

Sous le Manguier (p129) has internet access at lunchtime, as does Green Island Beach Restaurant (p130). Restaurant Gilda, at the turn-off to the Terrasses du Lagon restaurant, offers wi-fi access (Rs 50 per hour) for customers. Down a side street between Chez Tino and Soleil des Z'Iles, **Les Hollandais Cybercafé** (Map p127; ☎ 480 0138; www.leshollandais.com; Le Maho; per 10min Rs 15; ☒ 9am-7pm Mon-Sat) has computer terminals and doubles as a patisserie.

#### TOURIST INFORMATION

**Mauritius Tourism Promotion Authority** (MTPA; Map p127; ☎ 480 0925; Royal Rd; ☒ 9am-5pm Mon-Sat) Has a kiosk at the public beachfront near Le Four à Chaud restaurant but is of very little help as it only provides general information about the island and does not have details about getting to Île aux Cerfs.

### Sights & Activities

The actual 'trou d'eau douce' for which the town is named can be found in a man-made stone hole next to the national coast guard's office. To find the **natural spring**, follow the fork in the main road away from the Gothic church as it slopes down the hill to the docks – the well is on the right side. Locals visit the stash of fresh water when the government supply gets corrupted after a strong storm.

Worth a look, **Victoria 1840** (Map p127; ☎ 480 0220; Victoria Rd; ☒ noon-3pm & 7-10pm Mon-Sat) is an old sugar mill that has been lovingly refurbished to house some of the works of Yvette Maniglier, a bewitching French painter who spent a year under the wing of Matisse. The juxtaposition of industrial brick and splashy modern art works surprisingly well and is best appreciated while dining at the in-house restaurant, Le Café des Arts (p130). To reach the mill-gallery, drive along the main road west out of town away from the stone Gothic church. Then, follow the path towards the Touessrok turning at the signposted entrance on the right side.

Two of the island's best golf courses are located in the area – the Touessrok's fairway masterpiece on Île aux Cerfs (p130) and the Ernie Els–designed dreamscape in the Anahita complex (p129).

For information on getting to Île aux Cerfs, see p130. For details about the popular forest reserve Domaine de l'Étoile, see p126.

### Sleeping

There's more choice in Trou d'Eau Douce than anywhere else on the east coast, and you'll find a decent range of budget and midrange accommodation. The area's upmarket sleeps can be found to the south – and if you're interested in sticking around for a while, why not buy a villa in the Anahita development.

#### APARTMENTS & VILLAS

Unlike the rest of the island, most of the apartments in Trou d'Eau Douce are family run – many have a certain ramshackle charm. If you're looking for a private villa, try **EasyRent** ( ☎ 452 1010; www.easyrent.mu).

**Le Dodo** (Map p127; ☎ 480 0034; christa0307@hotmail. com; Royal Rd; apt €20-30; ⊠ ) Le Dodo is like an orphanage for outdated furniture, with decor that is horribly mismatched, but somehow it all seems to work. The owner is kind and the apartments come fully outfitted with retro fixtures. Ask for one of the apartments higher up – although there's no elevator, the views over the cluttered village and azure sea are memorable.

**Villa La Fourche** (Map p127; ☎ 480 1194; www.villala fourcheltee.blogspot.com; 2-bedroom apt from €45; ⊠ 🖳 ) Tucked down a back street away from the coastal buzz, this quiet option is a good deal for large families, but the furnishings need updating.

**Cilaos Beach Resort** (Map p127; ☎ 480 2985; lalloosa rah@hotmail.com; Royal Rd; studios €50-60, apt €85-110; ⊠ ) This complex of fully equipped apartments and studios sits right on the beach just north of Trou d'Eau Douce. It's a bit of a hike into town unless you have a car, but it's a friendly and relaxed place – rooms, however, are very simple, if a bit faded. The studios are better value for money.

**Villa Mahé** (Map p127; ☎ 452 1010; www.easy rent. mu; Royal Rd; villa €150-350; ⊠ 🛜 ) For a spot of luxury at a very reasonable price, go for this endearing holiday home owned by the Montocchio family. There's a certain beachy charm about the place with its weathered white-wood exterior and slap-shut colonial shutters. The semidetached house sleeps 10 people and has stunning sea views from the wooden balconies.

### GUESTHOUSES & CHAMBRES D'HÔTES
In Trou d'Eau Douce it's hard to draw the line between apartments and *chambres d'hôtes* as most places are quite congenial and privately run.

**Sous le Manguier** (Map p127; ☎ 419 3855; 748 7347; www.slm-online.org; Royal Rd; apt €15-45; ⊠ ) The owners of the like-named restaurant rent out two self-catering apartments (for up to four people) and a small studio.

**Chez Mariella Manguiller** (Map p127; ☎ 480 0320, 780 3988; mariellamanguillier@hotmail.com; d/q incl breakfast €30/50; ⊠ 🛜 ) Although technically a stack of self-service studios, this place feels much more like a welcoming *chambre d'hôte*, since the owner, Mariella – with her big smile and mane of dreads – is one of the friendliest folks you'll meet in town. Rooms have benefited from an eclectic sense of style and boast

generous balconies sprouting seaward. The owner's husband is a fisherman and guests often snap up his daily catch to cook in their kitchens.

**Les Toits Verts** (Chez Roseline Duvivier; Map p127; ☎ 480 0503, 752 5552; rduvivier@intnet.mu; studios/apt €40/90; ⊠ ) There are no signs directing travellers to this address – you'll have to keep your eyes peeled for the signature *toits verts* (green roofs). And boy will you be glad you made the effort! This is one of the best deals in Trou d'Eau Douce, and not just because of its seaside location (a rarity in the area). The charmingly decorated rooms have all the mod cons and sit between the lapping waves and a lush, well-tended garden.

### HOTELS & RESORTS
And so begins the endless parade of luxury hotels that march along the east coast all the way up to the northern part of the island.

**Four Seasons Resort at Anahita** (Map p127; ☎ 402 3100; www.fourseasons.com/mauritius; villas incl breakfast €450-4000; ⊠ 🖳 🛜 🖳 ) Located in Beau Champ, slightly south of Trou d'Eau Douce, the Four Seasons Resort is part of a vast luxury complex known as Anahita. The draw at Anahita is the clutch of IRS bungalows, which offers foreigners the chance to purchase their very own piece of paradise. For those who are looking for something a bit more temporary, the resort features a beautiful assortment of holiday villas. The design scheme plays with local materials, like tropical timber and volcanic rock, while seamlessly integrating every modern convenience. Four stone-cut pools, a spa and a stunning golf course are also big draws.

**Le Touessrok** (Map p127; ☎ 402 7400; www.letouess rokresort.com; s/d/ste incl half board from €610/900/1010; ⊠ 🖳 🛜 🖳 ) Where to begin? Le Touessrok has one of the best resort reputations on the island, and the accolades are well deserved. Rambling across a sandy peninsula, the hotel blends Moorish-inspired architecture to the thick patches of surrounding jungle. While amenities are undoubtedly aplenty, the resort distinguishes itself from the rest of the five-stars with its two offshore islands: the famous Île aux Cerfs (p130) and the totally exclusive, Robinson Crusoe–style hideaway, Îlot Mangénie. Don't forget to ask a staff member where the name 'Touessrok' comes from – we're pretty sure you'll be as surprised with the down-the-earth answer as we were.

MAURITIUS

## Eating

Trou d'Eau Douce is the kind of place where you'll do perfectly fine just grabbing a chair and table at the first joint you stumble upon. It's a town of fishermen after all, so stick with the seafood. If you're looking for a more up-market experience, you can't go wrong with any of the restaurants at Le Touessrok or the famous breakfast buffet at Anahita.

**Green Island Beach Restaurant** (Map p127; ☎ 251 7152; Royal Rd; mains Rs 175-525; ☒ lunch & dinner Tue-Sun) The decor may be sparse, but the uberfriendly staff and delicious assortment of international faves more than make up for it. Have some *rougaille saucisses* with a slice of pizza – the menu is vast and everything's well priced. There's free wi-fi and an informal internet terminal for diners.

**Le Four à Chaud** (Map p127; ☎ 480 1036; Royal Rd; mains Rs 215-875; ☒ noon-3pm & 7.30pm-midnight) This is the smartest place in central Trou d'Eau Douce – head here for an evening of feasting on *fruits de mer* and a fantastic list of matched wines. Reserve ahead to get one of the few balcony tables with sea views, and note that the menu is exclusively seafood. The name is a play on words (it's opposite the old lime kiln, or *four à chaux*).

**Chez Tino** (Map p127; ☎ 480 2769; Royal Rd; mains Rs 300; ☒ 10.30am-10pm Mon-Sat, lunch Sun) Pufferfish hanging in vast numbers from the ceiling characterise this brilliant, quirky little place. Reserve a table on the wonderful terrace for the best views and enjoy a superb meal of Mauritian cooking with a heavy focus on seafood (langouste in particular). Tino also has a few rooms (without/with breakfast Rs 800/1000) on offer if you're looking for a place to spend the night. Delivery available.

**Terrasses du Lagon** (Map p127; ☎ 480 0223; Coastal Rd, Le Maho; mains Rs 300-550; ☒ noon-10pm Tue-Sun) Yes, the food is pretty good (skip the pizza though), but the real draw here is the stunning setting on a pirogue-filled lagoon. The cerulean water gently laps near the dining terrace as visitors clink their aperitifs. It's quite a romantic spot at sunset.

**Sous le Manguier** (Map p127; ☎ 419 3855, 748 7347; Royal Rd; tables d'hôtes Rs 700; ☒ lunch, dinner on reservation only) Opposite the Gothic church, this delightful *table d'hôte* is, as its name suggests, 'under the mango tree'. The downstairs restaurant is open during the day, and in the evening the owners invite you to join them for some fantastic home-cooked specialities on their upstairs terrace.

**Le Café des Arts** (Map p127; ☎ 480 0220; Victoria Rd; menu Rs 3400; ☒ noon-3pm & 7-10pm Mon-Sat) For those with wider wallets, this intriguing dining option is located within an old mill that has been transformed into Victoria 1840 (p128), an oddly charming gallery space. Crisp white cloths are draped over the tables and canvases of wicked brush strokes adorn the cracked brick walls. The food, a modern nod to traditional island flavours, mirrors the old-meets-new surrounds.

## Getting There & Around

There are no direct buses between Port Louis and Trou d'Eau Douce. You'll need to change at Centre de Flacq, from where onward services to Trou d'Eau Douce run roughly every half-hour. Taxis cost around Rs 500 from Centre de Flacq, Rs 1700 to the airport and Rs 1500 to Port Louis.

For information about transport to Île aux Cerfs, see p131.

## ÎLE AUX CERFS

Like Marilyn Monroe and Cleopatra, Île aux Cerfs' killer looks have triggered its demise. Once sparsely populated by *cerfs* (stags; imported for hunting from Java), this picturesque island is now overrun with touts and tourists baking under the tropical sun or lazing in the perfect, gin-clear waters. The obtrusive crowds and general summer-camp vibe may be off-putting at first, but few people realise that the island boasts over 4km of sandy bliss. Hike a mere kilometre down the beach and you'll uncover an idyllic ocean vista all to yourself.

Much of the island's interior belongs to the Touessrok's stunningly manicured 18-hole golf course – perhaps one of the most scenic spots to tee off in the world. Nonguests are welcome to play, although advance bookings are essential. Island guests are politely asked to stay off the greens and fairways lest they be conked in the head by a soaring Titleist.

There's no need to pack a picnic when visiting Île aux Cerfs – the island has four eating options, three of which are very reasonably priced considering the luxurious Touessrok (p130) owns the land deed.

**Sands Snack Bar** (mains Rs 250; ☒ 9am-5pm) A great place for light bites, sandwiches and juicy hamburgers. Tasty cocktails are served between noon and 4pm.

**La Chaumière Masala** (mains Rs 250-360; ☒ noon-3pm) This memorable dining experience offers Indian dishes refined to the European palate. Tables are perched in trees.

**Paul & Virginie** (mains Rs 400; 🕑 noon-3.30pm) A sociable spot at the watersports centre serving a scrumptious assortment of fresh fish and seafood. Popular with tour groups.

**Clubhouse Restaurant** (mains Rs 600-700; 🕑 breakfast & lunch) Classic (and pricey) international fare served at the golf course's clubhouse. Fairway fuel rather than a culinary endeavour.

## Getting There & Away

Despite what the signs say, there is no public ferry to Île aux Cerfs. Guests of Le Touessrok get whisked over to the island for free on the hotel launch. Lesser mortals must choose from a variety of dizzying transport options. If you have a private vehicle, the cheapest way to reach the island is by taking Le Touessrok's public boat from the Embarquadère de Pointe Maurice (drive past the entrance to Le Touessrok and follow the signs for the golf course). The journey costs Rs 250 round trip and boats depart every 20 minutes between 9am and 5pm.

Dozens of boat operators run by former fishermen in Trou d'Eau Douce offer a water-taxi service to the island for Rs 350 round trip. Ask at your accommodation to be set up with a reliable option or try **Bateaux Vicky** (Map p127; ☎ /754 5597; bateauxvicky@yahoo.com; Royal Rd; 🕑 9am-5pm). The taxi boats run roughly every 20 to 30 minutes between 9am and 4pm, with the last boat back at 5pm (the island 'closes' to visitors at 5pm sharp). The trip takes between 15 and 30 minutes depending on your point of departure. It's not necessary to book ahead. Many of these local operators also offer a side trip to the waterfalls at Grande Rivière Sud-Est (Rs 600) or a beachside barbecue on the island (Rs 1000).

The other way to reach the island is on a popular catamaran day trip, which usually includes snorkelling, sunbathing and a belly-widening barbecue lunch. Check out www.mauritiuscatamaran.com for a list of day-trip options.

# BELLE MARE & PALMAR

North of Trou d'Eau Douce as far as Pointe de Flacq, a 10km-long beach includes some of the best white sand and azure ocean in Mauritius. Unsurprisingly, the area is also home to an impregnable string of luxury resorts.

## Information

The small junction township of Belle Mare has a few services, including a bank and several superettes. You'll also find banking services along the coastal road leading to Le Saint Géran resort along the dead-end Pointe de Flacq.

## Sights & Activities

### HINDU TEMPLE

Besides the endless vistas of azure, the area doesn't boast a whole lot when it comes to sights other than a gorgeous **Hindu temple** (🕑 dawn-dusk) that sits on a teeny islet tenuously tethered to the mainland by a thin landbridge. The views of the dazzling white bastion are best appreciated from Rasoi (p133), the Indian restaurant at Le Saint Géran.

### WATERSPORTS

Mauritius' east coast has a few notable dive sites, including **Belmar Pass** nearby. The area's five-star hotels – including Le Saint Géran, Beau Rivage and Belle Mare Plage – all have reputable scuba outfits. See p28 for more information about diving in the area, or visit www.msda.mu for a complete list of insured operators.

For a fun half-day away from the beach, swing by **Le Waterpark & Leisure Village** (Map p127; ☎ 415 2626; www.lewaterpark.intnet.mu; Coastal Rd; adult/child Rs 300/160; 🕑 10am-5.30pm), which offers rides, slides and thrills aplenty spread across 10 hectares of an old sugar estate.

### GOLF

The endless proliferation of top-end sleeps means that there are plenty of places to tee off in the area. In addition to the golf courses

---

**SATURDAY NIGHTS ON ÎLE AUX CERFS**

Taking a cue from Ibiza and Nikki Beach, the management of Le Touessrok turns the sands of Île aux Cerfs into a raging dance floor every Saturday night between October and March. The all-night romp fest starts at 11pm and DJ-ed beats blare until 5am. Admission costs Rs 500 and includes boat service and one drink.

further south at Anahita and Le Touessrok, you'll find greens at Belle Mare Plage and Le Saint Géran.

## SPA

Most of Mauritius' top-end resorts have an on-site spa, but if you're looking for a unique pampering experience try the **Pedi:Mani:Cure Studio** (Map p127; ☎ 401 1688; Le Saint Géran, Pointe de Flacq; ⊙ 9am-8pm) at the Saint Géran. Developed by renowned French podiatrist Bastien Gonzalez, the not-to-be-missed treatment (Rs 5500) invigorates and revives tired hands and feet, giving them a radiant glow.

## Sleeping

The sandy beaches of Belle Mare and Palmar offer the highest density of upmarket hotels on the island – each one an opulent attempt to outdo the next. In addition to the endless row of top-end resorts, vacationers will be delighted to find a cache of stately seaside villas.

### APARTMENTS & VILLAS

Tucked betwixt the five-star grandeur of rambling resorts is a noteworthy selection of private villas – the perfect choice for those seeking solitude. Like the hotels next door, the villas come equipped with daily maid and concierge services (you can even request an in-house chef for an additional fee).

The following agencies manage a wide selection of properties, and costs range from €150 to €1000:

**EasyRent** ( ☎ 452 1010; www.easyrent.mu) Ask about the newly built Villa Bali (€500).

**Idyllic Villas** (www.idyllic-mauritius.com)

### HOTELS & RESORTS

The following selection includes our favourite hotels in the area and should not be considered exhaustive. All of these resorts should be booked well in advance through a travel agent – the public rates (listed here) are downright scary.

**Emeraude** (Map p127; ☎ 415 1107; www.emeraude mauritius.com; Belle Mare; d incl half board €145; ✴ 🖵 ⏺ ) Set in a breezy garden facing the public beach in Belle Mare, Emeraude is breath of fresh air from the sky-high walls of the neighbouring five-star compounds. Some 20 semidetached cottage units with gabled roofs frame a sociable pool area, an open-air restaurant and a bar.

**La Palmeraie** (Map p127; ☎ 401 8500; www. palmeraie-hotel.com; Palmar; s/d incl half board €205/304;

✴ 🖵 ⏺ 🔲 ) It may seem a bit strange to travel all the way to Mauritius in order to visit Morocco, but La Palmeraie's lavish kasbah theme seems to be a hit with tourists. Gossamer drapery and stylish adobe turrets reek of 'boutique chic' as they play up the idea of an Arabian mirage. We much prefer the common spaces to the private suites – the design scheme in the rooms feels tacked on rather than seamlessly incorporated into the architecture.

**Belle Mare Plage** (Map p127; ☎ 402 2600; www.bel lemareplagehotel.com; Pointe de Flacq; d incl half board €540; ✴ 🖵 ⏺ 🔲 ) One of Mauritius' most delightful and exclusive hotels, the Belle Mare Plage quite simply ticks every box. Pass through the inviting lobby – scented with vanilla and ylang-ylang, no less – before uncovering an enviable beach and cache of top-notch amenities. Golfers relish the two championship-level courses and well-respected academy, spa fanatics purr like a kitten while being pummelled by expert massage therapists, and gourmet buffs are sated at the superb Blue Penny Café.

**our pick Le Saint Géran** (Map p127; ☎ 401 1688; www.oneandonlylesaintgeran.com; Pointe de Flacq; ste incl half board €1045; ✴ 🖵 ⏺ 🔲 ) There's no other way to say it, Le Saint Géran is classic Mauritian luxury at its finest. And the clientele seems to agree. The resort sees more repeat customers than any other top-end hotel on the island (and these aren't your average vacationers – the guest list is a veritable who's who of movie stars and politicos). Spacious rooms, under the signature bright-blue roofs, are arranged along the seemingly endless oceanfront – everyone has a to-die-for view. Watersports are aplenty, there's a charming kids club for the little ones, and the top-notch butler service caters to every request. Le Saint Géran has set the bar unobtainably high in the dining category as well. Two of the three on-site restaurants were created by Michelin-star chefs – Rasoi (p133), an Indian eatery set on a stunning pavilion, and Spoon des Îles (p133), the inventive masterpiece by well-known chef Alain Ducasse. An extensive renovation is planned in the near future.

**our pick Le Prince Maurice** (Map p127; ☎ 413 9130; www.princemaurice.com; Pointe de Flacq; s/d incl half board €720/960; ✴ 🖵 ⏺ 🔲 ) The sense of grace and perfect tranquillity is immediately striking as you pass through the entryway – this is a world unto itself that knows no limit to luxury. The lobby's seamless melange of marble architecture and flowing infinity pools can only be described as sublime, and the opulent suites, hidden just beyond, continue the timeless elegance. The abundance of open-air pavilions and elegant thatch is meant to elicit the ancient days of the spice trade – modern amenities are cleverly hidden and butlers are dressed in muted tones as they move across the grounds catering to every whim. Swimming pools, spas, access to Belle Mare Plage's golf courses and a floating restaurant (you'll see) round out the amenities list.

Also worth a look:

**Beau Rivage** (Map p127; ☎ 402 2000; www.naiade. com; Belle Mare; s/d incl half board from €468/694; 🕸 🖵 🛜 🔊 ) A stylish hotel and jewel in the crown of the Naiade group. The three-storey thatched villas, grouped around a huge pool, blend seamlessly with the abounding palms. Perfect for romance.

**Residence** (Map p127; ☎ 401 8888; www.theresidence. com; Belle Mare; s/d incl half board from €405/582; 🕸 🖵 🛜 🔊 ) Evoking the forgotten grandeur of colonial India, the Residence's vast complex of hotel rooms occupies an enviable stretch of sand. Rooms are simply decorated – white drapery everywhere and framed Darwin-esque animal sketches on the walls.

## Eating

As the hotels here are so all-encompassing, there is little incentive for guests to leave their resorts and dine elsewhere. All of the hotels, however, welcome nonguests to dine at their à la carte restaurants, and the choice is superb. Prices are consummately high, but it's well worth stopping by for a special occasion.

**Symon's Restaurant** (Map p127; ☎ 415 1135; Belle Mare; mains Rs 230-900; 🕑 10am-10pm) The best (and pretty much only) option in Belle Mare beyond the all-star line-up of in-house hotel restaurants, Symon serves up a variety of Indian, Mauritian and Chinese dishes. The views are ho-hum, but at least you won't break the bank.

**Rasoi** (Map p127; ☎ 401 1688; Le Saint Géran, Pointe de Flacq; mains Rs 600-1300; 🕑 12.30-3.30pm & 7-10pm) Rasoi is the brainchild of Vineet Bhatia, a Michelin-star chef who made a name for himself in the London restaurant scene. The dining area is situated upon an open-air verandah made of slatted jungle trunks tucked under a generous awning of thatch. While appreciating the views of the lagoon, cane-draped hills and a Taj Mahal–like temple, guests savour a dynamic assortment of Indian-inspired

dishes. The lunch menu features a more casual selection of *naan* wraps and seafood samplers (the salmon is breathtaking); dinner is decidedly more sophisticated. Reservations required.

**our pick** **Spoon des Îles** (Map p127; ☎ 401 1688; Le Saint Géran, Pointe de Flacq; mains Rs 1300-2200; 🕑 dinner Tue-Sun) If the name Alain Ducasse doesn't ring a bell, then how about the term 'Michelin-star chef'? Undoubtedly the island's finest dining address, this ode to *haute cuisine* is Ducasse's first out-of-France avatar of the award-winning Spoon franchise. The parade of dishes and expertly matched wines rolls out like a pitch-perfect performance. The first act features an intriguing assortment of entrées that play with taste, temperature and texture. The bombastic second act focuses on signature main dishes like seared tuna, grilled venison and flavourful lamb. Dessert is a seemingly unending set of curtain calls: a triple-chocolate platter, a box of bite-sized treats, home-baked madeleines and a giant meringue to take home as a souvenir. If you're celebrating any event during your holiday in Mauritius, make sure you do it here (and make sure you come with an empty stomach – this isn't one of those upmarket restaurants that serves two-bite dishes!). Reservations required.

## Getting There & Around

For information on transport, see p128.

## POSTE DE FLACQ & ROCHES NOIRES
pop 7100

Even quieter and more rugged than the sandy streamers of Belle Mare, this calm area bordering the island's north still has a distinctive Creole vibe and feels generally unmarred by upmarket developers. Holidaymakers seeking tranquillity should look no further than the lovely selection of private villas dotting the stone-strewn coast.

## Sleeping
### APARTMENTS & VILLAS

With a noticeable lack of resorts, Poste de Flacq is a haven for upscale villa rentals that work out to be a much better deal than many of the luxury hotel packages (especially if you're travelling with friends and/or family). Contact **EasyRent** ( ☎ 452 1010; www.easyrent.mu) or **CG Villas** ( ☎ 262 5777; www.villas-maurice.com) to organise your stay – they manage a sizeable collection of beach houses in the area.

The following villas are worth a special mention:

**Villa Lafayette** (Map p127; ☎ 262 5777; www.villas-maurice.com; Royal Rd, Poste Lafayette; villas €360; ☒ ☒ ) This traditional Mauritian beach house feels slightly Mediterranean with its white-and-blue colour scheme. The pool is tucked within an interior courtyard and the backyard faces a wild stretch of sand and sea.

**Villa La Mauricienne** (Map p127; ☎ 262 5777; www.villas-maurice.com; Royal Rd, Poste Lafayette; villas €500; ☒ ☒ ) Sheltered by a massive roof of thatch and bamboo, this opulent retreat feels decidedly Asian in theme with abounding bursts of fuchsia and orange. The master suite is lofted above the open-air terrace, which looks out over the enormous swimming pool and giant strip of private sand.

**our pick** **L'Ilot** (Map p127; ☎ 452 1010; www.easyrent.mu; Royal Rd, Roches Noires; villas €780-1080; ☒ ☎ ) If you've got money to burn, let this be your pyre. Go one better than staying at a five-star resort and rent out your own private island! This stunning four-bedroom masterpiece sits on its own islet attached to the mainland by a concreted bridge made from boulders.

### GUESTHOUSES & CHAMBRES D'HÔTES

**our pick** **La Maison d'Été** (Map p127; ☎ 410 5039; www.lamaisondete.com; Poste Lafayette; d incl breakfast Rs 2100; ☒ ☐ ☎ ☒ ) La Maison d'Été is ranked as one of Mauritius' top B&Bs on a certain trip-advising website, and we can definitely understand why. The Franco-Mauritian owners have hit the nail on the head; an effortless tropical charm pervades the collection of poolside rooms, each one decorated with tasteful tributes to island life. The property also has an inviting restaurant, Auberg'inn.

### Eating

Besides the *case*-like superettes dotting the coastal road, there's only one restaurant of note in this area of the east coast. If you're staying at a villa and are interested in freshly caught seafood, ask your villa operator to contact one of the local fishermen – they'll deliver whole fish and langoustes directly to your door.

**Auberg'inn** (Map p127; ☎ 410 5039; Poste Lafayette; pizzas Rs 230, mains Rs 390-1600; ☺ lunch & dinner Tue-Sat, dinner Sun-Mon) La Maison d'Été's in-house restaurant is run like a stand-alone establishment serving up an enticing assortment of pasta, fish, and 'fusion food'. The inn's owner often moonlights as the chef and takes special care when preparing locally sourced dishes matched with international wines. The menu is limited to pizza on Sunday evenings.

### Getting There & Around

For details on transport, see p128.

## CENTRE DE FLACQ
pop 17,700

Centre de Flacq is a world away from the east's postcard-perfect coast. This chaotic junction feels much more like the other inland townships and offers relatively little to tourists.

If you venture 5km west of Centre de Flacq along the Rte A7 towards Quartier Militaire, you'll come across **Flacq Union of Estates Limited** (FUEL; Map p127; ☎ 413 2583), the largest and most modern sugar mill on the island. It may be possible to tour the facility during harvest season (July to November) – call for details.

Also on Rte A7 in the town of St Julien is **Chez Manuel** (Map p127; ☎ 418 3599; mains Rs 200-900; ☺ lunch & dinner Mon-Sat), a popular restaurant with smiling staff and scrumptious Chinese cuisine.

### Getting There & Away

For transport information, see p128.

# Rodrigues

Blissfully isolated over 600km northeast of the mainland, this tiny volcanic outcrop is a stunning mountainous gem that barely feels connected to its big sister, Mauritius, let alone the wider world.

Often billed as the 'Mauritius of 25 years ago', Rodrigues actually bears little resemblance to its neighbour beyond the scenic strips of peach-tinged sand. The island's population of 37,000 is predominantly African and Creole – a far cry from the ethnic melting pot next door. You won't find a stalk of sugar cane here either – Rodrigues' hilly interior is clothed with fruit-bearing trees and vast acreages of vegetable patches. While the pace of life is undeniably slow – which gives the island its time-warped vibe – the atmosphere is friendly and relaxed, rather than incorrigibly boring. In fact, visitors can partake in a variety of blood-pumping activities from kitesurfing in the turquoise lagoon to hiking through the lush interior.

While Mauritius uses its manmade spoils to attract the jetset crowd, Rodrigues hopes to play its 'green' card and lure a different subset of travellers. Over the last few years, locals have started to address the island's environmental issues in earnest. Shoals Rodrigues, a local NGO, is working with the native fishermen to curb unsustainable catching practices. The François Leguat Reserve has jumpstarted a successful program to repopulate the island with giant tortoises. Strict construction laws forbidding rambling beachside resorts have already begun to preserve the charming constellation of local *chambres d'hôtes* (family-run B&Bs).

Although the island will never be the untouched kingdom discovered some 400 years ago, Rodrigues is nonetheless a fabulous hideaway whose star attraction – the idyllic lagoon – will remain a cherished memory for every visitor.

**HIGHLIGHTS**

- Snapping photos of the azure lagoon and hunting for hidden treasure along the rugged **east-coast beaches** (p139)
- Savouring traditional Rodriguan eats at a local **table d'hôte** (p142)
- Hitching a ride with a local fisherman for a picnic lunch or an overnight camping trip on one of the lagoon's glittering **offshore islets** (p140)
- Cavorting with hundreds of curious tortoises at the **François Leguat Reserve** (p137)
- Gliding across the sea while enjoying the thrills and spills of **kitesurfing** (p140)

RODRIGUES

# HISTORY

Rodrigues is named after the Portuguese navigator Don Diégo Rodriguez, who was the first European to discover the uninhabited island in 1528. Dutch sailors were the next to pay a call, albeit very briefly, in 1601, followed a few years later by the French.

At first Rodrigues was simply a place where ships could take refuge from storms and replenish their supplies of fresh water and meat. Giant tortoises were especially prized since they could be kept alive on board for months. Over the years thousands were taken or killed until they completely died out. Rodrigues also had a big flightless bird, the solitaire, which went the same sorry way as its distant cousin, the dodo.

The first serious attempt at colonisation occurred in 1691 when Frenchman François Leguat and a band of seven Huguenot companions fled religious persecution at home in search of a 'promised land'. They made a good stab at it. Crops grew well and the island's fauna and flora were a source of wonder. Even so, after two years, life on a paradise island began to pall, not least due to the lack of female company. With no boat of their own (the ship they arrived on failed to return as promised), Leguat and his friends built a craft out of driftwood and eventually made it to Mauritius.

The next group to arrive were far more determined. In 1735, the French founded a permanent colony on Rodrigues as part of a European power struggle to control the Indian Ocean. They established a small settlement at Port Mathurin, but a lack of leadership coupled with the difficult climate meant the colony never really prospered. When the British – who wanted a base from which to attack French-ruled Mauritius – invaded in 1809, they were met with little resistance.

One of the more important events under British rule was the arrival of telecommunications in 1901. Rodrigues was one of the staging posts for the undersea cable linking Britain and Australia. The old Cable & Wireless offices are still to be seen at Pointe Canon above Port Mathurin.

Then, in 1967, Rodriguans distinguished themselves by voting against independence from Britain by a whopping 90% (the rest of Mauritius voted strongly in favour). It was a dramatic illustration of the difference in outlook between the two islands. Following independence, Rodriguans continued to argue that their needs were significantly different from the rest of the country and that, in any case, they were being neglected by the central government. What they wanted was a greater say in their own future.

The campaign was led by Serge Clair and his Organisation du Peuple de Rodrigues (OPR), founded in 1976. His patience and political skill eventually paid off. In 2001 it was announced that Rodrigues would be allowed a degree of autonomy, notably in socioeconomic affairs and in the management of their natural resources. The following year 18 counsellors were elected; the Regional Assembly was formally inaugurated in 2002 with Serge Clair as Chief Commissioner. The assembly is now trying to tackle the overriding problems of population growth and poverty. In addition, complete independence is still a fervent desire for many. In April 2010, the Muvman Independantis Rodriguais (MIR) was launched when two candidates ran for government positions as 'Rodriguans' rather than 'Mauritians' – their claims were denied. Efforts to break away will undoubtedly continue as the movement gains momentum.

Today the economic mainstays of Rodrigues are fishing and agriculture, with tourism and handicrafts playing an increasingly important role. Plans for the island's own air carrier, the aptly named SolitAir, are well underway – locals remain positive that the island will become a hotspot for 'green' tourism.

## ORIENTATION

The island of Rodrigues is 8km wide and 18km long, with a steep, hilly interior and a series of shallow bays that scallop the island's edge like crocodile teeth. A shimmering lagoon – over three times the size of the island itself – surrounds the island like an azure halo.

The airport is located in the island's west end – a tract of land that is generally unpopulated and mostly visited by curious tourists coming to check out a series of caves and a turtle conversation centre. Port Mathurin, located in the middle of the northern coast, is the main economic centre of the island and the unofficial capital. Most visitors stay at accommodation further east in the Anse Aux Anglais area and inland around Grande Montagne. As the shoreline curves down to form the east coast, Rodrigues reveals its stunning cache of bleach-blonde sand. Quiet beaches and scenic trails dot the landscape in the southeast as well.

## INFORMATION

### Emergency

**Port Mathurin Pharmacy** (Map p139; ☎ 831 2279; Rue de la Solidarité; ☿ 7.30am-4.30pm Mon-Fri, 7.30am-3pm Sat, 7.30-11am Sun) The only pharmacy on the island.

**Queen Elizabeth Hospital** (Map p138; ☎ 831 1628) The island's main hospital is at Crève Coeur, immediately east of Port Mathurin.

### Internet Access

Only a couple of hotels and guesthouses have internet connections.

**RodNet** (Map p138; ☎ 831 0747; Rue Johnston, Port Mathurin; per min Rs 3; ☿ 8.30am-4pm Mon-Fri, 8.30am-noon Sat) Discounts for longer surfing time (Rs 300 for five hours). Turtle-speed connection.

### Money

Most of the island's banks are in Port Mathurin and flank Rue Max Lucchesi. Mont Lubin and La Ferme also have banks, and there's an ATM at the airport.

**Barclays** (Map p139; ☎ 831 1553; Rue de la Solidarité, Port Mathurin)

**Mauritius Commercial Bank** (MCB; Map p139; ☎ 831 1833; Rue Max Lucchesi, Port Mathurin)

**State Bank** (Map p139; ☎ 831 1642; Rue Max Lucchesi, Port Mathurin)

### Post

**Central Post Office** (Map p139; ☎ 831 2098; Rue de la Solidarité, Port Mathurin; ☿ 8.15-11.15am & noon-4pm Mon-Fri, 8.15-11.45am Sat) There are tiny satellite offices in Mont Lubin, La Ferme and Grande Montragne.

### Tourist Information

There's a small but helpful **tourist office** (Map p139; ☎ 832 0867; www.rodrigues-island.org; Rue de la Solidarité, Port Mathurin; ☿ 8am-4pm Mon-Fri, 8am-noon Sat) in La

Résidence. Pamphlets and brochures offer information on tours and *chambres d'hôtes*. The Carte Verte (p139) is not available here.

## SIGHTS

Besides Rodrigues' golden beaches – the best of which flank the island's eastern ridges – there are several interesting sights to take in, including a couple of caves and several noteworthy architectural contributions.

### Port Mathurin

This tiny port is the island's hub and, for want of a better word, its capital. The island is run from the local legislative assembly here, although it feels very far from being an administrative centre. The word 'soporific' may come to mind, but during the day the town has a friendly and happening vibe – especially around the buzzing market stalls.

One of the oldest buildings still standing in Port Mathurin, **La Résidence** (Map p139; Rue de la Solidarité) dates from 1897, when it provided a fairly modest home for the British Chief Commissioner. Its facilities are now used as function rooms for the new Regional Assembly.

For fine views over Port Mathurin and the lagoon, there's an easy 1km walk from the end of Rue Mamzelle Julia to a lookout atop Mt Fanal. At dusk this is a good place to see Rodrigues fruit bats.

### François Leguat Reserve

In 1691, François Leguat described Rodrigues as a 'paradise island', and this **giant tortoise and cave reserve** ( ☎ 832 8141; www.tortoisecavereserve-rodrigues. com; adult/child Rs 265/130; ☿ 9am-5.30pm, tours at 10.30am, 12.30pm & 2.30pm) has grand plans to re-create the veritable Eden described in the logbooks of

---

**THE LAGOON ISLANDS**

There are 17 small islands sprinkled around Rodrigues' lagoon. **Île aux Cocos**, barely 1km in length, is a nature reserve and bird sanctuary populated by small colonies of noddies and lesser noddies. It is only possible to visit Île aux Cocos on a guided tour (Rs 900 to Rs 1000 per person including park admission and a picnic lunch), which can be arranged through hotels and tour agents. The boat trip takes at least an hour each way and usually runs between 10am and 3pm. During high tide, when the waves cover up the marshy areas, the island feels like a magical sandbar floating in the blue.

**Île Hermitage**, a tiny island renowned for its beauty (and possible hidden treasure), and **Île aux Chats** are both accessible by boat from Port Sud-Est. The latter is rather unremarkable, but the surrounding reef makes it a popular destination for snorkellers and divers.

Sunday is the most ideal time to visit these islets since most businesses are closed on Rodrigues.

# RODRIGUES

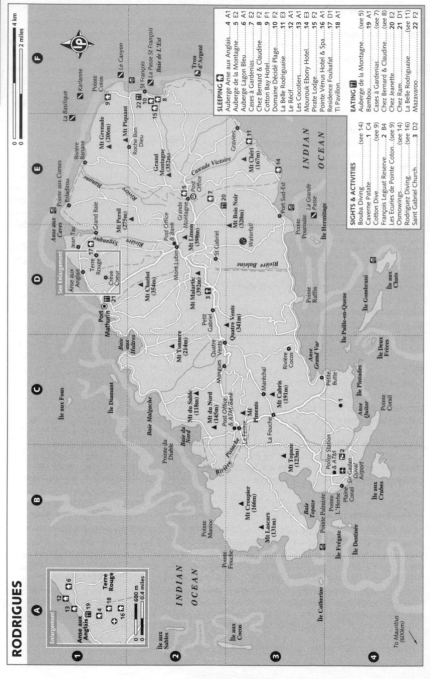

**SLEEPING**
Auberge Anse aux Anglais......4 A1
Auberge de la Montagne.........5 E2
Auberge Lagon Bleu...............6 A1
Cases à Gardenias..................7 E2
Chez Bernard & Claudine.......8 F2
Cotton Bay Hotel...................9 F1
Domaine Décidé Plage.........10 F2
La Belle Rodriguaise............11 E3
Le Récif.............................12 A1
Les Cocotiers.....................13 A1
Mourouk Ebony Hotel..........14 E3
Pirate Lodge.......................15 F2
Pointe Vénus Hotel & Spa....16 A1
Residence Foulsafat.............17 D1
Ti Pavillon.........................18 A1

**EATING**
Auberge de la Montagne.....(see 5)
Bambou...............................1 C4
Cases à Gardenias.............(see 7)
Chez Bernard & Claudine...(see 8)
Chez Jeanette....................19 A1
Chez Ram..........................20 E2
La Belle Rodriguaise.........21 D1
Mazavaroo.........................22 F2

**SIGHTS & ACTIVITIES**
Bouba Diving.....................(see 14)
Caverne Patate....................1 C4
Cotton Dive......................(see 7)
François Leguat Reserve.......2 B4
Les Écuries de Pointe Coton..(see 9)
Osmowings.......................(see 14)
Rodriguez Diving................(see 16)
Saint Gabriel Church............3 D2

the island's early explorers. The project is well underway – hundreds of Malagasy tortoises roam the grounds (the outcome of a successful breeding program); there's a small enclosure with several giant fruit bats (the island's only endemic mammal); and roughly 115,000 indigenous trees have been planted over the last four years (sadly the island does not have any remaining old-growth forest). The on-site museum is also worth a look, as it recounts the history and settlement of the island, and offers detailed information about the extinct solitaire, cousin of the like-fated dodo. Don't miss the guided tours of the on-site caves. Spirited tour leaders point out quirky rock shapes and discuss the island's interesting geological history. Keep an eye out for the tibia bone of a solitaire that juts out from the cavern's stone ceiling.

## Caverne Patate

Caverne Patate, in the southwest corner of the island, is an impressive cave system with a few stalagmite and stalactite formations. There are four **guided tours** (admission Rs 75) daily, usually at 9am, 11am, 1pm and 3pm, during which a guide points out formations with uncanny resemblances to a dodo, Buckingham Palace and even Winston Churchill! The 700m tunnel is an easy walk, but gets slippery in wet weather; wear shoes with a good grip and take a light jacket or pullover.

The track to the caves is signposted off the road from La Ferme to Petite Butte. Buses en route to La Fourche can drop you off at the turn-off.

## Saint Gabriel Church

This surprisingly grand church, situated in the middle of the island, has one of the largest congregations in the Port Louis diocese. Constructed between 1936 and 1939, the impressive place of worship was built by local volunteers who arduously lugged stone, sand and coral from all corners of the island. Christianity is an integral part of life on the island – hundreds upon hundreds of Rodriguans gather here every Sunday.

## ACTIVITIES
### Hiking

Hiking is the best way to uncover the island's natural treasures – most notably, its wild,

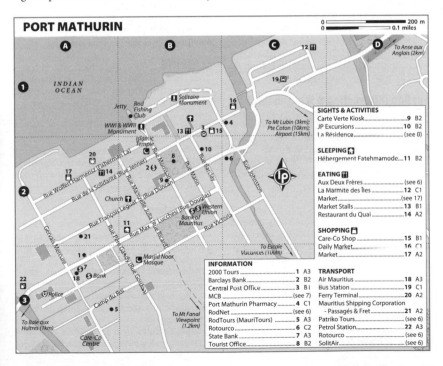

**PORT MATHURIN**

0 ____ 200 m
0 ____ 0.1 miles

INDIAN OCEAN

To Anse aux Anglais (2km)

To Mt Lubin (3km);
Pte Coton (10km);
Airport (15km)

To Escale Vacances (100m)

To Mt Fanal Viewpoint (1.2km)

To Baie aux Huîtres (1km)

Care-Co Centre

**SIGHTS & ACTIVITIES**
Carte Verte Kiosk................9 B2
JP Excursions.....................10 B2
La Résidence.................(see 8)

**SLEEPING**
Hébergement Fatehmamode...11 B2

**EATING**
Aux Deux Frères...............(see 6)
La Marmite des Îles..........12 C1
Market..........................(see 17)
Market Stalls...................13 B1
Restaurant du Quai...........14 A2

**SHOPPING**
Care-Co Shop...................15 B1
Daily Market....................16 C1
Market...........................17 A2

**INFORMATION**
2000 Tours.......................1 A3
Barclays Bank....................2 B2
Central Post Office..............3 B1
MCB...........................(see 6)
Port Mathurin Pharmacy.........4 C1
RodNet........................(see 6)
RodTours (MauriTours)..........5 A3
Rotourco.........................6 C2
State Bank.......................7 A3
Tourist Office...................8 B2

**TRANSPORT**
Air Mauritius....................18 A3
Bus Station......................19 C1
Ferry Terminal..................20 A2
Mauritius Shipping Corporation
- Passagés & Fret..............21 A3
Patriko Tours................(see 6)
Petrol Station..................22 A3
Rotourco....................(see 6)
SolitAir.......................(see 6)

undeveloped beaches. The newly conceived Carte Verte de Rodrigues, published by the Association Rodrigues Entreprendre Au Féminin, charts the island's eight most popular hikes and provides detailed information on how to access each trailhead using public transportation.

The island's most famous walk (No 4 on the Carte Verte) is the classic coastal trail from St François down to Graviers. On the way you'll pass the island's most stunning stretches of sand, including Trou d'Argent, the supposed location of a pirate's hidden booty.

The Carte Verte is available for purchase (Rs 75) at a kiosk in central Port Mathurin (see Map p139); call ☎ 832 4240 if you're interested in hiring a guide. Any of the local tour agencies can provide guides as well.

### Diving

In general, Rodrigues' marine environment is still remarkably well preserved, making the island an excellent spot for divers. The best sites lie off the east and south coasts (see p30).

The three main dive centres are **Cotton Dive** (Map p138; ☎ 831 8001, 831 8208; diverod@intnet.mu) at the Cotton Bay Hotel, **Bouba Diving** (Map p138; ☎ 832 3063; http://www.boubadiving.com) at the Mourouk Ebony Hotel and **Rodriguez Diving** (Map p138; ☎ 831 0957; http://rodriguez-diving.tripod.com/) at Pointe Vénus Hotel & Spa and Les Cocotiers. Nonguests are always welcome – just ring ahead. Figure on Rs 1700 for a dive and equipment.

### Surfing (Kitesurfing & Windsurfing)

All the pros agree – Rodrigues is one of the best places in the world to kite surf. The top outfitter is **Osmowings** (Map p138; ☎ 832 3051; www.kitesurf-rodrigues.com) based at the Mourouk Ebony Hotel. A two-hour 'initiation' course costs €65 per person. Kitesurf buffs can rent equipment for €19 an hour.

### Fishing

The island's leading deep-sea fishing experts are the **Rod Fishing Club** ( ☎ 875 0616; www.rodfishingclub.com; Terre Rouge) run by Yann Colas, skipper of the Black Marlin, which makes frequent jigging sorties from Port Mathurin. Book via the website or the operator, and meet at the pier.

### Horseback Riding

Rodrigues' rugged landscape is perfect for an afternoon on horseback. The island's best stables are **Les Ecuries de Pointe Coton** (Map p138; ☎ 831 8537, 875 5540; Pointe Coton), located adjacent to the Cotton Bay Hotel. The friendly team can cater to all levels.

## TOURS

Guided tours led by friendly locals are the best way to explore Rodrigues. The most popular outing is a half-day trip to Île aux Cocos (p137) followed by hiking excursions along the wild beaches and hilly interior.

There are several excellent travel agencies in town offering a range of activities, accommodation, tours and vehicle rentals. The tourist office has a small photocopied sheet with the phone numbers of a dozen boatswains willing to take tourists out to the various islets in the turquoise lagoon.

**2000 Tours** (Map p139; ☎ 831 1894; 2000trs@intnet. mu; Rue Max Lucchesi)

**Beraca** ( ☎ 831 2198; tropicalguy17@caramail.com; Baie aux Huitres)

**JP Excursions** (Map p139; ☎ 831 1162; www.jpexcursion -rodrigues.com; Rue Barclay)

**Patriko Tours** (Map p139; ☎ 831 2044; patrikotours@yahoo. com; Rue François Leguat)

**RodTours** (Map p139; ☎ 831 2249; www.mauritours. net; Mont Venus) Part of MauriTours.

**Rotourco** (Map p139; ☎ 831 0747; www.rotourco.com; Rue François Leguat) Offers adorable studio accommodation in Baie Malagache (Rs 2500). Highly recommended.

## SLEEPING

Your choice of accommodation will largely affect your experience on Rodrigues. While Port Mathurin and Anse aux Anglais are convenient to activities and 'nightlife' (we're using that term *very* loosely here), the guesthouses in the quieter parts of the island offer the getaway-from-it-all experience par excellence. While we highly recommend the *chambres d'hôtes*, there are a couple of lovely upmarket hotels for those seeking a pinch of luxury.

### Port Mathurin

Port Mathurin makes a convenient base if you are travelling by bus, but frankly it lacks the characterful *chambres d'hôtes* you'll find elsewhere on the island.

**Hébergement Fatehmamode** (Map p139; ☎ 831 2607; mahmood@intnet.mu; Rue Max Lucchesi; apt from Rs 500; 🖾) Right in the centre of town, these no-frills rooms are about as cheap as things get on the island.

**Escale Vacances** (Map p139; ☎ 831 2555; www. escalevacances-rodrigues.com; Rue Johnston, Fond La Digue;

s/d incl breakfast €74/120, incl half board Rs 84/140; ⚇ ▣ )
Located just outside the town centre, Port
Mathurin's most upmarket option lives in a
converted colonial mansion that feels somewhat like an old schoolhouse. There is, however, something rather elegant and country
club-esque about the pool area out the back
– you just have to ignore the exposed air-con
units tacked on to the facade.

## North Coast

The main concentration of hotels and guesthouses is found 2km east of Port Mathurin at
Anse aux Anglais, although this isn't the best
place to truly get away from it all.

### ANSE AUX ANGLAIS

The tourist hub of Anse Aux Anglais is a
15-minute walk from the bus station in Port
Mathurin.

**Auberge Lagon Bleu** (Map p138; ☎ 831 0075;
www.aubergelagonbleu.com; Caverne Provert; s/d/tr
Rs600/800/1000; ⚇ ) Wicker baskets and colourful paintings abound at this very casual guesthouse on the road towards Jean Tac. Guests
congregate in the sociable eating area tucked
under tin roofing and drooping laundry lines.
Fresh coats of paint have spruced up the otherwise Spartan bedrooms. It's an additional
Rs 420 per person for half board.

**Ti Pavillon** (Map p138; ☎ 875 0707; www.tipavillon.
com; s/d incl breakfast €26/35; ⚇ ▣ 🛜 ) This friendly
spot welcomes guests with wallet-pleasing
prices and simple digs painted in bright primary colours. The common spaces are cluttered with wonderful bits and bobs – Chinese
lanterns and handmade woodcuts dangle
over head, tropical fish blow bubbles in the
aquarium, furnishings are made from a ragtag
assortment of tree stumps and patio furniture,
and staircases seem to ramble off in different
directions much like an Escher drawing.

**Auberge Anse aux Anglais** (Map p138; ☎ 831 2179,
832 0537; www.rodrigues-vacances.com; Anse aux Anglais;
s/d incl half board €34/50; ⚇ ▣ ) Tucked down a
side street behind Auberge Les Filaos, this
well-positioned guesthouse is in need of a
designer's touch. The basic rooms feel prison-
esque and the unattractive lobby has sterile
linoleum tile that orbits the small trapezoidal
swimming pool. Nevertheless, travellers still
seem to gravitate towards this place since the
price tag is quite reasonable.

**Le Récif** (Map p138; ☎ 831 1804; lerecif@intnet.mu;
Caverne Provert; s/d incl half board Rs 1250/2100; ⚇ )

Perched on the cliff just east of Anse aux
Anglais, Le Récif was under massive renovation at the time of research, but things
look promising – rooms are set to have all
the mod cons and the new restaurant will
offer postcard-worthy views of the emerald
lagoon. Sadly the in-house discotheque has
been closed down.

**Les Cocotiers** (Map p138; ☎ 831 1058; resa@otentik.
mu, www.mauritours.net; s/d with half board from €123/176;
⚇ ▣ ) A great choice at the end of the coastal
road, this friendly resort comes with an airy
restaurant, an inviting swimming pool and a
popular on-site dive centre. Vaco paintings
adorn the walls in the rooms, and the beds
have colourful duvets to match. The hotel
hides a small selection of cheaper sleeps usually reserved for customers from Réunion –
ask about these if you're on a tighter budget.

**Pointe Vénus Hotel & Spa** (Map p138; ☎ 832 0104;
marketing@otentik.mu; Crève Coeur; s/d incl half board
€162/232; ⚇ ▣ ▣ ) Up on a hill in Crève
Coeur, the Pointe Vénus is the area's best attempt at high-end luxury. While the public
areas are charming and well manicured, the
rooms are rather ho-hum, sporting standard
catalogue furniture. The hotel is a consider-
able distance from the sea, but the pool area
(with a charming gazebo) is very welcoming
and has great views out over the village and
lagoon. If you're eyeing an upmarket option,
go for the Mourouk or Cotton Bay instead.

### GRAND BAIE

**Residence Foulsafat** (Map p138; ☎ 831 1760; www.
residencefoulsafat.com; Jean Tac; d incl half board €60) High
up in the hills with memorable views of the
infinite blue, this friendly option has three
charming houses each with a unique design
and theme. Our favourite was the adorable
honeymooners' cottage with stone walls and
attached gazebo covered with gingerbread
trim. The owner moonlights as the island's
consular agent to France.

## Interior

Rodrigues' jungley interior features some of
the most memorable lodging options on the
island. Prince William often stays at the rustic
Domaine de Décidé, hidden deep within the
bush, and frankly not worth hunting down.

**Auberge de la Montagne** (Map p138; ☎ 831 4607;
http://aubergedelamontagne.net.tc; Grande Montagne;
d incl half board €50; ⚇ ) Right at the island's
mountainous heart, this long-established

and much-loved *chambre d'hôte* is run by the charming Baptiste family and set overlooking a wonderful fruit orchard. Twisting hallways – the byproduct of several expansions – lead to three upstairs bedrooms that feel cosy if a bit dated. The meals here are a real highlight here.

**our pick** **Cases à Gardenias** (Map p138; ☎ 832 5751; www.casesagardenias-rodrigues.com; Montagne Bois Noir; d incl half board from €120; ☒ ▣ ) Cases à Gardenias is, without a doubt, the most stylish and unique guesthouse on the island. It's the pride and joy of the lovely owners, a Belgian-Mauritian couple, who have built up their entire property from scratch. The beautiful plantation-inspired bedrooms have lovely stonewashed furniture (made by hand), and in the morning guests can wander the orchards in search of fresh fruit or help the beekeeper tease out the sticky honey from the colourful apiary. At the time of research a second set of rooms was under construction.

### East Coast

#### SAINT FRANÇOIS

**Chez Bernard & Claudine** (Map p138; ☎ 831 8242; cbmoneret@intnet.mu; d incl half board €30; ☒ ) When Saint François was known for its end-of-the-world seclusion, this charming Tudor-style lodge was the only place to hang your hat. Now there are several options in the area, but the well-maintained rooms at Bernard and Claudine's house are still perennially popular among tourists on tighter budgets. Meals here are delicious, and you're well placed for walks along the east coast.

**Domaine Décidé Plage** (Map p138; ☎ 728 7159; www.villarodrigues.com; r/studio from €40/90; ☒ ) Not to be confused with Domaine de Décidé tucked away in the island's interior, this pleasant seaside option has a long, two-storey row of comfortable rooms and less appealing apartments.

**Pirate Lodge** (Map p138; ☎ 831 8775; www.pirate-lodge.com; ste incl breakfast €120; ☒ ) Still sporting that new-car smell, these attractive apartments are set in a scenic palm grove visited by chirping birds. The outside design incorporates colourful Creole-inspired details while the interiors are much more modern – IKEA-esque knickknacks dot the living rooms and fully equipped kitchens.

#### POINTE COTON

**Cotton Bay Hotel** (Map p138; ☎ 831 8001; www.cottonbayhotel.biz; d incl half board €202; ☒ ☒ ) Still going strong after 18 years in the biz, charming Cotton Bay is the island's oldest hotel. The design scheme has a lovely Creole motif – floral trim and tropically inspired prints adorn rooms. Perks include a lovely pirogue-themed restaurant, outings on a private catamaran and endless streamers of honey-tinged sand. Significant discounts are available for guests staying more than five nights. A renovation and expansion is planned for the future – the hotel will be adding several rooms and a high-end spa.

### South Coast

**La Belle Rodriguaise** (Map p138; ☎ 832 4040; www.labellerodriguaise.com; Graviers; d incl half board €70; ☒ ☒ ) Françoise Baptiste's newest endeavour is this inviting seaside retreat near the quaint township of Graviers. Sun-drenched rooms sit in charming *case*-style abodes and have wonderfully unobstructed sea views. Up the hill guests will find an inviting amoeba-shaped pool and a breezy dining room set on a sweeping veranda.

**Mourouk Ebony Hotel** (Map p138; ☎ 832 3351; www.mouroukebonyhotel.com; Mourouk; s/d incl half board €134/199; ☒ ☒ ) The Mourouk Ebony is completely isolated at the end of a wiggling mountain road, and easily recognised from afar by its bright-orange roofing. The grounds feature gorgeous gardens full of orchids and wildflowers that abut the out-of-this-world beach. Gentle Creole beats waft over the lobby's hand-dyed wicker lounge chairs. The rooms, however, could use a little sprucing up; the furniture is a bit worn and the off-white colour scheme evokes coffee-stained teeth.

## EATING

The highlight of any visit to Rodrigues is sampling the unique local cuisine at one of the island's many *tables d'hôtes*. Rodriguans cook a variety of recipes that are quite different from their Mauritian neighbours – less emphasis is placed on spiciness and most meals are cooked with minimal amounts of oil.

### Table d'Hôtes

The following options represent the best and most well known 'hosts' tables' on the island. Meals range from Rs 350 to Rs 700, and you should always call at least one day ahead to make a reservation.

**Auberge de la Montagne** (Map p138; ☎ 831 4607; Grande Montagne) Françoise Baptiste, the delightful author of an eminent Rodriguan cookbook, prepares lip-smacking local specialities.

**Cases à Gardenias** (Map p138; ☎ 832 5751; Montagne Bois Noir) Fantastic hosts serve a smorgasbord of homemade goodies: wine, honey, fresh fruit, preserves and cured meats.

**Chez Bernard & Claudine** (Map p138; ☎ 831 8242; Saint François) This is a great place to break up the journey if you're walking to Trou d'Argent. The speciality is seafood grilled on an open wood fire.

**Chez Jeanette** (Le Tropical; Map p138; ☎ 831 5860; Montagne Bois Noir) Traditional Rodriguan flavours is what you'll get at this friendly spot hidden in the hills. Dishes always feature an assortment of vegetables grown in the property's gardens.

**our pick** **La Belle Rodriguaise** (Map p138; ☎ 832 4040; Graviers) The newest venture by the talented Françoise Baptiste, owner of Auberge de la Montagne. Perfected recipes are served on a breezy verandah with never-ending ocean views.

## Restaurants
### PORT MATHURIN

Self-caterers will find several small grocery stores on Rue de la Solidarité and Rue Mamzelle Julia. You can buy fresh fruit from stalls near the post office (mornings only from Monday to Saturday). On Saturday there is an excellent **street market** (Rue Wolfert Harmensz) down by the ferry terminal, with a smaller version

---

**THE GOURMAND'S CHECKLIST**

A list of Rodrigues' must-eats according to Françoise Baptiste; author, hostess and chef extraordinaire:

■ *Ourite* – octopus salad with lemon juice, olive oil, pepper, onions and salt. The dried variety has a rather pungent taste and admittedly isn't for everyone.

■ *Vindaye d'ourite* – boiled tender octopus flavoured with grated curcuma (any of a genus – Curcuma – of tropical plants of the ginger family, with thick, tuberous rootstocks that yield starch, including turmeric), garlic, vinegar, lemon juice and a sprinkle of local spices.

■ *Saucisses Créole* – a variety of meats that are dried and cured locally.

■ *La Torte Rodriguaise* – a small cake of papaya, pineapple or coconut mixed with a cream made from a local root called *corn-floeur*.

---

on Wednesday. For quick eats, outlets on Rue de la Solidarité sell *pain fouré* (filled rolls) and noodles for a handful of rupees.

Port Mathurin has several restaurants; the following are our favourites.

**Restaurant du Quai** (Map p139; ☎ 831 2840; Fisherman Lane, Rue Wolfert Harmensz; mains Rs 175-475; ⌚ lunch & dinner Tue-Sun) This friendly place by the harbour is always full in the evenings with local families and visitors enjoying its fine seafood and lobster dishes. The charming staff are very keen to please and make a damn fine punch cocktail as an aperitif.

**La Marmite Des Îles** (Map p139; ☎ 832 1279; mains Rs 240-300; ⌚ lunch & dinner) Waitresses donning flowery Creole dresses serve up delicious local specials like zesty *ourite* (octopus) salad and mouth-watering grilled fish. The restaurant is located along the sea, behind a rather derelict building near the bus station. There are no signs leading the way, so you'll have to snoop around until you hear the island tunes punctuating the humid tropical air.

**Aux Deux Frères** (Map p139; ☎ 831 0541; Patriko Bldg, Rue François Leguat; mains Rs 250-350; ⌚ 8.30am-2.30pm Mon-Sat & 6.30-10pm Fri & Sat) Perched above a plaza of tour operators, Port Mathurin's newest haunt serves local and international dishes in swish surrounds.

### AROUND RODRIGUES

Beyond Port Mathurin, most eating establishments operate from locals' homes; there are, however, a couple of full-fledged eateries. The Mourouk (p142) and Cotton Bay (p142) restaurants are also open to the public. Self-caterers will find small superettes (a small self-service grocery store) dotting each fishing village.

**Chez Ram** (Map p138; ☎ 832 0736; Baie Lascars; mains Rs 175-475; ⌚ lunch & dinner, closed Wed) The fanned white napkins do little to give this place any sense of charm or character, and the four outdoor tables sit rather unceremoniously beside the parking and main road, but Chez Ram does offer up excellent local cuisine – it has the *exact* same menu as Restaurant du Quai (owned by the same family). The dining room closes at 9.30pm.

**Bambou** (Map p138; ☎ 832 0701; pizza Rs 160-360, mains Rs 225-275; ⌚ dinner Wed-Mon) The most sociable spot in Anse aux Anglais, this popular restaurant earns high points for its friendly, dread-headed staff who serve up the usual assortment of local seafood and chicken. Grab one of the tiny tables outside and watch island life roll by at the public beach across the street.

**Mazavaroo** (Map p138; ☎ 716 2292; mains Rs 300-400; ⊙ lunch, dinner by reservation only) Hikers tackling a scenic east-coast jaunt can take a lunch break at this very casual affair. Hunker down on chopped palm trunks to savour home-cooked seafood (smoked marlin, grilled fish, prawns and lobster) served on painted pastel tables.

## ENTERTAINMENT

Apart from a couple of places in Port Mathurin, nightlife on the island is virtually nonexistent. The exception is live folk-music performances. Rodriguans are known as skilled accordionists, who play versions of old colonial ballroom and country dances such as the 'Scottish', the waltz and the mazurka. They also play a distinctive version of the *séga*, known as *séga tambour,* where the drum is unusually prominent. Popular groups include Racines, Cardinal Blanc, Cascavelles and Ambience Tropicale. They often perform at the big hotels, all of which have folk evenings to which nonguests are welcome (it's a good idea to phone ahead).

## SHOPPING

Rue de la Solidarité and Rue Mamzelle Julia are the main shopping streets. Here you'll find a number of outlets selling handicrafts, especially baskets and hats made from dried *vacoa* (pandanus) leaves. Items made from coconut fibres and coconut-shell jewellery are also popular souvenirs. Look out, too, for local foodstuffs such as preserved lemons, chillies and honey. The Saturday market is reasonably cheap and a pleasantly relaxed place to shop for fresh produce and some souvenirs. During the rest of the week there's a **daily market** (Map p139; ⊙ 8am-5pm Mon-Sat) next to the bridge near the post office that's well worth a visit.

**Care-Co** (Map p139; Rue de la Solidarité) sells coconut-shell items, honey and model boats made by people with disabilities.

## GETTING THERE & AWAY
### Air

The island's main **Air Mauritius office** (Map p139; ☎ 831 1632; fax 831 1959; ADS Bldg, Rue Max Lucchesi) is in Port Mathurin. There is also an office at the **airport** ( ☎ 832 7700), which is open for all arrivals and departures. It's a good idea to phone the airline the day before you leave anyway, just to make sure there's been no change to the schedule. See p157 for flight details.

There is a luggage limit of 15kg per person, with excess charged at Rs 35 per kilo. When checking in at the Mauritius end, you may be asked how much you weigh. Don't worry, you won't have to go through the indignity of being weighed like a sack of potatoes – an approximation is fine.

### Sea

The *Mauritius Pride* makes the voyage from Port Louis to Rodrigues every fortnight, docking at the passenger terminal on Rue Wolfert Harmensz in Port Mathurin. See p158 for more information.

## GETTING AROUND
### To/From The Airport

Flights arrive at **Sir Gaetan Duval airport** (Plaine Corail Airport; ☎ 831 6301) at the southwest tip of the island. A public bus runs between the airport and Port Mathurin roughly every 30 to 40 minutes from 6am to 4pm. The most hassle-free away to get to and from the airport is to pre-organise a ride with your accommodation of choice. Some hotels and guesthouses will include the price of a pick-up in their room rate. Figure on Rs 500 for a taxi to Port Mathurin.

### Bus

The main bus station is in Port Mathurin. In addition to the airport bus, the most useful bus routes are those to Grand Baie and Pointe Coton in the east of the island, and to Gravier, Port Sud-Est and Rivière Cocos on the south coast. All apart from the Grand Baie buses pass through Mont Lubin in the centre of the island. Most buses operate every 30 to 60 minutes from about 7am to 4pm Monday to Saturday on most routes. The Sunday service is fairly sporadic. Expect to pay Rs 10 to Rs 30 depending on your destination.

### Car

The road system in Rodrigues has improved enormously and sealed roads now lead to most parts of the island. Though 4WD vehicles are no longer strictly necessary, most hire cars are still sturdy pick-ups.

Car rental can be arranged through most hotels and guesthouses and local tour operators (p137), who will deliver all over the island. Expect to pay at least Rs 1200 per day. Most importantly, make sure you have sufficient petrol before setting off for the day –

the island's only **petrol station** (Map p138; Rue Max Lucchesi; ☻ 6am-6.30pm Mon-Sat, 6am-3pm Sun) is in Port Mathurin.

## Bicycle & Motorcycle

If your hotel or guesthouse doesn't offer bike or motorcycle rental, contact **Rotourco** (Map p139; ☎ 831 0747; www.rotourco.com; Rue François Leguat) or one of the other travel agencies in Port Mathurin. The going rate is around Rs 200 per day for a bike and Rs 600 to Rs 650 for a scooter. It costs Rs 350 to fill a scooter's petrol tank. Note that we recommend a scooter over a bicycle, as many of the interior roads can be discouragingly hilly.

## Taxi

Most taxis on Rodrigues are 4WD pick-ups. Expect to pay between Rs 500 and Rs 1000 depending on location. You can also hire taxis by the day for an island tour; expect to pay in the region of Rs 2000 to Rs 2800.

# Mauritius Directory

## CONTENTS

## ACCOMMODATION

By sheer volume alone, Mauritius offers the greatest range of sleeping options among the islands featured in this guide. There are three main types of accommodation: fully equipped vacation rentals, locally run guesthouses, and larger hotels and resorts.

In general, high season runs from around October to April, with a focus on the European winter months. Prices soar at the end of December and beginning of January. From May to September travellers can expect prices to dip during the low-season months, often called 'green season'. For budget digs, you can expect to pay under €60 (or Rs 2000). Expect to spend between €60 to €150 (Rs 2000 to Rs 10,000) for midrange accommodation, and top-end resorts and villas are priced above €150 (Rs 10,000).

### Apartments & Villas

Renting a holiday apartment or villa is by far the most economical option in Mauritius. There are hundreds of rental options available for tourists ranging from small studios in factory-sized complexes to lavish seaside mansions fit for a movie star. If you're travelling with your family or friends, a large high-end property can cost as little as €15 per person,

---

**PRACTICALITIES**

- Mauritius uses the metric system for weights and measures.

- Electric current is 220V, 50Hz; British-style three-pin sockets are most common, though you'll also find the continental two-pin variety.

- The two most important, widely read dailies are the French-language *L'Express* (www.lexpress.mu) and *Le Mauricien* (www.lemauricien.com). The *News on Sunday* and the *Mauritius Times* are English-language weeklies.

- There are three free television channels in Mauritius run by the state Mauritius Broadcasting Corporation (MBC) – MBC1, MBC2 and MBC3. There are also numerous pay channels. Programming is mainly in Creole but with foreign imports in French, English and numerous Indian languages.

- Radio is a more popular medium, with a huge number of local commercial stations broadcasting in Creole and Hindi, and the BBC World Service and Voice of America readily available. A couple of the most popular radio stations include Kool FM 89.3 Mhz and Taal FM 94.0 Mhz.

which more than rivals the hostel-esque relics from an earlier era of travel on the island. But remember, even though rentals represent a better price-value ratio on the whole, you always get what you pay for.

Most of the accommodation in this category is privately owned and managed by an umbrella agency that markets a large pool of crash pads. We've included lists of reputable rental agencies within the Sleeping sections of each destination. While choices can vary greatly, you should always expect (make sure to double-check) that your home-away-from-home comes with daily maid service, a fully equipped kitchen, air-con and concierge service provided by the property manager.

## Guesthouses & Chambres d'Hôtes

If you're looking for an island experience that doesn't involve the term 'all-inclusive', Mauritius' guesthouses and *chambres d'hôtes* (B&Bs) are well worth a gander. This category of accommodation is managed by locals – often families – who dote on their guests with genuine hospitality. It's a fantastic way to learn about the *real* Mauritius hidden from package-deal tourists. In fact, you'll usually have the chance to dine with your accommodation's proprietors at their *tables d'hôtes*.

Over the last few years the government has begun issuing security mandates for all tourism-related properties. Panic buttons and 24-hour security have become a compulsory expense for owners, forcing guesthouses to jack up their prices beyond the budget range to pay the bills. As a result, the island's *chambres d'hôtes* are starting to go the way of the dodo, especially since all-inclusive resorts have been known to offer bargain-basement prices to stay competitive during the economic downturn. Nonetheless, there's still a scatter of charming spots sprinkled around the island that are, now more than ever, promoting a 'local experience'. You'll find a clus-

ter in Pointe d'Esny, though *chambres d'hôtes* are particularly popular in Rodrigues.

## Hotels & Resorts

Rounding out the sleeping circuit is Mauritius' best-known brand of accommodation – the dreamy resorts found on the pages of magazines and in TV commercials for credit cards. And, despite the global economic recession, dozens of these opulent properties continue to spring up each year. There are, however, two distinct categories of hotels in Mauritius – the luxury over-the-top resorts that stretch along the sea, and the old-school midrangers that need some serious TLC. It's best to avoid the latter as many of the posh properties offer vacation incentives that rival the has-beens, and the guesthouses (which are often cheaper) are generally in better shape. Upscale properties come in various tiers of luxury – there are three-, four- and five-star resorts. You'll do perfectly well with a three-star charmer, and while the five-star price tags may be out of reach for most travellers, it is well worth checking with travel agents about hotel-and-flight vacation packages. In fact, no upmarket sleeps should be booked with the public rates – agency rates are always cheaper. If you have your sights set on a luxury vacation, expect to pay €100 per person per night (including half board) at the very minimum. Prices quickly climb all the way up to €1000.

## ACTIVITIES

There's much more to Mauritius than sun worship – you'll find plenty of ways to get the blood pumping after one too many days of baking on the beach.

### Canyoning & Abseiling

Explore Mauritius' gorges and waterfalls from a completely different angle – splash straight through 'em! **Vertical World** ( ☎ 697 5430; www.verticalworldltd.com) and **Otélair** ( ☎ 696 6750; www.otelair.

com) offer half- and whole-day excursions in the western part of the island. The highlight is Tamarin Falls (p108) on the cusp of the Black River Gorges National Park. Vertical World also offers rock climbing in Albion (p97).

## Catamarans & Yacht Cruises

A catamaran day trip is one of the most popular activities in Mauritius. Hundreds of tourists each day board speedy boats to zoom around the azure lagoon and wavy seas or stop at offshore islets and shallow reefs. The most popular trip is to Île aux Cerfs (p130) on the east coast. Grand Baie is the major hub of cruise activity – dozens of vessels head for the wee islands in the north, including Îlot Gabriel and Île Plate (p86). On the west side of the island, the popular cruising option is a half- or full-day trip to Île aux Bénitiers (p111) with a side of dolphin-watching (p104). In general, the best cruising option is the northern islets – the reefs are more pristine, the beaches quieter and prices less inflated. Île aux Cerfs is a good option for those who suffer from motion sickness as the boat never leaves the calm lagoon waters. The most romantic option is the sunset cruises offered by most operators. If you're looking for something a bit more traditional, you'll find myriad fishermen in Mahébourg (p115) and the surrounding beaches (p119) who have transformed their vessels into mini leisure crafts. Most operators include buffet lunches, alcohol and snorkelling. Make sure to shop around before choosing your cruise – some catamarans are not licensed to stop on any islands. Most cruises can be booked through tour agents and hotels. Check out www.mauritius catamaran.com for more information.

## Cycling & Mountain Biking

The tourism authority of Mauritius is currently pushing 'cyclo-tourism' as one of the island's new draws. Cycling is slowly starting to build steam, and although we don't advise a round-the-island bike tour just yet (the traffic can be downright scary!), there are some great opportunities for mountain biking in the island's hilly centre. **Yemaya** ( ☎ 752 0046, 283 8187; www.yemayaadventures.com) offers mountain-biking trips in Chamarel (p109) and the neighbouring Black River Gorges National Park. If you wish to rent some wheels and blaze your own trail, we recommend contacting **Fit For Life** ( ☎ 452 2005; www.fflmauritius.com) in Bambous, a township between Quatres Bornes and Flic en Flac. High-quality all-terrain bicycles go for Rs 250 per day.

## Deep-Sea Fishing

The fisheries around Mauritius support large predators such as marlin, wahoo, tuna and sharks, luring big-game anglers from around the world. Annual fishing competitions are held in Black River in November and February. See p104 for information about fishing seasons.

Game fishing has far less environmental impact than commercial fishing, but the weight and the number of fish caught has shown a marked decline since its heyday in the 1970s. It's now rare to catch anything over 400kg. Using the practice of 'tag-and-release' is an option for those who want the thrill without depriving the ocean of these magnificent creatures.

Anglers get to take home a trophy such as the marlin's nose spike, or a couple of fillets, but the day's catch belongs to the operator, who sells it to be served up at local restaurants.

Most of the big hotels run boats, and there are several private operators based at Black River, Trou aux Biches and Grand Baie. Most outfits have a minimum hire time of around six hours, and each boat can normally take three anglers and three guests. Expect to pay upwards of Rs 13,000 per boat.

## Diving & Snorkelling

Diving and snorkelling are very well established in Mauritius. There are roughly 45 diving outfits spread across the island. See www.msda.com for a list of insured operators and check out p28 for details about the area's top scuba spots. Although diving through interesting rock formations and schools of colourful fish is undoubtedly a holiday highlight, Mauritius' sites won't inspire devotion like those in the Maldives or the Philippines.

The success of your diving experience will largely depend on your guide or instructor. If you're going to dive with the outfit operating at your hotel, make sure to stop by the day before and get a feel for the place. If you don't feel comfortable, there's nothing stopping you from diving with the operator at the next hotel down the road.

For snorkellers, nothing tops the reefs at Blue Bay. Rodrigues also gets a thumbs up in the diving and snorkelling categories namely due to the complete lack of scuba-donning tourists (or the complete lack of tourists in general!).

## Golf

No leisure island would be complete without a handful of world-class golf courses. In fact, the oldest fairway in the Indian Ocean, the Mauritius Gymkhana Club (p77), can be found on the island. Several five-star resorts in the island's east have excellent golfing facilities, including Belle Mare Plage (p132), Le Saint Géran (p132), Four Seasons Resort at Anahita (p129) and Le Touessrok's shmancy greens on Île aux Cerfs (p130). The course at Tamarina (p105) is the highlight in the west. Check out the stunningly maintained Domaine de Bel Ombre (p124) along the south coast.

## Hiking

For those interested in more than the usual beach activities, Mauritius offers some attractive hikes. Most are in the areas where the Central Plateau meets the coastal plains. The Black River Gorges National Park (p107) has several scenic trails, and further north, you'll find Le Pouce and Corps de Garde (p74) – both make an excellent introduction to hiking in Mauritius. Many of the *domaines* in the southeastern part of the island (see p125) offer beautiful trails through the island's oldest forests.

As a general rule, when hiking you should pay attention to 'Entrée Interdit' (Entry Prohibited) signs – they may mean you're entering a hunting reserve. 'Chemin Privée' (Private Rd) signs are generally there for the benefit of motorists; most landowners won't object to the odd pedestrian. It's best to ask if you're unsure about where you should and shouldn't walk.

If you plan on tackling any of these hikes alone, make sure to check out **Fitsy** (www.fitsy. com), an excellent website with detailed GPS and satellite imagery that maps out the course of each trail. We highly recommend, however, hiring a guide for any of the island's major hikes. A knowledgeable guide provides invaluable insight into the region's flora and fauna. There are four main outdoor outfits on the island: **Yemaya** ( ☎ 752 0046, 283 8187; www.yemaya adventures.com), **Yanature** ( ☎ 785 6177; www.yanature. com), **Vertical World** ( ☎ 697 5430; www.verticalworld ltd.com) and **Otélair** ( ☎ 696 6750; www.otelair.com).

Yanature is the only company that has permission to ascend Le Morne. On Rodrigues, the east-coast beaches make for a splendid half-day hike, which can be tackled solo. Any of the local tour operators can arrange guided hikes through the rugged centre.

## Horseback Riding

Mauritius has some lovely rambling countryside, which is perfect for riding excursions. There are heaps of equestrian outfits throughout the island – you'll find a couple of ranches in the west (p105 and p109), an interesting farm in the south that rescues old race horses (p122), and several outfits in the north (p80 and p81). Domaine Les Pailles (p74) on the Central Plateau and Domaine de l'Étoile (p126) in the southeast also offer horseback-riding excursions.

For information about horse racing and betting, see p70.

## Kayaking

The azure lagoon surrounding Mauritius has calm waters perfect for sea kayaking. **Yemaya** ( ☎ 752 0046, 283 8187; www.yemayaadventures.com) offers kayak outings to Île Ambre, an attractive offshore islet; see p94 for details.

## Skydiving

If surfing and abseiling don't get the blood flowing quite enough, it is now possible to jump out of an airplane soaring 3000km above the island. See p85 for details.

## Surfing, Kitesurfing & Windsurfing

A small scene led by Australian and South African surfers built up in the 1970s around Tamarin (p103) on the west coast (the surf movie *The Forgotten Island of Santosha* was made here), but the wave crashed during the 1980s.

These days, the scene around Tamarin comprises a small community of local and Réunionnais surfers. You can plug into what's happening and rent surfboards from one of the old-school establishments in Tamarin, like the Tamarin Hotel or Chez Jacques.

The kitesurfing and windsurfing movements have grown in leaps and bounds over the last decade – you'll find hundreds of wave hunters gathering along the west coast just south of Tamarin. Several kitesurfing and windsurfing outfits offer beginner courses at 'Kite Lagoon' on the west side of Le Morne (see p112 for details); the infamous 'One Eye', on the south side, is for experts. When the wind changes in the winter months, you'll find great breaks in the southeast near Pointe d'Esny and Mahébourg (p115). There's also a highly regarded kitesurfing school at Cap Malheureux in the north (p94).

### Undersea Walks & Submersibles
One popular but environmentally ruinous way to enjoy the underwater world if you don't dive is to take an 'underwater walk' – available at a number of places but most commonly found in the tourist hub of Grand Baie (see p86). Participants don a weight belt and a diving helmet and stroll along the seabed feeding the fish in a Jules-Verne-journey-beneath-the-sea kinda way. Oxygen is piped down from the surface – using solar-powered compressors, no less – and divers are on hand in case there are any problems.

Undersea walks carry a greater risk of damaging the sensitive marine environment and they're absolutely no substitute for diving or even snorkelling.

## BUSINESS HOURS
Post offices in Mauritius generally operate from 8.15am to 4pm Monday to Friday, and 8.15am to 11.45am Saturday; note that the last 45 minutes are available for stamp sales only. Government offices usually open from 9am to 4pm Monday to Friday and 9am to noon Saturday, although you can expect them to be closed during religious and public holidays. Banks are generally open from 9am to 3.15pm on weekdays, though you'll find extended hours in the tourist hubs of Grand Baie and Flic en Flac. Restaurants usually open for lunch from around noon to 3pm, and dinner starts around 7pm. Many restaurants are closed on Sunday. Shops typically open from 9am to 5pm Monday to Friday, and 8am to noon on Saturday. Most stores – especially the ones located on the Central Plateau – will also close early (around 1pm) on Thursdays. On Rodrigues shops and offices are known to close much earlier than 4pm; to be on the safe side it's best to do all your business in the morning.

## CHILDREN
Travelling with children in Mauritius presents no particular problems. In fact, kids generally have a ball. Most of the high-end hotels

featured in this book have dedicated facilities (like 'kids clubs') for children – most include babysitting services as well. The proliferation of villa leases has made it easy to bring the entire family on vacation.

Besides the seaside, the biggest attractions on the island are the animal preserves at La Vanille (p121) and Casela Nature & Leisure Park (p99; though note you must be of a certain height to participate in the popular lion walks). Many of the island's *domaines,* like Domaines Les Pailles (p74) and Domaine de l'Étoile (p126), have activities tailored to youngsters like quad-biking and archery. Horseback riding (p149) and dolphin-watching day trips (p104) are also popular options for the little ones.

To put their holiday in context, there's a wonderful series of cartoon books by Henry Koobes (published locally by Editions Vizavi Ltd). The English-language titles include *In Dodoland, SOS Shark* and *Meli-Melo in the Molasses.*

For more information, see Lonely Planet's *Travel with Children.*

## CLIMATE CHART
For further information on choosing the best time of the year for visiting Mauritius, see p64.

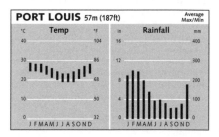

## CUSTOMS REGULATIONS
In Mauritius, visitors aged 16 years and over may import 200 cigarettes or 250g of tobacco; 1L of spirits; 2L of wine, ale or beer; 250mL of *eau de toilette;* and up to 100mL of perfume.

There are restrictions on importing food, plants and animals, for which import permits are required. Other prohibited and restricted articles include spear guns and items made from ivory, shell, turtleshell or other materials banned under the Convention on International Trade in Endangered Species

(CITES); it is also illegal to take such items out when you leave.

## DANGERS & ANNOYANCES

As with most destinations, dangerous actions beget dangerous consequences, and Mauritius is no different. Your biggest annoyances is likely to be environmental (mosquitoes in some places, sunburn and the occasional upset stomach).

The Indian Ocean is a warm tropical ocean, so there are several aquatic nasties to watch out for. Fortunately, few travellers encounter anything more serious than the odd coral cut. For more information, see p327.

All beaches below the high-tide line are public property, so you are entitled to plop your towel down on the sand, whatever some over-officious security guard might tell you.

### Coconuts

Lying under a coconut palm may seem like a tropical idyll, but, as silly as it may sound, there have been some tragic accidents. Take care when walking under coconut trees and don't lie (or park your car) beneath them.

### Cyclones

Mauritius lies within the cyclone belt. Most cyclones occur between December and March. While direct hits are relatively uncommon, storms miles away can bring very strong winds.

As soon as a cyclone is detected, a system of alerts is used to inform the public of the level of danger. In Mauritius there are four levels of alert. The alerts and then regular bulletins are broadcast on radio and TV.

### Taxis

Taxi drivers in Mauritius usually earn up to 20% commission from certain shops, hotels, restaurants and other businesses to which they take clients. Keep this in mind if a taxi driver tells you that the place you want to go to is full or closed or more expensive than one he knows. Insist first on going to your chosen destination. It would be ideal to rent your own vehicle to explore the island at your leisure. For more on hiring taxis, see p160.

### Theft

Petty theft and break-ins can be somewhat of a common occurrence beyond the walls of your resort. Favourite haunts for thieves are the beaches. Île aux Cerfs is a particular hot spot. The best strategy is not to take any valuables to the beach – and never tempt a passing thief by leaving your belongings unattended.

Be extra careful in crowded places such as markets and avoid walking around with your valuables casually slung over your shoulder. When travelling on public transport, keep your gear near you.

If you hire a car, it's best not to leave anything valuable in it at all. If you must do so, hide everything well out of sight. Wherever possible, park in a secure car park or at least somewhere busy – never park in an isolated spot, especially at night.

Don't leave vital documents, money or valuables lying about in your room. Many hotels provide room safes, which are well worth using. Otherwise, leave your valuables in the safe at reception and get a receipt. While most hotels are reliable, to be extra sure, pack everything in a small, double-zippered bag that can be padlocked, or use a large envelope with a signed seal that will reveal any tampering. Count money and travellers cheques before and after retrieving them from the safe.

If you do have something stolen, report it to the police. The chances of them recovering anything are remote, but you'll need a statement proving you have reported the crime if you want to claim insurance.

## EMBASSIES & CONSULATES

Many countries do not have representatives in Mauritius, and usually refer their citizens to the embassy in Pretoria, South Africa. Countries with diplomatic representation in Mauritius include the following:

**Australia** (Map p66; ☎ 202 0160; www.mauritius. embassy.gov.au; 2nd fl, Rogers House, 5 President John Kennedy St, Port Louis; ◷ 8am-3.30pm Mon-Fri)

**Canada** (Map p66; ☎ 212 5500; canada@intnet.mu; 18 Jules Koenig St, Port Louis; ◷ 10am-noon Mon-Fri)

**France** (Map p66; ☎ 202 0100; www.ambafrance-mu. org; 14 St Georges St, Port Louis; ◷ 8am-noon Mon-Fri)

**Italy** (Map p66; ☎ 207 7844; 2nd fl, Air Mauritius Bldg, President John Kennedy St, Port Louis; ◷ 8.30am-noon Mon-Fri)

**Russia** ( ☎ 696 1545; rusemb.mu@intnet.mu; 10 Queen Mary St, Floréal; ◷ 8.30am-noon & 2-5pm Mon-Fri)

**Seychelles** (Map p66; ☎ 211 1688; gfok@intnet.mu; 616 St James Ct, St Denis St, Port Louis)

**Sweden** (Map p66; ☎ 206 3203; marieandre.boulle@ taylorsmith.mu; Aqualia Bldg, Old Quay D Rd, Port Louis; ◷ 8.30am-4.30pm Mon-Fri)

UK (Map p66; ☎ 202 9400; bhc@intnet.mu; 7th fl, Les Cascades Bldg, Edith Cavell St, Port Louis; ☒ 7.45am-3.45pm Mon-Thu, 7.45am- 1.30pm Fri)
USA (Map p66; ☎ 202 4400; http://mauritius.usembassy.gov; 4th fl, Rogers House, 5 President John Kennedy St, Port Louis; ☒ 7.30am-4.45pm Mon-Thu, 7.30am-12.30pm Fri)

# FESTIVALS & EVENTS

Given the range of beliefs and customs in Mauritius, hardly a week goes by without some celebration (and a day off work!). You can usually find out about the latest *cavadee*, *teemeedee* or other ceremonies on Mauritius' government website (www.gov.mu).

On Rodrigues, the main cultural event is the Festival Kréol, which takes place over three days at the end of October. Concerts, craft exhibitions and other events – including lots of eating – break out all over the island.

The Fête du Poisson, held on Rodrigues in the first week of March, marks the opening of the fishing season. It is celebrated with all sorts of festivities, including fishing expeditions – and lots more eating.

Regattas featuring traditional wooden fishing boats are popular in Rodrigues. Most take place in the lagoon off Port Sud-Est between January and December, but the most prestigious event of the year is the regatta held off Pointe de l'Herbe in May.

## Chinese Festivals

The Chinese New Year is celebrated with the Chinese Spring Festival, which is a public holiday and falls in late January or early February. On New Year's Eve, homes are spring cleaned and decked out in red, the colour of happiness, and firecrackers are let off to protect against evil spirits. The next day, cakes made of rice flour and honey are given to family and friends. No scissors or knives may be used in case someone is hurt and begins the New Year with bad luck.

## Christian Festivals

The most important date for many Mauritian Christians is 9 September, Père Laval Feast Day, which marks the anniversary of the priest's death. Pilgrims from around the world come to his shrine at Ste-Croix to pray for miracle cures (p68).

## Hindu Festivals

### CAVADEE

One of the more unusual Mauritian festivals, the Thaipoosam Cavadee takes place in January or February each year at most Hindu temples and features acts of self-mutilation by devotees. Honouring a vow to Subramanya, the second son of Shiva, pilgrims pierce their tongues and cheeks with skewers. They then march from their chosen temple to the banks of a river carrying the *cavadee* (a wooden arch decorated with flowers and palm leaves, with pots of milk suspended from each end of its base) on their shoulders.

The Thaipoosam Cavadee is a public holiday, but other small *cavadees* occur during the rest of the year at selected temples.

### TEEMEEDEE

This is a Hindu and Tamil fire-walking ceremony in honour of various gods. The ceremonies occur throughout the year, but mostly in December and January. After fasting and bathing, the participants walk over red-hot embers scattered along the ground. The Hindu temples in Quatre Bornes, Camp Diable (near Rivière des Anguilles) and the Vale (near Goodlands) are noted for this event. A feat along similar lines is sword climbing, seen mostly between April and June. The best demonstrations occur at Mont Choisy and in the towns of Triolet and Solitude (between Port Louis and Trou aux Biches).

### OTHER HINDU FESTIVALS

Each year, most of the island's Hindus make a pilgrimage to Grand Bassin, a crater lake in the south of the island, for the festival Maha Shivaratri. For information about the celebration, see p109.

Hindus also celebrate the victory of Rama over the evil deity Ravana during Divali (Dipavali), which falls in late October or early November. To mark this joyous event, countless candles and lamps are lit to show Rama (the seventh incarnation of Vishnu) the way home from his period of exile.

Holi, the festival of colours, is known for the exuberant throwing of coloured powder and water, and tourists are not exempt from the odd dousing. The festival symbolises the victory of divine power over demonic strength. On the night before Holi, bonfires are built to symbolise the destruction of the evil demon Holika. This festival is held in February or March.

Other major public festivals include Pongal (January or February), Ougadi (March or April) and Ganesh Chaturti (August or September). The latter celebrates the birthday of Ganesh, the elephant-headed god of wisdom and prosperity.

### Muslim Festivals

Muslims celebrate Eid al-Fitr to mark the end of the fasting month of Ramadan, which is the ninth month of the lunar year. Eid al-Fitr is always a public holiday.

## FOOD

Food is likely to be a highlight of any visit with the huge choice of cuisine available and some excellent restaurants throughout the country. If you're staying at an all-inclusive resort, there is little incentive to venture out and explore; however, a lunch at a Creole *table d'hôte* (host's table) can be a very enlightening experience for you and your palate. Read through our selection of eateries and choose your restaurants carefully – many places offer up uninspiring, drab food simply because they're guaranteed customers from big resorts nearby.

Street eats cost around Rs 5 to 10 for snacks like rotis, *dhal puris* and *boulettes* (meatballs) served at markets, along public beaches and in the capital. A budget meal at a local restaurant away from the tourist circuit will cost Rs 200 to 300. Moving up a notch, you can expect to pay around Rs 500 in a midrange place, while the bill at a classier establishment will be at least Rs 1000 per head for two or three courses and alcohol. For information about some of the culinary delights in store in Mauritius, see p56.

## GAY & LESBIAN TRAVELLERS

Mauritius has a paradoxical relationship to homosexuality. While gay and lesbian rights are legally guaranteed and much of the population is young and progressive, there remains a rigidly conservative streak to the Mauritian character. As a result gay life remains fairly secretive – mainly existing on the internet, in private and at the occasional party. While there were no gay or lesbian bars or clubs on the island at the time of writing, there are monthly underground club nights organised by text message.

For gay and lesbian travellers there's little to worry about. We've never heard of any problems arising from same-sex couples sharing rooms during their holidays. You're still best to avoid public displays of affection outside your hotel and generally to be aware that what might not be abnormal at home may be considered shocking here.

## HOLIDAYS

The following public holidays are observed in Mauritius:

**New Year** 1 & 2 January
**Thaipoosam Cavadee** January/February
**Chinese Spring Festival** January/February
**Abolition of Slavery** 1 February
**Maha Shivaratri** February/March
**Ougadi** March/April
**National Day** 12 March
**Labour Day** 1 May
**Assumption of the Blessed Virgin Mary** 15 August
**Ganesh Chaturti** August/September
**Divali** (Dipavali) October/November
**Arrival of Indentured Labourers** 2 November
**Eid al-Fitr** November/December
**Christmas Day** 25 December

## INSURANCE

A travel-insurance policy to cover theft, loss and medical problems is a good idea. Some policies specifically exclude dangerous activities, which can include scuba diving, motorcycling and even hiking. Always check the small print and make sure that the policy covers ambulances or an emergency flight home. If you plan on diving, we strongly recommend purchasing dive-specific insurance with **DAN** (www.diversalertnetwork.org). For more information on health insurance, see p323.

Worldwide travel insurance is available at www.lonelyplanet.com/travel_services. You can buy, extend and claim online anytime – even if you're already on the road.

## INTERNET ACCESS

Most towns have at least one internet cafe and access can be found at most resorts, hotels

---

**TOP 5 TABLES D'HÔTES**

*Tables d'hôtes* are a great way to experience the local culture through home-cooked meals and chit-chat with the affable hosts. These are our favourites:

- **La Clef des Champs** (Central Plateau; p77)
- **Cases à Gardenias** (Rodrigues; p142)
- **La Belle Rodriguaise** (Rodrigues; p143)
- **Les Lataniers Bleus** (West; p105)
- **St Aubin** (South; p122)

and guesthouses. Despite the mind-numbing room rates at some of the four- and five-star getaways you'll probably have to pay an additional fee to check your email. At the time of research, villa operators were starting to add wi-fi connections in their properties.

## LEGAL MATTERS

Foreigners are subject to the laws of the country in which they are travelling and will receive no special consideration because they are tourists. If you find yourself in a sticky legal predicament, contact your embassy (p151). In general, travellers have nothing to fear from the police, who rarely harass foreigners and are very polite if you do need to stop them. Talking on your mobile phone while driving will definitely get you pulled over (it happened to us!) – it's best to play up your tourist naiveté and you'll be let off the hook (speaking in English helps even more).

## MAPS

Although Mauritius markets itself heavily as a major tourism destination, the island has a frustrating lack of decent maps (a ploy to keep you within the walls of your resort!). The best map of the island is the satellite imagery on Google Earth. If you don't have printing facilities on hand, try the map produced by the **Institut Géographique Nationale** (IGN; www.ign. fr). The Globetrotter travel map is also a good choice. Both are available from local bookstores and supermarkets.

There are no decent maps of Rodrigues, but the Ti Boussol, the best one available, can be found all over the island.

## MONEY

The Mauritian unit of currency is the rupee (Rs), which is divided into 100 cents (¢). There are coins of 5¢, 20¢ and 50¢, and Rs 1, Rs 5 and Rs 10. The banknote denominations are Rs 25, Rs 50, Rs 100, Rs 200, Rs 500, Rs 1000 and Rs 2000. While the Mauritian rupee is the only currency accepted on the island, almost all villas, guesthouses and hotels (and several high-end restaurants usually affiliated with hotels) tether their prices to the euro to counterbalance the rupee's unstable fluctuations.

For exchange rates, see the inside front cover. For information on costs, see p18.

### ATMs

Armed with your PIN, it's perfectly possible to travel on plastic in Mauritius since ATMs are widespread. Even Rodrigues has a smattering of them. They're mostly located outside banks, though you'll also find them at the airports, at larger supermarkets and in some shopping malls. The majority of machines accept Visa and MasterCard, or any similar cards in the Cirrus and Plus networks, while Amex now has a tie-in with Mauritius Commercial Bank (MCB).

### Credit Cards

Visa and MasterCard are the most commonly accepted cards, though Amex is catching up quickly. Nearly all tourist shops, restaurants and accommodation accept payment by credit card, as do car-hire companies, tour agents and so forth. Any establishment well outside the tourist bubble will still expect payment in cash.

A few places add on an extra fee, typically 3%, to the bill to cover 'bank charges'. The cheaper car-hire companies are the worst offenders. To be on the safe side, always ask. Cash advances on credit cards are available from most major banks, including MCB, Barclays, the State Bank and HSBC. Just remember to take your passport.

### Moneychangers

Major currencies and travellers cheques can be changed at the main banks, exchange bureaus and the larger hotels. Bureaux de change sometimes offer slightly better rates than banks, but there's usually little difference. Hotels tend to have the worst rates and may add an additional service commission. As a general rule, travellers cheques bring a better rate than cash. There is no black market in Mauritius.

Banks don't charge commission on changing cash. As for travellers cheques, the system varies. Some banks, such as HSBC, charge 1% of the total, with a minimum of Rs 200, while MCB and the State Bank levy Rs 50 for up to 10 cheques. Don't forget to take along your passport when changing money. And make sure you hang on to the encashment form, which will have to be presented if you want to change Mauritian rupees back into foreign currency at the end of your stay.

### Taxes

Most items apart from unprepared food are subject to 15% VAT. There's no clear rule about whether this tax is included in prices quoted for meals, rooms and activities. If it's not clear, be sure to ask or you may be in for a shock.

### Tipping

Tipping is not generally practiced in Mauritius and is never an obligation. Top-end hotels and restaurants sometimes add a service charge of about 10% to 15% to the bill.

## POST

The postal service in Mauritius is quick and reliable. Poste restante is available at central post offices. You usually have to pay a small fee to collect letters and may be asked for your passport. See p150 for post office hours. In general, mailing services end about 45 minutes before closing and the bureau becomes a retail shop for stamps and envelopes.

## SHOPPING

If the beaches begin to pall, you can shop till you drop in Mauritius. Given such a wide choice, there is no reason to purchase items made from endangered species – avoid any seashell, coral or turtleshell products.

Bargaining is very much part of life in Mauritius. It's usual to bargain in markets and anywhere prices aren't marked, and sometimes even on marked prices if you're a big spender. As a tourist, however, you'll need well-honed bargaining skills to get much of a discount.

### Clothing

Although the textile industry has been eclipsed by China, it is still one of Mauritius' biggest earners. Many of the brand-name clothes on sale in Europe, Australia and the USA are produced in the factories around Curepipe, Floréal and Vacoas. Shoppers can save by buying at the source, and many of the bigger suppliers have outlet stores where you can snap up items at a fraction of their usual retail price. Those really watching the rupees can opt for convincing – and not-so-convincing – copies of well-known designer brands. One of the best places to pick up genuine seconds is the market at Quatre Bornes (p76). Other vendors tend to congregate on President John Kennedy St in Port Louis, and in the Rose Hill and Curepipe markets in central Mauritius. Check carefully for minor flaws and dodgy stitching.

Floreal Knitwear in Floréal is renowned for its stylish sweaters and other knitted garments. The company supplies Gap, Next and other international outfitters, but you can buy the same items before the branded labels have been added for a fraction of the final cost at their Floréal emporium (p77).

Shibani and Maille St are two other local companies producing high-quality knitwear. Maille St specialises in cashmere sweaters in colours to die for. For kids there's Gecko, while Habit and the fetchingly named IV Pl@y target teens with up-to-the-minute streetwear. You'll find branches of these shops in Port Louis' Caudan Waterfront complex (p72), Grand Baie's Sunset Boulevard (p90) and other upmarket shopping malls.

### Handicrafts & Souvenirs

Locally produced basketry, essential oils, sugar, spices, teas and T-shirts all make very portable souvenirs. The Craft Market (p72) in Port Louis' Caudan Waterfront complex offers perhaps the widest choice. Most of the crafts and souvenirs sold at Port Louis' Central Market (p72) and the Grand Baie Bazaar (p90) are of Malagasy origin, like leather belts and bags, masks, embroidery and semiprecious-stone solitaire sets.

From Rodrigues you can take home a very natty *vacoas*-leaf hat or basket. The island is also famous for its honey and lemon and chilli preserves. Jewellery and other items made from coconut shell by people with disabilities are available from Care-Co in Port Mathurin. For details, see p144.

### Model Ships

Whether or not you could conceive of having one at home, it is difficult not to be impressed by the skill that goes into producing Mauritius' famous model ships. Small-scale shipbuilding has become a huge business and you'll see intricate replicas of famous vessels, such as the *Bounty, Victory, Endeavour, Golden Hind* and even the *Titanic,* for sale all over the island; it's hard to believe that model shipbuilding dates back to only 1968, when an unknown Mauritian carved a model ship for fun and launched a whole new industry.

The models are made out of teak or mahogany (cheaper camphor wood is liable to crack), and larger ships take up to 400 hours to complete. Men usually work on the structure and the women do the rigging and sails, which are dipped in tea to give them a weathered look.

One of the best model-ship builders is **Voiliers de L'Océan** (Map p75; ☎ 676 6986, 674 6764; www.voiliersocean.intnet.mu; Sir Winston Churchill St; ☺ 9am-6pm), in Curepipe. The company also has an outlet, MAST, in Port Louis' Caudan Waterfront complex. The biggest factory is **Historic Marine** ( ☎ 283 9404; www.historic-marine.com; ☺ 8am-5pm Mon-Fri, 9am-noon Sat & Sun) in Goodlands, in the north of the island. In both cases the staff will be happy to show you around the workshop (weekdays only) without any pressure to buy.

To get your goods home safely, shops will pack the models for carry-on luggage or in sturdy boxes to go in the hold, and deliver them to your hotel or the airport at no extra charge.

## SOLO TRAVELLERS

Mauritius is very much a couple's vacation destination and the island markets itself to honeymooners and those seeking a romantic getaway. Although there are no taboos about travelling alone, the holiday infrastructure isn't tailored to those looking to make new friends. In general, single travellers will pay 70% to 90% of the price of a double room, making a solo trip quite an expensive venture. Signing up for activities like catamaran day trips, guided hikes and diving are good ways of meeting other people – and try staying at *chambres d'hôtes* rather than big-name resorts in order to meet a few locals.

## TELEPHONE

Although Mauritius may feel lost in the Indian Ocean, the island's telephone services are definitely up to snuff. In fact, Mauritius offers some of the cheapest mobile-phone services in the world.

The state-controlled Mauritius Telecom has a virtual monopoly on landlines, although there's an open market for mobile services – Cellplus (owned by Mauritius Telecom) and Emtel compete with each other for every mobile-phone user in the country.

The rate for a call to Australia, Europe or the USA is about Rs 20 per minute. These rates fall by around 25% during off-peak hours (10pm to 6am from Monday to Friday and noon on Saturday to 6am the following Monday).

When phoning Mauritius from abroad, you'll need to dial the international code for Mauritius ( ☎ 230), followed by the seven-digit local number. There are no area codes in Mauritius.

## Mobile Phones

Coverage on Mauritius and Rodrigues is generally excellent and mobile phones are a cheap way to communicate with others. In fact, many Mauritians have more than one mobile phone. If you have a GSM phone and it has been 'unlocked', you can keep costs down by buying a local SIM card from either **Cellplus** (Map p66; ☎ 203 7649; www.cellplus.mu; Mauritius Telecom Tower, Edith Cavell St, Port Louis) or **Emtel** (Map p66; ☎ 212 5400; www.emtel-ltd.com; Air Mauritius Bldg, President John Kennedy St, Port Louis). A starter pack costs around Rs 140 including Rs 125 worth of calls. To top-up your credit you can buy prepaid cards almost anywhere. When buying a SIM card you'll usually need to bring along your passport and a sponsor's signature.

Local calls are charged at between Rs 1.50 and Rs 5 per minute depending if you're calling someone on the same network or not. International calls cost a couple of rupees per minute on top of the standard Mauritius Telecom rates.

Purchasing a SIM card package – even for one call to home – is much less costly than buying a local phonecard.

## TIME

Mauritius is GMT+4 hours, both on the mainland and on Rodrigues. When it's noon in Port Louis, it's 8am in London, 9am in Paris, 3am in New York and 6pm in Sydney. Mauritius does not operate a system of daylight savings; being equatorial its sunset and sunrise times vary only slightly throughout the year.

## TOURIST INFORMATION

Although independent travellers are definitely in the minority, there are two corporate entities dedicated to those who don't fall into the package-getaway category. The **Mauritius Tourism Promotion Authority** (MTPA; ☎ 208 6397; www.tourism-mauritius.mu) is a government-run body essentially responsible for promoting the island and its virtues to foreign markets. The other organisation is the recommended **Association des Hôteliers et Restaurateurs de l'île Maurice** (AHRIM; ☎ 637 3782; www.mauritiustourism.org), an association of high-quality hotels, guesthouses and restaurants. AHRIM is starting to offer guesthouse-plus-airfare packages – an attempt to empower tourists to have a local experience while also benefiting from discounted airfares. Check out its website for details.

Both AHRIM and MTPA have desks in the arrivals hall at the airport, which operate from the first flight until around 1pm. They can assist with hotel bookings and general island information. MTPA also has a constellation of kiosks peppered across the island, although, to be perfectly frank, we found these stations disappointing – many were empty during prime business hours, and when we did find someone manning a booth they tossed us an outdated island map and offered very limited information. You're better off asking tour operators, hotel staff or anyone else accustomed to dealing with the usual onslaught of traveller's queries.

Also useful is Mauritius Telecom's 24-hour phone service, **Tourist Info** ( ☎ 152). At any time of day or night you can speak to someone (in English) who will at least try to answer your questions.

## TRAVELLERS WITH DISABILITIES

Mauritius makes a relatively decent provision for those with mobility problems. Modern buildings conform to international standards for disabled access, although public toilets, pavements and lifts tend not to be as good. Most top-end hotels have wheelchair access, lifts and specially equipped bathrooms. In big hotels, there are always plenty of staff around to help and it is often possible to hire an assistant if you want to go on an excursion or a boat trip. With a bit of extra warning, some riding stables, dive centres and other sports operators can cater for people with disabilities.

None of the public transport systems offer wheelchair access. Anyone using a wheelchair will be reliant on private vehicles.

## VISAS

You don't need a visa to enter Mauritius if you are a citizen of the EU, the USA, Australia, Canada, Japan, New Zealand or a number of other countries. You can find more information on the government website (www.gov.mu). Initial entry is granted for a maximum of three months and proof of a planned and paid-for departure is required. If you change your departure plans, make sure you don't exceed your permitted stay.

Extensions for a further three months as a tourist are available from the **Passport & Immigration Office** (Map p66; ☎ 210 9312; fax 210 9322; Sterling House, Lislet Geoffrey St, Port Louis). Applications must be submitted with one form, two passport-size photos, your passport, an onward

ticket and proof of finances. Two letters may also be necessary – one from you explaining why you want to stay longer, and one by a local 'sponsor' (it can be someone providing accommodation). Providing you can satisfy these demands there should be no further problems, but since the police are responsible for passport control, and quite a few visitors overstay their entry permits, there are 'get tough' periods.

## WOMEN TRAVELLERS

There are no particular dangers for women in Mauritius, and you won't feel out of place travelling solo either. It's still sensible to avoid walking alone along heavily forested trails and roaming around late at night outside of resorts, particularly as most places have very poor or nonexistent street lighting. Port Louis is one extreme example where it really would be foolish to walk about alone after dark, especially near the Jardins de Compagnie (a favoured hang-out of pimps, drug addicts and prostitutes).

# TRANSPORT AROUND MAURITIUS

## AIR

Mainland Mauritius has only one airport, the well-run **Sir Seewoosagur Ramgoolam International Airport** (http://aml.mru.aero). **Air Mauritius** (www.airmauritius.com), the country's one main domestic airline, connects mainland Mauritius with the island of Rodrigues. At the time of research the secondary Catovair had one aircraft in its 'fleet' and Rodrigues was cutting the ribbon on its very own airline, SolitAir, which will offer direct service to both mainland Mauritius and Réunion starting in the near future.

Air Mauritius also offers helicopter tours and charters from SSR international airport to a number of major hotels. A full one-hour island tour costs Rs 32,000 for up to two passengers; a quick 15-minute jaunt will set you back Rs 12,000. For information and reservations, contact **Air Mauritius Helicopter Services** ( ☎ 637 3754; www.airmauritius.com/helicopter) or ask your hotel to organise a transfer or trip.

## BICYCLE

Cycling isn't really a practical means of long-distance transport in Mauritius – there is simply too much traffic and drivers can be unwieldy – but bikes are fine for short hops along the coast. Given that the coast is pleasantly flat, it's amazing how much ground you can cover in a day. The coast roads are also quieter than those in the interior, so you can relax and take in the landscape.

In general, the roads are well maintained, but look out for potholes along country lanes, especially in the western part of the island. Avoid cycling anywhere at night, as most roads are poorly lit and traffic can be erratic.

Most hotels and guesthouses can help you arrange bike rentals (usually mountain bikes), or try **Fit For Life** ( ☎ 452 2005; www.fflmauritius.com). Expect to pay Rs 250 for a quality bike. You'll usually be asked for a deposit of Rs 5000, either in cash or by taking an imprint of your credit card. Most bikes are in pretty reasonable condition, but be sure to check the brakes, gears and saddle (some are mighty uncomfortable) before riding off into the blue beyond. The bike should have a lock; use it, especially if you leave your bike at the beach and outside shops.

## BOAT

The only scheduled domestic passenger service is between Port Louis and Port Mathurin in Rodrigues. The *Mauritius Pride* sails between both ports every fortnight and the journey takes around 25 hours. Tickets and information are available through travel agents or direct from the Mauritius Shipping Corporation: in Mauritius, contact **Coraline Shipping Agency** (off Map p66; ☎ 217 2285; msc@coraline.intnet.mu; Nova Bldg, 1 Military Rd, Port Louis); on Rodrigues, the **Mauritius Shipping Corporation** (Map p139; ☎ 831 0640; www.mauritiusshipping.intnet.mu; Rue François Leguat, Port Mathurin). Return fares are available and there is a choice of either a seat/cabin. These are popular services, so it is advised that you book ahead.

Various private operators offer cruises to offshore islands, or snorkelling and fishing excursions. See p148 and the listings under individual towns for more information about these services.

## BUS

Anyone on a budget will fare well using the network of bus routes that criss-cross the island. Bus travel is cheap and fun – you'll usually find yourself chatting to gregarious locals – and although you won't set any landspeed records, it's generally a fairly easy and reliable way to get around.

It's best to stick to express buses whenever possible, as standard buses seem to stop every few metres and can take up to twice as long to reach the same destination. To give an idea of journey times, it takes approximately an hour by standard services from Mahébourg to Curepipe, an hour from Curepipe to Port Louis, and an hour from Port Louis to Grand Baie.

Long-distance buses run from around 6am to 6.30pm, though there is a late service between Port Louis and Curepipe until 11pm. Generally there are buses every 15 minutes or so on the major routes, with less frequent buses on the express services. Buses in country areas can be few and far between.

As an indication, fares range from Rs 15 for a short trip to a maximum of Rs 35 for the run from Port Louis to Mahébourg. Air-conditioned express buses may be a couple of rupees extra. Tickets are available from the conductor or porter (the conductor's 'assistant'); keep some small change handy. Retain your tickets, as inspectors often board to check them, and press the buzzer when you want to get off.

The buses are single-deck vehicles bearing dynamic names such as 'Road Warrior', 'Bad Boys' and 'The Street Ruler'. It's perhaps not surprising that some drivers harbour Formula One racing fantasies; fortunately, the frequent stops slow things down a touch. Though the buses are in varying states of disrepair, the fleet is gradually being upgraded.

The buses are almost always packed, especially on the main routes, but turnover is quick at all the stops. If you start the trip standing, you're likely to end up sitting.

Be warned that you could have problems taking large bags or backpacks on a bus. If it takes up a seat, you will probably have to pay for that extra seat. A few travellers have even been refused entry to a full bus if they have a large bag.

There is no countrywide bus service for Mauritius. Instead there are several large regional bus companies and scores of individual operators. Unfortunately, there are no published timetables available. Your best source of information is to phone the umbrella body, the **National Transport Authority** ( ☎ 202 2800). Locals also usually know the best way to get from A to B.

## CAR & MOTORCYCLE

By far the easiest and quickest way to get around Mauritius and Rodrigues is to hire a car. Prices aren't as low as they could be, considering the numbers of visitors who rent vehicles, but you should be able to negotiate a discount if you're renting for a week or more.

Mauritian roads range from the one stretch of polished motorway – running from SSR international airport to Port Louis and Grand Baie – to heavily potholed minor roads riddled with debris. Even on the motorway you'll find people wandering across the road and a generally relaxed attitude. As in most places, the greatest danger comes from other drivers, not the roads. Mauritian drivers tend to have little consideration for each other, let alone for motorbikes. Buses are notorious for overtaking and then pulling in immediately ahead of other vehicles to pick up or drop off passengers; always show extra caution when a bus comes in sight. At night be aware that you'll face an assault course of ill-lit oncoming vehicles, totally unlit bikes and weaving pedestrians. If you sense that you've hit something while driving at night in a quiet, dimly lit area, do not stop your vehicle to check it out. If you think that you have hit something, proceed to the nearest police station. Motorcyclists should also be prepared for the elements, as sudden rain showers can come out of clear skies.

## Car Hire

Generally, drivers must be more than 23 years of age (some companies only require a minimum age of 21) and have held a driving licence for at least one year, and payment must be made in advance. You can pay by credit card (Visa and MasterCard are the most widely accepted), though small companies might add a 3% 'processing fee' for this service. All foreigners are technically required to have an International Driving Licence. Few rental agencies enforce this, but it's safest to carry one as the police can demand to see it.

Rates for the smallest hatchback start at around Rs 900 a day (including insurance and unlimited mileage) with one of the local operators. Expect rates to start at Rs 1200 when using an international chain. On top of that you will be required to pay a refundable deposit, usually Rs 15,000; most companies will take an imprint of your credit card to cover this. Policies usually specify that drivers are liable for the first Rs 10,000 of damage in the event of an accident. Note that if you are renting a private apartment or villa you can usually ask the management company to help you sort out a lease.

Although there are dozens of operators on the island, it is best to book ahead during the high-season months (the European winter holidays). The following car hire companies have airport desks or can deliver to the airport.

**ABC** ( ☎ 216 8889; www.abc-carrental.com; 3B)
**ADA** ( ☎ 675 2626; www.adamaurice.net, in French; 14)
**Avis** ( ☎ 405 5200; www.avismauritius.com; 4B)
**Budget** ( ☎ 467 9700; www.budget.com.mu; 1A)
**Europcar** ( ☎ 637 3240; www.europcar.com; 3A)
**First** ( ☎ 213 9290; www.firstcarrental.mu; 8)
**Hertz** ( ☎ 670 4301; www.hertz.com; 17A)
**Sixt** ( ☎ 427 1111; www.sixt.com; 7B)

## Motorcycle Hire

There are only a few places where you can hire motorbikes, which is a shame as this is a great way to explore the quiet coastal roads – especially in traffic-free Rodrigues. While you'll occasionally find a 125cc bike, most are 100cc or under; the smaller models are referred to as scooters.

Expect to pay upwards of Rs 500 per day (Rs 600 in Rodrigues). As with car hire, payment is requested in advance along with a deposit of Rs 5000 or so.

Towns offering motorcycle hire include Grand Baie, Flic en Flac, Mahébourg and Port Mathurin. You should be aware that most motorcycle hire is 'unofficial' so you may not be covered in case of a collision.

## Parking

Parking is free and not a problem in most of Mauritius, though it's best not to leave your car in an isolated spot. City parking requires payment. There are supervised car parks in Port Louis, but elsewhere you'll have to park on the street, which involves buying parking coupons. These are available from petrol stations and cost from Rs 50 for 10 coupons, with each coupon valid for 30 minutes. The same coupons can be used all over the island. Street parking is generally free at night and on weekends; the exact hours, which vary from one town to another, are indicated on signposts.

## Road Rules

Local motorists seem to think they'll save electricity by not switching on their headlights, and the police are better at people control than traffic control. Traffic congestion is heavy in Port Louis. There are many pedestrian zebra crossings, but cross with care. Don't expect courtesy and don't expect drivers to be worried about insurance – you'll get knocked over.

Driving is on the left and the speed limit varies from 30km/h in town centres to 110km/h on the motorway – speed limits are usually marked. Even so, not many people stick to these limits and the island has its fair share of accidents.

Drivers and passengers are required to wear seat belts. For lack of sufficient breathalysers, the alcohol limit (legally 0.5g/L) is defined by the police as one glass of beer.

## HITCHING

Hitching is never entirely safe in any country in the world, and we don't recommend it. Travellers who decide to hitch should understand that they are taking a small but potentially serious risk. People who choose to hitch will be safer if they travel in pairs and let someone know where they are planning to go.

Getting a lift in Mauritius is subject to pretty much the same quirks of luck and fate that you experience hitching anywhere. The only place where it really does come in handy is Rodrigues. Since few people there own cars, hitching is a popular way to get around, especially on Sundays, when buses are few and far between. Those driving in Rodrigues will make friends by offering lifts to locals who'll try and flag you down almost anywhere. Obviously, proceed with caution and don't offer lifts to groups if you're alone.

## TAXI

It's sometimes possible to imagine that every adult male in Mauritius is a taxi driver. Taxi drivers will often shout out at travellers they see wandering around Port Louis or Grand Baie, while ranks outside hotels usually overflow with drivers. Negotiation is key – meters are rarely used and you'll usually be ripped off if you get in a taxi without agreeing on a price first. During the journey most drivers will also tout for future business; if you aren't careful, you may find that you've agreed to an all-day island tour. If you aren't interested, make this very clear, as many drivers won't take no for an answer.

Many guesthouse managers/owners have attempted to mitigate their guests' constant frustration with rip-offs by arranging prices with local taxi drivers. The quotes given under such arrangements, particularly those from small guesthouses, are often acceptable; they can usually arrange competitively priced airport pick-ups as well. Once you've got a feel for the rates, you can venture into independent bargaining. Check the Getting There & Away sections in the destination chapters for details regarding how much you should pay for a lift. You'll find that these prices are fairly standard throughout – you may be able to knock off Rs 100 or Rs 200 here and there, though don't be crestfallen if you can't whittle the driver down to the exact price marked on the pages (after all, they have had more practise at the taxi game than you!).

Taxis charge slightly more at night and may ask for an extra fee if you want the comfort of air-con. It's also worth remembering that some taxis charge around Rs 1 per minute waiting time. It seems minimal, but it adds up if you stop for lunch or do some sightseeing on foot. Your best bet is to negotiate a set fare with the driver that includes waiting time.

### TAXI HIRE

For around Rs 2000 you can hire a taxi for a full-day tour of sights along one or two coasts of the island. You can cut costs by forming a group – the price should *not* be calculated per person. If you want to squeeze a tour of the whole island into one day, keep in mind that this won't leave much time for sightseeing. You're better off splitting the island tour into two days. Once you've agreed to a price and itinerary, it helps to get the details down in writing. Although most drivers can speak both French and English, double-check before setting off to ensure you won't face a day-long communication barrier. If you're lucky, you'll get an excellent and informative guide, but note that most drivers work on a commission basis with particular restaurants, shops and sights. If you want to go to a restaurant of your choice, you may have to insist on it. Again, small guesthouses can usually recommend a reliable driver.

### SHARE TAXI

When individual fares are hard to come by, some taxis will cruise around their area supplementing the bus service. For quick, short-haul trips they pick up passengers waiting at the bus stops and charge just a little more than the bus. Their services are called 'share taxis' or 'taxi trains'. Mind you, if you flag down a share taxi, you'll only be swapping a big sardine can for a small one, and if you flag down an empty taxi, you may have to pay the full fare.

# Réunion

JEAN-BERNARD CARILLET

# Réunion Snapshots

After having faced a major health crisis in 2006 and 2007 due to the mosquito-borne Chikungunya virus, Réunion is back on its feet. By mid-2007 the 'Chik', as it's dubbed in Réunion, was eradicated. The future looks brighter now. Despite the worldwide downturn in tourism, the sector has been slowly picking up again. Local authorities lay emphasis on the island's 'green' image and its fantastic opportunities for ecotourism and outdoor activities. Their aim is to tap into new markets, especially the German and Anglophone ones, in order to reduce the dependence on the French market.

Paradoxically, one of the greatest immediate concerns is not the environment but the ever-growing population. Recent estimates suggest that the population of Réunion will reach one million by 2020. Housing and transport are the main problems. Already there is tremendous pressure on building land. Most of the population is concentrated on the coastal strip, where the towns are gradually beginning to merge into one continuous urban 'ring'. Houses are also spreading slowly up the hillsides and traffic congestion is becoming a major headache. To relieve some of this pressure, the government invested in an ambitious expressway, the Route des Tamarins, between St-Paul and Étang-Salé-les-Bains, which was inaugurated in June 2009 after six years of work. Another mammoth project, the 'Tram-Train', was in the pipeline until May 2010, when it was dropped for lack of funding. It was a sort of tramway, which would have connected Ste-Marie to St-Paul (40km) via St-Denis. That said, environmentalists still hope that this project will be reactivated.

## HISTORY

Réunion has a history similar to that of Mauritius. It was colonised by the French after the mid-17th century but later fell briefly under British rule. As in Mauritius, the colonisers introduced plantation crops and African slaves. Later came Indian indentured labourers and Chinese merchants, creating an ethnic diversity which is one of these islands' most distinctive characteristics. While Mauritius gained its independence in 1968, Réunion remains an overseas department of France.

### WELCOME TO PARADISE

The first visitors to the uninhabited island were probably Malay, Arab and European mariners, none of whom stayed. Then, in 1642, the French took the decision to settle the island, which at the time was called Mascarin. The first settlers arrived four years later, when the French governor of Fort Dauphin in southern Madagascar banished a dozen mutineers to the island.

On the basis of enthusiastic reports from the mutineers, King Louis XIV of France officially claimed the island in 1649 and renamed it Île Bourbon.

However appealing it seemed, there was no great rush to populate and develop the island. It was not until the beginning of the 18th century that the French East India Company and the French government took control of the island.

### COFFEE, ANYONE?

Coffee was introduced between 1715 and 1730 and soon became the island's main cash crop. The island's economy changed dramatically. As coffee

**FAST FACTS**

Population: 820,000 (estimated)

Territory size: 2512 sq km

Languages: French, Creole

Capital: St-Denis

Highest point: Piton des Neiges (3070m)

Distance from Réunion to Mauritius: 220km

Unemployment: 30%

Estimated number of cars: 350,000

Lychee season: Dec-Feb

The most ruthless hunter of runaway slaves was François Mussard, whose name is now remembered only because it has been given to a dank, dark cave near Piton des Neiges.

required intensive labour, African and Malagasy slaves were brought by the shipload. During this period, cereals, spices and cotton were also introduced as cash crops.

Like Mauritius, Réunion came of age under the governorship of the visionary Mahé de Labourdonnais, who served from 1735 to 1746. However, Labourdonnais treated Île de France (Mauritius) as a favoured sibling, and after the collapse of the French East India Company and the pressure of ongoing rivalry with Britain the governance of Île Bourbon passed directly to the French crown in 1764.

After the French Revolution, the island's name was changed to La Réunion (meaning 'Joining' or 'Meeting').

From around 1685, Indian Ocean pirates began using Île Bourbon as a trading base.

## THE BRITISH MOVE IN...

In 1810, during the Napoleonic Wars, Napoleon Bonaparte lost the island to the *habits rouges* (redcoats). Under British rule, sugar cane was introduced to Réunion and quickly became the primary crop. The vanilla industry, introduced in 1819, also grew rapidly.

The British didn't stay long: five years later, under the Treaty of Paris, the spoils were returned to the French as Île Bourbon. The British, however, retained their grip on Mauritius, Rodrigues and the Seychelles.

## ... AND THE FRENCH COME BACK TO STAY

In 1848, the Second Republic was proclaimed in France, slavery was abolished and Île Bourbon again became La Réunion. Like Mauritius, Réunion immediately experienced a labour crisis and, like the British in Mauritius, the French 'solved' the problem by importing contract labourers from India, most of them Hindus, to work the sugar cane.

Réunion's golden age of trade and development lasted until 1870, with the country flourishing on the trade route between Europe, India and the Far East. Competition from Cuba and the European sugar-beet industry, combined with the opening of the Suez Canal (which short-circuited the journey around the Cape of Good Hope), resulted in an economic slump.

After WWI, in which 14,000 Réunionnais served, the sugar industry regained a bit of momentum, but it again suffered badly through the blockade of the island during WWII.

Réunion became a Département Français d'Outre-Mer (DOM; French Overseas Department) in 1946 and has representation in the French parliament. Since then there have been feeble independence movements from time to time but, unlike those in France's Pacific territories, these have never

---

### BLACK HISTORY

The late 18th century saw a number of slave revolts, and many resourceful Malagasy and African slaves, called *marrons*, escaped from their owners and took refuge in the mountainous interior. Some of them established private utopias in inaccessible parts of the Cirques, while others grouped together and formed organised communities with democratically elected leaders. These tribal chieftains were the true pioneers of the settlement of Réunion, but most ultimately fell victim to bounty hunters who were employed to hunt them down. The scars of this period of the island's history are still fresh in the population's psyche; perhaps from a sense of shame, there's surprisingly little record of the island's Creole pioneers except the names of several peaks (Dimitile, Enchaing, Mafate, Cimendef) where they were hunted down and killed. The Espace Culturel Muséographique Dimitile (ECM; see p201) at Entre-Deux provides excellent introductions to these sensitive subjects, tracing the history of slavery and *marronage* (the act of escaping plantation life) and celebrating the achievements of these unsung heroes of the Cirques.

amounted to much. While the Réunionnais seemed satisfied to remain totally French, general economic and social discontent surfaced in dramatic anti-government riots in St-Denis in 1991.

In March 1998, there was a major eruption at the Piton de la Fournaise – the longest eruption of the volcano in the 20th century, with a total of 196 days of volcanic activity. In April 2007, another major eruption resulted in the RN2 expressway being closed for several months.

The turn of the century marked a new era for Réunion; the local authorities managed to sign a few agreements with the French state, which confirmed the launching of subsidised *grands chantiers* (major infrastructure works), including the expressway called the Nouvelle Route des Tamarins, the Tram-Train between Ste-Marie and St-Paul and the enlargement of the Route du Littoral (the expressway between St-Paul and St-Denis). These huge civil engineering works are expected to sustain growth on the island. So far, only the Route des Tamarins has been completed. Delays in finalising financial agreements have prevented the works of the Tram-Train and Route du Littoral from starting.

# THE CULTURE

## THE NATIONAL IDENTITY

For a general introduction to the island, pick up Catherine Lavaux's classic *La Réunion: Du Battant des Lames au Sommet des Montagnes*. It covers everything from the geography and flora of Réunion to its history.

The physical and cultural distinctions between the various ethnic groups are far less apparent in Réunion than in Mauritius. In Réunion there has been much more interracial mixing over the years. Ask the Réunionnais how they see themselves and the chances are they'll say 'Creole' – not in the narrow sense of having Afro-French ancestry, but simply meaning one of 'the people'. That is, someone who speaks Creole, who was born and bred on the island and is probably – but not necessarily – of mixed ancestry. This sense of community is the gel that holds society together.

The Réunionnais are in general more reserved than the Mauritians, but within this overall pattern there are local differences: southerners are reckoned to be more relaxed and friendly, while perhaps not surprisingly the people living in the Cirques are the most introverted.

While the Réunionnais do also regard themselves as French, they don't really identify with people from the mainland. There is even a slight undercurrent of resentment towards the 100,000 or so mainlanders who dominate the island's administration and economy. The locals refer to them very slightly derogatorily as Zoreilles (the Ears); the usual explanation is that they are straining to hear what's being said about them in the local patois.

## LIFESTYLE

Contemporary Réunionnais are a thoroughly 21st-century people. The vast majority of children receive a decent standard of education and all islanders have access to the national health system, either in Réunion or in France. There are traffic jams, everyone is on a mobile (cell) phone, and flashy cars are ubiquitous. But beneath this modern veneer, there are many more traditional aspects.

One of the strongest bonds unifying society, after the Creole language, is the importance placed on family life. It's particularly made evident at the *pique-nique du dimanche en famille* (Sunday family picnic; see p166). Religious occasions and public holidays are also vigorously celebrated, as are more personal, family events, such as baptisms, first communions and weddings.

**PATRICK LOUAISIEL**

This Zoreille has been studying Réunion's cultural fabric for more than 30 years and is married to a Tamil lady.

**What makes Réunion unique, culturally speaking?** Sadly, the cultural riches of our island remain underrated. Visitors head straight to the west coast, the cirques and the volcano. It's a shame, because they miss out on lots of cultural facets. We have a fascinating Creole, African, Indian, Chinese and French heritage. There's a wealth of religious buildings on this island – mosques, churches, temples, pagodas – that testify to our rich past, and tourists are positively surprised to see how diverse Réunion is.

**How can visitors get to know better Réunionnais culture?** It's a good idea to make your trip coincide with fire walks (September to January), or the Cavadee and Dipavali festivals. The tourist offices can provide exact dates and locations. The Abolition of Slavery Day, on December 20, is also a great occasion to immerse yourself in local culture, with lots of local music and dancing. And be sure to take time to discover Creole architecture in St-Denis, St-Pierre, Entre-Deux, and Hell-Bourg, where you'll find a flurry of well-preserved *cases créoles* (traditional Creole houses).

*Patrick Louaisiel leads cultural tours around Réunion, with a focus on religious and traditional beliefs.*

Though Réunion can't be mistaken for, say, Ibiza, Réunionnais share a zest for the fest. On weekends St-Gilles-les-Bains, L'Hermitage-les-Bains and St-Pierre are a magnet for Réunionnais from all over the island. The towns turn wild on those evenings as flocks of night owls arrive en masse to wiggle their hips and guzzle pints of Dodo beer and glasses of rum.

On a more mundane level, you'll quickly realise that the possession of a brand new car is a sign of wealth and respect. The 'car culture' is a dominant trait; small wonder that traffic jams are the norm on the coastal roads. Many Réunionnais spend up to two hours daily in their car going to and from work! One favourite topic of conversation is the state of the roads, especially the tricky Route du Littoral between St-Paul and St-Denis, which is sometimes closed due to fallen rocks.

Another noticeable (though less immediately so) characteristic is the importance of *la di la fé* (gossip). If you can understand a little bit of French (or Creole), tune in to *Radio Free Dom* – you'll soon realise that gossip's a national pastime.

A cagier issue is the RMI (see Economy, p165). For the French mainlanders, the Réunionnais are *assistés* (spoiled children) who get a lot of funds from Paris and from the generous welfare system. For the Réunionnais, it's just resourcefulness and a way to improve their standard of living.

People are relatively tolerant of homosexuality, though by no means as liberal as in mainland France; open displays of affection may be regarded with disdain, especially outside St-Denis.

There's a refreshingly liberal attitude towards women, and younger Réunionnais women especially are quite outspoken and emancipated. Divorce, abortion and childbirth outside marriage are all fairly uncontentious issues. However, it's not all rosy: women are poorly represented in local government and politics, and domestic violence is prevalent. This is closely connected to high rates of alcoholism.

Despite the social problems that blight any culture, on the whole it's a society that lives very easily together.

## ECONOMY

Réunion is one of the richest islands in the Indian Ocean. The standard of living is fairly high, and it's no surprise. As a French department, the island receives a lot from mainland France *(la métropole)*. However, Réunion faces

---

**SUNDAY PICNIC: A RÉUNIONNAIS INSTITUTION**

At the weekend there's nothing the Réunionnais like better than trundling off to the seaside or the mountains for a huge family picnic – think giant-sized rice cookers replete with hearty *carris* (curries) in the company of *gramounes* (grandparents) and *marmailles* (children). To get the most sought-after picnic shelters, some members of the family sometimes arrive at 4am to reserve them! Visitors are welcome, and are usually invited to share a meal.

---

numerous challenges. The unemployment rate, for example, currently hovers around 30%, way above the national average (about 8% at the time of writing), but at least it's down from the peak of 38% in 1998. It's particularly problematic for women and young people without qualifications. Why isn't there any major social outburst? It's simple: the generous French social system, especially the RMI (Revenu Minimum d'Insertion; an allowance that any unemployed person aged over 26 can claim), acts as a lifesaver for many individuals – not to mention the high level of *travail au noir* (moonlighting) on top of the RMI. You won't see homelessness in Réunion, not simply because of the existence of the RMI but also because of family ties, which remain strong.

Réunion imports around 60% of its needs from *la métropole*. In turn, mainland France accounts for some 70% of Réunion's exports. The vast majority is sugar, with other agricultural and marine products coming a distant second.

For the present, Réunion's sugar producers have managed to hang on to their European quotas and guaranteed prices but, following EU enlargement and with the reform of the EU sugar sector that was adopted in 2006, they may not be able to do so for much longer. As a result, the movers and shakers of Réunion's economy are increasingly looking to closer ties with Mauritius and the rest of Africa for their financial future.

Tourism is another major source of income, but it plummeted to 278,000 visitors in 2006 (down from 410,000 tourist arrivals in 2005) as a result of the Chikungunya epidemic. Since 2007, the sector has been picking up again (400,000 tourist arrivals in 2008) but the vast majority of visitors are French. There's a huge potential for growth, but there are a few hurdles: it's underpromoted in the Anglophone markets; English is not widely spoken on the island (to say the least); and the cost of flights is still prohibitive.

## POPULATION

Cultural diversity forms an integral part of the island's social fabric. Réunion has the same population mix of Africans, Europeans, Indians and Chinese as Mauritius, but in different proportions. Cafres (people of African ancestry) are the largest ethnic group, comprising about 45% of the population. Malbars (Hindu Indians) comprise about 25% of the population, white Creoles (people of French ancestry) 15%, Europeans (also known as Zoreilles) 7%, Chinese 4% and Z'arabes (Muslim Indians) 4%.

Creoles of African origin are called Cafres locally. The mainland French are called Zoreilles or Métro, and the French who have adopted the island's lifestyle and can speak Creole are called Zoréol.

The bulk of the island's population lives in coastal zones, with Malabars living predominantly in the east. The rugged interior is sparsely populated. Because the birth rate has remained quite high, a third of the population is under 20 years of age.

Réunion also sees a continual tide of would-be immigrants. With a system of generous welfare payments for the unemployed, the island is seen as a land of milk and honey by those from Mauritius, the Seychelles and some mainland African countries. In recent years there has been significant immigration from neighbouring Comoros and Mayotte Islands.

## RELIGION

An estimated 70% of the population belongs to the Catholic faith, which dominates the island's religious character. It's evidenced in the many saints' days and holidays, as well as in the names of towns and cities. Religious rituals and rites of passage play an important part in the lives of the people, and baptisms, first communions and church weddings are an integral part of social culture.

About a quarter of Réunionnais are Hindus, which is the dominant faith in the east. Traditional Hindu rites such as *teemeedee,* which features fire-walking, and *cavadee,* which for pilgrims entails piercing the cheeks with skewers, often take place. (For more information on these rites, see p152.) Muslims make up roughly 2% of the population; as in Mauritius, Islam tends to be fairly liberal, though a number of Muslim women wear the veil.

Interestingly, a great deal of syncretism between Hinduism, Islam and Catholicism has evolved over the years. In fact, many of the Malabar-Réunionnais participate in both Hindu and Catholic rites and rituals.

Apart from celebrating the Chinese New Year, the Sino-Réunionnais community (making up about 3% of the population) is not very conspicuous in its religious or traditional practices.

As in Mauritius, religious tolerance is the norm. Mosques, churches, Hindu temples and pagodas can be found within a stone's throw of each other in most towns.

It's estimated that almost one-third of all Réunionnais, about 450,000 people, live in *la métropole* (mainland France).

## ARTS

One of the greatest pleasures of visiting Réunion is experiencing Creole-flavoured French culture or French-flavoured Creole culture, depending on how you look at it. For news of cultural activities on the island, keep an eye on the local press and visit local tourist offices, where you can pick up flyers, theatre programs and a number of free events guides such as the monthly *Azenda* (www.azenda.fr, in French).

### Literature

Few Réunionnais novelists are known outside the island and none are translated into English. One of the most widely recognised and prolific contemporary authors is the journalist and historian Daniel Vaxelaire, who has written a number of evocative historical novels. His *Chasseurs des Noires,* an easily accessible tale of a slave-hunter's life-changing encounter with an escaped slave, is probably the best to start with.

Jean-François Sam-Long, a novelist and poet who helped relaunch Creole literature in the 1970s, also takes slavery as his theme. *Madame Desbassyns*

---

**THE ODD CULT OF ST EXPÉDIT**

St Expédit is one of Réunion's most popular saints, though some scholars argue there never was a person called Expédit. Whatever the truth, the idea was brought to Réunion in 1931 when a local woman erected a statue of the 'saint' in St-Denis' Notre-Dame de la Délivrance church in thanks for answering her prayer to return to Réunion. Soon there were shrines honouring St Expédit all over the island, where people prayed for his help in the speedy resolution of all sorts of tricky problems.

Over the years, however, worship of the saint has taken on the sinister overtones of a voodoo cult: figurines stuck with pins are left at the saint's feet; beheaded statues of him are perhaps the result of unanswered petitions. The saint has also been adopted into the Hindu faith, which accounts for the brilliant, blood-red colour of many shrines. As a result the Catholic Church has tried to distance itself from the cult, but the number of shrines continues to grow.

was inspired by the remarkable life story of a sugar baroness. In *La Nuit Cyclone* he explores the gulf between whites and blacks in a small village, against a backdrop of black magic and superstition.

Other well-established novelists to look out for are Axel Gauvin *(Train Fou, L'Aimé* and *Cravate et Fils)* and Jules Bénard.

There are several up-and-coming writers who deal with contemporary issues. Joëlle Ecormier spins her first novel, *Plus Légér que l'Air,* around a young islander living in France who returns to Réunion to face her past. *Les Chants des Kayanms* by Agnès Gueneau also revolves around Zoreilles–Réunionnais relationships, in this case a love affair between a local woman and a man from the mainland. It's a lyrical tale, evoking the rhythms of *maloya* (traditional slave music).

## Music & Dance

Réunion's music mixes the African rhythms of reggae, *séga* (traditional slave music) and *maloya* with French, British and American rock and folk sounds. Like *séga, maloya* is derived from the music of the slaves, but it is slower and more reflective, its rhythms and words heavy with history, somewhat like New Orleans blues; fans say it carries the true spirit of Réunion. *Maloya* songs often carry a political message and up until the 1970s the music was banned for being too subversive.

Instruments used to accompany the *séga* and the *maloya* range from traditional homemade percussion pieces, such as the hide-covered *rouleur* drum and the maraca-like *kayamb*, to the accordion and modern band instruments.

The giants of the local music scene, and increasingly well known in mainland France, are Daniel Waro, Firmin Viry, Gramoun Lélé, Davy Sicard, Kaf Malbar and the group Ziskakan. More recently, women have also emerged on the musical scene, including Christine Salem and Nathalie Nathiembé. All are superb practitioners of *maloya*. Favourite subjects for them are slavery, poverty and the search for cultural identity.

As for Creole-flavoured modern grooves, the Réunionnais leave those to their tropical cousins in Martinique and Guadeloupe, although they make popular listening in Réunion. It's all catchy stuff, and you'll hear it in bars, discos and vehicles throughout the islands of the Indian Ocean.

Stay tuned – the website www.runmuzik.fr (in French) is your chaperone to Réunionnais music.

## Architecture

The distinctive 18th-century Creole architecture of Réunion is evident in both the grand villas built by wealthy planters and other *colons* (settlers/colonists) and in the *ti' cases,* the homes of the common folk.

Local authorities are actively striving to preserve the (few) remaining examples of Creole architecture around the island. You can see a number of beautifully restored houses in St-Denis and in the towns of Cilaos, Entre-Deux, Hell-Bourg and St-Pierre, among other places. They all sport *lambrequins, varangues* and other ornamental features.

---

### KABARS

If you're passionate about Creole music (and we're sure you will be), try to attend a *kabar.* A *kabar* is a kind of impromptu concert or ball that is usually held in a courtyard or on the beach, where musicians play *maloya*. It's usually organised by associations, informal groups or families, but outsiders are welcome. There's no schedule; *kabars* are usually advertised by means of word of mouth, flyers or small ads in the newspapers. You can also inquire at the bigger tourist offices.

# FOOD & DRINK

Réunionnais like to eat and their food is a pleasure on the palate, with a balanced melange of French cuisine (locally known as *cuisine métro*) and Creole specialities and flavours, not to mention Indian and Chinese influences. A good number of eateries, *chambres d'hôte* (family-run B&Bs) and cafes offer a wide variety of quality food, and not just in the larger towns, with the added bonus of a great choice of drinks.

## STAPLES & SPECIALITIES

It's impossible to visit Réunion without coming across *carri* (curry), also spelt *cari* locally, which features on practically every single menu. The sauce comprises tomatoes, onions, garlic, ginger, thyme and saffron (or turmeric) and accompanies various kinds of meat, such as chicken *(carri poulet)*, pork *(carri porc)*, duck *(carri canard)* and guinea fowl *(carri pintade)*. Seafood *carris*, such as tuna *(carri thon)*, swordfish *(carri espadon)*, lobster *(carri langouste)* and freshwater prawn *(carri camarons)* are also excellent. Octopus *carri*, one of the best *carris* you'll eat, is called *civet zourite* in Creole. Local vegetables can also be prepared *carri*-style – try *carri baba figue* (banana-flower *carri*) and *carri ti jaque* (jackfruit *carri*) – but they incorporate fish or meat. *Carris* are invariably served with rice, grains (lentils or haricot beans), *brèdes* (local spinach) and *rougail*, a spicy chutney that mixes tomato, garlic, ginger and chillies; other preparations of *rougail* may include a mixture of green mango and citrus.

The word *rougail* is a bit confusing, though. It's also used for some variations of *carris*. *Rougail saucisses* is in fact sausages cooked in tomato sauce, while *rougail boucané* is a smoked pork *carri* (without saffron), and *rougail morue* is cod *carri* (also without saffron). You'll also find *civet*, which is another variety of stew. A widespread Tamil stew is *cabri massalé* (goat *carri*). On top of this, you'll find excellent beef meat (usually imported from South Africa) prepared in all its forms (steak, sirloin, rib).

Seafood lovers will be delighted to hear that the warm waters of the Indian Ocean provide an ample net of produce: lobster, prawns, *légine* (toothfish), swordfish, marlin, tuna and shark, among others. Freshwater prawns, usually served in *carri*, are highly prized.

Réunionnais love vegetables, eating them in salads or in *gratins* (a baked dish). You'll certainly come across *chou chou* (choko; a speciality in the Cirque de Salazie), lentils (a speciality in the Cirque de Cilaos), *bois de songe* and *vacoa* (a speciality in the Wild South), not to mention *bringelles* (aubergines) and *baba figue* (banana flower).

Snacks include samosas, *beignets* (fritters) and *bonbons piments* (chilli fritters).

Fruits also reign supreme. Two iconic Réunionnais fruits are litchis (lychees) and *ananas Victoria* (pineapple of the Victoria variety). Local mangoes, passionfruit and papaya are also fabulously sweet. The local vanilla (see the boxed text, p238) is said to be one of the most flavoured in the world.

Breakfast is decidedly French: *pain-beurre-confiture* (baguette, butter and jam) served with coffee, tea or hot chocolate is the most common threesome. Added treats may include croissants, *pain au chocolat* (chocolate-filled pastry), brioches and honey.

What about desserts? If you like carb-laden cakes and pies, you'll be happy in Réunion. They might knock five years off your life but they taste so good you won't care. Each family has its own recipe for *gâteaux maison* (homemade cakes), which come in various guises. They are usually made from vanilla, banana, sweet potato, maize, carrot, guava… Our favourite is *macatia* (a variety of bun), which can also be served at breakfast.

The tourist office in St-Denis has put together a guide to 12 *villages créoles*, including Cilaos, Hell-Bourg and Entre-Deux, chosen for their particularly rich architectural heritage and traditional way of life.

Drool over your keyboard while checking out the recipes on the following websites (all in French): www.cuisinereunion naise.com; www.creole .org/cuisine.htm; www .goutanou-cuisine-reunionnaise.org; and www.iledelareunion.net/ cuisine-reunion.

## DRINKS

Rum, rum, rum! Up in the hills, almost everyone will have their own family recipe for *rhum arrangé,* a heady mixture of local rum and a secret blend of herbs and spices. In fact, not all are that secret. Popular concoctions include *rhum faham,* a blend of rum, sugar and flowers from the faham orchid; *rhum vanille,* made from rum, sugar and fresh vanilla pods; and *rhum bibasse,* made from rum, sugar and tasty *bibasse* (medlar fruit). The family *rhum arrangé* is a source of pride for most Creoles; if you stay in any of the rural *gîtes* or *chambres d'hôte* you can expect the proprietor to serve up their version with more than a little ceremony.

Réunion being French territory, wine is unsurprisingly taken seriously. Along with French wines, you'll find a good choice of South African reds and whites. The island also has a small but blossoming viniculture in Cilaos, where you can do a tasting (see the boxed text, p205).

The local brand of beer, Bourbon (known as Dodo), is sold everywhere. It is a fairly light, very drinkable beer. Foreign beers are also available. For a refresher, nothing beats a fresh fruit juice or a glass of Cilaos, a high-quality sparkling water from Cirque de Cilaos.

The French take their coffee seriously and it's a passion that hasn't disappeared just because they're now in the Indian Ocean. A cup of coffee can take various forms but the most common is a small, black espresso called simply *un café.*

> Unlike *rhum arrangé,* punch is made of only one fruit (most commonly banana, vanilla or lychee) and is served as an aperitif. *Rhum arrangé* is usually served as a *digestif* (post-meal drink).

## WHERE TO EAT & DRINK

There is a wondrous array of eateries in Réunion, from snack-bar-cum-cafes to high-class restaurants serving fine French cuisine, to *tables d'hôte* (home-cooked meals served at *chambres d'hôte*) and beach restaurants. For self-caterers, there's no shortage of very well-stocked supermarkets, not to mention numerous markets, where you can stock up on delicious, fresh ingredients. On Sunday, most Réunionnais opt for a picnic on the beach or in the Hauts.

On top of *la carte* (menu), most restaurants have *menus* (set courses) and daily specials. You'll also find numerous roadside stalls selling fruits, especially during the lychee season from December to February.

The service charge is included in the bill, and tipping is not necessary. If you want to leave something extra, that's up to you.

## HABITS & CUSTOMS

There are relatively few strict rules of dining and etiquette. Though formal restaurants certainly exist, a casual atmosphere and boisterous families are the norm, especially at weekends.

---

**TRAVEL YOUR TASTE BUDS**

If you're a gastronomic adventurer, start your culinary odyssey with *salade de palmiste,* a delectable salad made from the bud of the palmiste palm tree, known as the 'heart of palm'. The palm dies once the bud is removed, earning this wasteful salad delicacy the title 'millionaire's salad'. For something a bit more unusual, try *carri bichiques* (a sprat-like delicacy), which is dubbed *le caviar réunionnais* (Réunionnais caviar). You might need to seek out *larves de guêpes* (wasps' larvae), another local delicacy that is available from April to October. Fried and salted, they reputedly increase sexual stamina.

You may also want to learn the terms for *carri pat' cochons* (pig's trotter *carri*) and *carri anguilles* (eel *carri*) so you don't accidentally order them in a restaurant. Réunionnais also drool over *carri tang* (hedgehog *carri*), which you're not likely to find served in restaurants. If you happen to eat it at a private home, let us know if you've survived it…

---

**RÉUNION'S TOP FIVE**

**Les Letchis** (p239) An ode to Creole cuisine and 'riverfood'. Eel curry, anyone?
**L'Igloo** (p182) Addictive ice creams.
**Table Paysanne Chez Fiarda** (p231) Superb Creole dishes prepared with produce from the farm.
**Ferme-Auberge Chez Éva Hannibal** (p237) The dinner menu will have you walking out belly-first.
**Le Vieux Port** (p232) Fabulous *salade de palmiste* ('heart of palm' salad) enjoyed in a bucolic setting.

See also p233 for our favourite picnic spots.

---

Table manners are more or less the same as those in mainland France. And, as in France, lunches are taken seriously in Réunion – long, lingering midday meals are de rigueur.

## VEGETARIANS & VEGANS

Despite the Indian influence, Réunion is an island of meat lovers. To our knowledge, there aren't any dedicated vegetarian restaurants. That said, vegetarians won't go hungry. Salads, rice and fruits are ubiquitous. In Chinese restaurants, menus feature vegetarian dishes, such as chop suey and noodles. Most supermarkets have vegetarian fare too, and *chambres d'hôte* owners will be happy to cook vegetarian dishes if you let them know well in advance. And there's always dessert!

# ENVIRONMENT

Réunion lies about 220km southwest of Mauritius, at the southernmost end of the great Mascarene volcanic chain. Réunion's volcano, Piton de la Fournaise, erupts with great regularity, spewing lava down its southern and eastern flanks. The last major eruption occurred in 2007, when lava flows reached the sea and added another few square metres to the island. Since 1998 there have been spectacular eruptions almost every second year – an attraction in its own right. But don't worry: the volcano is expertly monitored by local authorities and there are strict security measures when it's erupting.

## THE LAND

There are two major mountainous areas on Réunion. The older of the two covers most of the western half of the island. The highest mountain is Piton des Neiges (3070m), an alpine-class peak. Surrounding it are three immense and splendid amphitheatres: the Cirques of Cilaos, Mafate and Salazie. These long, wide, deep hollows are sheer-walled canyons filled with convoluted peaks and valleys, the eroded remnants of the ancient volcanic shield that surrounded Piton des Neiges.

The smaller of the two mountainous regions lies in the southeast and continues to evolve. It comprises several extinct volcanic cones and one that is still very much alive, Piton de la Fournaise (2632m). This rumbling peak still pops its cork relatively frequently in spectacular fashion, and between eruptions quietly steams and hisses away. No one lives in the shadow of the volcano, where lava flowing down to the shore has left a remarkable jumbled slope of cooled black volcanic rock, known as Le Grand Brûlé.

These two mountainous areas are separated by a region of high plains, while the coast is defined by a gently sloping plain which varies in width. Numerous rivers wind their way down from the Piton des Neiges range,

Piton de la Fournaise is undoubtedly the island's most iconic attraction and one of the world's most accessible active volcanoes. The website www.fournaise.info (in French) will keep even nonvulcanologists enthralled.

through the Cirques, cutting deeply into the coastal plains to form spectacular ravines.

# WILDLIFE
## Animals

Because it was never part of a continental land mass, Réunion has relatively few animal species. The island's only indigenous mammal species are two types of bat, both of which can sometimes be seen around the coast at night. The mammals which you are far more likely to see are introduced hares, deer, geckoes, rats and, if you're lucky, chameleons. Tenrecs (called *tang* in Creole), which resemble hedgehogs, were a species introduced from Madagascar.

The most interesting creepy crawlies are the giant millipedes – some as long as a human foot – which loll around beneath rocks in more humid areas. Another oversized creature is the yellow-and-black *Nephila* spider whose massive webs are a common sight. You'll also find the *Heteropoda venatoria* or huntsman spider, called *babouk* in Creole.

As far as bird life is concerned, of the original 30 species endemic to the island, only nine remain. The island's rarest birds are the *merle blanc* or cuckoo shrike – locals call it the *tuit tuit*, for obvious reasons – and the black petrel. Probably the best chance of seeing – or, more likely, hearing – the *tuit tuit* is directly south of St-Denis, near the foot of La Roche Écrite. Only an estimated 160 pairs remain.

Bulbuls, which resemble blackbirds (with yellow beaks and legs but grey feathers) and are locally known as *merles*, are also common. The Mascarene paradise flycatcher is a pretty little bird with a small crest and a long, flowing red tail.

Birds native to the highlands include the *tec-tec* or Réunion stonechat, which inhabits the tamarind forests. There's also the *papangue*, or Maillardi buzzard, a protected hawklike bird which begins life as a little brown bird and turns black and white as it grows older. It is Réunion's only surviving bird of prey and may be spotted soaring over the ravines.

The best-known sea bird is the white *paille-en-queue* or white-tailed tropicbird, which sports two long tail plumes. It can often be seen riding the thermals created by the Piton de la Fournaise volcano. Other sea birds include visiting albatrosses, petrels and shearwaters.

Mynahs, introduced at the end of the 18th century to keep the grasshoppers under control, are common all over the island, as are the small, red cardinal-like birds known as fodies.

The best spots to see bird life are the Forêt de Bébour-Bélouve above Hell-Bourg, and the wilderness region of Le Grand Brûlé at the southern tip of the island.

## Plants

Now this is Réunion's strong point! Thanks to an abundant rainfall and marked differences in altitude, Réunion boasts some of the most varied plant life in the world. Parts of the island are like a grand botanical garden. Between the coast and the alpine peaks you'll find palms, screw pines (also known as pandanus or *vacoa*), casuarinas *(filaos)*, vanilla, spices, other tropical fruit and vegetable crops, rainforest and alpine flora.

Réunion has no less than 700 indigenous plant species, 150 of which are trees. Unlike Mauritius, large areas of natural forest still remain. It's estimated that 30% of the island is covered by native forest; some areas – particularly in the ravines – have never been touched by man.

Meet Réunion's feathered creatures in Nicolas Barré and Armand Barau's beautifully illustrated field guide, *Oiseaux de la Réunion*.

Find information on local birds and where to spot them at www.seor.fr (in French).

Gnarled and twisted and sporting yellow, mimosa-like flowers, the *tamarin des Hauts* or mountain tamarind tree, is a type of acacia and is endemic to Réunion. Locals compare them to oak trees because the timber is excellent for building. One of the best places to see these ancient trees is in the Forêt de Bébour-Bélouve, east of the Cirque de Salazie.

At the other extreme, the lava fields around the volcano exhibit a barren, moonlike surface. Here the various stages of vegetation growth, from a bare new lava base, are evident. The first plant to appear on lava is the heather-like plant the French call *branle vert (Philippia montana)*. Much later in the growth cycle come tamarind and other acacia trees.

Afforestation has been carried out mainly with the Japanese cryptomeria, *tamarin des Hauts,* casuarina and various palms.

Like any tropical island, Réunion has a wealth of flowering species, including orchids, hibiscus, bougainvillea, vetiver, geranium, frangipani and jacaranda. Flower-spotters will enjoy the several excellent botanical gardens on the island, including the Conservatoire Botanique National de Mascarin (p197), the Jardin d'Eden (p189) near St-Gilles-les-Bains and the Jardin des Parfums et des Épices (p231) in St-Philippe.

> A number of traditional distilleries continue to produce essential oils from geranium and vetiver leaves – a great gift for envious friends back home.

## NATIONAL PARKS

It is estimated that nearly a third of the 25km-long lagoon along the west coast from Boucan Canot south to Trois Bassins has already suffered damage from a variety of causes: sedimentation, agricultural and domestic pollution, cyclones, fishermen and divers. To prevent the situation deteriorating further, a marine park was set up in 1997. In addition to educating local people on the need to keep the beaches and the water clean, the **Association Parc Marin Réunion** (http://parcmarin.chez.com, in French) has been working with local fishermen and various water-sports operators to establish protection zones. A fully fledged nature reserve was created – at last! – in 2007.

There are big plans afoot to protect the interior of the island, too. The **Parc National des Hauts de la Réunion** (www.reunion-parcnational.fr, in French) was established in early 2007, resulting in half of Réunion's total land area being now under protection. There's a tightly regulated core area of 1000 sq km, including the volcano, the mountain peaks and the areas around Mafate and Grand Bassin, surrounded by a buffer zone of some 700 sq km to encompass most of the ravines. The plans envisage a totally integrated approach, not only to protect the animal and plant life, but also to preserve traditional ways of life and to encourage sustainable development, including initiatives linked to ecotourism.

## ENVIRONMENTAL ISSUES

As in Mauritius, the central problem confronting Réunion is how to reconcile environmental preservation with a fast-growing population in need of additional housing, roads, jobs, electricity, water and recreational space.

Unlike Mauritius, however, the authorities here have access to greater financial resources, backed up by all sorts of European rules and regulations. In general, they have been able to adopt a more coordinated approach, introducing measures to improve water treatment and reduce nitrate use by farmers, for example, at the same time as cleaning up the lagoon.

Despite the establishment of the Parc National des Hauts de la Réunion and the Parc Marin Réunion (see p173), the island is facing major issues, all related to two massive engineering works. The 'smaller' is the new Route des Tamarins, which was completed in 2009. This 34km expressway that slices across the hills above St-Gilles-les-Bains required numerous bridges over the ravines. According to local environmentalists, the road cut across the only remaining savannah habitat on the island.

The second major engineering project is a piece of technical prowess. The idea behind this herculean scheme is to transfer water from the east coast, where supply exceeds demand, to the dry and heavily populated west coast. The solution someone came up with was to drill a tunnel 30km long and 3.5m high right through the island! Tunnelling began in 1989, but needless to say they hit a few hitches along the way. It is reckoned that the project should be completed by 2013.

# Réunion

RÉUNION

*Oh la la!* After a long-haul flight, you step off the plane and you're greeted with a *bonjour*. Then you breakfast on croissants and *chocolat chaud* (hot chocolate). At first glance, Réunion is like a chunk of France teleported to the tropics. But beyond the Gallic panache, you'll soon realise it's a resplendent tapestry, which also blends Indian, African and Chinese influences.

Jutting out of the ocean like a basaltic shield cloaked in green, Réunion is a mini-Hawaii, with astounding geographical diversity. Within an hour or two, the landscape morphs from lava fields to lush primary forest, from jagged peaks to sprawling coastal cities. Among the not-to-be-missed Réunion experiences are Piton de la Fournaise, one of the world's most accessible active volcanoes, and the scenically magical Cirque de Mafate, which is only accessible by foot and feels like the world's end. This extraordinarily varied terrain provides an incredible stage for the stimulus-needy. Hiking is the number-one activity, but canyoning, paragliding, rafting, horseback riding and climbing are also available. Seafaring types will appreciate the good diving and surfing opportunities along the west coast.

Réunion has its cultural gems as well, with stunning Creole architecture, as well as colourful religious buildings and festivals. And food lovers can expect a taste-bud-teasing culinary scene. Accommodation-wise, there are no showy resorts, just a number of locally owned hotels and family-run *chambres d'hôtes* (B&Bs) – the perfect way to immerse yourself in local culture.

---

## HIGHLIGHTS

- Gorging your senses on the Martian landscapes of the **Plaine des Sables** (p217) and the volcano of **Piton de la Fournaise** (p217)

- Exploring the mystical, rugged topography of **Cirque de Mafate** (p214), **Cirque de Cilaos** (p202) and **Cirque de Salazie** (p209)

- Going heritage-hunting among the Creole buildings of **Hell-Bourg** (p210), **Entre-Deux** (p200) and **St-Denis** (p176)

- Finding the perfect picnic spot at the aptly named **Belvédère de l'Eden** (p236)

- Swapping stress for bliss in the valley-village seclusion of **Grand Bassin** (p215)

- Surfing and paragliding by day in **St-Leu** (p196) before diving into **L'Hermitage-les-Bains'** steamy nightlife (p193)

---

- Telephone code: 262     ▪ Population: 820,000     ▪ Area: 2512 sq km

## CLIMATE & WHEN TO GO

Because of the high mountains, Réunion's climate varies more than that of Mauritius. It still, however, experiences only two distinct seasons: the hot, rainy summer from December to April and the cool, dry winter from late April to November. The east coast is considerably wetter than the west, but wettest of all are the mountains above the east coast – around Takamaka, Plaine-des-Palmistes and the northern and eastern slopes of the volcano. As with Mauritius, the cyclone season is roughly December to March.

Temperatures on the coast average 22°C during winter and 27°C in summer. In the mountains, they drop to 11°C and 18°C respectively. Clouds generally cover the peaks and high plains from mid-morning. The drier winter months are the most favourable for hiking (see p242 for more information), as some of the trails are simply impassable when it's wet.

The peak tourist seasons are during the French school holidays from July to early September. From October through to the New Year holidays is also busy, but after this everything eases down during cyclone-prone February and March. The weather normally changes for the better in April, which isn't a bad time to a visit.

See p260 for the climate chart for St-Denis.

# ST-DENIS

pop 140,000

Francophiles will feel comfortable in St-Denis (san-de-*nee*), the capital of Réunion. Except for the palms and flamboyant trees to remind you that you're somewhere sunnier (and hotter), St-Denis could be easily mistaken for a French provincial enclave, with a flurry of trendy shops, brasseries, bistros and *boulangeries* (bakeries). Mmmmm…those little *pains au chocolat* (chocolate-filled pastries) will linger long on the palate!

With most of Réunion's tourist attractions located elsewhere on the island, most visitors only stay long enough to book *gîtes de montagnes* (mountain lodges), pick up a few tourist brochures and rent a car before dashing off to more magnetic locations. But St-Denis warrants more than a fleeting glance. Scratch beneath the French polish and you'll soon realise that the city also boasts an undeniably Creole soul, with a portfolio of delightful colonial and religious buildings and a casual multi-ethnic atmosphere.

If that's not enough, there are always epicurean indulgences. Sip a black coffee at a chic pavement cafe listening to a *séga* or *maloya* soundtrack or indulge in fine dining at a gourmet restaurant. *Bon appétit!*

## HISTORY

St-Denis was founded in 1668 by the governor Regnault, who named the settlement after a ship that ran aground here. But St-Denis didn't really start to develop until the governor Mahé de Labourdonnais moved the capital here from St-Paul in 1738; the harbour was in general more sheltered and easier to defend, and water more abundant.

The 19th century ushered in St-Denis' golden age. As money poured in from the sugar plantations, the town's worthies built themselves fine mansions, some of which can still be seen along Rue de Paris and in the surrounding streets. But in the late 1800s the bottom dropped out of the sugar market and the good times came to a stuttering end. St-Denis' fortunes only began to revive when it became the new departmental capital in 1946. To cope with the influx of civil servants, financiers and office workers, the city expanded rapidly eastwards along the coast and up the mountains behind. Even today the cranes are much in evidence as St-Denis struggles to house its ever-growing population.

## ORIENTATION

The centre of St-Denis is built on a grid pattern on a coastal plain dropping gently northwards towards the sea. Life revolves around the seafront Barachois area, and Ave de la Victoire, the main thoroughfare heading inland.

The main shopping area stretches along the semi-pedestrianised Rue Maréchal Leclerc, which strikes east from Ave de la Victoire, and spills over into the surrounding streets.

## INFORMATION

### Emergency

**Ambulance** ( ☎ 15)
**Fire services** ( ☎ 18)
**Police** ( ☎ 17)

### Internet Access

**B@bookcafé** ( ☎ 0262 90 90 65; 82-88 Rue Juliette Dodu; per hr €9; 🕐 10am-5.45pm Tue, Thu & Fri, 10am-

3.45pm Wed & Sat) Pleasant atmosphere upstairs in the Librairie Autrement. Also has wi-fi.

## Medical Services

**Centre Hospitalier Régional** ( ☎ 0262 90 50 50; Allées des Topazes, Bellepierre) Réunion's main hospital has 24-hour medical and dental treatment and English-speaking staff.

## Money

Bring your credit card or stock up with euros beforehand! There's no money changing service – it has been superseded in favour of ATMs. You'll find a cluster of banks with ATMs near the junction of Rue Jean Chatel and Rue Labourdonnais; all the main banks and the central post office have ATMs.

## Post

**Central post office** (60 Rue Maréchal Leclerc; 7.30am-6pm Mon-Fri, to noon Sat)

## Tourist Offices

**Centrale de Réservation – Île de la Réunion** ( ☎ 0262 90 78 78; www.reunion.fr; 5 Rue Rontaunay; 8am-noon & 1-5pm Mon-Thu, 8-11am Fri) Same location as Gîtes de France. This tourist office provides information and does bookings for activities, B&Bs, hotels and *gîtes de montagnes*. It also offers hiking information.

**Gîtes de France** ( ☎ 0262 72 97 81; www.gitesde france.re; 5 Rue Rontaunay; 8am-noon & 1-5pm Mon-Thu, 8am-noon & 1-4pm Fri) Information on *chambres d'hôtes*.

**Office du Tourisme** ( ☎ 0262 41 83 00; otinord@wana doo.fr; 14 Rue de Paris; 9am-6pm Mon-Sat) Housed in a historic building, the St-Denis tourist office has English-speaking staff and can provide plenty of information, maps and brochures. You can also book *gîtes de montagnes* here.

## SIGHTS

St-Denis' most important sights are concentrated along the main road running from Le Barachois in the north to the Jardin de l'État (botanical gardens) a couple of kilometres inland.

## Colonial Architecture

St-Denis is devoid of beach, but it boasts a gaggle of well-preserved colonial buildings harking back to the city's heyday in the 19th century. The larger colonial piles are mainly strung out along Rue de Paris, Ave de la Victoire, Rue Pasteur and Rue Jean Chatel.

One of the grandest is the **Préfecture** (Place de la Préfecture), which began life as a coffee ware-house in 1734 and later served as the head-quarters of the French East India Company. Many, however, consider the neoclassical **Former Hôtel de Ville** (Town Hall; Rue de Paris), at the north end of Rue de Paris, to be the city's most beautiful building; it's certainly more imposing, with its regimented columns, balustrades and jaunty clock tower. Along Rue de Paris, the eye-catching Villa Carrère (p180), which houses the tourist office, L'Artothèque (p180), the Musée Léon Dierx (p180) and the mansion that houses the **Conseil Général de la Réunion – Direction de la Culture** (18 Rue de Paris) are also well worth a gander.

Also of interest are **Palais Rontaunay** (Rue Rontaunay), built in 1854, and the stunning **Maison Deramond-Barre** (15 Rue de Paris), which was the family home of former French prime minister Raymond Barre and the birthplace of the poet and painter Léon Dierx. On Rue Jean Chatel you'll stumble across **Anciens Magasins Aubinais** (37 Rue Jean Chatel), a former warehouse, and the **Ancienne Maison des Notaires** (18 Rue Jean Chatel). Along Rue Labourdonnais you can't miss two elegant Creole buildings, **Villa Fock Yee** (41 Rue Labourdonnais) and, across the road, the 18th-century **Villa Kichenin** (42 Rue Labourdonnais).

Many of these palatial residences feature elaborate verandahs and intricate *lambrequins* (ornamental window and door borders).

If given advance notice, the tourist office can organise guided tours in English (€8, minimum two persons).

## Religious Buildings

St-Denis is home to a smattering of attractive religious buildings, including the eye-catching **Grande Mosquée** (121 Rue Maréchal Leclerc; 9am-noon & 2-4pm), also known as the Noor-E-Islam mosque. The cool white-and-green interior is a haven of peace. The Islamic community in St-Denis is very traditional, so if you wish to visit, dress and behave with respect.

Ambling down Ave de la Victoire, you'll come across the fairly unassuming, Tuscan-style **Cathédrale de St-Denis** (Place de la Cathédrale). Notre-Dame de la Délivrance (1893), which sits on the hillside across the usually dry Rivière St-Denis, is noteworthy for the statue of St Expédit just inside the door, dressed as a young Roman soldier. For more information about this unusual saint see the boxed text, p167.

Thread your way back to the centre until you come across the discreet **Pagode Guan Di**

RÉUNION

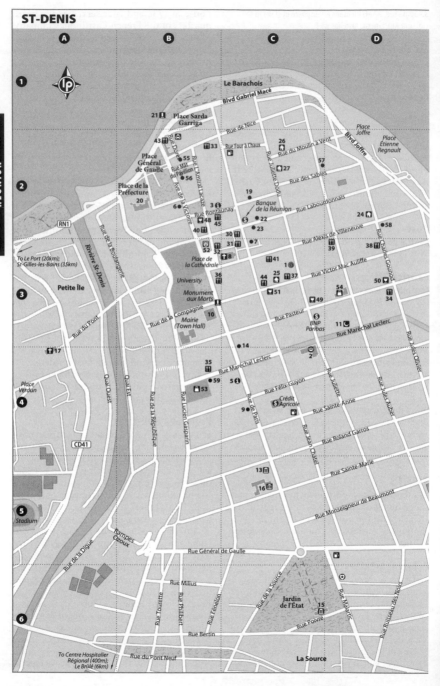

ST-DENIS

**INFORMATION**
B@bookcafé ........................................ **1** C3
Central Post Office ......................... **2** C4
Centrale de Réservation - Île de
   la Réunion ................................... **3** B2
German Consulate ......................... **4** G5
Gîtes de France ......................... (see 3)
Office du Tourisme ....................... **5** C4
Service des Étrangers .................. **6** B2

**SIGHTS & ACTIVITIES**
Ancienne Maison des Notaires ..... (see 30)
Anciens Magasins Aubinais ........ **7** C3
Cathédrale de St-Denis ............... **8** C3
Conseil Général de la Réunion -
   Direction de la Culture ............ **9** C4

Former Hôtel de Ville (Town Hall) .... **10** B3
Grande Mosquée ........................... **11** D3
Hindu Temple ................................ **12** E4
L'Artothèque ................................. **13** C5
Maison Deramond-Barre .............. **14** C3
Musée d'Histoire Naturelle .......... **15** C6
Musée Léon Dierx ......................... **16** C5
Notre-Dame de la Délivrance ...... **17** A4
Pagode Guan Di ............................ **18** E4
Palais Rontaunay .......................... **19** C2
Préfecture ...................................... **20** B2
Roland Garros Monument ........... **21** B1
Villa Carrère ............................ (see 5)
Villa Fock Yee ............................... **22** C2
Villa Kichenin ............................... **23** C2

**SLEEPING**
Austral Hôtel ................................ **24** D2
Central Hôtel ................................ **25** C3
Hôtel Phoenix ............................... **26** C2
Le Juliette Dodu ........................... **27** C2
Les Loges du Park ........................ **28** F5
Pension Zoulékan Limbada .......... **29** E3

**EATING**
Ancienne Maison des Notaires ....... **30** C2
B@bookcafé ............................ (see 1)
Café-Restaurant Le K-T Dral ....... **31** C3
Clos St-Jacques ............................ **32** B3
Entre Vous et Nous ...................... **33** B2
Helios ............................................ **34** D3
Kim Son ......................................... **35** B4

La Récré ......................................... **36** B3
Le Castel Boulanger ..................... **37** C3
Le Caudan ...................................... **38** D3
Le DCP ............................................ **39** D3
Le Labourdonnais .......................... **40** B2
Le Massalé ..................................... **41** C3
Le Reflet des Îles .......................... **42** E3
Le Roland Garros .......................... **43** B2
L'Igloo ........................................... **44** C3
L'Instant Pitti ............................... **45** B2
Petit Marché .................................. **46** E4

**DRINKING**
Café-Restaurant Le K-T Dral .... (see 31)
Le Boy's .......................................... **47** E3
Le Fashion ...................................... **48** B2
Le Zanzibar .................................... **49** C3
Moda Bar ....................................... **50** D3
O'Bar ............................................... **51** C3

**ENTERTAINMENT**
Jazzy Bar ....................................... **52** B3

**SHOPPING**
Grand Marché ............................... **53** B4
Petit Marché ............................ (see 46)
Soredisc ......................................... **54** D3

**TRANSPORT**
Air Austral ..................................... **55** B2
Air France ...................................... **56** B2
Air Madagascar ............................. **57** C2
Air Mauritius ................................. **58** D2
Car Jaune ................................. (see 60)
Corsairfly ....................................... **59** B4
L'Océan Bus Terminal .................. **60** E3

RÉUNION

(Rue Sainte-Anne), which is used by the Chinese community. If you haven't run out of stamina, make your way to St-Denis' small but wildly colourful **Hindu temple** (Rue Maréchal Leclerc), which stands out among a row of shops. Visitors are not allowed inside the temple.

### Museums

St-Denis' strong point is its buildings, rather than its museums, but it's worth popping your head into the rewarding **Musée Léon Dierx** ( ☎ 0262 20 24 82; 28 Rue de Paris; admission €2; ⊗ 9.30am-5pm Tue-Sun). Housed in the former bishop's palace, built in 1845, it hosts Réunion's most important collection of modern art. The more high-profile works may include paintings, sculptures and ceramics by Picasso, Renoir, Gauguin and Matisse (the works exhibited change every three months). You can also see a few paintings by the Réunionnais poet and painter Léon Dierx (1838–1912). The handsome pale-yellow villa next door to the Musée Léon Dierx contains **L'Artothèque** ( ☎ 0262 41 75 50; 26 Rue de Paris; admission free; ⊗ 9.30am-5.30pm Tue-Sun). This contemporary art gallery hosts changing exhibitions of works by local artists and those from neighbouring countries.

The recently renovated **Villa Carrère** ( ☎ 0262 41 83 00; 14 Rue de Paris; admission free; ⊗ 9am-6pm Mon-Sat) houses a permanent exhibition on the colonial past of St-Denis.

Go eye to eye with lemurs and other stuffed specimens in the **Musée d'Histoire Naturelle** ( ☎ 0262 20 02 19; admission €2; ⊗ 9.30-5.30pm Tue-Sun), which is located in the Jardin de l'État. Besides impressive lemurs, you'll see a good insect and bird collection on the 1st floor.

### Other Sights

A good place to catch the sea breeze in St-Denis is **Le Barachois**. This seafront park, lined by cannons facing out to sea, has an area set aside for *pétanque* (a game similar to bowls), cafes and a **monument** to the Réunion-born aviator Roland Garros, leaning nonchalantly on a propeller. Shady Place Sarda Garriga, across the road, was named after the governor who abolished slavery in Réunion in 1848.

The attractive **Jardin de l'État** (botanical gardens; admission free; ⊗ 7am-6pm), at the southern end of Rue de Paris, is a good place to be introduced to a variety of tropical plants and trees. The Musée d'Histoire Naturelle stands at the far end of the gardens.

## SLEEPING

The accommodation scene in St-Denis is a bit disappointing. Most hotels tend to be dull multistorey blocks that are designed with business travellers in mind. Budget beds are an endangered species and the choice of up-market accommodation is limited.

### Budget

**Pension Zoulékan Limbada** ( ☎ 0262 41 05 00; 35 Rue de l'Est; d with shared bathroom €24) This Indian-run guesthouse occupying a virginal-white building has a quiet location. The four tidy but low-key rooms tick all the right boxes, but party animals take note that guests are asked to be quiet at all times and respect prayer times. Some Zoreilles (French people from mainland France) use this as a landing pad before finding an apartment, so it's wise to book well in advance.

**Les Loges du Park** ( ☎ 0692 96 48 17; leslogesdupark@ wanadoo.fr; 34 Rue Voltaire; d €35-45; ☒ ☎ ) It may not be the most memorable stay of your trip, but Les Loges du Park is an economic option for anyone in need of a good night's rest with fixings like air-con, satellite TV, salubrious bathrooms, back-friendly mattresses and free wi-fi. There's also a kitchen for guests' use. It's in a quiet area, about 10 minutes' walk from the centre.

### Midrange

**Hôtel Phoenix** ( ☎ 0262 41 51 81; phoenix.dupont@wana doo.fr; 1 Rue du Moulin à Vent; s €45, d €48-50, all incl breakfast; ☒ ☎ ) A well-run little number with a central location, the Phoenix offers neat rooms, sparkling bathrooms and a small, flower-filled garden. Some rooms face a concrete wall; try for rooms 5, 6 or 7, which have a balcony. Note that the air-con is on from 7pm to 7am only. Advance reservation is recommended.

**Central Hôtel** ( ☎ 0262 94 18 08; www.centralhotel.re; 37 Rue de la Compagnie; s €54-93, d €73-105, all incl breakfast; ℗ ☒ ☎ ) The Central gets by on its handy location, a waddle away from restaurants, bars and shops. It offers bland, fairly identical looking hotel rooms without much island flavour. Warning: there are no elevators.

**Austral Hôtel** ( ☎ 0262 94 45 67; www.hotel -austral.com; 20 Rue Charles Gounod; s €76-82, d €87-93; ℗ ☒ ☎ ☲ ) Distinctly unimpressive for the price, the Austral is not quite the three-star heavyweight it thinks it is, but the rooms have the requisite comforts, location is tip-top and there's a pool.

## Top End

**Le Juliette Dodu** ( ☎ 0262 20 91 20; www.hotel-jdodu
.com; 31 Rue Juliette Dodu; s €90, d €110-160, ste €195;
Ⓟ Ⓧ 🛜 🛠 ) Escape the plebeian hordes and
live like a colonial administrator in this stylish
Creole building dating from the early 19th
century. Although the rooms are unextraor-
dinary, there are still enough vintage touches
in the reception area – period furnishings,
plump armchairs and old-fashioned tiles – to
satisfy the snob within, with the added lure of
a small pool and a cosy restaurant. It's a two-
minute strut south of the Barachois.

**Mercure Créolia** ( ☎ 0262 94 26 26; www.accor.com;
14 Rue du Stade, Montgaillard; d incl breakfast €115-190;
Ⓟ Ⓧ 🛜 🛠 ) Located some way south of
the city centre in a tranquil neighbourhood,
your efforts in getting up here are rewarded
with splendid views over the coast. Rooms
are functional and unflashy, but you'll be too
busy lounging by the pool and drinking up
the view to mind.

## EATING

Thanks to the French passion for gastronomy,
St-Denis is a nirvana for food-lovers, with a
smorgasbord of eateries to suit all palates and
budgets. French or Creole? Chinese or Indian?
Fusion or traditional? Throw budgetary caution to the wind and splurge. Most places
accept credit cards.

## Restaurants

Note that many bars (see Drinking &
Entertainment) also serve food.

**Le Roland Garros** ( ☎ 0262 41 44 37; 2 Place Sarda
Garriga; mains €11-25; 🕑 lunch & dinner) *Oh la la*, this
heavenly place has the feel of a true Parisian
bistro – packed, buzzing and full of attitude.
You can't really go wrong – everything is
pretty good – but if you want a recommendation, go for the *tartare d'espadon* (tuna
tartare).

**Le DCP** ( ☎ 0262 20 10 14; 46 Rue Jules Auber; mains
€11-25, menus €22-27; 🕑 lunch & dinner) If you have
a weakness for ultrafresh fish, Le DCP is
the place to indulge. The decor is another
clincher: it occupies a restored Creole building with an agreeable terrace. Inside, aquatic
murals and shades of blue and white create a
*20,000 Leagues Under the Sea*–like ambience.

**ourpick Le Reflet des Îles** ( ☎ 0262 21 73 82; 27
Rue de l'Est; mains €11-36; 🕑 lunch & dinner Mon, Tue &
Thu-Sat) This much-lauded eatery specialising
in Creole food is the perfect place to try out

*cuisine lontan* (traditional dishes). Dip into
one of 20 cracking *carris* (curries) and *civets*
(stews). The menu is translated into English –
a rarity in Réunion. The waiters play the
tropical-island card with their snazzy shirts.

**Café-Restaurant Le K-T Dral** ( ☎ 0692 95 92 00; 5
Ruelle Saint Paul; mains €14-16; 🕑 lunch & dinner Mon-
Sat) The trendiest choice in the centre at the
time of writing, K-T Dral is part cafe and
part restaurant. The range of daily specials
on offer – mostly *métro* dishes prepared with
local ingredients – is well priced and filled
with subtle flavours.

**La Récré** ( ☎ 0262 23 83 41; 21 Ave de la Victoire;
mains €14-18; 🕑 lunch & dinner) Set in a courtyard
that opens onto a busy street (but a hedge of
tropical plants protects you from the hustle
and bustle), La Récré is a popular joint for
informal dining, with a wide-ranging menu
focussing on fish and meat dishes.

**L'Instant Pitti** ( ☎ 0262 51 63 94; 18 Rue Rontaunay;
mains €15-32, lunch menu €15; 🕑 lunch & dinner Tue-Sat).
This upscale restaurant turns out an ever-
changing menu of items that transgress all
culinary boundaries. It's been recommended
to us for its good-value lunch menu. The atmosphere hums good-naturedly at lunchtime
but is rather more subdued and romantic in
the evening.

**Entre Vous et Nous** ( ☎ 0262 30 54 68; 12 Rue de
Nice; mains €21-30, menus €18-23; 🕑 lunch Mon-Fri, dinner
Mon-Sat) A surprisingly hip restaurant inside a
Creole house complete with dark-wood interior, this cool culinary outpost specialises
in high-flying creative dishes, such as an excellent *pavé d'autruche en croûte de pistache*
(pistachio-encrusted ostrich fillet).

**ourpick Clos St-Jacques** ( ☎ 0262 21 59 09; 5 Ruelle
Édouard; mains €23-26, menus €23-27; 🕑 lunch Mon-Fri,
dinner Tue-Sat) Subdued lighting, elegant furnishings and a smattering of fancy decorative touches, including colourful posters and
quirky replicas of cicadas hanging on the
walls, provide the perfect setting for a romantic dinner. A neoclassical French menu
puts the emphasis on Provençal cuisine with
the addition of Réunion grown (or fished)
ingredients.

Other temptations:

**Kim Son** ( ☎ 0262 21 75 00; 13 Rue Maréchal Leclerc;
mains €9-23; 🕑 lunch Mon-Fri, dinner Mon, Tue & Thu-
Sat) Offers well-prepared Vietnamese and Chinese fare in
rustic surrounds.

**Helios** ( ☎ 0262 20 21 50; 88 Rue Pasteur; mains €12-26;
🕑 lunch & dinner Tue-Sat) This St-Denis icon has a good

**RÉUNION**

repertoire of flavoursome *métro* dishes, best enjoyed on the flowery terrace.

**Le Labourdonnais** ( ☎ 0262 21 27 66; 14 Rue L'Amiral Lacaze; mains €16-26; ☸ lunch & dinner Mon-Sat) It's the decor that's the pull here, blending rustic beams and stone walls with colonial-era elegance.

## Quick Eats

our pick **Le Castel Boulanger** ( ☎ 0262 21 27 66; 43 Rue de la Compagnie; ☸ 6am-7pm Mon-Sat, 7am-noon Sun) Hands down the best bakery-deli in St-Denis, with such a tantalising array of brioches, croissants, *macatias* (a variety of bun) and sandwiches that we almost made ourselves a nuisance here. Excellent breakfasts too (from €8).

**Le Massalé** ( ☎ 0262 21 75 06; 30 Rue Alexis de Villeneuve; ☸ 10am-8pm Mon-Thu & Sat, 2-8pm Fri, 11am-8pm Sun) This teeny outlet tempts you with its colourful array of Indian snacks and sweets to eat in or take away. Perennial favourites include samosas as well as candy-pink or apple-green *balfi*. Wash it down with a glass of cardamom tea.

**Le Caudan** ( ☎ 0262 94 39 99; 38 Rue Charles Gounod; mains €7-12; ☸ lunch & dinner) Tasty Indo-Mauritian snacks and light meals are the order of the day at this under-the-radar neighbourhood venture set in a small Creole house. The homemade biryani is the speciality here. A side order of *beignets banane* (banana fritters) and a glass of *alouda* (sweet, milky drink) will round things off nicely.

**B@bookcafé** ( ☎ 0262 90 90 65; 82-88 Rue Juliette Dodu; mains €7-13; ☸ lunch Tue-Sat) A snazzy spot upstairs in the Librairie Autrement. Good salads.

our pick **L'Igloo** ( ☎ 0262 21 34 69; 67 Rue Jean Chatel; ice creams from €2, mains €8-12; ☸ 11am-midnight) You say you're itching for an ice-cream fix? Good, because it's hard to resist the fresh fruit sorbets and creamy delights at this iconic ice-cream parlour. Try the outstanding *fruits des bois* (fruits of the forest berries) and you'll imagine you're eating the pulped fruits on a cold day. Also serves up snack options and light meals, including salads and omelettes, at lunchtime.

## Self-Catering

For fresh fruit and vegetables, there is a wide range of cheap produce at the **Petit Marché** (Rue Maréchal Leclerc; ☸ 6am-6pm Mon-Sat, 6am-noon Sun).

## DRINKING & ENTERTAINMENT

If it's Ibiza-style nightlife you're after, you're barking up the wrong tree here. Most of Réunion's action is down the coast at

L'Hermitage-les-Bains (p193) and St-Pierre (p223). However, there's a handful of OK nightspots to keep you entertained in the centre of St-Denis.

**Le Zanzibar** ( ☎ 0262 20 01 18; 41 Rue Pasteur; ☸ lunch Mon-Sat, bar & dinner 5pm-midnight) Le Zanzibar, a bar and a restaurant, is the hang-out of well-connected locals and serves devilishly good tropical potions. The menu also gets a nod from the city's roaming stomachs.

**O'Bar** ( ☎ 0262 52 57 88; 32 Rue de la Compagnie; ☸ 8am-midnight Mon-Sat) A funky drinking spot right in the centre. The streetside terrace allows for a dash of people-watching. Food is only so-so.

**Café-Restaurant Le K-T Dral** ( ☎ 0692 95 92 00; 5 Ruelle Saint-Paul; ☸ 8am-midnight Mon-Sat) Tucked in an alley behind the cathedral, this congenial bar is an essential landmark on the St-Denis nightlife scene. It's packed to the rafters on weekends and you come here as much for a cocktail as for the trendy atmosphere.

**Le Fashion** ( ☎ 0262 46 17 06; 12 Rue Rontaunay; ☸ Thu-Sat) This snazzy lounge bar is also a dancing place that gets the thumbs up from St-Denis regulars.

Alternatives:

**Jazzy Bar** ( ☎ 0262 21 85 01; 20 Rue Labourdonnais; ☸ 7pm-2am Tue-Sat) A jazz lounge and a great late-night haunt for aspiring insomniacs.

**Le Boy's** ( ☎ 0692 66 25 53; 108 Rue Pasteur; ☸ 9pm-4am Thu-Sat) Gay-friendly – you guessed it.

**Moda Bar** ( ☎ 0262 58 76 14; 75 Rue Pasteur; ☸ 7pm-2am Thu-Sat) A formulaic but friendly place. Partygoers grind away to loud salsa rhythms on Friday and Saturday, while Thursday is for karaoke.

## SHOPPING

The main shopping streets are the semi-pedestrianised Rue Maréchal Leclerc and Rue Juliette Dodu.

**Grand Marché** (2 Rue Maréchal Leclerc; ☸ 8am-6pm Mon-Sat) This place has a mishmash of items for sale, including Malagasy wooden handicrafts, fragrant spices, woven baskets, embroidery, T-shirts, furniture and a jumble of knick-knacks.

**Petit Marché** (Rue Maréchal Leclerc) On the east side of town, this is mainly a fresh-produce market, but you can buy herbs and spices and local *rhums arrangés* (flavoured rums) here at competitive prices.

**Soredisc** ( ☎ 0262 21 68 29; 61 Rue Pasteur) For tapes and CDs of *maloya*, *séga* and other local music, this store has far and away the biggest selection.

## GETTING THERE & AWAY
### Air
The vast majority of flights come in to **Roland Garros International Airport** ( ☎ 0262 28 16 16; www. reunion.aeroport.fr), about 10km east of St-Denis.

Airlines with offices in St-Denis:

**Air Austral** ( ☎ 0825 01 30 12; 4 Rue de Nice)
**Air France** ( ☎ 0820 82 08 20; 7 Ave de la Victoire)
**Air Madagascar** ( ☎ 0892 68 00 14; 31 Rue Jules Auber)
**Air Mauritius** ( ☎ 0262 94 83 83; 13 Rue Charles Gounod)
**Corsairfly** ( ☎ 0820 04 20 42; 2 Rue Maréchal Leclerc)

All airlines also have an office at the airport. For further information regarding air travel see p318.

### Bus
L'Océan bus terminal, the main long-distance bus station, is on the seafront. From here **Car Jaune** ( ☎ 0810 12 39 74) operates various services. Information for Car Jaune including all its routes and *horaires* (timetables) around the island and the airport bus service is available from the information counter at the bus terminal. You can also pick up timetables at the tourist office. Some of the more useful routes include the following:

**Line A** West to St-Pierre via Le Port, St-Paul, St-Gilles-les-Bains, St-Leu, Étang-Salé-les-Bains and St-Louis (€4.20, two hours, about 10 daily).
**Lines F or G** East to St-Benoît via Ste-Suzanne and St-André (€2.80, one hour, about 12 daily).
**Z'éclair** (express) East to St-Benoît via St-André (€3.50, one hour, about 10 daily).
**Z'éclair** (express) West to St-Pierre, direct (€7, one hour, about 18 daily).

### Car & Motorcycle
There's not much point in having a car in St-Denis unless you're using it as a base to explore the rest of the island. If that's the case, you can either pick a car up at the airport or avoid paying the airport surcharge (around €22) by having it delivered to your hotel. For more information on car hire, see p265.

### Ferry
St-Denis' ferry terminal is at Le Port, located 20km west of St-Denis. For information on ferries to/from Mauritius, see p322.

## GETTING AROUND
St-Denis is relatively small and getting around the centre on foot is a breeze.

### To/From the Airport
Taxis between St-Denis and Roland Garros International Airport cost around €20 during the day and €30 at night. Cheaper and almost as convenient is the regular Navette Aéroport service, which runs from L'Océan bus terminal to the airport about once an hour between 7am and 7.45pm (between 7.30am and 7.15pm coming from the airport). The fare is €4 and the journey takes a minimum of 20 minutes.

### To/From the Port
The terminal for passenger ferries to Mauritius is in Le Port, 20km west of St-Denis. There are no bus services direct to the terminal. All non-express buses between St-Denis and St-Pierre stop at the bus station in Le Port, from where locally operated buses depart roughly every 30 minutes for the Gare Maritime, Port Est. You're better off splashing out on a taxi (€45 from St-Denis).

There is a small information desk at the ferry terminal, open for arrivals, but no other facilities for tourists. Taxis wait on arrival.

### Taxi
Taxis around town are generally expensive. A trip across town will set you back at least €8.

During the day you should have no problem finding a taxi. It gets more difficult at night, when you might have to phone for one. A reliable company offering a 24-hour service is **Taxis Paille-en-Queue** ( ☎ 0262 29 20 29).

# THE WEST

Welcome to Réunion's Sunshine Coast, or Réunion's Riviera, or the leeward coast. However you label it, say hello to this 45km-long string of seaside resorts and suburbs running from St-Paul to St-Louis. It does have a wealth of developed tourist facilities and attractions, including the best of the island's beaches (which is not saying a lot).

Sea, sand and sun are not the only *raison d'être* on the west coast. There's also a superfluity of activities on land and sea. Big surf breaks issue a siren's call to surfers, steep drop-offs tempt divers, spectacular slopes beckon mountain bikers, while paragliders soar over the lagoon.

Despite the fact that tourist development has got a little out of hand to the south of

RÉUNION

St-Paul, there remain hidden corners of untouched wonder in this most populous, most visited region. It's easy to leave the new Route des Tamarins (see p265) that zips along the flanks of the mountains and explore the glorious hinterland and its bucolic offerings – think sugar-cane fields, lush orchards, geranium plantations and cryptomeria forests swathing the slopes of the mountains, studded with character-filled villages that retain a palpable rural air. Oh, and charming *chambres d'hôtes* where you can retreat in homely comfort.

With the exception of St-Louis and the Hauts (Hills), this region is predominantly Zoreilles territory and feels closer to mainland France than South Africa. Brush up on your French!

## DOS D'ANE & AROUND
### pop 26,000 (incl La Possession)

After braving St-Denis' busy streets and before tackling the seaside resorts further south, a drive up to the isolated village of Dos d'Ane, in the hills above Le Port (take the D1), will give you a breath of fresh air. It's an excellent base for **hikes** in the interior; from here you can walk to the Plaine d'Affouches and La Roche Écrite, as well as into the Cirque de Mafate via the Rivière des Galets route. For a shorter ramble, there are superb views to be had from the Cap Noir kiosk, about 20 minutes from the Cap Noir car park above Dos d'Ane (it's signposted), or from the Roche Verre Bouteille lookout, less than an hour's walk from the car park. It's possible to do a loop combining the two lookouts (about 1½ hours).

If you like peace, quiet and sigh-inducing views, you'll have few quibbles with **Chambre d'hôte et Gîte Les Acacias – Chez Axel et Patricia Nativel** ( ☎ 0262 32 02 34; Rue Germain Elisabeth, Dos d'Ane; dm €17, d incl breakfast 44), which offers two *chambres d'hôtes* and three spick-and-span six-bed dorms. The hearty evening meals (dinner €18) go down well after a day's tramping and the views from the terrace are stupendous. If you're after some serious cosseting and privacy, **Village Nature – Lodge Roche Tamarin** ( ☎ 0262 44 66 88; www.villagenature.com; 142 Chemin Boeuf Mort, La Possession; d €155-255; ⚇ ⬙ ⬚) is the answer, with a cluster of plush wooden chalets ingeniously deployed on a jungle-clad hillside. It also offers two swimming pools, a gourmet restaurant and, the real clincher, a full-service

spa. The ethos here is one of relaxation, so don't expect tacky entertainment programs. It's in La Possession, about 400m off the D1 that climbs to Dos d'Ane (it's signposted).

To get to Dos d'Ane by public transport you'll have to change buses in Le Port. All nonexpress and most express buses between St-Pierre and St-Denis stop at the Le Port bus station. From Le Port, there are six buses a day from Monday to Saturday but only three on Sunday.

## ST-PAUL
### pop 20,000

Lively if not jaw-dropping in beauty, Réunion's second-largest *commune* after St-Denis deserves a quick stop if you're into history. It's also an obvious transit point if you plan to reach Le Maïdo (p186) by public transport.

Most tourists who do come here visit the bright and well-kept **Cimetière Marin**, the cemetery at the southern end of town. It contains the remains of various famous Réunionnais, including the poet Leconte de Lisle (1818–94) and the pirate Olivier 'La Buse' Levasseur (The Buzzard), who was the scourge of the Indian Ocean from about 1720 to 1730.

You'll also find a few well-preserved **colonial buildings** along the seafront. On a street running parallel to the seafront lies the colourful **Hindu temple** (Rue St-Louis), built in 1871.

Make sure you save energy for the animated **market** on the seafront promenade. It's held all day on Friday and on Saturday morning. With heaps of local vegetables, fruits and spices, it makes for a colourful experience.

### Sleeping

**La Case Passion** ( ☎ 0262 57 19 15, 0692 05 17 94; www.lacasepassion.fr; 37 Ave des Moutardiers, Plateau Caillou; s/d €25/40; ⚇ ⬙ ⬚) Life feels less hurried at this sweet establishment located in Plateau Caillou, about 4km south of St-Paul. The French owners are friendly and the two airily spruced-up, but still very small, rooms won't leave you wanting too much, but it's the verdant setting, the copious breakfast (€7) and the swimming pool that make this place special. Evening meals (€16) are available by request. Note that the shared shower is outdoors.

**Le Quai Ouest** ( ☎ 0262 45 57 17; 8 Blvd du Front de Mer; d with shared bathroom €50, d €60; ⬚) The price is steep for such functional doubles, but it's

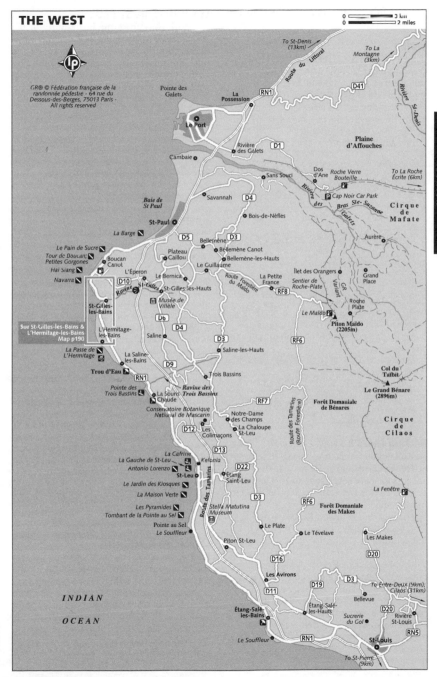

# THE WEST

0 — 3 km
0 — 2 miles

GR® © Fédération française de la
randonnée pédestre - 64 rue du
Dessous-des-Berges, 75013 Paris -
All rights reserved

RÉUNION

To St-Denis
(13km)

To La
Montagne
(3km)

Route du Littoral

RN1

D41

Rivière St-Denis

Pointe des
Galets

La
Possession

Le Port

Rivière
des Galets

D1

Plaine
d'Affouches

Cambaie

Sans Souci

Dos
d'Ane

Roche Verre
Bouteille

To La Roche
Écrite (6km)

Baie de
St-Paul

Savannah

D4

Cap Noir Car Park

Rivière des

Bras Ste-Suzanne

Cirque
de
Mafate

St-Paul

Bois-de-Nèfles

La Barge

D5

Bellemène

D3

Aurère

Le Pain de Sucre
Tour de Boucan
Petites Gorgones
Haï Siang
Navarra

Boucan
Canot

L'Éperon

D10

Ravine St-Gilles

Plateau
Caillou

Bellemène Canot

Bellemène-les-Hauts

Le Guillaume

Le Bernica

St-Gilles-les-Hauts

Route Forestière
du Maïdo

La Petite
France

RF8

Îlet des Orangers

Sentier de
Roche-Plate

GR Variant

Grand
Place

St-Gilles-
les-Bains

Musée de
Villèle

D6

Le Maïdo

Roche
Plate

See St-Gilles-les-Bains &
L'Hermitage-les-Bains
Map p190

L'Hermitage-
les-Bains

D4

Saline

Piton Maïdo
(2205m)

La Passe de
L'Hermitage

La Saline-
les-Bains

D3

Saline-les-Hauts

RF6

Col du
Taïbit

Trou d'Eau

RN1

D9

Trois Bassins

Le Grand Bénare
(2896m)

Pointe des
Trois Bassins

La Souris
Chaude

Ravine des
Trois Bassins

RF7

Route des Tamarins (Route Forestière)

Forêt Domaniale
de Bénares

Cirque
de
Cilaos

Conservatoire Botanique
National de Mascarin

D12

Notre-Dame
des Champs

Les
Colimaçons

La Chaloupe
St-Leu

La Cafrine

D13

Kelonia

La Gauche de St-Leu
Antonio Lorenzo
Le Jardin des Kiosques

St-Leu

D22

Étang
Saint-Leu

La Fenêtre

La Maison Verte

Stella Matutina
Museum

D3

RF6

Forêt Domaniale
des Makes

Les Pyramides
Tombant de la Pointe au Sel

Pointe au Sel
Le Souffleur

Piton St-Leu

Le Plate

Le Tévelave

Les Makes

D16

D20

*INDIAN*

*OCEAN*

Les Avirons

D11

D19

D3

To Entre-Deux (9km);
Cilaos (31km)

Bellevue

D20

Étang-Salé-
les-Bains

Étang-Salé-
les-Hauts

Sucrerie
du Gol

Rivière
St-Louis

Le Souffleur

RN1

St-Louis

RN5

To St-Pierre
(9km)

conveniently located, opposite the seafront market place.

## Eating

The *camions-snacks* (snack vans) on the seafront market place are St-Paul's best bargain for cheap eats. They operate from late morning until late at night. Grilled fish, *entrecôte frites* (beef ribsteak with fries), salads and *carris* are the order of the day, but there are also pizzas, crêpes and sandwiches.

**Le Grand Baie** ( ☎ 0262 22 50 03; 14 Rue des Filaos; mains €10-16; ☯ lunch & dinner Tue-Sun) This excellent local haunt rarely registers on St-Paul's tourism radar because it's tucked behind the Cimetière Marin. Big mistake. Munch on well-prepared Creole and *métro* dishes (as well as pizzas at dinnertime) while the ocean crashes just feet away.

**Restaurant de l'Étang** ( ☎ 0262 45 29 68; 1 Blvd Jacob de la Haye; mains €13-17; ☯ lunch Mon-Sat, dinner Wed-Sat) North of the centre, this haven of peace is blessed with a lush garden that's a perfect spot for a relaxed feed or tipple. There's nothing unorthodox on the menu, just the usual Creole suspects cooked to perfection: *cabri massalé* (goat *carri*) and *canard combava* (duck with a variety of aromatic citrus), among others.

**Terranga** ( ☎ 0262 45 03 24; 323 Chaussée Royale; mains €16-18; ☯ lunch & dinner Tue-Sat) This upscale eatery prepares delectable French-inspired dishes with a tropical twist served in verdant surrounds. The *canard à la mangue* (duck in a mango sauce) will certainly win your heart.

## Getting There & Away

St-Paul lies on Car Jaune's bus route between St-Denis (€2.70) and St-Pierre (€4.30). There are express buses every one to two hours in either direction (fewer on Sunday) and much more frequent nonexpress services.

The local bus company **Kar'Ouest** ( ☎ 0262 45 72 30) operates fairly infrequent services from the central bus station to villages up in the hills such as Le Bernica, La Petite France, Villèle, Le Guillaume and L'Éperon, among others. Walkers, take note: there's also a special bus to Le Maïdo (that takes you to the start of the Sentier de Roche Plate, the footpath into the Cirque de Mafate, which strikes off the road about 4km below the summit) three times daily except Sunday (€1.50, one hour); the first bus leaves at 6am and the last one down is at 5.20pm.

## LES HAUTS DE ST-PAUL

A world away from the hurly-burly of the coast, the verdant Hauts de St-Paul is wonderful country for exploring off the beaten track, but unless you have a lot of time, you need a vehicle. Buses serve most places from St-Paul, but they aren't really convenient for the Hauts. We won't suggest any set itinerary, for this area lends itself to a DIY approach – from St-Paul, use the D5 as a launchpad, then follow your nose (but bring a good map). You'll come across hamlets with such charming names as **Bellemène-les-Hauts**, **Bois-de-Nèfles**, **Le Bernica**, **Le Guillaume**… It's as cute as it sounds! Start early morning to get the best views of the coast.

### Sleeping & Eating

**Chambre d'hôte Chez Suzy et Gaia** ( ☎ 0262 32 45 14, 0692 52 82 59; www.chez-gayaetsuzie.fr.st; 197 Route Hubert-Delisle, Bellemène Canot; d incl breakfast €40) This mellow *chambre d'hôte* run by a hospitable Indian couple has two rooms – be sure to ask for the *'vue mer'* (room with a sea view). The dinner menu (€23) is based on good-quality local produce, including home-grown vegetables.

**Villa La Clé des Champs** ( ☎ 0262 32 37 60, 0692 20 17 04; www.lacledeschamps.re; 154 Chemin des Barrières, Bellemène-les-Hauts; d €130, ste €160, all incl breakfast; ☍ ) Looking for a night at some place extra special? Make a beeline for this lovely *maison d'hôte*, the pride and joy of friendly owners Martine and Léon. Set high in the hills above Bellemène-les-Hauts, it has five rooms done out in chic warm Provençal or oriental colours, with sensational views over the coast thrown in for free. Food is a big thing here (dinner from €45); Martine is a real cordon bleu chef, mastering such gourmet dishes as *carpaccio de camarons aux fruits de la passion* (freshwater prawns carpaccio-style with passion fruit). Oh, and there's a jacuzzi in the garden.

## LE MAÏDO & AROUND

Be prepared to fall on your knees in awe: far above St-Paul and St-Gilles-les-Bains on the rim of the Cirque de Mafate, Le Maïdo is one of the most impressive viewpoints in Réunion. The lookout is perched atop the mountain peak at 2205m and offers stunning views down into the Cirque and back to the coast. As with other viewpoints, you should arrive early in the day – by 7am if possible – if you want to see anything other than cloud.

Getting there is half the fun. The sealed Route Forestière du Maïdo winds all the way up to the viewpoint from Le Guillaume (14km) in the hills above St-Gilles-les-Bains, offering a scenic drive through majestic cryptomeria forests. You'll also find a smattering of attractions along the way to keep you entertained.

A word of warning: expect traffic snarls on Sunday when hundreds of picnicking families set up base in the shade of trees along the road.

## Sights & Activities
### MOUNTAIN BIKING
The Maïdo area, with its thrillingly steep descents and spectacular mountain scenery, is a top two-wheel destination. The Megavalanche Mountain Race – the biggest downhill race in the Indian Ocean region – takes place here each year. It is a 2205m descent using a mass start and draws riders from across Réunion and the world.

Fancy a downhill ride at your own pace? See the boxed text, below.

### HIKING
Hiking options abound near Le Maïdo. The peak is the starting point for the tough walk along the Cirque rim to the summit of **Le Grand Bénare** (2896m), another impressive lookout (allow at least six hours for the return trip). Hikers can also descend from Le Maïdo into the Cirque de Mafate via the Sentier de Roche-Plate, which meets the GR R2 variant that connects the villages of Roche-Plate and Îlet des Orangers (allow three hours to reach Roche-Plate). See p242 for more information on hiking in Mafate.

### HORSE RIDING
The **Centre Équestre du Maïdo** ( ☎ 0692 67 54 47; Route du Maïdo, La Petite France; horse riding per hr €20, pony rides €5-10; ☺ 9am-noon & 1.30-5pm Wed, Sat & Sun school term, daily school holidays) organises gentle jaunts around La Petite France. Recommended is the three-hour ride (€50), which takes in viewpoints over the bay of St-Paul. Pony rides are available for children.

### PARC AVENTURE
For Tarzan types, **La Forêt de L'Aventure** ( ☎ 0692 30 01 54; Route Forestière des Cryptomérias, La Petite France; adult/child €20/15; ☺ 9.30am-5pm daily school holidays, by reservation school term) has set up two wonderful adventure circuits in a 3-hectare perimeter, with a variety of fixtures, including Tyrolean slides. There's a 'Mini Forêt' for the kiddies (over five). It's signposted, about 500m to the north of La Petite France, after L'Alambic Bègue (see p188).

### OTHER ATTRACTIONS
The hamlet of **La Petite France** (1000m) is famous for its traditional **distilleries** producing essential oils from geranium, cryptomeria and vetiver leaves (nice smell!). They run small shops where you can stock up on perfumes, soaps and other natural health products. Stop off at the following places, all scattered along the main road in La Petite France:

**Distillerie du Maïdo – Chez Nanou Le Savoyard** ( ☎ 0692 61 75 43; www.ladistilleriedumaido.com; La Petite France; ☺ 8.30am-6pm)

---

### THRILLING DOWNHILLS

The spectacular flanks of Le Maïdo will prove a sort of nirvana for mountain bikers who prefer sitting back and letting gravity do the work. The 35km, 2205m descent follows trails that wind through tamarind and cryptomeria forests and sugar-cane fields. Throughout the ride you're presented with astounding views of the lagoon and the coast.

**Rando Réunion Passion** (Map p190; ☎ 0262 24 26 19, 0692 21 11 11; www.descente-vtt.com; 3 Rue du Général de Gaulle, St-Gilles-les-Bains) in St-Gilles-les-Bains is a professional set-up that offers a range of mountain-bike trips for riders of all levels. The most popular ride is the 'Classique du Maïdo' descent, from the lookout to the coast. If you're a beginner, fear not! You won't ride at breakneck speed, and various stops are organised along the way, where the guide will give you the lowdown on flora and fauna. Half-day packages including bike hire, transport to the start (by minivan) and a guide cost around €55 per person (minimum four). Children over 12 are welcome.

If you want to open up the throttle a little more, opt for the 'Maïdo Sportif' (€55) or the 'Méga, Tête Dure' (€90) descents.

The ultimate is the 'Rando du Volcano' (Volcano Ride), which takes in the southern flank of Piton de la Fournaise down to St-Joseph (€150). Memorable!

RÉUNION

**La Maison du Géranium Rosat** (☎ 0692 82 15 00; La Petite France; 🕑 8.30am-5pm daily except Wed & Fri afternoon)
**L'Alambic Bègue** (☎ 0692 64 58 25; La Petite France; 🕑 8.30am-6pm)

Further up, at an altitude of 1500m, the **Relais du Maïdo** (☎ 0262 32 40 32; Route du Maïdo; 🕑 Tue-Sun) is a kind of theme park, with a smattering of attractions, mostly geared to children, including pony rides (€5), quad bikes (€5 to €10) and archery (€6). There's also an onsite restaurant.

### Sleeping & Eating

La Petite France makes a convenient base for an early-morning start up to Le Maïdo.

**Chambre d'hôte Chez Rose Magdeleine** (☎ 0262 32 53 50; Chemin de l'École, La Petite France; d incl breakfast €40, dinner €20) A simple yet well-run B&B with four neat rooms, just off the main road.

**Chez Ary et Lucette** (☎ 0262 32 40 69; Route du Maïdo, PK3; d €45; 🕑 Jul-May) Here you'll find six robust, wood-panelled rooms in a low-slung building. A few metres further up, the restaurant (mains €10 to €15, open for lunch Saturday to Monday, Wednesday and Thursday, closed June) whips up comforting Creole *carris* served with all the traditional accompaniments. Bag a seat near the windows (views!).

**Chez Doudou** (☎ 0262 32 55 87; Route de Maïdo, PK 3; mains €12-13; 🕑 lunch Thu-Tue) Opposite Chez Ary et Lucette. With its barnlike surrounds, Chez Doudou boasts a kind of ramshackle charm but has no views to speak of. It also specialises in Creole classics.

Both Chez Ary et Lucette and Chez Doudou are full to bursting at weekends – reservations are advised.

### Getting There & Around

Kar'Ouest (line 2) runs three buses a day (Monday to Saturday) taking walkers from St-Paul to the start of the Sentier de Roche Plate, the footpath into the Cirque de Mafate, which strikes off the road about 4km below the summit. The first bus up the hill leaves at 6am and the last one down is at 5.20pm (€1.50, one hour).

## BOUCAN CANOT

**pop 2000**

In this attitude-fuelled little resort town dubbed the Réunionnais St-Tropez, the obvious focus is the **beach**. It's been listed as one of Réunion's best, and once you get a glimpse of the gentle curve of the bright white sand, lined with palms and casuarina trees and framed with basalt rocks and cliffs, you'll see why. It gets packed on weekends. Caveat: currents can be strong.

### Sleeping

**La Villa Du Soleil** (☎ 0262 24 38 69; www.lavilladusoleil.com; 54 Route de Boucan Canot; s €43-47, d €50-54; ❄ 📶 🏊) Wedged between the highway (noise!) and the beach, this family-run hotel is the most affordable establishment in Boucan Canot, with 13 ordinary rooms arranged around a courtyard. It feels a tad compact, but at this price we're not complaining.

**Résidence Les Boucaniers** (☎ 0262 24 23 89; www.les-boucaniers.com; 29 Route de Boucan Canot; d from €70; 🅿 ❄) Rumbling with the heavyweight hotels in this neck of the woods, these self-catering studios and apartments are a tad long in the tooth but have lovely views of the beach. Breathe in the sea air and sun-splashed hedonism from the balcony.

If you want to do Boucan Canot in style, opt for the following:

**Le Saint-Alexis** (☎ 0262 24 42 04; www.hotelsaintalexis.com; 44 Route de Boucan Canot; d €160-275, ste €265-550; ❄ 📶 🏊) A four-star venue with all the luxury trappings.

**Le Boucan Canot** (☎ 0262 33 44 44; www.boucancanot.com; 32 Route de Boucan Canot; s €160-195, d €198-244, ste €245-310, all incl breakfast; ❄ 📶 🏊) Another four-star bigwig (though ageing a bit) at the other end of the beach.

### Eating

There's a clutch of snack stands and laid-back cafe-restaurants along the seafront promenade, including **Ti Boucan** (☎ 0262 24 85 08; Route de Boucan Canot; mains €7-15, menu €13; 🕑 lunch), which has a brilliant-value *formule* (lunch set menu), **La Boucantine** (Route de Boucan Canot; mains €12-21; 🕑 lunch & dinner) and the unmissable **Bambou Bar** (☎ 0262 24 59 29; Route de Boucan Canot; mains €10-25; 🕑 lunch Tue-Sun, dinner daily), which scores high on atmosphere, with a thatched roof and plenty of wood and greenery. Its menu is translated into English.

### Getting There & Away

Car Jaune's lines B and C between St-Denis and St-Pierre run through the centre of Boucan-Canot.

## ST-GILLES-LES-BAINS & L'HERMITAGE-LES-BAINS

pop 6000

Robinson Crusoe–style beaches and pristine wilderness, oh no no! The tourism machine shifts into overdrive in the large resort complex of St-Gilles and L'Hermitage (as they are usually known), with white sands, restaurants, nightclubs and a boisterous atmosphere on weekends. During the week, however, the atmosphere is much more relaxed and you shouldn't have to fight for a space to lay your towel. There are numerous water activities on offer, from diving to deep-sea fishing. The surf here isn't bad either; many amateurs hone their skills in St-Gilles before attempting the more challenging swells at St-Leu.

Let's be frank: it's got that generic resort feel and there's no discernible Creole character. If you're after more authenticity, clunk in your seat belt, jump on a serpentine country road and drive up to some rustic and authentic villages in the Hauts.

### Information

ATM-clad commercial banks can be found along the main drag in St-Gilles.

**Hotwave** ( ☎ 0262 24 04 04; 37 Rue du Général de Gaulle, St-Gilles-les-Bains; internet access per hr €7; ⊗ 10am-7pm Mon-Sat) Internet cafe. Also has wi-fi.

**Office du tourisme** ( ☎ 0810 79 77 97; www. saintpaul-lareunion.com; 1 Place Paul-Julius Bénard, St-Gilles-les-Bains; ⊗ 10am-1pm & 2-6pm) Has helpful English-speaking staff.

**Post office** (Rue de la Poste, St-Gilles-les-Bains; ⊗ 8.15am-5pm Mon-Fri, 8am-noon Sat) Has an ATM.

### Sights

The attractive **Plage des Roches Noires** is obviously the biggest pull at St-Gilles. Further south, **Plage de L'Hermitage**, lined with casuarina trees, is another alluring place to fry in the sun. Both beaches are safe for swimming and extremely popular on weekends. Snorkelling is better at Plage de L'Hermitage.

In the modern Port de Plaisance complex, the quite engaging **Aquarium de la Réunion** ( ☎ 0262 33 44 00; www.aquariumdelareunion.com; adult/child €8/5; ⊗ 10am-5.30pm Tue-Sun) houses a series of excellent underwater displays, including tanks with lobsters, barracudas, groupers and small sharks.

Appealing to a wider audience than just plant lovers and gardeners, **Le Jardin d'Eden** ( ☎ 0262 33 83 16; www.jardindeden-ethnobotanique.com;

RN1; adult/child €7/3.50; ⊗ 10am-6pm Sat-Thu), across the main road from L'Hermitage, is definitely worth an hour or so for anyone interested in tropical flora. Sections of the gardens are dedicated to interesting concepts such as the sacred plants of the Hindus, medicinal plants, edible tropical plants, spices and aphrodisiac plants.

### Activities

#### BOAT EXCURSIONS

The best way to discover St-Gilles' iridescent lagoon is by joining a boat excursion. Various operators offer *promenades en mer* (boat excursions) and *observation sousmarine* (glass-bottomed tours) along the coast towards St-Leu or St-Paul. 'Safaris dauphin' (dolphin encounters), sunset cruises and daylong catamaran cruises are also available. Depending on the duration of the cruise (the shortest tours last 30 minutes) and the type of boat, rates range from €12 to €90 per adult and from €7 to €50 per child. Tours go every day but are weather-dependent.

The following outfits have a booth at the jetty beside the aquarium:

**Le Grand Bleu** ( ☎ 0262 33 28 32; www.reunioncroisieres. com) Has the largest range of tours.

**Visiobul** ( ☎ 0262 24 37 04; www.visiobul-reunion.com)

#### SURFING

Hawaii it ain't, but Plage des Roches Noires has respectable waves that are suitable for beginners. **École de Surf et de Bodyboard des Roches Noires** ( ☎ 0262 24 63 28, 0692 86 00 59; bertrand.surf@ wanadoo.fr) is a 'travelling' surfing school that runs lessons (€30 for two hours) and courses (€122 for 10 hours). Children are welcome.

#### DIVING

The waters off St-Gilles offer plenty of scope for diving (including the chance to explore a few wrecks), whatever your level. See p31 for more information about diving.

Reputable dive operators in St-Gilles:

**Bleu Marine Réunion** ( ☎ 0262 24 22 00; www.bleu -marine-reunion.com; Port de Plaisance)

**Corail Plongée** ( ☎ 0262 24 46 38; www.corail-plon gee.com; Port de Plaisance)

**Ô Sea Bleu** ( ☎ 0262 33 16 15; www.reunion-plongee. com; Port de Plaisance)

#### MOUNTAIN BIKING

Downhill rides from Le Maïdo (p187) can be arranged with **Rando Réunion Passion** ( ☎ 0262

RÉUNION

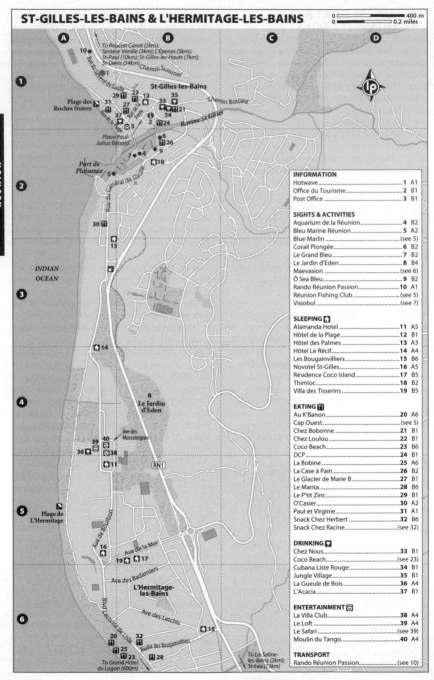

# ST-GILLES-LES-BAINS & L'HERMITAGE-LES-BAINS

45 18 67, 0692 21 11 11; www.descente-vtt.com; 3 Rue du Général de Gaulle).

## SPORTFISHING

St-Gilles is a good base for fans of Ernest Hemingway. The waters off the west coast are a pelagic playpen for schools of marlin, swordfish, sailfish, shark and tuna. A fishing trip (four to six people) costs from €350/600 per half-/full day. Three recommended outfits: **Blue Marlin** ( ☎ 0692 65 22 35; www.bluemarlin.fr; Port de Plaisance)
**Maevasion** ( ☎ 0262 33 38 04; www.maeva-fishing. com; Port de Plaisance)
**Réunion Fishing Club** ( ☎ 0262 24 36 10; www. reunionfishingclub.com; Port de Plaisance)

## Sleeping

There's plenty of accommodation in the area, but almost everything is booked out during holiday periods and on weekends. The more appealing hotels and *chambre d'hôte* are in the countryside just north of town or to the south in L'Hermitage-les-Bains.

### ST-GILLES-LES-BAINS

**Hôtel de la Plage** ( ☎ 0262 24 06 37; www.hoteldela plage.re; 20 Rue de la Poste; d with shared bathroom €38-43, d €45-54; 🟦 🛜) The highlights of this long-established and well-run hostel-like venture are its ultra-central location and colourful communal areas. The nine rooms are nothing special but get the job done. Some have bathrooms, some don't, some are spacious, some are boxy, some open onto a terrace, some don't. Rooms 114, 115 and 116 are the best.

**our pick Senteur Vanille** ( ☎ 0262 24 04 88, 0692 78 13 05; www.senteurvanille.com; Route du Théâtre; bungalow €79-156, chalet €134-156; 🟦 🛜) A true find for peace seekers, Senteur Vanille makes you feel you've stepped into a Garden of Eden, with mango, lychee and papaya trees all over the grounds (the owner is a major fruit producer in Réunion). Curl up in a well-equipped chalet or in a cute-as-can-be Creole bungalow. The wonderful setting makes it easy to meet the three-night minimum stay. The nearest beach is a 15-minute walk down a path. It's a few kilometres east of the centre, in the direction of St-Gilles-les-Hauts; it's signed down a lane beside the Total petrol station.

Other places to rest your head:
**Hôtel des Palmes** ( ☎ 0262 24 47 12; fax 0262 24 30 62; 205 Rue du Général de Gaulle; d €50-65; 🟦 🖥) This two-star offers good-sized villas, but its location ain't

so great – it's sandwiched between the highway and the main road to L'Hermitage.
**Thimloc** ( ☎ 0262 24 23 24; www.thimloc.fr; 165 Rue du Général de Gaulle; d €54-64, 🟦 🛜) Six adjoining rooms in a shady garden.

### L'HERMITAGE-LES-BAINS

**Villa des Tisserins** ( ☎ 0262 33 15 23; villa.des.tis serins@wanadoo.fr; 25 Ave de la Mer; d €35-50, bungalow €80; 🛜 🖥) If you're looking to save and be close to the beach, this laid-back villa with five rooms and three bungalows – all with self-catering facilities – is a bonanza. Mellow out in the garden or take a dip in the kidney-shaped pool. Excellent value.

**Résidence Coco Island** ( ☎ 0262 33 82 41; www.chez -cocoisland.com; 21 Ave de la Mer; d €40-65; 🟦 🛜 🖥) A few doors from Villa des Tisserins, this is another popular budget option, with 16 unimaginative rooms of varying size and shape – have a look before committing. Cheaper rooms share bathrooms. Guests can use the communal kitchen. Prices drop for stays longer than five nights.

**Les Bougainvilliers** ( ☎ 0262 33 82 48, 0692 22 15 23; www.bougainvillier.com; 27 Ruelle des Bougainvilliers; d €53-59; 🅿 🟦 🛜 🖥) For something personal, try this jolly, hospitably run little bolt-hole with 14 rooms. Firm mattresses, colourful walls, flat screen TVs, a pool, plus a communal kitchen and a flower-filled garden, all just a stroll from the beach. The catch? It's a wee compact – the pool almost licks the terrace of the downstairs room.

**Grand Hôtel du Lagon** ( ☎ 0262 70 00 00; www.naiade. com; 28 Rue du Lagon; s €200-305, d €300-395, ste from €360, all incl breakfast; 🟦 🖥 🖥) Simply stunning, du Lagon pays elegant homage to luxurious colonial architecture, with a gaggle of Creole-style villas scattered amid a verdant property overlooking the beach. At the very south end of the beach at L'Hermitage.

Other options:
**Alamanda Hotel** ( ☎ 0262 33 10 10; www.alamanda.fr; 81 Ave de Bourbon; 🟦 🛜 🖥 ) The tired rooms of this two-star were about to be overhauled when we visited. Call to check the latest prices.
**Novotel St-Gilles** ( ☎ 0262 24 44 44; www.accorhotels. com; Ave de la Mer; d from €130; 🟦 🛜 🖥 ) Accor's flagship Réunionnais resort offers plenty of amenities. Internet discounts of up to 30% are often available.
**Hôtel Le Récif** ( ☎ 0262 70 01 00; www.naiade.com; 50 Ave du Bourbon; s €195-205, d €286-300, all incl breakfast; 🟦 🛜 🖥 ) Though playing second fiddle to the Grand Hôtel du Lagon, it's still an excellent property, with 146 rooms and plenty of amenities.

**RÉUNION**

## Eating

St-Gilles is well endowed with eating places, and new restaurants are constantly opening up. Standards tend to be more variable than elsewhere on the island.

### ST-GILLES-LES-BAINS

The *camions-pizzas* (mobile pizza vans) on the main street are a good bargain. They operate in the evening.

our pick **La Case à Pain** (☎ 0262 33 27 89; 27 Rue du Port; 7am-7pm Tue-Sun) Hmm! We can still smell the scent of freshly baked *pain frotté à la vanille* (a variety of bread flavoured with vanilla) wafting from the door (available on certain days only). Its other offerings, including brioches, are worth the dental bills, too.

**Le Glacier de Marie B** (☎ 0262 24 53 06; 13 Rue de la Poste; ice creams from €1.80; 11am-7pm Tue-Sun) You'll lose all self-control at this drool-inducing ice-cream parlour. Amid a mind-boggling array of flavours, the electric purple pitaya screams 'try me'. Good pancakes and smoothies, too.

**Chez Loulou** (☎ 0262 24 40 41; 86 Rue du Général de Gaulle; mains €5-8; 7am-1pm & 3-7pm Mon-Sat, 7am-1pm Sun) The most iconic Creole *case* (house) for miles around, with a distinctive turquoise facade on the main drag. The belt-bustingly good samosas and *macatias* continue to torment us! Good sandwiches and takeaway meals at lunchtime, too.

**O'Casier** (☎ 0262 33 17 38; 190 Rue du Général de Gaulle; mains €10-23; lunch & dinner Tue-Fri & Sun, dinner Sat) This sassy *bistrot chic* (gastropub) churns out excellent charcuterie and cheese platters, as well as *métro* dishes. Since wine also features high here, get stuck into the list of well-chosen French tipples, available by the glass.

**DCP** (☎ 0262 33 02 96; Place du Marché; mains €11-25, menus €22-27; lunch & dinner) Fish lovers, you'll find nirvana here: the DCP has a wide assortment of fish delivered daily from the harbour. Order it grilled, *à la vapeur* (steamed) or raw, accompanied with a curcuma, pineapple or Roquefort sauce.

our pick **Le P'tit Zinc** (☎ 0262 24 07 50; 58 Rue du Général de Gaulle; mains €14-20, menus €10-15; dinner Mon-Sat) This venue has a tantalising menu showcasing all the classics of Creole cuisine, served in snug surrounds complete with wood beams, elegant furnishings and tropical plants. Feeling adventurous? Go for the *carri pat' cochon* (pig's trotter *carri*). The spiffing balcony on the 1st floor (two tables only) is a good place to linger over a meal.

**Chez Bobonne** (☎ 0262 39 27 96; 3 Rue St-Alexis; mains €22-25; dinner) Indulge in delicious, flawlessly prepared dishes at this fine-dining restaurant with a contemporary decor. It's tucked away from the main drag.

Other recommendations:

**Cap Ouest** (☎ 0262 33 21 56; Port de Plaisance; mains €13-25; 9am-midnight) Light meals are available at this buzzing eatery overlooking the harbour. Live music on weekends.

**Paul et Virginie** (☎ 0262 33 04 53; 15 Rue de la Plage; mains €17-23, menus €12-30; lunch Wed-Sun, dinner Tue-Sun) Top-notch location on the seafront, with a breezy terrace. Budget tip: the two-course lunch special is just €12.

### L'HERMITAGE-LES-BAINS

**Snack Chez Herbert** (☎ 0262 32 42 96; 40 Blvd Leconte de Lisle; mains €2-6; lunch & dinner Tue-Sun) This popular joint is worth visiting for its good, cheap and wholesome Creole staples. Snacks, salads, sandwiches and other nibbles are also available. Take your plunder to the beach or grab a (plastic) table on the shaded pavement.

**Snack Chez Racine** (42 Blvd Leconte de Lisle; mains €3-8; lunch & dinner Mon-Sat) Another casual hang-out with a light satisfying menu, next door to Chez Herbert.

**Coco Beach** (☎ 0262 33 81 43; Blvd Leconte de Lisle; mains €13-24; lunch & dinner) This eatery overlooking the beach has garnered high praise for its grills and ultra-fresh fish, salads and tapas. It's also a good place to hang out and just enjoy the tropical atmosphere and fashionable buzz with a fresh Dodo beer in hand.

**Au K'Banon** (☎ 0262 33 84 94; Blvd Leconte de Lisle; mains €14-18; lunch daily, dinner Fri & Sat) This friendly restaurant with a casual atmosphere occupies a privileged spot on the beach. The menu runs the gamut from fish dishes and grilled meats to salads and ice creams. What sets it apart, though, is the *formule petit déjeuner au bord du lagon* (lagoonside breakfast; €7). Hmm, croissants and baguette metres from the turquoise waters…

**Le Manta** (☎ 0262 33 82 44; Blvd Leconte de Lisle; mains €16-23; lunch & dinner) Concealed in a wonderfully overgrown garden, this well-respected restaurant has a great selection of fish and meat dishes, as well as a few Creole classics and salads. Toothsome specialities include *salade manta*, comprising smoked marlin and tuna, and *lasagne d'espadon* (lasagne with swordfish). No, it's not right on the beach – it's just across the road.

**our pick** **La Bobine** ( ☎ 0262 33 94 36; Blvd Leconte de Lisle; mains €16-40; ☺ lunch & dinner) This sprightly restaurant with an exotic feel – the wood and thatch are imported from Madagascar – enjoys a perfect location, slap bang on the beach. The wide-ranging menu features delicious fish or meat dishes, such as *assiette de poissons fumés* (a combo platter of smoked fish). There's also a snack section (until 5pm), with a choice of sandwiches, salads and light meals.

## Drinking

St-Gilles is one of the top places in Réunion (on an equal footing with St-Pierre) for barhopping. The atmosphere is very Zoreilles – you could be mistaken for thinking you're in the French Côte d'Azur. Most places are scattered along Rue du Général de Gaulle and the chichi seafront. L'Hermitage is noted more for its beachside venues. As the bars fade from about midnight on, the centre of pleasurable gravity shifts to L'Hermitage (see Entertainment). Most bars also serve food.

### ST-GILLES-LES-BAINS

**Cubana Liste Rouge** ( ☎ 0692 10 76 31; 122 Rue du Général de Gaulle; ☺ 6pm-2am) Kick off the night with a few shots at this salsa-inspired venue featuring bordello-red curtains.

**Jungle Village** ( ☎ 0262 33 21 93; Rue du Général de Gaulle; ☺ 7pm-2am Mon-Sat) Big, bold and cheesy – it's hard to miss the log-cabin exterior and the ugly monkey mannequin above the entrance – sums up this popular bar on St-Gilles' main drag.

**L'Acacia** ( ☎ 0262 27 36 43; 1 Rue de la Poste; ☺ 11am-midnight) The terrace at this fashionable open-air bar and restaurant on the seafront is perfect for watching the surfers frolicking in the waves. There's a pool too.

**Chez Nous** ( ☎ 0262 24 08 08; 122 Rue du Général de Gaulle; ☺ 7pm-2am) A hip bar and restaurant with a loungey feel.

### L'HERMITAGE-LES-BAINS

**Coco Beach** ( ☎ 0262 33 81 43; Blvd Leconte de Lisle; ☺ lunch-midnight) This beachside restaurant in L'Hermitage is packed on Friday and Sunday evening, when there's live music. There's also plenty of Dodo beer with which to lubricate your gullet.

**La Gueule de Bois** ( ☎ 0262 22 90 06; 5 Rue des Îles Éparses; ☺ 6pm-midnight Tue-Sun) The name of this cheerful den is a French expression meaning 'hangover', which is pretty appropriate given

the incendiary rums on offer. It hosts live bands certain evenings. Food is also served.

## Entertainment

Party, party, party! L'Hermitage rocks on weekends. By far the capital of Réunion's club scene, it has the greatest density of discos on the island. The fun starts late – after 11pm – and places typically close around 4am. Cover charges vary between €10 and €15 at most venues (but some are free). You don't need to be completely dolled up but if you're wearing shorts or flip-flops you'll be turned away. Check the flyers posted around town or ask the locals to find out which clubs are the flavour of the month.

**Le Safari** ( ☎ 0262 25 99 13; http://lesafari.net; 1 Rue des Îles Éparses) A local place that pulls in just about everybody on the island on weekends, when a DJ cranks up the salsa, R&B and other soundtracks.

**Moulin du Tango** ( ☎ 0262 24 53 90; www.moulin-du-tango.fr; Ave de Bourbon) Bump your hips with a more mature crowd in this legendary dance club in L'Hermitage. Famous for its Bal des Célibataires ('singles' ball') on Wednesday and its themed nights, such as 'Tu es mon soleil' ('You're my sun').

Other staunch favourites:

**La Villa Club** ( ☎ 0692 60 19 00; www.lavilla-club.com; 71 Ave de Bourbon) Another crowd-puller in L'Hermitage. Latin and dance music dominate the play list.

**Le Loft** ( ☎ 0262 24 81 06; 1 Rue des Îles Éparses) Another hot spot that's cookin' after 2am, with scantily clad clubbers posturing on podiums.

## Getting There & Away

Car Jaune's nonexpress buses between St-Denis and St-Pierre (lines B and C) run through the centre of St-Gilles down Rue du Général de Gaulle. Buses run about every 45 minutes or so in either direction from 5am to 6pm. The trip to St-Denis takes at least one hour and costs €2.80.

## Getting Around

### CAR & MOTORCYCLE

There are numerous local operators and a few international outlets in St-Gilles. Find them along Rue du Général de Gaulle.

### BIKE

**Rando Réunion Passion** ( ☎ 0262 45 18 67; www.descente-vtt.com; 3 Rue du Général de Gaulle) rents out mountain bikes (€35 per day).

RÉUNION

**RÉUNION**

## ST-GILLES-LES-HAUTS & AROUND

**pop 2000**

If all these beaches start to overwhelm and you need a break from the commercialism of the coast, a 20-minute drive from St-Gilles-les-Bains transports you to yet another world up in the hills, in St-Gilles-les-Hauts. For some cultural sustenance, head to the **Musée de Villèle** ( ☎ 0262 55 64 10; admission €2;  10am-12.30pm & 1.30-5pm Tue-Sun), south of St-Gilles-les-Hauts on the D6. It's set in the former home of a wealthy coffee- and sugar-baroness who, among other things, owned 300 slaves. Legend has it that she was a cruel woman and that her ghost inhabits the Piton de la Fournaise; supposedly her tormented screams can be heard from the hellish fires whenever the volcano is erupting. She died in 1846 and her body lies in the **Chapelle Pointue**, on the D6 by the entrance to the museum. The house itself, which is only accessible on a guided tour (in French only), was built in 1787 and is full of elegant period furniture. After the tour, you're free to wander the outbuildings and the 10-hectare park, which contains the ruins of the sugar mill.

You could also stop off in the village of L'Éperon and visit the **Village Artisanal de L'Éperon**. Housed in a picturesque old grist, it's home to a small community of artists and artisans. There are also a number of boutiques selling ceramics, locally tanned leather and other *objets d'art*.

The villages of St-Gilles-les-Hauts, Villèle and L'Éperon can all be reached by fairly infrequent minibuses out of St-Paul (see p186).

## LA SALINE-LES-BAINS & AROUND

**pop 2750**

If you find the scene in St-Gilles and L'Hermitage a little too much, head to La Saline-les-Bains. Though immediately to the south of L'Hermitage along the coast, it has a distinct atmosphere. Here it's more mellow, more alternative, more nonconformist, and the beach of **Trou d'Eau** is usually less crowded. Not a fan of tan lines? Head further south and lay your towel on **Plage de la Souris Chaude**, a 'maverick beach', which is a favourite among nudists (only just tolerated) and gay men (head to the northern tip of the beach).

The area is also popular for **surfing**, especially for beginners. To the south of La Saline, surfers gather at the **Pointe des Trois Bassins**, where the waves are generally easier and more

consistent than around St-Leu. A number of operators park their vans on the clifftop and offer lessons for adults and children (see p196).

**Kayaking** is a great way to explore the lagoon at a gentle pace. The beachfront restaurant Planch'Alizé (right) rents canoes, kayaks and paddleboats (from €5 per hour).

### Sleeping

#### LA SALINE-LES-BAINS

**Le Vacoa** ( ☎ 0262 24 12 48; www.levacoa.com; 54 Rue Antoine de Bertin; d €52-56;  ) A five-minute stroll from the beach, this little two-storey *résidence hôtelière* (mini-resort) contains 15 modern, well-appointed (albeit hanky-sized) rooms arranged around a central courtyard. There's a kitchen for guests' use. Prices drop after three nights.

**La Maison du Lagon** ( ☎ 0262 24 30 14; www.lamaisondulagon.com; 72 Rue Auguste Lacaussade; s €66-100, d €86-121, ste €190;  ) This villa has a compact but respectable collection of various-sized rooms – try to snaffle a sea-facing one. The real bonus here is the location – it's *les pieds dans l'eau* (right by the beach). The pool is a bit of a joke, though.

**our pick** **La Closerie du Lagon** ( ☎ 0262 24 12 56, 0692 86 32 47; www.closerie-du-lagnon.fr; 78ter Rue Lacaussade; d €100;  ) A splendid villa with all mod cons in a peaceful property by the beach. It's fully equipped. Intimate, chic and gay-friendly.

**Hôtel Swalibo** ( ☎ 0262 24 10 97; www.swalibo.com; 9 Rue des Salines; s €105-130, d €130-165;  ) This small (some would say 'cramped') two-storey hotel is a good deal if you can get online specials. The rooms are well appointed and are arranged around a gleaming pool. There's an onsite restaurant. It's 200m away from the beach.

#### LA SOURIS CHAUDE

With your own wheels, you'll need a code to enter La Souris Chaude residential area – phone your accommodation ahead and they will give you the code.

**Kitouni Guesthouse** ( ☎ 0262 34 05 82, 0692 44 30 58; kitounicase@hotmail.com; 5 Allée des Tuits Tuits; d with shared bathroom €25;  ) Kitouni means, er, 'naked bum' in Creole. Fear not, this is a respectable port of call on top of being a cast-iron bargain for budget travellers and surfies, with three tidy rooms, a kitchen for guests' use, a lounge with TV and DVDs and a lovely garden to snooze under swaying palms. You're only steps from the beach.

**Le Dalon Plage** ( ☎ 0262 34 29 77, 0692 04 94 26; le.dalon@wanadoo.fr; 6 Allée des Tuits Tuits; d €65; ✹ ▣ ☞ ) It's *au naturel* at this hedonistic, gay-friendly place almost next door to Kitouni. Guests are allowed (if not incited) to swim naked in the gleaming pool. Well, we were too prudish to get our kit off and instead preferred to slumber in the fully equipped, solar-heated bungalow – a wonderful retreat.

## Eating & Drinking

**La Bonne Marmite** ( ☎ 0262 39 82 49; Route du Trou d'Eau; mains €8-16, dinner buffet €15; ✹ lunch daily, dinner Mon-Sat) Pounce on La Bonne Marmite's excellent-value dinner buffet, which features 10 wholesome *carris*, and you'll leave perfectly sated. It's a coconut's throw from the beach (with the sea just out of sight, alas), almost next door to La Petite Vague.

**ourpick La Petite Vague** ( ☎ 0262 59 79 73; Route du Trou d'Eau; mains €9-14; ✹ lunch daily, dinner Wed-Sun) Sweet! La Petite Vague is right on the beach, and it serves good, fresh food at competitive prices given the five-star location.

**Planch'Alizé** ( ☎ 0262 24 62 61; Rue des Mouettes; mains €12-19; ✹ lunch daily, bar 9am-7pm daily) For a decent beach munch or a drink, nothing can beat this casual eatery.

**Le Copacabana** ( ☎ 0262 24 16 31; Rue Lacaussade; mains €17-22; ✹ lunch daily, dinner Fri & Sat, bar 9am-late daily) Simple meals are the order of the day at this trendy little bar-restaurant right on the beach. It's also a laid-back spot to sip a *rhum arrangé* or a refreshing fruit juice any time of the day. Cover bands perform here on Friday evening. You'll find it about 150m further south from La Maison du Lagon.

## ST-LEU
pop 25,000

Since the good old days of the sugar industry ended, forward-looking St-Leu has transformed itself into a mecca for outdoor enthusiasts. This is the place to get high – legally: no doubt you'll be tempted to join the paragliders who wheel down from the Hauts to the lagoon. Scuba divers swear that the drop-offs here are the best on the island and surfing fiends rave about the tremendous Gauche de St-Leu.

And culture? St-Leu has a smattering of handsome stone buildings dating from the French colonial era, such as the *mairie* (town

hall) and the church opposite. Other attractions are the shady park along the seafront and a protected beach that is popular with families.

St-Leu is also optimally placed for explorations of the coast and forays into the Hauts.

## Information

**Office du Tourisme de St-Leu** ( ☎ 0262 34 63 30; www.saintleureunion.com; 1 Rue Le Barrelier; ✹ 1.30-5.30pm Mon, 9am-noon & 1.30-5.30pm Tue-Fri, 9am-noon & 2-5pm Sat) At the north end of the main road passing through the centre of town. It has brochures galore and helpful, English-speaking staff. *Gîtes de montagnes* can also be booked here.

## Sights

Don't miss **Kelonia** ( ☎ 0262 34 81 10; www.kelonia .org; Pointe des Châteaux; adult/child €7/5; ✹ 9am-5pm), an ecologically conscious marine and research centre dedicated to sea turtles, about 2km north of St-Leu. It features exhibits, interactive displays and big tanks where you can get a close-up look at the five different varieties of turtle found in the waters around Réunion, especially the green turtle *(Chelonia mydas)*. Kids love the place but adults will also be blown away by this well-organised venture. Guided tours are available.

The little white **chapel of Notre-Dame de la Salette**, perched on the side of the hill to the east of town, was built in 1859 as a plea for protection against the cholera epidemic sweeping the entire island. Whether by luck or divine intervention, St-Leu was spared from the epidemic, and thousands of pilgrims come here each year on 19 September to offer their thanks.

On the cliffs at Pointe au Sel, between St-Leu and Étang-Salé-les-Bains, the **Musée du Sel** ( ☎ 0262 34 67 00; www.selreunion.com; Pointe au Sel; admission free; ✹ 9am-noon & 1.30-5pm Tue-Sun), housed in an old salt warehouse, traces the local salt-harvesting history. It's flanked by salt evaporation ponds. After visiting the museum, follow the path that leads to **La Caverne** (no sign), a large, wonderful rock pool with turquoise waters only known to locals. It's ideal for splashing about, sunbathing or picnicking.

## Activities
### DIVING

The dive spots off Pointe au Sel to the south of St-Leu offer some of the best underwater landscapes in Réunion, while the lagoon

RÉUNION

closer to St-Leu is good for coral. See p31 for more information about diving.

Reputable dive centres:

**Abyss Plongée** ( ☎ 0262 34 79 79; www.abyss-plongee .com; 17 Blvd Bonnier)

**Bleu Océan** ( ☎ 0262 34 97 49; www.bleuocean.fr; 25 Rue du Général Lambert)

**Excelsus** ( ☎ 0262 34 73 65; www.excelsus-plongee .com; Pointe des Châteaux)

**Plongée Attitude** ( ☎ 0692 07 88 99; www.lrun.fr; 37 Rue du Lagon) Same location as L Run (see p197).

**Réunion Plongée** ( ☎ 0262 34 77 77; www.reunion plongee.com; 13 Ave des Artisans)

### PARAGLIDING

St-Leu is one of the world's top spots for paragliding, with excellent uplifting thermals year-round. If you're new to dangling yourself in the air, you can tandem paraglide with one of the many operators offering flights (from €75 for a 15- to 25-minute aerial buzz). They also run introductory courses from €260. The most popular launch pad is at an altitude of 800m, high above the town. There's another launch pad at 1500m. The descent from the mountain is amazing, with heart-stopping views over the lagoon and the coast. Children over six are welcome.

Operators with good credentials and professional staff:

**Airanx** ( ☎ 0692 68 81 81; www.airanx.com; 38 Rue du Général Lambert)

**Azurtech** ( ☎ 0262 34 91 89; www.azurtech.com; Pointe des Châteaux)

**Bourbon Parapente** ( ☎ 0262 34 18 34, 0692 87 58 74; www.bourbonparapente.com; Rue du Général Lambert)

**Parapente Réunion** ( ☎ 0262 24 87 84; www .parapente-reunion.fr; 1 Route des Colimaçons)

### SURFING

One word: awesome. The surf break known as **La Gauche de St-Leu** ('the Left of St-Leu') has achieved cult status among surfies from all over the Indian Ocean. Certainly not for the faint-hearted, it instils profound respect (if not fear) even in the most seasoned surfers. The best season runs from May to October.

Beginners should make for a spot called **La Cafrine**, which is a bit more innocuous, or head to Pointe des Trois Bassins (see p196) or St-Gilles-les-Bains (p189).

To brush up on your surfing skills or try a first lesson, contact **École de surf Cyril Theveneau** ( ☎ 0692 04 40 40; www.ipomea-surf.com) or **École de surf de St-Leu** ( ☎ 0692 65 44 92). Both outfits offer tuition and courses for all levels (from €20 per hour). They don't have shops – call ahead for an appointment.

## Sleeping

**Dodo Spot** ( ☎ 0262 34 76 98; www.dodospot.com; 67 Rue du Général Lambert; d with shared bathroom €30, studios €44-54; 🛜 ) On the northern edge of town, this is an acceptable standby, if you can forgive some flagrant omissions in the brochure and on the website. Sure, it's almost 'two steps away from the lagoon', but there's no mention of the noisy highway in between! Despite being in a plant-filled property, the whole place feels a bit cramped, especially the coffin-sized rooms; it's worth dropping the extra €14 to grab a more spacious studio.

**Palais d'Asie** ( ☎ 0262 34 80 41, 0692 86 48 80; 5 Rue de l'Étang; d €32-45; 🍴 🛜 🏊 ) One of St-Leu's best bargains, though the 'Palais' bit is a gross misnomer. It's comfortably central, with minimally furnished but functional rooms. And no, that icon's not a misprint – it really does have its own (small) swimming pool.

**Résidence des Alizés** ( ☎ 0262 34 82 31; www. residencealizes.com; 48bis Rue des Alizés; studios €36-48; 🍴 🏊 ) On the southern outskirts of town, this white villa shelters six self-catering studios of varying shapes and sizes. Ask for the Paille En Queue or the L'Horizon, which boast the best views (and are justifiably dearer). They all feel a bit worn, but when you factor in the pool, the serene setting and the ample views of the coast, this establishment offers great value. There's a three-night minimum stay.

**Iloha** ( ☎ 0262 34 89 89; www.iloha.fr; Pointe des Châteaux; d €85-98, bungalow €116-165; 🍴 🛜 🏊 ) It's not quite the upscale option it thinks it is, but the pool, the onsite restaurant and mature gardens do add a resort flavour. Views take in the lagoon. Good for families. It's on Route des Colimaçons, north of town.

**our pick** **Blue Margouillat** ( ☎ 0262 34 64 00; www. blue-margouillat.com; Impasse Jean Albany; r €135-220; 🍴 🛜 🏊 ) This delightful, small hotel on the southern outskirts of St-Leu adds a welcoming touch of glam to the local hotel scene, with just 14 artfully designed and sensitively furnished rooms, a romantic restaurant that serves dinner (mains €24 to €31) daily and smashing views.

Other places:

**Ti Som** ( ☎ 0692 24 18 12; 228 Rue du Général Lambert; dm €16, d with shared bathroom €35) The cheapest place to stay for miles, with a brightly painted 10-bed dorm. If privacy is a priority, opt for the no-frills but OK doubles. The shared kitchen is a plus.

**Repos Laleu** ( ☎ 0262 34 93 84; http://pagesperso -orange.fr/repos.laleu; 249 Rue du Général Lambert; d €55; 🐾 🛜 ) Offers eight fully equipped apartments, smack dab in the centre. Prices drop to €41 from the fourth night onward

## Eating

**Our pick** **L Run** ( ☎ 0692 05 55 49; 37 Rue du Lagon; mains €3-12; 🕙 lunch Tue, Wed, Fri-Sun, dinner Fri & Sat) Brimming with good cheer, this inviting eatery run by a gang of Zoreilles ladies offers crunchy salads, zesty pastas and copious omelettes. Make sure you save a corner for the crêpes.

**L'Orange Givrée** ( ☎ 0262 34 89 53; Rue Le Barrelier; mains €4-9; 🕙 8am-5pm Mon-Sat) Blink and you'll miss the tiny entrance of this funky little den next to the tourist office. It whips up appetising salads, sandwiches and other treats at wallet-friendly prices. Good breakfast too (€6).

**Le Zat** ( ☎ 0262 42 20 92; 14 Rue de la Compagnie des Indes; mains €13-17; 🕙 lunch daily, dinner Sat) Overlooking the beach, this small venture majors in fish and meat dishes.

**Villa Vanille** ( ☎ 0262 34 03 15; 69 Rue du Lagon; mains €14-22; 🕙 lunch & dinner Wed-Mon) No plastic chairs (sweet mercy!) but teak furnishings and an agreeable terrace. Choose from frondy salads, meat and fish dishes – the *thon mi-cuit et son médaillon de foie gras* (semicooked tuna served with a medallion-shaped serving of duck liver) was delicious – and ice creams. Lounge on the beach across the road once you've finished your meal – this is the life!

Other recommendations:

**Rondavelle Les Filaos – Chez Jean-Paul** (sandwiches from €3; 🕙 7.30am-9pm) A very popular beach shack.

**Palais d'Asie** ( ☎ 0262 34 80 41, 0692 86 48 80; 5 Rue de l'Étang; mains €5-9; 🕙 lunch & dinner Wed-Sun) Cheap Creole and Chinese nosh. Eat in or take away.

**Le Lagon – Tilbury** ( ☎ 0262 34 79 13; 2 Rue du Lagon; mains €8-22; 🕙 lunch & dinner daily) This beachfront place won't start a revolution but the menu covers enough territory to please most palates.

## Drinking & Entertainment

**Le Comptoir** ( ☎ 0262 33 55 36; 228 Rue du Général Lambert; 🕙 8am-midnight Mon-Sat) St-Leu's best drinking spot (an easy distinction, given the lack of competitors). Take a seat in the room or join the happy din at the main bar. Chances are that you'll bump into your div-

ing/paragliding/surfing instructor. Live music on Thursday.

**Le K** ( ☎ 0262 34 79 69; www.lesechoir.com; 125 Rue du Général Lambert) One of Réunion's venues for contemporary theatre, dance and music, as well as puppet shows, circus acts and other cultural activities. The organisers also put on open-air concerts and film shows in the area. Contact the tourist office to find out about the latest shows.

## Getting There & Away

Car Jaune buses between St-Denis and St-Pierre run through the centre of St-Leu (€4.20 , about 15 daily). The bus station is near the town hall. From there, Ti' Car Jaune minibuses have services for most villages in the Hauts.

## AROUND ST-LEU

After all that exertion in St-Leu, there's no better way to wind down than by exploring the villages that cling to the sloping hills high above the town. The zigzagging roads are scenic to boot and the atmosphere wonderfully laid-back.

To the north of St-Leu, take the D12, known as Route des Colimaçons – a series of intestine-like S-curves – then veer due south on the D3 to **La Chaloupe St-Leu** before plunging back to the coast via **Piton St-Leu**, where the brightly painted **Hindu temple** is worth a gander. If you really want to get away from it all, you could continue to drive uphill from the village of **Les Colimaçons** until you reach the Route Forestière des Tamarins, which threads for 36km across the slopes from Le Tévelave to Le Maïdo – sensational. Whatever your itinerary, a good road map is essential as it's easy to get disorientated.

Aside from the scenery and the astounding vistas, there are a few not-to-be-missed attractions in the area. On the Route des Colimaçons, on the slopes north of St-Leu, you'll find the **Conservatoire Botanique National de Mascarin** ( ☎ 0262 24 92 27; 2 Rue du Père Georges, Les Colimaçons; adult/child €6/3; 🕙 9am-5pm Tue-Sun). This attractive garden is in the grounds of a 19th-century Creole mansion and contains an impressive collection of native plant species, all neatly labelled, as well as many from around the Indian Ocean. Spitting distance from the Conservatoire is the **Église du Sacré-Coeur**. This majestic church was built in 1875, using lava stones.

RÉUNION

Another must-see is the well-organised **Stella Matutina museum** ( ☎ 0262 34 16 24; www.stella matutina.fr; 10 Allée des Flamboyants; adult/child €7/2.50; ⊙ 9.30am-4.45pm Tue-Sun), which lies 4km south of St-Leu on the D11 to Piton St-Leu and Les Avirons. It's dedicated primarily to the sugar industry, but also provides fascinating insights into the history of the island and has exhibits on other products known and loved by the Réunionnais, such as vanilla, orchids, geraniums and vetiver.

Many of the villages in the hills above St-Leu, including Piton St-Leu and Les Colimaçons, lie on the Car Jaune bus route E from St-Pierre to La Chaloupe St-Leu. They can also be reached from the bus station in St-Leu.

## Sleeping & Eating

There are several peaceful villages within 10km of St-Leu that offer accommodation in a relaxed, rural setting. All the places listed below boast bird's-eye views down to the coast.

**Chambre d'hôte Caz' Océane** ( ☎ 0262 54 89 40; www.creole.org/cazoceane; 28 Chemin Mutel, Notre-Dame des Champs, La Chaloupe St-Leu; s/d incl breakfast €28/30, dinner €20) Run by a friendly Zoreilles couple, this B&B in the hamlet of Notre-Dame des Champs offers good value for money. No one would accuse the three rooms of being over-decorated but they are neat and spacious and guests can use a terrace with million-dollar views – perfect for an *apéro* (apéritif) after a bout of sightseeing. Excellent breakfast too (the homemade fruit salad, served in season, is a killer).

**Chambre d'hôte Le Moutardier – Chez Mélanie Darty** ( ☎ 0262 54 01 94; 16 Chemin des Avocats, Le Plate, Piton St-Leu; d incl breakfast €35, meals from €22) Ideally sited on a hillside with swoony ocean views, this mellow, down-to-earth B&B offers four neat, well-scrubbed rooms at a price that won't make you flinch. Tip: avoid the two rooms at the rear, which have obstructed views. Madame Darty can cook some reputedly good Creole meals, prepared with fresh produce from the farm.

**Chambre d'hôte Chez François et Michèle Huet** ( ☎ 0262 54 76 70, 0692 67 62 54; www.gitehuet-reunion .fr; 202 Chemin Potier, Les Colimaçons; d incl breakfast €50, dinner €20) The four rooms here are sparkling, fresh and colourful, but only two rooms come with a sea view. Ask for the spacious Creole-style *gîte* in the flower-filled garden if you

intend to stay more than three nights. When it comes to preparing fish dishes, the Huets know their stuff. It's signposted, uphill from the botanical garden.

**Chambre d'hôte Bardzour – Chez Marie-Claire Vion** ( ☎ 0262 34 13 97; www.bardzour.com; 22 Chemin Georges Thénor, Piton St-Leu; d incl breakfast €50-65; ❷ ⓓ ⓦ) This is a lovely option if you're looking for a secluded, rural atmosphere, though it cops some noise from the Route des Tamarins below. These well-equipped rooms set among orchards provide a very cushy landing after a hard day's driving. *Table d'hôtes* (€20) meals are available twice a week. To find it, take the D11 towards Stella Matutina and Piton St-Leu, then continue to the very end of the lane.

## LES AVIRONS & LE TÉVELAVE

pop 1500

Les Avirons is nothing inspirational but Le Tévelave, about 10km up an impossibly twisty road in the hills above Les Avirons, is a gem of a village. It offers a real taste of rural life and is a great base for walkers. You can really feel a sense of wilderness and seclusion here, light years away from the bling and bustle of the coast. At the top of the village is the starting point for the **Route Forestière des Tamarins**. This road leads through a cryptomeria forest and emerges 36km later below Le Maïdo. Picnic sites abound along the road.

## Sleeping & Eating

**Ferme-Auberge L'Écorce Blanc** ( ☎ 0262 38 31 52; 46 Rue Francis Rivière; d with shared bathroom incl breakfast €30, meals €20) The 600m-long access road is dreadfully steep, but you'll be rewarded with sensational views over the coast. Perched on the side of a hill, way above town, this friendly *ferme auberge* (farm inn) is beloved by locals for its authentic home cooking (by reservation). Sadly, the indoor dining room is as atmospheric as a dentist's waiting room. There are also four simple rooms in the same building as the dining room (noisy at meal times).

**Chambre d'hôte Case Namasté** ( ☎ 0262 24 38 33; http://casenamaste.reunion.fr; 17 Rue Francis Rivière; s/d with shared bathroom incl breakfast €35/40, meals €25; ⓦ) With its large communal area, open fireplace and exposed beams, this B&B is cosy to boot, as are the three shiny-clean rooms, with wood-panelled walls and feminine touches. There's also a fully equipped bungalow in the garden

(€80 for two nights). The owners run cooking courses – and what cooking: chocolate and bread! It's near the *terrain de pétanque* (pétanque pitch). It's not signposted.

**Domaine des Fougères** ( ☎ 0262 38 32 96; www
.domainedesfougeres.com; 53 Route des Merles; s/d €50/62, mains €16-22; ⊗ lunch & dinner; ⊚ ) The panoramic views and the secluded location, right at the start of the forest road, are the biggest perks to staying in this rural hotel with Creole architecture. Otherwise, the atmosphere is a bit staid with functional rooms. Angle for a room with a sea view.

## ÉTANG-SALÉ-LES-BAINS
pop 12,000

Miles away from the hullabaloo around St-Gilles, Étang-Salé-les-Bains is more a low-key resort for locals than foreign tourists, though its superb black-sand beach is no longer a secret for in-the-know sunbathers, swimmers and surfers.

### Information

**Office du Tourisme** ( ☎ 0892 70 22 01; otsi.run@
wanadoo.fr; 74 Rue Octave Bénard; ⊗ 9am-noon & 1-4.30pm Mon-Sat) It's housed in the old train station on the roundabout that marks the town centre. *Gîtes de montagnes* can be booked here.

---

**TOP DIY CULTURAL IMMERSIONS**

- Visit the colourful Tamil temples on the east coast (p233), and attend a religious festival (p236)

- Bed down in B&Bs, preferably in the Hauts (p224), for a whiff of local life

- Hike through the unspoiled Cirque de Mafate (p242)

- Forget your dietician and enjoy hearty, wholesome *carris* at local-style restaurants (p169)

- Spend a Sunday afternoon at a popular picnic spot – you may be invited to share a meal (p233)

- Visit a working distillery and learn how rum is made (p235)

- Wander the streets of Hell-Bourg (p210), St-Denis (p176) and St-Pierre (p220) looking for the most attractive Creole buildings

---

### Sights & Activities

The generous stretch of ash-coloured **beach** on the northern outskirts of town is great for sunbathing, swimming and ogling unfortunate tan lines, and offers excellent sunset vistas. Most of the beach has a shallow bottom with a gradual slope. To the south, near the harbour, there's a smaller beach known as **Bassin Pirogue**, which is ideal for kids – a shallow reef close to shore makes for calm, protected waters – but this sandy stretch was not super clean when we visited.

On the southern outskirts of Étang-Salé-les-Bains, **Le Souffleur** (The Blowhole) is a rocky crevice that spurts up a tower of water as the waves crash against it.

Very few visitors know that **diving** is available at Étang-Salé-les-Bains. And what diving! The owners of **Plongée Salée** ( ☎ 0262 91 71 23; www.plongeesaleereunion.com; Centre Carine) take only small groups. The sites are almost untouched.

Étang-Salé-les-Bains also has good **surfing** year-round, with large offshore waves for experienced surfers and gentle beach breaks that are suitable for beginners. On the main street, **École de Surf Extreme Sud** ( ☎ 0262 26 67 02; www.extremesud.re; 67 Rue Octave Bénard) offers surfing lessons for all levels. Rates for a two-hour group/private lesson start at €25/100.

Wanna keep the kids happy? Take a small detour to **Croc Parc** ( ☎ 0262 91 40 41; www.crocparc .re; Route Forestière; adult/child €8/6; ⊗ 10am-5pm), near Étang-Salé-les-Hauts (it's signposted). There are about 160 reptiles at this complex. Admission is steep, but worthwhile if your visit coincides with a feeding demonstration, held at 4pm on Wednesday and Sunday.

### Sleeping & Eating

**Camping Municipal de l'Étang-Salé-les-Bains** ( ☎ 0262 91 75 86; camping.es@civis.re; Rue Guy Hoarau; camp site per night €13-16) The island's only official camp site. Facilities are a bit worn but it's located in a shady spot a short walk back from the beach.

**Résidence Les Sables Noirs** ( ☎ 0262 38 04 89, 0692 08 06 28; www.lessablesnoirs.com; 88b Ave Raymond Barre; dm €15, d with shared bathroom €30; ⊗ ⊚ ) If being near the beach isn't a must, this hostel-like venture efficiently run by Guy and Evelyne is manna from heaven for thrifty travellers. It shelters one eight-bed dorm, one 12-bed dorm and eight doubles, which are all squeaky clean and well appointed. Air-con is extra in the doubles (€5). It's in Étang-Salé-les-Hauts,

RÉUNION

about 4km away from Étang-Salé-les-Bains, near the church.

**Le Floralys – Caro Beach** ( ☎ 0262 91 79 79; www .hotel-floralys.com; 2 Ave de l'Océan; d €90-180; 🕱 🛜 🄌 ) This well-run three-star abode is set in a 3-hectare garden beside the roundabout in the middle of town. There's an onsite restaurant.

**L'Été Indien** ( ☎ 0262 26 67 33; 1 Rue des Salines; mains €10-22; 🕑 lunch & dinner Tue-Sun) This outfit gets kudos for its expansive menu that will satisfy even the pickiest eater. Bring an empty tum. Your belly will be more than happy after you've heroically wolfed down a Frisbee-sized pizza.

You'll find a few *camions-snacks* along the beach.

## ST-LOUIS
pop 44,000

If St-Gilles and L'Hermitage are very Westernised and touristy, St-Louis, by contrast, is very Indian and falls below many travellers' radars. This is the heart of Tamil culture on the west coast, and it won't take long to feel that the city exudes an undeniably exotic atmosphere. The town doesn't have anything fantastic to offer, but it is certainly worth a stop to admire a handful of religious buildings, including a Tamil temple, a splendid mosque and the biggest church on the island.

A highlight (and a major landmark, with its big chimneys) is the **Sucrerie du Gol** ( ☎ 0262 91 05 47; www.gqf.com; adult/child €5/3), about 1.5km west of St-Louis. You can tour this old sugar refinery, one of only two on the island still functioning, during the cane harvest (July to December). Visits take place Tuesday to Saturday with prior reservation.

**our pick** **Chambre d'hôte Case Tatave** ( ☎ 0262 39 72 54; www.location-gite-ile-reunion.com; 55 Rue Hubert Delisle, Rivière St Louis; d incl breakfast €50, dinner €18; 🛜 🄌 ) is a peach of a B&B. Picture this: a lovely Creole house that has been renovated with a happy respect for the spirit of the place shelters two oh-so-inviting rooms complete with parquet flooring, period furniture, Creole ceilings and rich fabrics. One minus: bathrooms are not en suite. The French owners rent cars at unbeatable rates. It's in Rivière St-Louis, about 6km from St-Louis.

Car Jaune buses between St-Denis and St-Pierre run through St-Louis (about 10 daily). Buses to Cilaos run from the bus station (€1.50, 10 daily).

## LES MAKES
pop 2500

One of Réunion's best-kept secrets, Les Makes boasts a wonderful bucolic atmosphere and a lovely setting. Snuggled into the seams of the Hauts, it's accessible via a tortuous secondary road from St-Louis (12km). At almost 1200m, breathing in the fresh alpine air here is enough therapy for a lifetime.

The area is ideal for stargazing. The **Observatoire astronomique** ( ☎ 0262 37 86 83; www .ilereunion.com/observatoire-makes/; 18 Rue Georges Bizet; adult/child €9/5) offers stargazing programs from 9pm to midnight. It's best to call ahead to confirm the program is on.

It's a sin to visit Les Makes and not take the forest road that leads to **La Fenêtre** (The Window), another 10km further uphill. Hold on to your hat and lift your jaw off the floor as you approach the viewpoint: the view over the entire Cirque de Cilaos and the surrounding craggy summits that jab the skyline will be etched in your memory forever. La Fenêtre is also a wonderful picnic spot. Hint: arrive early, before it gets cloudy.

Horse riding is also a terrific way of exploring the surrounding forests. It can be arranged through **Centre Équestre de la Fenêtre** ( ☎ 0262 37 88 74; Route de la Fenêtre, Les Makes; per hr €16; 🕑 Tue-Sat).

Should you fall under the spell of this charming area (no doubt you will), you can bunk down at the **Chambre d'hôte Le Vieil Alambic – Chez Jean-Luc d'Eurveilher** ( ☎ 0262 37 82 77; www .levieilalambic.com; 55 Rue Montplaisir, Les Makes; d incl breakfast €50, meals from €20), an adorable B&B on the road to La Fenêtre, with four uninspiring but tidy rooms (no views) and highly respected traditional meals. Rejoicing begins with, say, *beignets de papaye verte au fromage* (papaya fritters with cheese), followed by *lapin au vin blanc et à la vanille* (rabbit in wine sauce flavoured with vanilla). Save room for desserts – the *fondant des anges* (a homemade cake with sweet potato, papaya and coconut milk) is a victory for humanity. Self-caterers will opt for **Bungalows des Makes** ( ☎ 0262 37 80 10, 0692 77 28 38; www.bungalowsrun.com; 5 Rue Raisins Marrons, Les Makes; d from €50), which comprises four chalet-like bungalows in flowering gardens and a small spa. Meals are available on request.

## ENTRE-DEUX
pop 5170

This sweet little village high in the hills 18km north of St-Pierre got its name (which means 'between two') because it is situated on a ridge between two valleys – the Bras de Cilaos and the Bras de la Plaine. Entre-Deux is a delightful place to stay and get a taste of rural life. It boasts a wealth of *cases créoles*, traditional country cottages surrounded by well-tended and fertile gardens, many of which are being restored. There's also a strong tradition of local crafts, including natty slippers made from the leaves of an aloe-like plant called *choca*.

## Information

**Tourist office** ( ☎ 0262 39 69 80; www.ot-entredeux .com; 9 Rue Fortuné Hoareau; 🕙 8am-noon & 1.30-5pm Mon-Sat) Occupies a pretty *case créole* on the road into the village. Staff can arrange guided visits (usually in French) of the village (adult/child €9/5) and can provide leaflets on walks in the region (including climbing Le Dimitile) and on local artisans.

## Sights & Activities

Opportunities for **hiking** abound. Many visitors come here for the tough hike up the slopes of iconic **Le Dimitile** (1837m) to a sensational view over the Cirque de Cilaos. This summit is also endowed with a strong historical significance; *marrons* (runaway slaves) took refuge in the area in the late 19th century. Just before the summit, the modest yet well-organised **Espace Culturel Muséographique Dimitile** (ECM; www.ecmdimitil.com; admission €3, with an audio guide €7; 🕙 9am-3pm) does a good job of explaining *marronage* and tracing the history of slavery in Réunion.

There are several options to reach the summit. The shortest route starts from the end of the D26 (there's a small parking area), about 10km from Entre-Deux, at an altitude of 1100m. Count on a four- to five-hour return slog. To soak up the atmosphere, it's not a bad idea to overnight at one of the *gîtes* near the summit.

The tourist office can provide information and sketch maps detailing the various routes.

Feeling lazy? Join a 4WD tour. **Kreolie 4x4** ( ☎ 0262 39 50 87, 0692 86 52 26; www.kreolie4x4.com; 4 Impasse des Avocats) runs day trips that include Entre-Deux and the viewpoint at Le Dimitile (€95, including lunch). Guides are informative, providing interesting titbits on the area's flora and fauna (in French).

## Sleeping

**Auberge de Jeunesse** ( ☎ 0692 33 74 18, 0692 28 35 69; 120 Chemin Defaud, Ravine des Citrons; dm €14; 🅿 ) The

most obvious choice if funds are short, this youth hostel occupies an enticing villa in a tranquil neighbourhood, about 3km from the centre (follow the Ravine des Citrons sign). Inside, it's much less eye candy, with monastically plain two- to eight-person rooms.

**Chambre d'hôtes Mirest – Lucienne Clain** ( ☎ 0262 39 65 43; 1 Chemin Sources-Raisin; d incl breakfast €40) What sets this *chambre d'hôte* apart is the stunning architecture – no plain, concrete building, but a cheerful mix of wood and lava stones. Its three rooms are airy and comfortable and open onto a flourishing garden. The dining room serves up panoramic views along with *table d'hôtes* (dinner €23).

**Le Dimitile** ( ☎ 0262 39 20 00; www.dimitile.eu; 30 Rue Bras Long; d incl breakfast €130-205; 🅿 🛜 🏊 ) This beautifully manicured haven is run with care by a couple from Alsace – saffron yellows on the facade, cosy reds on the floors, natural stones, a lovely pool – but it's missing something to bring it all together… something like soul. It has a well-regarded onsite restaurant (mains €16 to €26, *menus* €35 to €58, open for lunch Saturday and Sunday, and dinner daily).

Up on Le Dimitile, you'll find a couple of *gîtes:*

**Gîte Émile** (Map p225; ☎ 0262 57 43 03, 0682 67 24 54; dm incl half board €32) Has basic accommodation in five- to 12-person dorms. From the *gîte* to the viewpoint, it's a 30- to 45-minute walk.

**Gîte Le Chalet** (Map p225; ☎ 0692 27 33 22, 0692 27 33 24; nadegejosian.legros@wanadoo.fr; dm incl half board €35) At La Cape, about 2km south of Gîte Émile. Digs are in three- to eight-bed dorms. Transfers by 4WD from the end of the D26 can be arranged (€15 per person). It's usually open on weekends only.

## Eating

**Le Longanis** ( ☎ 0262 39 70 56; 9bis Rue du Commerce; mains €6-13; 🕙 lunch Mon-Sat, dinner Mon, Tue & Thu-Sat) This venue right in the centre boasts a happy buzz at lunchtime and whips up lip-smacking, dirt-cheap meals. Grab a dish from the daily specials, add a salad and you're sorted.

**Le Chocas** ( ☎ 0692 69 56 06; 12 Rue de l'Église; mains €9-14; 🕙 lunch Tue-Sun) Don't know what *chocas* is? It's time to get a hands-on education. Nestled in a lush garden, this reputable eatery specialises in this quirky-tasting vegetable, prepared in all its forms (with pork, shrimp etc). You can also pick up the usual Creole suspects.

**L'Arbre à Palabres** ( ☎ 0262 44 47 23; 29 Rue Césaire; mains €12-16; 🕙 lunch Thu-Sun, dinner Thu-Sat) For a menu that strays a little off the familiar 'sausage *rougail* and chicken curry' path, try this cute eatery in a Creole house, near the tourist office. The menu changes daily, according to what's available at the market. There's often live music on weekends.

### Getting There & Away

Car Jaune operates a bus service between Entre-Deux and the *gare routière* in St-Pierre. There are five buses a day from Monday to Saturday and two on a Sunday.

# THE CIRQUES

A trip to the Cirques is an iconic Réunion experience. No amount of hyperbole could ever communicate the astonishingly guileless beauty of the island's heart and soul. Knitted together like a three-leaf clover, the Cirques of Cilaos, Salazie and Mafate are different in spirit from the rest of the island – more inward-looking, more secretive, more austere. Quintessentially Réunionnais. The fast-paced and hedonistic coastal life seems light years away. The few roads daring to traverse the gorges and ranges are more crooked than a politician, winding in and out of tortuous valleys.

The whole island was once the dome of a vast prehistoric shield volcano, centred on Piton des Neiges, but the collapse of subterranean lava chambers formed the starting point for the creation of the Cirques. Millions of years of rainfall and erosion did the rest, scouring out the amphitheatres that are visible today.

No prize for guessing that this rugged region is a fantastic playground for the stimulus-needy, with staggering mountain scenery, a mesh of well-marked trails and jaw-dropping canyons that beg to be explored. But if all you need is to decompress, there are always epicurean delights, including a robust cuisine scene and welcoming accommodation options where you can rejuvenate mind and body.

Nature is not the only drawcard. The Cirques are also of strong historical interest. They first began to be settled by *marrons* (see p163) in the 18th century, and their descendants still inhabit some of the wild remote villages of the Cirques. The people residing here are an independent and unhurried lot, adamantly tied to their *îlet* (village) and their traditions.

Each Cirque has its own personality – try to include the three of them in your itinerary.

## CIRQUE DE CILAOS

The setting couldn't be more grandiose. Think snaggle-toothed volcanic peaks, deep ravines and forests that are straight out of a Brothers Grimm fairy tale. At times, swirling banks of cloud add a touch of the bizarre. A sweet sprinkling of secluded hamlets top off this area's indisputable 'wow!' effect.

Thrill-seekers, rejoice: the Cirque de Cilaos is the mother of all canyoning experiences on the island, with three iconic canyons that are set in some of the most impressive scenery in Réunion. Hiking is also extraordinary. Another pull is the smattering of well-priced hotels and B&Bs.

To get here, clunk in your seatbelt and take a deep breath: the RN5, which connects

---

**THE CIRQUES & THE VOLCANO FROM ABOVE**

The helicopter dilemma: you're loath to add to noise and air pollution. But your heart is set on a bird's-eye view of the magnificent Cirques and the volcano. While they aren't cheap (between €85 to €260, depending on the duration of the tour), most travellers rate such a trip as a highlight of their visit to Réunion. Ultimately you'll go with your gut (and budget). Contact **Helilagon** ( ☎ 0262 55 55 55; www.helilagon.com) or **Corail Hélicoptère** ( ☎ 0262 22 22 66; www.corail-helicopteres.com).

If you really want to feel the wind in your hair, several outfits offer tandem microlight flights with a qualified instructor. They run about 10 different tours around the island, starting at €40 for a gentle tour above the lagoon. Needless to say, all flights are dependent on the prevailing weather conditions. For more information, contact the following:

**Felix ULM** ( ☎ 0262 43 02 59; www.felixulm.com)
**Les Passagers du Vent** ( ☎ 0262 42 95 95; www.ulm-reunion.com)
**Mascareignes Air Lines** ( ☎ 0262 32 53 25; www.mascareignes.fr)
**Papangue ULM** ( ☎ 0692 08 85 86; www.fransurf.com/papangue-ulm)

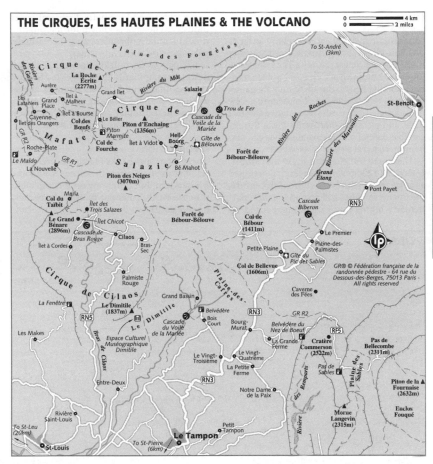

**THE CIRQUES, LES HAUTES PLAINES & THE VOLCANO**

St-Louis with Cilaos, 37km to the north, is Réunion's premier drive (and that is saying a lot). Snaking steeply around more than 400 twists and turns along the way up into the amphitheatre, it provides vista-point junkies with a steady fix. *Bon voyage!*

## Getting There & Away
Cilaos is located 112km from St-Denis by road and 37km from the nearest coastal town, St-Louis.

Buses to Cilaos depart from St-Louis. There are about 10 buses daily, and eight on Sunday (€1.50, 1½ hours). The last service up to Cilaos leaves St-Louis at 6.30pm (5.30pm on Sunday); going down again, the last bus leaves Cilaos at 5pm.

There are nine buses a day (four on Sunday) from Cilaos to Bras Sec (€1) between 6am and 7pm. For Îlet à Cordes (€1) there are about nine buses daily (four on Sunday) from 5.50am to 7pm, with the last bus back at 6pm. The tourist office in Cilaos has timetables.

Another option is the minibus service offered by the **Société Cilaosienne de Transport** (☎ 0262 31 85 87, 0692 66 13 30), which costs €28 for two people for Îlet à Cordes. The same outfit provides transport from Cilaos to Le Bloc on the GR R1 to the Piton des Neiges and Hell-Bourg (€15 for two people) and to the trailhead for the Col du Taïbit on the GR R1/GR R2 to Mafate (€15 for two people), saving you at least an hour's walking time in each case.

RÉUNION

## Cilaos

**pop 6000**

Cilaos is ensnared by scenery so mind-blowingly dramatic it's practically Alpine. One name says it all: Piton des Neiges (3070m). The iconic peak towers over the town of Cilaos, acting like a magnet to hiking fiends. But there's no obligation to overdo it: a smattering of museums, a slew of underrated vineyards, regenerative thermal baths and plenty of short walks mean this incredible dose of natural magnificence can also be appreciated at a more relaxed pace.

The largest settlement in any of the Cirques, Cilaos sits 1200m above sea level. Developed as a spa resort at the end of the 19th century, the town's fortunes still rest on tourism, particularly hiking and canyoning, backed up by agriculture and the bottled mineral-water industry. The area is known for the production of lentils, embroidery and, increasingly, palatable rosé and white wines.

Cilaos fills up quickly on weekends. But despite its popularity it manages to stave off changes that would detract from its appeal as an 'ecotourism' destination – there are no massive hotels or blaring discos, only low-key, small-scale operations. Enjoy it to the hilt.

### INFORMATION

There aren't any banks in Cilaos. There is an ATM at the post office that accepts Visa and MasterCard, but don't rely on it completely: it occasionally runs out of euros, especially on weekends.

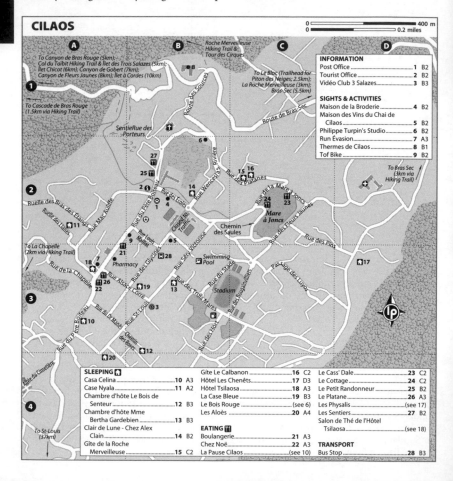

CILAOS

0 .................. 400 m
0 .................. 0.2 miles

**INFORMATION**
Post Office ......................................... **1** B2
Tourist Office .................................... **2** B2
Vidéo Club 3 Salazes ....................... **3** B3

**SIGHTS & ACTIVITIES**
Maison de la Broderie .................... **4** B2
Maison des Vins du Chai de
  Cilaos ............................................. **5** B2
Philippe Turpin's Studio ............... **6** B2
Run Évasion ...................................... **7** A3
Thermes de Cilaos ........................... **8** B1
Tof Bike ............................................. **9** B2

**Post office** (76 Rue du Père Boiteau; 8am-4pm Mon-Fri, 8-11.30am Sat)

**Tourist Office** ( ☎ 0892 70 22 01; mmocilaos@wanadoo.fr; 2bis Rue Mac Auliffe; 8.30am-12.30pm & 1.30-5pm Mon-Sat, 9am-noon Sun) The tourism office is particularly helpful, with multilingual staff who provide reliable information about local and long-distance walks and dispense lists of accommodation, restaurants and activities. Has pamphlets on bus schedules in the Cirque. You can also book *gîtes de montagnes* here.

**Vidéo Club 3 Salazes** (40 Rue St-Louis; internet access per hr €12; 10am-noon & 3-9pm Tue-Sun) Internet access, and has wi-fi.

## SIGHTS

### Maison de la Broderie

The originator of Cilaos' embroidery tradition was Angèle Mac Auliffe, the daughter of the town's first doctor of thermal medicine. Looking for a pastime to fill the long, damp days in the Cirque, Angèle established the first embroidery workshop with 20 women producing what later evolved into a distinctive Cilaos style of embroidery.

Nowadays, the **Maison de la Broderie** ( ☎ 0262 31 77 48; Rue des Écoles; admission €1; 9.30am-noon & 2-5pm Mon-Sat, 9.30am-noon Sun) is home to an association of 30 or so local women dedicated to keeping the craft alive. They embroider and sell children's clothes, serviettes, place settings and tablecloths. It's laborious work: a single placemat takes between 12 and 15 days to complete.

### Thermes de Cilaos

The *sources thermales* (thermal springs) of Cilaos were first brought to the attention of the outside world in 1815 by a goat hunter from St-Louis, Paulin Técher. A track into the Cirque was constructed in 1842, paving the way for the development of Cilaos as a health spa for rich colonials. The spring is heated by volcanic chambers far below the surface. It's said to relieve rheumatic pain, among other bone and muscular ailments.

The old thermal station was opened in 1896, but the spring became blocked in a cyclone that occurred in 1948. The project was revived in 1971, only to close in 1987 because of damage to the buildings caused by the chemicals in the spa water. The latest incarnation of the Cilaos spa is the **Thermes de Cilaos** ( ☎ 0262 31 72 27; thermes-cilaos@cg974.fr; Route de Bras-Sec; 1-6pm Mon-Sat, 9am-5pm Sun) at the north end of town. All manner of health treatments are offered, including a 20-minute hydromassage (€15). This is a perfect way to rejuvenate tired and sore muscles after your hike.

### Maison des Vins du Chai de Cilaos

You can learn more about Cilaos wine at the **Maison des Vins du Chai de Cilaos** ( ☎ 0262 31 79 69; 34 Rue des Glycines; 9am-noon & 2-5.30pm Mon-Sat). A short film (in French) is followed by a guided tour of the modern vinification plant and a wine tasting. Take home a bottle from about €12.

### Philippe Turpin's Studio

The sculptor, painter and printmaker Philippe Turpin, who etches on copper and then rolls the prints off the inky plates, has a **studio** ( ☎ 0262 31 73 64, 0692 28 03 03; 2 Route des Sources; 9am-noon & 2-6pm) that is open to the public. Turpin captures the wonder of Réunion in a fantastical, almost medieval way; his renditions of the Cirques resemble illustrations of fairy kingdoms.

### La Roche Merveilleuse

Head to the 'Marvellous Rock' for an eagle-eye panorama of Cilaos. It's accessible on foot (see p206) or by road. From Cilaos, take the road to Bras-Sec. The turn-off to La Roche Merveilleuse is signposted on the left, after about 2km. It's not a bad idea to get there

---

**RÉUNION** (side tab)

---

> ### A TOAST IS IN ORDER
>
> You mustn't leave Cilaos without sampling a glass (or three) of *vin de Cilaos* (Cilaos wine). Not to be deprived of their wine, the French brought vines with them to Réunion in the 17th century. They were originally grown along the west coast, but in the late 19th century settlers introduced vines into the Cirques, cultivating them on trellises outside their houses or on tiny terraces hacked out of the hillside. For years, the wines they produced were sugary sweet whites, reminiscent of sherry and tawny port. In the late 1970s, however, a few enterprising growers in Cilaos upgraded their vine stock and began producing something far more palatable. In addition to sweet and dry whites, growers now produce reds and rosés. They are not necessarily the most distinguished of wines but they're improving in quality, especially the rosés.

by bike. **Tof Bike** ( ☎ 0692 01 90 80; 68 Rue du Père Boiteau; ☽ 8.30am-noon & 2.30-6pm Mon-Fri) rents out mountain bikes for €14 per half-day.

Bring a picnic – the setting is enchanting and there are a few kiosks (wooden shelters) to protect picnickers from any rain.

## ACTIVITIES
### Canyoning

Of the stellar spots for canyoning in Réunion, the Cilaos area tops the list, with three major canyons that draw action-seekers like bees to a honey pot: Canyons de Gobert, Fleurs Jaunes and Bras Rouge. All are very atmospheric; you can expect various jumps, leaps into natural pools and jaw-dropping rappelling. Access to the canyons involves a preliminary five- to 45-minute hike. The time spent in the canyon is about three to five hours. The most suitable canyons for beginners and families are Canyon de Gobert and Mini Fleurs Jaunes (which is a section of Fleurs Jaunes). All canyoning outings are led by a qualified instructor. Plan on €45 to €70 per person, depending on the duration of the outing. The major operators include the following (some don't have offices but can be reached by phone):

**Bouisset Fabrice** ( ☎ 0692 66 22 73; bouisset.fabrice@wanadoo.fr)

**Canyon Ric a Ric** ( ☎ 0692 86 54 85; www.canyonreunion.com)

**Cilaos Aventure** ( ☎ 0692 66 73 42; www.cilaosaventure.com)

**Run Évasion** ( ☎ 0262 31 83 57; www.runevasion.fr; 23 Rue du Père Boiteau)

### Hiking

There are fabulous hiking options in the vicinity of Cilaos, with well-marked trails suitable for all levels of fitness. The tourist office produces a small leaflet that gives an overview of the walks in the Cirque. The most popular walks include the following:

**Bras Rouge** About 2½ hours return. An easy walk to the top of a waterfall.

**Col du Taïbit** About 4½ hours return, with 830m of altitude gain. An iconic climb to the pass that separates the Cirque de Cilaos from the Cirque de Mafate. From the pass you can walk down to Marla (p214) in the Cirque de Mafate in about 45 minutes. The starting point is signposted on the D242 (the road to Îlet-à-Cordes), 5km from Cilaos.

**Îlet des Trois Salazes** At an altitude of 1500m, this small settlement (right) on the way to the Col du Taïbit (see above) requires a 30- to 45-minute steep walk from the D242; the height gain is 240m. Even if you don't continue

to the Col du Taïbit, it's worth making it here to enjoy the scenic location, the ample views and the community atmosphere – not to mention a rejuvenating cup of herbal tea; try 'L'Ascenseur' (The Lift) or 'La Descente' (The Descent).

**La Chapelle** This path connects Cilaos to Îlet-à-Cordes (about four hours return). You can skip the return walk by taking the bus from Îlet-à-Cordes.

**La Roche Merveilleuse** About two hours return. A gentle ramble to a lookout, with lofty views over Cilaos. Also accessible by car.

**Piton des Neiges** A mind-boggling ascent to Réunion's highest point (3070m). It's usually done in two days, with an overnight stay in Gîte de la Caverne Dufour, reached after three hours from the start of the path at Le Bloc. Hard-core hikers may want to complete the round trip in one day (about nine hours). See p250 for a full description.

**Sentier Botanique** An easy 90-minute loop with a focus on local flora (most species are labelled). Perfectly suitable for families. It starts at La Roche Merveilleuse.

For guided walks, contact **Aparksa Montagne** ( ☎ 0692 66 50 09; www.aparksa-montagne.com). The owner, Thomas Percheron, has lived in South Africa and is fluent in English.

### Rock Climbing

Rock climbing is becoming increasingly popular in Cilaos, where there is no shortage of awesome cliffs and gorges, particularly the stunning Fleurs Jaunes area, which is home to dozens of mind-boggling ascents, graded 4 to 8 (easy to difficult). For novices, there are also *falaise-écoles* (training cliffs that are specially equipped for beginners). Run Évasion and Cilaos Aventure (see left) employ qualified instructors. Plan on €45 per person.

### SLEEPING

Cilaos has ample choice of accommodation options, but it can become crowded at weekends and during the tourist season.

### Budget

`our pick` **La Case Bleue** ( ☎ 0692 65 74 96; www.gitecasebleue.com; 15 Rue Alsace Corré; dm €15, d €40) An excellent choice, this *gîte d'étape* occupies an attractive Creole house painted in blue. Top marks go to the light-filled dorm, the back-friendly mattresses, the salubrious bathrooms and the impeccable communal kitchen. There's also a cosy double with its own entrance – ideal for couples. Meals come in for warm praise, too (€16), and the owners are well clued up on hiking in the Cirque. There are only 10 beds, so book ahead.

**GO GREEN IN THE CIRQUE DE CILAOS**

You can get a better understanding of the environment and traditional life of the Cirque de Cilaos by visiting two 'eco-villages' that can be reached by foot only.

**Îlet des Trois Salazes** ( ☎ 0692 90 04 62, 0693 02 01 00; www.3salazes.com; ☒ 7am-4pm) is perched on a small plateau at an altitude of 1500m on the path to Col du Taïbit (left), which involves a 30- to 45-minute walk. No language barrier here: the community is run by Ian Winkless, an Irishman who settled a few decades ago in Cilaos. With his family-in-law, he has rehabilitated this patch of land using natural methods. The farm operates a volunteer-work program that emphasises medicinal-herb cultivation, community outreach and childhood education. Pause here to sample a tisane, a melt-in-your-mouth *gâteau ti son* or a Creole lunch (€20, by reservation). There's also a lookout with stupendous mountain vistas.

At **Îlet Chicot** ( ☎ 0692 72 27 17; admission €2, hut incl breakfast €12; ☒ 10am-3pm Tue-Sat) the Hoarau family aims to give you a sensitive introduction to the *vie lontan* (traditional life of yore). Their property is reached after an easy 10-minute walk from the D242, about 6km from Cilaos (look for the sign on the right). It features an organic garden with fruit-bearing trees, medicinal herbs and aromatic plants. Creole meals can be arranged by reservation (from €20). Wanna go bush? Stay in one of the three *ti cases* (huts), which are constructed using vetiver straw. They're simple, but it's wonderful to be able to linger amid the beauty of the natural surroundings and enjoy the jaw-dropping views over Cilaos. The lack of electric lights makes for great stargazing.

**Gîte de la Roche Merveilleuse** ( ☎ 0262 31 82 42; 1 Rue des Platanes; dm €15, d €36-40) This all-wood *gîte* looks like a Canadian chalet transplanted to Cilaos. Opt for one of the four snug doubles, which feel like cosy birds' nests, but the real appeal is the panoramic view from the terrace. Meals (€17) can be arranged if there's a minimum of five persons.

**our pick Clair de Lune – Chez Alex Clain** ( ☎ 0262 31 88 03, 0692 82 47 13; 10 Rue Wenceslas Rivière; dm incl breakfast €17) Run by Alex, who knows a thing or 50 about Cilaos and adopts all guests like stray kittens, this congenial spot has rooms of varying size and shape, with three- to 10-bed dorms and one double. Bathrooms are shared. The living area is a good place to swap tales with like-minded travellers.

Other options:

**Gîte Le Calbanon** ( ☎ 0692 09 27 30; www.lecalbanon .fr; 9 Rue des Platanes; dm €15) This neat *gîte d'étape* in a modern building boasts a quiet location and ample views of Cilaos. It offers simple accommodation in quads, which can also be used as doubles for €35, or in a 12-bed dorm.

**Chambre d'hôte Mme Bertha Gardebien** ( ☎ 0262 31 72 15; 50 Rue St-Louis; s/d with shared bathroom incl breakfast €30/40) Close to everything, this unassuming B&B run by a Creole grandma provides three no-frills rooms.

**Midrange & Top End**

**Les Aloès** ( ☎ 0262 31 81 00; www.hotel-aloes.com; 14 Rue St-Louis; s/d incl breakfast €54/68; ☒ ) Friendly two-star hotel on the edge of town. Bright blues, yellows and ochres colour the well-tended rooms. The upstairs ones have the best views. The owner is very knowledgeable about hiking.

**Chambre d'hôte Le Bois de Senteur** ( ☎ 0262 31 91 03, 0692 29 81 20; www.leboisdesenteur.com; 4 Chemin des Roses; d incl breakfast €60; ☒ ) Providing a restful retreat, this trim place is brought to life with lashings of colourful paint on the facade. Inside the 10 rooms are pleasingly if modestly furnished. The upstairs rooms have balconies and afford dashing views of the Piton des Neiges (especially rooms 6, 7 and 10). It's in a peaceful cul-de-sac.

**Case Nyala** ( ☎ 0262 31 89 57, 0692 87 70 14; www .case-nyala.com; 8 Ruelle des Lianes, d incl breakfast €70-80) On a quiet back street close to the centre, this little Creole place with lemon-yellow walls and green shutters harbours a clutch of small-ish rooms and a well-appointed communal kitchen. The complimentary rum in the glass flasks on the shelves will help you forget that this place is a tad overpriced. Families will opt for the larger, self-contained bungalow at the rear.

**Casa Celina** ( ☎ 0262 40 19 02, 0692 60 27 62; http:// hotel-casa-celina.emonsite.com; 12 Rue du Père Boiteau; d incl breakfast €79; ☒ ) Opened in 2009, this well-run place occupies a skilfully refurbished house. The five rooms border on diminutive but the architect has maximised limited space. There's a 20% discount if you stay two nights or more. The restaurant La Pause Cilaos is downstairs.

RÉUNION

**our pick Le Bois Rouge** ( ☎ 0262 31 73 64; www.ile reunion.com/leboisrouge; 2 Route des Sources; s/d incl breakfast €70/90; 🛜 ) Character and charm. Somewhere between a boutique hotel and B&B, the Bois Rouge has five immaculate rooms that are uniquely decorated with works of Philippe Turpin (see p205) and boast parquet flooring made of precious wood as well as terraces overlooking Cilaos. Bonuses: complimentary bicycles, a well-stocked DVD library, and free transfers to the start of most hiking trails near Cilaos. Discounts are available in low season.

**Hôtel Tsilaosa** ( ☎ 0262 37 39 39; www.tsilaosa.com; Rue du Père Boiteau; s €83-92, d €102-122, all incl breakfast; 🛜 ) This well-run three-star abode in a restored Creole home offers a smooth stay, with 15 rooms that are imaginatively decked out in local style; those upstairs boast mountain views (rooms 15 and 16 are the best). The owner has set up a wine cellar in the basement and offers tastings of Cilaos tipples (€5).

**Hôtel Les Chenêts** ( ☎ 0262 31 85 85; www.hotel leschenets.fr; Rue des Trois Mares; s/d incl breakfast €88/116; 📖🍴) Cilaos' biggest hotel is a colourful place with a touch of a hunting lodge about its foyer. The rooms are spacious and come with gleaming bathrooms. There's a heated pool, a sauna, a bar and a restaurant, Les Physalis.

## EATING

We'll be honest: despite the choice of eateries on offer, don't expect gastronomic thrills in Cilaos. Most places tend to rest on their laurels, with rather stodgy fare served in generic surrounds. On the bright side, Cilaos holds a few surprises up its sleeves. It's noted for its lentils, grown mainly around Îlet à Cordes, and its wines (see p205).

Self-caterers will find grocery stores along the main street.

**Boulangerie** (64 Rue du Père Boiteau; pastries & sandwiches from €0.70; 🕒 6.30am-7pm Mon-Sat, to noon Sun) Ask a local where they go for the best *macatias* and croissants and they point to this delectable little bakery. It has a wide variety of cavity-inducing goodies, as well as excellent sandwiches made with baguettes (from €2.50).

**Salon de Thé de l'hôtel Tsilaosa** ( ☎ 0262 37 39 39; Rue du Père Boiteau; cakes €4; 🕒 2-6pm) This delightfully peaceful venue in the hotel's tea room will torment the sweet-toothed and weak-willed with homemade cakes and pies, including a *tarte à la confiture de pêche* (tart with peach jam), and about 15 varieties of tea. Enough said, we're drooling on the keyboard!

**La Pause Cilaos** ( ☎ 0262 31 27 92; 12 Rue du Père Boiteau; mains €4-18; 🕒 noon-9pm) The most eclectic menu in town. Choosing the main course is a real nail-biter – should it be lasagne, mussels, pizzas, crepes or pork rib? Whatever you choose you can't go wrong, though it does suffer slightly from being a jack-of-all-trades.

**Le Petit Randonneur** ( ☎ 0262 31 79 55; Rue du Père Boiteau; mains €10-17; 🕒 lunch Sat-Thu) A favourite haunt of hungry walkers, this family-run restaurant serves up hearty local dishes such as smoked sausages and chicken in a vanilla sauce, as well as moderately priced *plats du jour* (daily specials) and crêpes, best enjoyed on the terrace, with plastic tables.

**Les Sentiers** ( ☎ 0262 31 71 54; 63 Rue du Père Boiteau; mains €12-14, menu €22; 🕒 lunch & dinner Thu-Mon) Come lunch and dinner, this cute *case créole* is alive with action. Tables spill from inside out onto a breezy terrace. Food-wise, the menu features all the Creole classics plus a few Chinese dishes. The rustic decor is easy on the eye, with exposed beams and flashing laminate floors.

**Le Cottage** ( ☎ 0262 31 70 38; 2 Chemin des Saules; mains €12-17; 🕒 lunch Tue-Sun, dinner Tue-Sat) The all-wood surrounds boast a kind of rustic charm and the dining room overlooks the Mare à Joncs (reserve a table near the windows). Has a good repertory of palate-pleasing Creole dishes.

**Chez Noë** ( ☎ 0262 31 79 93; mains €13-15, menus €24-28; 🕒 lunch Tue-Sun, dinner Tue-Sat) A long-standing institution, Chez Noë is almost a rite of passage in Cilaos, but some say it rests on its laurels. It churns out invigorating Creole favourites such as sausage with lentils and *gratin de chouchou* (choko; a green squash-like vegetable that is served baked).

Other places to get your fill:

**Le Cass' Dale** ( ☎ 0262 31 84 29; Mare à Joncs; mains €5; 🕒 10am-7pm) This open-air kiosk overlooking the Mare à Joncs is a great place to chill with regulars over a sandwich or a *poulet frites* (chicken with fries).

**Le Platane** ( ☎ 0262 31 77 23; Rue du Père Boiteau; mains €10-22; 🕒 lunch & dinner Thu-Tue) Here you can wrap your mandibles around omelettes, salads and *carris*, but skip the unexceptional pizzas. There's a shady terrace at the back.

**Les Physalis** ( ☎ 0262 31 85 85; Rue des Trois Mares; mains €11-25; 🕒 lunch & dinner) A well-regarded venue, at the Hôtel Les Chenêts. Sadly, the sterile dining room seriously detracts from the atmosphere.

## Îlet à Cordes

Îlet à Cordes is a marvellous 'stop the world and get off' place and you'll leave with reluctance. The setting is truly photogenic: wherever you look, this tiny *écart* (settlement) is cradled by soaring mountains, with major peaks looming on the horizon. Vineyards and fields where lentils are grown complete the picture.

### SLEEPING & EATING

**Gîte d'étape et chambre d'hôte de l'Îlet** ( ☎ 0262 25 38 57, 0692 64 74 48; 27 Chemin Terre-Fine; dm/d incl breakfast €18/40, dinner €20; ⌨ ) No typo – here the *coup de grâce* is the sparkling pool (one of only two swimming pools in the Cirques), which is even heated during the colder months! The wood-panelled rooms, which can sleep two to six, are nothing fancy but well maintained. Solange Grondin, your amenable hostess, prides herself on her farm cooking, which usually means pork with cauliflower, *brèdes chouchou* (a mix of local vegetables) and homemade cakes.

**Au P'tit Bout du Monde – Chambre d'hôte Chez Carole Maillot** ( ☎ 0262 25 74 57, 0692 86 17 70; 18bis Chemin Terre-Fine; s/d incl breakfast €36/40) Offers two neat rooms (aim for the upstairs one) in a modern house at the far end of the village. The secluded location makes for great stargazing and the views over Le Grand Bénare and Piton des Neiges never fail to impress. No meals are served but there's a communal kitchen. You can also have dinner at Chez Hélène Payet (by reservation), a five-minute jog away.

**Au Petit Coin Charmant – Chambre d'hôte Chez Hélène Payet** ( ☎ 0262 35 18 13, 0692 68 49 68; 13 Chemin Terre-Fine; d incl breakfast €40, dinner €20) Madame Payet has four reassuringly Air-Wicked rooms in an alluring tropical garden. The food is more poultry with homegrown vegetables than creative concoctions, but it gets rave reviews from travellers.

**Snack Le Reposoir** ( ☎ 0262 25 14 36; Chemin Terre-Fine; ☻ 7am-7pm Mon-Sat, 7am-1pm & 5-7pm Sun) Across the road from Gîte d'étape et Chambre d'hôte de l'Îlet, this modest cafe-bar serves snacks and sandwiches, and has a limited selection of goods if you're fixing your own food.

## Bras-Sec

As in Îlet à Cordes, you've reached *le bout du monde* (the end of the Earth) in Bras-Sec, about 6km from Cilaos. This is a place to just kick back and enjoy the get-away-from-it-all atmosphere. If you've got itchy feet, a recommended **hike** is the Tour du Bonnet de Prêtre, a 4½-hour loop that skirts around

the bizarrely shaped peak that lies south of the village.

### SLEEPING & EATING

**Gîte d'étape Les Mimosas** ( ☎ 0262 96 72 73; 29 Chemin Saül; dm €17, s/d €25/35 all incl breakfast) This is an unflashy but homey place with functional two-to six-person rooms. Dinners (€20) are ultra copious and come in for warm praise.

**Les Calumets** ( ☎ 0262 35 40 63; http://calumets .neuf.fr; Chemin Saül; s/d with shared bathroom incl breakfast €20/40) Bridging the gap between *gîte d'étape* and B&B, this quirky affair run by an affable Breton couple is a good deal if you're after a bucolic setting. There's a pristine cryptomeria forest and a gurgling river at the back. Angle for one of the two rooms in the all-wood building at the front; the two other rooms at the back of the main house feel rather claustrophobic.

## CIRQUE DE SALAZIE

If you need a break from beach-bumming and want to cool off in forested mountains, head to the Cirque de Salazie. Like the Cirque de Cilaos, the Cirque de Salazie has bags of natural panache, with soaring peaks, soul-stirring vistas, thundering waterfalls, tortuous roads and a spattering of rural hamlets thrown in for good measure.

The winding mountain road that slithers into the Cirque from St-André on the northeast coast offers awesome views and is reason enough to make the trip. Yet the prize at the end of it is golden too: with its Creole colour, Hell-Bourg is the crowning glory of the Cirque.

The Cirque de Salazie is a bit 'flatter' (although 'flat' is not the first word that will spring to mind when you see it!) than the Cirque de Cilaos, but the scenery as you approach is nearly as awesome. The vegetation is incredibly lush and waterfalls tumble down the mountains, even over the road in places – Salazie is the wettest of the three Cirques.

For detailed information on the Tour des Cirques, a hiking route that takes in the Cirque de Salazie, see p242.

### Getting There & Away

There are seven buses daily from St-André to Salazie (€1.60) between 6.10am and 5.45pm (in the opposite direction, buses run from 5.30am to 4.40pm). On Sunday buses leave St-André at 8.40am, 1.30pm and 5.45pm (8am, 12.40pm and 3.45pm from Salazie).

RÉUNION

Buses from Salazie to Hell-Bourg run about every two hours from 6.45am to 6.20pm. In the opposite direction, there are services from 6.15am to 5.45pm. There are four buses in each direction on Sunday.

There are eight buses a day (four on Sunday) from Salazie to Grand Îlet and Le Bélier between 6.45am (9.15am on Sunday) and 6.20pm. Heading back to Salazie services depart from Le Bélier between around 5.45am and 5pm (7am to 5.20pm on Sunday), calling at Grand Îlet 10 minutes later.

From Le Bélier to Col des Bœufs, there are two buses per day on Monday, Wednesday and Friday at 7.35am and 2.35pm, as well as two buses on Sunday (at 10am and 4.25pm). In the opposite direction, buses leave at 8.05am and 3.05pm (10.25am and 4.55pm on Sunday).

There's only one petrol station, in Salazie – fill up in St-André.

## Salazie
### pop 2400
The road alongside the gorge of the Rivière du Mât from St-André to Salazie, which lies at the eastern entrance to the Cirque, winds past superb waterfalls. There's not much to detain you in Salazie, though, and most visitors press on to Hell-Bourg. You'll have to change buses here if you're heading further up into the Cirque.

Further along the road to Hell-Bourg, just north of the turn-off to Grand Îlet, you'll see the **Cascade du Voile de la Mariée** (Bridal

Veil Falls) on your left. These towering falls drop in several stages from the often cloud-obscured heights into the ravine at the roadside. You get an even better view from the Grand Îlet road.

## Hell-Bourg
### pop 2200
The town of Hell-Bourg emerges like a hamlet in a fairy tale after 9km of tight bends from Salazie. You can't but be dazzled by the fabulous backdrop – the majestic mountain walls that encase Hell-Bourg like a grandiose amphitheatre. No prize for guessing that this rugged terrain offers fantastic hiking opportunities. It offers plenty to more sedentary types as well. Culture aficionados will get their fill in this quintessential Réunionnais town with its enchanting centre, where old Creole mansions line the streets.

Hell-Bourg takes its curious name from the former governor Amiral de Hell; the town itself is anything but! It served as a thermal resort until a landslide blocked the spring in 1948. Visitors can still see the ruins of the old baths.

### INFORMATION
There are no banks in Hell-Bourg, but the post office has an ATM.

**L'Orchidée Rose** ( ☎ 0262 47 87 22; 26 Rue Olivier Manès; internet access per hr €7.60; ☺ 10am-9pm) Internet access.

**Maison du Tourisme** ( ☎ 0262 47 89 89; pat.salazie@ wanadoo.fr; 47 Rue Général de Gaulle; ☺ 9am-noon &

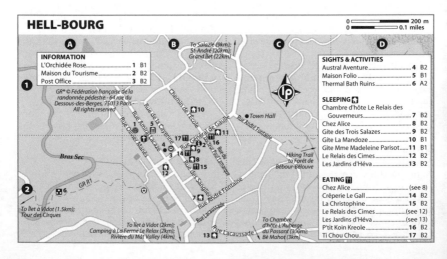

1-5pm) Has pamphlets on hiking options and bus schedules in the Cirque. Can also arrange bookings at *gîtes de montagne* and guided tours in English if given advance notice.

**Post office** (Rue du Général de Gaulle; ☺ 8.30am-noon & 1-2.45pm Mon-Fri, 8-11am Sat) Has an ATM.

## SIGHTS

First up, architecture and history buffs should take a look at the town's appealing **Creole buildings**, which date back as far as the 1840s, when Hell-Bourg was a famous resort town that attracted a rather well-heeled crowd. You can go on a guided tour organised by the tourist office; it takes about an hour and costs €9 (by reservation).

One of the loveliest of Hell-Bourg's Creole houses is **Maison Folio** ( ☎ 0262 47 80 98; 20 Rue Amiral Lacaze; admission €5; ☺ 9-11.30am & 2-5pm), a typical 19th-century bourgeois villa almost engulfed by its densely planted garden. The owners show you around, pointing out the amazing variety of aromatic, edible, medicinal and decorative plants, and give insights into local culture – unfortunately, only in French.

The **thermal bath ruins** are found in the ravine a 10-minute walk west of town. There's not much left now, but it's a quiet and leafy spot.

The landscape surrounding the hamlet of **Îlet-à-Vidot**, about 2km from Hell-Bourg, is little short of breathtaking. The iconic, flat-topped **Piton d'Enchaing**, covered with thick vegetation, seems to stand guard over the town.

From Îlet-à-Vidot, the asphalted road continues for about 2km until a small parking lot. From here, a steep footpath leads in about 15 minutes to the **Rivière du Mât valley**. Cross the footbridge and you'll soon reach a lovely picnic site by the river.

Another cute hamlet that's well worth visiting is **Bé Mahot**, about 3.5km from Hell-Bourg. With its clunky, colourful Creole houses clinging on the hillside and fantastic vistas of the Cirque, it's scenic to boot. There are several picnic sites along the road.

## ACTIVITIES
### Hiking
Not surprisingly, the Hell-Bourg area is an adventure playground for hiking enthusiasts, with a good selection of day hikes.

**Hell-Bourg–Gîte de Bélouve** About four hours return, with 570m of altitude gain. From Gîte de Bélouve, you can continue to the Trou de Fer viewpoint (p219).

**Îlet-à-Vidot–Piton d'Enchaing** This soaring 1356m peak is a popular but challenging five- to six-hour hike (return), with 670m of altitude gain.

**Hell-Bourg–Terre Plate–Source Manouilh–Îlet-à-Vidot–Hell-Bourg** An exhilarating five-hour loop, with a net altitude gain of about 600m.

**Hell-Bourg–Gîte du Piton des Neiges** A pleasant alternative to Cilaos if you're planning to hike up to Piton des Neiges. Expect a tough six- to seven-hour climb (one way), with a net altitude gain of 1470m.

Hikers doing the Tour des Cirques route will have to pass through Hell-Bourg as they cross the Cirque de Salazie. For more information on Tour des Cirques, see p242.

For hikes into the Cirque de Mafate, see p213.

### Canyoning
Just thinking of the canyoning options available in the Cirque makes our spine tingle. Get wet at Trou Blanc, which is said to be the most 'aquatic' canyon in Réunion, with lots of *toboggans* (plunging down water-polished chutes) and leaps. Some sections are appropriately named 'The Washing Machine', 'The Bath', 'The Aquaplaning'... Another reputable canyon is Voile de la Mariée, near Salazie, which is a more aerial circuit that includes a 50m rappel. Note that these canyons are not accessible during the rainiest months (from December to March). Count on €45/65 for a half-/full-day excursion.

Reliable operators:

**Alpanes** ( ☎ 0692 77 75 30; www.alpanes.com, in French) Doesn't have an office in Hell-Bourg.

**Austral Aventure** ( ☎ 0262 32 40 29; www.creole.org/austral aventure; Rue Amiral Lacaze, Hell-Bourg)

## SLEEPING

**Camping à La Ferme Le Relax** ( ☎ 0692 31 29 52; 21 Chemin Bras Sec, Îlet à Vidot; camp site per person €12) Head to this homely camp site, in the hamlet of Îlet à Vidot, about 2km northwest of Hell-Bourg, if you're after a peaceful setting to pitch your tent, within a grassy property. The ablution block is in good nick and there's a kitchen for guests' use. Laurent, the sporty owner (he's the local fireman and has run the Grand Raid race), can take you to various scenic spots in the area and provide you with a wealth of information (alas, in French) about local plants and architecture (€13).

**our pick Gîte La Mandoze** ( ☎ 0262 47 89 65, 0692 65 65 28; Chemin de l'École; dm/d €15/36) This *gîte* set in a

Creole house has all the hallmarks of a great deal: renovated, well-maintained (if a bit boxy) rooms that can sleep six people, well-scrubbed bathrooms, a tranquil location and a tab that won't burn a hole in your pocket. For those wanting more privacy, three doubles, with wood-panelled walls, are available. The owner, Patrick Manoro, is a mine of local knowledge and occasionally plays guitar for his guests in the evening. Dinner is available (€19).

**Gîte Mme Madeleine Parisot** ( ☎ 0262 47 83 48; 16 Rue Général de Gaulle; dm €16) The energetic Madame Parisot runs a homely *gîte d'étape* with two- to four-bed rooms in the centre of town. Some rooms can charitably be termed 'compact', so ask to see a few before committing. Dinner is available (€18).

**Gîte des Trois Salazes** ( ☎ 0692 46 78 48; tatiana .hck@hotmail.fr; Rue Général de Gaulle; dm incl breakfast €17) This well-run *gîte* is a secure spot to hang your rucksack, the rates are good and it's handily set on the main drag. It features four salubrious five- to six-bed rooms with well-scrubbed bathrooms. Tatiana is your friendly host.

**Chez Alice** ( ☎ 0262 47 86 24; 1 Rue des Sangliers; d incl breakfast €35) Clad in more wood than a Swedish sauna, this is a good option if you're counting the pennies. The seven rooms feel a tad hanky-sized but are perfectly acceptable and have private bathrooms. It's behind the restaurant.

**Chambre d'hôte L'Auberge du Passant** ( ☎ 0262 47 86 28; Rue du Stade; d incl breakfast €45) Peacefully positioned on the outskirts of town, this *chambre d'hôte* features two adjoining rooms occupying a neat bungalow surrounded by lots of greenery. Bail out if you're offered a darker room in the main house. *Table d'hôte* meals (dinner €17) come in for warm praise.

**Chambre d'hôte Le Relais des Gouverneurs** ( ☎ 0262 47 76 21; calouboyer@wanadoo.fr; 2bis Rue Amiral Lacaze; d incl breakfast €45-70; ☎ ) If you have a soft spot for romantic places, you need look no further. Park your backpack (or your suitcase) in one of the two Nuptiale rooms complete with four-poster beds, wooden floors and pastel-coloured walls. The cheaper Standard and Familiale rooms are more ordinary but excellent value. Excellent dinners (€20).

**Le Relais des Cimes** ( ☎ 0262 47 81 58; www.relais descimes.com; 67 Rue Général de Gaulle; s/d incl breakfast €59/73; ☎ ) The rooms in the motel-like building lack character and the furniture shows serious signs of hard use, but it's tidy enough and renovation plans are in the air. Most up-

stairs rooms have mountain views. There's a second building across the street, which was being refurbished at the time of research and should feature comfy rooms by the time you read this.

**our pick Les Jardins d'Héva** ( ☎ 0262 47 87 87; www .lesjardinsdheva.com; 16 Rue Lacaussade; d incl breakfast €90; ☎ ) This is a wonderfully relaxing option with five handsomely designed bungalows; each has a theme and is decorated differently. One glitch: they turn their back on the fantastic views of the Cirque. The real steal is the little spa, where you can reinvigorate weary feet after a busy day's walking. There's an onsite restaurant if you're feeling too lazy to travel elsewhere.

## EATING

While Cilaos is known for its lentils, Hell-Bourg is synonymous with *chouchou*, a green, pear-shaped vegetable imported from Brazil in 1834. It comes in salads, gratins and as *chouchou* gateau to finish. You can stock up on basic provisions at the grocers and other food shops along the main road.

**Crêperie Le Gall** ( ☎ 0262 47 87 48; 55 Rue Général de Gaulle; mains €3-10, menus €10-16; ☺ lunch & dinner) The only place for miles around that serves succulent pancakes. Yes, pancakes! Wash it all down with a *bolée de cidre* (bowl of cider). Lovely.

**Ti Chou Chou** ( ☎ 0262 47 80 93; 42 Rue Général de Gaulle; mains €8-23, menus €17-24; ☺ lunch & dinner Sat-Thu, closed Jun) This small restaurant with its appealing colourful facade on the main drag is run by a friendly young team. Herbivores will opt for the *assiette ti chouchou*, which offers a combination of *chouchou*, *cresson* and *capucine* (all local vegetables). There's a shady terrace at the back.

**La Christophine** ( ☎ 0692 52 15 46; Rue des Sangliers; mains €9-11, menu €15; ☺ lunch & dinner Thu-Tue) Located in a Creole house right behind Chez Alice, this family-style eatery serves up great cheap eats and local ambience. Excellent *carris* are served in little pots.

**Chez Alice** ( ☎ 0262 47 86 24; 1 Rue des Sangliers; mains €10-15, menu €18; ☺ lunch Tue-Sun, dinner Tue-Thu & Sat) The fare at this family-run veteran is certainly not gourmet but has a temptingly pronounced regional flavour. Among the many winners are the Hell-Bourg trout, the *gratin de chouchou* (choko gratin) and the *carri porc aux pommes de terre* (pork with potatoes), all served at affordable prices in rustic surrounds. Portions are large enough to satisfy the most voracious hiker.

**Le Relais des Cimes** ( ☎ 0262 47 81 58; 67 Rue Général de Gaulle; mains €11-18, menus €16-19; ⊙ lunch & dinner) At this Hell-Bourg stalwart the eclectic food is well presented and served in rustic surrounds, with wooden ceilings and red tablecloths. Try the trout with vanilla flambéed in rum, the house speciality.

**Les Jardins d'Héva** ( ☎ 0262 47 87 87; 16 Rue Lacaussade; mains €19, menus €20-25; ⊙ dinner) Superb setting: central Hell-Bourg at your feet, the jagged peaks of the Cirques in the distance. Tuck into well-prepared *carris* and fish dishes.

**P'tit Koin Kréol** ( ☎ 0693 92 62 00; Rue du Général de Gaulle; mains €5-10; ⊙ Thu-Sun) This little restaurant in a cute Creole house is a good place to sample authentic Réunionnais fare prepared mamma-style. Tour your taste buds with a *gratin de chouchous* (*chouchou* with melted cheese) or a chicken curry.

## Grand Îlet & Col des Bœufs

This is a sweet, picturesque spot. About 17km west of Salazie, accessed by a scenic white-knuckle road, Grand Îlet really feels like the end of the line. The village sits at the base of the ridge separating the Cirque de Salazie and the Cirque de Mafate. Above the village are the mountain passes of Col des Bœufs and Col de Fourche, which form the main pedestrian routes between the two Cirques; access is via the village of **Le Bélier**, 3km above Grand Îlet, where you'll find the start of the tarred *route forestière* that leads to Col des Bœufs. The *route forestière* is dotted with a number of *kiosques* (picnic shelters) that are popular at weekends.

About 500m before the guarded car park at Col des Bœufs, there's a sign indicating the path to **Piton Marmite** on the left. Follow it and after about 10 minutes you'll reach a lookout with fabulous views of the Cirque de Salazie.

You'll find several *chambres d'hôtes* in Grand Îlet as well as a few shops selling basic foodstuffs.

### SLEEPING & EATING

**Chambre d'hôte Liliane Bonnald** ( ☎ 0262 41 71 62; liliane.bonnald@wanadoo.fr; Chemin Camp-Pierrot; d €40, meals €20) In a modernish house on the road to Le Bélier, the five rooms upstairs won't be selected for a *Wallpaper* photo shoot but are kept tickety-boo and boast a few fancy touches, such as Creole ceilings and wood

---

**FORAYS INTO THE CIRQUE DE MAFATE**

If you have a day to spare, do not miss the opportunity to hike into the Cirque de Mafate. From the car park just below Col des Bœufs, it takes only two hours to descend to La Nouvelle, dubbed 'the capital of Mafate' – it makes a great half-day hike, and you can have lunch in La Nouvelle. A longer option is to take the Sentier Scout which branches off the *route forestière* (it's signposted, about 2.3km before the car park at Col des Bœufs) and leads to Aurère in Bas Mafate; you can spend the night in Aurère and walk back to the *route forestière* the next day by following the recently upgraded Sentier Augustave – a lovely loop.

---

panelling on the walls. Liliane Bonnald, your affable host, is a good cook too (ah, the *porc à la patate douce*; pork and sweet potato).

**Chambre d'hôte La Campierelle – Chez Christine Boyer** ( ☎ 0262 47 70 87; Chemin Camp-Pierrot; d €40, meals €20) Cross the road from Chambre d'hôte Liliane Bonnald and you'll be greeted by an old lady wearing a straw hat, Madame Boyer, the mother of Liliane Bonnald. She rents out four humble rooms in a small Creole house just off the road. It's no great shakes and the bathrooms feel a bit dated, but it's OK and when it comes to concocting traditional *carris* at dinner, Madame Boyer knows her stuff.

**Chambre d'hôte Le Cimendef – Chez Noeline et Daniel Campton** ( ☎ 0262 47 73 59; www.chambresdhote cimendef.com; Route du Bélier; s/d/ste €38/45/85, meals €20; 🛜 ) All five rooms are pleasing and are graced with ravishing views over the Cimendef (2226m), but we were smitten by the darling Prestige suite, which features a jacuzzi, timber floor, a luminous bathroom with well-chosen tiles, Creole ceilings, flat-screen TV, teak furniture, an enticing orange colour scheme and your own terrace. You'll also eat well here.

**Snack Le Grand Îlet – Chez Serge** ( ☎ 0262 47 71 19; Route du Bélier; mains €10; ⊙ lunch & dinner) This economical, neon-lit eatery set in a modern house by the main road is worth stopping at for its copious daily dishes (beef or chicken with vegetables, sausage *rougail*).

### GETTING THERE & AROUND

If you're coming here to hike and have your own car, you can leave it in the guarded car park (parking one/two days €2/10) at Le Petit Col, 6.5km up the *route forestière* and only 20 minutes' walk below the Col des Bœufs.

## CIRQUE DE MAFATE

We only need to say one word: mesmerising. Nothing can prepare you for that first glimpse of this geologic wonder, with its dramatic scenery, shifting colours, blissful serenity (except for the occasional whirring of choppers) and unsurpassed grandeur. No cars, no towns, no stress. Just soaring mountains, jagged peaks, giddily deep ravines, thick forests and a sprinkle of tiny *écarts* where time seems to have stood still.

Apart from its grandiose topography, what sets the Cirque de Mafate apart is its relative inaccessibility, despite being very close to the coastal fleshpots. There are no roads that lead into the Cirque (although a *route forestière* runs right up to the pass at Col des Bœufs), so the villages that are scattered in this giant extinct volcano are accessible only by foot.

Unsurprisingly, the Cirque de Mafate is a walker's paradise, with a good network of paths connecting the villages.

The Cirque was named after a runaway slave, the chieftain and sorcerer Mafate, who took refuge among its ramparts. He was hunted down and killed in 1751 by a hunter of runaway slaves.

See p249 for sleeping and eating options in the Cirque de Mafate.

### Sights & Activities

Despite its remoteness and seclusion, the Cirque de Mafate is populated. In the valleys, plateaus and spurs that slice up the jaw-dropping terrain are scattered discreet little Creole settlements that retain a rough-diamond rural edge. Not much happens in these villages but it's hard not to fall under the spell of their phenomenal setting. They provide a few trappings of civilisation if you're walking through the Cirque.

The southern part of the Cirque is called Haut Mafate (Higher Mafate) and receives the bulk of visitors. It comprises peaceful **Marla**, the highest hamlet of the Cirque at an altitude of 1621m; **La Nouvelle**, dubbed the 'capital of Mafate' and one of the main gateways to the Cirque, perched on a plateau at an altitude of 1421m; and **Roche-Plate**, at the foot of the grandiose Maïdo.

The northern part of the Cirque is called Bas Mafate (Lower Mafate) and is considered even more secretive than Haut Mafate. It comprises **Îlet à Bourse**, **Îlet à Malheur**, **Aurère**, **Grand Place**, **Cayenne**, **Les Lataniers** and **Îlet des Orangers**. Aurère is perched Machu Picchu–like above the precipitous canyon of the Bras Bémale. The two tiny communities of Grand Place and Cayenne lie above the rushing Rivière des Galets near the Cirque's main outlet.

Mafate offers some of the most inspirational **hiking** trails in Réunion, so pack your sturdy shoes and delve into the Cirque (see the chapter Hiking in Réunion, p242). If you'd prefer to take it easy and see all this fantasyland from the air, book a **helicopter** or an **ultralight aircraft tour** (see p202).

# LES HAUTES PLAINES & THE VOLCANO

Réunion's only cross-island road passes through the Plaine-des-Cafres and the Plaine-des-Palmistes, collectively known as Les Hautes Plaines. At an altitude of about 1000m, the air is refreshingly crisp and often swathed in misty fog – a blessing if you're coming from the scorching coastal cities.

These relatively large open areas actually form the saddle that separates the massif (comprising the three Cirques) from the volcano, Piton de la Fournaise. And what a volcano! It ranks as one of the most active volcanoes on Earth, playing in the same league as Hawaii. It's also one of the most accessible ones – you can trek up the caldera.

Because there's a road from the Hautes Plaines that approaches within a few kilometres of the summit of the volcano, nearly all visitors approach it from this side.

## PLAINE-DES-CAFRES & AROUND

Velvet-green hills and pastures undulating off into the horizon. Fresh air. Mist. Conifers. Filled with iconic pastoral landscapes, the Plaine-des-Cafres area bears an unexpected likeness to Bavaria. It is cool, relaxing and oxygenated. Chalk that up to altitude and attitude. It sits 1200m above sea level and is regularly massaged by cool breezes. Once a refuge for runaway slaves from the coast, the Plaine-des-Cafres is a vast, gently rolling area that spreads between the Cirques and Piton de la Fournaise.

As you make the approach from the south (St-Pierre), the Plaine-des-Cafres begins shortly after the sprawling, nondescript town of Le Tampon and ends at Col de Bellevue, at the top of the winding road that plunges down to Plaine-des-Palmistes. North of Le Tampon on RN3 (the cross-island road) are numerous small settlements that are named for their distance from the sea – Le Vingt-Quatrième (24th), for example, is 24km from the ocean.

The most interesting place on the Plaine-des-Cafres from a visitor's perspective is **Bourg-Murat**, which is the obvious launch pad for the volcano. It's in this rural settlement where the Route Forestière du Volcan turns off to Piton de la Fournaise. The town and the surrounding area have a wealth of accommodation and dining choices, making it a handy base.

## Information

**Office du Tourisme** ( ☎ 0262 27 40 00; www.tampon tourisme.re; 160 Rue Maurice Krafft, Bourg-Murat; ⏰ 9am-12.30pm & 1.30-5pm Mon-Sat) Near the Caltex petrol station. Bookings for *gîtes de montagnes* can be made here.

## Sights & Activities

Everything you need to know about Piton de la Fournaise and volcanoes in general should become clear at the excellent **Maison du Volcan** ( ☎ 0262 59 00 26; www.maisonduvolcan.fr; RN3, Bourg-Murat; adult/child €6.50/3; ⏰ 9.30am-5pm Tue-Sun). Unfortunately, most of the information is in French, but some interactive displays are in English and the videos of eruptions are self-explanatory. There's a 40-minute film on the 2007 eruption and a shorter one on the 2010 eruption.

**Horse riding** is a fun and ecofriendly way to commune with the pastoral wilderness around Bourg-Murat. The ultimate is a two- to three-day excursion that takes in the eerie landscape around the volcano – highly recommended. Rates range from €17 for a one-hour jaunt to about €110 per day for a multiday trek. Among reputable operators:
**Centre Équestre Alti Merens** ( ☎ 0262 59 18 84, 0692 04 12 38; 120 Rue Maurice Kraft, PK26; ⏰ closed Mon morning & Fri morning) On the southern edge of Bourg-Murat.

---

### DETOUR TO GRAND BASSIN – THE LOST VALLEY

The utterly picturesque valley of Grand Bassin, known as *la vallée perdue* (the lost valley) or *Mafate en miniature* (Mafate in miniature), is one of the few areas in Réunion that is only accessible on foot. Thanks to its splendid isolation, this little morsel of paradise is a dream come true for those seeking to get well and truly off the beaten track.

To get there, follow the road D70 to Bois Court from Vingt-Troisième village. At the end of the road you can look down into the valley from the **Belvédère** viewpoint. The path down to Grand Bassin begins about 800m south of the Belvédère (it's signposted). It plunges almost straight down to the river 600m below; allow 1½ hours for the descent and at least 2½ hours to get back up again. You can leave your car at a private home about 100m before the trailhead (look for the sign 'P'). It costs €3 (€8 for overnight parking).

Grand Bassin is formed by the confluence of three rivers. Near to where they join is a quiet hamlet with a handful of *gîtes*. From the hamlet, follow the river towards the west and you'll soon reach a few rock pools where you can dunk yourself – just blissful. Further west, you can descend at the base of the impressive **Cascade du Volle de la Mariée** waterfall.

Grand Bassin is a terrific place to kick off your shoes for a few days and sample authentic rural Réunionnais life. Digs are in rustic dorms or in doubles, but that's part of the fun. Prices are the same at all *gîtes*: €35 per person including half board. Day-trippers will fork out €16 to €20 for a meal, usually a wholesome *carri* made with locally grown products.

**Auberge de Grand-Bassin** ( ☎ 0262 59 10 34, 0692 11 13 90) Has two doubles.

**La Vieille Tonnelle** ( ☎ 0262 27 51 02, 0262 59 20 27) Has three doubles. Luc, the friendly owner, will treat you to a wicked *rhum bois* (rum flavoured with an endemic wood). Good homemade jams.

**Le Paille-en-Queue** ( ☎ 0262 59 03 66, 0692 70 86 03) A few doubles.

**Le Randonneur** ( ☎ 0692 78 04 50; http://grandbassin.skyrock.com) A chalet-like venue with good views. One double, one triple and four quadruples, all tiled.

**Les Orchidées** ( ☎ 0262 38 02 73) On the eastern outskirts of the hamlet. Has two quadruples. Good homemade honey.

**RÉUNION**

**Écuries du Volcan** ( ☎ 0692 66 62 90; 9bis Domaine Belle-vue, Bourg-Murat; ⌚ daily by reservation) On the northern edge of Bourg-Murat. Offers an interesting day trip (€73) that includes a visit to a traditional farm and a Creole lunch.

## Sleeping

**Gîte de la Fournaise** ( ☎ 0262 59 29 75; gitedelafournaise@wanadoo.fr; RN3, Bourg-Murat; dm €15/34) The two dorms downstairs are OK, but the renovated double room upstairs really cuts the mustard, with its own terrace and views of Piton des Neiges. The French owner is extra nice and offers to pick up walkers from the GR R2 (and drop them off the next morning), which passes a few kilometres north of Bourg-Murat. Dinner costs €20.

**Gîte de Bellevue** ( ☎ 0262 59 15 02, 0692 07 80 83; Domaine Bellevue, Bourg-Murat; dm €15, bungalow €100) A good find in a bucolic property, behind the equestrian centre Écuries du Volcan (p215). Has two doubles and two quads, all scrubbed attentively. The bungalow can sleep five. Bar breakfast (€5), no meals are provided but there are kitchen facilities.

**Gîte Marmite Lontan** ( ☎ 0262 57 46 09, 0692 60 51 38; www.marmitelontan.com; s incl half board €38; ⌚ Tue-Sat) Not your average *gîte*, this little cracker is isolated on the Route du Volcan about 2km from the centre of Bourg-Murat. Entering the property, you feel as if you've stumbled onto the set of *Little House on the Prairie*. In the role of Charles Ingalls you have amiable Pilou. The five dorms are neat and can sleep two to four people. The whole place radiates a ramshackle air – from the quirky facade, which is entirely covered with thongs, to the dining room, which is a Pandora's box of *objets lontan* (utensils and other knick-knacks from the old days). It also serves *plat du jour* (daily special) at lunchtime.

**La Ferme du Pêcher Gourmand** ( ☎ 0262 59 29 79; http://pagesperso-orange.fr/pecher.gourmand; RN3, PK25; d incl breakfast €48, bungalow €70) This modern *auberge* is run by a friendly couple and is surrounded by a pleasant garden. The six adjoining rooms are a bit of a squeeze, but the setting more than compensates. There's also a stand-alone bungalow, which offers more privacy.

**Hôtel-Restaurant Les Géraniums** ( ☎ 0262 59 11 06; hotelgeranium@wanadoo.fr; RN3, PK24; s/d €66/82; ⌚ ) The Géraniums is a tad overrated but nonetheless of a good standard, especially if you nab a room with mountain views; avoid the rooms that overlook the parking lot. It's in Le Vingt-Quatrième on the main road south of Bourg-Murat.

Other options:

**Hôtel-Auberge Le Volcan** ( ☎ 0262 27 50 91; aubvolcan@wanadoo.fr; RN3, PK27, Bourg-Murat; s/d €29/40) Features stock-standard rooms in various pavilions smack-bang in the middle of Bourg-Murat. The mattresses will keep your chiropractor happy.

**Hôtel l'Ecrin** ( ☎ 0262 59 02 02; www.hotel-ecrin.fr.st; RN3, PK27, Bourg-Murat; s/d incl breakfast €60/82; ⌚ ) A cluster of small cottages scattered amid gardens that carpet a knoll. The furnishings are tired but it's functional and serviceable.

## Eating

Most lodging options offer half board.

**Palais des Fromages** ( ☎ 0262 59 27 15; Route du Volcan; cheese & waffles €3-4; ⌚ 9am-5pm Thu, Fri & Sun, to 3pm Sat) This unassuming dairy farm on the outskirts of Bourg-Murat has a lot to answer for – namely our raging addiction to *fromage crémeux au combava* (creamy goat cheese flavoured with combava), best enjoyed at a picnic table in the cryptomeria forest nearby. Also concocts waffles on Sunday.

**Hôtel-Auberge du Volcan** ( ☎ 0262 27 50 91; RN3, PK27, Bourg-Murat; mains €11-18; ⌚ lunch Tue-Sun, dinner Tue-Sat) You'll find all the usual Creole favourites and a sprinkling of *métro* dishes served in hearty portions in this country inn in the centre of Bourg-Murat. Last orders are at 8pm.

**Le QG** ( ☎ 0262 38 28 55; 60bis rue Alfred Picard, Bourg-Murat; mains €12-18; ⌚ 7am-9.30pm Fri-Tue, to 2pm Wed) What do you get if you cross a Réunionnais chef (André), a Senegalese waiter (Abdou) and a snug dining room? The QG! If the thought of *rougaille zandouille* (sausage stew Creole-style) or *carri poulet* (chicken curry) exquisitely cooked in the hearth doesn't make you dribble then you've started pushing up daisies. Also serves breakfast.

**Le Vieux Bardeau** ( ☎ 0262 59 09 44; RN3, PK24; mains €12-18, menus €12-20; ⌚ lunch Tue-Sun, dinner Wed-Sat) Recapture the atmosphere of the colonial era in this gracefully ageing diva occupying a lemon-yellow Creole mansion beside the main road in Le Vingt-Quatrième. The Creole buffet is excellent value, but you'll also find *métro* specialities à la carte.

**Relais Commerson** ( ☎ 0262 27 52 87; 37 Bois Joly Potier, Bourg-Murat; mains €13-37, menus €15-35; ⌚ lunch Thu-Tue) A rustic dining room and a menu laden with inspired Creole fare, including *escalope d'espadon à la crème de palmiste* (tuna steak in a palm-hearts sauce).

**Le Panoramic** ( ☎ 0262 59 36 12; RN3, PK27, Bourg-Murat; mains €15-25, menus €16-30; ⌚ lunch & dinner)

Do swordfish fillet, minced duck with guava sauce, and kangaroo fillet (!) in wine sauce tickle your fancy? Enjoy a long list of well-prepared *métro* and Creole specialities in this modern abode behind Hôtel l'Ecrin.

**La Ferme du Pêcher Gourmand** ( ☎ 0262 59 29 79; RN3, PK25; menus €22-31; ⏱ lunch Sat & Sun, dinner Mon-Sat) Homegrown produce rules the roost of this delightful *ferme-auberge* (farm restaurant) on the main road south of Bourg-Murat. The set menu is a culinary feast revolving around duck preparations and organic vegetables. A *crème brûlée à la vanille* (cream pie with a caramelised topping and flavoured with vanilla) will finish you off sweetly.

### Getting There & Away

There are three buses daily (two on Sunday) each way between St-Benoît and St-Pierre via Plaine-des-Cafres and Plaine-des-Palmistes. From St-Pierre to Bourg-Murat, the fare is €2.80. Coming from St-Benoît, it's €4.20.

## PITON DE LA FOURNAISE (THE VOLCANO)

The magnum opus of Mother Nature in Réunion, Piton de la Fournaise is the island's most famous natural attraction. Simply dubbed *le volcan* (the volcano) by Réunionnais, Piton de la Fournaise is not a dormant monster, but an active geological wonder that erupts with great regularity; in April 2007 the central, 900m-wide crater collapsed by 300m, and new lava fields were formed on its southeastern flanks, down to the coast. Early January 2010 a new eruption occurred, though less powerful. Scientists keep a close watch on the volcano's moods, and are poised to issue warnings if things look to be gathering steam. At the first sign of an eruption, the paths near the volcano and the road up to it will be closed.

The good news is that it's one of the world's most accessible active volcanoes, and it's possible to hike up to the crater rim (though this is subject to change depending on current conditions, so ask while you're there). You can also fly over the volcano (see p202), approach the area from the saddle of a horse (see p215) or simply enjoy the scenery from a viewpoint at **Pas de Bellecombe** (2311m), the 'entrance' to the volcanic area, right on the crater's outer rim, where the road ends.

The main gateway to the volcano is Bourg-Murat (p215), where you can visit the Maison

**LIVE FROM THE VOLCANO**

A webcam has been positioned on the outer crater rim, due north of Piton de la Fournaise. It allows walkers to check out the weather conditions that prevail near the volcano and curious travellers to simply admire the monster in its full grandeur. The images update every five minutes. Log on to www.fournaise.info/webcam.php.

du Volcan. From there, a scenic, zigzagging secondary road leads to Pas de Bellecombe, about 30km southeast of Bourg-Murat. The gradual change of scenery is mind-boggling. The grassy meadows and cryptomeria forests typical of the Hautes Plaines progressively change to scrubland and Martian landscape. Be sure to pause at **Belvédère du Nez-de-Bœuf** (viewpoint), blessed with unsurpassable views over the valley gouged by the Rivière des Remparts. About 22km from Bourg-Murat, there's another fabulous viewpoint at **Pas des Sables** (2360m), from where you can gaze at a wide windswept plain, made of ashes, **Plaine des Sables**. With its lunar landscape, it could form a perfect backdrop for a new version of *Mad Max*. The road plunges down to the plain and becomes a dirt road with wicked potholes (but it's OK with a car) before continuing uphill to Pas de Bellecombe and Gîte du Volcan. You've reached the end of the world.

From the viewpoint at Pas de Bellecombe you'll be rewarded with mesmerising views of the volcano and its outer crater, known as **Enclos Fouqué**. The very photogenic, small scoria cone with bizarre ochre hues you can see to the east in Enclos Fouqué is **Formica Leo**. The main crater, the 900m-wide **Dolomieu Crater**, is active; the 2632m-high, 200m-wide **Bory Crater**, to the east, is inactive.

### Sleeping & Eating

There's a modest **cafeteria** ( ⏱ 9am-5pm) selling snacks and refreshments at Pas de Bellecombre.

If you wish to stop overnight to soak up this grandiose scenery, the 65-bed **Gîte du Volcan** ( ☎ 0692 85 20 91; www.legiteduvolcan.com; dm €16, bungalow incl breakfast €60-80, lunch €13-16, dinner €19) boasts a stunning location, a 15-minute walk from Pas de Bellecombe. Digs are in four- to 12-bed dorms. There are also two

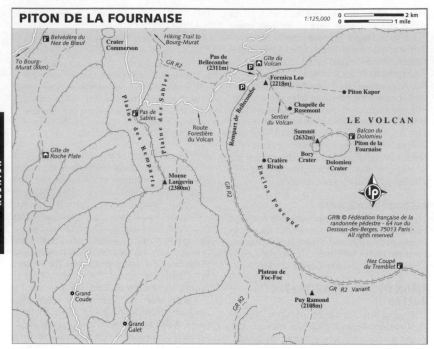

PITON DE LA FOURNAISE

bungalows that come with bathrooms. Hot water is limited and is token-operated (€1.50). In principle, bookings are to be made through Centrale de Réservation – Île de la Réunion (see p177) or through any tourist office, but the caretakers usually accept travellers who haven't reserved if the *gîte* is not full (but reservations are recommended, especially during the trekking season). The restaurant is open at lunch for day trippers and serves up five different dishes. The real clincher are the picture-windows with lovely mountain views. Water is recycled. Credit cards are accepted.

### Getting To/From Piton de la Fournaise

For those with a vehicle, getting to the volcano couldn't be easier because of the all-weather Route Forestière du Volcan, which climbs 30km from Bourg-Murat all the way to Pas de Bellecombe.

Without your own car, the 5½-hour hike to the volcano from Bourg-Murat via the Sentier Josémont (GR R2) is regarded as something of a walk for masochists, as it's easy to pick up a ride along the Route Forestière du Volcan instead.

## PLAINE-DES-PALMISTES

There were once large numbers of palm trees on the Plaine-des-Palmistes (hence the name), but as a result of heavy consumption of palm-heart salad, few now remain. The town itself is spread out along the highway and is a good base for Forêt de Bébour-Bélouve. Its only specific sight is the **Domaine des Tourelles**, a lovely 1920s Creole building just south of the town centre, which now houses a shop selling local crafts and produce, and a small **tourist office** ( ☎ 0262 51 47 59; www.domaine-tourelles .com; 260 Rue de la République; ☷ 9am-5.30pm Mon-Fri, 10am-5pm Sat & Sun).

If you want to commune with nature, be sure not to miss the walk to the **Cascade Biberon**, a 240m-high waterfall to the north of Plaine-des-Palmistes (it's signposted). It's an easy one-hour return walk along a well-marked path.

Plaine-des-Palmistes has a slew of reliable accommodation options, including the **Gîte du Pic des Sables** ( ☎ 0262 51 37 33; 2 Allée des Filaos; dm/d €20/50, breakfast/dinner €5/20), a cleanish but cramped *gîte d'étape* on the road to Forêt de Bébour-Bélouve, about 4km from the highway

---

### HIKING UP PITON DE LA FOURNAISE

Réunion's iconic feature, Piton de la Fournaise is simply a must-do for walkers. From Pas de Bellecombe, it's possible to hike up to **Balcon du Dolomieu**, a viewpoint on the southeastern side of the Dolomieu Crater rim, from where you can gaze down upon the bottom of the caldera, some 350m down. Balcon du Dolomieu is a five-hour, 14km out-and-back walk. It's graded moderate and has an altitude gain of about 500m. It can get very busy, but the eerie landscape more than makes up for the crowds of people. Note that since the 2007 eruption it's no longer possible to do a circuit around the Dolomieu Crater and the Bory Crater; ignore all maps showing this circuit, as they're not up to date.

From the car park at Pas de Bellecombe, follow the path to the northeast that leads to a door (closed when the volcano is active). This is where the path starts in earnest by plunging 527 steps to the floor of the immense Enclos Fouqué, reached after about 15 minutes. You're now walking on a field of solidified lava. The route across the lava plain is marked with white paint spots. At times it can feel like you are walking on Mars, with only the dry crunch of the cinders underfoot for company. You'll first pass the very photogenic Formica Leo and, about 45 minutes from the start, a spectacular cavern in the lava known as **Chapelle de Rosemont** comes into view. From here, the path veers to the left and takes a gradual route up the eastern wall of the cone until it reaches the Balcon du Dolomieu viewpoint. Caveat! There's no guardrail, just a white line.

While the volcano walk is popular and is not technically demanding, it shouldn't be undertaken lightly. The landscape here is harsh and arid, despite the mist that can drench hikers to the skin. The chilly wind whips away moisture, leaving walkers dehydrated and breathless.

Early morning is the best time to climb the volcano, as you stand a better chance of clear views, but this is when everyone else hits the trail as well.

Since the eruption of April 2007, two new walks in the Enclos Fouqué have been established. They do not lead to Dolomieu Crater, but to **Piton Kapor** (about three hours return), a small volcanic cone north of Piton de la Fournaise, and to **Cratère Rivals** (about four hours return), in the southwestern part of the Enclos. Leaflets detailing these routes are available at the tourist office in Bourg-Murat.

Many people get a head start by staying at the Gîte du Volcan (p217) and leave at the crack of dawn, so be sure to book well in advance.

---

(direction Petite Plaine). It has mountain bikes for rent (€5 per hour). In a quiet location on the eastern edge of town, **La Ferme du Pommeau** ( ☎ 0262 51 40 70; www.pommeau.fr; 10 Allée des Pois de Senteur; s €54, d €71-79; 🛜 🔲 ) is a rambling two-star hotel consisting of several nicely maintained buildings. Inside, it's a bit disappointing, with clean but unadventurous rooms and Ikea-minimalist decor. There's a pool and a reliable **restaurant** (mains €14-29, menus €24-38; 🕑 Mon-Sat) on-site, which features Creole cuisine and *métro* dishes. On the main drag, **Les Platanes – Chez Jean-Paul** ( ☎ 0262 51 31 69; mains €11-19, menu €17; 🕑 lunch Wed-Sun) is always full with Réunionnais families at lunch on Sunday – a good sign.

### Getting There & Away

Plaine-des-Palmistes is situated on the cross-island highway between St-Benoît and St-Pierre. There are three buses a day (two on Sunday) in each direction. The fare from St-Pierre is €4.20.

## FORÊT DE BÉBOUR-BÉLOUVE

An absolute must-see, the majestic Forêt de Bébour-Bélouve could set the stage for a new version of *Jurassic Park*, with a mix of tamarind trees, huge *fanjan* (fern trees) and moss. It lies to the northwest of Plaine-des-Palmistes, and is accessible via a surfaced forest road which begins at La Petite Plaine, just southwest of Plaine-des-Palmistes, and finishes 20km further on, 400m from the **Gîte de Bélouve** ( ☎ 0692 85 93 07; Forêt de Bébour-Bélouve; dm/d with shared bathroom €16/€40, breakfast/meal €5/€17), which is scenically wedged onto a bluff lording over the Cirque de Salazie. Digs are in six- to 12-bed dorms. Bookings are essential.

You'll find some excellent picnic spots at the beginning of the forest. It's also a popular **walking** area, with a network of footpaths of varying levels of difficulty. The tourist office at Plaine-des-Palmistes has a leaflet on walks in the forest. Some favourites:

**Sentier Botanique de la Petite Plaine** A 45-minute loop with interpretative panels about flora.

**Sentier de la Tamarineraie** A 1½-hour loop, from the Gîte de Bélouve.

**Sentier du Trou de Fer** An easy 3.5km walk that leads to a lookout from where you can marvel at horseshoe-shaped falls known as the Trou de Fer, hailed as one of the most spectacular natural sights in Réunion – it has graced the covers of many books. The path starts at the Gîte de Bélouve.

**Tour du Piton Bébour** An easy 1¼-hour loop.

You can also rent a mountain bike at Gîte du Pic des Sables (p218) and explore the area at your leisure.

Note that the forest road is at times closed to traffic 2.5km below the Gîte de Bélouve from noon on Friday to 7am on Monday. Just leave your car at the car park and walk to the *gîte*.

# ST-PIERRE

**pop 26,000**

If you need to let off steam before (or after) heading off into the Cirques, you've come to the right place. St-Pierre pulses with an energy unknown elsewhere on the island, especially at weekends. Havana it ain't, but this vibrant, feisty, good-natured city knows what really counts in life: having a good time.

If St-Denis is Réunion's administrative and business capital, enchanting St-Pierre is its throbbing heart. Basking in the clear light of the southwest, the 'capital of the south' has an entirely different feel from its northern counterparts. It remains unmistakably more Creole than cosmopolitan and rather staid St-Denis.

St-Pierre's attractions include a slew of colonial-era edifices scattered in the centre and an attractive seafront. The picturesque Terre Sainte district is also worth a stroll.

## ORIENTATION

The centre of St-Pierre consists of a compact grid of streets. Most places are easily walkable, though the bus station for long-distance buses, at the junction of Rue de Presbytère and Rue Luc Lorion, is a bit of a hike.

## INFORMATION

There are ATMs at the central post office and at most banks in the town centre.

**BRED** (Rue du Four à Chaux; ☾ 8am-4.15pm Mon-Wed & Fri, to 3.30pm Thu) Has an ATM.

**Central post office** (Rue des Bons Enfants; ☾ 7.30am-5.30pm Mon-Fri, to noon Sat)

**Jet Set Bar** (32 Blvd Hubert-Delisle; internet access per hr €4.80; ☾ 9am-midnight Mon-Thu, to 2am Fri & Sat, 2pm-midnight Sun) Internet cafe. Also offers wi-fi access. Fast, friendly, high-tech and reliably open late.

**Tourist office** ( ☎ 0892 702 701; ot-saint.pierre@wanadoo.fr; 26 Rue Amiral Lacaze, Terre Sainte; ☾ 9am-noon & 1-4.45pm Mon-Sat) Has English-speaking staff and can provide useful brochures and a town map. You can also book *gîtes de montagnes* here.

## SIGHTS

Compact, colourful St-Pierre is easily seen in a day on foot. You'll find a scattering of colonial buildings in the centre, including the old **Hôtel de Ville** (Rue Méziaire Guignard), which started life as a coffee warehouse for the French East India Company during the 18th century. The old **colonial-era train station** is now occupied by a cafe. Another must-see is the **Entrepôt Kervéguen** (Rue du Four à Chaux), which was also used as a warehouse by the French East India Company. In the same area, keep your eyes peeled for the **médiathèque Raphaël Barquisseau** (off Rue des Bons Enfants), another building dating from the thriving era of the French East India Company. There are many other Creole mansions and houses that beg to be admired, especially along Rue Marius et Ary Leblond. One of the grandest is **école St-Charles** (Rue Marius et Ary Leblond), which was built in the late 18th century. To the east, the neoclassical **Hôtel de la Sous-Préfecture** (Rue Augustin Archambaud) is also worthy of interest.

The **cemetery** at the western end of Blvd Hubert-Delisle is worth the wander. The grave of African sorcerer Le Sitarane is still a popular pilgrimage spot for Réunionnais who believe in *gris gris* (black magic). It is covertly used for black-magic rites by people looking to bring misfortune upon others. The grave is on the right-hand side at the west end of the cemetery.

If you still have energy to burn, it's well worth exploring the **Terre Sainte** district, situated to the east of the centre. Though no longer the traditional fishing village it used to be, this area has its own peculiar appeal, especially along the seashore, where fishermen can be seen playing dominoes in the late afternoon.

Those who want to understand how the ambrosia called rum starts in the sugar-cane fields and ends on their palates should really

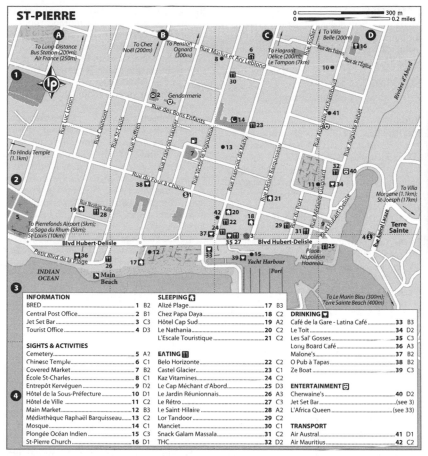

**ST-PIERRE**

0 ——————— 300 m
0 ——————— 0.2 miles

RÉUNION

| INFORMATION | | | SLEEPING | | | |
|---|---|---|---|---|---|---|
| BRED | 1 | B2 | Alizé Plage | 17 | B3 | |
| Central Post Office | 2 | B1 | Chez Papa Daya | 18 | C2 | |
| Jet Set Bar | 3 | C3 | Hôtel Cap Sud | 19 | A2 | **DRINKING** |
| Tourist Office | 4 | D3 | Le Nathania | 20 | C2 | Café de la Gare - Latina Café ... 33 B3 |
| | | | L'Escale Touristique | 21 | C2 | Le Toit ... 34 D2 |
| | | | | | | Les Sal' Gosses ... 35 C3 |
| **SIGHTS & ACTIVITIES** | | | **EATING** | | | Long Board Café ... 36 A3 |
| Cemetery | 5 | A2 | Belo Horizonte | 22 | C1 | Malone's ... 37 B2 |
| Chinese Temple | 6 | C1 | Castel Glacier | 23 | C1 | O Pub à Tapas ... 38 B2 |
| Covered Market | 7 | B2 | Kaz Vitamines | 24 | C2 | Ze Boat ... 39 C3 |
| École St-Charles | 8 | C1 | Le Cap Méchant d'Abord | 25 | D3 | |
| Entrepôt Kervéguen | 9 | D2 | Le Jardin Réunionnais | 26 | A3 | **ENTERTAINMENT** |
| Hôtel de la Sous-Préfecture | 10 | D1 | Le Rétro | 27 | C2 | Cherwaine's ... 40 D2 |
| Hôtel de Ville | 11 | C2 | Le Saint Hilaire | 28 | A2 | Jet Set Bar ... (see 3) |
| Main Market | 12 | B3 | Lor Tandoor | 29 | C2 | L'Africa Queen ... (see 33) |
| Médiathèque Raphaël Barquisseau | 13 | C2 | Manciet | 30 | C1 | |
| Mosque | 14 | C1 | Snack Galam Massala | 31 | C1 | **TRANSPORT** |
| Plongée Océan Indien | 15 | C3 | THC | 32 | D2 | Air Austral ... 41 D1 |
| St-Pierre Church | 16 | D1 | | | | Air Mauritius ... 42 C2 |

come to the museum called **La Saga du Rhum** ( ☎ 0262 35 81 90; www.sagadurhum.fr; Chemin Fredeline; adult/child €7/5; ☀ 10am-5pm Sat-Thu, to 6pm Fri), which is set on the site of the Isautier estate, one of the oldest rum distillers on Réunion. It's northwest of Saint-Pierre (direction Bois d'Olives).

No trip to St-Pierre would be complete without a wander through the **main market**, which takes place on Saturday morning (7am to noon) and sprawls along the seafront at the west end of Blvd Hubert-Delisle. During the week (8am to 6pm Monday to Saturday) there's a smaller **covered market** (Rue Victor le Vigoureux) under a hall in the town centre. Alongside fresh fruit and vegetables, stalls sell souvenirs such as local spices and

herbs, *vacoa* bags and the usual assortment of Malagasy crafts.

After having succumbed to all-night carousing and luscious cuisine in St-Pierre, you might want to repent your sins. Head straight to the charming **St-Pierre church** (Rue Auguste Babet) if you are Catholic, to the splendid **mosque** (Rue François de Mahy) if you're Muslim, to the impressive **Hindu temple** (Ravine Blanche) if you are Hindu, and to the discreet **Chinese temple** (Rue Marius et Ary Leblond) if you are Buddhist. But if, like us, you are a hedonist beyond redemption, you might rather lounge on the white-sand **main beach**! Hint: there's a lesser-known, more intimate **beach** in Terre Sainte, an espadrille's throw from Marin Bleu restaurant.

## ACTIVITIES

There's excellent **diving** off St-Pierre (see p32 for more information). Contact **Plongée Océan Indien** (☎ 0262 31 03 91, 0692 69 41 57; Harbour) at the yacht harbour.

## SLEEPING

Reservations are essential at weekends.

### Budget

**Chez Papa Daya** (☎ 0262 25 64 87; www.chezpapadaya .com; 27 Rue du Four à Chaux; s with shared bathroom €25-30, s €30-35, d with/without bathroom €35/30; ❄ ☎) Papa Daya is something of an institution for bargain-hunters, but its standing has been challenged in recent years by two newcomers whose owners are members of the same family as Monsieur Daya. Overall it's more homely, if a bit more cramped, than its competitors, with lots of greenery and jolly murals around, and facilities include a simple kitchen, a laundry room and a TV lounge. No air-con in the cheaper rooms.

**Le Nathania** (☎ 0262 25 04 57, 0692 70 87 60; www .hotelnathania.com; 12 Rue François de Mahy; s/d with shared bathroom €25/40, d €45-55; ℗ ❄ ☎) Another traveller-friendly stalwart. What it lacks in style is made up for by an ace location and tidy rooms with TV. The cheapest have shared facilities and are fan-cooled. There's also a kitchen (for breakfast only) and laundry area. Prices drop by €5 to €10, depending on the rooms, after two nights.

**L'Escale Touristique** (☎ 0262 35 20 95, 0692 72 58 58; 14 Rue Désiré Barquisseau; s with shared bathroom €30, d with shared bathroom €30-35, d €40; ℗ ❄ ☎) Almost a carbon copy of Le Nathania (same family, same ambience, and probably the same architect). Rooms are well scrubbed, but a bit compact, though it's hard to argue with the prices. Ask for rooms 101, 102 or 103, which come with a balcony. Air-con is only available in the dearer rooms. Added perks include free parking, a communal kitchen (for breakfast only) and a laundry area. Don't expect dollops of atmosphere. Prices drop by €5 if you stay two nights or more.

**Pension Ognard** (☎ 0262 25 89 72, 0262 21 95 98; 113 Rue François Isautier; d €30; ℗) A simple guesthouse, with only eight rooms that share bathrooms and kitchen facilities. Best asset is the tropical garden.

### Midrange & Top End

**Hôtel Cap Sud** (☎ 0262 25 75 64; www.hotel-capsud -reunion.com; 6 Rue Caumont; d €45; ❄ ☎) Middle-of-the-road sums up this two-star venture with a handy location and unmemorable rooms.

**Alizé Plage** (☎ 0262 35 22 21; www.ilereunion.com/ alizeplage; 17bis Blvd Hubert-Delisle; d €95; ❄ ☎) The Alizé thinks it is irresistible because its position right on the beach is peerless. Hubris: only three rooms come with sea views, and though they are nicely appointed, they won't contend for a design Oscar.

**Villa Morgane** (☎ 0262 25 82 77; www.villamorgane .re; 334 Rue de L'Amiral Lacaze; d incl breakfast €110-400; ❄ ☎ ⚐) You'll go giddy over the exuberant, ever-so-slightly OTT interior of this *maison d'hôte* in Terre Sainte. The themed suites have been creatively designed, some with Italian flair, some with Asian touches. The Pompéi suite, complete with frescoes, parquet floor and ornate stucco ceilings, has to be seen to be believed (check out the website).

**our pick Villa Belle** (☎ 0692 65 89 99; www.villabelle .net; 45 Rue Rodier; s/d/ste €160/170/350; ℗ ❄ ☎ ⚐) If you could smell charm, this super-smooth boutique B&B in a converted Creole mansion would reek of it to high heaven. It's the epitome of a refined cocoon, revelling quietly in minimalist lines, soothing colour accents and well-thought-out decorative touches, including contemporary artworks by the owner himself. Like the rest of the place, the communal areas are a sensory interplay of light, wood and stone. After a day of turf pounding, relax in the stress-melting pool. Gay-friendly.

## EATING

The excellent Creole, French, Italian and Asian restaurants make this town as pleasing to the belly as it is to the eye; you won't want to be skipping any meals here. Many bars also double up as restaurants.

### Quick Eats

**Castel Glacier** (☎ 0262 22 96 56; 38 Rue François de Mahy; ice creams €2-6, mains €8-16; ☷ 11am-6pm Mon, 11am-11pm Tue-Thu, to midnight Fri & Sat, 2-11pm Sun) Generous scoops and about 30 flavours are the trademarks of this drool-inducing ice-cream parlour opposite the mosque. Also serves up salads, pancakes and *plats du jour*.

**Kaz Vitamines** (☎ 0262 25 30 86; 6 Rue François de Mahy; mains €4-5; ☷ 10am-5pm Tue-Sat) If you've reached your *carri*-eating limits, head down to this quirky den for a cold veggie soup or a salad (€5), just off the main drag.

**Lor Tandoor** (☎ 0262 01 24 24; Rue du Port; mains €6-9, menu €9.50; ☷ lunch Tue-Sun, dinner Tue-Sat) Lor

Tandoor keeps things plain and simple: ordinary decor, brisk service and a good range of freshly prepared light meals to eat in or take away.

**Snack Galam Massala** ( ☎ 0692 37 12 98; 5 Rue du Four à Chaux; mains €6-9; ☺ lunch Mon-Sat, dinner Sat) You wouldn't guess it from the humble surrounds, but this family-run place concocts tasty Indian dishes, including fish curry and chicken marinated with ginger.

**Belo Horizonte** ( ☎ 0262 22 31 95; 10 Rue François de Mahy; mains €9-19; ☺ lunch Mon-Sat, dinner Thu-Sat) Walls saturated in cheery coloured accents – baby pink, citrus, apple green – and other fancy decorative touches set the tone of this zinging joint where you can tuck into salads, hot tarts and pasta dishes. Excellent homemade desserts, too.

You didn't think we would forget the carb lovers and chocoholics? If, like us, you think life is unbearable without a croissant or a chocolate tart, bookmark **Manciet** ( ☎ 0262 25 06 73; 64 Rue Victor le Vigoureux; ☺ 6.30am-12.30pm & 2.30-6.30pm Tue-Sat, 6.30am-12.30pm Sun).

## Restaurants

**Le Rétro** ( ☎ 0262 25 33 06; 34 Blvd Hubert-Delisle; mains €9-25, menus €12.50-25; ☺ lunch & dinner) Of all the things you might not expect to see on the seafront, an 'authentic' Parisian brasserie ranks quite highly. But that's exactly what this is, except that *serveurs* are less surly than in the City of Light. Pastas, salads, seafood and meat dishes grace the menu.

**Chez Noël** ( ☎ 0692 70 51 47; 104 Rue de Suffren; mains €9-21; ☺ lunch & dinner Mon-Sat) Occupying an atmospheric Creole house, Chez Noël earns top marks across the board for great Creole specialities and competitive prices. Choosing a wood-fired *carri* is a real cliff-hanger – should it be the *rougail saucisse* (sausage stew Creole-style) or the *cabri massalé* (goat stew)? Get both. Pizzas are also available.

**Le Cap Méchant d'Abord** ( ☎ 0262 91 71 99; Blvd Hubert-Delisle; mains €12-20; ☺ lunch & dinner Tue-Sun) Commanding an enviable location directly on the seafront, this large and lively restaurant is usually packed with Réunionnais familles at weekends. Don't let its popularity put you off. It's a good spot for Chinese specialities and Creole dishes at economical prices.

**Le Jardin Réunionnais** ( ☎ 0262 91 15 28; 9 Petit Blvd de la Plage; mains €12-22; ☺ lunch Tue, Wed & Fri-Sun, dinner Tue-Sun) A mix of Creole and *métro* flavours is at work here. Diners are treated to exemplary

dishes that will bring you back for seconds. Colourful paintings on the walls brighten the dining room, while various tropical plants shade the pleasant terrace.

**ourpick Flagrant Délice** ( ☎ 0692 87 28 03; 115 Rue François de Mahy; mains €21-25, menu €20; ☺ lunch Tue-Fri, dinner Tue-Sat) Hip Flagrant Délice is a gourmand's playpen. Be good to yourself with kangaroo fillet, salmon fillet in a vanilla sauce and luscious wines. Try to nab a seat at the 'Petit Coin Exotique' (little exotic corner), complete with cushions, by the pool.

**Le Saint-Hilaire** ( ☎ 0692 68 86 03; 1 Rue Ibrahim Vally; mains €26-30, menus €45-90; ☺ dinner Mon-Sat) This upscale restaurant west of the centre is a gastronomic delight. The menu drips with panache and is highlighted by delectable dishes such as *canard mariné aux épices et patates douces* (duck marinated with spices and sweet potatoes) – *bon appétit*!

Other flavoursome feeds:

**THC** ( ☎ 0262 59 66 94; 7 Rue Auguste Babet; mains €18-20, menus €16-20; ☺ lunch Tue-Fri, dinner Tue-Sat) Sick of stodgy *carris*? Then head here for lovable fusion fare served in a strong design-led interior.

**Le Marin Bleu** ( ☎ 0262 35 61 65; 45 Rue de L'Amiral Lacaze; mains €17-27; ☺ lunch & dinner Mon-Sat) This immutable seafood favourite in the Terre Sainte district gets the thumbs up for its choice of fish dishes.

## DRINKING & ENTERTAINMENT

Night owls, rejoice: St-Pierre has a well-established party reputation. The best buzz can be found on the seafront and in the vicinity of the town hall. Most places open from 6pm and close at around 2am or later. Most drinking spots also serve food.

**Malone's** ( ☎ 0262 25 02 22; 36 Blvd Hubert-Delisle; ☺ daily) St-Pierre's long-standing hip, hot (it gets congested) and happening spot on weekends. Swill a beer or two to imbibe the feel-good vibe before hitting the clubs.

**Café de la Gare – Latina Café** ( ☎ 0262 35 24 44; 7 Blvd Hubert-Delisle; ☺ daily) One of the most atmospheric spots for a drink (or a light meal) is the terrace of this cafe in the old train station. In the evening it transforms into a convivial bar.

**L'Africa Queen** (7 Blvd Hubert-Delisle; ☺ Fri & Sat) If there's a constant here, it's the promise that the music, whatever the style, will get you groovin'. DJs roll through salsa, hip hop, house, electro and soul but always find a way to keep the dance floor filled. Heart-start the night with a few shots at Café de la Gare, in the same building.

RÉUNION

**Jet Set Bar** ( ☎ 0262 32 83 86; www.jetset-bar.com; 32 Blvd Hubert-Delisle; ◷ daily) A chill-out bar by day, this place heats up to club temperature at night on weekends when groovy DJs take over with deep and chill house, electronica and other beats.

**Cherwaine's** ( ☎ 0262 35 69 49; 6 Rue Auguste Babet; ◷ daily) This bar is a pillar of St-Pierre's gay scene. Sets aside certain nights for entertainment offerings, including karaoke.

**Long Board Café** ( ☎ 0262 96 34 12; Petit Blvd de la Plage; ◷ daily) Spiffing setting, in a Creole house with a terrace opening onto the seafront – a great place for quaffing a sunset beverage. Offers live entertainment and karaoke on selected evenings.

**Les Sal' Gosses** ( ☎ 0262 96 70 36; 38 Blvd Hubert-Delisle; ◷ daily) Next door to DCP, this cool den hosts gigs from local bands. Good blend of jazz, soul and funk. Also has a tempting menu, tapas and billiards.

**Le Toit** ( ☎ 0262 35 32 45; 5 Rue Auguste Babet; ◷ Tue-Sat) Attracting mostly Zoreilles regulars, this hanky-sized bar is well worth a gander for its quirky decor, with an onslaught of postcards, posters and murals. Great value beers and cocktails are two more reasons to stay. Skip the food.

**O Pub à Tapas** ( ☎ 0262 34 61 94; 53 Rue du Four à Chaux; ◷ Tue-Sat) No rock 'n' roll and no R&B here – this popular venture is famed for the quality of its live-music sessions featuring *maloya* (traditional dance music of Réunion), salsa and African sounds. And yes, it serves tapas.

**Ze Boat** ( ☎ 0693 33 44 33; Harbour; ◷ 6pm-midnight) The concept of a lounge bar in a boat has reached St-Pierre. As you would expect, Ze Boat is full of attitude and atmosphere, but cocktails are reasonably priced (around €3.50).

## GETTING THERE & AWAY
### Air
Air Mauritius and Air Austral operate daily flights between **Pierrefonds Airport** ( ☎ 0262 96 77 66; www.grandsudreunion.org), 5km west of St-Pierre, and Mauritius. See p318 for more information.

Airlines with offices in St-Pierre:

**Air Austral** ( ☎ 0825 01 30 12; 14 Rue Augustin Archambaud)

**Air France** ( ☎ 0820 82 08 20; 72 Rue Luc Lorion)

**Air Mauritius** ( ☎ 0262 96 06 00; 7 Rue François de Mahy)

### Bus
Car Jaune's long-haul buses stop at the long-distance bus station beside the junction of Rue Presbytère and Rue Luc Lorion, west of town. Buses to/from St-Denis (€7) run frequently along the west coast via St-Louis and St-Gilles-les-Bains or direct via the Route des Tamarins if it's a Z'éclair service. There are also two or three services a day to St-Benoît via Plaine-des-Palmistes (€7.50) and the same number around the south coast through St-Joseph and Ste-Philippe (€7). For Cilaos, change in St-Louis.

# THE WILD SOUTH

Aaaah, the *Sud Sauvage* (Wild South), where the unhurried life is complemented by the splendid scenery of fecund volcanic slopes, occasional beaches, waves crashing on the rocky shoreline and country roads that twist like snakes into the Hauts. In both landscape and character, the south coast is where the real wilderness of Réunion begins to unfold. Once you've left St-Pierre, a gentle splendour and a sense of escapism become tangible. The change of scenery climaxes with the Grand Brûlé, where black lava fields slice through the forest and even reach the ocean at several points.

## ST-PIERRE TO ST-JOSEPH
Life – and travel – becomes more sedate as one heads west through some of the south coast's delicious scenery. With only a few exceptions urban life is left behind once the road traverses **Grand Bois** and snakes its way along the coastline.

Beach lovers should stop at **Plage de Grande Anse**, which is framed with basaltic cliffs and features a white-sand beach, a protected tide pool and picnic shelters (take the D30 that branches off the RN2 and winds down for about 2km to the beach). On weekends, the beach is often swamped with locals.

Pick up some brochures and maps at the small **tourist office** ( ☎ 0892 702 201; Plage de Grande Anse; ◷ 9am-noon & 1-5pm Mon, Wed, Thu & Sat), at the end of the parking lot.

Backtrack to the RN2 and drive east until you reach the turn-off for **Petite Île**. From Petite Île, a scenic road wobbles slowly up to some charming villages in the Hauts. Continue uphill until the junction with the

# THE SOUTH

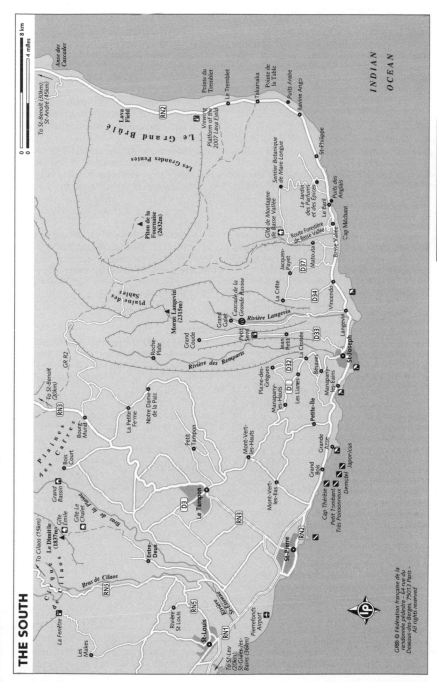

D3. If you turn left, you'll reach **Mont-Vert-les-Hauts**, approximately 5km to the west (and from then it's an easy drive downhill to the coast via Mont-Vert-les-Bas); if you turn right, you will cross **Manapany-les-Hauts** before reaching Les Lianes for St-Joseph.

Seeing the area from the saddle of a horse is a fun way to experience the visual appeal of the region, even if you're not an experienced rider. **L'Écurie du Relais** ( ☎ 0262 56 78 67, 0692 00 42 98; www.ecuriedurelais.com; 75 Chemin Léopold Lebon, Manapany-les-Hauts; ☽ by reservation Tue-Sun) has guided trips in the Hauts as well as day tours to Grande Anse. Expect to pay around €18 for an hour and €110 for a day tour. The two-hour ride (€32) takes you to rarely visited points in the Hauts with stunning views of Plaine-des-Grègues.

Back on the coastal road, head to **Manapany-les-Bains**. This charming spot lies at the mouth of an impressive ravine and boasts a protected tide pool where you can splash about.

## Sleeping & Eating

Despite some signs on the road, many places are not easy to find, but that's part of the charm. Check locations on the website (if any) or call ahead. Of course, some words in French for directions always helps.

### MONT-VERT-LES-BAS

**Chambre d'hôte La Cour Mont Vert** ( ☎ 0262 88 38 95; www.courmontvert.com; 18ter Chemin Roland Garros; d €65, dinner from €25; � ) Your heart will lift at the dreamy views over the coast; your body will rejuvenate with the Valatchy's healthy meals; your soul will find peace in the four button-cute Creole bungalows set in rural grounds awash with mangoes and lychees. Simply arrive, absorb and enjoy. Rates drop to €60 if you stay at least two nights.

**L'Araucaria** ( ☎ 0262 31 10 10; www.hostelleriearaucaria.fr; 2 Chemin de L'Araucaria; s €65-70, d €70-75; ☇ ☒ ) This small complex features three pavilions shaped like cubic Tetris pieces, which sit on a grassy patch of land. The seven rooms are bright and tidy, but don't have air-con. The real draws are the ocean vistas – straight from heaven – and the gleaming pool. There's an onsite restaurant.

### GRANDE ANSE

**Palm Hotel & Spa** ( ☎ 0262 56 30 30; www.palm.re; Grande Anse; d incl breakfast €230-650; ☒ ☇ ☒ ) If you're really looking to push the boat out in the Wild South, then to be honest there's only this four-star resort. Peacefully reposed on a promontory overlooking the cerulean ocean, it sports spacious villas and lodges that are designed with finesse but, frustratingly, not all face out towards the sea. Bask lizard-like by the turquoise pools (yes, two pools), recharge the batteries in the luxurious spa or treat yourself to a sophisticated meal at one of the two restaurants (open to nonguests by reservation).

**Les Badamiers** ( ☎ 0262 56 97 53; 22 Chemin Neuf; mains €11-12; ☽ lunch & dinner Mon-Sat) This family-run eatery in a private house spins tasty *carris* at puny prices. Wash it all down with a glass of rum (€2). It's about 100m away from the beginning of the road that descends to Grande Anse.

**Le Vacoa** ( ☎ 0262 56 95 17; 25 Route de Grande Anse; mains €12-22, menu €22; ☽ lunch & dinner Tue-Sun) Strategically positioned on the road to Plage de Grande Anse, this modest eatery offers a full menu of familiar favourites, including Creole and Chinese dishes. Bag a seat on the breezy terrace or take away and eat on the beach.

### PETITE ÎLE

**Chambre d'hôte Chez Maoul** ( ☎ 0262 56 82 26; 6 Rue du Piton; d incl breakfast €50, dinner €23; ☒ ☒ ) The four wood-clad rooms in this homely B&B nestled in a jungle-like garden have a cabin-in-the-woods feel but offer a fine sense of originality, as testified by the cute Do-Myel room: walls are bedecked with newspapers (as in old Creole houses). The upstairs rooms get more light. The tiny pool is an added bonus. Maoul is a former *maloya* musician and is known to break out in song at dinnertime. The food is great and varied, with homegrown vegetables.

**Chambre d'hôte Vérémer** ( ☎ 0262 31 65 10; www.chambre-gite-veremer.com; 40 Chemin Sylvain Vitry; d incl breakfast €50-60; ☒ ☇ ☒ ) Three cocoon-like rooms in two neat Creole buildings nestled in a well-tended tropical garden, with superlative views and a splendid pool that guests can use in the morning and in the afternoon. Aim for the Mer room, which opens onto the garden and the pool. Coming from St-Pierre, it's signposted off the main road just beyond the turning for Petite-Île. Grande Anse beach is 3.5km away. Gay-friendly.

### MANAPANY-LES-BAINS

**L'Eau Forte** ( ☎ 0262 56 32 84; www.eau-forte.fr; 137bis Blvd de L'Océan; d €40; ☒ ☇ ) Bargain! Perfect for self-caterers, this fully equipped, spick-and-span villa boasts an ace location, right above Plage de Grande Anse. If hunger beckons, Chez Jo is a coin's toss down the road. There's a two-night minimum stay. Air-con is extra (€5).

**Gandalf Safari Camp** ( ☎ 0692 40 78 39; www.gandalfsafaricamp.de; 87 Blvd de l'Océan; d incl breakfast €60; ✕ ▢ ☎) Christina and Claus, the German owners, have long lived in Africa – hence the name. Their B&B with an eco bent (it's solar heated and rainwater is recycled) features five rooms that are individually designed, but feel a tad compact due to the cubicle shower plonked in the corner. Perks include a kitchen for guests' use, a TV lounge, a jacuzzi and a relaxing garden, plus 4WD tours can be organised (€50). Good English is spoken. Air-con is extra (€5). Rates drop to €55 if you stay two nights minimum. It's a two-minute stroll from the beach.

**Restaurant Chez Jo** ( ☎ 0262 31 48 83; 143 Blvd de l'Océan; mains €7-22; ✆ lunch Thu-Tue, dinner Fri & Sat) In this buzzy eatery overlooking the tide pool in Manapany-les-Bains, you're bound to find something on the menu that takes your fancy. Treat yourself to kangaroo steak, salads or chicken with *pleurotes* (mushrooms), or just pop in for an exquisite fruit juice (from €3). Takeaway meals, too.

## ST-JOSEPH
**pop 13,000**

The Wild South's hub, modernish St-Joseph (say 'St-Jo' if you want to sound local) won't leap to the top of your list of preferred destinations in Réunion but it offers useful services, including a tourist office and banks with ATMs. While it oozes the kind of sunny languor you'd associate with the tropics, the snarled traffic and bustling shopping streets at peak hours impart the energy (and stress) of a city.

If you can, plan to be in St-Jo on a Friday morning, when the streets spill over with numerous stalls.

The **Maison du Tourisme du Sud Sauvage** ( ☎ 0262 37 37 11; www.sudsauvage.com; 3 Rue Paul Demange; ✆ 9am-5pm Mon-Sat) is near the bus station in the centre. English is spoken.

One of the best-kept secrets in the Wild South is a secluded cove with a splendid black-sand **beach**, at the entrance of St-Jo (coming from St-Pierre). Drive past the first roundabout (where the Quick lies), then take the first right (direction 'Déchèterie'). Follow the road for about 300m until you reach a skate park. Leave your car here and walk for about five minutes down a path to the shore… Enjoy!

For a bird's-eye view of St-Jo and the coast, you can walk up to **Piton Babet**, the knoll that lies between the main road and the ocean. It shouldn't take more than 10 minutes.

### Sleeping

Accommodation options are thin on the ground in St-Jo.

**La Case** ( ☎ 0262 56 07 50; www.case.fr; 2 Rue Jean Bart; d €37, studio €50; P ✕ ☎ ▣ ) If it weren't located on the main road, this laid-back venture set in a well-groomed garden of colourful vegetation would feel like a little oasis. The three rooms are fan-cooled and tread a fine line between

---

### GO SHOP!

Petite Île is a source of inspiration for many artists and artisans who sell their *objets d'art* and crafts. Their workshops are open to the public (but it's best to call them beforehand). Don't miss the opportunity to buy original, locally made souvenirs and get an insight into local traditions. Most places are signposted.

You can't go wrong if you visit the following places:

**Bam Rouge** ( ☎ 0692 57 50 89; 1 Impasse des Plumosas, Petite Île) Fabrice Payet carves bamboo and turns out small pots, pens, key rings and ashtrays.

**Dekocéan** ( ☎ 0692 04 05 25; 41 Rue Joseph Suacot, Petite Île) Next door to Chambre d'hôte Chez Maoul. Isabelle Biton specialises in porcelain painting. She paints Réunion-inspired designs (Creole *cases,* people, fruits, flowers and chameleons) on plates, cups and bowls.

**Maison de L'Abeille** ( ☎ 0262 56 95 03; 68 Chemin Laguerre, Petite Île) Not a craftshop but a bee farm, the Maison de L'Abeille sells hive natural products, including honey and gingerbread. Also has *légumes lontan* (traditional vegetables).

**Roche et Couleurs** ( ☎ 0262 98 92 55; 9 Chemin Denis Leveneur, Petite Île) Marie Thérèse Mussard focuses her work on enamel and does colourful objects.

'minimal' and sparse; toilets are shared. At the back of the compound, the five impeccably maintained studios open onto a rectangular pool. There isn't much atmosphere but it's a good base to explore the area. There's a green ethos: waste is recycled, water is solar heated and the pool uses a salt filtration system. On the eastern edge of town.

**Chambre d'hôte L'Arpège Austral** ( ☎ 0262 56 36 89, 0692 70 74 12; arpegeaustral@orange.fr; 53 Rue des Prunes, St-Joseph; d €52, bungalow €55, all incl breakfast; ☎ ) Wonderful to be so near St-Joseph (2.5km), yet in such a serene spot. Sylvie, your hostess, offers two rooms with sloping ceilings and teak furniture. For more privacy, the adjoining bungalow, sheathed with soothing ochres and decked out with a small private terrace, fits the bill. Book in for a *table d'hôte* meal (dinner €20) and you may sample a low-calorie *carri* on the shady terrace. It's on the road to Grand Coude (follow the D33).

### Eating

**Art Thé** ( ☎ 0692 83 47 68; 1 Rue Marius et Ary Leblond; mains €9-12; ☺ 10.30am-5.30pm Mon-Fri) Part tea lounge and restaurant, part art gallery, this uber-cool venture brings a refreshing dash of originality in St-Jo. And, mercifully, Marie's cuisine is low on cholesterol; here it's more easy-to-digest salads and homemade lasagne than stodgy *carri*.

**L'Ambroisie** ( ☎ 0262 31 51 99; 306 Rue Raphaël Babet; mains €10-26; ☺ lunch Tue-Sun, dinner Tue-Sat) This no-nonsense eatery on the main road has a standard selection of *carris*, *métro* staples and Chinese dishes. If the food doesn't put a smile on your face, the naive murals featuring Greek gods will. There's a takeaway counter as well.

### Getting There & Away

St-Joseph lies on Car Jaune's coastal bus route between St-Pierre and St-Benoît. In addition to the central bus station, buses stop in Petite Île, Vincendo and Manapany-les-Bains.

## AROUND ST-JOSEPH

Lose yourself in the Hauts! Starting from St-Joseph you can cherry-pick an itinerary in the hinterland that takes in drowsy hamlets where locals all know each other, green-velvet mountains cloaked in layers of wispy cloud, rolling sugar-cane fields, twisting roads and panoramas to make the heart beat faster.

Follow the picturesque D3 that cuts inland before swinging northwestwards to Manapany-Les-Hauts. You'll pass **Bésaves** and **Les Lianes**. You could also drive up to **Plaine-des-Grègues** (follow the D32, which branches off the D3 in La Croisée), the highest village of the area, which crouches in a bowl of mountains. This village is famed for its plantations of curcuma and vetiver, which are both used in perfumery. Learn more about the virtues (and fragrances) of these plants at the **Maison du Curcuma** ( ☎ 0262 37 54 66; www.maisonducurcuma .fr; 14 Chemin du Rond, Plaine-des-Grègues; admission free; ☺ 9am-noon & 1.30-5pm). It also sells delicious homemade marmalades and jams as well as locally grown spices.

### Sleeping & Eating

**Chambre d'hôte Chez Nathalie Hoareau** ( ☎ 0262 37 61 92; http://monsite.wanadoo.fr/giterunsud; 205 Rue Edmon Albius, Bésaves; d incl breakfast €45) A village address in the gently rolling Hauts de St-Joseph. There are three plain rooms at the back, but with one of the most delightful gardens you'll find in this price category. The owner, Didier

---

**GETTING AWAY FROM IT ALL: RIVIÈRE DES REMPARTS**

Grand Bassin is not enough for you? Treat yourself by checking out the Rivière des Remparts, an easily overlooked splendour immediately north of St-Joseph. This valley – one of the wildest in the south – is accessible on foot (or by 4WD). The classic **hike** is along the river, up to the hamlet of **Roche-Plate**, about 18km to the north, and on to Nez de Bœuf on the road that leads to Piton de la Fournaise. Allow about four hours to reach Roche-Plate from St-Joseph, and another four hours to Nez de Bœuf.

In Roche-Plate, you can break up your journey at the following *gîtes* (both have doubles):
**Gîte de la Rivière des Remparts** ( ☎ 0692 68 35 32; dm incl half board €38)
**Gîte Le Mahavel** ( ☎ 0692 20 76 52, 0692 76 97 23; dm incl half board €40)

Note that 4WD transfers from St-Joseph can be arranged by the *gîtes* (€150 return, up to 10 people), but we don't really encourage it – the best way to get a feel for the valley is to explore it on foot.

Hoareau, is a sugar-cane producer and grows a high-quality variety of coffee and is happy to lead guests in this Garden of Eden.

## ST-JOSEPH TO GRAND COUDE

The timeless hamlet of Grand Coude, perched on a plateau at an altitude of 1300m, boasts a marvellous setting, with the soaring Morne Langevin (2315m) as the backdrop. Here you'll be smitten by mellow tranquillity and laid-back lifestyle.

From St-Joseph, take the narrow D33, which passes through **Jean Petit** and twists its way across splendidly rugged scenery of looming peaks and deep gorges. Pull over for a picnic at **Petit Serré**, where a narrow ridge divides two valleys, the valley of the Rivière Langevin on your right and the valley of the Rivière des Remparts on your left. At one point the ridge is little wider than the road itself – you have the feeling of driving on a razor's edge!

At the end of the D33, about 15km north of St-Joseph, Grand Coude appears like a mirage. At the entrance of the village, **Le Labyrinthe En Champ Thé** ( ☎ 0692 60 18 88; Grand Coude; adult/child €5/4; ☽ 9am-5pm Sat & Sun, by reservation weekdays) is definitely worth an hour or so for anyone interested in tropical flora, with an emphasis on tea. This botanical garden is the only place in Réunion where tea is cultivated. A 50g bag costs €10.

And now, coffee. Caffeine-addicts should make a beeline for **La Maison de Laurina** ( ☎ 0692 68 78 72; 24 Chemin de la Croizure; admission €12; ☽ by reservation), whose owner grows a top-quality variety of coffee, the Bourbon Pointu. Price is a bit steep but it includes tastings of various homemade delicacies flavoured with coffee (biscuits, liquor, rum). It's in the same location as Chambre d'hôte L'Eucalyptus.

### Sleeping & Eating

**our pick** **Chambre d'hôte Au Lapin d'Or** ( ☎ 0262 56 66 48, 0692 70 09 18; rolande.sadehe@hotmail.fr; 55bis Chemin Concession, Jean Petit; s/d incl breakfast €42/50, dinner €23) Do you like rabbit? We dare ask because the owners of this pert little B&B (which translates as 'Golden Rabbit') in Jean Petit raise rabbits, meaning you'll enjoy them prepared Creole-style at dinner. Accommodation-wise, the three rooms are outfitted with cheerful pastels and glistening bathrooms. Our favourite thing about Au Lapin d'Or is the warm welcome and the genuine smiles. Don't miss

out on their homemade *rhum tisane* (aromatic rum) – incendiary (you'll see).

**Domaine de Malmany** ( ☎ 0692 20 48 49; Chemin des Géraniums, Grand Coude; dm incl half board €42) If you want to feel close to nature, this isolated mountain getaway couldn't be more perfect. Sitting on a sloping terrain and clad in wood, it feels like a hunting chalet. It's often booked by groups at weekends but the owners welcome visitors any time of the week provided you call ahead (they live in Jean Petit). Digs are in two- to eight-bed dorms, each with its own bathroom.

**Chambre d'hôte L'Eucalyptus – Chez Marie-Claude Grondin** ( ☎ 0262 56 39 48; 24 Chemin de la Croizure, Grand Coude; s/d incl breakfast €32/43, dinner €23) Absolute peace and quiet prevail at this unfussy B&B. Choose between the dinky all-wood bungalow or one of the two simple rooms in a white-and-yellow Creole building. Unwind in the generous garden, where coffee and geranium fill the air (ask for a cup of Bourbon Pointu coffee). Creole meals are served at dinner.

## ST-JOSEPH TO ST-PHILIPPE

The coastline between St-Joseph and St-Philippe is definitely alluring: a string of rocky coves and dramatic cliffs pounded by crashing waves and backed by steep hills clad with dense forests and undulating sugar-cane fields, with a few black-sand beaches thrown in for good measure.

Inland, it's no less spectacular. Abandon your map and follow the sinuous *départementales* (secondary roads) that wiggle up to the Hauts and creep through beguiling settlements, which warrant scenic drives and boast killer views over the ocean and plunging canyons.

### Rivière Langevin

About 4km east of St-Joseph, you'll reach the coastal town of **Langevin**. From the coast, the Rivière Langevin valley slithers into the mountains. A narrow road follows the wide stony bed of the river and leads to **Cascade de la Grande Ravine**, an impressive waterfall about 9km from the junction with the coastal road. If you need to cool off, there are plenty of natural pools along the river where you can dunk yourself. Our favourites include Trou Noir (it's signposted) and a pool that lies about 200m before the Cascade de la Grande Ravine (you can't miss it). Come prepared:

this valley is extremely popular with picnicking families on Sunday.

If you haven't brought a picnic, there's a bevy of cheap and cheerful eateries along the river at the entrance of the valley. They're pretty much of a muchness and serve up Creole classics, which you can eat inside or take away.

Recommended options:

**Le Benjoin** ( ☎ 0262 56 23 90; Route de la Passerelle; mains €6-12; 🕙 lunch Tue-Sun) Famed for its *thé dansant* (tea dance) on Wednesday and Sunday (from 9am) – a great way to immerse in local culture.

**Les Pieds dans L'Eau** ( ☎ 0262 37 13 64; Route de la Passerelle; mains €6-12; 🕙 lunch Tue-Sun) Cheap Creole staples.

## Vincendo & Les Hauts

In Vincendo, few visitors get wind of the black-sand **beach** fringed by *vacoa* trees a few kilometres south of the RN2. There are some dangerous currents at certain times of the year, so ask around before diving in.

Back in the village, follow the D34 that goes uphill to the north and takes you to the hamlet of **La Crête**. From there, the D37 leads due east to another peaceful settlement, **Jacques-Payet**, before zigzagging downhill until the junction with the coastal road.

### SLEEPING & EATING

**ourpick** **Rougail Mangue** ( ☎ 0262 31 55 09; www.rougailmangue.com; 12 Rue Marcel Pagnol, Vincendo; dm/s/d/tr/q €16/33/43/53/64; 🛜 🖳 ) You'd never guess it from the road but this unfussy abode is as welcoming as an old friend's hug thanks to its Italian owner, Cosimo. The ground floor is occupied by a smart communal room, one eight-bed dorm, two squeaky-clean quads and a cheery double opening onto a well-tended garden. They all come with their own bathroom. The *coup de grâce* is the glorious pool, with the ocean as a backdrop (look at the picture on the website – no Photoshopping). Breakfast is extra (from €5) and can be enjoyed alfresco under a gazebo. There's also a kitchen. It's on the main road, between Langevin and Vincendo.

**Gîte La Table des Randonneurs** ( ☎ 0692 61 73 47; 17 Chemin des Barbadines, Jacques-Payet; dm/d incl breakfast €20/40, dinner €22) Way up in the hills, 'The Hikers' Table' is a safe bet, with two doubles, one quad and one six-bed room. They're in no danger of appearing in *House Beautiful*, but everything is in immaculate shape and

functional. The menu features local delicacies like smoked duck with *vacoa*. It's about 7km northeast of Vincendo (follow the D37).

**Ferme-Auberge Desprairies** ( ☎ 0262 37 20 27; www.ferme-auberge-desprairies.com; 44 Route de Matouta, Matouta; d incl breakfast €35, dinner €20) One of the best things about this inoffensive inn is the road to it, which travels through sugar-cane fields despite being only a couple of kilometres from the coast. There are signs of wear and tear in the six rooms but they're kept tidy and in this location for this price, you won't hear anyone complaining. Follow the D37 to the east to get here.

**La Médina du Sud** ( ☎ 0262 37 32 51; www.lamedina-loc.com; 23 Chemin de la Marine, Vincendo; d €45-65; 🞰 🖳 ) There's nothing Moorish in this modern building by the turn-off for the beach, except the owner's origins. The six flats are characterless but fully equipped, well proportioned and perfectly serviceable, with the added bonus of a pool.

**Le Tagine** ( ☎ 0262 37 32 51; 23 Chemin de la Marine, Vincendo; mains €12-21; 🕙 lunch daily, dinner Thu-Sat) Next door to La Médina du Sud (same owner), Le Tagine is a good place to give your tastebuds something new to sing about, with toothsome Moroccan couscous and tajines. Traditional Creole dishes and salads also feature on the menu.

## Basse-Vallée & Cap Méchant

And now, Basse-Vallée. The area is known for its production of baskets, bags (called *bertels*), hats and other items from *vacoa* fronds. You can see them being made and learn more about this versatile palm at **Maison d'Artisanat Local – Association Vacoa Sud** ( ☎ 0262 37 16 96; RN2; 🕙 9am-5pm). Then head to **Cap Méchant**, one of the eeriest landscapes in the Wild South, with huge lava fields, windswept black cliffs, rows of *vacoa* trees and the mandatory picnic shelters. There's an excellent coastal path along the sea cliffs (bring sturdy shoes).

### SLEEPING & EATING

The following places to stay are all along the Route Forestière de Basse Vallée.

**Gîte de Montagne de Basse Vallée** ( ☎ 0262 37 36 25; Route Forestière, Basse-Vallée; dm €16, dinner €17) This simple *gîte de montagne* is about 8km above the village of Basse Vallée, along the Route Forestière de Basse Vallée. Bookings must be made through the Centrale de Réservation – Île de la Réunion (p177) or any tourist office on the island, but if you turn up without a reservation and there's space, the caretaker will probably let you in.

**OUR PICK** **Gîte de Théophane** ( ☎ 0262 37 13 14, 0692 18 86 84, 0692 87 25 43; Route Forestière, Basse-Vallée; dm incl half board €40, dinner €20) This rural paradise, lost in the middle of the forest, is accessible on foot (about 20 minutes) via a scenic *sentier forestier* (forest dirt track) or by 4WD only from the Route Forestière (signed at the junction, about 5.5km above the village of Basse-Vallée). Digs are in six-bed dorms, each with its own bathroom. At dinner the owners will treat you with the freshest island ingredients. It can't get more Wild South than this.

**Ferme-Auberge Le Rond de Basse Vallée** ( ☎ 0692 85 40 37, 0692 69 65 51; Route Forestière, Basse-Vallée; d incl breakfast €40, dinner €22) Another great place to commune with nature, further up the Route Forestière. There are four rooms with virginal-white walls and spick-and-span bathrooms in a Creole-style building in harmony with the environment. The restaurant is across the road and features regional dishes with authentic flavours, including – you guessed it – *vacoa*.

On the seafront in Cap Méchant, locals disagree about which outpost does the best *carris*, chop sueys and *porc au palmiste* (pork with palm hearts) – you'll just have to try them all for yourself. They are mobbed at weekends but almost deserted on weekdays:

**Le Cap Méchant** ( ☎ 0692 85 39 28; Cap Méchant; mains €10-16; ☯ lunch Tue-Sun)

**L'Étoile de Mer** ( ☎ 0262 37 04 60; mains €10-17; Cap Méchant; ☯ lunch)

**Le Pinpin** ( ☎ 0262 37 04 19; Cap Méchant; mains €12-17; ☯ lunch Thu-Tue)

## Le Baril

Le Baril is the last settlement before St-Philippe. The main attraction here is the **Puits des Anglais** (the Wells of the British), a splendid saltwater pool that has been constructed into the basaltic rock. It's mobbed at weekends but you'll have the whole place to yourself during the week.

### SLEEPING & EATING

**Chambre d'hôte Le Pinpin d'Amour** ( ☎ 0262 37 14 86; www.pinpindamour.com; 56 Chemin Paul Hoareau, Le Baril; d €55, dinner €27; ☐ ) Spending a night at this original *chambre d'hôte* makes a good story to tell the folks back home. Your hosts have a passion for *vacoa* and pinpin (the palm's

edible artichoke-like fruit), meaning you'll be guaranteed to taste them at dinner (and sometimes at breakfast), prepared in all their forms. Accommodation-wise, the five appealing, if a bit itty-bitty, rooms sport pastel-coloured walls and honey-boarded floors. It's amid the sugar-cane fields above Le Baril, about 2km from the coastal road. Alas, no sea views from the rooms. There's a 10% discount for stays of two nights and more.

**Hôtel-Restaurant Le Baril** ( ☎ 0262 37 01 04; www.anthurium.com; RN2, Le Baril; d €55-60; ☯ ) It's a shame. This hotel boasts a sensational location, right above the rocky shoreline, but it's in dire need of an overhaul and, as it is, can't be recommended. There are plans to renovate it extensively – check while you're there.

**OUR PICK** **Table Paysanne Chez Fiarda** ( ☎ 0692 69 03 48; 21 Chemin Ceinture, Le Baril; menu €25; ☯ lunch by reservation Tue-Sun) Plenty of smiles from the owners, recipes plucked straight out of grandma's cookbook, a serene setting in the Hauts and lovely views from the terrace – if you're after an authentic Creole experience, this place is hard to beat. 'Here we can eat local specialities that are hard to find elsewhere, such as chicken with palm hearts', says an aficionado. It's signposted from the main road.

## ST-PHILIPPE
### pop 5000

Vegetarians will reach Shangri-la in St-Philippe, the self-proclaimed capital of *vacoa*. No joke – no less than 5000 visitors turn up to join St-Philippois townsfolk for the 10-day Fête du Vacoa in August.

The only town of consequence in the Wild South (along with St-Joseph), St-Philippe has a wonderfully down-to-earth, unfussy ambience. Although this friendly little town is devoid of overwhelming sights, it has a slew of (good) surprises up its sleeves and is optimally placed for explorations of the coast and forays into the Hauts. Oh, and St-Philippe lies in the shadow of Piton de la Fournaise.

### Sights

Inland between Le Baril and St-Philippe, don't miss the 3-hectare garden, **Le Jardin des Parfums et des Épices** ( ☎ 0262 37 06 36; adult/child €6.10/3.05; ☯ tours 10.30am & 2.30pm). It contains over 1500 species in a natural setting in the Mare Longue forest, 3km west of St-Philippe. Knowledgeable and enthusiastic guides present the island's history, economy and

**RÉUNION**

culture through the plants; tours are in French. Continue a few kilometres further up to the **Sentier Botanique de Mare Longue**. This pristine forest has an end-of-the-world feeling that will appeal to those in search of hush. From the car park you can tackle one of the three interpretative trails in the primary forest.

The small **Eco-Musée de St-Philippe – Au Bon Roi Louis** ( ☎ 0262 37 16 43; adult/child €5/2; ☺ 9am-noon & 2-4.30pm Mon-Sat), a few doors down from St-Philippe's town hall, makes for a perfect introduction to the area's history and culture. The little Creole house is stuffed with an eclectic assortment of antiques and agricultural equipment.

With its handful of colourful fishing boats, the teensy **fishing harbour** is also worth a peek.

## Sleeping & Eating

**Chambre d'hôte Le Palmier** ( ☎ 0262 37 04 11, 0692 02 85 71; nicole_97442@yahoo.fr; 8 Rue de la Pompe; d incl breakfast €50; ☺ ⓦ ) Lacking excitement, maybe, but this friendly B&B down a little lane at the east end of St-Philippe is a safe bet. Rooms are neat, with immaculate tiles, prim bathrooms and colourful bedspreads for a dash of panache. Avoid the larger one at the back, which has obstructed views. Guests can use the pool in front of the owners' house if they stay at least two nights – a good incentive, indeed.

**Chambre d'hôte Au Domaine du Vacoa** ( ☎ 0262 37 03 12, 0692 64 89 89; marieanna.bigot@mediaserv.net; 12 Chemin Vacoa; d incl breakfast €55, dinner from €23) This B&B set in a pert little *case créole* features two spacious rooms enhanced with splashes of colour, back-friendly mattresses, crisply dressed beds and spotless bathrooms. And sea views. At dinner warm your insides with duck, *vacoa* and other vegetables from the garden – all organic, of course.

**La Bicyclette Gourmande** ( ☎ 0262 31 94 63; 43 Rue Leconte de Lisle; mains €8-16; ☺ lunch Thu-Tue, dinner Fri & Sat) It's hardly haute cuisine at the 'Greedy Bicycle' but the fine choice of salads and pizzas alongside the mainstream Creole dishes ensure an easy midday fuel. It's opposite the Ecomusée de St-Philippe.

**Marmite du Pêcheur** ( ☎ 0262 37 01 01; 18A Ravine Ango; mains €12-37, menu €17; ☺ lunch Thu-Tue) Stuffed to the gills with *vacoa*? Can't stomach one more morsel of *carri poulet*? Then opt for this eatery where cuisine is predominantly fishy – crab, shrimps, fish, and mussels, climaxing with a gargantuan *marmite du pêcheur* (€30), a kind of seafood stew. Downside: the din-

ing room doesn't register even a blip on the charm radar. It's just off the main road, east of St-Philippe.

## LE GRAND BRÛLÉ

The crowning glory of the Wild South, the arid, eerie landscape of Le Grand Brûlé is a 6km-wide volcanic plain formed by the main lava flow from the volcano. This is where the action goes when the volcano is erupting. The steep slopes above, known as Les Grandes Pentes, have funnelled lava down to the coast for thousands of years.

Leaving St-Philippe to the east, you'll first come across **Puits Arabe** (Wells of the Arabs), a manmade hole in the basaltic rock. It's a popular picnic site, with shelters scattered amid rows of vacoa trees.

In 1986, the lava unusually flowed south of Le Grand Brûlé to reach the sea at **Pointe de la Table**, a few hundred metres north of Puits Arabe. Part of the magmatic flow also reached **Pointe du Tremblet**, to the north. This eruption added over 30 hectares to the island's area, and more than 450 people had to be evacuated and several homes were lost. An interpretative trail has been set up at Pointe de la Table and makes for a lovely hike on the basaltic cliffs pounded by the ocean. Previous lava flows have been colonised by various kinds of plants, including ferns and shrubs.

In April 2007, in one of the most violent eruptions ever recorded, another impressive lava flow was formed, about 2km north of Pointe du Tremblet. The road was cut off for several months. It's a primal experience to drive through the barren moonscape that is this huge expanse of solidified, pure black lava field. Three years after the eruption, some patches were still warm and belched off steam when it rained. It's forbidden to walk across the lava flow, but a **viewing platform** has been built just off the RN2.

### Eating

A number of so-called 'restaurants' (in fact, private homes turned into casual eateries) have recently sprung up along the RN2 between St-Philippe and Le Grand Brûlé, but they're nothing to sing praise about. The only place that we recommend is **Le Vieux Port** ( ☎ 0692 15 79 31, 0692 59 09 23; RN2, Le Tremblet; mains €10-20; ☺ lunch), a fine specimen of a restaurant, ideally situated in a tropical garden about 500m south of the 2007 lava flow. It is strictly local cuisine – albeit of a refreshingly creative nature. Locals rave about the *rôti de porc palmiste* (pork with palm heart) – so tender! – and the delicious palm-heart salad. It also features a repertoire of fish dishes that you won't find elsewhere, such as *maccabit* (a kind of grouper). Reservations are advised on weekends. It also does takeaway.

# THE EAST

The east coast is everything the west coast is not: low-key, unpretentious and luxuriant (yes, it *does* get much more rain). While this coast lacks the beaches of the west, the region makes up for it with spectacular waterfalls, lush tropical vegetation and fantastic picnic spots. The main produce of the area is sugar cane, but the region is also known for its vanilla plantations and fruit orchards, including lychees.

This coastal stretch is also considered to be 'other', partially as it's the bastion of Tamil culture in Réunion. Here you'll find a distinctive atmosphere, with numerous temples and colourful religious festivals. For visitors it's an opportunity to discover a Réunion you never imagined.

Tourism in this area remains on a humble scale, with no star attractions. However, it's worth taking a few days to explore the quiet recesses of this less-visited part of the island where you can experience Réunion from a different perspective.

## STE-SUZANNE & AROUND
pop 20,000

The seaside town of Ste-Suzanne is usually glimpsed in passing by most tourists on the route down the coast, which is a shame because there are charming pockets in the area that beg discovery, including the splendid Rivière Ste-Suzanne, which is both a playground for outdoorsy types and a hot spot for sunbathers and picnickers.

## Information

**Tourist office** ( ☎ 0262 52 13 54; www.ot-nordreunion .com; Rue du Phare; ☿ 9am-noon & 2-5pm). Beside the lighthouse. *Gîtes de montagnes* can be booked here.

## Sights & Activities

Next to the tourist office, the small **lighthouse** (1845) – the only one on the island – is worth a gander. It's no longer in operation. Notable

### TOP FIVE PICNIC SPOTS

- **The beach at L'Hermitage-les-Bains** (p189) – fun and casual
- **Belvédère de l'Eden** (p236) – our favourite (shh…)
- **Anse des Cascades** (p241) – in a lovely coconut grove
- **Le Maïdo** (p186) – fresh air galore
- **Rivière Langevin** (p229) – wildly popular at weekends

religious buildings include the **Chapelle Front de Mer**, an ornate Tamil temple built on a pebbly beach north of town (it's unsigned).

Garden fans and architecture buffs will especially enjoy a visit to the classic **Domaine du Grand Hazier** ( ☎ 0262 52 32 81; tours €5; ☿ daily by reservation), a superb 18th-century sugarplanter's residence 3km southwest of Ste-Suzanne. It's an official French historical monument with a 2-hectare garden planted with a variety of tropical flowers and fruit trees. On the same property you'll also find **La Vanilleraie** ( ☎ 0262 23 07 26; www.lavanilleraie .com; tours €5; ☿ 9am-noon & 2-5pm Mon-Sat), where you can see vanilla preparation and drying processes and also purchase vanilla pods. The manager speaks English.

If you need to cool off, the **Bassin Boeuf waterfall** beckons. From Ste-Suzanne, follow the D51 in the direction of Bagatelle for about 7km until you see the signpost 'Bassin Boeuf'. Leave your car at the small parking area and walk for a few minutes down a dirt road to the Rivière Ste-Suzanne. It presents a series of enticing natural pools fringed with stone slabs, ideal for picnicking and sunbathing. To get to the waterfall, cross the river and follow the path on the right for about five minutes.

Just beyond the church towards the southern end of town is a road signposted inland to **Cascade Niagara**, a 30m waterfall which is also on the Rivière Ste-Suzanne. At the end of the road, about 2km further on, you wind up at the waterfall. On weekends it's a popular picnic site. If you want to see the waterfall from a different perspective, contact **Niagara Vertical** ( ☎ 0692 48 55 54; www.niagara-vertical.net; adult/couple €20/30; ☿ 9am-3pm Wed, Sat & Sun school term, daily school holidays), which has set up three **Via Ferrata** circuits of varying degrees of

RÉUNION

difficulty. Canyoning outings can also be arranged through **Alpanes** ( ☎ 0692 777 530; www.alpanes.com; from €45; ☑ by reservation).

In the Quartier-Français district, **Cascade Délices** is another easily accessed waterfall. It's only 4m high, but the jungle-like setting will appeal to nature lovers, and you can dunk yourself in the cool water.

## Sleeping & Eating

**Le Pharest** ( ☎ 0262 98 91 10; www.pharest-reunion .com; 22 Rue Blanchet; s €29-56, d €42-79, all incl breakfast; ☒ ☎ ☒ ) We're suckers for the relaxing atmosphere that prevails in this oasis of calm, near the lighthouse. The four wooden bungalows are kept in good nick and are set in a well-tended tropical garden. Added pluses

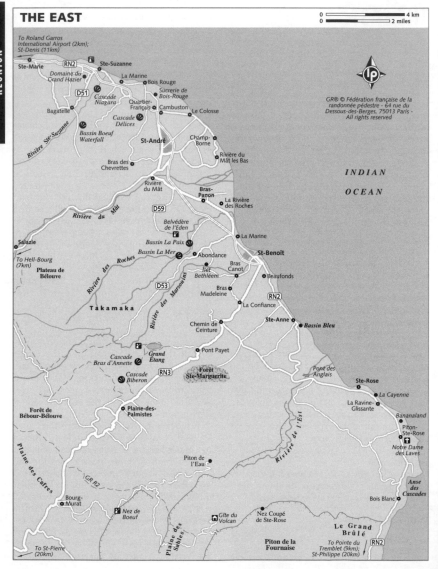

**THE EAST**

0 — 4 km
0 — 2 miles

To Roland Garros International Airport (2km); St-Denis (11km)

Ste-Marie

RN2   Ste-Suzanne

Domaine du Grand Hazier

La Marine

D51   Bois Rouge

Cascade Niagara   Sucrerie de Bois-Rouge

Bagatelle   Quartier-Français   Cambuston   Le Colosse

Cascade Délices

Bassin Boeuf Waterfall   **St-André**

Champ-Borne

Rivière Ste-Suzanne

Bras des Chevrettes

Rivière du Mât les Bas

Rivière du Mât

Bras-Panon

La Rivière des Roches

D59

**INDIAN**

**OCEAN**

GR® © Fédération française de la randonnée pédestre - 64 rue du Dessous-des-Berges, 75013 Paris - All rights reserved

Belvédère de l'Eden

Salazie

Bassin La Paix

La Marine

To Hell-Bourg (7km)

Bassin La Mer   Abondance   **St-Benoît**

**Plateau de Bélouve**

Rivière des Roches

Bras Canot

Îlet Bethléem   Beaufonds

D53

Bras Madeleine

**Takamaka**   Rivière des Marsouins

La Confiance   RN2

Chemin de Ceinture   Ste-Anne   Bassin Bleu

Cascade Bras d'Annette   Grand Étang   Pont Payet

Pont des Anglais

Cascade Biberon   RN3   Forêt Ste-Marguerite   Ste-Rose

**Forêt de Bébour-Bélouve**   **Plaine-des-Palmistes**   La Cayenne

La Ravine-Glissante   Bananaland

Rivière de l'Est   Piton-Ste-Rose

Notre Dame des Laves

Piton de l'Eau

Plaine des Cafres   GR R2

Anse des Cascades

Bourg-Murat   Bois Blanc

Nez de Boeuf   Gîte du Volcan   Nez Coupé de Ste-Rose

To St-Pierre (20km)   Plaine des Sables   **Le Grand Brûlé**

Piton de la Fournaise   To Pointe du Tremblet (9km); St-Philippe (20km)   RN2

**RÉUNION**

include a swimming pool and a restaurant. The kitchen features salads made with local produce and locally caught fish. Air-con is extra (€4).

**Chambre d'hôte La Cuisine de Clemencia** ( ☎ 0262 47 52 78, 0692 80 01 47; 18 Chemin des Galets, Bras Pistolet; d incl breakfast €45, dinner €25) This B&B is a winner, not least for the marvellous sense of peacefulness that wraps the property, in a secluded hamlet up in the Hauts. The standalone bungalow feels like a cosy doll's house and proffers ample coastal views. At the end of the day, make sure you treat yourself to a copious *table d'hôtes*; the delicious Creole specialities are made using local produce. From Quartier-Français, take the D46 in the direction of Deux Rives, then follow *Route des Hauts, Église du Père Laval.*

**Les Berges du Bocage** ( ☎ 0692 55 61 50; 1 Chemin du Bocage; lunch buffet €11; ⊗ lunch Mon-Sat) The lunch buffet, with five different Creole and Chinese dishes, is brilliant value, and the location, in a verdant property by the river, is ace. It's at the southern end of town.

## Getting There & Away
Ste-Suzanne is served by Car Jaune bus routes F and G running between St-Denis and St-Benoît.

## ST-ANDRÉ & AROUND
pop 44,000

St-André is the anti-St-Gilles. While St-Gilles (and the northwestern coast) is appropriately dubbed 'Zoreille-Land', St-André is the epicentre of Tamil culture in Réunion, and you'll see more women draped in vividly coloured saris than Zoreilles wearing designer glasses and trendy shirts. Busy streets transport you to a city somewhere in India with curry houses, sari shops and bric-a-brac traders. You'll definitely feel closer to Bombay than Paris.

The mainly Tamil population in the area is descended from indentured labourers who were brought from India to work in the sugarcane fields and factories after slavery was abolished in 1848.

## Orientation & Information
St-André is very spread out – it's best to get around by car.

You'll find banks with ATMs in the centre. The **Office Municipal du Tourisme de St-André** ( ☎ 0262 46 91 63; Maison Martin Valliamé, 1590 Chemin du Centre; ⊗ 9am-5pm Mon-Sat) is housed in Maison Valliamé.

## Sights
St André's Indian atmosphere is most apparent in the Hindu temples dotted around the town. The most imposing are the **Temple of Colosse** (Chemin Champ-Borne) and **Temple du Petit Bazar** (Ave de l'Île de France). It's not possible to visit the interior, but guided tours can be arranged; contact the tourist office.

Also worth a look is **Maison Martin Valliamé** (1590 Chemin du Centre; ⊗ 9am-5pm Mon-Sat), a handsome colonial villa dating from 1925, northeast of the centre. Guided tours in French (€3) are available from 10am to 4pm on the hour.

If you're after Réunion's Vanille Bourbon, head to **Plantation de Vanille Roulof** ( ☎ 0262 46 01 15; www.lavanilledelareunion.com; 470 Rue des Chanets; guided tours €5; ⊗ 9am-5pm Mon-Sat), a small family-run operation where you can buy vanilla pods at reasonable prices (€10 for 25g). You can also find out about the technique of 'marrying' the vanilla, a delicate operation in which the flowers are fertilised by hand.

The **Sucrerie de Bois-Rouge** ( ☎ 0262 58 59 74; www.bois-rouge.fr; 2 Chemin du Bois Rouge; guided tour adult/child €8/4, distillery €3.50/1.75; ⊗ by reservation Mon-Sat) is on the coast 3km north of St-André. During the cane harvest (July to December) visitors are shown around the huge, high-tech plant, following the process from the delivery of the cut cane to the final glittering crystals. The two-hour tour includes the neighbouring distillery, where the by-products (cane juice and molasses) are made into rum. From January to June, you can only visit the distillery. Children under seven years aren't allowed into the refinery. English-language tours are available. There's a shop, **Tafia et Galabé** (www.distillerie savanna.com; ⊗ 9.15am-12.30pm & 2.30-6pm Mon-Sat), where you can sip (and buy) the good stuff.

## Sleeping
**Chambre d'hôte Véronique Savriama** ( ☎ 0262 46 69 84; auberge-savriama@wanadoo.fr; 1084 Chemin Quatre-Vingt; s/d incl breakfast €38/41, dinner €18-20; ❄ ) This place is efficiently run but the four upstairs rooms are a tad sombre and smallish but come with air-con and have their own entrance. Best asset is the tasty *table d'hôtes* meals, with an Indian emphasis. Pity about the very ordinary dining room, though. It's in the district of Rivière du Mât les Bas on the coast southeast of St-André.

RÉUNION

RÉUNION

---

## LITTLE INDIA

If you happen to be around Ste-Suzanne and St-André at certain periods of the year, you'll discover a very exotic side of the island, with lots of colourful festivals organised by the Tamil community. If you're about, be sure to join in the heady hype of these local festivals. In January, don't miss **Tamil fire-walking** ceremonies, when participants enter a meditative state and then walk over red-hot embers as a sign of devotion to various deities. Thousands of goats are slaughtered as offerings and are distributed among the participants. Another must-see is the **Cavadee** festival, which usually takes place in January or February. In October or November, make a beeline for **Divali** (aka Dipavali), the Festival of Light. Dancers and decorated floats parade through the town centre. Visitors are welcome. Contact the tourist office in St-André for specific dates.

---

**Chambre d'hôte L'Auberge du Désert – Chez Éric Bédier** ( ☎ 0262 46 64 43; Bras-des-Chevrettes; d incl breakfast €40, dinner €20) Find this secluded B&B about 2.5km from the town centre (it's signposted). Featuring five tidy rooms (no air-con) in an imposing building ensnared in a tropical garden, its standout feature is the large pool at the back – bliss after a long day's driving.

**Le Domaine des Oiseaux** ( ☎ 0262 92 50 22, 0692 52 25 20; 300 Chemin Grand Canal, Champ-Borne; d incl breakfast €65, dinner €20; ✗ ▨ ) In this immaculate B&B occupying a massive villa not far from the seafront, the nine rooms exemplify functional simplicity with no knick-knacks to clutter things up, just painted walls as well as back-friendly beds. Some rooms offer glimpses of the sea. You can expect a warm welcome from the Agenors, who are *bons viveurs* (fun loving).

### Eating

**Ti Fred** ( ☎ 0692 62 57 76; 561 Chemin Colosse; mains €5-10; ✗ lunch & dinner Mon-Sat) No culinary acrobatics in this few-frills haunt near the Temple du Colosse, just keep-the-faith Creole staples and pizzas at puny prices. Eat in or take away.

**Le Sri Lankai** ( ☎ 0692 85 83 06; 1431 Ave de l'Île de France; mains €6-9; ✗ lunch & dinner Mon-Sat) This modest eatery whips out South Indian dishes and a few vegetarian options at prices that

won't make you flinch. It's across the road from the Temple du Petit Bazar.

**Le Beau Rivage** ( ☎ 0262 46 08 66; Chemin Champ-Borne; mains €10-40; ✗ lunch Tue-Sun, dinner Tue, Wed & Thu-Sat) True to its name ('the beautiful shore'), Le Beau Rivage boasts a fantastic location – it's on the seafront, beside the church ruins in Champ-Borne (ask for a table near the windows). The cuisine is predominantly Chinese.

### Getting There & Away

Buses from St-Denis to St-Benoît pass through St-André. If you're travelling to Salazie by bus, you will have to change here; there are seven buses daily in each direction (three on Sunday). From Salazie there are connections to Hell-Bourg.

## BRAS-PANON
pop 9800

Bras-Panon is Réunion's vanilla capital, and most visitors come here to see (and smell!) the fragrant vanilla-processing plant. The town is also associated with a rare sprat-like delicacy known as *bichiques*. In early summer (around November or December) these are caught at the mouth of the Rivière des Roches as they swim upriver to spawn.

### Sights

The **Coopérative de Vanille** ( ☎ 0262 51 70 12; 21 RN2; admission €5; ✗ 9am-noon & 2-5pm Mon-Sat), a working vanilla-processing plant, offers an introduction to the process of producing Réunion's famous Vanille Bourbon via a 45-minute guided tour and a film on the history of vanilla cultivation. You'll find various vanilla products at the factory shop. It's worth a visit just for the dreamy smell.

A fabulous place to chill out is the aptly named **Belvédère de l'Eden**, in upcountry Bras-Panon. From Bras-Panon, take the road to St-André, then turn left onto the D59 (in the direction of Vincendo, Bellevue) for about 9km (follow the signs) until you reach a car park. From there, follow the meandering trail signed L'Eden. After about 20 minutes, you'll discover a wonderfully secluded picnic spot locals wish you didn't. The views of the coast are incomparable.

Another blissful site is **Bassin La Paix**, in the Rivière des Roches valley, about 2.5km west from Bras-Panon (it's signposted). From the car park, a path quickly leads to a majestic waterfall tumbling into a large rock pool.

Swimming is forbidden, but it's an ideal picnic spot. For a more off-the beaten track experience, you can continue upstream to **Bassin La Mer**, another cascading delight that can be reached on foot only. The start of the trail is signposted from the car park, and it's an enjoyable (though exposed and hot) 40-minute walk. Reward yourself with a dip in the swimming holes at the bottom of the fall.

Car Jaune buses (lines F and G) stop outside the vanilla cooperative en route between St-André and St-Benoît.

### Sleeping & Eating

**ourpick** **Ferme-Auberge Chez Éva Annibal** ( ☎ 0262 51 53 76; Chemin Rivière du Mât; s/d with shared bathroom incl breakfast €20/35, dinner €23) Pack a hearty thirst and giant-sized appetite before venturing into this plain but feisty inn. The Full Monty feast comprises rum, *gratin de légumes* (baked vegetables), fish curry, duck with vanilla, and cakes, all clearly emblazoned with a Creole Mama stamp of approval. There are also three functional but clean rooms with sloping ceilings and communal facilities upstairs.

**Chambre d'hôte La Passiflore** ( ☎ 0262 51 74 68; www.lapassiflore.re; 3 Rue des Baies-Roses; d incl breakfast €48, dinner €28; 🅿 🛜 🐾 ) Run by a well-travelled *métro* couple, this B&B stands in a haven of tropical peace in a side street near the Coopérative. The three clinically clean rooms are embellished with a few exotic bits and bobs. Float in the scintillating pool or bask in the sunny garden. Air-con is extra (€5).

**Le Vani-La** ( ☎ 0262 51 56 58; 21 RN2; mains €10-18; 🅈 lunch Mon-Fri) Vanilla is king of the castle in this little restaurant right beside the Coopérative de Vanille. It turns up in both savoury and sweet dishes, including a wicked *crème brûlée à la vanille* (cream pie with a caramelised topping and flavoured with vanilla).

**Le Bec Fin** ( ☎ 0262 51 52 24; 66 RN2; mains €10-28; menu €13-18; 🅈 lunch daily, dinner Fri & Sat) Tickle your taste buds with a slurp of *planteur* (aromatic rum), then continue your indulgence with a feisty portion of *sarcives* (a variety of sausage) or *poisson sauce piquante* (fish in piquant sauce). On weekdays it lays on an excellent buffet lunch for just €13.

## ST-BENOÎT & AROUND
**pop 31,500**

Sugar-cane fields, lychee and mango orchards, rice, spices, coffee… Great carpets of deep-green felt seem to have been draped over the lower hills that surround St-Benoît, a major agricultural and fishing centre.

Bar a few impressive religious buildings – a mosque, a church and a Tamil temple on the outskirts of town – no one can accuse St-Benoît of being overburdened with tourist sights. The area's best features lie elsewhere; turn your attention from the coast and plant it firmly in the cooler recesses of the hills and valleys to the west. The Rivière des Marsouins valley in particular is a delight, with its plunging waterfalls and luxuriant vegetation. Small wonder that there is excellent white-water rafting here.

### Sights & Activities
#### FORÊT STE-MARGUERITE

For a complete change of pace and atmosphere, consider spending some time in the protected 159-hectare **Forêt Ste-Marguerite** ( 🅈 9am-4pm Tue-Sun), way up in the hills. Fans of flora will get their kicks here; there are over 150 indigenous species of plants. A network of easy walking trails snakes through the quiet forest.

Take the RN3 in the direction of Plaines-des-Palmistes until you reach a roundabout at Chemin Ceinture; Forêt Ste-Marguerite is signed on the left.

#### ÎLET BETHLÉEM

Very few visitors have heard about Îlet Bethléem, a magical spot by the Rivière des Marsouins that locals would like to keep for themselves. Reached after a 15-minute walk from the car park, it features an old chapel (1858) – still a pilgrimage site – and a smattering of picnic shelters amid lush vegetation. It's also an excellent swimming spot, with lots of natural rock pools. Unfortunately, the area was sprinkled with rubbish the day we visited. Follow the D53 in the direction of Takamaka, then turn left after about 1km (it's signposted).

#### TAKAMAKA

North of St-Benoît the D53 strikes southwest, following the Rivière des Marsouins 15km upstream to end beside the **Takamaka viewpoint**. Be prepared to fall on your knees in awe: despite a small power plant near the viewpoint, the overwhelming impression is of a wild, virtually untouched valley, its vertical walls cloaked with impenetrable forests. Here and there the dense green is broken by a silver ribbon of cascading water.

RÉUNION

RÉUNION

---

**VANILLA UNVEILED**

The vanilla orchid was introduced into Réunion from Mexico around 1820, but early attempts at cultivation failed because of the absence of the Mexican bee that pollinates the flower and triggers the development of the vanilla pod. Fortunately for custard lovers everywhere, a method of hand-pollination was discovered in Réunion in 1841 by a 12-year-old slave, Edmond Albius. Vanilla was highly prized in Europe at the time and Albius' discovery ushered in an economic boom, at least for the French 'vanilla barons'.

The vanilla bubble burst, however, when synthetic vanilla – made from coal – was invented in the late 19th century. Réunion's vanilla industry was almost wiped out, but in recent years the growing demand for natural products has led to something of a revival. You'll now find vanilla 'plantations' hidden in the forests from Ste-Suzanne south to St-Philippe.

The majority of Réunion's crop is exported (Coca-Cola is the world's single biggest buyer), but vanilla is still a firm favourite in local cuisine. It crops up in all sorts of delicacies, from cakes and pastries to coffee, liqueurs, even vanilla duck and chicken. Best of all is the sublime flavour of a vanilla-steeped *rhum arrangé* (a mixture of rum, fruit juice, cane syrup and a blend of herbs and berries).

---

## GRAND ÉTANG

Around 12km southwest of St-Benoît along the road towards Plaine-des-Palmistes, is the 3km road to Grand Étang (Big Pond). This pretty picnic spot lies at the bottom of an almost vertical ridge separating it from the Rivière des Marsouins valley. Most people simply walk around the lake, following a well-defined path. It's muddy in places, but shouldn't take more than three hours from the car park, including a side trip to an impressive **waterfall**.

Horse riding is another low-impact way to soak up the drop-dead gorgeous scenery. The **Ferme Équestre du Grand Étang** ( ☎ 0262 50 90 03; www.fermequestre.re; Pont Payet; half-/full day €45/110; ⏰ daily), just beyond the turn-off to Grand Étang, arranges half-day treks to Grand Étang; the full-day trek includes lunch. It's also possible to arrange longer excursions to Bras Canot (two days) and Takamaka (three days). One-day excursions in the area of Piton de la Fournaise – most notably in the far west-looking Plaine des Sables – are also on offer (€150; horses are transferred by van). Ask for Fanou, who can speak English.

## WHITE-WATER RAFTING

Réunion's best white water is found near St-Benoît. The Rivière des Marsouins offers magical white-water experiences for both first-time runners and seasoned enthusiasts. A half-day excursion will set you back €45.

The following companies are based by the river, close to Les Letchis restaurant (p239), and specialise in rafting trips on the Rivière des Marsouins and Rivière des Roches:

**Oasis Eaux Vives** ( ☎ 0692 00 16 23; www.oasisev.com)
**Run Aventures** ( ☎ 0262 64 08 22; www.runaventures.com)

## Sleeping & Eating

**Chambre d'hôte L'Orangeraie** ( ☎ 0262 50 97 60, 0692 01 18 87; http://monsite.orange.fr/orangeraie; Pont Payet; d incl breakfast €52, dinner €22; ☎ ) A good port of call if you want to get away from it all. The room and the bungalow are ordinary but the setting is fabulous – tropical plants everywhere – and Madame is a good cook. Much of the produce cooked up is straight from the *potager* (veggie patch). At breakfast, you can dip into eight varieties of homemade jams – hmm, the lychees. It's about 7km from St-Benoît along the road towards Plaine-des-Palmistes (take the RN3 in the direction of Plaine-des-Palmistes) and follow the signs from the Ferme Équestre at Pont Payet).

**Longanis Lodge** ( ☎ 0692 76 84 52; www.longanilodge .com; Chemin Harmonie, Abondance; lodge €100, weekend €300; ☎ ) The Longanis stuns with its design-led architecture and bucolic setting by a river shaded by majestic longani trees. The villa can accommodate up to six people, so it's a fantastic deal for friends or families. It's ecofriendly (water is solar heated, ventilation is natural and rainwater is recycled). It's in Abondance, about 5km from St-Benoît (take the road to Takamaka).

**Le Régal' Est** ( ☎ 0262 97 04 31; 9 Place Raymond Albius; mains €10-30, menu €15; ⏰ lunch & dinner Mon-Sat) Locals rave about this hip venture located upstairs in the covered market, but we found the prices inflated at dinner and the *brochettes* *de poisson* (skewered fish) a bit skimpy. Chef's bad day, maybe? The lunchtime menu (€15) is a better deal, though.

**Le Beauvallon** ( ☎ 0262 50 42 92; Rivière des Roches; mains €10-30; ☯ lunch) Le Beauvallon is well known to everyone in the area, not least for its location beside the mouth of the Rivière des Roches and its seasonal, scrumptious *carri bichiques*. On the flipside, the vast dining room doesn't contain one whit of soul or character.

**our pick Les Letchis** ( ☎ 0692 66 55 36; 42 Îlet Danclas; mains €12-35; ☯ lunch) Eastern Réunion's best-kept secret, Les Letchis boasts a fantastic location in a luxuriant garden by the Rivière des Marsouins. The menu is an ode to Creole classics and 'riverfood'; standouts include *carri bichiques* and *carri canard fumé* (smoked duck curry). If you want to explore new culinary territories, try *carri chevaquines* (a curry made from small freshwater prawns) or *carri anguilles* (eel curry). Reservations are advised.

## Getting There & Away

From St-Benoît a scenic road (the RN3) cuts across the Plaine-des-Palmistes to St-Pierre and St-Louis on the far side of the island. Alternatively, you can continue south along the coast road, passing through Ste-Anne, Ste-Rose, St-Philippe and St-Joseph to reach St-Pierre.

St-Benoît is a major transport hub. Bus services to and from St-Denis run approximately every half-hour. There are also two services linking St-Benoît and St-Pierre: line H follows the RN3 over the Plaine-des-Palmistes; line I takes the coast road via Ste-Philippe and St-Joseph. In both cases there are about four buses daily.

## STE-ANNE

The village of Ste-Anne, about 5km south along the coast from St-Benoît, is noted for its surprisingly extravagant **church**. The facade of the building is covered in stucco depictions of fruit, flowers and angels. The overall effect is flamboyant rather than tasteful, and is reminiscent of the mestizo architecture of the Andes in South America.

There's no beach in Ste-Anne, but if you need to cool off, there's no better place than **Bassin Bleu**, appropriately dubbed 'the lagoon of the east', at the mouth of a river, on the southern edge of town. It's a superb swimming spot, with crystal-clear water and big boulders. Take a plunge! Take note that it's mobbed at weekends.

Between Ste-Anne and Ste-Rose is the graceful **Pont des Anglais** suspension bridge over the Rivière de l'Est, now bypassed by the main highway but open to pedestrians. It was claimed to be the longest suspension bridge in the world at the time of its construction in the late 19th century.

The **tourist office** ( ☎ 0262 47 05 09; accueil@otst .re; Rue de l'Église; ☯ 9am-noon & 1-5.30pm Mon-Sat) is besides the church.

The nearest accommodation options are in St-Benoît or in Ste-Rose.

## Eating

**Il Etait Une Fois dans l'Ouest** ( ☎ 0692 64 60 11; 133 RN2; mains €5-10; ☯ lunch Mon-Sat) It's not cutting-edge cuisine at this humble place on the main road, but the daily specials are all flawlessly cooked. Don't be put off by the location on the main road; there's a peaceful dining room with sea views at the back.

**L'Auberge Créole** ( ☎ 0262 51 10 10; 1 Chemin Case; mains €8-34, menus €20-35; ☯ lunch Thu-Tue, dinner Tue & Thu-Sat) In this respected option, the menu roves from Creole dishes and *métro* classics to pizzas and Chinese specialities at prices that are more sweet than sour. Pity about the drab, neon-lit interior; take your order to go and eat under *vacoa* trees at Bassin Bleu.

## Getting There & Away

Ste-Anne is a stop on the coastal bus route from St-Benoît to St-Pierre.

## STE-ROSE & AROUND

pop 6600

South of St-Benoît, the landscape becomes more open and less populated as the road hugs the coast around Piton de la Fournaise, the volcano which regularly spews lava down its flanks. The small fishing community of Ste-Rose has its harbour at the inlet of La Marine.

South of Ste-Rose the first tongues of lava from Piton de la Fournaise start to make their appearance.

## Sights & Activities

At the picturesque **harbour** you'll see a **monument** to the young English commander Corbett, who was killed in 1809 during a naval battle against the French off the coast.

Further south you'll reach **La Cayenne**, which has a superb picnic area scenically perched on

RÉUNION

a cliff overlooking the ocean – well worth a pause. There's a snack bar, which does take away meals.

Continue on the RN2 and you'll soon come across **Bananaland** ( ☎ 0262 53 49 74; 371ter RN2; €3; 🕑 9am-4pm Sun-Thu), a family-run operation where you can visit a banana plantation and buy various banana products, including jam and cakes. Everything is homemade and organic.

**Notre Dame des Laves** is in **Piton Ste-Rose**, 4.5km south of Ste-Rose. The lava flow from a 1977 eruption went through the village, split when it came to the church and reformed again on the other side. Many people see the church's escape as a miracle of divine intervention. A wooden log 'washed up' by the lava now forms the lectern inside the church, while the stained-glass windows depict various stages of the eruption. Next to the church stands **La Vierge au Parasol**, a statue of the Virgin Mary optimistically holding an umbrella as protection against the volcano! A local planter set it up at the turn of the century in the hope of protecting his vanilla pods from volcanic hellfire and brimstone.

**Anse des Cascades** is beside the sea about 3km south of Piton Ste-Rose. The water from the hills drops dramatically into the sea near a traditional little fishing harbour. The coconut grove is splendid and is a hugely popular picnic spot.

Beyond Anse des Cascades, the main road continues south along the coast, climbs and then drops down to cross the 6km-wide volcanic plain known as Le Grand Brûlé (see p232).

Don't leave Ste-Rose without taking a **boat trip** along the craggy shores where you'll get different perspectives of the coastline. Trips can be arranged through **Le Grand Bleu** ( ☎ 0692 66 67 58; Port de Ste-Rose; adult/child €20/10; 🕑 by reservation Tue-Sun).

## Sleeping & Eating
### STE-ROSE
our pick **Ferme-Auberge La Cayenne** ( ☎ 0262 47 23 46; 317 Ravine Glissante; d incl breakfast €45, dinner €20) This well-run guesthouse scores points with its location – it's perched above the sea in La Ravine-Glissante, 1.5km south of Ste-Rose. The six sun-soaked rooms are as neat as a pin, and the views of the swishing indigo waters from the balcony are nothing short of charming. The owner, Madame Narayanin,

cooks beautifully, using mostly homegrown ingredients. Let the breeze tickle your skin while you eat authentic cuisine alfresco on the covered terrace. Breakfast is extra (€5).

**Chambre d'hôte La Roseraye – Chez M Adam de Villiers** ( ☎ 0262 47 21 33; christian.adv@wanadoo.fr; 206 RN2, Ste-Rose; d incl breakfast €45-50, dinner €20) La Roseraye's most memorable features are the riot of greenery all round the sprawling property, the five tastefully adorned rooms and the antiquated charm that wraps the place – it's a converted sugar-cane plantation, dating from 1832. One weak point: some rooms are a bit close to the main road.

our pick **Chambre d'hôte Matilona** ( ☎ 0692 85 86 86; http://monsite.orange.fr/matilona; 84 Chemin du Petit Brûlé; s/d incl breakfast €45/52, ste €65, dinner €25; 🅿 🛜 🖥 ) Formerly a supermarket, it's amazing what a renovation and an ownership change does for a place. Don't be put off by the peeling facade; push the door and you're in another reality – tastefully designed rooms, quality furnishings, generously sized communal areas and a seductive garden overflowing with colourful plants. And a killer pool. Monsieur is a former chef, so you can expect to eat well. Brilliant value.

**Hôtel-Restaurant La Fournaise** ( ☎ 0262 47 03 40; www.hotellafournaise.fr; 154 RN2; d €65; 🅿 🖥 🛜 ) There's a fresh feel in this modernish venture on the main road. Spruce rooms, shiny-clean toilets, air-con, an onsite restaurant and a pool are the order of the day here. The catch? It lacks charisma.

**Snack Chez Louiso** ( ☎ 0262 47 26 57; 112 Chemin du Petit Brûlé; mains €5-8; 🕑 lunch Tue-Sun) Chez Louiso is a casual open-air eatery overlooking the harbour. The menu is limited to a couple of daily specials, but they're well prepared and sizzling-hot value.

### PITON STE-ROSE
**Chambre d'hôte Le Joyau des Laves** ( ☎ 0262 47 34 00; www.joyaudeslaves.com; d incl breakfast €43-70, menus €11-28; 🕑 lunch Sat-Thu, dinner Mon-Thu & Sat; 🛜 ) On a headland 7km south of Ste-Rose, this is a comfortable *chambre d'hôte* run by a delightful young couple. Even if you're not staying, it's worth phoning ahead to eat in the restaurant and try local specialities such as palm hearts and *baba figues* (banana flowers) from the surrounding gardens.

**Les 2 Pitons de la Fournaise** ( ☎ 0262 47 23 16; RN2; mains €8-16; 🕑 lunch & dinner) Opposite the church. Creole and Chinese dishes.

## ANSE DES CASCADES

**Restaurant des Cascades** ( ☎ 0262 47 20 42; mains €10-32, menu €12; ☯ lunch Sat-Thu) A local and tourist favourite, this ramshackle beach restaurant in a lovely coconut grove bursts to the seams on weekends. It serves fresh fish and Creole dishes as well as sandwiches and a lovely palm-hearts salad. The lunch buffet (€12) served on weekdays is brilliant value. Nab a seat if it's not too busy, otherwise take your order to go and enjoy it in a quieter spot near the beach.

## Getting There & Away

Buses running from St-Benoît to St-Pierre make handy stops near Notre Dame des Laves, Anse des Cascades and La Vierge au Parasol.

RÉUNION

# Hiking in Réunion

Now we're talking. Hiking is *the* very best of what Réunion has to offer. Formed from one mighty dead volcano (Piton des Neiges) and one active volcano (Piton de la Fournaise), the island is a paradise for hikers, adventure-sports enthusiasts or indeed anyone who is receptive to the untamed beauty of a wilderness environment. The island is virtually unique in the Indian Ocean for offering both superb mountain scenery and excellent outdoor infrastructure, with more than a thousand kilometres of hiking trails, the best of which take you through an awe-inspiring landscape of jagged mountain crests, forested valleys, tumbling waterfalls and surreal volcanic tuff. Vast swathes of the interior of the island are accessible only by foot. As a result, the natural environment is remarkably intact, with a huge variety of flora, from tropical rainforest to gnarled thickets of giant heather. The good news is you don't need to be a masochist to enjoy this walking wonderland. Homely *gîtes* (lodges) and *chambres d'hôtes* (family-run B&Bs) are spaced at convenient distances along popular trails, offering simple accommodation and wholesome meals – sample a *rougail saucisses* (hearty sausage stew) in Cirque de Mafate and you'll know what we mean.

There are two major hiking trails, known as Grande Randonnée Route 1 (GR R1) and Grande Randonnée Route 2 (GR R2), with numerous offshoots. The GR R1 does a tour of Piton des Neiges, passing through Cilaos, the Forêt de Bébour-Bélouve, Hell-Bourg and the Cirque de Mafate. The GR R2 makes an epic traverse across the island all the way from St-Denis to St-Philippe via the three Cirques, the Plaine-des-Cafres and Piton de la Fournaise. A third trail, the Grande Randonnée Route 3 (GR R3), does a tour of Cirque de Mafate and overlaps with some sections of the GR R1 and GR R2.

The trails are well maintained, but the tropical rainfall can eat through footpaths and wash away steps and handrails. Even experienced hikers should be prepared for tortuous ascents, slippery mud chutes, and narrow paths beside sheer precipices. The routes are well signposted on the whole, but it's essential to carry a good map and you should check locally on the current situation; trails are occasionally closed for maintenance, especially following severe storms.

The trails described in this section – Tour des Cirques, Around Bas Mafate and Around Haut Mafate – are popular hikes, though there are countless variations, and they should be well within the capabilities of any reasonably fit adult; children with a sense of adventure and a good head for heights should be able to do the walks with a little extra time.

If you don't have time for a multiday trek, there are also plenty of great day hikes that will give you a taste of life in rural Réunion – we've outlined the most popular ones in the Réunion chapter.

The hiking times given are for an average hiker carrying a 10kg backpack and taking only brief breaks.

## WHEN TO HIKE

The best time to hike is during the dry season, from around late April to the end of October; May and June, as well as September and October, are probably the best months of all. July and August are a bit chilly, and during the rainy months a number of paths are not accessible. The weather is extremely changeable from one part of this small island to the other. For example, you can leave Col des Bœufs shrouded in mist and arrive at the village of La Nouvelle under a blazing sun.

The weather in Réunion has a tendency to become worse as the day goes on. As the hours pass, the island's uplands seem to delight in 'trapping' any cloud that happens to come their way. An early start is therefore one of the best defences against the vagaries of the elements.

The next day's weather forecast is shown on the two main TV channels after the evening news (generally around 8pm). You can also get the forecast by telephoning the **Météo France voice service** ( ☎ 0892 68 08 08; per min €0.45). Cyclone bulletins are available on ☎ 0897 65 01 01 (€0.51 per minute). Both these services are in French. Also check out the website www.meteo.re.

## WHAT TO BRING

Good shoes are essential for hiking the trails of Réunion, which are made of gravel and stone and often very steep, muddy or slippery. Hiking shoes with good ankle support are better than sneakers. If you're overnighting, take a pair of sandals for the evening – your feet will thank you.

Be sure to carry water (at least 2L for a day's hiking), wet-weather gear, a warm top, a hat, sunscreen, sunglasses, insect repellent, a whistle, a torch and a basic medical kit including plasters (Band-Aids), elastic bandages and muscle balm for blisters and minor muscle injuries. The *gîtes* provide sheets and blankets, but if you intend sleeping out at altitude, you'll need a decent sleeping bag, as temperatures in the Cirques can fall rapidly at night.

In most places to stay and places to eat, payment will be expected in cash, so bring a stash of euros with you. The only places to get euros in the Cirques are the ATMs at the post offices in Salazie and Cilaos, and these can't be depended on.

You will be able to buy most last-minute supplies at a sporting-goods store or one of the big supermarkets in Réunion as well as in Cilaos.

## INFORMATION SOURCES

Hiking information is provided by the headquarters of the **Centrale de Réservation – Île de la Réunion** (Map p178; ☎ 0262 90 78 78; www.reunion.fr; 5 Rue Rontaunay, St-Denis; 🕑 8am-noon & 1-5pm Mon-Thu, 8-11am Fri), formerly known as Maison de la Montagne et de la Mer, in St-Denis, and by associated tourist offices, including those in Cilaos, Salazie, Hell-Bourg, Ste-Suzanne, St-Gilles-les-Bains, St-Pierre, St-Leu, Plaine-des-Palmistes, Ste-Anne, St-Joseph and Bourg-Murat. All these offices organise bookings for *gîtes d'étape et de randonnée* (walkers' lodges) and can give advice as to which paths are currently closed. They can also arrange hiking tours.

By far the most useful website for hikers is that of the Centrale de Réservation – Île de la Réunion (see above). It allows you to book your accommodation online.

The websites http://runrando.free.fr (in French) and www.gites-refuges.com are also useful.

For information on *état des sentiers* (closed trails), phone the voice service at ☎ 0262 37 38 39 (in French).

The **Fédération Française de la Randonnée Pédestre** (FFRandonnée; www.ffrandonnee.fr) is responsible for the development and upkeep of the GR walking tracks.

For more information on walking, contact the **Comité départemental de la randonnée pédestre de la Réunion** ( ☎ 0262 94 37 16; 8 rue de la Caserne, 9002 HLM Chirico, Petite Ile, 97400 Saint-Denis).

## MAPS

Réunion is covered by the six 1:25,000 scale maps published by the **Institut Géographique National** (IGN; www.ign.fr). These maps are reasonably up-to-date and show trails and *gîtes*. Map number 4402 RT is one of the most useful for hikers, since it covers Cirque de Mafate and Cirque de Salazie as well as the northern part of the Cirque de Cilaos. It also covers the whole of the GR R1. The maps are sold all over the island, including at the Centrale de Réservation – Île de la Réunion in St-Denis.

## BOOKS

Several excellent route guides are available at the Centrale de Réservation – Île de la

Réunion and at most bookshops in St-Denis. Though only in French, they are still useful for their maps.

The definitive guide to the GR® R1, GR® R2 and GR® R3 is the *TopoGuides GR® Grande randonnée L'Île de la Réunion* (2010), published by the FFRandonnée. It uses 1:25,000 scale IGN maps and details the itineraries. The GR® R1 is described in six *étapes* (stages), the GR® R2 in 12 stages and the GR® R3 in five stages.

The FFRandonnée also publishes the *Topoguide PR® Sentiers forestiers de L'Île de la Réunion* (2007), which covers 25 walks varying from one-hour jaunts to six-hour hikes.

Published locally by Orphie, *52 Balades et Randonnées Faciles* is designed with children in mind and describes outings that can be covered in less than four hours. A broader range of walks is covered by *62 Randonnées Réunionnaises* (also by Orphie). The loose-leaf format, with one walk per page, is extremely practical.

For the volcano area and the Wild South, nothing can beat the excellent *Le Guide du Piton de la Fournaise* by Jean-Luc Allègre.

## TOURS & GUIDES

Réunion's hiking trails are well established and reasonably well signposted, but you may get more information about the environment you are walking through if you go with a local guide. The Centrale de Réservation – Île de la Réunion has a list of organised adventure trips on the island. Alternatively, contact one of the following operators.

Fully qualified mountain guides can be contacted through the Centrale de Réservation – Île de la Réunion and local tourist offices (see p243). Rates are negotiable and vary according to the length and degree of difficulty of the hike; an undemanding one-day outing should start at around €45 per person (minimum four people).

**Allons Bat Carré** ( ☎ 0692 43 06 79; http://abcrandos. feeling974.com, in French)

**Aparksa Montagne** ( ☎ 0692 66 50 09; www.aparksa -montagne.com) Run by Thomas Percheron, who has lived in South Africa and is fluent in English.

**Austral Aventure** ( ☎ 0692 87 55 50; www.creole.org/ austral-aventure; Rue Amiral Lacaze, Hell-Bourg)

**Kokapat Rando** ( ☎ 0262 33 30 14, 0692 69 94 14; www.kokapatrando-reunion.com)

**Randorun Trek** ( ☎ 0262 26 31 31; www.randorun. fr, in French)

**Réunion Mer et Montagne** ( ☎ 0692 83 38 68; www. reunionmeretmontagne.com, in French)

**Réunion Randonnées** ( ☎ 0692 64 45 26; www. reunion-randonnees.com)

**Run Évasion** ( ☎ 0262 31 83 57; www.runevasion.fr, in French; 23 Rue du Père Boiteau, Cilaos)

## SLEEPING & EATING

Most of the accommodation for hikers consists of *gîtes de montagnes* (mostly found in isolated locations on the trails themselves) or of privately run *gîtes d'étape* along the walking trails. Both offer dorm beds and meals. There's often very little to separate the two types of *gîte* in terms of comfort or facilities. Almost all *gîtes* provide hot showers (they're solar heated). A third option consists of small, family-run *chambres d'hôtes* (mostly found in the villages at the ends of the hiking trails). Your choice of where to stay will most likely be based on where you can find a room. There are also a few hotels in Hell-Bourg and Cilaos for that last night of luxury (and central heating) before you set out on your hike. See p256 for more information on accommodation and costs in Réunion.

Many visitors from mainland France book their accommodation before arriving in Réunion, so don't make the mistake of leaving it to the last minute. During July and August and around Christmas it's hard to find a bed in the Cirques for love or money. At other times it's best to book at least a couple of months in advance, particularly for popular places such as the *gîtes* at Caverne Dufour (for Piton des Neiges) and Piton de la Fournaise.

The *gîtes de montagnes* are managed by the Centrale de Réservation – Île de la Réunion and must be booked and paid for in advance. This can be done at the Centrale de Réservation – Île de la Réunion in St-Denis (or through its website) and at tourist offices (see p243). Most of these offices accept credit cards, though check beforehand to be sure this is the case. When you pay, you will receive a voucher to be given to the manager of the *gîte* where you will be staying. You must call the *gîte* to book your meals at least one day in advance; this can be done at the same time as the original booking if you'd rather, but meals still have to paid for on the spot. For the privately owned *gîtes*, it is less restrictive in terms of logistics; you can book directly through the *gîte*.

If all this organisation doesn't fit in with your idea of adventure, you can camp for free in some areas in the Cirques, but only for one night at a time. Popular spots in the Cirque

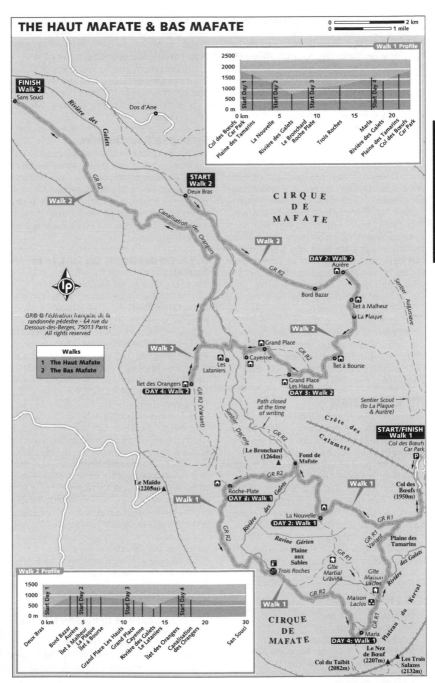

# THE HAUT MAFATE & BAS MAFATE

de Mafate include Trois Roches on the GR R2 between Marla and Roche-Plate, Plaine aux Sables between La Nouvelle and Trois Roches and Plaine des Tamarins on the GR R1 near La Nouvelle; Le Grand Sable on the GR R1 near Le Bélier; and at the *gîte* at Bébour-Bélouve, on the Cirque de Salazie's rim. Setting up camp on Piton de la Fournaise (the volcano) is forbidden for obvious reasons.

Most *gîtes* offer Creole meals, which are normally hearty, though a little rustic for some palates. The standard fare is *carri poulet* (chicken curry), *boucané* (smoked pork) or *rougail saucisses,* often with local wine or *rhum arrangé* (rum punch) thrown in. Breakfast usually consists of just a cup of coffee with *biscottes* (rusks) – or, if you're lucky, bread – and jam.

If you plan to self-cater, you will need to bring plenty of carbohydrate-rich food. Instant noodles are light and filling, while chocolate and other sugary snacks can provide the energy necessary to make it up that last mountain ridge. Note that only a few *gîtes* are equipped with cooking facilities; you are best off bringing a camping stove. Bear in mind that you are not allowed to light fires anywhere in the forest areas. Some villages in the Cirques have shops where you can purchase a very limited variety of food; few places stock anything more wholesome than biscuits, processed cheese and tinned food.

## THE HAUT MAFATE

Surrounded by ramparts, crisscrossed with gullies and studded with narrow ridges, Cirque de Mafate (p214) is the wildest and most remote of Réunion's Cirques. The following itinerary takes you through the most scenic areas of the southern part of the Cirque in four days. This is just a suggestion for an average walker; there are countless variations, which makes it easy to tweak your own itinerary depending on your time constraints and level of fitness.

There are several routes into Mafate, including Bord Martin (for the Sentier Scout, that leads to La Plaque and Aurère), Col de Fourche

and Cilaos via the Col du Taïbit (p206), but we've chosen to start this loop at the Col des Bœufs car park as it's the most convenient option. For sleeping information, see p251

This hike can also be combined with the Tour des Cirques (see p250) and Bas Mafate (see p247).

IGN's 1:25,000 topographic map 4402 RT covers the area.

### Getting to/from the Hike

There are regular buses from Salazie to Grand Îlet and Le Bélier (see p209). From Le Bélier to Col des Bœufs car park, services are more infrequent (see p211 for more details) but it's easy to hitch a ride to the car park. If you drive, take note that secure parking is available at the car park, but you'll have to fork out €10 per day.

### Day 1: Col des Bœufs Car Park to La Nouvelle
2hr, 4.5km, 100m ascent, 520m descent

The trail to La Nouvelle starts at the car park below **Col des Bœufs**, from where you'll get your first glimpse of the Cirque de Mafate (and what a glimpse!). Ahead, GR R1 plunges steeply to the forested **Plaine des Tamarins**. The *tamarin des Hauts* (mountain tamarind trees) are cloaked in a yellowish lichen called *barbe de capucins* (monks' beard), and the low cloud often creates a slightly spooky atmosphere like something from Tolkien's *The Lord of the Rings*.

Follow the path signposted to La Nouvelle (the other branch heads south to Marla), which meanders through the forest in a fairly leisurely fashion before dropping rapidly to the village of **La Nouvelle**. There are some fabulous views of **Le Grand Bénare** on the Cirque rim to the south as you descend.

La Nouvelle used to be a cattle-raising centre, but tourism has very much taken over as the village's main source of income. The village has several shops, a school, a helipad and an interesting shingle-roofed chapel.

La Nouvelle is well endowed with *gîtes d'étape*. It also boasts a bakery and no fewer than three *épiceries* (groceries) where you can buy basic provisions.

### Day 2: La Nouvelle to Roche-Plate via Le Bronchard
3hr, 4.7km, 450m ascent, 795m descent

The trail to Grand Place, Cayenne and Roche-Plate via Le Bronchard turns downhill just

## THE HIKE AT A GLANCE

| | |
|---|---|
| **Duration** | 4 days |
| **Distance** | 20.4km |
| **Difficulty** | moderate |
| **Start/Finish** | Col des Bœufs car park |
| **Nearest Town** | Grand Îlet (p213) |

after the La Nouvelle chapel and heads into the maize fields before plummeting into the valley of the **Rivière des Galets**. This steep and often treacherous descent is not for the faint-hearted, though reassuring handrails are provided for some of the steeper sections.

To make up for the risk, the views are to die for (figuratively speaking!) and an exhilarating two hours or so will get you to Fond de Mafate (the bottom of the Cirque), where you can take a well-deserved splash in the river. When you've recovered your energy, follow the red and white paint stripes on the rocks along the riverbanks for about 300m and start the arduous ascent up the far side of the valley.

When you reach the white metal cross at **Le Bronchard** after roughly one hour from the floor of the valley, the worst is over. The final stretch descends slowly down to the village of **Roche-Plate** (count on about 15 minutes). Ignore the turn-off to Marla, Trois Roches and La Nouvelle, which branches off to the left as you enter the village. The village of Roche-Plate sits at the foot of the majestic **Le Maïdo** (2205m).

## Day 3: Roche-Plate to Marla via Trois Roches
**5hr, 6.8km, 900m ascent, 370m descent**

The trail to Marla via Trois Roches begins where the trail from La Nouvelle enters Roche-Plate. The first section rises steadily through a dry landscape with *choka* (an agave species). Towering overhead are the peaks of Le Grand Bénare and Le Gros Morne. Apart from one significant drop, the path stays fairly level before descending to the waterfall at **Trois Roches** (about 2¾ hours from Roche-Plate).

This curious waterfall drops through a narrow crack in a bed of grey granite that has been perfectly polished into ripple patterns by aeons of erosion, and is a popular camping spot. The falls are named after the huge boulders (there are actually seven, not three) that were deposited here by prehistoric torrents.

Marla is about 2¼ hours beyond the falls. The trail crosses the river and then follows the left bank, passing through a rather arid landscape of eroded volcanic cinders from Piton des Neiges. After recrossing the river just downstream from a pile of vast alluvial boulders, the trail then climbs the far bank to Marla in about an hour.

At an altitude of 1640m, **Marla** is the highest village in Cirque de Mafate. Its name is said to be derived from a Malagasy term mean-

ing 'many people', but these days, the town consists of only a few houses. Hungry and haggard? Marla has a smattering of places to stay and eat. You can also elect to end your hike here by crossing the **Col du Taïbit** to Cilaos (see Day 5 of Tour des Cirques, p255).

## Day 4: Marla to Col des Bœufs Car Park
**3hr, 4.8km, 540m ascent, 280m descent**

This easy last day picks up the GR R1 at the north end of the village. The trail is signposted to La Nouvelle, Col de Fourche and Col des Bœufs, and should get you to **Maison Laclos** within about 20 minutes. This traditional dwelling – said to be one of the oldest in the Cirque – was abandoned in the aftermath of Hurricane Hyacinthe, which came through in 1980, and is now a ruin. From there, the main GR R1 trail returns to La Nouvelle, but you can take the right-hand fork, a GR R1 variant, which cuts straight back up (northward) to the Plaine des Tamarins (allow about one hour). This trail connects with the main GR R1 trail into the Cirque, from where it's roughly an hour back over the Col des Bœufs to the car park.

## THE BAS MAFATE

After (or before) a loop in the Haut Mafate, you might want to explore the Bas Mafate, which is even more secluded (and this is saying something) and less 'touristy' than Haut Mafate. The circuit we describe below starts from the Rivière des Galets valley and takes in all the îlets (hamlets) of Bas Mafate, including Aurère, Îlet à Malheur, La Plaque, Îlet à Bourse, Grand Place Les Hauts, Grand Place, Cayenne, Les Lataniers and Îlet des Orangers – a great way to immerse yourself in local culture and sample authentic rural Réunionnais life. It's a four-day hike, but you can design a longer or shorter itinerary depending on how pressed and how full of beans you are.

If time allows, you can rejoin the Haut Mafate itinerary (p246). A path connects

HIKING IN RÉUNION

| THE HIKE AT A GLANCE | |
| --- | --- |
| **Duration** | 4 days |
| **Distance** | 30km |
| **Difficulty** | moderate |
| **Start** | Deux Bras |
| **Finish** | Sans Souci |
| **Nearest Towns** | Rivière des Galets & Sans Souci |

---

### ECOWALKING

To help preserve the ecology and beauty of Réunion, consider these tips when hiking.

#### Rubbish

- Carry out all your rubbish. Don't overlook easily forgotten items, such as silver paper, orange peel, cigarette butts and plastic wrappers. Empty packaging should be stored in a dedicated rubbish bag. Make an effort to carry out rubbish left by others.

- Never bury your rubbish: digging disturbs soil and ground cover and encourages erosion. Buried rubbish will likely be dug up by animals, who may be injured or poisoned by it. It may also take years to decompose.

- Minimise waste by taking minimal packaging and no more food than you will need. Take reusable containers or stuff sacks.

- Sanitary products, condoms and toilet paper should be carried out despite the inconvenience. They burn and decompose poorly.

#### Human Waste Disposal

- Contamination of water sources by human faeces can lead to the transmission of all sorts of nasties. Where there is a toilet, use it. Where there is none, bury your waste. Cover the waste with soil and a rock.

#### Erosion

- Hillsides and mountain slopes, especially at high altitudes, are prone to erosion. Stick to existing tracks and avoid short cuts.

- If a well-used track passes through a mud patch, walk through the mud so as not to increase the size of the patch.

- Avoid removing any plant life – it keeps the topsoil in place.

---

Îlet des Orangers and Roche-Plate. From Les Lataniers, you can also get to Roche-Plate via the Sentier Dacerle. The path from Cayenne to La Nouvelle was closed at the time of writing.

IGN's 1:25,000 topographic map 4402 RT covers the area.

### Getting to/from the Hike

To get to the start of the walk, catch any bus heading to the west or the south coast from St-Denis, and get off at the 'Sacré Cœur' bus stop in Rivière des Galets, from where a 4WD taxi will pick you up (make sure you book in advance). Taxis follow the floor of the Rivière des Galets valley and will drop you off at Deux Bras, which will spare you a monotonous stretch of about 9km. It costs €20 for one or two passengers, or €7 per person if there are at least three people. Contact **Mr Thiburce** ( ☎ 0692 08 00 47), **Mr Legros** ( ☎ 0692 82 86 36) or **Mr Thomas** ( ☎ 0692 62 82 10). If driving, you'll need to arrange parking with a taxi driver (count on €10 per day for the service).

From Sans Souci, there are about 20 buses daily (except Sunday and bank holidays) to St-Paul (€1.50).

### Day 1: Deux Bras to Aurère
3hr, 4.5km, ascent 705m

From **Deux Bras**, follow the riverbank path for about 30 minutes, until you reach an intersection. This first section is flat, but be prepared for wet feet, as you'll have to cross the Rivière des Galets several times. At the intersection, follow the sign for Aurère and Îlet à Malheur. The path now climbs above the right bank of the river. The valley narrows and is unrelentingly rugged with steep cliffs. After about 1½ hours from the start, the path bends to the southeast and makes a sharp ascent before emerging at **Bord Bazar**. It's then an easy 15-minute stroll through a wood to the picturesque hamlet of **Aurère**.

### Day 2: Aurère to Grand Place Les Hauts
3¾hr, 5.5km, ascent 470m, descent 560m

Day 2 starts with a 20-minute drop to the Ravine du Bras Bémale, which is crossed on a

## SLEEPING & EATING IN BAS MAFATE

You'll find a slew of decent *gîtes* (*privés* or run by the Centrale de Réservation – Île de la Réunion) that offer soft drinks, alcohol (beer and wine) and meals. Don't expect gastronomic ecstasy, though – it's normally satisfying, wholesome *carris* and homemade cakes. Plan on €15 to €17 for a meal. Digs are in well-maintained dorms with solar-heated showers, but a number of *gîtes* also offer double rooms. A few places offer camp sites. You'll find water at every *gîte*, but between stops there are very few sources of drinking water.

### AURÈRE

**Auberge Piton Cabris – Charlemagne Libelle** ( ☎ 0262 43 36 83; dm €15, breakfast/meal €5/15) Four four-bed dorms. Good views from the terrace.

**Gîte Boyer Georget – Le Poinsettia** ( ☎ 0262 55 02 33, 0692 08 92 20; dm €14, breakfast/dinner €5/15) Beds are in five- to 11-bed dorms. Also has three doubles and a small grocery store.

**Gîte François Libelle** ( ☎ 0262 42 31 36; camp site €10, dm €15, breakfast/meal €5/15) Digs are in four- to six-bed dorms that feel a bit cramped. It's also possible to camp.

**Gîte Narcisse Libelle** ( ☎ 0262 43 86 38, 0692 09 18 86; dm €15, meals €15) A newish venture on the outskirts of Aurère, on the way to Îlet à Malheur. Two four-bed dorms.

### ÎLET À MALHEUR

**Camping Les Filaos** ( ☎ 0692 53 15 21; camp site €5, breakfast/dinner €5/15) You'd be hard pressed to find a more atmospheric setting to pitch your tent, with a property overflowing with tropical plants. Tents and sleeping mats can be rented for an extra €5.

**Gîte Guy Libelle** ( ☎ 0262 43 56 96; dm €15, breakfast/meal €5/15) An excellent *gîte* run by Centrale de Réservation – Île de la Réunion. Has a small grocery store too.

### LA PLAQUE

**Gîte L'Arbre du Voyageur** ( ☎ 0262 43 50 60, 0692 09 10 10; dm incl half board €45, camp site incl half board €30) Two adjoining seven-bed dorms and a lovely camp site in a property that feels like the world's end. A bit pricey, but the welcome is affable, the setting serene and the food is among the best in Mafate.

### ÎLET À BOURSE

**Gîte Christophe Thomas** ( ☎ 0262 43 43 93; d & q €15, breakfast/dinner €5/15) A comfy *gîte* with two doubles and four quadruples, all with private bathrooms. Bookings must be made with Centrale de la Réservation – Île de la Réunion.

### GRAND PLACE LES HAUTS

**Gîte Coeur de Mafate** ( ☎ 0262 55 01 68; dm €35, breakfast/meal €5/15) Three small houses with six beds and private bathrooms. Best assets are the location and the swoony views.

**Gîte Eloïse** ( ☎ 0262 43 31 05, 0692 29 13 70; d incl half board €35) A rather rustic place, with one eight-bed room and one 10-bed room.

**Gîte Le Pavillon** ( ☎ 0262 43 66 76, 0692 66 60 83; dm/s/d incl half board €35/41/76) A modernish place with three dorms, two doubles and a grocery store; the owner, Benoit Boyer, also runs a bakery. It's also possible to camp (for free) if you have dinner (€15).

### GRAND PLACE BOUTIQUE & CAYENNE

**Gîte Le Bougainvillier** ( ☎ 0262 43 40 08; dm incl half board €35) A simple venture near the school.

**Gîte Thomas** ( ☎ 0262 43 85 42; s/dm €16/15, breakfast/dinner €5/15) Has to be booked through Centrale de Réservation – Île de la Réunion.

### LES LATANIERS

There are three *gîtes* in Les Lataniers but they're really basic. You're better off staying at Îlet des Orangers.

### ÎLET DES ORANGERS

**Gîte des Orangers – Chez Christelle Hoareau** ( ☎ 0692 03 83 93; dm €15, breakfast/dinner €5/15) An attractive place near the chapel. Two six-bed dorms and two doubles.

**Gîte du Village** ( ☎ 0692 07 79 24; dm €15, breakfast/dinner €5/15) Opposite Gîte des Orangers. One 10-bed dorm and one double. You'll also find a bar/food store.

conducively atmospheric footbridge. Then it's a quick ascent to **Îlet à Malheur**, a lovely settlement with a cute chapel. Another 25 minutes will bring you to **La Plaque**. Leaving La Plaque, the path then descends to Grande Ravine, which you'll cross on a footbridge, and climbs again on the other side. After about 30 minutes **Îlet à Bourse** comes into view. This hamlet is famous for its magnificent alley of casuarina trees. From Îlet à Bourse the path descends sharply for about 15 minutes until it reaches Bras d'Oussy. After fording the river, it's 30 minutes of tough ascent until an intersection; follow signs for Gîte Cœur de Mafate, Gîte Le Pavillon, Gîte Elodie and Roche Plate. Ten minutes later you reach the top of a forested ridge, from where you can easily make out **Grand Place Les Hauts**, reached after a 20-minute steep descent.

### Day 3: Grand Place Les Hauts to Îlet des Orangers
3½hr, 6.5km, ascent 645m, descent 500m

This is a challenging day, with one major descent followed by one long ascent that require some heavy legwork. The ample rewards for all this effort are the sensational landscapes and the lovely *îlets* (hamlets) you'll traverse along the way. From your *gîte* in Grand Place Les Hauts, the path plummets down to the floor of the Rivière des Galets valley via **Grand Place** and **Cayenne**, with an altitude loss of about 500m. Allow one hour for the descent. One minute beyond the footbridge over the river, fork left for Les Lataniers, Les Orangers. Now the climb begins. About 40 minutes of switchback ascent brings you to a spur where **Les Lataniers** lies. Take the path that passes through the hamlet, then continue the ascent to **Îlet des Orangers** (after roughly 45 minutes, ignore the turn-off on the right to Canalisation des Orangers – this is for tomorrow), reached after about 1¼ hours. This last section features spectacular landscapes consisting of precipitous mountain slopes and steep-sided valleys. Îlet des Orangers is a delightful place that is perched on two split plateaus surrounded with near-vertical mountain slopes. Be sure to peek at the cosy chapel near the *gîtes*.

### Day 4: Îlet des Orangers to Sans Souci via Canalisation des Orangers
4hr, 13.5km, ascent 50m, descent 600m

This long stage begins by backtracking to the intersection with the Canalisation des Orangers trail, which involves a 30-minute descent. The next 2¾ hours, along the **Canalisation des Orangers**, are relatively easy. Past the intersection, the path levels out, enabling you to walk at a steady clip along the flank of the mountain, maintaining an average altitude of around 800m along a narrow ledge above the Rivière des Galets. Be sure to look back at the sheer, haunting bulk of the interior of the Cirque. The only landmarks along the path include a tunnel, about one hour from the intersection, and several waterfalls. After the Canalisation des Orangers trail, a dirt track leads downhill to **Sans Souci** in less than 45 minutes, where you can take the bus to the bright lights of the coast.

## TOUR DES CIRQUES
Simply magical. The Tour des Cirques (Round the Cirques) is a Réunion classic that is sure to leave you with indelible memories. Combining the best of the three Cirques, it will offer you three distinct atmospheres and various landscapes. As a bonus, you'll cross a few towns that are well equipped with cosy accommodation facilities.

The walk roughly follows the path of GR R1 and is best started in Cilaos, which has excellent facilities for walkers and the added advantage of a health spa (p205) where you can unwind after your hike. The hike overlaps with days 1 and 4 of the Haut Mafate hike (p246), so you can easily extend the walk by combining the two routes.

### Getting to/from the Hike
There are regular bus services between St-Louis on the west coast and Cilaos (see p203).

### Day 1: Cilaos to Caverne Dufour
4½hr, 5km, 1250m ascent

The trail starts just north of Cilaos, at the junction of the roads for Îlet à Cordes and Bras-Sec, and rises through the casuarina forest to the Plateau des Chênes. Take the right fork towards La Roche Merveilleuse (Marvellous Rock); the left fork leads along the ridge to Col du Taïbit. The trail crosses the forest road several times before it reaches **La Roche Merveilleuse**

| THE HIKE AT A GLANCE | |
|---|---|
| **Duration** | 5 days |
| **Distance** | 51.5km |
| **Difficulty** | demanding |
| **Start/Finish** | Cilaos (p204) |

## SLEEPING & EATING IN HAUT MAFATE

There's a good choice of *gîtes* in Haut Mafate, but be sure to book at weekends and during holidays, especially in La Nouvelle and Marla, which get overnighting walkers. La Nouvelle boasts the most comfortable *gîtes* in Mafate.

### LA NOUVELLE
**Camping Collet** ( ☎ 0692 45 59 33; camp site per person €5) Lovely grounds, with lots of shade, grassy areas and a clean ablution block.

**Gîte Joseph Cuvelier** ( ☎ 0262 43 49 63; dm €15, breakfast/dinner €6/17) Rustic, handkerchief-sized dorm.

**Gîte Oréo** ( ☎ 0262 43 58 57; dm €15, breakfast/dinner €5/15) Near the soccer field. A few compact dorms and one double. Book through Centrale de Réservation – Île de la Réunion.

**Gîte Georget Bègue** ( ☎ 0262 43 43 10, 0692 26 94 11; dm/d incl half board €38/86, dinner €20) Four- and eight-bed dorms and three doubles with private bathrooms. Excellent food.

**Gîte Yvon Gravina** ( ☎ 0262 43 38 72; d €35) Accommodation only. Six doubles.

**Relais de Mafate** ( ☎ 0262 43 61 77, 0692 23 60 60; dm/d €16/35, bungalow d/tr/q €60/80/100, breakfast €6, meals from €20) The largest venture in Mafate, with various types of accommodation for all budgets. Also has a restaurant, a bakery and a grocery store.

**Le Tamareo** ( ☎ 0692 32 08 28; dm/d €20/45, dinner €20; 🛜 ) Had just opened when we visited. Four doubles and three triples with shared bathrooms. Yes, there's wi-fi.

**Snack-Bar du Village** ( ☎ 0692 37 97 37; meals €8-12; 🕐 daily) Serves sandwiches and salads.

### PLAINE AUX SABLES
**Gîte Martial Gravina** ( ☎ 0262 43 01 73, 0692 14 57 06; dm/d €14/32, breakfast/meals €4/14) At Plaine aux Sables, a 45-minute walk from La Nouvelle, on the way to Marla. Has two doubles and four quadruples with private bathroom. Food comes in for warm praise.

### ROCHE-PLATE
**Auberge du Bronchard** ( ☎ 0262 43 83 66; dm/d €15/45, breakfast/meal €5/18) A very well-run establishment with five immaculate doubles, two dorms and a restaurant. There's also a food store.

**Gîte Chez Axel – Ti Kaz Bleue** ( ☎ 0692 29 37 58; dm incl half board €35) One small house with four beds and one bigger house with eight beds, each with its own ablution block. Excellent dinners.

**Gîte Chez Juliette** ( ☎ 0262 42 28 79; dm incl half board €35, meals €15) Three eight-bed dorms and lovely views.

**Gîte du Village – Thomas Judex** ( ☎ 0262 43 61 19; camp site €5-8, dm €16, breakfast/meals €6/18) On the way to Îlet des Orangers. Three itty-bitty, four-bed dorms opening onto a terrace with ample views.

### MARLA
**Gîte des Trois Roches** ( ☎ 0262 32 50 90; bungalows €45) The most comfortable abode in Marla. Lovely bungalows with private bathrooms and superb views.

**Gîte du Centre** ( ☎ 0692 34 25 34; dm incl half board €40) A recent, colourful *gîte* and a grocery store.

**Gîte Fanelie Cesar** ( ☎ 0692 03 26 15; dm/d €15/33, breakfast/dinner €5/16) Clean doubles and four-bed dorms.

**Gîte Maison Laclos** ( ☎ 0692 07 86 54; dm/d €16/37, breakfast/dinner €6/19) A neat place located a 20-minute walk from Marla, on the way to Col des Bœufs.

**Gîte Yolande Hoareau** ( ☎ 0262 43 78 31; dm/d €16/36, breakfast/dinner €6/16) Runs two *gîtes,* one private and one that has to be booked through Centrale de la Réservation – Île de la Réunion.

There's also the **Snack-Bar Le Marla**, near the school, and the **Epicerie du Village**, which sells bread and other supplies.

(avoid the Sentier de Découverte, a circular nature trail around the rock), and then descends to meet the Bras-Sec road.

The trail follows the Bras-Sec road for about 400m, then branches off to the left at **Le Bloc**.

Many walkers skip this first hour's walk by getting a bus up to Le Bloc from Cilaos (see p203).

From Le Bloc, it's a demanding ascent through a forest of cryptomeria (a cedar-like tree) to the **Plateau du Petit Matarum**,

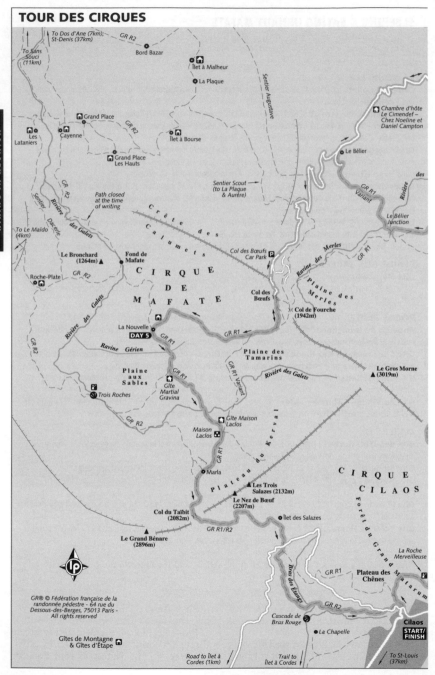

# TOUR DES CIRQUES

To Dos d'Ane (7km);
St-Denis (37km)

GR R2

Bord Bazar

To Sans
Souci
(11km)

Îlet à Malheur

La Plaque

Sentier Augustave

Chambre d'hôte
Le Cimendef –
Chez Noeline et
Daniel Campton

Grand Place

Les
Lataniers

Cayenne

GR R2

Îlet à Bourse

Le Bélier

Grand Place
Les Hauts

GR R1
Variant

Rivière

des

Sentier Scout
(to La Plaque
& Aurère)

Sentier

Rivière
Dacerie

des Galets

Path closed
at the time
of writing

Crête    des

Le Bélier
Junction

To Le Maïdo
(4km)

GR R2

Le Bronchard
(1264m)

Fond de
Mafate

Calumets

Col des Bœufs
Car Park

Ravine    des    Merles

GR R1

Roche-Plate

GR R2

Rivière    des    Galets

C I R Q U E

D E

M A F A T E

Col des
Bœufs

Plaine
des
Merles

Col de Fourche
(1942m)

GR R2

La Nouvelle

**DAY 5**

GR R1

GR R1

Ravine    Gérien

Plaine    aux
Sables

Trois Roches

GR R2

GR R1

Gîte
Martial
Gravina

GR R1 Variant

Plaine des
Tamarins

Rivière des Galets

Le Gros Morne
(3019m)

Gîte Maison
Laclos

Maison
Laclos

GR R1

Plateau    du    Kerval

C I R Q U E

Marla

Les Trois
Salazes (2132m)

C I L A O S

Le Nez de Bœuf
(2207m)

Col du Taïbit
(2082m)

GR R1/R2

Îlet des Salazes

Forêt    du    Grand    Matarum

La Roche
Merveilleuse

Le Grand Bénare
(2896m)

Plateau des
Chênes

GR © Fédération française de la
randonnée pédestre - 64 rue du
Dessous-des-Berges, 75013 Paris -
All rights reserved

GR R1

Bras    des    Étangs

GR R2

Gîtes de Montagne
& Gîtes d'Étape

Road to Îlet à
Cordes (1km)

Trail to
Îlet à Cordes

Cascade de
Bras Rouge

La Chapelle

Cilaos
**START/
FINISH**

To St-Louis
(37km)

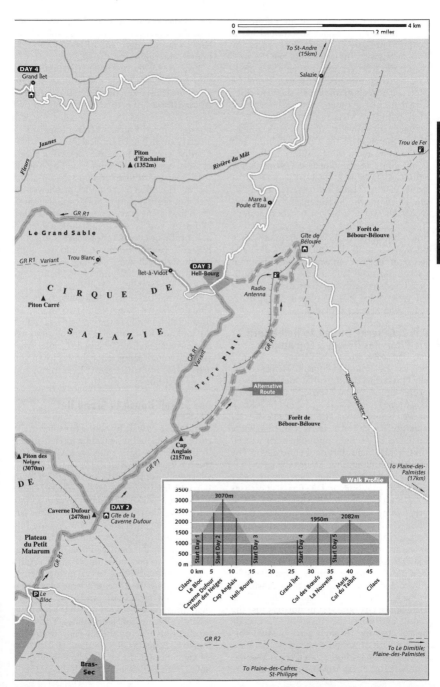

a flat area reached after about 1¼ hours. Here the forest changes to stunted giant heather bushes (known as *branles* or *brandes*) cloaked in wisps of lichen. Be prepared: the next section is even more challenging than the previous one from Le Bloc, with steep gradients all the way from here to the *gîte*; allow another two hours from Plateau du Petit Matarum to the *gîte*.

Once you gain the saddle, there's a turn-off on the right to the Col de Bébour and Le Dimitile, and a short distance further on, you'll come to the **Gîte de la Caverne Dufour** ( ☎ 0262 51 15 26; dm €17, breakfast/dinner €5/15) at nearly 2500m. Though still pretty rustic, this *gîte de montagne* boasts inside toilets and (cold) 'showers' (usually a trickle of water). You'll need to bring plenty of warm clothes and remember to book well in advance through Centrale de Réservation – Île de la Réunion (p243); even with 48 beds, it's often packed out, especially at weekends and holiday. It's also possible to camp for free beside the *gîte*, which has 24 sites in 'bungalow-tents'; blankets are provided.

## Day 2: Caverne Dufour to Hell-Bourg via Piton des Neiges & Cap Anglais
7hr, 11km, 600m ascent, 2140 descent

Because the summit of Piton des Neiges is usually cloaked in cloud by mid-morning, most people choose to stay overnight at the Gîte de la Caverne Dufour, starting out for the peak at, or even before, dawn. The path begins directly opposite the *gîte* and is clearly marked in white on the rock face, but you should bring a torch (flashlight) if you start out before dawn. The climb takes about three hours return.

The landscape becomes increasingly rocky the higher you climb, and the final section rises steeply over shifting cinders that make for slippery footing. At the summit there are few traces of vegetation, and the red, black and ochre rock leaves little doubt about the mountain's volcanic origins. On a clear day, the whole island is spread out beneath you. If you didn't beat the cloud to the summit, you may just be confronted by an enveloping cloak of white.

Back at the Caverne Dufour, the trail to Hell-Bourg (six hours) runs north across the saddle and skirts the rim of the Cirque de Salazie, passing through giant heather forest. It's a bit of a mud chute, so watch your footing. After 1¼ hours you'll reach a white-painted cross at **Cap Anglais**, from where there

are excellent views over the Cirque de Salazie. Take the GR R1 variant straight downhill from here to the southern end of Hell-Bourg (2¾ hours), emerging near the stadium.

Instead of getting straight to Hell Bourg from Cap Anglais, die-hards may choose to walk along the Cirque rim through the lush **Forêt de Bébour-Bélouve**. Just beyond the turn-off, the trail begins a series of slippery ascents and descents through a marshy area of heather forest. Then it enters an enchanted tropical forest, with primordial ferns and huge trees draped in sheets of moss. Around three hours from Cap Anglais you'll reach a radio antenna on the lip of the Cirque. This point offers spectacular views over Hell-Bourg and plenty of photo opportunities.

Following the gravel forest road for another kilometre, you'll come to the comfortable and beautifully situated **Gîte de Bélouve** (see p219). If you've got the time, you could overnight here and the following day take a side trip to the Trou de Fer viewpoint (p219) before hitting the bright lights of Hell-Bourg.

The final descent to **Hell-Bourg** from the Gîte de Bélouve takes around two hours. Cut through the garden of the *gîte* and bear left at the lookout. You emerge in Hell-Bourg near the town hall on Rue Général de Gaulle. Treat yourself to a meal and a hot shower when you arrive! (For information on places to stay and eat in Hell-Bourg, see p210.)

## Day 3: Hell-Bourg to Grand Îlet
5hr, 11km

Start this day's walk by taking the track at the end of Rue Général de Gaulle in Hell-Bourg to the thermal-bath ruins (see Map p210); this track connects with the Îlet-à-Vidot road, which will take you to the small parking lot in Îlet-à-Vidot, where the asphalted road ends.

From the parking lot, a dirt road descends into the valley, reaching a turn-off on the left to Trou Blanc after about 500m. Ignore this turn-off and continue straight ahead, passing a turning on the right to Piton d'Enchaing. The track ascends rather uneventfully for the next 1½ hours, crossing several ravines, before skirting along the edge of a large plantation of casuarina trees at Le Grand Sable. The trail then drops down to cross one of the tributaries of the Rivière des Fleurs Jaunes. There's an excellent bivouac on the far bank where the trail to Le Bélier (a GR R1 variant) strikes off to the right through the woods. Allow about three hours from Hell-Bourg to reach this point.

From there, take the GR R1 variant, following signs down to Le Bélier. You should reach the road at Le Bélier after 1½ to two hours. From there it's less than an hour's walk downhill to Grand Îlet, where you'll find grocers, a bread shop and overnight accommodation, including comfortable *chambre d'hôtes* (see p213). The closest B&B from Le Bélier is Chambre d'hôte Le Cimendef – Chez Noeline et Daniel Campton (p213), about 1.2km away (the other B&Bs are much further down).

## Day 4: Grand Îlet to La Nouvelle via Col des Bœufs
**2hr, 4.5km, 520m descent**

Tip: avoid the slog back uphill to Le Bélier and up the *route forestière* (forest road) to the Col des Bœufs; alternatively, take the bus from Grand Îlet to Le Bélier and on to Col des Bœufs car park just below the summit (see p209); if there's no bus when you set off, it's easy to get a ride up there. Thus you'll spare yourself a rather monotonous section.

From the Col des Bœufs it's an easy 2½-hour hike to **La Nouvelle**. This is the same as the first day of the Haut Mafate walk, crossing the atmospheric Plaine des Tamarins and descending on the far side to the village of La Nouvelle. (For more information on this part of the route, see p246.)

## Day 5: La Nouvelle to Cilaos
**8hr (or 6hr to the D242), 12.5km, 620m ascent, 870m descent**

This final day will take you back to the modern comforts of Cilaos, passing through some stunning countryside on the way.

The first section is a fairly easy two-hour walk to Marla, beginning with a steep descent into the Ravine Gérien and passing some nice views of the Cirque. Be sure to ignore the trails signed off to 'Marla par passerelle' and to the 'Plaine aux Sables'.

Marla consists only of a few houses, but the village shop sells snacks and drinks (for more information on Marla, see p217). From here,

---

**HIKING TIPS**

Safety is basically a matter of common sense and being prepared. Remember to do the following:

- Use a detailed and up-to-date map.
- Double-check the state of the paths before setting out.
- Check the weather report before setting out.
- Leave early enough to reach your destination before dark.
- Take plenty of water and energy-rich snacks.
- Wear comfortable hiking boots.
- Take wet-weather gear.
- Carry a basic medical kit.
- Tell people where you're going if you are hiking alone.

---

ignore paths off to the right for Trois Roches and Roche-Plate, but keep heading south towards the reservoir. The trail ascends steadily towards the obvious low point on the ridge, reaching **Col du Taïbit** in about 1½ hours. If you reach this viewpoint early in the morning, there are magnificent views over the Cirque de Mafate, and down the Cirque de Cilaos to St-Louis and the coast.

The trail (GR R1/R2) descends slowly to the plateau at **Îlet des Salazes** (see p207) where you can treat yourself to an invigorating tisane (herbal tea), before dropping steeply through drier country to cross the D242 – the Îlet à Cordes road – after about two hours. You could always pick up a lift or a bus to Cilaos here, but die-hards should continue across the road and descend into the valley. The trail divides just beyond. The easier and prettier option is to take the right fork, following the GR R2 along the west bank of the Bras des Étangs. It crosses the river near the Cascade de Bras Rouge and then climbs gradually to come out at the Thermes de Cilaos. From there you can take a shortcut up the Sentier des Porteurs for the final ascent into town.

Depending on how you feel, you could stop off at the spa in Cilaos for a massage, or hit one of the restaurants in town for a well-earned Bourbon beer!

---

**EMERGENCIES**

In a real emergency out on the trail, lifting both arms to form a 'V' is a signal to helicopter pilots who fly over the island that you need help. If you have a mobile phone, call the emergency services on ☎ 112.

# Réunion Directory

## CONTENTS

## ACCOMMODATION

While accommodation in Réunion might not reach the stellar heights of Mauritius and the Seychelles, there is still plenty of choice. The smarter hotels tend to be concentrated around the coast and in the attractive mountain towns of Cilaos and Hell-Bourg. In the midrange bracket, there's a smattering of small family hotels and lots of *chambres d'hôtes* (B&Bs), the best of which offer good value for money. Budget travellers will find it hard to keep costs down in St-Denis and the coastal towns around St-Gilles-les-Bains, but elsewhere *gîtes* and the cheaper *chambres d'hôtes* fit the bill. Generally, for a double room you can expect to pay under €40 for budget accommodation, between €40 to €100 for midrange, and over €100 for top-end accommodation.

It is wise to book well in advance, particularly in high season (the mainland France and local school holidays, particularly July, August and around Christmas), when the best places fill up weeks, if not months, ahead. If you're planning a hiking trip in September or October, it's also imperative to book *gîtes de montagnes* as early as possible (see p257), as these months are the busiest and there's only a limited number of places available.

Each year, the **Centrale de Réservation – Île de la Réunion** (Map p178; ☎ 0262 90 78 78; www.reunion.fr; 5 Rue Rontaunay), the former Maison de la Montagne et de la Mer, features updated listings of B&Bs, camp sites, *gîtes d'étape* and hotels.

Recommendations under Sleeping entries are in ascending order of price.

---

### PRACTICALITIES

- Réunion uses the metric system for weights and measures.

- Electric current is 220V, 50Hz AC; plugs have two round pins.

- Video recorders and players run on the PAL system.

- If your French is up to it, keep a finger on the pulse by reading the daily regional newspapers *Journal de l'Île de la Réunion* (JIR; www.clicanoo.com) and *Le Quotidien* (www.lequotidien.re), both good for features and events listings.

- TV viewers have the choice of two government channels, Télé Réunion and Tempo, as well as the independent Antenne Réunion and Canal + Réunion. Most of the programming on the public channels comes from mainland France.

- Tune in to RFO (www.rfo.fr), Kreol FM (www.radiokreol.com) or Radio Free Dom (www.freedom.fr) for local news (in French and Creole), reports and… gossip!

## Camping

Bad news for those who want to spend their holiday under canvas: at the time of writing, there was only one official camp site, on the southwest coast at Étang-Salé-les-Bains. There are plans to open a second camp site in L'Hermitage-les-Bains; check with the tourist office in St-Gilles-les-Bains. You'll also find a couple of *camping chez l'habitant* (informal, privately run camp sites) in Entre-Deux, Îlet-à-Vidot and Bélouve. The Cirque de Mafate also features a few simple camping spots.

You can camp for free in some designated areas in the Cirques, but only for one night at a time. Setting up camp on Piton de la Fournaise (the volcano) is forbidden for obvious reasons.

## Chambres d'Hôtes

*Chambres d'hôtes* are the French equivalent of B&Bs. They are normally tucked away in the hills or in scenic locations and offer a window into a more traditional way of life. Options include everything from restored Creole houses or modern buildings to rooms in family houses. On the whole standards are high, and rooms are generally excellent value. B&B rates are from around €40 for a double room. Breakfast is always included.

Many *chambres d'hôtes* also offer *table d'hôtes* (hearty evening meals) at around €17 to €28 per person (set menu), but this must be reserved in advance (usually the day before). This is a fantastic way to meet locals and sample the local cuisine.

Many *chambres d'hôtes* are members of **Gîtes de France** (Map p178; ☎ 0262 72 97 81; www.gites defrance.re; 5 Rue Rontaunay, St-Denis), which is represented in St-Denis. It has a brochure listing all the *chambres d'hôtes* in Réunion. They are also listed on the website. *Chambres d'hôtes* can be booked either through Gîtes de France or by phoning the owners directly.

## Gîtes de Montagnes

*Gîtes de montagnes* are basic mountain cabins or lodges, operated by the local authorities through the Centrale de Réservation – Île de la Réunion. It is possible to organise a walking holiday using the *gîtes de montagnes* only.

The *gîtes de montagnes* in Réunion are generally in pretty good condition. Thanks to solar power, they all now have electricity, although not all get as cushy as providing warm showers. The Gîte de la Caverne Dufour

---

**TOP FIVE BEST VALUE SLEEPS**

- **Chambre d'hôte Caz Océane** (The West; p198)
- **La Case Bleue** (The Cirques; p206)
- **Rougail Mangue** (The Wild South; p230)
- **Chez Papa Daya** (St-Pierre; p222)
- **Chambre d'hôte Matilona** (The East; p240)

---

at Piton des Neiges is the most basic: it has no hot water, but there are inside toilets.

*Gîtes de montagnes* must be booked and paid for in advance, and charges are not refundable unless a cyclone or a cyclone alert prevents your arrival. In practice, you won't be denied access if you just turn up without your voucher, but you may not have a bed if it's full. Last-minute reservations may be accepted, as there are often last-minute cancellations.

You can book through the **Centrale de Réservation – Île de la Réunion** (Map p178; ☎ 0262 90 78 78; www.reunion.fr; 5 Rue Rontaunay) in St-Denis or through any tourist office on the island, including those in St-Denis, Cilaos, Salazie, Hell-Bourg, St-Gilles-les-Bains, St-Pierre, St-Leu, St-André, Ste-Anne, and Bourg-Murat (see individual town entries for contact details). It's highly recommended that you book well in advance, especially during the busy tourist seasons. One night's accommodation without food costs around €15 per person.

When staying in a *gîte de montagne*, you have to call the *gîte* at least one day ahead to book your meals (or you can ask for this to be done for you when you make the original booking). Dinner costs from €15 to €17, and usually consists of hearty *carris* (curries). Breakfast costs around €5 and normally consists of coffee, bread and jam. Payment is made directly to the caretaker, in cash.

Sleeping arrangements usually consist of bunk beds in shared rooms, so be prepared for the communal living that this entails, although the newer *gîtes* usually have a few private rooms. Sheets and blankets are provided, though you might want to bring a sheet sleeping bag (a sleep sheet).

It's not a bad idea to also bring along toilet paper and a torch. It can get quite chilly at night, so warm clothing will be in order. Some places will let you cook, but many kitchens are so basic – and sometimes grimy – that you probably won't bother.

On arrival and departure you must 'book' in and out with the manager, who will collect your voucher and payment for meals. In theory, you're not meant to occupy a *gîte* before 3pm or remain past 10am. For more information about these *gîtes* and for hiking-related information, see the Hiking in Réunion chapter (p242).

## Gîtes d'Étape

*Gîtes d'étape*, sometimes simply called *gîtes*, are privately owned and work in roughly the same way as the *gîtes de montagnes*, offering dorm beds and meals. Some places even have doubles. One main difference is that you can book these places directly with the owners. There are numerous *gîtes d'étape* in the Cirque de Mafate, and others dotted around the island; most are in the vicinity of walking trails. The host will often offer meals or cooking facilities.

Local tourist offices can provide lists of *gîtes d'étape* in their area. Also check out the website www.reunion.fr.

## Meublés de Tourisme & Gîtes Ruraux

*Gîtes ruraux* and *Meublés de Tourisme* are private houses and lodges that families and groups can rent for self-catering holidays, normally by the week or weekend. There are dozens of *gîtes ruraux* scattered all over the island.

Most offer lodging for four or more people, with facilities of varying standards. Costs vary from around €300 to €500 per week and from €100 to €250 for a weekend (note that not all offer bookings for just a weekend). If you average out the per-person, per-week price and factor in cooking several meals in the house, *gîte* stays can actually be quite economical. Plus, the *gîte* owner often lives nearby and can be a mine of local information.

Contact **Gîtes de France** (Map p178; ☎ 0262 72 97 81; www.gitesdefrance.re; 5 Rue Rontaunay, St-Denis), local tourist offices or check out the websites www.reunion.fr, www.clevacances.re and www.iha.fr. *Gîtes ruraux* and *Meublés de Tourisme* can be booked by phoning the owners directly. A deposit of some sort is usually required in advance.

## Youth Hostels

Réunion has only two operating *auberges de jeunesse* (youth hostels), which are located in Bernica and Entre-Deux. Bookings can be made directly with the hostel.

## Hotels

If you're after serious cosseting and ultraposh digs, you've opened this book on the wrong page. Most hotels on the island are rated as one-, two- or three-star, and lots are unclassified. There is only a sprinkling of four-star hotels.

Réunion isn't flush with hotels, so getting a room can sometimes be difficult. Primarily, they're found in St-Denis and around the beach resorts of the west coast, especially St-Gilles-les-Bains, though you'll also find some scattered in the interior.

Most room rates include breakfast, but check when booking to be sure.

# ACTIVITIES

Want to get the heart pumping and the lungs gasping? You've come to the right place. Réunion offers a smorgasbord of activities for the adventure-seeker all over the island. Do you want to shoot down a river in a raft? Explore the countryside on horseback? No problem: it's all here, plus more; surfing, canyoning, paragliding and mountain biking are yours for the doing.

And if you need to recharge the batteries after all that exertion, rest easy: good restaurants serving wholesome *carris* are never far away.

High standards of professionalism are pretty uniform whatever the activity you choose. Just one quibble: the operators don't have much experience in dealing with English-speaking clients – brush up your French!

## Canyoning

If walking, sliding, rappelling, diving, jumping and swimming down canyons is your thing, Réunion's canyoning hot spots are found in the Cirque de Salazie and Cirque de Cilaos,

---

**BOOK YOUR STAY ONLINE**

For more accommodation reviews and recommendations by Lonely Planet authors, check out the online booking service at www.lonelyplanet.com/hotels. You'll find the true, insider low-down on the best places to stay. Reviews are thorough and independent. Best of all, you can book online.

which are famous for their deep throats, torrents and narrow gorges. For seasoned canyoners, Takamaka and Trou de Fer, accessible from the Hautes Plaines, are talismanic.

## Deep-Sea Fishing

As elsewhere in the Indian Ocean, the season for deep-sea fishing is tied to the feeding habits of bait-fish species; you stand the best chance of hooking a monster marlin from January to March. A boat with crew costs roughly €400/700 per half/full day (maximum of six people).

The main operators are based in St-Gilles-les-Bains (see p189).

## Diving

Réunion is not a hardcore diver's destination, but that doesn't mean you should give it a wide berth. The west coast boasts its fair share of underwater wonders and deserves attention for its number of relaxed sites, with the added lure of a few wrecks and wall dives. You'll find professional dive centres in St-Gilles-les-Bains, St-Leu, Étang-Salé-les-Bains and St-Pierre.

For further information, see p31.

## Hiking

Hiking is without a doubt the most rewarding activity in Réunion, with an excellent system of well-marked trails and an extraordinarily varied terrain. No visitor to the island should miss the superb rugged Cirques of Cilaos, Salazie and Mafate. For the less energetic, the volcano climb makes a manageable day trip and offers some of the most unusual and impressive scenery on the island.

For more information about hiking in Réunion, see p242.

## Horseback Riding

Saddling up is a fun and ecofriendly way to commune with the wilderness and enjoy the glorious hinterlands and lush forests. Horseback riding is commonplace on the island. You don't need any riding experience, as riding centres cater to all levels of proficiency. Rides range from one-hour jaunts (from around €16) to multiday, fully catered treks. Particularly good areas include the Hautes Plaines, the Wild South and even the volcano.

## Mountain Biking

There's only one active hot spot: Le Maïdo. But what a hot spot! An outfitter based in St-Gilles-les-Bains (see the boxed text, p187) organises downhill runs from the upper reaches of Le Maïdo down to the coast.

## Paragliding

On the west coast, the St-Leu area ranks as one of the best paragliding spots in the world, with consistently excellent thermals throughout the year. Local companies offer everything from tandem flights over the lagoon for beginners to longer outings soaring over the Cirques. Prices range from €65 to €130 depending on the length of the flight. Children are welcome.

## Rafting

The wealth of scenic rivers that decorate eastern Réunion make it a water-lover's dream destination. Rivière des Marsouins and Rivière des Roches offer top-class runs to get the blood racing.

The price for all these activities (with a guide and equipment) usually starts at around €40 for a half-day excursion.

## Rock Climbing

In recent years Réunion has seen a growing interest in rock climbing, and it's no wonder. With its sensational stone masses and vertiginous cliffs, it delivers all the goods. The majority of climbing options are concentrated in the Cirque de Cilaos. The most famous spot is Fleurs Jaunes, which boasts a wide range of bolted routes of varying difficulty.

Adventure centres in Cilaos run courses.

> ## TOP FIVE PLACES TO GET OUTDOORS
>
> - **Piton de la Fournaise** (p219) – Scale up Réunion's number-one attraction
> - **Le Maïdo** (p187) – Quicken your pulse with a rip-roaring mountain-bike descent
> - **St-Leu** (p196) – Try paragliding and see the lagoon from above
> - **St-Benoît** (p238) – Test your mettle on a white-water run on Rivière des Marsouins
> - **Cilaos** (p206) – Learn the ropes (literally) of canyoning in the gentle Canyon de Gobert

RÉUNION DIRECTORY

## Surfing

Réunion has a good mix of quality waves perfect for beginners and experienced surfers. Reefs, rocky shelves and hollow sandy beach breaks can all be found – take your pick! Surfing has become increasingly popular in Réunion and some of the breaks are internationally known, especially the tricky Gauche de St-Leu. Today there are surf schools up and running at most premier surf beaches, including Boucan Canot, St-Gilles-les-Bains, La Saline-les-Bains, Étang-Salé-les-Bains and St-Leu.

In general, there are good conditions from May to November.

## BUSINESS HOURS

Shop hours are usually from 8.30am to 5pm or 6pm Monday to Saturday, often with a break from noon to 1pm or 2pm. Some shops close on Monday.

Banks are usually open from 8am to 4pm, Monday to Friday or Tuesday to Saturday.

Government offices are open from 8.30am to noon and 2pm to 5pm Monday to Thursday, to 3pm Friday.

Restaurants open for lunch between noon or 12.30pm and 2pm and for dinner from 7.30pm; they are often closed on one or two days of the week.

## CHILDREN

Fire the babysitter and bring the kids: Réunion is an eminently suitable destination if you're travelling with the sticky-fingered set. With its abundance of beaches, picnic spots and outdoor activities, plus its healthy food, it offers plenty to do for travellers of all ages in a generally hazard-free setting.

Most locals have a number of children themselves and will not be troubled by a screaming child at the next table, should your little treasure throw a tantrum over dinner.

Few hotels offer kids clubs but many places provide cots for free and additional beds for children at a small extra cost. Most *chambres d'hôtes* welcome children.

Many restaurants have children's menus with significantly lower prices.

There are excellent medical facilities in the main cities.

Lonely Planet's *Travel with Children* (Brigitte Barta et al) is a great before-you-go resource containing general tips on vacationing with the kiddies.

## CLIMATE CHART

For further information on choosing the best time of the year for visiting Réunion, see p176.

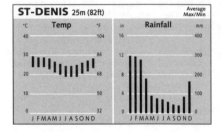

## CUSTOMS REGULATIONS

The following items can be brought into Réunion duty-free: 200 cigarettes, 50 cigars, 1L of strong liquor or 2L of liquor that is less than 22% alcohol by volume, 2L of wine, 50mL of perfume and 250mL of *eau de toilette*, and other goods up to the value of €880. Anything over the limit must be declared on arrival.

There are restrictions on importing plants and animals, for which import permits are required.

---

**BEACHED DREAMS**

Those who've come to Réunion buoyed by dreams of lounging on idyllic white-sand beaches with their beloved were badly advised by their travel agent. The island is quite lacking in those sandy excuses to laze about. Réunion is much more an outdoor and mountain destination than a beach destination. That said, there are a few good surprises on the west coast within the protective barrier of the lagoon. They include the beaches at St-Gilles-les-Bains, L'Hermitage-les-Bains, La Saline-les-Bains and Étang-Salé-les-Bains, all suitable for swimming. *The* beach as far as locals are concerned is Boucan Canot. All these beaches have lifeguards and designated safe swimming areas. There are also a few beaches in the south, including some black-sand ones. There are also dangerous currents, so take advice before plunging in.

With regards to currency, anyone entering or leaving the island must declare sums in excess of €7600.

## DANGERS & ANNOYANCES

Overall, Réunion is relatively safe compared with most Western countries, but occasional robberies do occur. Don't leave anything of value in a rental car or on the beach.

Violence is rarely a problem, and muggings are almost unheard of. Intoxicated people are the most likely troublemakers.

Hikers setting out into the wilderness should be adequately prepared for their trips.

### Driving

Unfortunately Réunion has a bad record when it comes to road safety, which means that you must drive defensively at all times. Potential dangers include drunk drivers, excessive speed, twisting roads and blind bends.

### Swimming

Swimmers should always be aware of currents and riptides. Drowning is a major cause of accidental death for visitors. If you're not familiar with water conditions, ask around. It's best not to swim alone in unfamiliar places.

Attacks by *les dents de la mer* (sharks) occasionally happen, and most years see a shark attack on a surfer or spear fisherman. This is no reason to be paranoid, though; the risks are statistically very low. The locals know their ocean, so it's best to seek their advice before entering the water.

## EMBASSIES & CONSULATES

Since Réunion isn't independent, only a few countries have diplomatic representation:

**Belgium** ( ☎ 0262 97 99 10; chatel@runnet.com; 80 Rue Adolphe Pegoud, 97438 Ste-Marie)

**Germany** (Map p178; ☎ 0262 21 62 06; h.mellano@ orange.fr; 9c Rue de Lorraine, 97400 St-Denis)

**Madagascar** (off Map p178; ☎ 0262 72 07 30; consulat -madrun@wanadoo.fr; 29 Rue St Joseph Ouvrier, 97400 St-Denis)

**Seychelles** ( ☎ 0262 57 26 38; hrop@wanadoo.fr; 67 Chemin Kerveguen, 97430 Le Tampon)

**Switzerland** ( ☎ 0262 45 55 74; poldestpol@wanadoo. fr; 107 Rue Crève Coeur, 97460 St-Paul)

## FESTIVALS & EVENTS

Major festivals in Réunion involve street parties, exhibitions, sports events, music, dancing and various other activities. Rural fairs are also hugely popular and usually celebrate local produce, which can be anything from *chou chou* (choko; a green squash-like vegetable) to sugar cane. For foreigners, they offer the chance to be immersed in local culture and to buy top quality regional specialities.

Abolition of Slavery Day (a national holiday) is taken very seriously, particularly among the Creole population, who still occupy a disadvantaged position in society.

The Indian community is principally made up of Tamil Hindus and they hold some amazing rites, including *cavadee* (in which pilgrims practise self-mutilation) and impressive firewalking ceremonies. The Hindu temple in St-André is the most popular location for these events. For more about these festivals, see p152.

To find out what's happening during your stay, contact any of the tourist offices in the relevant town.

Main festivals in Réunion:

### January
**Fête du Miel Vert** (Festival of Honey) Plaine-des-Cafres.
**Fête de la Vigne** (Wine Harvest Festival) Cilaos.
**Fire-walking ceremonies** Various locations.

### February
**Cavadee** Tamil procession; St-André.
**Chinese New Year** Various locations.

### April
**Tamil New Year** Dance displays; various locations.

### May
**Cross du Piton des Neiges** (Running race to the Piton des Neiges) Cilaos
**Fête du Choca** (Festival of Choca) Crafts made from choca leaves; Entre-Deux.
**Leu Tempo** Theatre festival; St-Leu.

### June
**Fête des Goyaviers** (Festival of Guava) Plaine-des-Palmistes.

### August
**Fête du Vacoa** (Festival of Vacoa) Crafts made from screw-pine fronds; St-Philippe.
**Pèlerinage à la Vierge au Parasol** (Pilgrimage to the Virgin with the Parasol) Ste-Rose.
**Sakifo** Festival of Creole music; St-Pierre.

### September
**Fête de Notre Dame de la Salette** (Festival of Notre Dame de la Salette) Fair and street events over 10 days; St-Leu.

**October**
**Fête de l'Ail** (Festival of Garlic) Petite Île.
**Fête des Bichiques** (Festival of Bichiques) Bras-Panon.
**Fête des Lentilles** (Festival of Lentils) Cilaos.
**Semaine Créole** (Creole Week) A week of cultural events; various locations.
**Grand Raid** Cross-country race in October or November; St-Philippe to St-Denis.
**Divali** (Dipavali) Tamil festival of light in late October or early November; St-André and other locations.

**November**
**Fête du Curcuma** (Festival of Curcuma) St-Joseph.
**Fête du Safran** (Festival of Saffron) Plaine-des-Grègues.

**December**
**Mégavalanche** Mountain-bike descent in late November or early December; Maïdo to St-Paul.
**Commémoration de l'Abolition de l'Esclavage** (Abolition of Slavery Day) Creole music and dancing; various locations.

## FOOD

Eating reviews listed in the Réunion chapter usually indicate the price of mains, followed by the price of *menus* (two- or three-course set menus). Set menus include all courses but no wine, except in some *chambres d'hôtes*, where wine may be included. Within each eating section, restaurants appear in order of ascending price.

You should be able to get a reasonable *plat du jour* (dish of the day) at lunchtime for between €8 and €13. For a full, midrange restaurant meal you should expect to pay €25 to €40 per person with wine.

For information on Réunionnais gastronomy, see p169.

## GAY & LESBIAN TRAVELLERS

French laws concerning homosexuality prevail in Réunion, which means there is no legal discrimination against homosexual activity and homophobia is relatively uncommon.

Throughout the island, but particularly on the west coast, there are restaurants, bars, operators and accommodation places that make a point of welcoming gays and lesbians. Certain areas are the focus of the gay and lesbian communities, among them St-Denis, St-Pierre and La Saline-les-Bains. Tourist offices have a leaflet that lists gay-friendly venues in Réunion. An overview of gay-friendly venues – accommodation, restaurants and activities – is available on www.reunion.fr.

## HOLIDAYS

Most of Réunion's offices, museums and shops are closed during *jours fériés* (public holidays), which are as follows:
**New Year's Day** 1 January
**Easter Monday** March/April
**Labour Day** 1 May
**Victory Day 1945** 8 May
**Ascension Day** late May or June
**Bastille Day** (National Day) 14 July
**Assumption Day** 15 August
**All Saints' Day** 1 November
**Armistice Day 1918** 11 November
**Abolition of Slavery Day** 20 December
**Christmas Day** 25 December

## INSURANCE

Insurance requirements for Réunion are the same as for Mauritius; see p153 for more information.

---

### RÉUNION FOR CRAZIES

If you want to work off any extra pounds gained in Réunion's fine restaurants, here's the solution: take part in the Grand Raid, one of the world's most challenging cross-country races. It's held every October or November. The route roughly follows the path of the GR R2 hiking trail, which traverses the island from St-Denis to Mare Longue, near St-Philippe, taking in parts of the Mafate and Cilaos Cirques, the Plaine-des-Cafres and the lunar landscape around Piton de la Fournaise.

Covering some 150km, the Grand Raid would be a challenging race over level ground, but runners also have to negotiate a total of some 9000m of altitude change, hence the race is nicknamed the 'Cross-Country for Crazies'! The pack leaders can complete this agonising run in 22 hours or less, but contestants are allowed up to 64 hours to finish.

Too difficult for you? Try the 'easier' Semi Raid, which starts from Cilaos and covers about 78km, with 'only' 4700m of altitude change.

For more information, contact the **Association Le Grand Raid** ( ☎ 0262 20 32 00; www.grandraid -reunion.com).

## INTERNET ACCESS

Wi-fi has spread across the island like a forest fire. Many midrange and all top-end hotels as well as B&Bs offer this service, usually without a charge. Coverage either extends throughout the hotel or may be restricted to public areas.

You will only find internet cafes in bigger towns and resort areas such as Cilaos, Salazie, St-Denis, St-Gilles-les-Bains, St-Leu and St-Pierre. The connection is generally good and rates are fairly standard at around €12 per hour.

## MAPS

For most purposes the IGN *Carte Touristique La Réunion* map, at a scale of 1:100,000 (1cm = 1km), which covers the island in one sheet, is perfectly adequate. The most detailed and accurate maps for hiking are the six-sheet 1:25,000 series (see p243).

## MONEY

As in France, the unit of currency is the euro (€), which is divided into 100 cents. Euro coins come in denominations of one, two, five, 10, 20 and 50 cents and one and two euros. Banknotes are issued in denominations of five, 10, 20, 50, 100, 200 and 500 euros.

For exchange rates, see the inside front cover. For information on costs, see p17.

### ATMs

Most banks and post offices have an ATM (known as a *guichet automatique de banque* or *gabier*) that honours major international credit cards. Visa and MasterCard are the most widely accepted. They are the easiest way to access funds while in Réunion. If you're heading off into the Cirques, it's wise to stock up with euros beforehand. There is only one ATM in Cilaos and three in Salazie.

### Credit Cards

Credit cards will prove the cheapest and easiest way to pay for major purchases in Réunion. Visa (Carte Bleue) and MasterCard (Eurocard) are the cards most widely accepted by hotels, restaurants, supermarkets, adventure centres, major petrol stations and stores. Credit cards are mandatory if you want to rent a car, as they'll be used as a form of *caution* (deposit). Smaller places, however, sometimes refuse cards for small amounts (typically under €15) and it's rare for *chambres d'hôtes* and *gîtes d'étape* to take credit cards.

### Money Changers

Changing money in Réunion? Dream on! The number of banks that have foreign-exchange facilities and do change cash has been dramatically reduced since the introduction of the euro. This service tends to be dropped in favour of ATMs. Consider yourself very lucky if you find a bank that changes foreign currencies on the island.

There are no exchange facilities at either Roland Garros International Airport or the ferry terminal in Le Port, though the airport does at least have an ATM.

As a general strategy, it's sensible to bring a fair supply of euros with you and to top up from the ATMs.

### Travellers Cheques

Travellers cheques are not widely accepted in Réunion; you'll find that most banks are reluctant to change them. Stash up on cash and rely on your credit card.

## TELEPHONE

Réunion's telephone system is efficient. For mobile phones, Réunion uses the GSM 900/1800 system, which is compatible with Europe and Australia (though not the USA). The network covers most towns and villages throughout the island, including the Cirque de Mafate. If your GSM phone has been 'unlocked', it is also possible to buy a SIM card with either of the two local network operators: Orange and SFR.

You'll usually find a public telephone in or near the post office and you can direct-dial international numbers on them. You can buy a *télécarte* (phonecard) at post offices and shops.

Alternatively, there are various prepaid calling cards (available at newsagents) that require you to dial a free number and enter a personal identity number (PIN) before you place your call.

All telephone numbers throughout Réunion consist of 10 digits; landline numbers start with ☎0262, and mobile-phone numbers start with ☎06. If calling a Réunion landline or mobile number from abroad (bar France), you'll need to dial the international access code (☎00), Réunion's country code (☎262), then the local number minus the first 0.

There are no area codes in Réunion.

## TOURIST INFORMATION

There are generally *offices du tourisme* (tourist offices) in most main towns across the island. Most of them have at least one staff member who speaks English.

Tourist-office staff provide maps, brochures and the twice-yearly magazine *Guide RUN*, which is a useful directory of hotels, restaurants, discos and other places of interest to visitors.

The **Centrale de Réservation – Île de la Réunion** (Map p178; ☎ 0262 90 78 78; www.reunion.fr; 5 Rue Rontaunay, St-Denis) is Réunion's regional tourist office.

You can also contact the French tourist office in your home country; these are listed on www.franceguide.com.

## TRAVELLERS WITH DISABILITIES

Independent travel is difficult for anyone who has mobility problems in Réunion. Only the newest of newly remodeled businesses have features specifically suited to wheelchair use.

Negotiating the streets of most towns in a wheelchair is frustrating given the lack of adequate equipment, and most outdoor attractions and historic places don't have trails suited to wheelchair use. Two notable exceptions are Kelonia in St-Leu (see p195), and the Maison du Volcan in Bourg-Murat (p215).

## VISAS

Though Réunion is a French department, it's not part of the Schengen treaty. The visa requirements for entry to Réunion are almost the same as for France, bar a few exceptions. For EU nationals, a national ID or a passport suffices. Citizens of a number of other Western countries, including Australia, the USA, Canada and New Zealand, do not need visas to visit Réunion as tourists for up to three months; they need only a passport.

Other nationals should check with the French embassy or consulate nearest your home address to find out if you need a visa. For example, Brazilian citizens do not need a visa to enter mainland France but do require a visa for Réunion.

## WOMEN TRAVELLERS

The sight of women travelling, be it in a group or alone, is not met with too much surprise or curiosity, and women travelling by themselves should encounter no difficulties, as long as sensible precautions observed in most Western countries are adhered to.

Women can enter most bars alone, but there are still a few places where this may attract unwanted attention – you'll get a pretty good idea when you enter.

It's not advisable to walk alone on the trails in the interior.

# TRANSPORT AROUND RÉUNION

## AIR

Réunion has two international airports. The vast majority of flights come into **Roland Garros International Airport** (off Map p234; ☎ 0262 48 80 68; www.reunion.aeroport.fr) about 10km east of St-Denis. Coming from Mauritius, you have the option of landing at **Pierrefonds Airport** (Map p225; ☎ 0262 96 80 00; www.pierrefonds.aeroport.fr), in the south of the island near St-Pierre.

For more information regarding air travel, see p318.

## BICYCLE

The traffic, the haste of most motorists and the steep and precarious nature of the mountain roads means that those considering cycling as a form of transport in Réunion should be prepared for some hair-raising and potentially dangerous situations.

## BUS

Réunion's major towns and many of the little ones in between are linked by bus. The island's bus service is knows as **Car Jaune** ( ☎ 0810 123 974) and has distinctive yellow buses. The main *gare routière* (bus station) is on Blvd Lancastel on the St-Denis seafront.

Buses on most routes run between about 6am and 7pm, with a limited number of services on Sunday. For a few sample fares, you'll pay €7 from St-Denis to St-Pierre, €3.50 from St-Denis to St-Benoît and €4.20 from St-Benoît to St-Pierre via Plaine-des-Cafres. You can pay the driver as you board. To get the bus to stop, you ring the bell or clap your hands twice loudly.

Car Jaune provides regional minibus services for several areas on the island; they run from St-Benoît, St-Joseph, Ste-Rose, St-Leu and St-Paul. These convoluted local routes can be fairly confusing, particularly if you don't speak much French. Of most use to travellers are the buses from St-André to Salazie, Salazie to Hell-Bourg, Grand Îlet and Le Bélier, and the buses from St-Louis to Cilaos, Îlet à Cordes and Bras-Sec.

## CAR

With most attractions located in the hills, we strongly recommend hiring a vehicle. No other form of transport lets you explore the island's secret backwaters as a set of motorised wheels. There are some gorgeous runs, cruising along the island's dramatic roads; heading into the mountains via the Cirques roads is a magnificent experience. The superbly engineered roads snake through hairpin bends, up steep slopes and along sheer drops, surrounded all the while by glorious – and distracting – scenery. This said, be prepared for traffic jams near the main cities.

The road system on the island is excellent and well signposted. The new Route des Tamarins, the main road to the west of the island, is an amazing feat of engineering (see below) and boasts international motorway standards.

*Routes départementales*, whose names begin with the letter D (or RD), are tertiary local roads, many of them very tortuous (use your horn!).

The experience is likely to be marred somewhat by the local drivers, who insist on driving these roads at breakneck speeds.

Petrol stations are very easy to come by. A litre of unleaded costs about €1.30. Most stations accept credit cards.

## Hire

Good news: *location de voitures* (car hire) is extremely popular in Réunion, and rates are reasonable. Most companies stipulate that the driver must be at least 21 (sometimes 23) years of age, have held a driving licence for at least a year, and have a passport or some other form of identification. EU citizens can drive on their national driving licence; from elsewhere, you'll need an international driving licence.

Prices and regulations don't vary much between the main international rental companies. Rates start at €45 per day (including third-party liability insurance and unlimited mileage) and can drop as low as €30 per day or €25 if you rent for several weeks. Most companies require a credit card, primarily so that you can leave a *caution* (deposit). They'll probably ask you to leave a signed credit-card slip without a sum written on it as a deposit.

Collision-damage waivers (CDW, or *assurance tous risques*) are not included and vary greatly from company to company. The *franchise* (excess) for a small car is usually around €800. You can reduce it to zero (or at least to a half) by paying a daily insurance supplement of around €10.

Arranging your car rental before you leave home is usually cheaper than a walk-in rental. Deals can be found on the internet through companies like **DriveAway Holidays** (www.driveaway.com.au) in Australia, **Holiday Autos** (www.holidayautos.co.uk) in the UK and **Location de Voiture** (www.elocationdevoitures.fr, in French) in France.

All major firms have a desk at the airports, and most offer delivery. They also have representatives in St-Gilles-les-Bains and St-Pierre.

There are also plenty of independent operators around the island. They are cheaper than international companies but their rental cars are usually older. Reputable ones include the following (websites all in French):

**Degrif' Loc – Bonne Route** ( ☎ 0262 26 29 44, 0692 05 18 32, 0692 27 17 19; www.degrifloc.re, www.bonneroute.re)

RÉUNION DIRECTORY

---

### ROUTE DES TAMARINS

'It's a major change for the island, because the horrendous traffic jams that plagued the west coast are now a thing of the past', says one inhabitant from St-Paul. Inaugurated in June 2009 after six years of work, the Route des Tamarins is a four-lane expressway that connects Saint-Paul to Étang-Salé – 34km – and branches onto the existing RN1. It creates a direct route between the two biggest cities, St-Denis in the north and St-Pierre in the south. This vital link can now be completed in less than an hour. Before the completion of the Route des Tamarins, it could take up to three hours. Built on slopes at a medium-altitude level, the road is a masterpiece of civil engineering, with four impressive viaducts, three tunnels, 23 bridges and nine interchanges, which all blend fairly unobtrusively into the environment. For tourists, this means easier, quicker access to the beaches in the west and St-Pierre, as well as safer road conditions.

**ITC Tropicar** ( ☎ 0262 24 01 01; www.itctropicar.com)
**Location Saint-Leusienne** ( ☎ 0262 34 77 12, 0692 86 44 90; www.locationsaint-leusienne.com)
**Mik Location** ( ☎ 0262 35 30 63; www.mik-location. com)
**Multi Auto** ( ☎ 0262 29 01 66, 0692 70 37 03; multi auto@wanadoo.fr)

## Road Rules

Like mainland France, Réunion keeps to the right side of the road. Speed limits are clearly indicated and vary from 50km/h in towns to 110km/h on dual carriageways. Drivers and passengers are required to wear seat belts. The alcohol limit is 0.5g/L.

# Seychelles

HOLGER LEUE

# Seychelles Snapshots

The Seychelles is a paradise for tourists, no doubt about it, and most tourists leave with a very positive impression of the country. Whether or not the Seychelles is heaven for its own population is another story. Politically, the situation has barely evolved in 30 years. The ruling party, the Seychelles People's Progressive Front (SPPF), led by President James Michel, has been governing the country since 1977. The Seychellois aspire to *sanzman* (change). Freedom of the press is still quite limited. The opposition newspaper, *Regar,* had to close down in 2006, and the SPPF continues to exert a firm grip on the media.

Economically, the country is in a transition period. The Seychelles is the richest country in Africa, but it has also long been one of the most highly indebted countries in the world, according to the World Bank. The year 2008 marked a turning point: due to increasing international pressures, local authorities decided to float the Seychelles rupee and deregulate the economy. Prices immediately rose by about 30%. Surprisingly, it didn't result in rioting and protests. Even better, it paid off; the country has achieved growth in a climate of global recession. Foreign investors are back. Tourism remains a major source of income for the nation, although visitor numbers fell by 5% in 2009 compared with 2008. That said, some Seychellois feel increasingly concerned about the repercussions of tourism development on their daily lives. Large tracts of unspoiled beaches have been more or less privatised by recent hotels. 'We fear that direct access to our beaches may be made more and more difficult', locals said to us. Others fear that their country is being 'sold' to foreign investors, who buy large tracts of land.

With the increase in acts of piracy in the entire Western Indian Ocean, the Seychelles found itself exposed to attacks led by Somali pirates in 2009 and 2010. The government called on the international community for assistance and has signed an agreement with the USA to combat piracy in the Seychellois territorial waters. At the time of writing, the Outer Islands were off-limits to foreigners.

# HISTORY

Until the 18th century the Seychelles was uninhabited. The islands were first spotted by Portuguese explorers, but the first recorded landing was by a British East India Company ship in 1609. Pirates and privateers used the Seychelles as a temporary base during lulls in their marauding.

## THE COLONIAL PERIOD

In 1742, Mahé de Labourdonnais, the governor of what is now Mauritius, sent Captain Lazare Picault to investigate the islands. Picault named the main island after his employer (and the bay where he landed after himself) and laid the way for the French to claim possession of the islands 12 years later.

It took a while for the French to do anything with their possession. It wasn't until 1770 that the first batch of 21 settlers and seven slaves arrived on Ste Anne Island. After a few false starts, the settlers began growing spices, cassava, sugar cane and maize.

In the 18th century, the British began taking an interest in the Seychelles. The French were not willing to die for their colony and didn't resist British attacks, and the Seychelles became a British dependency in 1814. The British did little to develop the islands except increase the number of slaves. After abolition in 1835, freed slaves from around the region were also brought here. Because few British settled, however, the French language and culture remained dominant.

Over the years the islands have been used as a holding pen for numerous political prisoners and exiles.

In 1903 the Seychelles became a crown colony administered from London. It promptly went into the political and economic doldrums until 1964, when two political parties were formed. France Albert René, a young lawyer, founded the Seychelles People's United Party (SPUP). A fellow lawyer, James Mancham, led the new Seychelles Democratic Party (SDP).

## INDEPENDENCE

Mancham's SDP, made up of businesspeople and planters, won the elections in 1966 and 1970. René's SPUP fought on a socialist and independence ticket. In June 1975 a coalition of the two parties gave the appearance of unity in the lead-up to independence, which was granted a year later. Mancham became the first president of the Republic of Seychelles and René the prime minister.

The flamboyant Sir Jim (as James Mancham was known) – poet and playboy – placed all his eggs in one basket: tourism. He jet-setted around the world with a beautiful socialite on each arm, and he put the Seychelles on the map.

The rich and famous poured in for holidays and to party, party, party. Adnan Khashoggi and other Arab millionaires bought large tracts of land, while film stars and celebrities came to enhance their romantic, glamorous images.

According to René and the SPUP, however, the wealth was not being spread evenly and the country was no more than a rich person's playground. René stated that poor Creoles were little better off than slaves.

## THE LONG ROAD TO DEMOCRACY

In June 1977, barely a year after independence, René and a team of Tanzanian-trained rebels carried out an almost bloodless coup while Mancham was in London attending a Commonwealth Conference. In the following years, René consolidated his position by deporting many supporters of the outlawed SDP. Opposed to René's one-party socialist state, these *grands blancs* (white landowners) set up 'resistance movements' in Britain, South Africa and Australia.

The country fell into disarray as the tourist trade dried to a trickle. The 1980s saw a campaign of civil disruption by supporters of the SDP, two army mutinies and more foiled coup attempts.

Finally, facing growing international criticism and the threatened withdrawal of foreign aid, René pulled a political about-face in the early 1990s; he abandoned one-party rule and announced the return to a multiparty democracy.

Elections were held in 1992 under the watchful eye of Commonwealth observers. René and his renamed Seychelles People's Progressive Front won 58.4% of the votes; Mancham, who had returned to the Seychelles, fielded 33.7% for his SDP and claimed the results were rigged.

René maintained his grip on power, while the SDP's star continued to wane. Even Mancham himself abandoned the SDP in favour of the centrist Seychelles National Party (SNP) in 1999. In the 2002 elections, the SNP, led by Wavel Ramkalawan, an Anglican priest, confirmed its stand as the main opposition party by winning over 42% of the vote.

In April 2004, René finally relinquished the presidency to the former vice president, James Michel, who had stood by René through thick and thin. After a close race with Wavel Ramkalawan, the opposition leader, Michel won the 2006 presidential election, gaining 53.5% of the vote.

William McAteer's *Rivals in Eden* and *Hard Times in Paradise* trace the islands' history from the first French landing in 1740 up to 1919. Deryck Scarr brings things up to date in *Seychelles since 1770*, which covers the 20th century.

Michel doesn't seem willing to cede his power to any of his opponents; he prematurely dissolved the National Assembly in March 2007, following the boycott of assembly proceedings by the opposition party, and the general elections in May 2007 returned 18 SPPF members as against seven members of the SPF opposition party led by Wavel Ramkalawan (exactly the same numbers as before the dissolution). Though these elections were held democratically, the opposition claimed that the government bought votes. The next presidential elections are due in 2011.

While René has been much criticised over the years, there's no denying that overall standards of health, education and housing have improved, and annual per capita income has grown from around US$1000 in 1976 to close on US$7000 today.

# THE CULTURE

## THE NATIONAL IDENTITY

Seychellois may appear somewhat indifferent to strangers at first meeting (at least by comparison with people in other African nations), but once the ice has been broken you will find intense friendliness and warmth. There's not much anticolonial feeling evident – it has long been replaced with a sense of national pride that developed after independence.

As in Mauritius and Réunion, it is the Creole language, cuisine and culture that helps bind the Seychelles society. Over 90% of the population speak Creole as their first language, though most also speak English – the language of government and business – and French.

The government has worked hard to promote social cohesion. As a result, racism is extremely rare, though there are concerns that the number of immigrant workers, particularly Indian labourers brought in to work on construction sites, may upset the balance.

On the whole, however, the Seychellois are pretty relaxed, and traditional work patterns are very different from Western ones.

Despite the apparently easygoing existence, the living standards of many Seychellois are lower than you might expect, mostly because of the disproportionately high cost of living. The islands may seem Westernised, but the minimum wage is around Rs 2000 (€325) per month. As prices creep up and more people struggle to make ends meet, burglaries and petty theft are on the rise. Crime levels are still extremely low, but it's a favourite topic of conversation among islanders.

> The Freedom Sq monument known to locals as Twa Zwazo (meaning 'three birds') is said to represent the continents of Africa, Europe and Asia, each of which has played a part in the development of the Seychellois.

## LIFESTYLE

Thanks to the islands' close links with Europe, the contemporary face of the Seychelles is surprisingly modern. The main island of Mahé is a rather sophisticated place, characterised as much by Western-style clothing, brand-new cars, mobile phones and modern houses as by any overt signs of traditional Creole culture. But beneath this strongly Westernised veneer, many aspects of traditional Creole culture survive. They live on in dance, music, hospitality, ancient beliefs, the language, the carefree attitude, and in many other day-to-day ways of doing things.

> Since 1982, when Creole was made the language of education, literacy rates have risen to nearly 90%.

The society continues to be largely male dominated. Fortunately for women, the tourism industry is regarded as an equal-opportunity employer.

Most Seychellois are Catholic, but marriage is an unpopular institution. The reasons cited are that not marrying is a relic of slavery, when marriages simply didn't take place, and that marriage is expensive. As a result an estimated 75% of children are born out of wedlock. There's no taboo about illegitimacy, however. Though the children tend to stay with the mother, fathers are legally obliged to support their offspring.

Since the age of consent is only 14 years, there are a large number of teenage mothers. Pregnant girls are not allowed to attend school, and after the birth few bother to return. This obviously has a negative impact on education levels and job options for a certain number of women.

The Seychellois are generally tolerant of gay and lesbian relationships as long as couples don't flaunt their sexuality. Indeed, there are few rules and regulations to be followed, beyond respecting local attitudes towards nudity and visiting places of religious worship (see below).

## ECONOMY

The economy is heavily reliant on tourism, which now employs at least 20% of the labour force, with exclusive resorts replacing the spice and coconut plantations. Despite the worldwide downturn in tourism, the sector has been picking up in recent years and the number of arrivals to the Seychelles is on the increase, with more than 160,000 visitors per year at the time of writing.

The other mainstay of the economy is industrial fishing, which actually overtook tourism as the country's biggest foreign-exchange earner in 2002.

Nevertheless, the economy remains extremely vulnerable to external events. Despite attempts to strengthen its agricultural base and use more locally manufactured products, the Seychelles continues to import 90% of its needs. As a result, even a slight dip in export earnings causes major ructions in the economy.

In 2008, the highly indebted country was forced to turn to the IMF for assistance. A package of reforms was passed, including the free floating of the rupee, the abolition of all exchange restrictions and massive cuts in public spending. The debt was frozen and the economy quickly rebounded.

The chronic foreign-exchange shortage has pushed the government to encourage foreign investments with tax incentives and other benefits. Sectors targeted include offshore banking and insurance, trans-shipment and shipping registration.

## POPULATION

The population of the Seychelles is more strongly African than in Mauritius or Réunion, but even so you'll see almost every shade of skin and hair imaginable, arising from a mixture of largely French and African genes, together with infusions of Indian, Chinese and Arab blood. Distinct Indian and Chinese communities make up only a tiny proportion of the ethnic mix, however, the rest being Creole. As for the *grands blancs,* most were dispossessed in the wake of the 1977 coup.

About 90% of Seychellois live on Mahé and nearly a third of these are concentrated in and around the capital. Most of the remaining 10% live on Praslin and La Digue, while the other islands are either uninhabited or home to tiny communities.

## RELIGION

Nearly 90% of Seychellois are Roman Catholic, 7% are Anglican and 2.5% belong to the rapidly expanding evangelical churches. The remainder belong to the tiny Hindu, Muslim and Chinese communities largely based in Victoria.

Most people are avid churchgoers. On a Sunday, Victoria's Catholic and Anglican cathedrals as well as the smaller churches scattered around the main islands are full to bursting. Note that both men and women should dress modestly and conservatively when visiting a place of worship; shorts or sleeveless tops are inappropriate.

There is also a widespread belief in the supernatural and in the old magic of spirits known as *gris gris*. Sorcery was outlawed in 1958, but a few *bonhommes* and *bonnefemmes di bois* (medicine men and women) still practise their cures and curses and concoct potions for love, luck and revenge.

## ARTS

Since these islands were originally uninhabited, the Creoles are the closest the country has to an indigenous population. Many aspects of their African origins survive, including the *séga* and *moutia* dances.

### Literature

Among the most important local authors writing in Creole are the poet-playwright Christian Sevina, short-story author and playwright Marie-Thérèse Choppy, poet Antoine Abel and mystery writer Jean-Joseph Madeleine. Unfortunately their works are not yet available in English.

In fact there is surprising little English-language fiction about these islands. Most authors go in for travelogues and autobiographies. The one exception is long-time resident Glynn Burridge, who mixes fact and fiction in his short stories. They are published locally in two volumes under the title of *Voices: Seychelles Short Stories* and are available in bookshops in Victoria.

### Music & Dance

The Indian, European, Chinese and Arabic backgrounds of the Seychellois are reflected in their music. The accordion, banjo and violin music brought to the islands by the early European settlers has blended with that of the *makalapo*, a stringed instrument with a tin soundbox; the *zez*, a monochord sitar; African skin drums; and the *bom*, a bowed instrument.

You may also come across roving *camtole* bands, which feature fiddle, banjo, accordion and drums. It is the sombre *moutia*, however, with its strong African rhythms, that is the traditional dance of the Seychelles. The slow, repetitive dance routines were originally accompanied by prayers that the slaves turned into work chants, similar to the early black gospel music of the USA. The *moutia* is normally danced around an open fire and serves as the primary evening entertainment.

The Seychelles version of the *séga* differs little from that of Mauritius. Many of the large hotels hold *séga* dance displays at least one night a week.

Patrick Victor and Jean-Marc Volcy are two of the Seychelles' best-known musicians, playing Creole pop and folk music. Other local stars are Emmanuel Marie and the late Raymond Lebon, whose daughter Sheila Paul made it into the local charts with an updated rendering of her father's romantic ballads.

### Visual Arts

David André's *Esper Sa Sanson*, some of which is sung in English, and Jean Ally's *Welcome* (an entirely English-language recording of *séga*) are both good introductions to local music and should be available in music stores in Victoria.

Over recent decades, more and more artists have settled in the Seychelles and spawned a local industry catering to souvenir-hungry tourists. While shops are full of stereotypical scenes of palm trees and sunsets, there are also some innovative and talented artists around.

Michael Adams is the best-known and most distinctive contemporary artist. He has a studio near Baie Lazare in South Mahé. George Camille is another highly regarded artist who takes his inspiration from nature. He has a gallery on Praslin. Other notable artists are Barbara Jenson, who has a studio on La Digue, Gerard Devoud at Baie Lazare and Nigel Henry at Beau Vallon.

Look out, too, for works by Leon Radegonde, who produces innovative abstract collages; Andrew Gee, who specialises in silk paintings and watercolours of fish; and the sun-drenched paintings of Christine Harter. The painter and sculptor Egbert Marday produces powerful sketches of fisherfolk and plantation workers, but is perhaps best known for the statue of a man with a walking cane, situated outside the courthouse on Victoria's Independence Ave. Lorenzo Appiani produced the sculptures on the roundabouts at each end of 5th June Ave in Victoria.

# FOOD & DRINK

Meat lovers, come prepared: the cuisine of the Seychelles is heavily influenced by the surrounding ocean, with fish appearing as the main ingredient in many dishes. Cultural influences are also distinctive, with a blend of European (mostly French and Italian) and African gastronomic delights.

## STAPLES & SPECIALITIES

Fish, fish, FISH! And rice. This is the most common combination (*pwason ek diri* in Creole patois) in the Seychelles, and we won't complain – fish is guaranteed to be served ultrafresh and literally melts in your mouth. You'll devour *bourgeois, capitaine,* shark, *job,* parrotfish, caranx, grouper and tuna, among others. To bring variety, they are cooked in innumerable guises: grilled, steamed, minced, smoked, stewed, salted, baked, wrapped in a banana leaf; the list goes on and on.

Seafood lovers will have found their spiritual home in the Seychelles; lobster, crab, seashells (especially *trouloulou* and *teck teck,* two local varieties of shells) and octopus are widely available.

The Seychelles is dripping with tropical fruit, including mango, banana, breadfruit, papaya, coconut, grapefruit, pineapple and carambole. Mixed with spices, they make wonderful accompaniments, such as the flavourful *chatini* (chutney). Vanilla, cinnamon and nutmeg are used to flavour stews and other preparations.

Gastronauts might consider trying *civet de chauve souris* (bat curry), which is considered a delicacy. You'll also find meat, mostly beef and chicken, but it's imported.

## DRINKS

Freshly squeezed juices and coconut water are the most natural and thirst-quenching drinks around. If you want to put some wobble in your step, Seybrew, the local brand of beer, is sold everywhere. Eku, another locally produced beer, is a bit harder to find. Wine is available at most restaurants, but be aware that some bottles will have been exposed to the heat.

Feeling adventurous? Try the infamous *calou,* a kind of palm wine – devilish. It's not sold in restaurants, but most families prepare their own poison.

## WHERE TO EAT & DRINK

There's a full gamut of restaurant types, from funky shacks and burger joints to ritzy restaurants. Larger hotels have a choice of restaurants, with one always serving buffets (usually Creole or seafood). There is not a vast selection of street snacks to choose from in the Seychelles, but street vendors sell fresh fruit and fish – a good option if you're self-catering. Grocery stores are also widely available in Mahé and Praslin. The Victoria market is another good place to stock up on fresh food.

## EATING WITH KIDS

If you're travelling with the tykes, you'll find that children's menus are not normally offered in restaurants. However, most local eateries will accommodate

Did you know that the film *Goodbye Emmanuelle* was filmed on La Digue?

The huge Indian Ocean Tuna plant in Victoria is one of the world's largest tuna canneries.

Traditional Seychelles cuisine is the focus of *Dekouver Marmit,* compiled by the Ministry of Local Government, Sports & Culture.

---

**SEYCHELLES' TOP FIVE**

This is a quick selection of some of our favourite places to indulge in fine dining, chosen for palate pleasure over price considerations. Turn to the appropriate page to initiate salivation.
**Coco Rouge** (p300) Unfussy and laid-back; killer smoked-fish salad.
**Le Corsaire** (p286) Style meets substance.
**Lanbousir** (p306) A beach shack near the most glamorous beach of the Seychelles.
**Laurier Hotel & Restaurant** (p301) Phenomenal Creole buffet.
**Café des Arts** (p301) Romantic to boot.

---

two children splitting a meal or can produce child-size portions on request. You can also ask for restaurant staff to bring you simple food.

## VEGETARIANS & VEGANS

Restaurant menus in the Seychelles are dominated by fish, seafood and meat dishes, though there are actually a few salad and pasta dishes that are meat-free. If you're self-catering, you'll have much more choice, with a good selection of fruits and vegetables.

## HABITS & CUSTOMS

Dining habits and customs in the Seychelles are similar to those elsewhere in the region, and in the home countries of most Western travellers. Lunch is usually the main meal of the day and is typically served around noon. Dinner tends to be a lighter version of lunch and is eaten around 7pm. Meals are central to family life on weekends.

# ENVIRONMENT

The Seychelles is a haven for wildlife, particularly birds and tropical fish. Because of the islands' isolation and the comparatively late arrival of humans, many species are endemic to the Seychelles.

> The Seychellois are said to be the biggest fish-eaters in the world, with an average annual consumption of 90kg per person.

## THE LAND

The Seychelles lies about 1600km off the east coast of Africa and just south of the equator. It is made up of 115 islands, of which the central islands (including Mahé, Praslin and La Digue) are granite and the outlying islands are coral atolls. The granite islands, which do not share the volcanic nature of Réunion and Mauritius, appear to be peaks of a huge submerged plateau that was torn away from Africa when the continental plates shifted about 65 million years ago.

## WILDLIFE
### Animals

> Esmeralda is in the *Guinness World Records* as the oldest tortoise in the world. She is actually a he, weighs more than 300kg and is believed to be over 200 years old. He lives on Bird Island.

Common mammals and reptiles include the fruit bat or flying fox, the gecko, the skink and the tenrec (a hedgehoglike mammal imported from Madagascar). There are also some small snakes, but they are not dangerous.

More noteworthy is the fact that giant tortoises, which feature on the Seychelles coat of arms, are now found only in the Seychelles and the Galápagos Islands, off Ecuador. The French and English wiped out the giant tortoises from all the Seychelles islands except Aldabra, where happily more than 100,000 still survive. Many have been brought to the central islands, where they munch their way around hotel gardens, and there is a free-roaming colony on Curieuse Island.

---

**TOP 10 ANIMALS TO WATCH FOR**

- Whale sharks – Mahé
- Magpie robins – Cousin, Cousine, Aride, Denis
- Giant tortoises – all islands
- Flycatchers – La Digue
- *Sooglossus sardineri* frogs – Morne Seychellois National Park, Mahé
- Black parrots – Vallée de Mai, Praslin
- Fruit bats – Mahé, Praslin, La Digue
- Sooty terns – Bird Island
- Sea turtles – Bird, Cousin, Fregate, North, Aldabra
- Sharks – off most islands

---

Almost every island seems to have some rare species of bird: on Frégate, Cousin, Cousine and Aride there are magpie robins (known as *pie chanteuse* in Creole); on Cousin, Cousine and Aride you'll find the Seychelles warbler; La Digue and Denis have the *veuve* (paradise flycatcher); and Praslin has the black parrot. The bare-legged scops owl and the Seychelles kestrel live on Mahé, and Bird Island is home to millions of sooty terns.

For further information on marine life, see p34.

## Plants

The coconut palm and the casuarina are the Seychelles' most common trees. There are a few banyans and you're also likely to see screw pines, bamboo and tortoise trees (so named because the fruit looks like the tortoises that eat it).

There are about 80 endemic plant species. Virgin forest now exists only on the higher parts of Silhouette Island and Mahé, and in the Vallée de Mai on Praslin, which is one of only two places in the world where the giant coco de mer palm grows wild. The other is nearby Curieuse Island.

In the high, remote parts of Mahé and Silhouette Island, you may come across the insect-eating pitcher plant, which either clings to trees or bushes or sprawls along the ground.

On the floral front, there are plenty of orchids, bougainvilleas, hibiscues, gardenias and frangipanis.

The botanical gardens in Victoria provide a pleasant and interesting walk. The Vallée de Mai on Praslin is a must. For chance discoveries, get away from the beach for a day and head into the hills on Mahé, Praslin or La Digue.

## NATIONAL PARKS

The Seychelles currently boasts two national parks and seven marine national parks, as well as several other protected areas under government and NGO (nongovernmental organisation) management. In all, about 46% of the country's total landmass is now protected as well as some 45 sq km of ocean, providing an invaluable resource for scientific investigation and species protection.

The most important protected areas include those listed in the table, p277.

## ENVIRONMENTAL ISSUES

Overall the Seychelles has a pretty good record for protecting its natural environment. As early as 1968, Birdlife International set the ball rolling when it bought Cousin Island and began studying some of the country's

Cousin and Aride Islands support huge colonies of lesser (black) noddies. During the birds' elaborate courtship, the male bird offers his mate leaves until he finds one to her satisfaction (she indicates her approval by defecating on it!).

Arachnophobes may have a difficult time in the Seychelles. Almost every tree branch is draped in sheets of tough sticky silk belonging to the huge palm spider. Despite its size – up to 10cm – this obtrusive arachnid is harmless to humans.

critically endangered species. This was followed in the 1970s with legislation to establish national parks and marine reserves.

The Seychelles was also the first African country to draw up a 10-year environmental management plan, in 1990, which ushered in a more integrated approach. The second plan (2000–2010) was aimed at increasing the involvement of local communities in decision-making and day-to-day management. It also set strict guidelines for all new building and development projects. Details of the third plan (2010–2020) were not finalised at the time of research.

Not that the government's record is entirely unblemished. In 1998 it authorised a vast land-reclamation project on Mahé's northeast coast to provide much-needed space for housing. More recently, the construction of Eden Island, an artificial island with luxury properties off Mahé's east coast, has also raised concerns. Both projects have caused widespread silting, marring the natural beauty of this coast indefinitely, though the alternative was to clear large tracts of forest. A difficult choice.

Tourism has had a similarly mixed impact. Hotels have been built on previously unspoilt beaches, causing problems with waste management and increased pressure on fragile ecosystems, not to mention more difficult access to public beaches. Recent examples include Constance Ephelia Resort at Port Launay and Four Seasons at Petite Anse on Mahé, as well as the Raffles at Anse Possession (Praslin). On the other hand, tourist dollars provide much-needed revenue for funding conservation projects. Local attitudes have also changed as people have learned to value their environment.

Further impetus for change is coming from NGOs operating at both community and government levels. They have notched up some spectacular successes, such as the Magpie Robin Recovery Program, funded by the Royal Society for the Protection of Birds and Birdlife International. From just 23 magpie robins languishing on Frégate Island in 1990, there are now nearly 200 living on Frégate, Cousin, Denis and Cousine Islands. Similar results have been achieved with the Seychelles warbler on Cousin, Cousine and Aride Islands.

As part of these projects, a number of islands have been painstakingly restored to their original habitat by replacing alien plant and animal species with native varieties. Several islands have also been developed for ecotourism, notably Frégate, Bird, Denis, North, Silhouette and Desroches Islands, with the likelihood that Aldabra and other outer islands will follow. The visitors

The *Field Guide to the Birds of Seychelles*, by Adrian Skerrett, Ian Bullock and Tony Disley, offers the most comprehensive and informative guide to local bird life.

Get to know more about the Seychelles' fabulous environment and conservation programs at the Nature Seychelles site (www.natureseychelles.org).

## PARADISE UNDER THREAT?

Brochures may continue to paint the Seychelles as an unspoilt, green-and-blue paradise, but the environmental impact of construction projects that were underway when we visited cannot be swept under the carpet. Every year, more resort hotels and lodges pop up, most notably on formerly pristine beaches or secluded islands. By the time you read this, there will be new tourist developments on Round Island, Long Island, Mahé (Anse à la Mouche) and Praslin (Anse Possession). Sure, they have nothing on the concrete-and-glass horrors of, say, Hawaii or Cancun, but they still necessitate additional support systems, including roads and numerous vehicle trips, not to mention cutting down vegetation. So far the government has traditionally tried to balance tourist developments with the protection of the natural assets that attract the tourists (and therefore revenue) to the islands, but the rising population and the growing demands of tourism are putting a strain on that policy. How long will it resist the temptation of easy money?

Another problem is that many developers are foreigners, which means that the big money goes out of the country. It's of much greater benefit to locals when travellers stay in smaller hotels and guesthouses, rather than the large, foreign-controlled resorts.

## SEYCHELLES NATIONAL PARKS

| Park | Features | Activities | Best time to visit | Page |
|------|----------|-----------|--------------------|------|
| Aldabra Marine Reserve | raised coral atoll, tidal lagoon, birdlife, marine turtles, giant tortoises | diving, snorkelling, scientific study | Nov, Dec & mid-Mar–mid-May | p310 |
| Aride Island Marine Nature Reserve | granite island, coral reef, seabirds, fish life, marine turtles | birdwatching, snorkelling | Sep-May | p298 |
| Cousin Island Special Reserve | granite island, natural vegetation, hawksbill turtles, seabirds, lizards | birdwatching | year-round | p297 |
| Curieuse Marine National Park | granite island, coral reefs, coco de mer palms, giant tortoises, mangrove swamps, marine turtles, fish life | diving, snorkelling, walking | year-round | p297 |
| Morne Seychellois National Park | forested peaks, mangroves, glacis habitats | hiking, botany, birdwatching | May-Sep | p287 |
| Port Launay Marine National Park & Baie Ternay | mangrove swamps, fish life, coral reefs | diving, snorkelling | year-round | p292 |
| Praslin National Park (Vallée de Mai) | native forest, coco de mer palms, other endemic palms, black parrots | botany, birdwatching, walking | year-round | p295 |
| Ste Anne Marine National Park | marine ecosystems, marine turtles | glass-bottomed boat trips, snorkelling, diving | year-round | p288 |

not only help fund conservation work, but it is also easier to protect the islands from poachers and predators if they are inhabited. With any luck, this marriage of conservation and tourism will point the way to the future.

# Seychelles

Raise your hands, who wants to go to the Seychelles? We thought so. Mother Nature was very generous with these 115 islands scattered in the Indian Ocean and has spoiled them rotten. Undeniably, the beaches are the big attraction, and what beaches: exquisite ribbons of white sand lapped by topaz waters and backed by lush hills and big glacis boulders. And hardly a soul in sight.

With such a dreamlike setting, the Seychelles is unsurprisingly a choice place for a honeymoon. But there's much more to do than simply cracking open a bottle of champagne with your loved one in a luxurious hotel. Having earned a reputation as a paradigm of ecotourism, the Seychelles is a top spot to watch birds and giant tortoises in their natural habitat. And a vast living world lies just below the turquoise waters, beckoning divers of all levels. When you tire of beaches you can venture inland on jungle trails, indulge in fine dining or enjoy the sublime laid-back tempo. What you shouldn't expect, though, is a thriving nightlife. These are quiet islands; those looking for an Ibiza-style party atmosphere were badly advised by their travel agent.

This paradise is more affordable than you think. On top of ultraluxurious options, the Seychelles has plenty of self-catering facilities and family-run guesthouses that are easier on the wallet and offer local colour.

Which island should you go for? Try to visit at least two of the three main islands (Mahé, Praslin and La Digue), which are easy to combine (and have their own personality), and a private island, such as ecofriendly Bird Island or dramatic Silhouette – you deserve it.

---

**HIGHLIGHTS**

- Scratching the leathery neck of a giant tortoise on **Curieuse Island** (p297)
- Splashing around in the jewelled waters of **Anse Source d'Argent** (p302), **Anse Soleil** (p291), **Petite Anse** (p292) or **Grande Anse** (p292) – absolute heaven
- Diving with toothy critters at **Shark Bank** (p33)
- Taking a guided walk in **Morne Seychellois National Park** (p287) to mug up on botany
- Living out that stranded-on-a-desert-island fantasy on secluded **Bird Island** (p308)
- Hearing yourself screaming 'Oh, these coconuts are so sexy!' in the **Vallée de Mai** (p295)

SEYCHELLES

MAURITIUS

RODRIGUES

REUNION

---

| ■ Telephone code: 248 | ■ Population: 87,000 | ■ Area: 455 sq km |

## CLIMATE & WHEN TO GO

The seasons in the Seychelles are defined by the trade winds. These bring warmer, wetter airstreams from the northwest from October to April. From May to September the southeast trades usher in cooler, drier weather but the winds whip up the waves and you'll want to find protected beaches. The turnaround periods (April to May and October to November) are normally calm and windless.

The rain generally comes in sudden, heavy bursts. Mahé and Silhouette, the most mountainous islands, get the highest rainfall. January is the wettest month by far, and July and August the driest. Temperatures range between 24°C and 32°C throughout the year.

Although the Seychelles lies outside the cyclone zone, cyclone activity elsewhere in the Indian Ocean can still bring unseasonably grey, windy weather between December and March.

Hotel prices shoot up and accommodation can be hard to find during the peak seasons from December to January and July to August. Easter can also get busy.

See p313 for the climate chart for Victoria, the capital of Mahé.

# MAHÉ

When it comes to wishing for the archetypal idyllic island, it's impossible to think past the glorious bays caressed by gorgeously multihued waters (the ones you see in travel mags) of Mahé. To the northeast, a range of granite peaks, including Mahé's highest point, Morne Seychellois (905m), adds to this vivid panorama.

By far the largest and most developed of the Seychelles islands, Mahé (named by the French in honour of the 18th-century governor of Mauritius, Mahé de Labourdonnais) is home to the country's capital, Victoria, and to about 90% of the Seychelles' population. Small wonder that it has excellent vacation and adventure opportunities, from exploring the mountainous jungle of the interior to diving pristine sites and snorkelling with whale sharks. Or just do nothing at all and flake out on porcelain-sand beaches. Your ideal holiday spot is surely here somewhere.

That said, Mahé has its fair share of the mundane, as testified by industrial development on the northeast coast. Yet paradise lies close at hand – a bus or car ride of no more than 20 minutes will bring you to fabulous natural attractions.

## VICTORIA

**pop 23,300**

Victoria may be the country's main economic, political and commercial hub, but peak hour here lasts an unbearable five minutes! It is home to about a third of the Seychelles' population, but even so Victoria retains the air of a provincial town. While it may not fulfil all fantasies about tropical paradises, the city still has a little charm and a little promise when you scratch beneath the surface. There's a bustling market, manicured botanical gardens and a fistful of attractive old colonial buildings sidling up alongside modern structures and shopping plazas. It's also a good place to grab last-minute gifts before heading home.

Oh, and there's the setting. Victoria is set against an impressive backdrop of hills that seem to tumble into the turquoise sea.

### Information

You'll have no trouble finding banks with ATMs and exchange facilities as well as bureaux de change in the centre.

**Behram's Pharmacy** ( ☎ 225559; Victoria House, Francis Rachel St; ⏰ 8.30am-4.45pm Mon-Fri, 8.15am-12.30pm Sat)

**Cable & Wireless** (Francis Rachel St; internet access per hr Rs 60; ⏰ 7.30am-4.30pm Mon-Fri, 7.30am-noon Sat) Internet access.

**Central post office** (Independence Ave; ⏰ 8am-5pm Mon-Fri, to noon Sat)

**Creole Travel Services** ( ☎ 297000; www.creoletravel services.com; Albert St) This reputable travel agency offers the full range of services, including ticketing, car hire, yacht charter and tours around Mahé and to other islands.

**Double Click** ( ☎ 610590; Palm St; internet access per hr Rs 140; ⏰ 8am-9pm Mon-Sat, 9am-8pm Sun) Internet cafe and moneychanger. Also offers wi-fi.

**Mason's Travel** ( ☎ 288888; www.masonstravel.com; Revolution Ave) Another well-established travel agency.

**Tourist office** ( ☎ 610800; www.seychelles.travel; Independence Ave; ⏰ 8am-5pm Mon-Fri, 9am-noon Sat)

---

**TOP FIVE BEST-VALUE SLEEPS**

**Anse Sévère Bungalow** (Praslin; p304)
**Chalets Anse Possession** (Praslin; p299)
**Devon Residence** (Mahé; p290)
**Lalla Panzi Beach Guesthouse** (Mahé; p290)
**Maison du Soleil** (Praslin; p300)

# MAHÉ

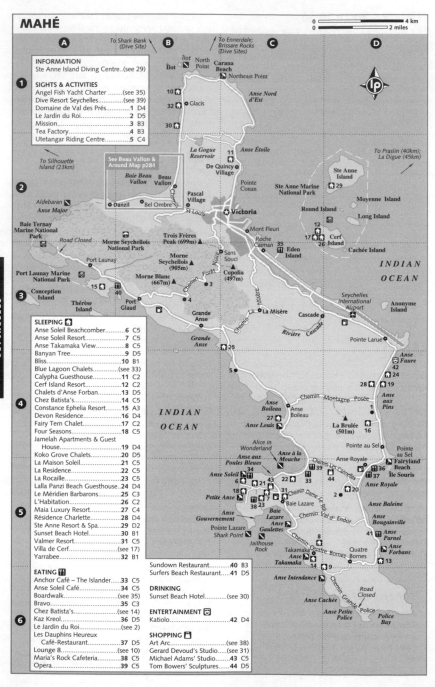

0 ————— 4 km
0 ————— 2 miles

**A** · **B** · **C** · **D**

To Shark Bank (Dive Site)
To Ennerdale; Brissare Rocks (Dive Sites)

**INFORMATION**
Ste Anne Island Diving Centre..(see 29)

**SIGHTS & ACTIVITIES**
Angel Fish Yacht Charter .......(see 35)
Dive Resort Seychelles..........(see 39)
Domaine de Val des Prés..........**1** D4
Le Jardin du Roi..................**2** D5
Mission.........................**3** B3
Tea Factory.....................**4** B3
Utetangar Riding Centre.........**5** C4

Îlot
Îlot
North Point
North Point
Carana Beach
Northeast Point
Anse Nord d'Est
Glacis
Anse Étoile
La Gogue Reservoir
De Quincy Village
Pointe Conan
Ste Anne Marine National Park
Ste Anne Island
To Praslin (40km); La Digue (45km)
Moyenne Island
Long Island
Round Island
Cerf Island
Cachée Island

To Silhouette Island (23km)

See Beau Vallon & Around Map p284

Baie Beau Vallon
Beau Vallon

Aldebaran
Anse Major
Danzil
Bel Ombre
Pascal Village
St Louis
Victoria
Mont Fleuri
Roche Caiman
Eden Island

INDIAN OCEAN

Baie Ternay Marine National Park
Road Closed
Morne Seychellois National Park
Trois Frères Peak (699m)▲
Morne Seychellois▲ (905m)
Morne Blanc (667m)▲
Sans Souci
Copolia (497m)
Seychelles International Airport
Anonyme Island

Port Launay
Port Launay Marine National Park
Conception Island
Thérèse Island
Port Glaud
Grande Anse
Grande Anse
La Misère
Cascade
Rivière Cascade
Pointe Larue

**SLEEPING**
Anse Soleil Beachcomber..........**6** C5
Anse Soleil Resort...............**7** C5
Anse Takamaka View...............**8** C5
Banyan Tree.....................**9** D5
Bliss..........................**10** B1
Blue Lagoon Chalets.............(see 33)
Calypha Guesthouse..............**11** C2
Cerf Island Resort..............**12** C2
Chalets d'Anse Forban...........**13** D5
Chez Batista's..................**14** C5
Constance Ephelia Resort........**15** A3
Devon Residence.................**16** D4
Fairy Tern Chalet...............**17** C2
Four Seasons....................**18** C5
Jamelah Apartments & Guest
   House.........................**19** D4
Koko Grove Chalets..............**20** D5
La Maison Soleil................**21** C5
La Residence....................**22** C5
La Rocaille.....................**23** C5
Lalla Panzi Beach Guesthouse....**24** D4
Le Méridien Barbarons...........**25** C3
L'Habitation...................**26** C2
Maia Luxury Resort..............**27** C4
Résidence Charlette.............**28** D4
Ste Anne Resort & Spa...........**29** D2
Sunset Beach Hotel..............**30** B1
Valmer Resort...................**31** C5
Villa de Cerf..................(see 17)
Yarrabee.......................**32** B1

Anse Faure

Anse aux Pins

Anse Boileau
Anse Boileau
Anse Louis
La Brûlée (501m)

Alice in Wonderland
Anse à la Mouche
Anse aux Poules Bleues
Anse Soleil
Petite Anse
Baie Lazare
Baie Lazare
Pointe au Sel
Pointe au Sel
Anse Royale
Fairyland Beach
Île Souris
Anse Royale
Anse Baleine

INDIAN OCEAN

Anse Gouvernement
Pointe Lazare
Shark Point
Anse Gaulettes
Jailhouse Rock
Takamaka
Quatre Bornes
Anse Takamaka
Anse Intendance
Anse Cachée
Anse Petite Police

Anse Bougainville
Anse Parnel
Anse Forbans
Quatre Bornes

Road Closed
Police
Police Bay

**EATING**
Anchor Café – The Islander.....**33** C5
Anse Soleil Café................**34** C5
Boardwalk......................(see 35)
Bravo..........................**35** C3
Chez Batista's.................(see 14)
Kaz Kreol......................**36** D5
Le Jardin du Roi...............(see 2)
Les Dauphins Heureux
   Café-Restaurant..............**37** D5
Lounge 8.......................(see 10)
Maria's Rock Cafeteria.........**38** C5
Opera..........................**39** C5

Sundown Restaurant.............**40** B3
Surfers Beach Restaurant.......**41** D5

**DRINKING**
Sunset Beach Hotel.............(see 30)

**ENTERTAINMENT**
Katiolo........................**42** D4

**SHOPPING**
Art Arc........................(see 38)
Gerard Devoud's Studio........(see 31)
Michael Adams' Studio..........**43** C5
Tom Bowers' Sculptures.........**44** C5

SEYCHELLES

Competent staff hand out booklets detailing all the country's accommodation options, lists of car-rental outlets, and decent maps of Mahé, Praslin and La Digue.

**Victoria Hospital** ( ☎ 388000; Mont Fleuri) The country's main hospital.

## Sights & Activities

The focal point of the city centre is a down-sized replica of the **clock tower** on London's Vauxhall Bridge. The replica was brought to Victoria in 1903 when the Seychelles became a crown colony. The **old courthouse** (Supreme Court; Francis Rachel St) beside the clock tower will appeal to fans of Creole architecture, as will the colonial buildings that are scattered along Francis Rachel and Albert Sts. Make a beeline for **Kanti House** (Albert St), an atmospheric shop that has been restored.

Victoria is home to a smattering of enticing religious buildings, including a **cathedral** (Olivier Marandan St) dating from the 19th century, an **Anglican church** (Albert St), a small **mosque** (Francis Rachel St) and a colourful **Hindu temple** (Quincy St).

When it first opened, the revamped covered **market** (Market St; ⏰ 5.30am-5pm Mon-Fri, to noon Sat) was something of a tourist gimmick, but over the years it's evolved into quite a lively, bustling place. Early morning is the best time to come, when fishmongers display an astonishing variety of seafood, from parrot fish to barracuda.

The **Natural History Museum** ( ☎ 321333; Independence Ave; admission Rs 20; ⏰ 8.30am-4.30pm Mon-Thu, to noon Fri & Sat) is worth a quick visit to learn about the islands' curious creatures, such as the Seychelles crocodile and the giant tortoise, both now sadly vanished from the main islands.

For respite, the manicured **botanical gardens** ( ☎ 670500; admission Rs 100; ⏰ 8am-5pm), full of streams and birdsong, are about 10 minutes' walk south of the centre. This is a good place to mug up on native plant life before venturing further afield. Star attractions are the coco de mer palms (see the boxed text, p297) lining the main alley. There's also a spice grove, a pen of giant tortoises, a patch of rainforest complete with fruit bats, and a cafeteria.

## Sleeping

Victoria's range of accommodation is disappointingly slim, especially considering it's the capital, but it does make sense to stay elsewhere, for instance in nearby Beau Vallon, and visit the town on day trips.

If you really want to be in Victoria, the closest hotel to the centre is **Hotel Bel Air** ( ☎ 224416; www.seychelles.net/belair; Bel Air Rd), on the road to Sans Souci, about 500m south of Revolution Ave, but it was scheduled for renovation at the time of writing (check the website). Further up on the road to Sans Souci, about 3km north ride from the centre), **Mountain Rise** ( ☎ 225308; mountainrise@seychelles.net; Sans Souci Rd; s/d incl breakfast €90/120; 🏊 ) is a good place to dawdle in and soak up the tranquil charm. It's in an atmospheric, airy heritage home that offers five spacious and comfortable rooms (the 'Heaven', cosy as a bird's nest, is a hot favourite among couples). There's also a good restaurant and a swimming pool. No air-con, but the location benefits from cooling breezes.

And now, a bargain. About 3km north of Victoria, off the coastal road, **Calypha Guesthouse** (Map p280; ☎ 241157; www.seychelles.sc/calypha; Ma Constance; s/d incl breakfast €40/60; 🍴 🛜 ) – look at the rates! – sports eight rooms. They're very simple but get the job done. What sets this place apart is the family-run atmosphere. Creole-style dinners are available on request (€15). Air-con is extra (€10 per day).

## Eating

Victoria is relatively well endowed with places to eat. In addition to the following, there are many takeaway outlets offering Creole staples such as grilled fish and chicken curry in the streets around the market.

**Lai Lam's Bread & Food Shop** (Benezet St; mains Rs 25-50; ⏰ 8am-5pm) If you're a carb seeker, head straight to that lively island of yeasty goodness smack dab in the centre. You won't be able to resist the aroma of freshly baked bread and cakes! It also has a takeaway outlet next door, which teems with locals filling up on good, cheap eats.

**Double Click** ( ☎ 610590; Palm St; mains Rs 50-90; ⏰ 8am-9pm Mon-Sat, 9am-8pm Sun) This buzzy eatery popular with students rustles up light and healthy meals, including salads and soups. Sandwiches will quell greater hunger pangs. Keep your fluids up with a zesty smoothie or a juice concoction.

**News Café** ( ☎ 322999; Trinity House, Albert St; mains Rs 50-100; ⏰ breakfast & lunch Mon-Fri) This cheerful cafe-bar overlooking the main drag is an excellent venue to devour a comforting breakfast (muesli!) and read the daily newspapers, or to take a lunchtime break from town. The generous sandwiches and colourful salads are best

SEYCHELLES

# VICTORIA

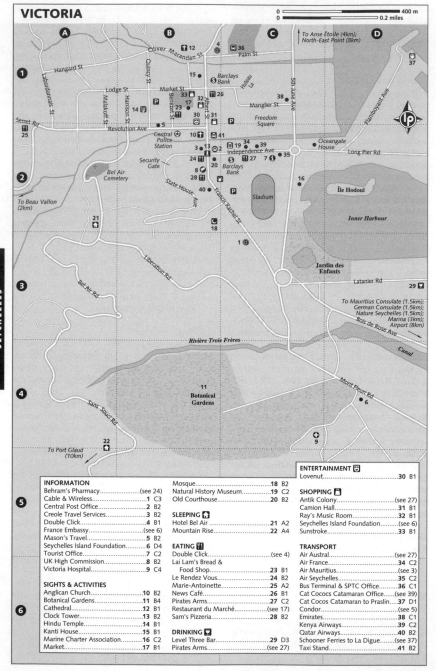

0 ——————— 400 m
0 ——————— 0.2 miles

enjoyed at the tables out front, allowing premium views of the people parade going past.

**ourpick** **Pirates Arms** ( ☎ 225001; Independence Ave; mains Rs 90-220; ☷ 9am-11pm Mon-Sat, noon-11pm Sun) Legendary to the point where it has become *the* meeting point in Victoria, this central cafe-restaurant veritably thrums the minute it opens its doors for breakfast (served until 11am). The menu is as long as your arm and runs from salads and sandwiches to pizzas and meat or fish dishes, all well prepared and well priced.

**Restaurant du Marché** ( ☎ 225451; Market St; mains Rs 110-250; ☷ breakfast & lunch Mon-Sat) The food is fresh and tasty at this appealing eatery within the market (upstairs). It's a good place to catch local vibes and enjoy plenty of local colour.

**Sam's Pizzeria** ( ☎ 322499; Francis Rachel St; mains Rs 140-300; ☷ lunch & dinner) Step into this cool spot for an escape from the busy street. Walls are adorned with paintings by local artist George Camille, which gives the place a splash of style. Get things going with pizzas cooked in a wood-fired oven, salads, pasta or grilled fish and meat. Takeaway is available.

**Le Rendez Vous** ( ☎ 323556; Francis Rachel St; mains Rs 180-375; ☷ 9am-10pm Mon-Sat) The Balinese-meets-Amazonian decor of this 1st-floor eatery overlooking the main square is easy on the eye, with darkwood furnishings, tropical plants and candlelit tables. Launch into French-influenced dishes (mostly prepared with local ingredients) and pizzas, but don't expect huge portions. An ice cream will finish you off sweetly.

**Marie-Antoinette** ( ☎ 266222; Serret Rd, St Louis; menu Rs 265; ☷ lunch & dinner Mon-Sat) This Creole restaurant in a beautiful old colonial house is a good place to test your stomach capacity. The set *menu* includes fish and aubergine fritters, grilled fish, chicken curry, fish stew, rice and salad, though to be fair you do probably come here more for the sense of history than for the food. It's on the road to Beau Vallon.

## Drinking & Entertainment

The most popular drinking hole is the Pirates Arms, which doubles as a bar and offers live music (a crooner with a guitar) several nights a week. The **Level Three Bar** (Latanier Rd; ☷ daily) is another hot spot, but it's not conveniently located.

Need to let off steam and rub shoulders with locals? Showcase your dance-floor repertoire at the **Lovenut** (Revolution Ave; men/women Rs 100/50; ☷ Wed, Fri & Sat), slap bang in the centre.

A cafeteria by day, Lovenut becomes a trendy discotheque at night.

## Shopping

The majority of craft and gift shops are concentrated in and around the market. **Camion Hall** (Albert St) is a crafts centre with a range of upmarket shops, including the jeweller Kreolor.

Another souvenir shop worth browsing is **Antik Colony** ( ☎ 321700; Pirates Arms Bldg, Independence Ave). George Camille's lovely paintings can be found at **Sunstroke** ( ☎ 224767; Market St).

For a wide selection of Creole music, visit **Ray's Music Room** ( ☎ 322674; Premier Bldg, Albert St).

If you want to buy a *coco fesse* (p297), head to the **Seychelles Island Foundation** (SIF; Mont Fleuri Rd), which has some stock and will issue you the required export permit. Be prepared to fork out about €150.

## Getting There & Around

Victoria is the main transport hub for buses around Mahé and for boats to Praslin and La Digue. For information about these services and for flights around the islands, see p315. For further information regarding air travel see p318.

Coming from the airport, a taxi into town costs around Rs 200. Alternatively, cross the road and pick up any bus heading north. See p316 for more about local buses.

The following airlines have offices in Mahé. **Air Austral** ( ☎ 323262; Independence Ave) Represented by Horizon Travel.

**Air France** ( ☎ 322414; Kingsgate House, Independence Ave)

**Air Mauritius** ( ☎ 297000; Albert St) Represented by Creole Travel Services.

**Air Seychelles** ( ☎ 381000; Independence Ave)

**Condor** ( ☎ 322642; Revolution Ave) Represented by Mason's Travel.

**Emirates** ( ☎ 292700; 5th June Ave)

**Kenya Airways** ( ☎ 322989; Kingsgate House, Independence Ave)

**Qatar Airways** ( ☎ 224518; Francis Rachel St)

## BEAU VALLON & THE NORTH COAST

A long, brilliant white arc of sands laced by palms and takamaka trees, Beau Vallon (Map p284; on Mahé's northwest coast, 3km from Victoria) boasts the most popular **beach** in Mahé. Here the water is deep enough for swimming, but watch out for large swells between June and November. It's overbuilt by

Seychellois standards (the ugly architecture of the Coral Strand hotel, which was closed at the time of writing, doesn't help), but you'll find it remarkably low-key and quiet if you have experienced other tropical destinations. The seaside ambience, with fishermen selling fresh fish late in the afternoon in the shade of takamaka trees, adds a dash of real life to the area.

Beau Vallon is the main destination on the northwest coast because of its beach and tourist infrastructure, but there's also some great scenery north, up the coast to **Glacis** and **North Point** (Map p280). With your own wheels, it's a scenic drive on a narrow road that hugs the coastline, with intermittent, lovely views over secluded coves at the foot of the cliffs. Here's a secret, only known to locals (whisper it softly): **Carana Beach** (Map p280). This tiny, dreamlike cove lapped by lapis lazuli waters offers a small patch of sand framed by big boulders, with a couple of palm trees leaning over the shore. It's at Northeast Point; look for a cement road on the left, in a high gradient descent of the road, or ask locals.

From Northeast Point, you can head down to Victoria via **Anse Étoile** (Map p280).

West of Beau Vallon, the coastal road goes past **Bel Ombre** (Map p280), which has a few good accommodation options and a little fishing harbour, and ends at **Danzil** (Map p280), where La Scala restaurant lies. From there, you can walk to Anse Major (see p289). Ah, Anse Major…

## Information

In Beau Vallon village, where the road from Victoria forks west to Bel Ombre and northeast to Glacis, there is a petrol station, a Barclays Bank ATM, a couple of bureaux de change, the police station and **Skynet** (Bel Ombre; internet access per hr Rs 30; 9.30am-8pm Mon-Sat, 10.30am-7pm Sun), which shelters an internet cafe, a call centre and a bureau de change.

You'll find convenience stores supplying basic foodstuffs and other necessities on the beach road and around the junction with the Bel Ombre road.

## Activities

### DIVING & SNORKELLING

There's plenty of great diving within the bay of Beau Vallon, including a few wrecks, as well as some top-notch dive sites well outside the

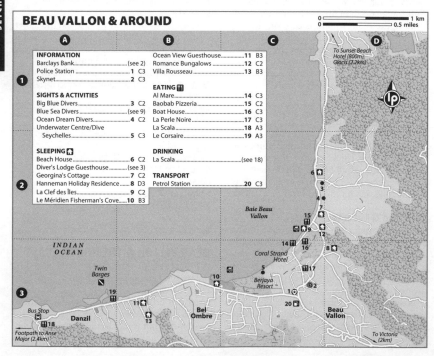

**BEAU VALLON & AROUND**

0 — 1 km
0 — 0.5 miles

**INFORMATION**
Barclays Bank ........................... (see 2)
Police Station ................................ 1 C3
Skynet ............................................. 2 C3

**SIGHTS & ACTIVITIES**
Big Blue Divers ............................... 3 C2
Blue Sea Divers ........................... (see 9)
Ocean Dream Divers ..................... 4 C2
Underwater Centre/Dive
    Seychelles .................................... 5 C3

**SLEEPING**
Beach House .................................... 6 C2
Diver's Lodge Guesthouse ........ (see 3)
Georgina's Cottage ....................... 7 C2
Hanneman Holiday Residence ..... 8 D3
La Clef des Îles .............................. 9 C2
Le Méridien Fisherman's Cove ... 10 B3

Ocean View Guesthouse ............ 11 B3
Romance Bungalows .................... 12 C2
Villa Rousseau ............................... 13 B3

**EATING**
Al Mare ........................................... 14 C3
Baobab Pizzeria ............................ 15 C2
Boat House .................................... 16 C3
La Perle Noire ............................... 17 C3
La Scala .......................................... 18 A3
Le Corsaire .................................... 19 A3

**DRINKING**
La Scala ....................................... (see 18)

**TRANSPORT**
Petrol Station ............................... 20 C3

To Sunset Beach Hotel (800m); Glacis (2.2km)

INDIAN OCEAN

Baie Beau Vallon

Coral Strand Hotel

Berjaya Resort

Twin Barges

Bus Stop

Footpath to Anse Major (2.4km)

Danzil

Bel Ombre

Beau Vallon

To Victoria (2km)

bay (see p33). Established dive shops include the following:

**Big Blue Divers** (Map p284; ☎ 261106; www.bigblue divers.net) North of Beau Vallon.

**Blue Sea Divers** (Map p284; ☎ 526051; www. blueseadivers.com) A French-run operation, next door to La Clef des Îles.

**Ocean Dream Divers** (Map p284; ☎ 248385; www. oceandreamdivers.com) North of Georgina's Cottage.

**Underwater Centre/Dive Seychelles** (Map p284; ☎ 247165, 542877; www.diveseychelles.com.sc) This English-run, well-oiled PADI five-star dive centre is in the Berjaya Resort.

The bay of Beau Vallon also hosts a few good snorkelling spots, especially along the rocky shore up the coast to North Point. It's also the main launching pad for **boat excursions** and snorkelling trips to Baie Ternay (p292) at the northwestern tip of the island, where the reefs are healthy and marine life plentiful. Full-day excursions can be organised for about €85 per person, including entry fees to the park, barbecue lunch and snorkelling gear. The best season is from April to October. A minimum of four to six persons is required. Contact the following operators (or ask your hotel or guesthouse to do it for you):

**Jimmy Mancienne** ( ☎ 510269) A reputable operator.

**Teddy's Glass Bottom Boat** ( ☎ 511125, 511198) Good credentials. Half-day trips can be arranged. Prices include transfers from most places in the Beau Vallon area.

**Underwater Centre/Dive Seychelles** (Map p284; ☎ 247165, 542877; www.diveseychelles.com.sc) At the Berjaya Resort. Fits snorkelling (Rs 250 to Rs 450) in during its dive outings to L'Îlot, Baie Ternay Marine National Park and the Lighthouse.

### WHALE-SHARK SPOTTING

Between August and October it's common to see whale sharks offshore from Mahé's north and west coasts. **Underwater Centre/ Dive Seychelles** (Map p284; ☎ 247165, 542877; www. diveseychelles.com.sc) runs dedicated snorkelling trips focusing on whale sharks in September and October (€110). It also runs whale-shark monitoring programs.

## Sleeping

Beau Vallon and Bel Ombre offer the widest range of accommodation in north Mahé.

### BUDGET

**Georgina's Cottage** (Map p284; ☎ 247016; georgina@ seychelles.net; Beau Vallon; s/d incl breakfast €55/75; ☒ )

This friendly operation has catered to budget travellers for years. As we speak, the people running Georgina's Cottage are jackhammering away for what promises to be a pretty serious makeover. The whole process is expected to be completed by 2011. It will feature comfortable rooms in a brand-new Creole building. Let's hope it will keep its prices reasonable ('less than €100', the manager assured us) and facilities hospitable. What won't change, though, is the prime location: a 20m Frisbee throw from the beach, it's also very close to dive centres, restaurants and shops. Eddy, the manager, is full of local info.

**OUR PICK** **Ocean View Guesthouse** (Map p284 ☎ 522010, 261039; www.choicevilla.sc; Bel Ombre; d incl breakfast €65-85; ☒ ) Another great-value port of call (same owner as the Beach House). Above the road in Bel Ombre, this jolly good villa shelters five immaculate rooms with balcony. The upstairs ones proffer splendid views of the bay. The cheaper Vakwa room, at the back, has no view. It's a 20-minute walk to Beau Vallon beach.

**Beach House** (Map p284; ☎ 522010, 261039; www. choicevilla.sc; Beau Vallon; d incl breakfast €75; ☒ ) In an area where economical options are on the verge of extinction, the Beach House deserves a pat on the back for quoting reasonable rates. The four functional and spacious rooms ensure a decent, if unmemorable, night's sleep for guests keen to roll out of bed and onto Beau Vallon beach, just across the road.

**Diver's Lodge Guesthouse** (Map p284; ☎ 261222; www.diverslodge.sc; Glacis; d incl breakfast €90-125; ☒ ) Just above the main coast road, next to Big Blue Divers, these four rooms in a modern villa are large, pathologically clean and equipped to a high standard. The ones upstairs are significantly dearer but offer fleeting glimpses of the ocean through the foliage of exotic trees. The owner's husband runs Teddy's Glass Bottom Boat – convenient if you plan to arrange a boat trip.

Other options:

**Yarrabee** (Map p280; ☎ 261248; www.seychelles -yarrabee.com; Glacis; studios €80-160; ☒ ) Two fully equipped studios and a three-bedroom unit with heavenly views of the bay. Pluses: it's near a tiny beach and a small supermarket.

**Villa Rousseau** (Map p284; ☎ 520646; arousseau@ seychelles.net; Bel Ombre; d/q €80/160; ☒ ) A three-bedroom villa with all mod cons, in a quiet property above Ocean View Guesthouse. Prices are for the whole villa – a bargain for couples.

SEYCHELLES

## MIDRANGE

**Romance Bungalows** (Map p284; ☎ 410382, 247732; www.romancebungalows.com; Beau Vallon; s/d incl breakfast €105/116; ⊠) We could tell you that the 'Romance Bungalows' live up to their name and are suitable for a cuddle with your sweetheart, but we won't. At least they provide all the home comforts, assuming you live in a spacious, well-appointed flat with a spotless kitchen (but no maid). The beach is only steps away and all amenities are within easy reach.

**Hanneman Holiday Residence** (Map p284; ☎ 425000; www.hanneman-holidays.com; Beau Vallon; d/q incl breakfast €175/375; ⊠ ⊑ ⓢ) This muscular villa was certainly not conceived by the most inspired architect on the island but inside it's much more welcoming, with seven impeccable apartments equipped to a very high standard. Bathrooms are so meticulous you could eat off the floor. There's a nifty pool, too. Discounts are available when it's slack – call Manfred Heinkelen, the German owner. It's a five-minute jog to the beach.

**La Clef des Îles** (Map p284; ☎ 537100; www.clefdes iles.com; Beau Vallon; d/tr/q €250/310/370; ⓢ) Pro: it's right on Beau Vallon beach, just next door to Blue Sea Divers and Baobab Pizzeria – location is irresistible and you're right in the thick of things. Con: it's right on Beau Vallon beach, just next door to Blue Sea Divers and Baobab Pizzeria – it lacks privacy. Four creatively designed, generously sized, fully equipped apartments have a terrace or a balcony that look onto the beach. You'll feel a bit lonely here, for the owners don't live on the premises. No air-con.

**ourpick Bliss** (Map p280; ☎ 413169; www.bliss-hotel. net; Glacis; d incl breakfast €250; ⊠ ⓢ) You wouldn't guess from the outside but this fashionably boho-chic venture is one of those places that make staying in North Mahé such a treat: eight rooms thoughtfully decorated with natural materials enjoy ocean views that will leave you speechless. Precious perks include a little spa (where locally made products are used), a scrumptious breakfast served on a great wooden sundeck, direct access to a small beach and superb snorkelling just metres offshore. Guests get a special rate for dinner at Lounge 8, which is right next door. Bliss, indeed.

## TOP END

**Sunset Beach Hotel** (Map p280; ☎ 261111; www.sunset -beach.com; Glacis; d incl breakfast €350-965; ⊠ ⊑ ⊑) This sunset-friendly seducer boasts an ace location on a little headland. The 28 units, divided into three categories (the best ones are the Junior suites), are in good nick (minus a couple of bumps and bruises on the wooden furniture) and hide coolly among rocks and trees. The pool shows some signs of wear and tear, but after one sundowner in the bar overlooking the ocean all will be forgiven. Best of all, there's direct beach access and excellent snorkelling options just offshore. There's a minimum stay of four nights.

**Le Méridien Fisherman's Cove** (Map p284; ☎ 677000; www.lemeridienfishermanscove.com; Bel Ombre; d incl breakfast from €520; ⊠ ⊑ ⓢ) A reliable resort with plush rooms and a staggering bow-shaped lobby. The beach is disappointingly thin, though.

## Eating

Whatever you think of this coastal stretch, you are sure to have memorable eating experiences here.

**Baobab Pizzeria** (Map p284; ☎ 247167; Beau Vallon; mains Rs 80-140; ⓨ lunch & dinner) Madame Michel presides over this unpretentious, sand-floored eatery right on the beach. After a morning spent in the waves, re-energise with a piping-hot pizza, a plate of spag or fish and chips.

**ourpick Al Mare** (Map p284; ☎ 620240; Beau Vallon; mains Rs 160-300; ⓨ 1-10pm) Large, well-spaced tables, potted plants and high ceilings put diners in the right mood to settle down for a big night sampling the ambitious dishes on offer – mostly seafood and pastas. Or you could simply park yourself with a cocktail (from Rs 120) on the concrete terrace to watch the sunset on Silhouette Island – soul-stirring. Sandwiches are also available in the afternoon.

**Le Corsaire** (Map p284; ☎ 247171; Bel Ombre; mains Rs 165-340; ⓨ dinner Tue-Sun) Le Corsaire is an atmospheric place just perfect for that special meal. And you could lose yourself in the homemade chocolate mousse that arrives at the end of the meal. Judging by the *tagliolini gorgonzola* (pasta with gorgonzola), the beautifully presented mains are just as yummy though, so don't worry *too* much about saving room for dessert. Gastronauts could opt for bat in white-wine sauce. Le Corsaire occupies a half-timbered mansion that seems to have come straight out of rural Normandy. Strong wine list, too.

**La Scala** (Map p284; ☎ 247535; Bel Ombre; mains Rs 180-360; ⓨ dinner Mon-Sat) An old favourite of visitors and locals alike, this restaurant specialises in Italian cooking. It might feel weird to sit down for *lasagne al forno* and breaded veal on a tropical Indian Ocean island, but go with the flow – the fare is well prepared and the low-lit ambience on the breezy terrace suitably romantic. A respectable selection of wines stands at your beck and call. At the end of the coast road near Danzil.

**La Perle Noire** (Map p284; ☎ 620220; Bel Ombre; mains Rs 190-320; ☽ dinner Mon-Sat) The 'Black Pearl' scores high on atmosphere, with an eye-catching nautical theme and seafaring paraphernalia liberally scattered around the dining rooms (can we borrow your superb model ships?). The food – mostly fish and meat dishes – doesn't quite live up to the promise of the surrounds, though.

**Boat House** (Map p284; ☎ 247898; Beau Vallon; buffet Rs 250; ☽ dinner) This long-standing venture has seen better days and its massive buffet is only so-so, but it does a good job of quelling hunger pangs, with about 20 different dishes on offer, including stodgy Creole curries, salads and barbecued fish (usually tuna and, if you're lucky, red snapper). The vaguely barnlike surrounds ooze a ramshackle charm, but please dump the plastic chairs.

**Lounge 8** (Map p280; ☎ 746808; Glacis; menu Rs 720; ☽ dinner) It seems that everybody goes gaga for the surprise five-course *menu* concocted at this hip eatery with a strong design-led decor. The food is imaginatively prepared and beautifully presented, but we found it a bit bland the day we came and the prices somewhat inflated. Chef's bad day? You be the judge.

### Drinking & Entertainment

Beau Vallon is the most 'happening' (by Seychellois standards, which isn't saying much) area on Mahé. The bars at La Scala (p286) and Sunset Beach Hotel (p286) are great for a sunset cocktail.

On Wednesday evening don't miss **Bazar Labrin** (☽ Wed), which injects a bit of vitality and excitement into the neighbourhood. Numerous food and craft stalls take position along the seafront, with impromptu live bands or sound systems. It's popular with local families and flirting youngsters. For tourists, it's a great opportunity to catch local vibes.

### Getting There & Away

Buses leave regularly from Victoria for Beau Vallon, either straight over the hill via St Louis, or the long way round via Glacis. The last bus to Victoria leaves around 7.30pm; it's a Rs 150 taxi ride if you miss it.

## MORNE SEYCHELLOIS NATIONAL PARK

While the dazzling coastline of Mahé is undoubtedly the main attraction, it's crucial that you take the time to explore the island's mountainous interior. One of Mahé's highlights, the splendid Morne Seychellois National Park (Map p280) encompasses an impressive 20% of the land area of Mahé and contains a wide variety of habitats, from coastal mangrove forests up to the country's highest peak, the Morne Seychellois (905m). Choked in thick forest formation, the enigmatic, central part of the park is virtually deserted and can only be reached by walking trails; you don't have to go very far before the outside world starts to feel a long, long way away. Without a doubt, the best way to appreciate the area is on a guided walk; see the boxed text, p289, for more information.

The road over the mountains from Victoria to Port Glaud (take the road to Bel Air, which branches off Liberation Ave, and continue on Sans Souci Rd), which cuts through the Morne Seychellois National Park, is a stunning scenic drive. At **Mission** (Map p280) you can see the ruins of a school that was built by the London Missionary Society in 1875. There's also a superb lookout with spectacular views of central Mahé and the west coast.

Tealovers will pause at the working **tea factory** (Map p280; ☎ 378221; Sans Souci Rd; admission Rs 25; ☽ 7am-4pm Mon-Fri), about 3km above Port Glaud. Free 20-minute tours showing the tea-making process are conducted during opening hours, but it's best to visit before noon, when you can see the whole process from drying to packing. There's also a gift shop where you can sample and purchase the fragrant SeyTé and *citronnelle*.

## EAST COAST

Let's face it: much of the east coast is given over to housing, so there are only a few spots that fit the picture-postcard ideal. And swimming is not *that* tempting, with very shallow waters and a profusion of algae – hardcore beach-hounds may be disappointed. This is not to say the east coast isn't a worthwhile place to visit. South of the airport are a number of small enclaves and undeveloped areas, where travellers looking for peace and isolation will find both

**ESCAPES TO STE ANNE MARINE NATIONAL PARK**

A definite must-see, Ste Anne Marine National Park (Map p280), off Victoria, consists of six islands. Of these, day-trippers are permitted to land on Cerf and Moyenne Islands. For a complete escape, you can stay on Cerf and Ste Anne Islands (and on Round and Long Islands by the time you read this). The park is fantastic for swimming and snorkelling. Sadly, the coral in the park is no longer as awesome as it was. Silting from construction works in the bay has led to significant coral damage, compounded by several episodes of coral 'bleaching'.

The park is primarily visited on glass-bottomed boat tours offered by the main travel agencies in Victoria (see p279) and some boat operators based in Beau Vallon (p284). The cost of a full day's outing including snorkelling and lunch starts at €85/50 per adult/child. You can also contact the **Marine Charter Association** (MCA; Map p282; ☎ 322126; mca@seychelles.net; 5th June Ave, Victoria), which charges only €60/30 per adult/child. And yes, there's diving in the park! There are about 10 dive sites, scattered off the various islands. Contact **Ste Anne Island Diving Centre** (Map p280; ☎ 570043; pal@seychelles.net; day trip from €70) at the Ste Anne Resort & Spa.

Note that the park authorities charge a fee of €10 per person (free for children under 12 years) to enter the marine park. Tour operators usually include this in their prices.

## Cerf Island

About 60 people live on Cerf Island, including Wilbur Smith, the South African novelist. As with Moyenne and Round Islands, there's good snorkelling and the beaches are seriously alluring.

You can stay at a comfortable little colonial-style hotel, **L'Habitation** (Map p280; ☎ 323111; habicerf@seychelles.net; s/d incl half board €210/252; ✷ ✷ ), just a 10-minute boat ride from Victoria. Run by the friendly Delta, this 12-room charmer is right on the beach and welcomes families. If you're looking for a place for romance, head to the more exclusive **Cerf Island Resort** (Map p280; ☎ 294500; www.cerf-resort.com; s/d incl half board from €290/362; ✷ ), or the newish **Villa de Cerf** (Map p280; ☎ 523161; www.villadecerf.com; d incl half board from €252; ✷ ✷ ✷ ), which occupies an elegant Creole mansion with an unparalleled location on the beach. Another recommended option is **Fairy Tern Chalet** (Map p280; ☎ 321733; www.fairyternchalet.sc; d €140; ✷ ). Digs are in two squeaky-clean bungalows overlooking the beach.

If there's enough demand the restaurants at L'Habitation, Cerf Island Resort and Villa de Cerf will usually offer a package including transport and lunch or dinner.

## Moyenne Island

Moyenne is owned by Brendon Grimshaw, who has spent the last 40 years hacking back the jungle to create his own tropical paradise. The native fauna and flora have been carefully regenerated and everything is neatly labelled, giving it the air of a botanical garden.

A stop on Moyenne is usually included in the tours, but it costs an extra €10.

## Round Island

This island was once home to a leper colony, but these days it's better known for the offshore snorkelling. A 10-villa luxury resort was under construction at the time of writing.

## Ste Anne Island

The largest of the six islands, and only 4km east of Victoria, Ste Anne boasts two ravishing beaches, along which spreads the super-swanky **Ste Anne Resort & Spa** (Map p280; ☎ 292000; www.sainteanne-resort.com; s/d from €635/905; ✷ ✷ ✷ ), with 87 glorious villas and top-notch amenities, including a spa, a dive centre and a kids club.

## Long Island & Cachée Island

Long Island has long been home to the prison but should welcome a new type of inmate with the opening of a swish hotel in 2011. The smallest island of the lot, Cachée, lies southeast of Cerf. It's uninhabited.

SEYCHELLES

## TOP NATURE WALKS IN THE MORNE SEYCHELLOIS NATIONAL PARK

If you've got itchy feet, there are excellent walks in the Morne Seychellois National Park, with a number of hiking trails through the jungle-clad hills. These are detailed in a series of leaflets that are available at the botanical gardens (p281) in Victoria (Rs 25). The trails are poorly signed, though, and muggings have been reported, so it's not a bad idea to hire a guide, who will also provide natural and cultural insights. **Jacques Barreau** ( ☎ 242386, 579191; www.naturetourguide.com) and **Basile Beaudoin** ( ☎ 241790, 514972) lead hiking and bird-watching trips into the Mahé back country and charge from €60 for an informative day's walk with lunch and transport (from €35 for a half-day). Bring plenty of water. Following is a selection of inspirational hikes.

### Danzil to Anse Major

The walk to this secluded beach takes you along a coast fringed by impressive glacis rock formations. The path starts at the end of the road heading west from Beau Vallon, a few hundred metres further up from La Scala restaurant. It's a fairly easy one-hour romp, but most of the path is exposed to the sun. Before descending to the beach, the path goes past a lookout that affords fantastic vistas of Anse Major. The beach is blissfully quiet, and is good for swimming, though there can be strong currents. You'll have to return by the same route.

### Tea Factory to Morne Blanc

The imposing white bulk of Morne Blanc (667m) and its almost sheer 500m face make a great hiking destination. Although the track is only 600m long, it is quite steep – climbing 270m from start to finish. Plan on roughly an hour for the ascent. The reward is a tremendous view over the west coast. The path starts 250m up the road from the tea factory on the cross-island road from Victoria to Port Glaud. You have to descend the same way.

### Copolia

This is the most popular walk on Mahé, and possibly the easiest. It also has a pleasant Indiana Jones feel – you walk almost all the way amid a thick jungle, with lots of interesting fauna and flora. Now is your chance to spot leaf insects and the *Sooglossus gardineri*, the smallest frog on earth. The trail starts on the cross-island Chemin Forêt Noire about 5km above Victoria. It's only just over 1km to the granite platform of Copolia (497m), but the final section is quite steep; allow roughly two hours there and back. The views of Victoria and Ste Anne Marine National Park are sensational.

### Trois Frères

Trois Frères (Three Brothers) refers to the three cliffs that tower over Victoria. The path is signed from the Sans Souci forest station on the Chemin Forêt Noire, about 4km from Victoria. The first part of the walk, until a kiosk from which you get ample views, is fairly easy and can be covered in about one hour. The second leg, until the cross on the summit (699m), is tricky to follow and involves some scramble. Still game? Allow an extra two hours to reach the summit. You have to descend the same way.

in no short supply. Take the oft-overlooked, little-known **Fairyland beach** (Map p280): this gem of a beach offers shimmering waters and great snorkelling around tiny **Île Souris**, just offshore. Other good strips of sand are found at **Anse Royale**, **Anse Bougainville**, **Anse Parnel** and **Anse Forbans** (all Map p280), further south.

Once you've got your fill of working your tan, head to **Le Jardin du Roi** (Map p280; ☎ 371313; Anse Royale; adult/child Rs 110/55; ☺ 10am-5pm), located 2km up in the hills above Anse Royale.

This lush spice garden owes its existence to Pierre Poivre, the French spice entrepreneur. There is a self-guided walk around the 35-hectare orchard-crossed-with-forest. The planter's house contains a one-room **museum** and there's a pleasant cafe-restaurant (p290) with smashing views down to the coast. Homemade jams, marmalade and spices are available at the gift shop.

The **Domaine de Val des Prés** (Map p280; ☎ 376100; admission free; ☺ 9.30am-5pm) at Anse aux Pins consists of a cluster of craft shops grouped around an old plantation house with a few bits of memorabilia. The rather motley assortment of crafts on offer includes model boats, pottery, paintings, clothing and products fashioned from the hugely versatile coconut tree.

There's an ATM at Anse Royale.

## Sleeping

The east coast may not be the sexiest part of the island, but we've unearthed a smattering of excellent-value (by Seychellois standards), family-run ventures from where you can easily reach the western coast, by bus or by car.

**Lalla Panzi Beach Guesthouse** (Map p280; ☎ 376411; lpb@seychelles.sc; Anse aux Pins; s/d/tr incl breakfast €45/60/80; 🏊) Lalla Panzi is not the beachfront paradise you were dreaming of, but it's a neat property leading down to the sea. This friendly guesthouse offers four scrupulously clean rooms arranged around a cosy lounge; rooms 2 and 3 have sea views. Furnishings are slightly dated but that's part of the charm. Though on the main road, it's quiet enough at night. The resident dogs are a bit intimidating at first sight but Thérèse, the affable owner, guarantees that 'they are well behaved'. Cash only.

**Résidence Charlette** (Map p280; ☎ 376204, 715746; d_charlette@yahoo.com; Le Cap; s €45, d €65-75; 🏊) An unfussy abode with an unpretentious appeal. Its dual attractions are its affordable rates and the spotlessness of the three self-catering apartments. They are set on grassy garden areas, behind the owners' house, which should seal you off from traffic noise. Bonuses: free transfers to/from the airport, free laundry service, and a Creole dinner for stays of one week or more. No meals, but there are a few stores nearby. Cash only.

**Jamelah Apartments & Guest House** (Map p280; ☎ 375429, 410819; jamelah@intelvision.net; Anse aux Pins; d/bungalows/apt incl breakfast €55/85/95; 🏊 🛜) The two uncluttered rooms (each with a balcony and sea views) are a cast-iron bargain, but if purse strings are a bit more relaxed or you're travelling with the kids in tow, opt for the bungalow or the four self-contained apartments in a separate building. They face a small 'beach', which is just adequate for a waist-high dip at high tide. The nearest stores and takeaway counters are just a 15-minute walk away. Cash only.

**ourpick Devon Residence** (Map p280; ☎ 510075, 710624; www.devonresidence.sc; Pointe au Sel; villas €85-110; 🏊 🛜) No, you're not hallucinating, the

view is real. Poised on a greenery-shrouded hillside, the five villas overlook Anse Royale – full frame. They're extremely well appointed, bright and immaculate. The cheaper villas are 'only' 90 sq metres, while the more expensive ones, at a whopping 145 sq metres, are fabulous for families or a group of friends. A flotilla of perks, including free transfers to/from the airport, daily cleaning service, air-con, free wi-fi, TV and washing machine make this one of the best-value stays you'll have. Bonus: the owner rents cars at unbeatable rates (you'll need wheels to stay here). It's in high demand (word of mouth, my friends), so book early. Cash is preferred.

**Koko Grove Chalets** (Map p280; ☎ 371538, 779808, 766574; www.kokogrove.nl; Anse Royale; chalets €95-150; 🏊) If you're after hush and seclusion, then these two timbered chalets, soothingly positioned in the velvety emerald hills above Anse Royale, are the answer. The two units are self-contained, with spacious living areas and private verandahs overlooking the swimming pool, with the ocean as a backdrop. Air-con is an extra €10 per day. If you're preparing your own food, there's a store 400m down the road. It's 400m before Le Jardin du Roi.

**ourpick Chalets d'Anse Forban** (Map p280; ☎ 366111; www.forbans.com; Anse Forbans; d €150; 🏊 🛜) 'Tranquillity; 12 sparklingly clean, fully equipped bungalows with tiled bathrooms; expansive lawns; family-friendly; lovely beach with good swimming; fishermen selling their catch on the beach in the afternoon' – this is what we scribbled on our notepad when we visited. Extra beds cost €15, and prices drop to €135 for stays of more than three nights. Add a few sunloungers and the proximity of a store, and you have a great deal.

## Eating & Drinking

**Le Jardin du Roi** (Map p280; ☎ 371313; Anse Royale; mains Rs 100-230; ⏰ 10am-4.30pm) The setting is wonderful at this cafe-restaurant way up the hills at the spice garden (see p289), and it puts you in the mood for a fruit juice or a crunchy salad as soon as you sit down. Seafood and sandwiches also feature on the menu. Save a cranny for ice creams: they are confected fresh on the premises with fruits from the garden. The Sunday *planteur* buffet (Rs 350) is a popular weekly event.

**Surfers Beach Restaurant** (Map p280; ☎ 781737; Anse Parnel; mains Rs 110-250; ⏰ noon-9.30pm Wed-Mon) A classic beachfront setting with a shady terrace characterises this delightful restaurant right on seductive Anse Parnel. Here the menu abounds in local flavour with everything from grilled fish to lobster and salads.

**Kaz Kreol** (Map p280; ☎ 371680; Anse Royale; mains Rs 120-380; ☺ noon-9pm) This family-run address sits right on the beach at Anse Royale. The menu strikes a good balance between seafood, pizzas and meat, not to mention a wide choice of Chinese specialities. Dining space is gaily decorated with fish and palm-tree murals, which matches the tropical atmosphere.

**Boardwalk** (Map p280; Eden Island; mains Rs 130-170; ☺ 11am-late) More a chilled-out bar than a restaurant, the Boardwalk is at the marina on Eden Island, almost next door to Bravo. Nab a seat on the wooden terrace, order a cocktail (Rs 100) and ogle over yachts you wished you owned.

**ourpick** **Bravo** (Map p280; ☎ 346020; Eden Island; mains Rs 150-330; ☺ lunch & dinner Mon-Sat) Four words: not to be missed. This breezy, open-air restaurant overlooking the marina at Eden Island provides an enchanting dining experience with delectable food. Everything's pretty good, but if you want a recommendation, go for the Mega Burger or the seared tuna salad. Save some room for an ice cream with chocolate sauce. Service is brisk and smiley.

**Les Dauphins Heureux Café-Restaurant** (Map p280; ☎ 430100; Anse Royale; mains Rs 160-300; ☺ lunch & dinner) Almost next door to Kaz Kreol, this eatery with a modernish feel also overlooks the beach. Chow down on subtly flavoured fish, seafood, curries and meat from an elaborate menu. Top marks go to the grilled red snapper, which melts in the mouth. The smoked fish salad is excellent but priccy (Rs 210).

## Entertainment

**Katiolo** (Map p280; ☎ 375453; Anse Faure; men/women Rs 100/50; ☺ Wed, Fri & Sat) If you still have some energy to burn, the east coast is home to one of Mahé's most popular nightclubs. It's a fairly hip venue, so dress up rather than down.

## Getting There & Away

Buses leave regularly from Victoria for the east coast. The last bus to Victoria leaves around 7.30pm.

# WEST COAST

The west coast is exquisite on the eyes. There are one or two sights to aim for, but it's the beaches and coastal scenery that are the star

---

attractions. Wilder than the east, this is the part of Mahé where green hills tumble past coconut-strewn jungles before sliding gently into translucent waters.

## Sights

The coastal drive between Anse Takamaka to the southwest up to Port Launay to the northwest provides tantalising glimpses of a number of beautiful spots. Throw away the guidebook for a day and go looking for your own slice of paradise.

The west coast is easily accessed from the east coast via several scenic roads that cut through the mountainous interior. Starting from Anse Forbans to the southeast, the road wiggles up through the mountain before reaching Quatre Bornes, from where a road leads to **Police Bay**, a splendid spot at the southern tip of the island. Sadly, the currents are too dangerous for swimming, but the beaches are great places to watch the surf (bring a picnic). Another road leads to the Banyan Tree hotel and the high-profile beach at **Anse Intendance** (from the police station at Quatre Bornes, take the 1.7km concrete road that leads down to the beach).

Coming up the west coast, **Anse Takamaka**, **Anse Gaulettes** and **Anse à la Mouche** all vie for the 'best beach' accolade, though most people plump for the idyllic little beach of **Anse Soleil**, a

**SEYCHELLES**

pocket-sized paradise where you can pause for lunch. It's accessible via a secondary road (it's signposted). Another top spot is **Petite Anse**. The pristine curve of white sand is accessible only to those who undertake the 20-minute walk down a hillside (clue: it's the beach below the Four Seasons). As the sun-low sky deepens to orange, this beach just might be heaven, despite the fact it has been partly privatised by the newly built Four Seasons hotel.

To the north of Anse à la Mouche the coast is a bit less glam but appealing nonetheless. If you can find access to **Anse Louis** (where the superswish Maia resort lies), you'll be rewarded with a superlative beach you never knew existed. You'll then go past **Grande Anse** – not suitable for swimming, due to strong currents – before reaching **Port Glaud**, a laid-back town that lazily spreads itself along the coast. Further north you'll reach **Port Launay** and **Port Launay Marine National Park**, which were considered the wildest areas on Mahé until the sprawling Constance Ephelia Resort opened recently. The road comes to an end at **Baie Ternay**, which is blessed with top **snorkelling** spots.

## Activities

There are excellent dive sites off the southwestern coast (see p33). Diving can be arranged through the reputable **Dive Resort Seychelles** (Map p280; ☎ 372057, 717272; www.seychelles diving.net), based in Anse à la Mouche.

**Whale-shark spotting** off Mahé's west coast is organised through **Underwater Centre/Dive Seychelles** (Map p284; ☎ 247165, 542877; www.divesey chelles.com.sc) in September and October.

We also recommend taking a one-hour horseback riding excursion with **Utetangar Riding Centre** (Map p280; ☎ 712355; Grande Anse; 1hr ride €50). There's nothing quite like galloping on Grande Anse beach with the wind in your hair. You'll also traverse some rainforest. Book one day in advance.

## Sleeping

Accommodation in west Mahé ranges from self-catering apartments offering various levels of comfort to big resort hotels with everything laid on.

### BUDGET

**La Rocaille** (Map p280; ☎ 524238; lelarocaille@gmail.com; Anse Gouvernement Rd, Anse Soleil; d/q €60/75) This is a pleasant find, but there's only one unit, on the

hill that separates Anse Gouvernement from Anse Soleil. It's very simple but well kept, and the grounds are nice enough, with lots of vegetation and birdsong. The friendly owners, who live next door, offer fruits to guests and are happy to drive them to the nearest village to stock up on food supplies (it's self-catering). The nearest beach is at Anse Gouvernement, about 400m down the hill.

**ourpick La Maison Soleil** (Map p280; ☎ 712677; www.maisonsoleil.info; Anse Soleil Rd; d or tr incl breakfast €85-120; ⚒) Seeking a relaxing cocoon with homey qualities without the exorbitant price tag? This champ of a self-catering option has all the key ingredients, with two tastefully done apartments, prim bathrooms and a colourful garden. It's also possible to rent the whole house. Anse Soleil is within walking distance.

**La Residence** (Map p280; ☎ 371733; www.laresidence. sc; Anse à la Mouche; d/q €90/170; ⚒) Perched on a hillside, the six fully equipped apartments and three villas are fresh and light-drenched yet simply furnished. The buildings are functional rather than whimsical but there are good views from the terrace (despite the odd power line).

**ourpick Anse Takamaka View** (Map p280; ☎ 510007; www.atv.sc; Takamaka; d €90-130, q €170; ⚒ ⚑ 🛜) No photo retouching on the website – we guarantee that the views from the terrace are *that* terrific, the pool *that* scintillating, and the three villas *that* roomy and comfortable. Run by a Seychellois German couple, this wonderfully soothing property has all the key ingredients. If you don't fancy cooking, meals are available on request (€12).

**Anse Soleil Resort** (Map p280; ☎ 361090; www.ans esoleil.sc; Anse Soleil; d/q €92/138; ⚒) Run by a hospitable family, this discreet number has just four self-catering apartments; the Kitouz is the best, but all are well equipped, nicely laid out and spacious, and come with a large terrace from where you can soak up the view over Anse à la Mouche (if you can ignore the power lines). We can hear you: 'Where's the nearest beach, darling?' – Anse Soleil is 1.6km down the road. Meals (€15) are available on request.

### MIDRANGE

**Chez Batista's** (Map p280; ☎ 366300; www.chez-batista. com; Anse Takamaka; s €76-94, d €135-170, villas €220-275, all incl breakfast; ⚒ 🛜) Your only concern here: whether to frolic on the beach *now* or first sip a cocktail at the restaurant. This long-standing venue on Takamaka beach features nine bland but tidy rooms (no sea views) as well as two luxurious villas. The whole property feels a bit compact and prices are a bit steep but, to be honest, it's the idyllic location that's the pull here.

**Blue Lagoon Chalets** (Map p280; ☎ 371197; www. seychelles.net/blagoon; Anse à la Mouche; d €125; 🔳) The friendly owner here offers four well-cared-for holiday units that are peppered across a well-tended park, a hop from the sea shore. They sleep up to four people and are fully equipped. Air-con is extra (€10).

**Anse Soleil Beachcomber** (Map p280; ☎ 361461; www.beachcomber.sc; Anse Soleil; d incl breakfast €140-220; 🔳 🛜) Among rocks on the idyllic cove of Anse Soleil, this small, family-run hotel with only 14 rooms is a perfect hideaway. The rooms are clean and simple with private terraces. Rooms 10 and 11 have the best setting – they offer more seclusion amid boulders and open onto the sea shore, but the more recent Premier rooms are not bad either. Half board is available. Anse Soleil Café is next door.

**Valmer Resort** (Map p280; ☎ 381555; www.valmer resort; Baie Lazare; d €180, chalets €310-420; 🔳 🛗 🛜) A cluster of well-organised villas cascades down a hillside cloaked in green, each enjoying stupendous ocean views. Apart from the very ordinary standard rooms, which are just off the main road, the 16 units are sun-filled, capacious and tastefully done out. A real hit is the pool, built at the foot of a big granite boulder. There's an onsite restaurant (by the pool) and an art gallery where you can marvel at (and buy) works by local painter Gerard Devoud. There's a minimum stay of three nights.

**Le Méridien Barbarons** (Map p280; ☎ 673000; www. lemeridien.com/barbarons; Barbarons; internet specials from €170, d incl breakfast €430-480; 🔳 🛗 🛜) The hotel is four-star average. But it's set along a pleasant stretch of beach. Don't expect much more from this 124-room resort than the standard amenities, including a small spa, a pool and tennis courts, as well as B-level restaurants and grounds. Bottom line: this is a decent deal if you can get internet specials (when we last checked, rooms cost €170) and like to socialise.

### TOP END

Mahé's swankiest hotels are scattered along the west coast. They're all set along the beach. Take your pick among the following:

**Constance Ephelia Resort** (Map p280; ☎ 395000; www.epheliaresort.com; Port Launay; d incl half board from €440; 🔳 🛗 🛜) High on ambitions, but low on atmosphere, this 264-room resort is not a bad option if you can get online promos.

**Four Seasons** (Map p280; ☎ 393000; www.fourseasons .com/seychelles; Petite Anse; d incl breakfast from €700; 🔳 🛗 🛜) With its stadium-sized villas perched on a hillside, swoony ocean views, sense of privacy and lovely spa, this five-star masterpiece, opened in 2009, is a fab place for honeymooners and loved-up couples, but it's a shame that it has partly privatised Petite Anse beach (boo!).

**Banyan Tree** (Map p280; ☎ 383500; www.banyantree. com; Anse Intendance; d incl breakfast from €1400; 🔳 🛗 🛜) Expect enormous villas, a wow-factor spa and a fabulous location on Anse Intendance.

**Maia Luxury Resort** (Map p280; ☎ 390000; www. maia.com.sc; Anse Louis; d incl breakfast from €1670; 🔳 🛗 🛜) Easily Mahé's most exclusive hotel, the Maia overlooks glorious Anse Louis. The spa is knock-out.

## Eating

**Sundown Restaurant** (Map p280; ☎ 378352; Port Glaud; mains Rs 120-240; ⏲ noon-5pm Mon-Sat) Well-prepared local seafood and a laid-back atmosphere make this a heart stealer. Light years away from the glitz usually associated with the Seychelles, it can't get more mellow than this.

**our pick** **Anse Soleil Café** (Map p280; ☎ 361700; Anse Soleil; mains Rs 150-300; ⏲ noon-8pm) Everyone adores this unfussy little eatery ideally positioned right on the beach at Anse Soleil. The menu is short and concentrates on simply prepared seafood served in generous portions. Fruit bat (yes, fruit bat, a local delicacy) had just been added to the menu when we visited. Digest all this over a drink afterwards.

**Maria's Rock Cafeteria** (Map p280; ☎ 361812; Anse Gouvernement Rd, Anse Soleil; mains Rs 165-230; ⏲ 10am-9pm Wed-Mon) Maria, the Seychellois spouse of artist Antonio Filippin (see p294), runs this quirky restaurant beside her husband's studio. The cavernous interior is discombobulating, with granite tabletops and concrete walls sprayed with paint. Food-wise, it majors on fish and meat dishes, grilled on a metal plate. Skip the pancakes, which taste like plastic.

**Chez Batista's** (Map p280; ☎ 366300; Anse Takamaka; mains Rs 170-500; ⏲ lunch & dinner) The impressive thatched canopy, the sand floor and the endless turquoise bay spread out in front of you help you switch to 'relax' mode. This is a great place for seafood, fish dishes or just a drink, but we met some tourists who found the place touristy and overrated. The eclectic lunch buffet (Rs 330) is the best option on the island on Sunday. It's wise to book on weekends.

**Anchor Café – The Islander** (Map p280; ☎ 371289; Anse à la Mouche; mains Rs 180-300; ☺ 10am-9pm Mon-Sat) Cafeteria-style eating is what you'll get during the day at this locale. Dinner is a more formal affair, with a wide assortment of fish and meat dishes. Try the grilled red snapper or the blackened fish. Eat alfresco, near a huge anchor in the garden.

**Opera** (Map p280; ☎ 372106; Anse à la Mouche; mains Rs 230-350; ☺ 11am-8.30pm Tue-Sun) Across the road from the beach, this lively eatery is high on atmosphere, with well-designed wooden tables and chairs. Alas, no views to speak of. How about the food? Spaghetti Creole-style, grilled beef tenderloin, and grilled tuna steak are examples of the tasty dishes on offer.

Most luxury hotels welcome outside guests at their restaurants (by reservation). For lunch, we've found the restaurant at Banyan Tree (p293) excellent value – think copious burgers, sandwiches, salads and pizzas for less than €20 in a five-star setting.

## Shopping

The glorious southwest seems to be an endless source of inspiration for a number of artists. Visit **Michael Adams' studio** (Map p280; ☎ 361006; www.michaeladamsart.com; Anse à la Mouche), where silkscreen prints burst with the vivid life of the forests. They are irresistible and highly collectable, so bring plenty of rupees if you're thinking of buying. Keep some cash for **Tom Bowers' sculptures** (Map p280; ☎ 371518; Anse à la Mouche) and for Antonio Filippin's somewhat risqué woodcarvings. Antonio's quirky studio, **Art Arc** (Map p280; ☎ 510977; Baie Lazare), is perched on a hill between Anse Gouvernement and Anse Soleil. Gerard Devoud's eye-goggling paintings are also sure to enliven your bedroom. **Gerard Devoud's studio** (Map p280; ☎ 381515; Baie Lazare) is at Valmer Resort.

## Getting There & Away

Buses leave regularly from Victoria for the west coast. The last bus to Victoria leaves around 7.30pm.

# PRASLIN

A wicked seductress, Praslin has lots of temptations: stylish lodgings, tangled velvet jungle, curving hills dropping down to gin-clear seas, gorgeous stretches of silky sand edged with palm trees and a slow-motion ambience. No, you're not dreaming!

Lying about 45km northeast of Mahé, the second-largest island in the Seychelles falls somewhere between the relative hustle and bustle of Mahé and the sleepiness of La Digue. Like Mahé, Praslin is a granite island, with a ridge of small mountains running east–west along the centre. The island is 12km long and 5km across at its widest point. The 5000 inhabitants of Praslin are scattered around the coast in a series of small settlements. The most important from a visitor's perspective are Anse Volbert (also known as Côte d'Or) and Grand Anse. At the southeast tip of the island is Baie Ste Anne, Praslin's main port.

Praslin has all you need to decompress. But if playing sardines on the strand ceases to do it for you, another world beckons at the Vallée de Mai, one of the most peculiar attractions in the Seychelles. Scuba diving, snorkelling and boat excursions to nearby islands famed for their bird life will also keep you buzzing.

## INFORMATION

All the major banks have ATMs and exchange facilities. There's a bureau de change at the airport and at Grand Anse. Praslin's two tourist offices can provide maps and basic information, and help with accommodation, car hire and excursion bookings. Praslin's travel agents all offer similar excursions at similar prices and can organise boat excursions, air tickets and the like. For car hire, it's best to negotiate directly with car-rental companies – tourist offices have a list.

**Barclays Bank** Baie Ste Anne ( ☎ 232218); Grand Anse ( ☎ 233344)

**Central post office** (Grand Anse; ☺ 8am-noon & 1-4pm Mon-Fri) Next to the police station in Grand Anse.

**Creole Travel Services** ( ☎ 294294; Grand Anse) Travel agency. Near the airstrip.

**D&B Medianet Services** (Anse Volbert; internet access per hr Rs 120; ☺ 10am-8pm Mon-Sat) Internet cafe. Next door to Gelateria de Luca.

**Mason's Travel** ( ☎ 288750; Grand Anse) Travel agency. In the Pension Complex.

**Mauritius Commercial Bank** (MCB) Anse Volbert ( ☎ 232602); Grand Anse ( ☎ 233940)

**Nadia's Internet Café** ( ☎ 233478; Grand Anse; internet access per hr Rs 30; ☺ 10am-5pm Mon-Thu, to 11.45am Sun) Inside Ocean Plaza building.

**Tourist office** airport ( ☎ 233346; stbpraslin@seychelles. sc; Praslin airport; ☺ 8am-noon & 2-4pm Mon-Fri, 8am-noon Sat); Baie Ste Anne jetty ( ☎ 232669; stbpraslin

**SEYCHELLES' BEST BEACHES**

It's gruelling work investigating which beaches qualify as the best of Seychelles. Here are a few of our favourites:

■ **Beau Vallon** (Mahé; p283) – Mahé's longest and most popular beach, sweeping blonde sand backed by takamaka trees. The best all-round choice for everyone, from singles to couples to families with kids

■ **Petite Anse** (Mahé; p292) – this beach with almost lagoon-still waters is hard to reach, which is its salvation

■ **Anse Intendance** (Mahé; p291) – famous for its hypnotically dramatic sunset. As the sun-low sky deepens to orange, the big granite boulders that frame the beach glow with muted copper tones and form a perfect backdrop for a romantic stroll

■ **Anse Takamaka** (Mahé; p291) – Mahé's sexiest beach is the perfect place for sunbathing

■ **Anse Lazio** (Praslin; p295) – excellent for sunbathing and snorkelling, and famous for its beach restaurants

■ **Baie Laraie** (Curieuse; p297) – an intimate paradise, accessible by boat

■ **Anse Source d'Argent** (La Digue; p302) – crystalline, glossy and framed with glacis boulders, this is the most photogenic of all the Seychelles' beaches

■ **Grand Anse** (La Digue; p302) – idyllic stretch of sand, excellent for frolicking in the crashing surf

■ **Anse Marron** (La Digue; p303) – a hidden gem on the isolated south coast, this virgin swathe of flaxen sand framed by ochre boulders is only accessible on foot

If you're looking for something ultra-exclusive, you can mark your footprints in pristine sand at Denis, Silhouette, Desroches, Frégate, North and Bird Islands (see p307).

@seychelles.sc; Baie Ste Anne; ☺ 8am-1pm & 2-4pm Mon-Fri, 8am-noon Sat)

## SIGHTS & ACTIVITIES
### Vallée de Mai
Praslin's World Heritage–listed **Vallée de Mai** (adult/under 12yr €15/free; ☺ 8am-5.30pm) is one of only two places in the world where you can see the rare coco de mer palms growing in their natural state (the other being nearby Curieuse Island) – not to mention more than 50 other indigenous plants and trees. If the entry price seems steep, remember this is a unique chance to experience a slice of Eden. Five **hiking** trails lead through this primeval, emerald-tinged forest, which remained totally untouched until the 1930s. The shortest is about 1km and the longest is 2km – perfect for families. As you walk amid the forest, the atmosphere is eerie, with the monstrous leaves of the coco de mer soaring 30m to a sombre canopy of huge fronds. Signs indicate some of the other endemic trees to look out for, including several varieties of pandanus (screw pines) and latanier palms. Bird-watchers also rate

Vallée de Mai as a top birding hot spot. Keep your eyes peeled for endemic species, including the Seychelles bulbul, the blue pigeon, the Seychelles warbler and the elusive black parrot, of which there are perhaps less than 100 left.

### Beaches
Is **Anse Lazio**, on the northwest tip of the island, the most enticing beach in the Indian Ocean? It's picture-postcard everywhere you look. Here, the long, broad pale-sand beach has lapis lazuli waters on one side and a thick fringe of palm and takamaka trees on the other, and it's framed by a series of granite boulders at each extremity. You won't find a better place for sunbathing and snorkelling.

The lovely, long stretch of sand at **Anse Volbert** is another stunner, but lacks the wild factor. At the island's southern tip, **Anse Consolation** and **Anse Marie-Louise** are also pretty spots. Continuing along the coastal road to the west, you'll find numerous coves and other beaches. **Grand Anse** has a long beach, but swimming is only average, with shallow waters and a profusion of algae.

SEYCHELLES

## PRASLIN

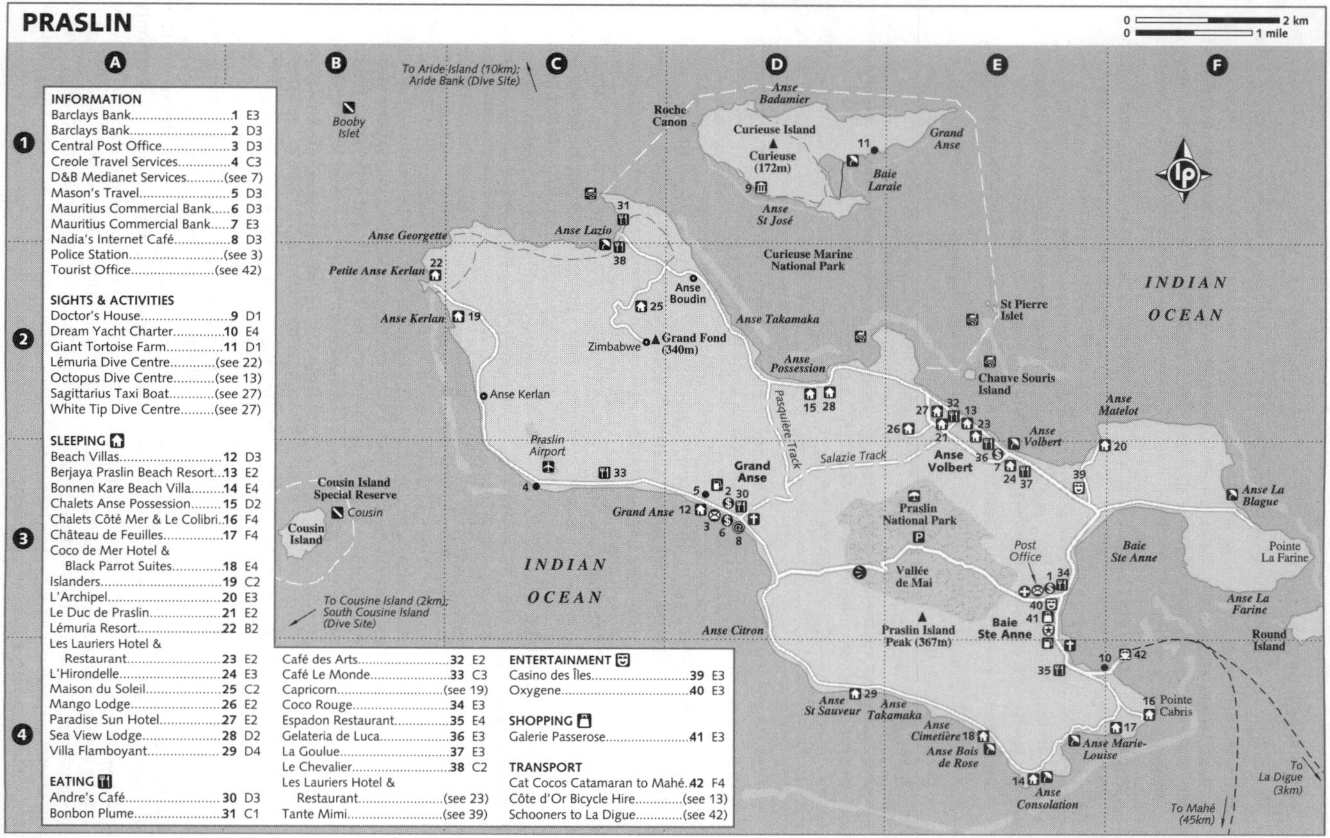

0 2 km
0 1 mile
A
B
C
D
E
F
1
2
3
4
To Aride Island (10km); Aride Bank (Dive Site)
Booby Islet
Roche Canon
Anse Badamier
Curieuse Island
Curieuse (172m)
Grand Anse
Baie Laraie
Anse St José
Curieuse Marine National Park
Anse Georgette
Anse Lazio
Petite Anse Kerlan
Anse Boudin
Anse Kerlan
Anse Takamaka
Grand Fond (340m)
Zimbabwe
St Pierre Islet
INDIAN OCEAN
Anse Possession
Chauve Souris Island
Anse Kerlan
Pasquière Track
Anse Matelot
Anse Volbert
Praslin Airport
Salazie Track
Anse Volbert
Grand Anse
Cousin Island Special Reserve
Cousin
Cousin Island
Grand Anse
Praslin National Park
Anse La Blague
Baie Ste Anne
Pointe La Farine
Post Office
Vallée de Mai
INDIAN OCEAN
To Cousine Island (2km); South Cousine Island (Dive Site)
Anse Citron
Praslin Island Peak (367m)
Baie Ste Anne
Anse La Farine
Round Island
Anse St Sauveur
Anse Takamaka
Anse Cimetière
Anse Bois de Rose
Pointe Cabris
Anse Marie-Louise
Anse Consolation
To La Digue (3km)
To Mahé (45km)

**INFORMATION**
- Barclays Bank ... 1 E3
- Barclays Bank ... 2 D3
- Central Post Office ... 3 D3
- Creole Travel Services ... 4 C3
- D&B Medianet Services ... (see 7)
- Mason's Travel ... 5 D3
- Mauritius Commercial Bank ... 6 D3
- Mauritius Commercial Bank ... 7 E3
- Nadia's Internet Café ... 8 D3
- Police Station ... (see 3)
- Tourist Office ... (see 42)

**SIGHTS & ACTIVITIES**
- Doctor's House ... 9 D1
- Dream Yacht Charter ... 10 E4
- Giant Tortoise Farm ... 11 D1
- Lémuria Dive Centre ... (see 22)
- Octopus Dive Centre ... (see 13)
- Sagittarius Taxi Boat ... (see 27)
- White Tip Dive Centre ... (see 27)

**SLEEPING**
- Beach Villas ... 12 D3
- Berjaya Praslin Beach Resort ... 13 E2
- Bonnen Kare Beach Villa ... 14 E4
- Chalets Anse Possession ... 15 D2
- Chalets Côté Mer & Le Colibri ... 16 F4
- Château de Feuilles ... 17 F4
- Coco de Mer Hotel & Black Parrot Suites ... 18 E4
- Islanders ... 19 C2
- L'Archipel ... 20 E3
- Le Duc de Praslin ... 21 E2
- Lémuria Resort ... 22 B2
- Les Lauriers Hotel & Restaurant ... 23 E2
- L'Hirondelle ... 24 E3
- Maison du Soleil ... 25 C2
- Mango Lodge ... 26 E2
- Paradise Sun Hotel ... 27 E2
- Sea View Lodge ... 28 D2
- Villa Flamboyant ... 29 D4

**EATING**
- Andre's Café ... 30 D3
- Bonbon Plume ... 31 C1
- Café des Arts ... 32 E2
- Café Le Monde ... 33 C3
- Capricorn ... (see 19)
- Coco Rouge ... 34 E3
- Espadon Restaurant ... 35 E4
- Gelateria de Luca ... 36 E3
- La Goulue ... 37 E3
- Le Chevalier ... 38 C2
- Les Lauriers Hotel & Restaurant ... (see 23)
- Tante Mimi ... (see 39)

**ENTERTAINMENT**
- Casino des Îles ... 39 E3
- Oxygene ... 40 E3

**SHOPPING**
- Galerie Passerose ... 41 E3

**TRANSPORT**
- Cat Cocos Catamaran to Mahé ... 42 F4
- Côte d'Or Bicycle Hire ... (see 13)
- Schooners to La Digue ... (see 42)

---

**SEXY COCONUTS**

This must be the sexiest fruit on earth, and it could be mistaken for some kind of erotic gadgetry in a sex shop. The *coco fesse* (the fruit of the coco de mer palm) looks like, ahem, buttocks with a female sex. It has been the source of many legends and erotic lore, given its peculiar shape. Now you can understand why these strange, sensual fruits excited the 17th-century sailors who first stumbled upon them after months at sea. Before 1768 the coconuts, which were occasionally found floating in the Indian Ocean, were believed to grow in a magic garden at the bottom of the sea. This rare palm grows naturally only in the Seychelles.

Only female trees produce the erotically shaped nuts, which can weigh over 30kg. The male tree possesses a decidedly phallic flower stem of 1m or longer, adding to the coco de mer's steamy reputation.

Harvesting the nuts is strictly controlled by the **Seychelles Island Foundation** (SIF; Map p282; www.sif.sc; Mont Fleuri Rd, Victoria), an NGO that manages the Vallée de Mai on behalf of the government. Money from the sale of nuts goes towards SIF's conservation work in the Vallée de Mai and on Aldabra.

If you want to lug one of these nuts home, be prepared to pay at least €150. They come in a husky state and will need to be polished; beware of ready-polished nuts, which are often fakes. The safest place to buy is directly from SIF, which will issue you with the required export permit.

---

Head to **Anse La Blague** on the east coast if you're after a secluded picnic spot. Very few tourists make it to this shady beach, which feels like the world's end. You might come across a few fishermen with their catch of *cordonnier* (job-fish).

Sadly, **Anse Georgette**, which is an indescribably lovely stretch of white sand at the northwestern tip of the island, has been engulfed by the Lémuria Resort. In theory it's a public beach that is accessible to anybody. In practice, you might be turned back at the gate of the Lémuria. Tip: get there by taxi boat from Anse Volbert.

## Boat Excursions to Nearby Islands

### CURIEUSE

Curieuse Island is a granite island 1.5km off Praslin's north coast and was a leper colony from 1833 until 1965. Curieuse is used as a breeding centre for giant Aldabra tortoises. The wardens at the **giant tortoise farm** (admission free; 9am-5pm) show visitors round the pens, after which you're free to explore the rest of the island. Nearby **Baie Laraie** is a fantastic place for swimming and snorkelling. From Baie Laraie, a path leads to Anse st José, where you can visit the **doctor's house** (admission free; 9am-5pm), which contains a small historical museum.

Most visitors to Curieuse Island arrive on an organised tour, usually in combination with Cousin and St Pierre Islet. Tours are arranged through Praslin's hotels or any tour operator. Day trips cost around €110/55 for an adult/child including lunch, landing fees and the marine-park entry fee.

The alternative is to charter your own boat from Anse Volbert. **Sagittarius Taxi Boat** (☎ 232234, 570454), on the beach beside the Paradise Sun Hotel, charges €35 for Curieuse, including fees; Curieuse with St Pierre costs €40. You'll also find taxi boats at Anse Possession.

### COUSIN

About 2km southwest of Praslin, Cousin Island is run as a nature reserve by **Nature Seychelles** (www.nature.org.sc). Seven species of seabirds nest here, including fairy terns, whitetailed tropicbirds and shearwaters. The bird population is estimated to exceed 300,000 on an island measuring just 1km in diameter. It's an amazing experience to walk through thick forest with birds seemingly nesting on every branch. Cousin is also home to five species of endemic land birds, including the Seychelles warbler and the magpie robin.

The island is also an important nesting ground for hawksbill turtles. As many as 100 turtles nest here between October and April. At any time of the year you're bound to see lizards: Cousin boasts one of the highest densities of lizards in the world.

Cousin can only be visited as part of an organised tour from Monday to Friday, usually in combination with Curieuse and St Pierre Islet. Day trips can be arranged through

SEYCHELLES

Praslin's hotels and tour operators for around €110/55 per adult/child. The adult price includes a €30 landing fee, which goes towards conservation efforts, and a barbecued lunch on Curieuse.

#### ST PIERRE ISLET

The glassy waters around St Pierre Islet, off Anse Volbert, are excellent for snorkelling and sloshing around.

Boat trips to St Pierre organised by hotels and private operators are usually offered in combination with Curieuse and Cousin (see p297). The alternative is to charter your own boat from Anse Volbert. Contact Sagittarius Taxi Boat (p297). It costs €30, including fees.

#### ARIDE

And now, Aride. The most northerly of the granite islands, this nature reserve lies 10km north of Praslin and supports the greatest concentration of sea birds in the area, including large colonies of noddies, terns and frigate birds, as well as lizards. From the summit (134m), the views are sensational.

Aride can be reached by boat between September and May only, as landing can be difficult at other times. During the season, the island is open to visitors three days a week.

Tours can be arranged through travel agencies, hotels and guesthouses in Praslin. A day trip costs about €110/50 per adult/child, including lunch and a guided tour of the island.

### Diving & Snorkelling

Whether you're an experienced diver or a novice slapping on fins for the first time, you'll find superb dive sites off Praslin. See p33 for more information on dive sites. A single dive costs from €40. There are three state-of-the-art dive shops on Praslin:

**Lémuria Dive Centre** (☎ 281281; Anse Kerlan) At the Lémuria Resort.

**Octopus Dive Centre** (☎ 232350, 512350; www.octopusdiver.com; Anse Volbert) Near the Berjaya Praslin Beach Resort.

**White Tip Dive Centre** (☎ 232282, 514282; www.whitetipdivers.com; Anse Volbert) Based at Paradise Sun Hotel.

The best snorkelling spots can be found at Anse Lazio (p295), around St Pierre Islet (p298) and off Baie Laraie on Curieuse (p297).

### Kayaking

It's not a bad idea to rent a kayak and explore Anse Volbert at your leisure and paddle round Chauve Souris Island. **Sagittarius Taxi Boat** (☎ 232234, 570454) handles rentals (from €10 per hour).

## SLEEPING

Demand for accommodation is high in Praslin. To avoid disappointment, particularly in high season, book your accommodation well in advance.

Truly budget options are nonexistent, but a number of guesthouses offer perfectly comfortable double rooms with private bathroom for around €100.

Anse Volbert, with its restaurants and other tourist facilities, makes a good base. Grand Anse is busier and less attractive, but less touristy, and there are some decent options within walking distance of the Baie Ste Anne jetty. If you're looking for a real hideaway, head for the wild and empty promontories to either side of Baie Ste Anne.

Most places offer their guests a free shuttle to Anse Lazio.

### Grand Anse & Anse Kerlan Area

**Beach Villas** (☎ 233445; martin@seychelles.net; Grand Anse; s/d incl breakfast €70/95; ❄) Nothing glam, but this venture boasts grassy garden areas, a beachfront location and nine well-kept rooms. Surprisingly, they don't face the sea. Dinner costs about €15. Good value.

**Islanders** (☎ 233224; www.the-islanders.com; Anse Kerlan; d incl breakfast €100-120; ❄ 📶) The good people at the Islanders are not setting out to win any 'best in its class' awards with their establishment but the virtue is that it's kept in good shape and you'll be made to feel at home. The four bungalows (eight rooms in total) are unpretentious but clean and the property opens onto Anse Kerlan. There's an onsite restaurant, Capricorn (see p300). One quibble: air-con is extra (€10).

**Lémuria Resort** (☎ 281281; www.lemuriaresort.com; Anse Kerlan; d incl breakfast from €660; ❄ 🏊 📶) Praslin's top-drawer establishment occupies the whole northwest tip of the island. If you're not bowled over by features such as the voluminous foyer and the soothing spa, you certainly will be by the three-tiered infinity pool, the three gorgeous beaches and the expansive grounds in which the villas blend in among the rocks and water features. Facilities include three restaurants, a kids club and an 18-hole golf course. One blemish: the property has engulfed the idyllic Anse Georgette, which is now a de facto part of the hotel, though it's a public beach by law.

### Anse St Sauveur Area

**ourpick Villa Flamboyant** ( ☎ 233036; vila@seychelles. net; Anse St Sauveur; d incl breakfast/half board €85/95, bungalows incl breakfast/half board €100/120) You'll be impressed by the large building (a converted planter's house) that merges effortlessly with a surrounding panoply of stately flamboyant trees. The six rooms are simply furnished yet comfortable. Also available are two modern, fully equipped bungalows. Rosemary, your charming host, is a good cook – ah, the banana fritters with coconut cream… Mooch around on the deserted beach, snooze in a hammock, or just listen to the cacophony of birds. One thing is sure: after several days here, you'll find it difficult to pack up and leave.

**Coco de Mer Hotel & Black Parrot Suites** ( ☎ 290555; www.cocodemer.com; Anse Bois de Rose; s €233-376, d €276-445, ste €380-548, all incl breakfast; ✖ ☎ ⑨ ) Choose the exclusive Black Parrot Suites, perched on a headland with fantastic ocean views, if you want some serious cosseting; the Coco de Mer, with 40 rooms, a gym, tennis court, a restaurant, shops and a bar, has more of a resort feel. There's no beach (bar an unimpressive artificial one) but you can cool off in the pool in the shape of a *coco fesse* (yes, they dared).

### Anse Consolation

**Bonnen Kare Beach Villa** ( ☎ 322457; www.bonnenkare. com; d/q €125/220) A lovely option for a group of friends or a family, this secluded four-room villa opening onto an idyllic sandy cove really fulfils the dreams of a private beach getaway. Don't fancy cooking? The maid can prepare meals on request. No air-con.

### Baie Ste Anne & Pointe Cabris Area

**Chalets Côté Mer & Le Colibri** ( ☎ 294200; www.chalet cotemer.com; Baie Ste Anne; d incl breakfast €126-170; ✖ ☎ ) A good deal at the southeastern tip of Baie Ste Anne. Features a clutch of A-framed bungalows and villas perched on a hillside cloaked in green, with glorious views over La Digue. The Colibri bungalows are slightly hipper than the no-frills Chalets Côté Mer. Aim for the Colibri, Magpie, Fairytern, Katiti or Kato, which are the best laid out. Lovers of fine food will enjoy the cooking here – the

French owner, René Parmentier, has made a name as an adept chef (half board from €140 for two). There's no beach but snorkelling is excellent along the rocky shore.

**ourpick Château de Feuilles** ( ☎ 290000; www. chateaudefeuilles.com; Pointe Cabris; d incl breakfast €435-630; ✖ ☎ ⑨ ) Paradise awaits you in this bijou hideaway sitting on an unfathomably beautiful headland near Baie Ste Anne. Nine luxurious villas are ingeniously deployed over several acres of tropical gardens. A serene symphony of earth tones and natural textures, elegant furnishings, sensational views, high-class amenities (including a complimentary car), an uber-romantic poolside restaurant – every detail is spot-on. The hotel's ultimate trump card, though, is its nifty hilltop Jacuzzi. There's a three-night minimum stay.

### Anse Volbert Area

**Mango Lodge** ( ☎ 232077, 570454; www.mango-lodge. com; Anse Volbert; s €75-95, d €125-150, all incl breakfast; ⑨ ) Efficiently run by South African Lesley, these digs offer something different, with a cluster of well-appointed bungalows and offbeat, stilt-raised A-framed chalets precariously perched on a greenery-cloaked hillside. What a hallucinogenic view! Enjoy dinner (available on request) on an open-air verandah overlooking the whole bay. Though it's only 600m from the beach, the access road is so steep that you definitely need wheels to stay here.

**Les Lauriers Hotel & Restaurant** ( ☎ 232241; www. laurier-seychelles.com; Anse Volbert; s/d incl breakfast €90/115, incl half board €115/165; ✖ ⑨ ) A pleasant oasis, despite the lack of sea views and the odd landscaping of the compound. Run by friendly Edwin and Sybille, it features six uncomplicated and smallish but neat rooms as well as eight bungalows. The woodcarved posts on the terrace are a nice touch. It's well worth opting for half board, given the attached high-quality restaurant (p301).

**L'Hirondelle** ( ☎ 232243; www.seychelles.net/hiron delle; Anse Volbert; r €95) The four rooms, although they won't knock your socks off, are comfortable and come fully equipped, and each has a balcony or a terrace that commands a blue-green lagoon vista. Downside: it's not shielded from the noise of the coast road. An extensive renovation is planned in the near future.

**Berjaya Praslin Beach Resort** ( ☎ 286286; www. berjayahotels-resorts.com; Anse Volbert; s/d incl breakfast from €125/140; ✖ ☎ ⑨ ) We've heard mixed reports

SEYCHELLES

about this midrange resort. Considering its brilliant location near the beach and solid amenities, we think it's good value if you can snag a promo deal and a renovated room (the old ones are best avoided).

**our pick** **Le Duc de Praslin** ( ☎ 232252; www.leduc -seychelles.com; Anse Volbert; s €215-300, d €245-350, all incl breakfast; ✖ ☒ ☎ ) After a massive refurbishment, this little island of subdued glamour, a *coco fesse*'s throw from the beach, now ranks as one of the most solid options on Praslin. The generous-sized, sensitively furnished rooms come with all mod cons and orbit around an alluring pool and a nicely laid-out tropical garden. If only it had ocean views, life would be perfect.

**L'Archipel** ( ☎ 284700; www.larchipel.com; Anse Gouvernement; d incl breakfast from €300; ✖ ☒ ☒ ) This resort occupies a large, nicely landscaped plot by the beach, at Anse Gouvernement (the eastern tip of Anse Volbert). Squeezed in between the spacious, stand-alone, split-level units are a swimming pool and a restaurant. The walk up to the highest bungalows may leave the terminally unfit short of breath. Naturally, you'll find all the usual resort facilities onsite.

**Paradise Sun Hotel** ( ☎ 293293; www.paradisesun. com; Anse Volbert; d incl half board €520-695; ✖ ☒ ☎ ) If you're looking for the classic Seychelles setting, complete with shady palms, lagoon views and a splendid china-white stretch of sand just steps from your door, then this resort-style operation won't disappoint. It offers 80 smartly finished bungalows with dark-wood fixtures and granite bricks, ample space and heaps of amenities, including a dive centre, a pool and a restaurant. It's kid-friendly.

## Anse Possession

Approximately halfway between Anse Lazio and Anse Volbert, Anse Possession is convenient to both. It's also a good, quiet base. There's a thin strip of sand but it can't rival with the beach at Anse Lazio or Anse Volbert.

**Chalets Anse Possession** ( ☎ 232180; tessalablache@ hotmail.com; Anse Possession; villas €70-110; ✖ ) Three two-bedroom villas are set in lush greenery off the coast road. Although not the height of luxury, they're clean, comfy, roomy and serviceable – perfect for the traveller who's not fussy. Meals (€15) can be served on request. Excellent value.

**Sea View Lodge** ( ☎ 711965, 780001; www.kokonet. sc/seaviewlodge; Anse Possession; d €90-110, q €130-170;

✖ ☒ ) This place has four bungalows, two of which are perched on a hillside. Needless to say the verandahs have stunning views over the bay and Curieuse Island. The newly built 'Banana' feels like a cosy bird's nest. All are fully equipped and very spacious.

## Anse Boudin

**Maison du Soleil** ( ☎ 576315, 598230; Anse Boudin; jean louis@seychelles.net; d/q €60/100) Almost too good to be true. A location scout's dream, this self-catering villa perched on a hilltop offers million-dollar views of Curieuse and Praslin's northern coastline. There's a second villa, a bit further down. OK, there's no air-con and you need wheels to stay here, but those are the only gripes. The property is secluded and slightly hard to find, off the steep road to Zimbabwe – just like paradise should be.

# EATING

Since most people eat in their hotels or guesthouses, there are relatively few independent restaurants on Praslin. You'll find takeaways at Grand Anse, Baie Ste Anne and Anse Volbert, and a clutch of smarter places scattered around the coast.

Most hotels have excellent restaurants that are open to all comers (by reservation).

## Grand Anse & Anse Kerlan

You can eat well without breaking the bank at the pleasantly informal **Andre's Café** ( ☎ 233001; Grand Anse; mains Rs 40-250; ☾ 9am-9pm Mon-Sat), which also does takeaway meals. The snazzier **Café Le Monde** (mains Rs 110-370; Grand Anse; ☾ lunch & dinner) is worth visiting for the good, wholesome food created from quality ingredients.

At Anse Kerlan, the Islanders (p298) has a good onsite restaurant, **Capricorn** ( ☎ 233224; mains Rs 150-300; ☾ lunch Mon-Sat). It's famous for its 'octopus Patrick-style' (octopus in a saffron sauce) and homemade ice creams.

## Baie Ste Anne

**our pick** **Coco Rouge** ( ☎ 232228; Baie Ste Anne; takeaways Rs 40-50, dinner menu Rs 275; ☾ lunch & dinner Mon-Sat) Coco Rouge is that easy-to-miss 'secret spot' that locals like to recommend. Run by Tony, a former English teacher, it serves up a good-value set *menu* at dinner, consisting of about six grandma-style Creole dishes prepared from fresh simple ingredients. The setting is refreshingly simple, with sturdy takamaka tables. It also has a takeaway counter.

**Espadon Restaurant** ( ☎ 582508; Baie Ste Anne; mains Rs 100, dinner menu Rs 300; ☷ lunch & dinner Mon-Sat) This tiny, typically Creole joint is a great place for a cheap and fast meal at lunchtime, or for a fixed *menu* come the evening. The naive fresco sporting colourful fish is amusing.

## Anse Volbert Area

**Gelateria de Luca** (Anse Volbert; mains Rs 80-160; ☷ 11am-8pm) Praslin's prime ice-cream parlour will leave you a drooling mess. Order a *coppa tropicale* (Rs 150), and you'll see why. It also whips up pasta dishes, pizzas and various snacks, and the vitamin-packed passionfruit juice is killer. Two minuses: the decor is as sexy as a parking lot and there's no view.

**La Goulue** ( ☎ 232223; Anse Volbert; mains Rs 150-300; ☷ lunch & dinner Mon-Sat) This little eatery doesn't have beach frontage but the terrace catches some breeze. The menu features Creole staples and various filling snacks.

**Tante Mimi** ( ☎ 232500; Anse Volbert; mains Rs 200-600; ☷ dinner Tue-Sun) Tante Mimi is a real heartbreaker. At the casino in Anse Volbert, you couldn't ask for a more atmospheric setting – think a lovely old colonial house, creaky parquet flooring, Creole furnishings throughout, silver cutlery, chandeliers and a wide-ranging menu featuring Creole classics. Unfortunately the food is hit-and-miss and the service utterly amateurish.

**our pick Café des Arts** ( ☎ 232252; mains Rs 450-800; ☷ dinner Tue-Sun) Praslin's most stylish restaurant is perfect for a *tête-à-tête*. Flickering candles, colourful paintings on the walls, swaying palms, a breezy terrace and the sound of waves washing the beach will rekindle the faintest romantic flame. The food is suitably refined; flavourful Seychellois favourites are whipped into eye-pleasing concoctions (think red snapper fillet in mango sauce or pumpkin soup with cinnamon).

**our pick Les Lauriers Hotel & Restaurant** ( ☎ 232241; Anse Volbert; buffet Rs 500; ☷ dinner Thu-Tue) Charismatic Edwin and his Belgian spouse prepare a spectacular buffet at dinner – we walked out belly first. Rejoicing begins with lip-smacking hors d'oeuvre displayed on a boat-shaped table (the avocado salad is to die for), followed by sizzling meat and expertly grilled fish morsels (usually red snapper, jack, job and shark). The dining room is atmospheric, especially the new wing, with wrought-iron furnishings. Make sure you reserve a table.

## Anse Lazio

**Le Chevalier** ( ☎ 560488; Anse Lazio; mains Rs 215-500; ☷ lunch) Can't get a table at Bonbon Plume? Don't despair. Here's an acceptable plan B. OK, it's not right on the beach and the setting is frustratingly bland (think a vast, tiled, open-air room on the ground floor of a modern villa), but the menu offers more variety than at Bonbon Plume. Prices are as high, though (burgers cost a whopping Rs 215).

**Bonbon Plume** ( ☎ 232136; Anse Lazio; mains Rs 280-450, menu Rs 400; ☷ lunch) Is it a tourist trap or a seafood mecca? Both, perhaps. With such a location – the palm-thatched canopy is right on the beach – tables are unsurprisingly in high demand. Anything from grilled crab in coconut sauce to the catch of the day, this is a simple seafood delight. For grilled lobster or *cigale de mer* (squill fish), you'll be looking at Rs 750.

## DRINKING & ENTERTAINMENT

Praslin's nightlife is not exactly buzzing. A good place to rub shoulders with locals is **Oxygene** (Baie Ste Anne; admission Rs 50; ☷ 10pm-4am Fri & Sat).

Other than that, most large hotels put on their own entertainment programs and have bars where you can enjoy the ocean breezes, or you can try your luck at the **Casino des Îles** ( ☎ 232500; Anse Volbert; ☷ slot machines noon-2am, gaming tables 7.30pm-3am).

## SHOPPING

**Galerie Passerose** (Baie Ste Anne; ☷ 10am-1pm & 3.30-6pm) A lovely art gallery run by knowledgeable Maureen Harter, who promotes the works of Seychellois artists including Michael Adams and Sheila Markham. She also makes beautiful jewels made of wood, shell or ceramic.

## GETTING THERE & AWAY

**Praslin airport** ( ☎ 284666) is 3km from Grand Anse and has flights every hour or so from Mahé. For further information, see p315.

It's almost as quick to take the Cat Cocos catamaran from Victoria. See p316 for routes, times and prices.

## GETTING AROUND

Praslin has a decent bus service as well as the usual taxis. A taxi ride from the airport to Anse Volbert will set you back Rs 200. For more information, see p316.

A car is a great way to see the island. Most travel agents and hotels will assist you in organising car hire.

**SEYCHELLES**

You can hire bikes through your accommodation or from **Côte d'Or Bicycle Hire** ( ☎ 232071) in Anse Volbert for Rs 100 per day.

Hopping around the small islands off Praslin is done by chartered boat; trips are usually organised through the hotels or tour operators.

# LA DIGUE

Remember that tropical paradise that appears in countless adverts and glossy travel brochures? Here it's the real thing, with jade-green waters, bewitching bays studded with heart-palpitatingly gorgeous beaches, and green hills cloaked with tangled jungle and tall trees. As if that wasn't enough, La Digue is ideally situated as a springboard to surrounding islands, including Félicité, Grande Sœur and the fairytale Île Cocos.

Despite its lush beauty, La Digue has managed to escape the somewhat rampant tourist development that affects Mahé and Praslin. Sure, it's certainly not undiscovered, but La Digue has a more laid-back feel than the other main islands, with only a few surfaced roads and virtually no cars, just the odd ox cart. The place is definitely more a back-to-nature than a jet-set-tourist kind of haven, making it possible to find that deserted *anse* (bay) where you really feel like you've been stranded in paradise.

Transport to La Digue is absurdly easy. It's only about 5km from Praslin, and getting by boat from one island to the other is simplicity itself, so you've no excuse not to spend a day or two at the very least on this island.

If money's any object, La Digue has a growing number of quaint family guesthouses and self-catering apartments in which to rest your head. While hardly glitzy, they usually boast loads of gracious charm.

## INFORMATION

All venues are in La Passe.

**Barclays Bank** ( ☎ 234148;  10am-2.30pm Mon-Fri) Has an ATM.

**Creole Travel Services** ( ☎ 234411;  8am-noon & 1-4pm Mon-Fri, 8am-noon Sat) An agent for Cat Cocos. Can arrange tours and boat excursions.

**La Digue Electronics** (internet access per hr Rs 60;  9am-noon & 2-6pm Mon-Sat) Internet cafe. Also offers wi-fi.

**La Digue Video & Internet Café** (internet access per hr Rs 120;  9am-9pm Mon-Sat, 1-8pm Sun)

**La Passe Moneychanger** (  9am-1pm & 2-5pm Mon-Fri, 9am-2.30pm Sat) At the jetty.

**Mauritius Commercial Bank** (MCB; ☎ 234560;  8.30-11.30am & 12.15-2.30pm Mon-Fri) Has an ATM.

**Mason's Travel** ( ☎ 234227;  8am-4.30pm Mon-Fri, 8am-noon Sat) Can organise tours and boat excursions.

**Nouvobanq** (  8.30am-2pm Mon-Fri, to 11.30am Sat) Has an ATM.

**Post office** (  8am-4pm Mon-Fri)

**Tourist office** ( ☎ 234393;  8am-4.30pm Mon-Fri, 9am-noon Sat) Provides basic information and helps organise tours.

## SIGHTS & ACTIVITIES
### La Passe

A visit to tiny La Passe almost feels like stepping back in time, so perfectly does it capture the image of a sleepy tropical port. Virtually no cars clog the streets. Men and women talk shop on the jetty while waiting for the schooner to arrive. Children ride bicycles on the tree-lined roads. Come Saturday night, most islanders head to Tarosa for some serious dancing and drinking.

Check out the few souvenir shops near the jetty, sign up for a boat excursion or hire a bicycle and just peddle around a bit.

### Beaches

Most new arrivals head straight for the beach at **Anse Source d'Argent**, and we don't blame them. *This* is the tropical paradise we've all been daydreaming about all winter: a dazzling white-sand beach backed by naturally sculpted granite boulders that would have made Henry Moore proud.

Alas, don't expect a Robinson Crusoe experience – it can get pretty crowded here, especially at high tide when the beach virtually disappears. Another downside: Anse Source d'Argent is scenic, but not that great for swimming due to the shallow water. 'We don't understand why tourists head en masse to Anse Source d'Argent; we have much more idyllic beaches around the island! For us, it's just an ideal flirting place because you can hide in the rocks', said one local tour operator.

Take note that the path down to Anse Source d'Argent runs through the old L'Union Estate coconut plantation. In other words, you'll have to pay the Rs 100 entry fee (valid for a day) to access the beach.

On the southeast coast, **Grand Anse** is a stunning beach to sun yourself on, and it sees fewer visitors because of the effort required to get there (though you can easily walk or cycle the 4km or so from La Passe). One caveat: swimming may be dangerous because of the strong offshore currents during the southeast monsoon, from April to October.

North of Grand Anse, two of the island's quietest beaches are **Petite Anse** and **Anse Cocos**. Both are accessible on foot only (see p304). Petite Anse is palm-fringed and idyllic, though there are strong currents to heed here, too. Anse Cocos is reached by a rather vague track at the north end of Petite Anse. At the southern tip of the island, little-known **Anse Marron** is a hidden morsel of tranquillity that can be reached on foot (see p304). Shh…

On the north coast, **Anse Sévère** and **Anse Patates** are good for snorkelling when the sea

is not too rough. On the northeast coast, locals recommend **Anse Grosse Roche** and **Anse Banane**, which are both very photogenic. Closer to La Passe, **Anse Réunion** is another alluring beach but there is usually algae drifting along the shore.

## L'Union Estate & Copra Factory

At one time, the main industry on La Digue was coconut farming, centred on L'Union Estate coconut plantation south of La Passe. These days **L'Union Estate** (admission Rs 100) is run as an informal 'theme park', with demonstrations of extracting oil from copra (dried coconut flesh). Also in the grounds are the Old Plantation House, a colonial-era graveyard, a boatyard and the obligatory pen of giant tortoises.

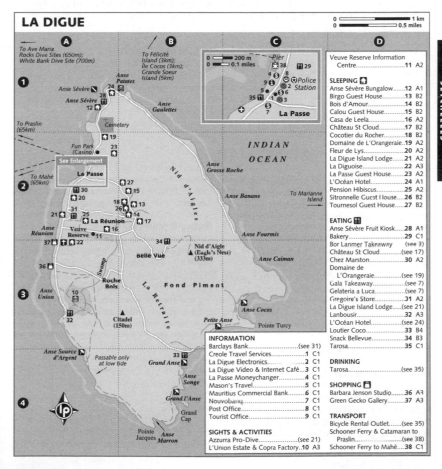

**LA DIGUE**

| | | |
|---|---|---|
| 0 | | 1 km |
| 0 | | 0.5 miles |

**SEYCHELLES**

Veuve Reserve Information Centre.............................**11** A2

**SLEEPING**
Anse Sévère Bungalow.........**12** A1
Birgo Guest House................**13** B2
Bois d'Amour........................**14** B2
Calou Guest House...............**15** B2
Casa de Leela.......................**16** A2
Château St Cloud..................**17** B2
Cocotier du Rocher...............**18** B2
Domaine de L'Orangeraie......**19** A2
Fleur de Lys..........................**20** A2
La Digue Island Lodge..........**21** A2
La Diguoise..........................**22** A3
La Passe Guest House...........**23** A2
L'Océan Hotel......................**24** A1
Pension Hibiscus...................**25** A2
Sitronnelle Guest House........**26** B2
Tournesol Guest House..........**27** B2

**EATING**
Anse Sévère Fruit Kiosk.........**28** A1
Bakery..................................**29** C1
Bor Lanmer Takeaway .....(see 7)
Château St Cloud............(see 17)
Chez Marston........................**30** A2
Domaine de
 L'Orangeraie................(see 19)
Gala Takeaway..................(see 7)
Gelateria a Luca.................(see 7)
Gregoire's Store....................**31** A2
La Digue Island Lodge......(see 21)
Lanbousir.............................**32** A3
L'Océan Hotel..................(see 24)
Loutier Coco.........................**33** B4
Snack Bellevue......................**34** B3
Tarosa..................................**35** C1

**DRINKING**
Tarosa.............................(see 35)

**SHOPPING**
Barbara Jenson Studio...........**36** A3
Green Gecko Gallery.............**37** A3

**TRANSPORT**
Bicycle Rental Outlet.......(see 35)
Schooner Ferry & Catamaran to
 Praslin...........................(see 38)
Schooner Ferry to Mahé........**38** C1

**INFORMATION**
Barclays Bank.......................(see 31)
Creole Travel Services...............**1** C1
La Digue Electronics..................**2** C1
La Digue Video & Internet Café...**3** C1
La Passe Moneychanger..............**4** C1
Mason's Travel..........................**5** C1
Mauritius Commercial Bank.........**6** C1
Nouvobanq...............................**7** C1
Post Office.................................**8** C1
Tourist Office.............................**9** C1

**SIGHTS & ACTIVITIES**
Azzura Pro-Dive.....................(see 21)
L'Union Estate & Copra Factory..**10** A3

**GOING BEYOND THE BEACH**

If your muscles are starting to shrivel after one too many days of beachbasking, take the time to explore the island's recesses that can only be reached by walking paths – you'll discover plenty of secret spots only known to locals. Tracks are not well defined and are difficult to find and to follow; it's advisable to go with a guide. Contact the tourist office for securing one or call **Rhondy** ( ☎ 590368), who charges €25/40 per half-/full day.

**Nid d'Aigle**

Ready to huff and puff? Tackle Nid d'Aigle (Eagle's Nest), the highest point on La Digue (333m), which commands sensational views. From La Passe, follow the inland concrete road that leads up to Snack Bellevue (it's signposted), then take the narrow path that starts behind the *snack*. After about 15 minutes, you'll reach an intersection on a ridge; turn right and follow the path until you reach Nid d'Aigle (no sign) after another 10 minutes. From Nid d'Aigle, it's possible to descend to Anse Cocos (add another 40 minutes), but a guide is mandatory for the path is overgrown.

**Grand Anse to Anse Cocos**

From Loutier Coco, it's an easy 15-minute walk to Petite Anse on a fairly well-defined path. From Petite Anse, it takes another 20 minutes to reach Anse Cocos, but the path is not clear – it's best to go with a guide.

**Grand Anse to Anse Marron (and on to Anse Source d'Argent)**

If you have time for only one walk, choose this option, because it's the most scenic. The coastline between Grand Anse and Anse Marron is extremely alluring: a string of hard-to-reach inlets lapped by azure waters, with the mandatory idyllic beach fringing the shore, and vast expanses of chaotic granite boulders. From Loutier Coco, it takes roughly 45 minutes to reach Anse Marron, a gem of solitude. It's poorly marked; you'll definitely need a guide. From Anse Marron, you can continue as far as Anse Source d'Argent at low tide, but there's a short section where you'll have to walk knee-deep in the water.

## Veuve Reserve

La Digue is the last refuge of the black paradise flycatcher, which locals call the *veuve* (widow). This small forest reserve has been set aside to protect its natural habitat. At the time of writing there were 14 pairs within the reserve. The male has long black tail feathers. The ranger claims that sightings are guaranteed if she goes on a small tour with you – we confirm. Other species include terrapins, fruit bats and moorhens. Several walking trails punctuated with interpretive panels about flora have been set up. Entry is free. There's a small **information centre** ( ☎ 783114; 🕙 8am-noon & 1-4pm Mon-Fri).

## Boat Excursions to Nearby Islands

Taking a boat excursion to nearby **Île Cocos**, **Félicité** and **Grande Sœur** will be one of the main highlights of your visit to the Seychelles and it's well worth the expense. Full-day tours typically stop to snorkel off Île Cocos and Félicité and picnic on Grande Sœur. The best snorkelling spots can be found off the iconic Île Cocos.

Most lodgings and travel agencies on La Digue can arrange such trips. Prices are about €95, including a barbecued fish lunch. Half-day tours can also be organised (€55).

## Diving & Snorkelling

La Digue has much to offer under the surface. Scuba divers should contact **Azzurra Pro-Dive** ( ☎ 292535; www.ladigue.sc) at La Digue Island Lodge. This PADI-certified dive centre organises a variety of dive trips and certification. See p33 for information on dive sites.

La Digue is billed as a snorkelling paradise. Sweet spots around the island include Anse Sévère and Anse Patates. Île Cocos and Félicité seem to be tailored to the expectations of avid snorkellers, with glassy turquoise waters and a smattering of healthy coral gardens around.

## SLEEPING

As more guesthouses and hotels open on La Digue it is becoming easier to find accommodation. Prices are usually negotiable if it's slack. Most places offer half-board options. The cheapest ones don't accept credit cards.

## Budget

**La Passe Guest House** ( ☎ /fax 234391; La Passe; s/d incl breakfast €30/60, incl half board €40/80) Unfussy, low-key and priced a hair lower than the competition – a bonanza for budget-conscious visitors. The three fan-cooled rooms (plus one which has air-con and costs an extra €10) won't have you writing 'wish you were here' postcards, but you can save the postage for sampling the good Creole dinners prepared by Marie-Anne, the friendly owner.

**Sitronnelle Guest House** ( ☎ 234230; La Passe; s/d incl breakfast €40/80; ✗ ) Quite a good deal for solo travellers, but less so for couples, this guesthouse on the inland road in La Passe offers five unadorned but well-kept rooms arranged around courtyard. Ambience is not this place's forte.

**Calou Guest House** ( ☎ 234083; www.calou.de; La Passe; s/d incl breakfast €55/110, incl half board €80/125; ✗ ) While the five bungalows with private terrace are far from fancy – think simple furnishings, old-style curtains and bedcovers, fake thatched roofs – the setting is the real draw, with an Eden-like garden replete with exotic fruit trees and soaring jungle-clad hills as the backdrop. The food is reputedly good, too. A *biergarten* (the owner, Klaus, is German) and a minuscule freshwater pool round out the fun.

**Pension Hibiscus** ( ☎ 234029, 575896; jealicei@seychelles.net; La Passe; d/q €70/120; ✗ ) Bargain! Tucked away in the interior of La Passe, this pension features a three-bedroom house with self-catering facilities. Nothing is fancy but it all feels very proper and immaculate, in a chilled-out setting. The owner, Jeanita, is a helpful gem and can prepare breakfast (€5) and dinner (€15) on request. Another house should be available by the time you read this.

**Bois d'Amour** ( ☎ 234490, 529290; www.boisdamour.de; La Passe; d/q €85/160) Three all-wood, fully equipped chalets in a garden overflowing with blossoming tropical flowers. They're amply sized and well spaced out, and may remind you of the little house on a Swiss cuckoo clock. The Kokoleo, at the far end of the property, is the best. The owners have plans to set up air-con.

**our pick Anse Sévère Bungalow** ( ☎ 247354; clemco@seychelles.net; Anse Sévère; house €92-98) An atmosphere of dreamlike tranquillity characterises this self-catering, two-bedroom house with a fab sea frontage. Your biggest quandary here: a bout of snorkelling (or swimming) or a snooze on the white-sand beach? If you don't fancy cooking, Agnelle, the maid, can prepare delicious Creole meals for about Rs 250. There's no air-con, but the location benefits from cooling sea breezes. Ideal for families. Book early.

Other options:

**Tournesol Guest House** ( ☎ 234155; www.ile-tropicale.com/tournesol; La Passe; s/d incl breakfast €45/90, incl half board €55/110; ✗ ) A no-frills option in a verdant compound.

**Casa de Leela** ( ☎ 234193, 512223; casadeleela@seychelles.sc; La Passe; d/q €95/175; ✗ ✗ ) Three recent, well-designed bungalows with all mod cons and a swimming pool set among a tropical garden. Breakfast (€7.50) on request.

## Midrange

**Birgo Guest House** ( ☎ 234518; www.birgo.sc; La Passe; s/d incl breakfast €55/110; ✗ ) A commendable guesthouse in a balmy garden setting. All eight rooms are clean, well organised (air-con, a private terrace, daily cleaning) and serviceable. There's a tiny pool, too.

**Fleur de Lys** ( ☎ 234459; www.fleurdelysey.com; La Passe; d €105-120; ✗ ) A chilled universe is created here by a lazy-day garden and a clutch of trim, Creole-style bungalows with spotless bathrooms and kitchenettes. Flake out in the serene setting or chatter with the knowledgeable Scottish owner. Breakfast is extra (€10).

**Cocotier du Rocher** ( ☎ 234489, 514889; cocoduroch@seychelles.sc; La Passe; d incl breakfast €110; ✗ ) Three houses with self-catering facilities. Although they're packed rather close together, they're sunny and comfortable enough. Dinner is available on request.

**La Diguoise** ( ☎ 234713; www.diguoise.net; La Passe; d incl breakfast €110-185; ✗ ✗ ) This B&B-style nest has you feeling like you've stepped into a Garden of Eden, with frangipani, banana, citrus, palm and ylang ylang trees throughout the well-tended grounds. The rooms in the two main houses are scrupulously clean and a healthy size; the superior rooms have access to the pool. There are also two smaller but cute rooms in a low-rise building at the back of the garden. An excellent breakfast menu gently eases you into the day. Dinner costs €20.

**Château St Cloud** ( ☎ 234346; www.seychelles.net/stcloud; La Passe; s €130-250, d €175-350, all incl breakfast; ✗ ✗ ✗ ) An agreeable place set in a former colonial estate. One of the most reliable bases on the island, it has well-appointed rooms of varying sizes and shapes, a restaurant and a pool. The superior rooms are dotted on a forest-clad hillside. If you're flush, book in to one of the deluxe rooms, which marry modern and Creole design influences.

**L'Océan Hotel** ( ☎ 234180; www.hotelocean.info; Anse Patates; d incl breakfast €185; ✸ ) One of our favourites for original character and oceanfront location (but no beach). Every bedroom boasts stupendous views of the sea and is decorated with driftwood, shells and paintings by local artist George Camille. Hint: aim for the Petite Sœur and Grande Sœur rooms (competition from honeymooners will be fierce, though). There's an onsite restaurant.

## Top End

**La Digue Island Lodge** ( ☎ 292525; www.ladigue.sc; Anse Réunion; s incl half board €210-330, d incl half board €300-500; ✸ ⚈ 🛜 ) This hodgepodge of a resort comprises A-frame chalets packed rather close together as well as an atmospheric plantation house, standard rooms, some with sea views. They're all set on exotic garden areas overlooking Anse Marron. Sunbathing is top-notch but swimming is not that enthralling, with very shallow waters and algae. Amenities are solid, with two restaurants, two bars, a dive centre and a pool.

**⟨our pick⟩ Domaine de L'Orangeraie** ( ☎ 299999; www.orangeraie.sc; Anse Sévère; d incl breakfast €250-600; ✸ ⚈ 🛜 ) Tropical luxury at its best. Dramatically deployed on hilly grounds in a sea of spruce greenery, Domaine de L'Orangeraie feels like heaven. No expense has been spared in dousing guests in sassy swank – creatively landscaped grounds, natural materials and high-class amenities (including a spa). Each villa is furnished in muted earth tones with subtle Asian accents. Step inside and let the Zen-like tranquillity envelop you, but make sure you bring along your airline's phone number – there's a good chance you'll be calling them to catch a later flight.

## EATING

If eating out in the evening, remember to take a torch with you as there are few street lights, and note that most restaurants close around 9pm.

**Gelateria a Luca** (La Passe; ✹ 11am-6pm) Has ice creams and fruit juices.

**Bor Lanmer Takeaway** (La Passe; mains Rs 40; ✹ lunch & dinner) If you're looking for a quick food fix,

check out the options at this cheap-and-cheerful eatery near the jetty.

**Gala Takeaway** (La Passe; mains Rs 40; ✹ lunch) This modest outlet dishes up excellent *barquettes* (carton) of octopus salad, goat curry, fish and other Creole staples at puny prices.

**Snack Bellevue** (Belle Vue; mains Rs 80-120; ✹ 11am-6pm) It's a hell of a hike or ride to get to this eagle's eyrie, but you'll be amply rewarded with cardiac-arresting views from the terrace. It serves up the usual suspects at very reasonable prices (not a mean feat, given the location).

**Tarosa** (La Passe; ☎ 234407; mains Rs 95-200; ✹ breakfast, lunch & dinner) This is La Digue's social hub, on the jetty. There's a little of everything for everyone, from satisfying breakfasts to sandwiches and smoked fish salad. It features a live band on Friday evening.

**Anse Sévère Fruit Kiosk** (Anse Sévère; fruit platter Rs 100; ✹ 11am-5pm) Recharge the batteries with a fresh fruit platter at this shack nudging pleasingly up Anse Sévère. Grilled fish is also available on certain days (Rs 200).

**⟨our pick⟩ Lanbousir** (Anse Union; mains Rs 110-140; ✹ 12.30pm-3.30pm) This sand-floored eatery run by three affable ladies is an ideal spot for a filling lunch after (or before) working your tan at nearby Anse Source d'Argent. Start things off with smoked fish salad, move on to a meltingly tender job fillet, then finish off with a rich banana pancake. Wash it all down with a lemon juice or a chilled coconut. A traveller's life is hard, isn't it?

**Chez Marston** ( ☎ 234023; La Passe; mains Rs 110-250; ✹ lunch & dinner) This institution serves some of the best food on the island. The wide-ranging menu features salads, sandwiches, prawns, fish or crab curries, pizzas and burgers, among other dishes.

**Loutier Coco** ( ☎ 514762; Grand Anse; buffet Rs 300; ✹ noon-3.30pm) Feel the sand in your toes at this oasis of a place on Grand Anse beach, but be prepared to share the experience with a raft of day-trippers here to enjoy the lavish buffet at lunchtime. The spread on offer includes grilled fish, traditional Creole curries and salads, fruit and coffee.

Other options worthy of interest include the hotel restaurants: L'Océan Hotel, Domaine de L'Orangeraie, Château St Cloud and La Digue Island Lodge all welcome visitors in their enchanting settings.

For self-caterers, **Gregoire's Store** ( ☎ 234024; La Passe; ✹ 8am-7.45pm Mon-Sat, to 1pm Sun) near La Digue Island Lodge is the best-stocked supermarket on the island. There's also a small **bakery** (La Passe; ⊗ 9am-6pm) near the pier where you can gnaw your way to carb bliss with fresh bread and cakes.

## DRINKING

The restaurant-meets-bar Tarosa is the most 'happening' spot in town and transforms itself into an open-air club on Saturday evening. This is your chance to rub shoulders with La Digue's movers and shakers and relive *Saturday Night Fever* island style!

## SHOPPING

You'll find various souvenir shops in La Passe, near the jetty.

**Barbara Jenson Studio** ( ☎ 234406; www.barbara jensonstudio.com; Anse Réunion; ⊗ 9.30am-6pm Mon-Sat) Barbara's work reflects the unique landscape and ethnically diverse people of the Seychelles.

**Green Gecko Gallery** ( ☎ 233302; Anse Réunion; ⊗ 10am-12.30pm & 1.30-6pm Mon-Sat) George Camille's paintings can be found at this gallery.

## GETTING THERE & AROUND

La Digue is easily reached by boat from both Mahé and Praslin. See p316 for details.

There are a few surfaced roads on the island. Given that it is less than 5km from north to south, by far the best – and most enjoyable – way to get around is on foot or bicycle. There are loads of bikes to rent. Operators have outlets near the pier, or you can book through your hotel. Most places charge around Rs 100 per day.

Ox carts used to be a popular mode of transport but are gradually being replaced by open-sided trucks.

There are only a handful of taxis on La Digue, as most people get around on bicycle or on foot. A one-way ride from the pier to Grand Anse costs around Rs 100.

# OTHER INNER ISLANDS

If you want to live out that stranded-on-a-deserted-island fantasy, consider staying at a private island resort. Rack rates are sky-high, but look out for internet deals.

Apart from the sense of exclusivity, what makes these hideaways so special is their green ethos. They're all involved in pioneering conservation projects and are sanctuaries for various rare species.

Transport is handled directly by the hotels on the islands.

## SILHOUETTE

Silhouette is the pyramid-shaped island you see looming on the horizon from Beau Vallon on Mahé. With steep forested mountain peaks rising from the ocean above stunning palm-shaded beaches, Silhouette is a truly magnificent island hideaway, though only 20km north of Mahé. The highest point is Mt Dauban (740m), and there are some truly wild stretches of beach at Anse Mondon,

**SEYCHELLES**

---

**ROBBIE BRESSON**

This Seychellois native has visited most islands of the Seychelles and has supervised numerous conservation projects, such as turtle and bird monitoring.

**Why do you think the Seychelles is a top destination for wildlife enthusiasts?** The Seychelles is a kind of Noah's ark. They're isolated and very far from any mainland, which has helped preserve species and habitats. We also have lots of protected areas and reserves, such as Morne Seychellois National Park, and most islands are predator-free. Our islands are an important stopover and breeding ground for multitudes of birds migrating between the two hemispheres.

**If friends came to the Seychelles to spot wildlife, where should I take them?** Try to include Cousin, Aride and Bird Islands in your itinerary – they all boast prodigious bird life and turtle populations, and are easily accessible. If money is no object, add Frégate, Denis or North Islands. The good thing is that most species are easily approached; you don't even need binoculars. Take Bird Island: hundreds of thousands of birds come each year to nest. You just have to sit on your verandah and birds land on your head! The giant turtles aren't aloof either; they just plod up to visitors to have their necks scratched. The ultimate is Aldabra, but it's currently not open to visitors due to acts of piracy.

*Robbie Bresson is the resident conservationist on Bird Island.*

Anse Lascar, Anse Patate and Grand Barbe. Silhouette is famed for its biological diversity and it's home to a variety of unique habitats and ecosystems. There's a small research station based in the village of La Passe that focuses on the conservation of giant tortoises and terrapins. Volunteers and tourists are welcome.

The five-star **Labriz Silhouette** ( ☎ 293949; www.labriz-seychelles.com; d incl breakfast €575; ☒ ☎ ⎙ ) comprises 110 opulent villas spread along a narrow sandy area east of the island, near La Passe. The list of facilities is prolific, with five restaurants, a wonderful spa and a state-of-the-art diving centre. Nature walks are available. One minus: the beach is no great shakes – it's too thin and too shallow at low tide – but you can take a tour to splendid Anse Mondon.

## NORTH

About 6km north of Silhouette, North Island is the last word in exclusivity and its hotel, **North Island** ( ☎ 293100; www.north-island.com; d incl full board €3500; ☒ ☎ ⎙ ), is generally lauded as a milestone in the 'couture castaway' Indian Ocean experience. The arrival by helicopter says it all: laid-back indulgence and James Bond glamour in a Bounty-licious paradise. Daz-white sandy coves? Tick. Award-winning spa and gourmet dining? Tick. Diving and snorkelling in one of the Seychelles' loveliest coral reefs? Tick. Your own butler to attend to your every whim? Tick. Shoes? Nah – the 11-ultra luxurious suites, which blend wood,

glass and stone, define the term 'barefoot chic'. There's a green ethos; natural habitats are being restored for the reintroduction of critically endangered species, and the resident ecologist takes guests on guided walks where they can witness sea turtles nesting on the beach. It's the kind of place where you expect to see corporate moguls and movie stars here to chill out. See you there!

## DENIS

Close your eyes. And just imagine. You land on a strip of coral by the sea. There's a white-sand beach lapped by luxuriously warm waters; a shimmering lagoon in every hue from lapis lazuli to turquoise; palm and casuarina trees leaning over the shore. Brochure material? No, just routine on Denis, a coral island that lies about 95km northeast of Mahé.

Many visitors come here simply to relax at the enchanting **Denis Lodge** ( ☎ 295999; www.denisisland.com; d incl full board from €1000; ☒ ☎ ⎙ ), but if working your suntan ceases to do it for you, there are nature walks along scenic pathways as well as fishing, snorkelling and diving trips that will keep you buzzing. Wildlife lovers will love it here, too; although Denis is small – barely 1.3km in length and 1.75km at its widest point – it's a sanctuary for a variety of species, including giant tortoises, magpie robins, paradise flycatchers and Seychelles warblers. From July to December you'll see turtles laying eggs on the beach. Food is organic and is prepared from produce grown on the island farm.

## BIRD

Bird is the ultimate in ecotourism and birdlife viewing. Hundreds of thousands of sooty terns, fairy terns and common noddies descend en masse between May and October to nest on this coral island that lies 95km north of Mahé. Hawksbill turtles breed on the island's beaches between October and February, while their land-bound relatives lumber around the interior.

It's very au naturel on Bird. No phones. No TV. No keys. No wi-fi. No infinity pool. Just you, 30 species of birds, 28 giant turtles, the inky-blue ocean and sensational beaches. Enjoy this slice of untouched paradise at **Bird Island Lodge** ( ☎ 323322, 224925; www.birdislandsey chelles.com; d incl full board from €420; ☒ ), which comprises 24 simple yet genuinely ecofriendly and

**SILHOUETTE ISLAND**

0 — 1 km
0 — 0.5 miles

Anse Mondon

INDIAN OCEAN

To Mahé (20km)

Labriz Silhouette
Jetty

Mt Dauban (740m)
Mt Pot à Eau (671m)
Research Station
La Passe

Anse Lascar
Pointe Ramasse

Grand Barbe

Anse Patate

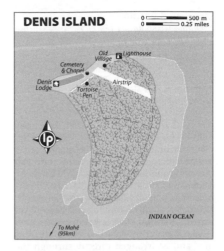

DENIS ISLAND

agreeably designed chalets. They rest in a leafy plot, a thong's throw from the beach. A host of activities is available. Why not take a dolphin-spotting cruise? Or snorkel over sensational reefs just offshore? Or join an ecotour of the island with the resident conservationist? Food is a definite plus, with copious meals using local ingredients.

## FRÉGATE

A 30-minute flight from Mahé brings you to fairytale Frégate, which is both a wildlife sanctuary and a hideaway for celebs and millionaires who find serenity in the exclusive **Fregate Island Private** ( ☎ 224925; www.fregate.com;

d incl full board from €3300; ⊠ ⊠ ⓐ ). Perched on a hillside, the seafacing villas feature a private pool and an open-air jacuzzi, and are reached by alleys that wind through the lush vegetation. Swim in the jewelled waters of Anse Macquereau, enjoy breakfast in the Treehouse (a dinky platform perched in the canopy), take a sailing cruise, sign up for a dive or enjoy a beauty treatment in the serene spa, which uses only local, edible products. Don't leave without taking a guided walk with the resident conservationist, who'll show you the organic farm, the hatchery for giant tortoises, the rare magpie robin and a giant tenebrionid beetle, a 4cm-long insect that's apparently found nowhere else on earth.

# OUTER ISLANDS

The majority of the Seychelles islands are scattered over hundreds of kilometres to the southwest of the main Mahé group. Sadly, most of these islands are accessible only to yachtsmen and those who can afford to stay at the extremely exclusive resorts.

The **Amirantes Group** lies about 250km southwest of Mahé. Its main island is **Desroches**, the only island that offers tourist infrastructure (see p310). Another 200km further south, the **Alphonse Group** is another cluster of coral islands that provides some of the best saltwater fly-fishing in the world. The largest of the group is the 1.2km-wide **Alphonse Island**.

BIRD ISLAND

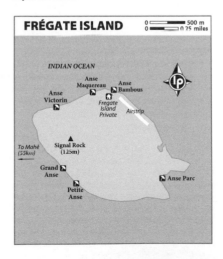

FRÉGATE ISLAND

The **Aldabra Group** is the most remote and most interesting of the outer-island groups. It includes **Aldabra Atoll**, the world's largest raised coral atoll, which is a Unesco World Heritage Site and nature reserve and lies more than 1000km from Mahé. Aldabra Atoll is home to about 150,000 giant tortoises, and flocks of migratory birds fly in and out in their thousands. Aldabra is managed by the **Seychelles Island Foundation** (SIF; Map p282; www.sif.sc; Mont Fleuri Rd, Victoria) in Victoria. Until now the islands have only really been accessible to scientists, volunteers and a very small number of tourists – mostly divers doing a cruise on the live-aboard dive boat *Indian Ocean Explorer* (www.ioexpl.com).

Unfortunately, the Aldabra Group was off-limits to foreigners at the time of writing, due to the presence of Somali pirates in the area. Check with the Seychelles Island Foundation for the latest information.

## Sleeping & Eating

**Desroches Island Resort** ( ☎ 376750; www.desroches -island.com; d incl full board from €1100; ☒ ☒ ☜ ) A great private island resort with a heavy focus on sportfishing enthusiasts and divers (there's an onsite dive centre), but families and honeymooners will also feel welcome here. Digs are in 20 sumptuous seafacing beach chalets as well as stadium-sized luxurious villas complete with their own private pools. The newly built spa is a killer, and world-class guided fly-fishing trips are available. The island itself is lovely, with dazzling white beaches almost all the way around it, as well as a turtle hatchery, a copra plantation, a tiny chapel, an old lighthouse and a small village of around 70 people. Desroches is only 6km long and barely 1km across – the stuff of castaway dreams.

The flight from Mahé takes about 45 minutes and is arranged directly through the resort.

# Seychelles Directory

## ACCOMMODATION

Glossy brochures focus on ultraswish resorts but the Seychelles actually has a pretty wide range of accommodation options. In addition to sumptuous island hideaways, it offers a range of affordable intimate hotels, picturesque Creole guesthouses and self-catering accommodation. Though the Seychelles remains an expensive destination, its tourist authorities are now promoting these more economical options.

For a double room, you can expect to pay under €100 for budget accommodation, €100 to €250 for midrange and over €250 for top-end rooms. Rates include all government taxes, and often include breakfast. Recommendations in our Sleeping entries are in ascending order of price.

Note that all accommodation in the Seychelles is registered and regulated by the Ministry of Tourism. This ensures a certain standard of service and facilities. Check out www.seychelles.com for the list of accommodation options. Other useful websites include www.seychelles-resa.com and www.seychellessecrets.com.

Camping is forbidden anywhere on the islands.

Virtually all the hotels charge higher rates during peak periods (Christmas to New Year and Easter). Book well ahead.

### Guesthouses & Self-Catering Accommodation

No, you don't need to remortgage the house to visit the Seychelles if you stay in one of the cheaper guesthouses or self-catering establishments that are burgeoning on Mahé, Praslin and La Digue. Self-catering options are private homes, villas, residences, studios or apartments that are fully equipped and can be rented by the night. The distinction between self-catering options and guesthouses is slim. Typically, rooms in guesthouses don't come equipped with a kitchen, and breakfast is usually offered. That said, at most self-catering ventures, breakfast and dinner are available on request. Standards are high – even in the cheapest guesthouse you can expect to get a room with a private bathroom and air-con, as well as a daily cleaning service. Both options are generally excellent value, especially for families or a group of friends. Most cost between €90 and €180. Many offer discounts for extended stays.

They also offer good opportunities for cultural immersion; they're mostly family-run operations and provide much more personal, idiosyncratic experiences than hotels.

### Resorts & Hotels

For those whose wallets overfloweth, there's no shortage of ultraswish options, such as the Banyan Tree, the Maia or the Four Seasons on Mahé, as well as the Lemuria on Praslin. They're straight from the pages of a glossy, designer magazine, with luxurious villas that ooze style and class, and fabulously lavish spas in gorgeous settings.

For those whose budget won't stretch quite this far, there are also a few good-value, moderate-

---

**PRACTICALITIES**

■ The Seychelles uses the metric system for weights and measures: kilometres, kilograms, litres and degrees in Celsius.

■ Electric current is 220V, 50Hz AC. The plugs in general use have square pins and three points.

■ The only daily paper is the government-controlled *Seychelles Nation* (www.nation.sc). Other newspapers include the weekly *People* (www.thepeople.sc), also government backed, and *Le Nouveau Seychelles Weekly* (www.seychellesweekly.com), the sole opposition paper.

■ The *Seychelles Broadcasting Corporation* (SBC; www.sbc.com) provides TV broadcasts from 6am to around midnight in English, French and Creole. The news in English is at 6pm. BBC World, France 24 and CNN can be received on satellite TVs.

■ SBC also runs the main radio station, which broadcasts daily from 6am to 10pm in three languages, as well as a 24-hour music station, Paradise FM. BBC World Service and Radio France International (RFI) broadcasts can be heard on the FM band on Mahé.

---

range affairs around Mahé, Praslin and La Digue, with prices around €170 for a double. Note that hotels commonly offer internet specials well below the advertised 'rack rates'.

All-inclusive, full-blown resorts featuring a wide range of recreational facilities and entertainment programs are quite rare in the Seychelles.

### Private Island Resorts

If you want to combine escapism with luxury, you've come to the right place. The Seychelles offers a clutch of ultra-exclusive hideaways that almost defy description. They include Bird, Desroches, Silhouette, North, Frégate and Denis Islands. This is where you really are buying into the dream. They offer every modern convenience but still preserve that perfect tropical-island ambience – the Robinson Crusoe factor – and feature an atmosphere of romance, rejuvenation and exotic sensuality. Each private-island resort has its own personality and devotees. There's minimal contact with the local people, though.

Expect to pay between a cool €420 to a whopping €3500 a night, full board.

## ACTIVITIES
### Bird-watching

Bird-watching in the Seychelles is a treat, and twitchers are sure to get a buzz – there are many desirable new ticks for their lists! The best bird-watching opportunities can be found in the Morne Seychellois National Park on Mahé, in the Vallée de Mai on Praslin, on Cousin, on Frégate, on Aride, and in Veuve Reserve on La Digue. And, of course, on Bird Island.

### Boating & Sailing

Experienced sailors and novices can charter sailboats, yachts and cruisers by the day or week. Charters can be arranged by calling a local charter company or a tour agent. Most companies offer boats with a skipper and crew, as well as 'bareboat' vessels on which you're your own skipper. The best months for cruising are April and October; the worst are January, July and August. Prices start at around €650 for a day trip.

Try the following charter companies:
**Angel Fish Yacht Charter** (Map p280; ☎ 344644; www.seychelles-charter.com; Eden Island, Mahé)
**Dream Yacht Charter** (Map p296; ☎ 232681; www.dream-yacht-seychelles.com; Baie St Anne, Praslin)
**Marine Charter Association** (Map p282; MCA; ☎ 322126; mca@seychelles.net; Victoria)
**Silhouette Cruises** ( ☎ 324026; www.seychelles-cruises.com)
**Water World** ( ☎ 514735; www.waterworld.sc)

### Diving & Snorkelling

The main draw here is undoubtedly the diving and snorkelling. The Seychelles provides superb dives for both experts and novices. Channels, drop-offs, seamounts, coral gardens, granite plateaus, wrecks and clouds of technicolour fish (and yes, sharks are part of the package) – what more could a diver hope for? Diving is available on Mahé, Praslin, La Digue, Bird, Frégate, Desroches, Denis, Silhouette and North.

Snorkelling is another popular choice with visitors. All islands have phenomenal snorkelling spots right offshore, but it's also well worth taking an organised snorkelling day trip to more remote islets, such as sensational St Pierre Islet (p298) and Île Coco (p304). It's not a bad idea to bring your own gear.

See the specialist diving chapter (p32) for more information.

### Fishing

The Seychelles supports extremely rich fisheries for big game fish such as giant barracuda, sailfish and marlin. There is also excellent saltwater fly-fishing around the Alphonse and Desroches Islands for the dedicated – and wealthy – angler.

A number of operators have jumped on the boat, so to speak, offering all-inclusive trips where they do everything for you but put the fish on the hook. They can be contacted through the **Marine Charter Association** (Map p282; MCA; ☎ 322126; mca@seychelles.net) in Victoria. Alternatively, most yacht charter companies (see p312) and tour companies also offer fishing expeditions. Expect to pay in the region of €600/900 for a half-/full day's outing. 'Tag and release' is widely practised.

### Hiking

Because the islands are relatively small and the roads little travelled (away from north Mahé), walking is a pleasurable activity just about anywhere in the Seychelles. There are still lots of wild, hilly and mountainous areas where you can escape the crowds, appreciate the islands' natural scenery and enjoy some of the many alternatives to beach-oriented activities.

### Whale Shark Spotting

Fabulous! From September to October, the waters off Mahé are one of the best places in the Indian Ocean to snorkel near a school bus–sized whale shark. This activity is professionally conducted by Underwater Centre/ Dive Seychelles in Beau Vallon (see p284). This ecologically sensitive dive centre also runs whale shark monitoring programmes.

## BUSINESS HOURS

In general, banks are open only from 8.30am to 2pm Monday to Friday, and 8.30am to 11am on Saturday. Government offices usually open from 8am to 4pm Monday to Friday. Restaurants are generally open from 11am to 3pm and 6pm to 9pm daily. Shop hours are typically 8am to 5pm Monday to Friday, and 8am to noon on Saturday.

## CHILDREN

The Seychelles is a very child- and family-friendly place. Most hotels cater for all age groups, offering baby-sitting services, kids clubs and activities especially for teenagers. While children will happily spend all day splashing around in the lagoon, boat trips around the islands should also appeal. Communing with giant tortoises is a sure-fire hit and visiting some of the nature reserves can be fun. Finding special foods and other baby products can be difficult, especially outside Victoria, so you might want to bring your favourite items with you.

Lonely Planet's *Travel with Children* gives you the lowdown on preparing for family travel.

## CLIMATE CHART

For more information on the best time of the year for visiting Seychelles, see p279.

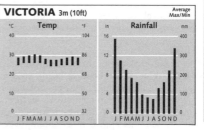

## DANGERS & ANNOYANCES

Beaches in the Seychelles may be true beauties but some are certainly moody, changing dramatically with the seasons. They can be tranquil and flat as a lake at certain times of the year, then savage with incredible surf and mean rip currents at other periods.

Don't leave your valuables unattended on the beach or in your car.

## EMBASSIES & CONSULATES

Countries with embassies and consulates in the Seychelles include the following:

**British High Commission** (Map p282; ☎ 283666; www.ukinseychelles.fco.gov.uk; PO Box 161, Oliaji Trade Centre, Francis Rachel St, Victoria)

**France** (Map p282; ☎ 382500; www.ambafrance-sc.org; BP478, La Ciotat, Mont Fleuri, Victoria)

**Germany** (☎ 601123; germanconsul@natureseychelles.org; Nature Seychelles, Roche Caiman, PO Box 1310, Mahé)

Mauritius ( ☎ 601122; nirmalshah@natureseychelles.org; Nature Seychelles, Roche Caiman, PO Box 1310, Mahé)

## FESTIVALS & EVENTS

The Seychelles may lack the range of festivals found in Mauritius and Réunion, but there are some lively cultural bashes during the year and a few fishing competitions and other sporting events.

### MARCH

**Semaine de la Francophonie** French culture takes over Mahé for a week of song recitals, films and art exhibitions in mid-March.

### MAY

**FetAfrik** The Seychelles celebrates its African origins with a weekend of music and dance in late May.

### OCTOBER

**SUBIOS Underwater Festival** (www.subios.com) Three day–long underwater-photography competition at Beau Vallon held in early October.

**Festival Kreol** (www.seychelles.net/festivalkreol) Week-long festival of Creole culture; last week of October.

## FOOD

For a full explanation of local cuisine and drinks, refer to the Food & Drink section (p273). We usually indicate the price of mains, followed by the price of menus (two- or three-course set menus). Within each eating section, restaurants appear in ascending order of prices. For a full, midrange restaurant meal you should expect to pay €25 to €35 per person, not including wine.

## GAY & LESBIAN TRAVELLERS

There is no open gay or lesbian scene in the Seychelles. The Seychellois are tolerant, but open displays of affection between gay or lesbian couples could raise eyebrows.

## HOLIDAYS

Public holidays in the Seychelles are observed as follows:

**New Year** 1 & 2 January
**Good Friday** March/April
**Easter Day** March/April
**Labour Day** 1 May
**Liberation Day** 5 June
**Corpus Christi** 10 June
**National Day** 18 June
**Independence Day** 29 June
**Assumption** 15 August
**All Saints' Day** 1 November
**Immaculate Conception** 8 December
**Christmas Day** 25 December

## INSURANCE

A travel-insurance policy to cover theft, loss and medical problems is a good idea. Some policies specifically exclude dangerous activities, which can include scuba diving. See also p153.

## INTERNET ACCESS

There's a couple of internet cafes in Victoria. Outside the capital, internet cafes are harder to find. At the time of writing, there were only two outlets with internet access in Praslin and two in La Digue. Expect to pay anywhere between Rs 40 and Rs 120 for an hour's access. Connection is still fairly slow by Western standards.

Wi-fi is increasingly available. Most mid- to top-range accommodation places as well as cafes offer wi-fi access to guests.

## MONEY

The unit of currency is the Seychelles rupee (Rs), which is divided into 100 cents (¢). Bank notes come in denominations of Rs 10, Rs 25, Rs 50, Rs 100 and Rs 500; there are coins of Rs 1, Rs 5, 1¢, 5¢, 10¢ and 25¢.

Euros are the best currency to carry. Prices for most tourist services, including accommodation, excursions, marine park fees, diving, car hire and transport are quoted in euros and can be paid in euros (and less frequently in US dollars), either in cash or by credit card. But you can also pay in rupees. In restaurants,

---

**FESTIVAL KREOL**

Held every year during the last week of October, the vibrant Festival Kreol is an explosion of Creole cuisine, theatre, art, music and dance. Creole artists from other countries are invited to participate, and the festival provides young artists with a platform from which to unleash their creative talents. There are various Creole handicrafts and foodstuffs on sale. Events take place on Mahé, Praslin and La Digue.

prices are quoted in rupees but you can also pay in euros. In this book, we quote rates as they are given in the Seychelles, whether it be in euros or in rupees.

The four main banks are Barclays Bank, Seychelles Savings Bank, Nouvobanq and Mauritius Commercial Bank (MCB). They have branches on Mahé, Praslin and La Digue. You'll also find numerous money-changers. There's no commission for changing cash. Don't lose time shopping around; rates are almost the same everywhere.

There are ATMs, which accept major international cards, at the airport and at all the major banks in Victoria. You'll also find ATMs at Beau Vallon and Anse Royale on Mahé and on Praslin and La Digue.

Major credit cards, including Visa and MasterCard, are accepted in most hotels, guesthouses, restaurants and tourist shops.

## SOLO TRAVELLERS
Solo travellers will have an easy time of it in the Seychelles; there are no specific dangers, worries or scams associated with travelling on your own. The only disadvantage solo travellers will face is accommodation costs – quite often single-room prices are only marginally cheaper than doubles, and if you're renting an apartment you'll be charged by the unit as a whole in most cases.

When eating out, be prepared to be the only single in the midst of honeymooners!

## TELEPHONE
The telephone system is efficient and reliable. There are public payphones on the three main islands from where you can make local and international calls. Telephone cards are available from Cable & Wireless and Airtel offices and from most retail outlets.

Local calls within and between the main islands cost around Rs 3 for up to three minutes. For an idea of international rates, calls to North America, Australia and the UK with Cable & Wireless cost roughly Rs 12 per minute.

Many foreign mobile services have coverage in the Seychelles, but roaming fees are high. If you have a GSM phone and it has been 'unlocked', you can use a local SIM card purchased from either Cable & Wireless or Airtel. Top-up cards are widely available. There is mobile reception on Mahé, Praslin, La Digue and Silhouette.

## TOURIST INFORMATION
The very well-organised **Seychelles Tourism Bureau** (STB; www.seychelles.travel) is the only tourist information body in the Seychelles. The head office is in Victoria. It has two offices on Praslin and one office on La Digue.

## TRAVELLERS WITH DISABILITIES
Most luxury hotels conform to international standards for disabled access, and it's usually possible to hire an assistant if you want to take an excursion.

Apart from that, special facilities for travellers with disabilities are few and far between in the Seychelles, and no beach is equipped with wheelchair access.

## VISAS
You don't need a visa to enter the Seychelles, just a valid passport, an onward ticket, booked accommodation and sufficient funds for your stay. On arrival at the airport, you will be given a visitor's visa for up to three months, depending on the departure date printed on your onward ticket.

## WOMEN TRAVELLERS
Generally speaking, women travellers should have few problems getting around solo in the Seychelles. As in any country, however, women should use their common sense when going to isolated stretches of beach and inland areas alone. Be wary of going to isolated stretches of beach alone.

# TRANSPORT AROUND SEYCHELLES
## AIR
The **Seychelles international airport** ( ☎ 384400), about 8km south of Victoria, is the only international airport in the Seychelles.

**Air Seychelles** ( ☎ 381000; www.airseychelles.com) takes care of all interisland flights, whether scheduled or chartered. The only scheduled services are between Mahé and Praslin, with around 20 flights per day in each direction. The fare for the 15-minute hop is €88 (return €176). The luggage limit is only 20kg (€1 per kilo for excess luggage). Air Seychelles also flies to Bird, Denis, Desroches, Frégate and North Islands, but on a charter basis – these flights are handled directly by the hotels on the island.

Note that Mahé is the only hub for flights within the Seychelles.

## BICYCLE

Bicycles are the principal form of transport on La Digue. On Praslin you can rent bikes at Anse Volbert or through your accommodation. Mahé is a bit hilly for casual cyclists and most visitors rent cars, so bike rental is hard to find there.

## BOAT

Travel by boat is very easy between Mahé, Praslin and La Digue, with regular and efficient ferry services. For all other islands you have to charter a boat or take a tour.

### Mahé to Praslin

The **Cat Cocos catamaran** ( ☎ 324843; www.catcocos.com) makes two to three return trips daily between Mahé and Praslin. Departing from Victoria, the journey takes about 50 minutes (not that much longer than the plane, if you include check-in time) and the fare is €43 one way (€57 in the upper, 'business' lounge); children under 12 pay half fare. In high season, it's advisable to book your ticket at least a day in advance with the ferry company or through a travel agent.

Another company, **Praslin Express** ( ☎ 225046, 225442), also has a service to Praslin (and La Digue) from Mahé (one way €30), but it's fairly unreliable; it was not functioning at the time of research, due to mechanical problems.

### Mahé to La Digue

Not afraid of seasickness? The schooner **La Belle Seraphina** ( ☎ 547168) is for you. This cargo boat runs between Mahé and La Digue from Monday to Friday and carries passengers if there is room. If you don't mind a bit of discomfort, it's a fun and cheap way to travel. The boat generally departs around 11.30am from Mahé, and around 5am from La Digue, but check when making the booking. The three-hour crossing costs just €10.

In principle, **Praslin Express** ( ☎ 225046, 225442) runs a daily direct service to La Digue from Mahé (one way €40).

### Praslin to La Digue

The **Inter-Island Ferry Co** ( ☎ 232329) operates a schooner and a catamaran service between Praslin and La Digue. There are about seven departures daily between 7am and 5.15pm

(5.45pm on Friday, Saturday and Sunday) from Praslin and between 7.30am and 5.45pm (6.15pm on Friday, Saturday and Sunday) from La Digue. The crossing takes about 30 minutes by schooner and about 15 minutes by catamaran.

The one-way/return fare is €10/20 per adult and €5/10 per child under eight.

## BUS

Good news: if you've got time, you don't really need to rent a car to visit the islands.

### Mahé

An extensive bus service operates throughout Mahé. Destinations and routes are usually marked on the front of the buses. There is a flat rate of Rs 7 whatever the length of journey; pay the driver as you board. Bus stops have signs and shelters and there are also markings on the road.

Timetables and maps of each route are posted at the terminus in Victoria, where you can also pick up photocopied timetables (Rs 5) at the **SPTC office** ( ☎ 280280; 🕑 7am-5pm Mon-Fri). All parts of the island are serviced. There's a bus roughly each hour on most routes from around 6am until 7pm (slightly later heading into Victoria).

### Praslin

Praslin also boasts an efficient bus service. The basic route is from Anse Boudin to Mont Plaisir (for Anse Kerlan) via Anse Volbert, Baie Ste Anne, Vallée de Mai, Grand Anse and the airport. Buses run in each direction every hour (every half-hour between Baie St Anne and Mont Plaisir) from 6am to 6pm. Anse Consolation and Anse La Blague are also serviced. For Anse Lazio, get off at Anse Boudin and walk to the beach (about 20 minutes; 1km). Timetables are available at the two tourist offices. There is a flat fare of Rs 7.

## CAR

If you want to be controller of your own destiny, your best bet is to rent a car. Most of the road network on Mahé and Praslin is sealed and in good shape. More of a worry are the narrow bends and the speed at which some drivers, especially bus drivers, take them.

Drive on the left, and beware of drivers with fast cars and drowsy brains – especially late on Friday and Saturday nights. The speed limit is supposed to be 40km/h in built-up

---

**VOLUNTEERING IN THE SEYCHELLES**

Wanna get involved in turtle tagging, whale-shark monitoring or researching certain animal species? **Nature Protection Trust of Seychelles** (http://islandbiodiversity.com), **Nature Seychelles** (www.natureseychelles.org), **Seychelles Island Foundation** (www.sif.sc) and **Marine Conservation Society Seychelles** (www.mcss.sc) all have volunteer programs.

---

areas, 65km/h outside towns, and 80km/h on the dual carriageway between Victoria and the airport. On Praslin the limit is 40km/h throughout the island.

## Rental

There are any number of car-rental companies on Mahé and quite a few on Praslin. Due to healthy competition, the cheapest you're likely to get on Mahé is about €35 to €40 a day for a small hatchback. Rates on Praslin are about €10 more expensive. The tourist office in Victoria has a list of car-rental outlets, but it's not a bad idea to book through your hotel or guesthouse. Most apartment and guesthouse owners have negotiated discounts with car-rental outlets for their clients. The major companies also have offices at the airport.

Drivers must be over 23 years old and have held a driving licence for at least a year. Most companies accept a national licence.

## TAXI

Taxis operate on Mahé and Praslin and there are even a handful on La Digue. Agree on a fare before departure.

# Regional Transport

## CONTENTS

# GETTING THERE & AWAY

## ENTERING THE COUNTRY

### Mauritius

When entering Mauritius you must have a passport valid for at least six months from the date of entry, a visa for Mauritius (if necessary; see p157) and a proof of departure, like an outbound ticket (together with a visa if necessary for your next port of call).

Immigration authorities will also require that you know the name, address and phone number of the place where you are staying in Mauritius (if you don't know just give them the name of any large hotel in this book). You will also be asked about the countries you've visited in the last six months, and if you've been to certain 'red-flag' countries, like several nations in Southeast Asia, the government may contact you during your stay to enquire about your health. They may also grill you on your finances, especially if you are staying more than the standard two weeks; possession of a valid credit card is usually fine.

### Réunion

As Réunion is a department of France, the formalities for entering the country are al-most the same as those for entering mainland France, bar a few exceptions (see p264 for details on visa requirements). All visitors must possess a passport valid for at least three months from the date of entry, a visa (if required) and a return or onward ticket (plus a visa if necessary for your next destination).

### Seychelles

'Titres de séjour' (a kind of tourist card/visa) of up to three months is issued free for all tourists on arrival. You just need to present a passport valid for at least six months from the date of entry and a return or onward ticket (with a visa for your next destination if required). Immigration officers will also require that you mention the name, address and phone number of the place where you are staying in the Seychelles (if you don't know just give them the name of any large hotel in this book). You may also be asked for evidence of sufficient funds to cover you during your stay; possession of a valid credit card is usually fine. For more information on visas, see p315.

### AIR

Expensive flights have always been the biggest deterrent to travellers interested in visiting this region, but this is gradually changing due to increased competition. Return flights from Europe to either of the three destinations at certain times of the year for less than €700? Yes, it's possible.

You can also buy a package deal that includes flight and hotel accommodation. This can actually work out cheaper than just buying a return scheduled flight, and as you're totally free to ditch the hotel after a few days and travel around yourself, this is an option you should consider.

---

**THINGS CHANGE...**

The information in this chapter is particularly vulnerable to change. Check directly with the airline or a travel agent to make sure you understand how a fare (and ticket you may buy) works and be aware of the security requirements for international travel. Shop carefully. The details given in this chapter should be regarded as pointers and are not a substitute for your own careful, up-to-date research.

The principal hubs for airlines flying to this region are Paris, Dubai and London.

## Airlines

**Aeroflot** (airline code SU; ☎ in Mauritius 211 9200; www.aerogroup.biz)

**Air Austral** (airline code UU; ☎ in Mauritius 202 6677, in Réunion 0825 013012, in Seychelles 323262; www.air-austral.com)

**Air France** (airline code AF; ☎ in Mauritius 202 6747, in Réunion 0820 820820, in Seychelles 297180; www.airfrance.com)

**Air Madagascar** (airline code MD; ☎ in Mauritius 203 2150, in Réunion 0892 68 00 14; www.airmadagascar.com)

**Air Mauritius** (airline code MK; ☎ in Mauritius 207 7070, in Réunion 0262 94 83 83, in Seychelles 297000; www.airmauritius.com)

**Air Seychelles** (airline code HM; ☎ in Mauritius 202 6727, in Seychelles 381000; www.airseychelles.com)

**British Airways** (airline code BA; ☎ in Mauritius 202 8000; www.britishairways.com)

**Cathay Pacific** (airline code CX; ☎ in Mauritius 212 4044; www.cathaypacific.com)

**Condor** (airline code DE; ☎ in Mauritius 208 4802, in Seychelles 322642; www.condor.com)

**Corsairfly** (airline code SS; ☎ in Réunion 0820 042042; www.corsairfly.com)

**Emirates** (airline code EK; ☎ in Mauritius 204 7700, in Seychelles 292700; www.emirates.com)

**Kenya Airways** (airline code KQ; ☎ in Seychelles 322989; www.kenya-airways.com)

**Qatar Airways** (airline code QR; ☎ in Seychelles 224518; www.qatarairways.com)

**South African Airways** (airline code SA; ☎ in Mauritius 208 6820; www.flysaa.com)

**Virgin Atlantic** (airline code VS; Mauritius only; ☎ in Mauritius 206 0900; www.virginatlantic.com)

## Tickets

The main point to remember when buying your air ticket is to start early. Mauritius, Réunion and the Seychelles are popular destinations and some flights are booked months in advance. Somewhat paradoxically, it's also worth looking last minute as that's when other good bargains sometimes become available; however, this can never be guaranteed of course.

If you are after a simple return ticket within fairly fixed dates, then it's easy to book online. Some of the better international online ticket websites include the following:

**Ebookers** (www.ebookers.com)

**Expedia** (www.expedia.com)

**Flight Centre International** (www.flightcentre.com)

**Flights.com** (www.flights.com)

**STA** (www.sta.com)

**Travelocity** (www.travelocity.com)

### INTERCONTINENTAL TICKETS

It is possible to include Mauritius, Réunion and the Seychelles as part of a Round-the-World (RTW) ticket. These can be bought through one of the three big airline alliances (Oneworld, Sky Team and Star Alliance) or through a travel agent. RTW tickets put together by travel agents tend to be more expensive but allow you to devise your own itinerary. In general RTW tickets are valid for up to one year and are calculated on the basis of either the number of continents or the distance covered.

Online ticket websites for intercontinental tickets:

**Airbrokers** (www.airbrokers.com)

**Airtreks.com** (www.airtreks.com)

**Oneworld** (www.oneworld.com)

**Sky Team** (www.skyteam.com)

**Star Alliance** (www.staralliance.com)

## Africa

You can fly to Mauritius direct from a number of cities in Africa, including Johannesburg, Cape Town and Durban (South Africa), Antananarivo (Tananarive; Madagascar) and Nairobi (Kenya). Airlines serving these routes include Air Mauritius, Air Madagascar and South African Airways (SAA).

The Seychelles is not particularly well connected with Africa. The only direct flights are to and from Johannesburg and Nairobi with Air Seychelles and Kenya Airways.

Réunion can be reached direct from Johannesburg, Madagascar, Comoros and Mayotte with Air Austral and Air Madagascar.

**Rennies Travel** (www.renniestravel.com) and **STA Travel** (www.statravel.co.za) have offices throughout southern Africa. Check their websites for branch locations.

## Australia

Air Austral flies direct from Sydney to Réunion, while Air Mauritius operates reasonably competitively priced direct flights from Melbourne and Perth to Mauritius. For the Seychelles, you can fly with Air Mauritius (via Mauritius) or Air Austral (via Réunion); another option is to fly via Singapore or Dubai. Two well-known agencies for discount fares with offices nationwide are **STA Travel** (☎ 134

782; www.statravel.com.au) and **Flight Centre** ( ☎ 133 133; www.flightcentre.com.au). For online bookings, try www.travel.com.au.

## Continental Europe

Most visitors from Europe arrive in Mauritius and Seychelles on hotel-flight package holidays, although this is much less the case for Réunion. Air Mauritius flies to a number of European destinations, including London, Paris, Zürich, Geneva, Rome, Milan, Munich, Frankfurt, Brussels and Vienna. Air Seychelles flies to Paris, London, Milan and Rome. All flights from Europe to Réunion go via Paris. Note that prices shoot up during July and August and over the Christmas and New Year holidays. However, flights to Mauritius and Seychelles on Emirates via Dubai (and on Qatar Airways to Seychelles via Doha) are both very competitively priced and worth investigating, with connections from all over Europe.

### FRANCE

Air Mauritius, Corsairfly and Air France operate frequent flights from Paris to Mauritius. Corsairfly offers continuing service to Lyon and Nantes.

Air France, Air Austral and Corsairfly all fly to St-Denis. Air Seychelles and Air France cover the Paris–Seychelles route.

Recommended agencies:
**Anyway** ( ☎ 0892 302 301; www.anyway.fr)
**Lastminute** ( ☎ 0899 70 01 70; www.fr.lastminute.com)
**Nouvelles Frontières** ( ☎ 0825 000 747; www.nouvelles-frontieres.fr)

### GERMANY

Condor flies direct from Frankfurt to Mauritius and the Seychelles, and from Munich to Mauritius. Air Mauritius flies direct from Frankfurt and Munich to Mauritius.

Recommended agencies:
**Expedia** ( ☎ 01805 007 146; www.expedia.de)
**Just Travel** ( ☎ 01805 055 559; www.jt.de)
**Lastminute** ( ☎ 01805 777 257; www.lastminute.de)
**STA Travel** ( ☎ 01805 456 422; www.statravel.de)

## UK & Ireland

Both Air Mauritius and British Airways operate direct flights between London and Mauritius.

Flights for Réunion generally connect through Paris. The return London–Réunion fare with Air France is no bargain, but you can sometimes get a cheaper deal by flying with one of the discount airlines on the London–Paris leg and buying a separate Paris–Réunion return.

Air Seychelles covers the London to Seychelles route and sometimes special

---

## CLIMATE CHANGE & TRAVEL

Climate change is a serious threat to the ecosystems that humans rely upon, and air travel is the fastest-growing contributor to the problem. Lonely Planet regards travel, overall, as a global benefit, but believes we all have a responsibility to limit our personal impact on global warming.

### Flying & Climate Change

Pretty much every form of motor travel generates CO2 (the main cause of humain-induced climate change) but planes are far and away the worst offenders, not just because of the sheer distances they allow us to travel, but because they release greenhouse gases high into the atmosphere. The statistics are frightening: two people taking a return flight between Europe and the US will contribute as much to climate change as an average household's gas and electricity consumption over a whole year.

### Carbon Offset Schemes

Climatecare.org and other websites use 'carbon calculators' that allow jetsetters to offset the greenhouse gases they are responsible for with contributions to energy-saving projects and other climate-friendly initiatives in the developing world – inlcuding projects in India, Honduras, Kazakhstan and Uganda.

Lonely Planet, together with Rough Guides and other concerned partners in the travel industry, supports the carbon offset scheme run by climatecare.org. Lonely Planet offsets all of its staff and author travel.

For more information check out our website: lonelyplanet.com.

deals make this route good value. Emirates via Dubai and Qatar Airways via Doha offer other good connections to Seychelles. All Irish travellers will need to connect through London or Paris.

Recommended travel agencies in the UK:

**Ebookers** (www.ebookers.com)

**Flight Centre** ( ☎ 0844 800 8660; www.flightcentre.co.uk)

**North-South Travel** ( ☎ 01245 608 291; www. northsouthtravel.co.uk) North-South Travel donates part of its profit to projects in the developing world.

**Quest Travel** ( ☎ 0845 263 6963; www.questtravel.com)

**STA Travel** ( ☎ 0871 230 0040; www.statravel.co.uk)

**Trailfinders** ( ☎ 0845 058 5858; www.trailfinders.com)

**Travel Bag** ( ☎ 0871 703 4698; www.travelbag.co.uk)

## USA & Canada

Given the huge distance involved in travelling from North America to the Indian Ocean, you'll be paying a handsome sum to travel this route. Nearly all flights to the Indian Ocean from the USA and Canada connect through London or Paris.

## SEA

Opportunities for sea travel to Mauritius, Réunion and the Seychelles are limited. The cruise liner *MS Mauritius Trochetia* (see p322) leaves Mauritius and Réunion for Toamasina in Madagascar approximately every two weeks. Contact **Coraline Shipping Agency** (Map p66; ☎ 217 2285; www.msclcoraline.com; Nova Bldg, Military Rd, Port Louis, Mauritius) for more information.

The only other alternatives are passing cruise liners, yachts and the occasional cargo-passenger ship. The cost is high, unless you can work your way as a crewmember. Cruise liners usually only stop for a day or two in each destination, but cruises do offer the opportunity of seeing the outer islands in the Seychelles group.

Companies offering Indian Ocean cruises:

**African Safari Club** (www.africansafariclub.com)

**P&O** (www.pocruises.com)

**Silversea** (www.silversea.com)

# TRANSPORT AROUND THE REGION

The following section covers transport between Réunion, Mauritius and the Seychelles. Be aware that if you're planning to travel to both Mauritius and Réunion, it makes much better financial sense to visit Mauritius first

and fly on to Réunion, as return flights work out around €100 cheaper when originating in Mauritius. The flat fare system of flights from Réunion to Mauritius hikes the fare by 40%.

## AIR
### Air Passes

If you're going to be island-hopping around the region, you can cut the cost of individual fares by buying an Indian Ocean Pass. The pass covers Air Mauritius, Air Austral and Air Seychelles flights between Mauritius, Réunion and the Seychelles and their services to Madagascar, Comoros, Mayotte and the Maldives. The pass, which is valid for two months, must be purchased outside the region from any of the three participating airlines. You must make a minimum of three different flights. Fares are discounted by about 30%. For details of prices contact the participating airlines.

### Mauritius to Réunion

Air Mauritius and Air Austral between them operate several flights a day from Réunion to Mauritius. Return fares hover between Rs 8500 and Rs 12,000 if you fly Mauritius–Réunion–Mauritius, but you may find special promotional rates for Rs 5500. The Réunion–Mauritius–Réunion fare usually hovers between €235 (or €205 if can get a promotional deal at certain times of the year) and €285. As well as the flights to St-Denis, there is a daily flight from Mauritius' Sir Seewoosagur Ramgoolam airport to Pierrefonds airport, Réunion's second airport in the south of the island near St-Pierre. Return fares start at around €160 for a round trip from Mauritius, and, again, are priced less competitively at €235 or €285 for a round trip when flying from Réunion.

At the time of writing there were no direct flights between Rodrigues and Réunion, although this may change soon; at the time of research, SolitAir, Rodrigues' airline, was just getting its wings, so to speak, and plans to offer direct flights between Réunion and Rodrigues starting in 2011.

### Mauritius to Seychelles

From the Seychelles, there's a choice between Air Mauritius and Air Seychelles, which between them operate four to five flights a week. Tickets cost from €300 for a return in low season.

### Réunion to Seychelles

Air Austral operates two weekly flights from Réunion to Seychelles. Tickets cost from €415.

## SEA

The Mauritius Shipping Corporation operates two boats between Réunion and Mauritius, with at least one sailing per week in low season, and up to three sailings per week in high season. The one-way journey takes about 11 hours. The newer and more comfortable boat is the *Mauritius Trochetia*. The return fare from Réunion in low/high season starts at roughly €200/240 for a berth in a 2nd-class cabin. From Mauritius, the price is Rs 4800/6700.

The sister ship, *Mauritius Pride*, has prices which are slightly cheaper. For a reclining seat in low/high season, you'll pay around €170/195 return from Réunion and Rs 3000/3600 from Mauritius.

Tickets and information are available through travel agents or direct from the Mauritius Shipping Corporation representative **Coraline Shipping Agency** (Map p66; ☎ 217 2285; msc@coraline.intnet.mu; Nova Bldg, Military Rd, Port Louis, Mauritius). In Réunion, contact **SCOAM** (☎ 0262 42 19 45; passagers@scoam.fr; 4 av. du 14-Juillet-1789, Le Port).

# Health

## CONTENTS

As long as you stay up to date with your vaccinations and take some basic preventive measures, you'd have to be pretty unlucky to succumb to most of the health hazards covered in this chapter. Mauritius, and to a lesser extent Réunion and the Seychelles, certainly have a fair selection of tropical diseases on offer, but you're much more likely to get a bout of diarrhoea or a sprained ankle than an exotic disease. One recent subject of concern in Mauritius and Réunion has been the Chikungunya epidemic of early 2006, which, while having returned to normal at the time of writing, is still something you should be aware of and a situation you should monitor.

## BEFORE YOU GO

A little planning before departure, particularly for pre-existing illnesses, will save you a lot of trouble later. Before a long trip, get a check-up from your dentist and from your doctor if you require regular medication or have a chronic illness, eg high blood pressure or asthma. You should also organise spare contact lenses and glasses (and take your optical prescription with you); get a first-aid and medical kit together; and arrange necessary vaccinations.

Travellers can register with the **International Association for Medical Advice to Travellers** (IAMAT; www.iamat.org). Its website can help travellers find a doctor who has recognised training. You might also like to consider doing a first-aid course (contact the Red Cross or St John's Ambulance) or attending a remote medicine first-aid course, such as that offered by the **Royal Geographical Society** (www.wildernessmedicaltraining.co.uk).

If you are bringing medications with you, carry them in their original containers, clearly labelled. A signed and dated letter from your physician describing all medical conditions and medications, including generic names, is also a good idea. If carrying syringes or needles, be sure to have a physician's letter documenting their medical necessity.

### INSURANCE

Find out in advance whether your insurance plan will make payments directly to providers or will reimburse you later for health expenditures (in many countries doctors expect payment in cash). It is vital to ensure that your travel insurance will cover the emergency transport required to get you to a good hospital, or all the way home, by air and with a medical attendant if necessary. Not all insurance policies cover this, so be sure to check the contract carefully. If you need medical care, your insurance company may be able to help locate the nearest hospital or clinic, or ask at your hotel. In an emergency, contact your embassy or consulate.

Membership of the **African Medical and Research Foundation** (AMREF; www.amref.org) provides

---

**RECOMMENDED VACCINATIONS**

The **World Health Organization** (www.who.int/en/) recommends that all travellers be adequately covered for diphtheria, tetanus, measles, mumps, rubella and polio, as well as for hepatitis B, regardless of their travel destination.

Although no vaccinations are officially required, many doctors recommend hepatitis A and B immunisations just to be sure; a yellow fever certificate is an entry requirement if travelling from an infected region (see p326).

an air-evacuation service in medical emergencies in some African countries, sometimes including Mauritius, Réunion and the Seychelles, as well as air-ambulance transfers between medical facilities. Money paid by members for this service goes towards providing grass-roots medical assistance for local people.

## MEDICAL CHECKLIST

It is a very good idea to carry a medical and first-aid kit with you, to help yourself in the case of minor illness or injury. Following is a list of items you should consider packing.

- antidiarrhoeal drugs (eg loperamide)
- acetaminophen (paracetamol) or aspirin
- anti-inflammatory drugs (eg ibuprofen)
- antihistamines (for hayfever and allergic reactions)
- antibacterial ointment (eg Bactroban) for cuts and abrasions (prescription only)
- steroid cream or hydrocortisone cream (for allergic rashes)
- bandages, gauze, gauze rolls
- adhesive or paper tape
- scissors, safety pins, tweezers
- thermometer
- pocket knife
- DEET-containing insect repellent for the skin
- sunblock
- oral rehydration salts
- iodine tablets (for water purification)
- syringes and sterile needles (if travelling to remote areas)

## INTERNET RESOURCES

There is a wealth of travel-health advice available on the internet. **Lonelyplanet.com** (www.lonelyplanet.com) is a good place to start. The World Health Organization publishes a superb book called *International Travel and Health*, which is revised annually and is available online at no cost at www.who.int/ith/. Other health-related websites of general interest are **MD Travel Health** (www.mdtravelhealth.com), the **Centers for Disease Control and Prevention** (www.cdc.gov) and **Fit for Travel** (www.fitfortravel.scot.nhs.uk).

You may also like to consult your government's travel-health website, if one is available:
**Australia** (www.dfat.gov.au/travel/)
**Canada** (www.hc-sc.gc.ca/pphb-dgspsp/tmp-pmv/pub_e.html)
**UK** (www.doh.gov.uk)
**USA** (www.cdc.gov/travel/)

## FURTHER READING

*A Comprehensive Guide to Wilderness and Travel Medicine* by Eric A Weiss (1998)
*Healthy Travel* by Jane Wilson-Howarth (1999)
*Healthy Travel Africa* by Isabelle Young (2000)
*How to Stay Healthy Abroad* by Richard Dawood (2002)
*Travel in Health* by Graham Fry (1994)
*Travel with Children* by Brigitte Barta et al (2009)

# IN TRANSIT

## DEEP VEIN THROMBOSIS (DVT)

Blood clots can form in the legs during flights, chiefly because of prolonged immobility. This formation of clots is known as deep vein thrombosis (DVT). Although most blood clots are reabsorbed uneventfully, some might break off and travel through the blood vessels to the lungs, where they could cause life-threatening complications.

The chief symptom of DVT is swelling or pain of the foot, ankle or calf. When a blood clot travels to the lungs, it may cause chest pain and breathing difficulty. Travellers with any of these symptoms should immediately seek medical attention.

To prevent the development of DVT during flights, walk about the cabin, perform isometric compressions of the leg muscles (ie contract the leg muscles while sitting), drink plenty of fluids and avoid alcohol.

## JET LAG & MOTION SICKNESS

If you're crossing more than five time zones you could suffer jet lag, resulting in insomnia, fatigue, malaise or nausea. To avoid jet lag, try drinking plenty of fluids (nonalcoholic) and eating light meals. Upon arrival, get exposure to natural sunlight and readjust your schedule (for meals, sleep etc) as soon as possible.

Antihistamines such as dimenhydrinate (Dramamine) and meclizine (Antivert, Bonine) are usually the first choice for treating motion sickness. The main side effect of these drugs is drowsiness. A herbal alternative is ginger (ginger tea, biscuits or crystallised ginger).

# IN MAURITIUS, RÉUNION & SEYCHELLES

## AVAILABILITY & COST OF HEALTH CARE

Health care in Mauritius and Réunion is generally excellent; the Seychelles is pretty good by African standards, but some travellers have been critical of the standard of the public health system. Generally, public hospitals offer the cheapest service, but may not have the most up-to-date equipment and medications; private hospitals and clinics are more expensive but tend to have more advanced drugs and equipment and better trained medical staff.

## INFECTIOUS DISEASES

It's a formidable list but, as we say, a few precautions go a long way…

### Chikungunya

This viral infection transmitted by certain mosquito bites was traditionally rare in the Indian Ocean until 2005 when an epidemic hit Réunion, Mauritius and Seychelles. Chikungunya (the unusual name means 'that which bends up' in the East African language of Makonde, a reference to the joint pain and physical distortions it creates in sufferers) is rarely fatal, but it can be, and it's always unpleasant. Symptoms are often flu-like, with joint pain, high fever and body rashes being the most common. It's important not to confuse it with dengue fever, but if diagnosed with Chikungunya, then expect to be down for at least a week, possibly longer. The joint pain can be horrendous and there is no treatment, those infected need simply to rest inside (preferably under a mosquito net to prevent reinfection), taking gentle exercise to avoid joints stiffening unbearably. Over 200 people died in Réunion from Chikungunya in 2005 to 2006, but at the time of writing the epidemic was over and should not be considered a major threat. Still, the best way to avoid it is to avoid mosquito bites, so bring plenty of repellent, use the anti-mosquito plug-ins wherever you can and bring a mosquito net if you're really thorough.

### Hepatitis A

Hepatitis A is spread through contaminated food (particularly shellfish) and water. It causes jaundice and, although it is rarely fatal, it can cause prolonged lethargy and delayed recovery. If you've had hepatitis A, you shouldn't drink alcohol for up to six months afterwards, but once you've recovered, there won't be any long-term problems. The first symptoms include dark urine and a yellow colour to the whites of the eyes. Sometimes a

fever and abdominal pain might be present. Hepatitis A vaccine (Avaxim, VAQTA, Havrix) is given as an injection: a single dose will give protection for up to a year, and a booster after a year gives 10-year protection. Hepatitis A and typhoid vaccines can also be given as a single dose vaccine (Hepatyrix or Viatim).

### Hepatitis B

Hepatitis B is spread through infected blood, contaminated needles and sexual intercourse. It can also be passed from an infected mother to the baby during childbirth. It affects the liver, causing jaundice and occasionally liver failure. Most people recover completely, but some people might be chronic carriers of the virus, which could lead eventually to cirrhosis or liver cancer. Those visiting high-risk areas for extended periods or those with increased social or occupational risk should be immunised. Many countries now routinely give hepatitis B as part of the routine childhood vaccination. It is given singly or can be given at the same time as hepatitis A (Hepatyrix).

A course will give protection for at least five years. It can be given over four weeks or six months.

### HIV

Human immunodeficiency virus (HIV), the virus that causes acquired immune deficiency syndrome (AIDS), is an enormous problem throughout Africa, but is most acutely felt in sub-Saharan Africa. The impact of the virus on South Africa's health system is devastating. The virus is spread through infected blood and blood products, by sexual intercourse with an infected partner and from an infected mother to her baby during childbirth and breastfeeding. It can be spread through 'blood to blood' contacts, such as with contaminated instruments during medical, dental, acupuncture and other body-piercing procedures, and through sharing used intravenous needles. At present there is no cure; medication that might keep the disease under control is available, but these drugs are too expensive for the overwhelming majority of Africans, and are not readily available for travellers either. If you think you might have been infected with HIV, a blood test is necessary; a three-month gap after exposure and before testing is required to allow antibodies to appear in the blood.

HEALTH

## Malaria

The risk of malaria in Mauritius and Réunion is extremely low; there is no risk in the Seychelles. The disease is caused by a parasite in the bloodstream spread via the bite of the female *Anopheles* mosquito. The early stages of malaria include headaches, fevers, generalised aches and pains, and malaise, which could be mistaken for flu. Other symptoms can include abdominal pain, diarrhoea and a cough. Several different drugs are used to prevent malaria, and new ones are in the pipeline – up-to-date advice is essential as some medication is more suitable for some travellers than others. There are antimalaria pills available and it is best to ask your doctor for further advice.

## Meningococcal Meningitis

Meningococcal infection is spread through close respiratory contact and is more likely in crowded situations, such as dormitories, buses and clubs. Infection is uncommon in travellers. Vaccination is recommended for long stays and is especially important towards the end of the dry season. Symptoms include a fever, severe headache, neck stiffness and a red rash. Immediate medical treatment is necessary.

## Rabies

Rabies is spread by receiving the bites or licks of an infected animal on broken skin. It is always fatal once the clinical symptoms start (which might be up to several months after an infected bite), so post-bite vaccination should be given as soon as possible. Post-bite vaccination (whether or not you've been vaccinated before the bite) prevents the virus from spreading to the central nervous system. Three preventive injections are needed over a month. If you have not been vaccinated, you will need a course of five injections starting 24 hours after being bitten or as soon as possible after the injury. If you have been vaccinated, you will need fewer post-bite injections, and have more time to seek medical help.

## Yellow Fever

Although not a problem in Mauritius, Réunion or the Seychelles, travellers should still carry a certificate as evidence of vaccination if they have recently been in an infected country. For a list of these countries visit the **World Health Organization website** (www.who.int/wer/) or the **Centers for Disease Control and Prevention website** (www.cdc.gov/travel/blusheet.htm). A traveller without a legally required, up-to-date certificate may be vaccinated and detained in isolation at the port of arrival for up to 10 days or possibly repatriated.

## TRAVELLERS' DIARRHOEA

Although it's not inevitable that you will get diarrhoea while travelling in the region, it's certainly possible. Sometimes dietary changes, such as increased spices or oils, are the cause. To avoid diarrhoea, only eat fresh fruits or vegetables if cooked or peeled, and be wary of dairy products that might contain unpasteurised milk. Although freshly cooked food can often be a safe option, plates or serving utensils might be dirty, so you should be highly selective when eating food from street vendors (make sure that cooked food is piping hot all the way through). If you develop diarrhoea, be sure to drink plenty of fluids, preferably an oral rehydration solution containing water (lots), and some salt and sugar. A few loose stools don't require treatment, but if you start having more than four or five stools a day, you should start taking an antibiotic (usually a quinoline drug, such as ciprofloxacin or norfloxacin) and an antidiarrhoeal agent (such as loperamide) if you are not within easy reach of a toilet. However, if diarrhoea is bloody, persists for more than 72 hours or is accompanied by fever, shaking chills or severe abdominal pain, you should seek medical attention.

## Amoebic Dysentery

Contracted by eating contaminated food and water, amoebic dysentery causes blood and mucus in the faeces. It can be relatively mild and tends to come on gradually, but seek medical advice if you think you have the illness, as it won't clear up without treatment (which is with specific antibiotics).

## Giardiasis

Giardiasis, like amoebic dysentery, is also caused by ingesting contaminated food or water. The illness usually appears a week or more after you have been exposed to the offending parasite. Giardiasis might cause only a short-lived bout of typical travellers' diarrhoea, but it can also cause persistent diarrhoea. Ideally, seek medical advice if you suspect you have giardiasis, but if you are in a remote area you could start a course of antibiotics.

# ENVIRONMENTAL HAZARDS
## Heat Exhaustion
This condition occurs following heavy sweating and excessive fluid loss with inadequate replacement of fluids and salt, and is particularly common in hot climates when taking unaccustomed exercise before full acclimatisation. Symptoms include headache, dizziness and tiredness. Dehydration is already happening by the time you feel thirsty – aim to drink sufficient water to produce pale, diluted urine. Self-treatment is by fluid replacement with water and/or fruit juice, and cooling by cold water and fans. The treatment of the salt-loss component consists of consuming salty fluids as in soup, and adding a little more table salt to foods than usual.

## Heatstroke
Heat exhaustion is a precursor to the much more serious condition of heatstroke. In this case there is damage to the sweating mechanism, with an excessive rise in body temperature; irrational and hyperactive behaviour; and eventually loss of consciousness and death. Rapid cooling by spraying the body with water and fanning is ideal. Emergency fluid and electrolyte replacement is usually also required by intravenous drip.

## Insect Bites & Stings
Mosquitoes in the region rarely carry malaria, Chikungunya and dengue fever, but they (and other insects) can cause irritation and infected bites. To avoid these, take the same precautions as you would for avoiding malaria, including wearing long pants and long-sleeved shirts, using mosquito repellents, avoiding highly scented perfumes or aftershaves etc. Bee and wasp stings cause major problems

only to those who have a severe allergy to the stings (anaphylaxis), in which case carry an adrenaline (epinephrine) injection.

Leeches may be present in damp rainforest conditions; they attach themselves to your skin to suck your blood. Salt or a lighted cigarette end will make them fall off. Ticks can cause skin infections and other more serious diseases. If a tick is found attached, press down around the tick's head with tweezers, grab the head and gently pull upwards.

## Marine Life
A number of Indian Ocean species are poisonous or may sting or bite. Watch out above all for sea urchins – while most hotel swimming areas have been carefully cleansed of these nasties, never take that for granted, and always check using a diving mask. Be extremely careful of urchins when swimming outside of roped-off areas – they can be very numerous where they exist and dwell in shallow as well as deep water. Other far rarer creatures to look out for include the gaudy lion fish with its poisonous spined fins, and for the cleverly camouflaged – and exceptionally poisonous – stonefish. Some shells, such as the cone shell, can fire out a deadly poisonous barb. The species of fire coral (in fact a type of jellyfish) packs a powerful sting if touched. Shark attacks are almost totally unheard of but very occasionally sharks do come into these waters, and while most are harmless, don't take that for granted.

## Water
As a general rule, tap water in Mauritius, Réunion and the Seychelles is safe to drink, but always take care immediately after a cyclone or cyclonic storm as mains water supplies can become contaminated by dead animals and other debris washed into the system. Never drink from streams as it might put you at risk of waterborne diseases.

HEALTH

# Language

## CONTENTS

## WHAT'S A CREOLE?

When people of differing native languages come into contact and develop a simple mode of communication that is based on both languages, the product is known as a pidgin. Once this 'neo-language' has become established to the point where it possesses a defined grammatical structure and writing system, and children learn it as a first language, it becomes a Creole.

The Creoles of Mauritius, Réunion and Seychelles are a blend of French and an assortment of African languages, with regional variations. Seychelles Creole is similar to that of Mauritius, but differs significantly from the Creole spoken in Réunion.

## MAURITIUS

It's said that when Mauritians have a community meeting, they speak Creole, take minutes in English and discuss the outcome with government officials in French.

The official languages of the country are English and French. English is used mainly in government and business. French is the spoken language in educated and cultural circles, and is used in newspapers and magazines. You'll probably find that most people will first speak to you in French and only switch to English once they realise you're an English speaker.

Creole derives from French and has similarities with Creoles spoken elsewhere. Ironically, the Creole spoken in Mauritius and Seychelles is more comprehensible to French people than that of Réunion, even though Réunion itself is thoroughly French. Most Indo-Mauritians speak Bhojpuri, derived from a Bihari dialect of Hindi.

There are major differences between the pronunciation and usage of Creole and standard French, but if you don't speak any French at all, you're doubly disadvantaged. *Parlez créole/Speak creole*, by Rose Hill (Mauritius: Editions de l'océan Indien) is a phrasebook in French and English.

For Mauritian Creole starters, you might like to try the following phrases:

| | |
|---|---|
| **How are you?** | *Ki manière?* |
| **Fine, thanks.** | *Mon byen, mersi.* |
| **I don't understand.** | *Mo pas comprend.* |
| **OK.** | *Correc.* |
| **Not OK.** | *Pas correc.* |
| **he, she, it** | *li* |
| **Do you have …?** | *Ou éna …?* |
| **I'd like …** | *Mo oulé …* |
| **I'm thirsty.** | *Mo soif.* |
| **Phoenix beer** | *la bière zarnier* (literally 'spider beer' – the label looks like one) |
| **Cheers!** | *Tapeta!* |
| **Great!** | *Formidabe!* |

## RÉUNION

French is the official language of Réunion, but Creole is the most widely spoken language. Few people speak English.

A word that means one thing in French can mean something completely different in Creole, and where a word does have the same meaning, it's usually pronounced differently in Creole.

Creole has a number of *bons mots* and charming idioms, which are often the result of Hindi, Arab and Malagasy influences or misinterpretations of the original French word. *Bonbon la fesse* (bum toffee) is a suppository, *conserves* (preserves) are sunglasses, and *cœur d'amant* (lover's heart) is a cardamom seed. *Coco* is your head, *caze* is your house, *marmaille* is your child, *baba* is your baby, *band* means 'family', *le fait noir* means 'night', and, if the stars are out, remember that *mi aime jou* means 'I love you'.

In Creole pronunciation there are two basic rules: **r** is generally not pronounced (when it is, it's pronounced lightly); and the soft **j** and **ch** sounds of French are pronounced as 'z' and 's' respectively. For example, *manzay* for 'manger' (to eat), *zamais* for 'jamais' (never) and *sontay* for 'chanter' (to sing).

## SEYCHELLES

English and French are the official languages of the Seychelles. Most people speak both, although French Creole (known as Kreol Seselwa) is the lingua franca. Kreol Seselwa was 'rehabilitated' and made semi-official in 1981, and is increasingly used in newspapers and literature. These days, most Seychellois will use English when speaking to tourists, French when conducting business, and Creole in the home.

Seychelles Creole is similar to that of Mauritius and Martinique, but differs remarkably from that of Réunion. The soft pronunciation of certain French consonants is hardened and some syllables are dropped completely. The soft **j** becomes 'z', for example. The following Creole phrases may help get you started:

| | |
|---|---|
| **Good morning./** | *Bonzour.* |
| **Good afternoon.** | |
| **How are you?** | *Comman sava?* |
| **Fine, thanks.** | *Mon byen, mersi.* |
| **What's your name?** | *Ki mannyer ou appel?* |
| **My name is ...** | *Mon appel ...* |
| **Where do you live?** | *Koté ou resté?* |
| **I don't understand.** | *Mon pas konpran.* |
| **I like it.** | *Mon kontan.* |
| **Where is ...?** | *Ol i ...?* |
| **How much is that?** | *Kombyen sa?* |
| **I'm thirsty.** | *Mon soif.* |
| **Can I have a beer,** | *Mon kapa ganny en labyer* |
| **please?** | *silvouplé?* |

# FRENCH

Along with the local Creoles, French is spoken in all three destinations. You'll find that menus on the islands are mostly in French, with English variations in some cases.

For a more comprehensive guide to the French language, pick up a copy of Lonely Planet's *French Phrasebook*.

## PRONUNCIATION

Most letters in French are pronounced more or less the same as their English counterparts. Below are a few that may cause confusion:

| | |
|---|---|
| **j** | as the 's' in 'leisure', eg jour (day); written as 'zh' in our pronunciation guides |
| **c** | before **e** and **i**, as the 's' in 'sit'; before **a**, **o** and **u**, as 'k' |
| **ç** | always pronounced as the 's' in 'sit' |
| **r** | pronounced from the back of the throat while constricting the muscles to restrict the flow of air |
| **n, m** | where a syllable ends in a single **n** or **m**, these letters are not pronounced, but the preceding vowel is given a nasal pronunciation |

## BE POLITE

An important distinction is made in French between *tu* and *vous*, which both mean 'you'; *tu* is only used when addressing people you know well, children or animals. If you're addressing an adult who isn't a personal friend, *vous* should be used unless the person invites you to use *tu*. In general, younger people insist less on this distinction between polite and informal, and you will find that in many cases they use *tu* from the beginning of an acquaintance.

The polite form is used in all instances in this guide unless indicated by 'inf' (meaning 'informal') in brackets.

## GENDER

All nouns in French are either masculine or feminine and adjectives reflect the gender of the noun they modify. The feminine form of many nouns and adjectives is indicated by a silent **e** added to the masculine form, as in *ami* and *amie* (the masculine and feminine for 'friend').

The gender of a noun is often indicated by a preceding article: 'the/a/some', le/un/du (m), la/une/de la (f); or one of the possessive adjectives, 'my/your/his/her', mon/ton/son (m), ma/ta/sa (f). In French, the possessive adjective agrees in number and gender with the thing in question: 'his/her mother', sa mère.

In the following phrases gender has been indicated where necessary. The masculine form comes first and is separated from the feminine by a slash.

## ACCOMMODATION

| | | |
|---|---|---|
| **I'm looking for a ...** | Je cherche ... | zher shersh ... |
| **camping ground** | un camping | un kom·peeng |
| **guesthouse** | une pension (de famille) | ewn pon·syon (der fa·mee·ler) |
| **hotel** | un hôtel | un o·tel |
| **youth hostel** | une auberge de jeunesse | ewn o·berzh der zher·nes |

**Where is a cheap hotel?**
Où est-ce qu'on peut
trouver un hôtel pas cher?
oo es·kon per
troo·vay un o·tel pa shair

**What is the address?**
Quelle est l'adresse?
kel e la·dres

**Could you write it down, please?**
Est-ce que vous pourriez
l'écrire, s'il vous plaît?
e·sker voo poo·ryay
lay·kreer seel voo play

**Do you have any rooms available?**
Est-ce que vous avez
des chambres libres?
e·sker voo·za·vay
day shom·brer lee·brer

| | | |
|---|---|---|
| **I'd like (a) ...** | Je voudrais ... | zher voo·dray ... |
| **single room** | une chambre à un lit | ewn shom·brer a un lee |
| **double-bed room** | une chambre avec un grand lit | ewn shom·brer a·vek un gron lee |
| **twin room** (with two beds) | une chambre avec des lits jumeaux | ewn shom·brer a·vek day lee zhew·mo |
| **room with a bathroom** | une chambre avec une salle de bains | ewn shom·brer a·vek ewn sal der bun |
| **to share a dorm** | coucher dans un dortoir | koo·sher don zun dor·twa |

| | | |
|---|---|---|
| **How much is it ...?** | Quel est le prix ...? | kel e ler pree ... |
| **per night** | par nuit | par nwee |
| **per person** | par personne | par per·son |

**MAKING A RESERVATION**
(for phone or email requests)

| | |
|---|---|
| To ... | A l'attention de ... |
| From ... | De la part de ... |
| Date | Date |
| I'd like to book ... | Je voudrais réserver ... (see the list under 'Accommodation' for bed and room options) |
| in the name of ... | au nom de ... |
| from ... (date) to ... | du ... au ... |
| credit card number | carte de crédit numéro |
| expiry date | date d'expiration |
| Please confirm availability and price. | Veuillez confirmer la disponibilité et le prix. |

**May I see the room?**
Est-ce que je peux voir
la chambre?
es·ker zher per vwa
la shom·brer

**Where is the bathroom?**
Où est la salle de bains?
oo e la sal der bun

**Where is the toilet?**
Où sont les toilettes?
oo son lay twa·let

**I'm leaving today.**
Je pars aujourd'hui.
zher par o·zhoor·dwee

**We're leaving today.**
Nous partons
aujourd'hui.
noo par·ton
o·zhoor·dwee

| | | |
|---|---|---|
| **air-conditioned** | climatisé | klee ma·tee zay |
| **a shower** | une douche | ewn doosh |
| **a washbasin** | un lavabo | un la·va·bo |
| **hot water** | eau chaude | o shod |
| **a window** | une fenêtre | ewn fe·netr |
| **a terrace** | une terrace | ewn tay·ras |
| **a sea view** | une vue sur la mer | ewn vue sewr la mair |
| **full board** | pension complète | pon·syon kom·plet |
| **half board** | demi-pension | day·mee pon·syon |
| **dining room** | la salle à manger | la sal a mon·zhair |

**kitchen**
*la cuisine*                la kwee·zeen
**television**
*une télévision*            ewn tay·lay·vee·zyon
**swimming pool**
*une piscine*               ewn pee·seen
**towel**
*une serviette*             ewn sair·vyet
**(not) included**
*(non) compris*            (non) kom·pree

## CONVERSATION & ESSENTIALS

| | | |
|---|---|---|
| **Hello.** | *Bonjour.* | bon·zhoor |
| **Goodbye.** | *Au revoir.* | o·rer·vwa |
| **Yes.** | *Oui.* | wee |
| **No.** | *Non.* | no |
| **Please.** | *S'il vous plaît.* | seel voo play |
| **Thank you.** | *Merci.* | mair·see |
| **You're welcome.** | *Je vous en prie.* | zher voo·zon pree |
| | *De rien.* (inf) | der ree·en |
| **Excuse me.** | *Excuse-moi.* | ek·skew·zay·mwa |
| **Sorry.** (forgive me) | *Pardon.* | par·don |

**What's your name?**
*Comment vous*             ko·mon voo
*appelez-vous?*            za·pay·lay voo
*Comment tu*               ko·mon tew
*t'appelles?* (inf)        ta·pel
**My name is ...**
*Je m'appelle ...*         zher ma·pel ...
**Where are you from?**
*De quel pays êtes-vous?*  der kel pay·ee et·voo
*De quel pays es-tu?* (inf) der kel pay·ee e·tew
**I'm from ...**
*Je viens de ...*          zher vyen der ...
**I like ...**
*J'aime ...*               zhem ...
**I don't like ...**
*Je n'aime pas ...*        zher nem pa ...
**Just a minute.**
*Une minute.*              ewn mee·newt

## DIRECTIONS

**Where is ...?**
*Où est ...?*              oo e ...
**Go straight ahead.**
*Continuez tout droit.*    kon·teen·way too drwa
**Turn left.**
*Tournez à gauche.*        toor·nay a gosh
**Turn right.**
*Tournez à droite.*        toor·nay a drwat
**at the corner**
*au coin*                  o kwun
**at the traffic lights**
*aux feux*                 o fer

---

| | | |
|---|---|---|
| **behind** | *derrière* | dair·ryair |
| **in front of** | *devant* | der·von |
| **far (from)** | *loin (de)* | lwun (der) |
| **near (to)** | *près (de)* | pray (der) |
| **opposite** | *en face de* | on fas der |
| | | |
| **beach** | *la plage* | la plazh |
| **bridge** | *le pont* | ler pon |
| **church** | *l'église* | lay·gleez |
| **island** | *l'île* | leel |
| **lake** | *le lac* | ler lak |
| **museum** | *le musée* | ler mew·zay |
| **sea** | *la mer* | la mair |
| **tourist office** | *l'office de* | lo·fees der |
| | *tourisme* | too·rees·mer |

## FOOD & DRINK
### Useful Phrases
**I'd like to reserve a table.**
*J'aimerais resérver*      zhay·mer·ray ray·zair·vay
*une table.*               ewn ta·bler
**A table for two, please.**
*Une table pour deux,*     oon ta·bler poor der
*s'il vous plaît.*         seel voo play
**Is service included in the bill?**
*Est-ce que le service*    es·ker ler sair·vees
*est inclu?*               et un·klew
**Do you have a menu in English?**
*Est-ce que vous avez*     es·ker voo a·vay
*la carte en anglais?*     la kart on ong·glay
**What's the speciality here?**
*Quelle est la spécialité ici?* kel ay la spay·sya·lee·tay ees·ee
**I'd like a local speciality.**
*J'aimerais une*           zhay·mer·ray ewn
*spécialité régionale.*    spay·sya·lee·tay ray·zhyo·nal
**Could you recommend something?**
*Est-ce que vous pouvez*   es·ker voo poo·vay
*recommender quelque*      re·ko·mon·day kel·ker
*chose?*                   shoz

LANGUAGE

**I'd like the dish of the day.**
Je voudrais avoir          zher voo·dray a·vwar
le plat du jour.           ler pla dew zhoor
**I'd like the set menu.**
Je prends le menu.         zher pron ler mer·new
**I'd like to order the ...**
Je voudrais commander ...  zher voo·dray ko·mon·day
**The bill, please.**
La note, s'il vous plaît.  la not seel voo play
**I'm a vegetarian.**
Je suis végétarien/        zher swee vay·zhay·ta·ryun/
végétarienne.(m/f)         vay·zhay·ta·ryen

| I don't eat ... | Je ne mange | zher ner monzh |
| | pas de ... | pa de ... |
| **meat** | viande | vyond |
| **fish** | poisson | pwa·son |
| **seafood** | fruits de mer | frwee der mair |

## Food Glossary
### BASICS
| | | |
|---|---|---|
| beurre | ber | butter |
| céréale | say·ray·al | cereal |
| gâteau | ga·to | cake |
| piment | pee·mon | chilli |
| sel | sel | salt |

### MEAT
| | | |
|---|---|---|
| agneau | a·nyo | lamb |
| bœuf | burf | beef |
| calamar | ka·la·mar | squid |
| camarons | ka·ma·ron | prawns |
| crevettes | krer·vet | shrimps |
| langouste | long·goost | lobster |
| mourgatte | moor·gat | squid |
| poisson | pwa·son | fish |
| porc | por | pork |
| poulet | poo·lay | chicken |
| poulpe | poolp | octopus |
| truite | trweet | trout |

### FRUITS & VEGETABLES
| | | |
|---|---|---|
| ananas | a·na·nas | pineapple |
| banane | ba·nan | banana |
| chou chou | shoo shoo | choko (squash) |
| combava | kom·ba·va | knobbly lime |
| goyave | go·yav | guava |
| noix de coco | nwa der ko·ko | coconut |
| pomme | pom | apple |
| pomme de terre | pom der tair | potato |

### COOKING TERMS
| | | |
|---|---|---|
| bouilli | boo·yee | boiled |
| frit/frite (m/f) | free/freet | fried |
| fumé | few·may | smoked |
| grillé | gree·yay | grilled |
| rôti | ro·tee | roasted |

### DRINKS
| | | |
|---|---|---|
| bière | bee·yair | beer |
| café | ka·fay | coffee |
| jus de fruit | zhew der fwee | fruit juice |
| pression | pre·syon | draft beer |
| thé | tay | tea |
| vin (rouge/blanc) | vun (roozh/blong) | wine (red/white) |

### MENU DECODER
*achards* (a·shar) – pickled vegetable salad
*alouda* (a·loo·da) – sweet, milky drink, popular in Mauritius
*baie rose* (bey roz) – pink pepper
*bhajas* (bha·yas) – fried balls of besan dough with herbs or onions
*bibasse* (bee·bas) – medlar fruit
*bichiques* (bee·sheek) – sprat-like seafood delicacy
*biryani* (beer·ya·nee) – curried rice; sometimes called *briani*
*bois de songe* (bwa der sonzh) – local vegetable
*bol renversé* (bol ron·vair·say) – rice with various toppings, such as chicken, beef or mixed vegetables
*bonbons piments* (bon·bon pee·mon) – see *dhal puris*
*boucané* (boo·ka·nay) – smoked pork
*bouillon brèdes* (boo·yon bred) – green vegetables cooked in a lightly spiced broth
*bouillon crabes* (boo·yon krab) – crabs cooked in broth
*brèdes* (bred) – leafy green vegetables similar to Chinese cabbage
*cabri massalé* (ka·bree ma·sa·lay) – goat curry
*caca pigeon* (ka·ka pee·zhon) – Indian nibbles (literally 'pigeon droppings')
*camarons d'eau douce* (ka·ma·ron daw doos) – freshwater shrimps
*carri coco* (ka·ree ko·ko) – mild meat curry with coconut cream
*carri poulet/poisson* (ka·ree poo·lay/pwa·son) – chicken/fish curry
*carri sauve souris* (ka·ree sov soo·ree) – bat curry
*cassoulet* (ka·soo·lay) – thick stew of duck meat and haricot beans
*catless* (kat·les) – Indian snack (cutlet in breadcrumbs)
*char siu* (char·syoo) – barbecue pork
*chatini* (cha·tee·nee) – finely chopped tomato, onion, chilli and coriander appetiser
*confit de canard* (kon·fee der ka·nar) – duck meat preserved in its own fat
*dhal puris* (dal poo·ree) – Indian snack (thin pancakes served with beans and chilli sauce)
*dosa masala* (do·sa ma·sa·la) – Indian snack (thin bread with spicy potato filling)
*faratta* (fa·ra·ta) – unleavened flaky flour pancakes

*foie gras* (fwa gra) – fattened duck liver
*gajacks* (ga·jaks) – predinner snacks
*Gâteau Napolitaine* (ga·to na po·lee·ten) – butter biscuits with jam and icing
*gâteaux piments* (ga·to pee·mon) – Indian snack (deep-fried balls of lentils and chilli)
*jalebies* (ja·le·bee) – fried batter spirals in syrup
*lassi* (la·see) – Indian yoghurt drink
*mazavaroo* (ma·za·va·roo) – chilli and prawn paste cooked in oil
*mine frit* (min freet) – fried Chinese noodles
*mojito* (mo·khee·to) – alcoholic drink made with mint, lemon, sugar and rum
*murg dopiaza* (murg do·pya·za) – chicken in an onion and tomato sauce
*murg makhani* (murg ma·ka·nee) – chicken with a tomato and cream sauce
*octopus vindaloo* (ok·to·poos vin·da·loo) – octopus in turmeric and mustard seed sauce
*pain fouré* (pun foo·ray) – filled bread rolls
*pasanda* (pa·san·da) – curry laced with almonds and sesame seeds
*phad thai* (paad tai) – mixed fried noodles
*porc à la sauce grand-mère* (por a la sos gron·mair) – dish of pork with chilli sauce (literally 'pork in grandma's sauce')
*rhum arrangés* (room a·ran·zhay) – mixture of rum, fruit juice, cane syrup and a blend of herbs and berries
*riz renversé* (ree ron·vair·say) – see *bol renversé*
*rogan josh* (ro·gan josh) – spiced lamb
*rosenberghis* (ro·zen·bur·gis) – tiger prawns
*rougail* (roo·gay) – spicy chutney popular in Réunion
*rougail saucisses* (roo·gay so·sees) – sausages in tomato and onion sauce
*salade ourite* (sa·laad oo·reet) – octopus salad, with seasoning including oil, vinegar and sliced onions
*samosa* – Indian snack (pastry triangle with various fillings)
*sauce rouge* (sos roozh) – brandy sauce
*tarte tatin* (tart ta·tan) – apple tart
*tom yum thalay* (tom yum ta·lay) – lemongrass-laced seafood soup
*vindaye* (vin·day) – turmeric-flavoured sauce with mustard seeds and vinegar
*waaria* (waa·ree·ya) – spicy vegetable snack

## HEALTH

**I'm ill.**
*Je suis malade.*       zher swee ma·lad
**It hurts here.**
*J'ai une douleur ici.*      zhay ewn doo·ler ee·see

| **I'm ...** | *Je suis ...* | zher swee ... |
|---|---|---|
| **asthmatic** | *asthmatique* | (z)as·ma·teek |
| **diabetic** | *diabétique* | dee·a·bay·teek |
| **epileptic** | *épileptique* | (z)ay·pee·lep·teek |

## EMERGENCIES

**Help!**
*Au secours!*       o skoor
**There's been an accident!**
*Il y a eu un accident!*      eel ya ew un ak·see·don
**I'm lost.**
*Je me suis égaré/e.* (m/f)   zhe me swee·zay·ga·ray
**Leave me alone!**
*Fichez-moi la paix!*      fee·shay·mwa la pay

| **Call ...!** | *Appelez ...!* | a·play ... |
|---|---|---|
| **a doctor** | *un médecin* | un mayd·sun |
| **the police** | *la police* | la po·lees |

| **I'm allergic** | *Je suis* | zher swee |
|---|---|---|
| **to ...** | *allergique ...* | za·lair·zheek ... |
| **antibiotics** | *aux antibiotiques* | o zon·tee·byo·teek |
| **nuts** | *aux noix* | o nwa |
| **peanuts** | *aux cacahuètes* | o ka·ka·wet |
| **penicillin** | *à la* | a la |
| | *pénicilline* | pay·nee·see·leen |

| **antiseptic** | *l'antiseptique* | lon·tee·sep·teek |
|---|---|---|
| **aspirin** | *l'aspirine* | las·pee·reen |
| **condoms** | *des préservatifs* | day pray·zair·va·teef |
| **contraceptive** | *le contraceptif* | ler kon·tra·sep·teef |
| **diarrhoea** | *la diarrhée* | la dya·ray |
| **nausea** | *la nausée* | la no·zay |
| **sunblock cream** | *la crème solaire* | la krem so·lair |
| **tampons** | *des tampons* | day tom·pon |
| | *hygiéniques* | ee·zhen·eek |

## LANGUAGE DIFFICULTIES

**Do you speak English?**
*Parlez-vous anglais?*      par·lay·voo ong·lay
**Does anyone here speak English?**
*Y u-t-il quelqu'un qui parle anglais?*      ya·teel kel·kung kee par long·glay
**How do you say ... in French?**
*Comment est-ce qu'on dit ... en français?*      ko·mon es·kon dee ... on fron·say
**What does ... mean?**
*Que veut dire ...?*      ker ver deer ...
**I understand.**
*Je comprends.*      zher kom·pron
**I don't understand.**
*Je ne comprends pas.*      zher ner kom·pron pa
**Could you write it down, please?**
*Est-ce que vous pouvez l'écrire?*      es·ker voo poo·vay lay·kreer
**Can you show me (on the map)?**
*Pouvez-vous m'indiquer (sur la carte)?*      poo·vay·voo mun·dee·kay (sewr la kart)

# NUMBERS

| 0 | zero | zay·ro |
|---|---|---|
| 1 | un | un |
| 2 | deux | der |
| 3 | trois | trwa |
| 4 | quatre | ka·trer |
| 5 | cinq | sungk |
| 6 | six | sees |
| 7 | sept | set |
| 8 | huit | weet |
| 9 | neuf | nerf |
| 10 | dix | dees |
| 11 | onze | onz |
| 12 | douze | dooz |
| 13 | treize | trez |
| 14 | quatorze | ka·torz |
| 15 | quinze | kunz |
| 16 | seize | sez |
| 17 | dix-sept | dee·set |
| 18 | dix-huit | dee·zweet |
| 19 | dix-neuf | deez·nerf |
| 20 | vingt | vung |
| 21 | vingt et un | vung tay un |
| 22 | vingt-deux | vung·der |
| 30 | trente | tront |
| 40 | quarante | ka·ront |
| 50 | cinquante | sung·kont |
| 60 | soixante | swa·sont |
| 70 | soixante-dix | swa·son·dees |
| 80 | quatre-vingts | ka·trer·vung |
| 90 | quatre-vingt-dix | ka·trer·vung·dees |
| 100 | cent | son |
| 1000 | mille | meel |

## QUESTION WORDS

| Who? | Qui? | kee |
|---|---|---|
| What? | Quoi? | kwa |
| What is it? | Qu'est-ce que c'est? | kes·ker say |
| When? | Quand? | kon |
| Where? | Où? | oo |
| Which? | Quel/Quelle? | kel (m/f) |
| Why? | Pourquoi? | poor·kwa |
| How? | Comment? | ko·mon |

## SHOPPING & SERVICES

**I'd like to buy ...**
Je voudrais acheter ...    zher voo·dray ash·tay ...
**How much is it?**
C'est combien?    say kom·byun
**I don't like it.**
Cela ne me plaît pas.    ser·la ner mer play pa
**May I look at it?**
Est-ce que je peux le voir?    es·ker zher per ler vwar

**I'm just looking.**
Je regarde.    zher rer·gard
**It's cheap.**
Ce n'est pas cher.    ser nay pa shair
**It's too expensive.**
C'est trop cher.    say tro shair
**I'll take it.**
Je le prends.    zher ler pron

| **Can I pay by ...?** | Est-ce que je peux payer avec ...? | es·ker zher per pay·yay a·vek ... |
|---|---|---|
| credit card | ma carte de crédit | ma kart der kray·dee |
| travellers cheques | des chèques de voyage | day shek der vwa·yazh |

| more | plus | plew |
|---|---|---|
| less | moins | mwa |
| smaller | plus petit | plew per·tee |
| bigger | plus grand | plew gron |

| **I'm looking for ...** | Je cherche ... | zhe shersh ... |
|---|---|---|
| a bank | une banque | ewn bonk |
| the hospital | l'hôpital | lo·pee·tal |
| the market | le marché | ler mar·shay |
| the police | la police | la po·lees |
| the post office | le bureau de poste | ler bew·ro der post |
| a public phone | une cabine téléphonique | ewn ka·been tay·lay·fo·neek |
| a public toilet | les toilettes | lay twa·let |

## TIME & DATES

| **What time is it?** | Quelle heure est-il? | kel er e til |
|---|---|---|
| **It's (8) o'clock.** | Il est (huit) heures. | il e (weet) er |
| **It's half past ...** | Il est (...) heures et demie. | il e (...) er e day·mee |

| in the morning | du matin | dew ma·tun |
|---|---|---|
| in the afternoon | de l'après-midi | der la·pray·mee·dee |
| in the evening | du soir | dew swar |

| today | aujourd'hui | o·zhoor·dwee |
|---|---|---|
| tomorrow | demain | der·mun |
| yesterday | hier | yair |

| Monday | lundi | lun·dee |
|---|---|---|
| Tuesday | mardi | mar·dee |
| Wednesday | mercredi | mair·krer·dee |
| Thursday | jeudi | zher·dee |
| Friday | vendredi | von·drer·dee |
| Saturday | samedi | sam·dee |
| Sunday | dimanche | dee·monsh |

| January | janvier | zhon·vyay |
|---|---|---|
| February | février | fayv·ryay |
| March | mars | mars |
| April | avril | a·vreel |
| May | mai | may |
| June | juin | zhwun |
| July | juillet | zhwee·yay |
| August | août | oot |
| September | septembre | sep·tom·brer |
| October | octobre | ok·to·brer |
| November | novembre | no·vom·brer |
| December | décembre | day·som·brer |

## TRANSPORT
### Public Transport

| What time does | À quelle heure | a kel er |
|---|---|---|
| ... leave/arrive? | part/arrive ...? | par/a·reev ... |
| boat | le bateau | ler ba·to |
| bus | le bus | ler bews |
| plane | l'avion | la·vyon |

| I'd like a ... | Je voudrais | zher voo·dray |
|---|---|---|
| ticket. | un billet ... | un bee·yay ... |
| one-way | simple | sum·pler |
| return | aller et retour | a·lay ay rer·toor |

**I want to go to ...**
Je voudrais aller à ...　zher voo·dray a·lay a ...
**The bus has been delayed.**
Le bus est en retard.　ler bews et on rer·tar
**The bus has been cancelled.**
Le bus a été annulé.　ler bews a ay·tay a·new·lay

| the first | le premier (m) | ler prer·myay |
|---|---|---|
| | la première (f) | la prer·myair |
| the last | le dernier (m) | ler dair·nyay |
| | la dernière (f) | la dair·nyair |
| ticket office | le guichet | ler gee·shay |
| timetable | l'horaire | lo·rair |

### Private Transport

| I'd like to hire | Je voudrais | zher voo·dray |
|---|---|---|
| a/an ... | louer ... | loo·way ... |
| 4WD | un quatre-quatre | un kat·kat |
| bicycle | un vélo | un vay·lo |
| car | une voiture | ewn vwa·tewr |
| motorbike | une moto | ewn mo·to |

**Is this the road to ...?**
C'est la route pour ...?　say la root poor ...
**Where's a service station?**
Où est-ce qu'il y a une　oo es·keel ya ewn
station-service?　sta·syon·ser·vees

| petrol/gas | essence | ay·sons |
|---|---|---|
| diesel | diesel | dyay·zel |
| mechanic | mécanicien | may·ka·nee·syun |

**The car/motorbike has broken down at ...**
La voiture/moto est　la vwa·tewr/mo·to ay
tombée en panne à ...　tom·bay on pan a ...
**I have a flat tyre.**
Mon pneu est à plat.　mom pner ay ta pla
**I've run out of petrol.**
Je suis en panne d'essence.　zher swee zon pan day·sons
**I had an accident.**
J'ai eu un accident.　zhay ew un ak·see·don

## TRAVEL WITH CHILDREN
**Are children allowed?**
Les enfants sont permis?　lay zon·fon son pair·mee

| I need (a) ... | J'ai besoin ... | zhay ber·zwun ... |
|---|---|---|
| car baby seat | d'un siège-enfant | dun syezh·on·fon |
| nappies/ | de couches- | der koosh· |
| diapers | culottes | kew·lot |
| highchair | d'une chaise haute | dewn shay zot |
| potty | d'un pot de | dun po der |
| | bébé | bay·bay |
| stroller | d'une poussette | dewn poo·set |

Also available from Lonely Planet:
*French Phrasebook*

LANGUAGE

# Glossary

**auberge** – farm inn
**auberge de jeunesse** – youth hostel

**baba figue** – the blossom of the banana tree
**bassins** – small lakes
**bibliothèque** – library
**bom** – stringed instrument with a bulbous gourd-shaped body
**bonhommes/bonfemmes di bois** – medicine men/women
**branles, brandes** – giant heather bushes

**Cafre** – person whose ancestors are black
**camaron** – freshwater shrimp
**camtole** – in the Seychelles, a traditional roving band featuring fiddle, banjo, drums and accordion
**carte de séjour** – residence permit
**case créole** – traditional Creole house
**cavadee** – Hindu festival featuring self-mutilating devotees
**cerfs** – stags
**chambre d'hôte** – family-run B&B
**colons** – colonial settlers
**commune** – administrative district
**Compagnie des Indes Orientales** – French East India Company
**contredanse** – dance similar to the quadrille

**dentelles** – decorative frieze on Creole houses

**écart** – settlement

**ferme-auberge** – farm restaurant
**filaos** – casuarina trees

**gare routière** – bus station
**gendarmerie** – police station
**gîte** – self-catering accommodation
**gîte d'étape** – walkers lodge
**gîte de montagne** – mountain lodge
**grains** – peas
**grands blancs** – rich white people
**gris gris** – black magic
**guichet automatique de banque (GAB)** – automated teller machine (ATM)

**hauts** – highlands
**hôtel de ville** – town hall; see also *mairie*

**îlet** – hamlet, in Réunion

**kanvar** – light wooden frame or arch decorated with paper flowers
**kotis** – dance similar to Scottish dancing

**le malaise Creole** – Creole people's anger at their impoverished status
**lambrequins** – ornamental window and door borders
**la métropole** – mainland France as known in Réunion
**le sud sauvage** – wild south (southern part of Réunion island)
**librairie** – bookshop
**location de voitures** – car hire
**lontan** – of yore

**mairie** – town hall
**makalapo** – stringed instrument with a tin sound-box
**maloya** – traditional dance music of Réunion
**Malbar** – persons of Tamil origin, in Réunion
**marmite** – traditional cooking pot
**marrons** – slaves who escaped from their owners
**Mascarene Islands** – the collective term for the group of volcanic islands in the West Indian Ocean consisting of Réunion, Mauritius and Rodrigues
**massalé** – Indian spice mix
**mazok** – dance reminiscent of the French waltz
**menu du jour** – set menu of the day
**merle blanc** – cuckoo shrike; Réunion's rarest bird
**métro cuisine** – cuisine of mainland France
**moutia** – sombre, traditional dance of the Seychelles
**MWF** – Mauritian Wildlife Foundation

**office du tourisme** – tourist office

**paille-en-queue** – white-tailed tropicbird
**papangue** – Maillardi buzzard, a protected hawklike bird
**plat du jour** – dish of the day
**pétanque** – game similar to bowls
**pie chanteuse** – magpie robins
**puja** – the burning of incense and camphor at the lake shore and offering of food and flowers

**ragga** – blend of reggae, house music and Indian music, popular in Mauritius
**ravanne** – primitive goatskin drum which traditionally accompanies the *séga* dance
**route forestière** – forestry road

**séga** – dance of African origin
**seggae** – combination of reggae and traditional *séga* music
**sentier botanique** – nature trail

**sentier forestier** – forest dirt track
**sentiers marmailles** – footpath suitable for children
**source thermale** – hot spring

**tabagie** – convenience store, in Mauritius
**table d'hôte** – meal served at a *chambre d'hôte*
**tamarin des Hauts** – mountain tamarind tree
**tec-tec** – bird native to Réunion's highlands; also known as Réunion stonechat
**télécarte** – telephone card
**teemeedee** – Hindu/Tamil fire-walking ceremony honouring the gods

**ti' cases** – homes of the common folk

**vacoa** – screw pines; also known as pandanus
**varangue** – verandah
**vélo tout terrain (VTT)** – mountain bike
**veuve** – widow (Seychellois name for the paradise flycatcher)

**zez** – monochord sitar
**Zoreilles** – name used in Réunion for people from mainland France (literally 'the ears')
**zourite** – octopus

# The Authors

### JEAN-BERNARD CARILLET
Coordinating Author

Paris-based journalist and photographer Jean-Bernard has clocked up numerous trips to the Indian Ocean and written extensively about Réunion and the Seychelles. Being a diving instructor, he was all too happy to don his mask to check out the best dive sites in the region, before putting on his hiking shoes to explore the rugged Cirques and scale up the iconic Piton des Neiges in Réunion. In the Seychelles he examined every burg, shore and cove searching for the perfect beach, the best grilled fish and the best-value hotels, and ended playing castaway for a week following an eruption of an unpronounceable volcano in Iceland.

Jean-Bernard has contributed to many Lonely Planet titles, both in French and in English.

### BRANDON PRESSER
Mauritius Snapshots, Mauritius, Rodrigues, Mauritius Directory

Dreams of island living started early for this landlocked Canadian, so naturally he jumped at the opportunity to explore some of the Indian Ocean's treasures. Armed with his non-Métropole French background, a penchant for spicy curries and a Divemaster certification, Brandon managed to fit right in – he even tricked a few Mauritians into showing him their secret haunts!

Brandon works as a full-time freelance travel writer and spends most of the year trotting the globe, pen in hand. He's authored around 20 Lonely Planet guides covering a variety of other far-flung island destinations such as Borneo, Iceland, the Caribbean and southern Thailand.

**LONELY PLANET AUTHORS**

Why is our travel information the best in the world? It's simple: our authors are passionate, dedicated travellers. They don't take freebies in exchange for positive coverage so you can be sure the advice you're given is impartial. They travel widely to all the popular spots, and off the beaten track. They don't research using just the internet or phone. They discover new places not included in any other guidebook. They personally visit thousands of hotels, restaurants, palaces, trails, galleries, temples and more. They speak with dozens of locals every day to make sure you get the kind of insider knowledge only a local could tell you. They take pride in getting all the details right, and in telling it how it is. Think you can do it? Find out how at **lonelyplanet.com**.

THE AUTHORS

# Behind the Scenes

## THIS BOOK

This 7th edition of Lonely Planet's Mauritius, Réunion & Seychelles was researched and written by Jean-Bernard Carillet and Brandon Presser. The Health chapter was written by Dr Caroline Evans. The 1st edition was researched and written by Robert Willox, the 2nd edition was updated by Robert Strauss and Deanna Swaney, the 3rd edition was updated by Sarina Singh. Joe Bindloss updated the 4th edition and Jann Dodd updated the 5th edition. The 6th edition was researched and written by Tom Masters and Jean-Bernard Carillet. This guidebook was commissioned in Lonely Planet's Melbourne office, and produced by the following:

**Commissioning Editors** Sasha Baskett, David Carroll, Stefanie Di Trocchio, Shawn Low
**Coordinating Editors** Erin Richards, Louisa Syme, Jeanette Wall
**Coordinating Cartographer** Anita Banh
**Coordinating Layout Designer** Wibowo Rusli
**Managing Editor** Brigitte Ellemor
**Managing Cartographers** Shahara Ahmed, Herman So
**Managing Layout Designer** Indra Kilfoyle
**Assisting Editors** Andrea Dobbin, Helen Koehne, Kristin Odijk, Gabrielle Stefanos
**Assisting Cartographer** Jacqueline Nguyen

**Cover Research** Naomi Parker
**Internal Image Research** Sabrina Dalbesio
**Language Content** Laura Crawford

**Thanks to** Lisa Knights, Katie Lynch, Annelies Mertens, Adrian Persoglia, Averil Robertson, Lyahna Spencer, Juan Winata

## THANKS
### JEAN-BERNARD CARILLET

A huge thanks to Stefanie Di Trocchio, Shawn Low, Sasha Baskett, Brigitte Ellemor, David Carroll and the editor team, especially Jeanette Wall, for their support throughout this challenging process. The carto team, especially Shahara Ahmed, Anita Banh and Herman So, also deserves credit. And it's been a joy to work with Brandon, my dynamic coauthor – bien vu, Brandon!

While researching this guidebook I was lucky enough to encounter plenty of helpful Réunionnais and Seychellois, including Jean-Paul Diana and Axelle, Amanda, Florie, Elsa, Robbie Bresson, Isabelle, Fabien, Oré, Jéjé-1, Jéjé-2 and Debo. Their assistance was invaluable, as were the countless pointers and tips I enjoyed from the travellers I met along the way.

As always, a phenomenal gros bisou to my daughter Eva.

---

### THE LONELY PLANET STORY

Fresh from an epic journey across Europe, Asia and Australia in 1972, Tony and Maureen Wheeler sat at their kitchen table stapling together notes. The first Lonely Planet guidebook, Across Asia on the Cheap, was born.

Travellers snapped up the guides. Inspired by their success, the Wheelers began publishing books to Southeast Asia, India and beyond. Demand was prodigious, and the Wheelers expanded the business rapidly to keep up. Over the years, Lonely Planet extended its coverage to every country and into the virtual world via lonelyplanet.com and the Thorn Tree message board.

As Lonely Planet became a globally loved brand, Tony and Maureen received several offers for the company. But it wasn't until 2007 that they found a partner whom they trusted to remain true to the company's principles of travelling widely, treading lightly and giving sustainably. In October of that year, BBC Worldwide acquired a 75% share in the company, pledging to uphold Lonely Planet's commitment to independent travel, trustworthy advice and editorial independence.

Today, Lonely Planet has offices in Melbourne, London and Oakland, with over 500 staff members and 300 authors. Tony and Maureen are still actively involved with Lonely Planet. They're traveling more often than ever, and they're devoting their spare time to charitable projects. And the company is still driven by the philosophy of Across Asia on the Cheap: 'All you've got to do is decide to go and the hardest part is over. So go!'

## SEND US YOUR FEEDBACK

We love to hear from travellers – your comments keep us on our toes and help make our books better. Our well-travelled team reads every word on what you loved or loathed about this book. Although we cannot reply individually to postal submissions, we always guarantee that your feedback goes straight to the appropriate authors, in time for the next edition. Each person who sends us information is thanked in the next edition and the most useful submissions are rewarded with a free book.

To send us your updates – and find out about Lonely Planet events, newsletters and travel news – visit our award-winning website: **www.lonelyplanet.com/contact**.

Note: We may edit, reproduce and incorporate your comments in Lonely Planet products such as guidebooks, websites and digital products, so let us know if you don't want your comments reproduced or your name acknowledged. For a copy of our privacy policy visit www.lonelyplanet.com/privacy.

### BRANDON PRESSER

First and foremost I'd like to thank Sebastien and Jacqueline (Jax of all trades) Bax for their gracious hospitality and wonderful support. Thanks also to Joelle Ng, Christine Rochecouste-Collet, Yannick and Verity, Georgina and Louis, Gregory Mayer, Josette Marchal-Vexlard, Gérald Rambert, Françoise Baptiste, Phanuel Lévèque and a special shout out to my doppelganger Olivier Cirendini. In Lonely Planet-land I'd like to thank my co-author, the illustrious Jean-Bernard Carillet, for his leadership, wisdom and words of encouragement. Thanks also to Stefanie Di Trocchio for commissioning the title, Shahara Ahmed (mapping guru!), Sasha Baskett, Jeanette Wall, Anita Banh, Shawn Low, Brigitte Ellemor and David Carroll. Lastly, a special shout out to Joanne for all her love and support!

## OUR READERS

Many thanks to the travellers who used the last edition and wrote to us with helpful hints, useful advice and interesting anecdotes:

Marie Elise Aarrestad, Ravi Baindur, Francoise Baptiste, Linda Barsová, Seyad Bhone, Sören Braun, Evelyne Bretagnolle, Yuliono Budianto, Louise Carroll, Soon Ling Chin, David & Elke Cottingham-Thijskens, Oliver de Lasti, Thomas Dupas, Igor Fabjan, Richard Faulkner, Nicole Henry Gardes, Dalila Haoua, Adrian Hermann, Jaap J Komen, Peter Jenkins, Jane Juif, Marie Kmetova, Claus Koehler, Gabriel Kostas, Louis Kwiatkowski, Alice La Pierre, Anette Ladage, Mike Long, Maud Maes, Ursa Mekis, Diana Morgan, Lynne Salkin Morris, William Oates, Mahantesh Pattanshetti, Rui Pereira, Terry Phippen, Mark Pickering, Anja Prinz, Yashir Ramessur, Annabelle Ritchie, Johannes Sauter

## ACKNOWLEDGMENTS

Many thanks to the following for the use of their content:

Globe on title page ©Mountain High Maps 1993 Digital Wisdom, Inc.

GR®, GRP® and PR® and their way markings (white/red, yellow/red and yellow) are the Fédération française de la randonnée pédestre's registered trademarks. All rights reserved – www.ffrandonnee.fr.

# Index

**000** Map pages
**000** Photograph pages

# GreenDex

The following is an index of the businesses and operators in Mauritius, Réunion and Seychelles that are doing their bit for sustainable travel. Our criteria for inclusion cover environmental (minimising negative environmental impacts), social or cultural (fostering authentic interaction and greater understanding between travellers and hosts) and economic (providing financial benefits for the host community). Our decisions about what to include were informed by the opinions of local experts. The index is not exhaustive but does provide a place to start for those who want to make informed choices.

Choosing sustainable travel products, just like running a business that is ecofriendly, is not an exact science and is also a continuous process. Because we know we haven't got it 100% right yet, we very much welcome feedback on our selection via lonelyplanet.com/feedback. For more information on travelling responsibly see p19 and lonelyplanet.com/responsibletravel.

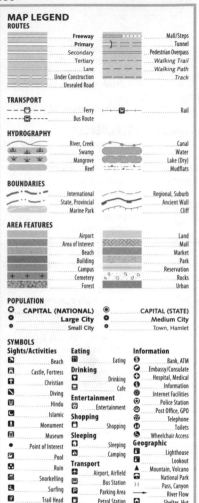

## MAP LEGEND

**ROUTES**

| | |
|---|---|
| Freeway | Mall/Steps |
| Primary | Tunnel |
| Secondary | Pedestrian Overpass |
| Tertiary | Walking Trail |
| Lane | Walking Path |
| Under Construction | Track |
| Unsealed Road | |

**TRANSPORT**

| | |
|---|---|
| Ferry | Rail |
| Bus Route | |

**HYDROGRAPHY**

| | |
|---|---|
| River, Creek | Canal |
| Swamp | Water |
| Mangrove | Lake (Dry) |
| Reef | Mudflats |

**BOUNDARIES**

| | |
|---|---|
| International | Regional, Suburb |
| State, Provincial | Ancient Wall |
| Marine Park | Cliff |

**AREA FEATURES**

| | |
|---|---|
| Airport | Land |
| Area of Interest | Mall |
| Beach | Market |
| Building | Park |
| Campus | Reservation |
| Cemetery | Rocks |
| Forest | Urban |

**POPULATION**

| | |
|---|---|
| CAPITAL (NATIONAL) | CAPITAL (STATE) |
| Large City | Medium City |
| Small City | Town, Hamlet |

**SYMBOLS**

| Sights/Activities | Eating | Information |
|---|---|---|
| Beach | Eating | Bank, ATM |
| Castle, Fortress | **Drinking** | Embassy/Consulate |
| Christian | Drinking | Hospital, Medical |
| Diving | Cafe | Information |
| Hindu | **Entertainment** | Internet Facilities |
| Islamic | Entertainment | Police Station |
| Monument | **Shopping** | Post Office, GPO |
| Museum | Shopping | Telephone |
| Point of Interest | **Sleeping** | Toilets |
| Pool | Sleeping | Wheelchair Access |
| Ruin | Camping | **Geographic** |
| Snorkelling | **Transport** | Lighthouse |
| Surfing | Airport, Airfield | Lookout |
| Trail Head | Bus Station | Mountain, Volcano |
| Zoo, Bird Sanctuary | Parking Area | National Park |
| | Petrol Station | Pass, Canyon |
| | Taxi Rank | River Flow |
| | | Shelter, Hut |
| | | Waterfall |

## LONELY PLANET OFFICES

**Australia** (Head Office)
Locked Bag 1, Footscray, Victoria 3011
☎ 03 8379 8000, fax 03 8379 8111
talk2us@lonelyplanet.com.au

**USA**
150 Linden St, Oakland, CA 94607
☎ 510 250 6400, toll free 800 275 8555
fax 510 893 8572
info@lonelyplanet.com

**UK**
2nd fl, 186 City Rd,
London EC1V 2NT
☎ 020 7106 2100, fax 020 7106 2101
go@lonelyplanet.co.uk

**Published by Lonely Planet Publications Pty Ltd**
ABN 36 005 607 983

© Lonely Planet 2010

© photographers as indicated 2010

Cover photograph: Pirogue (dugout canoe), Mauritius, Ethel Davies/ Photolibrary. Many of the images in this guide are available for licensing from Lonely Planet Images: lonelyplanetimages.com.

Printed through Colorcraft Ltd, Hong Kong
Printed in China

Mixed Sources
Product group from well-managed forests and other controlled sources
www.fsc.org  Cert no. SGS-COC-005002
© 1996 Forest Stewardship Council